THE AMERICAN NATION

Beginnings to 1877

THE AMERICAN NATION

Beginnings to 1877

James West Davidson

PRENTICE HALL
Upper Saddle River, New Jersey
Needham, Massachusetts

James West Davidson

James West Davidson is coauthor of *After the Fact: The Art of Historical Detection* and *Nation of Nations: A Narrative History of the American Republic.* Dr. Davidson has taught at both the college and high school levels and has consulted on curriculum design for American History courses.

Staff Credits

Editorial: Marion Osterberg, Rick Hickox, Anne Falzone

Marketing: Lynda Cloud, Laura Asermily

Production: Nancy Velthaus, Cleasta Wilburn, Greg Myers

Text Permissions: Doris Robinson

Art and Design: AnnMarie Roselli, Laura Bird, Kathryn Foot, Monduane Harris

Visual Research: Libby Forsyth, Emily Rose, Martha Conway

Pre-Press Production: Kathryn Dix, Annette Simmons, Carol Barbara

Manufacturing: Rhett Conklin

Historian Reviewers

Pedro Castillo, University of California, Santa Cruz, California

Judith Chesen, Wilberforce University, Wilberforce, Ohio

Robert H. Ferrell, Indiana University, Bloomington, Indiana

Stephen Middleton, North Carolina State University, Raleigh, North Carolina

Teacher Consultants and Reviewers

Sandra Eades, Ridgely Middle School, Lutherville, Maryland

Thomas P. Fusco, South Woods Middle School, Syosset, New York

Brian Gibson, Highland East Junior High School, Moore, Oklahoma

Judy Myers, West Junior High School, Boise, Idaho

Marilyn Renger, Balboa Middle School, Ventura, California

Reading Specialist

Barbara Mackie, Valley Stream Schools, K–12, Valley Stream, New York

Multicultural Reviewers and Consultants

David Beaulieu, Minnesota Department of Human Rights, St. Paul, Minnesota

Pedro Castillo, University of California, Santa Cruz, California

Judith Chesen, Wilberforce University, Wilberforce, Ohio

Charles Hancock, Ohio State University, Columbus, Ohio

Aida A. Joshi, University of San Francisco, San Francisco, California

Accuracy Panel

Susan Smulyan, Brown University, Providence, Rhode Island

With Lucy Barber, Laura Briggs, Crista De Luzio, Konstantin Dierks, Ruth Feldstein, Kathleen Franz, Carol Frost, Sarah Leavitt, Miriam Reumann

ISBN: 0-13-411083-8

5 6 7 8 9 10   00 99 98

PRENTICE HALL
SIMON & SCHUSTER EDUCATION GROUP
A VIACOM COMPANY

Acknowledgments and Illustration Credits appear on page 686.

UNIT 1 A Meeting of Different Worlds 1

UNIT 3 The New Republic 240

UNIT 4 An Expanding Nation 324

UNIT 5 The Nation Torn Apart · 424

SOURCE READINGS AND ART

SPECIAL FEATURES

★ *Lively features connect main ideas of American history to other subject areas.*

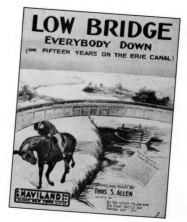

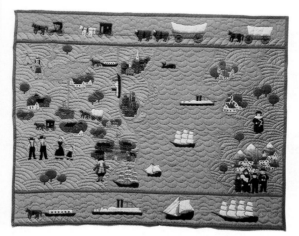

History Through LITERATURE

Art Gallery OUR COMMON HERITAGE

★ *In-depth stories offer a vivid close-up look at an important person or event.*

Picturing the Past

★ Picture essays provide a glimpse of the daily life of young Americans at different times in our history.

★ Pairs of pictures show how important events and ideas from the past influence our lives today.

SKILL LESSONS

Map, Graph, and Chart Skills

Critical Thinking Skills

Research Skills

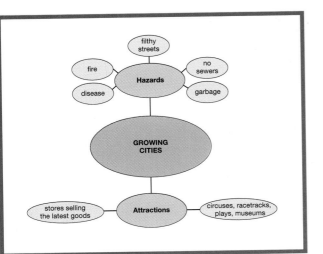

MAPS

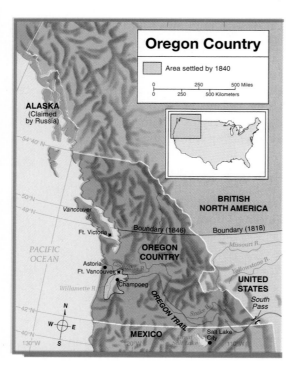

CHARTS, GRAPHS, AND TIME LINES

Causes and Effects

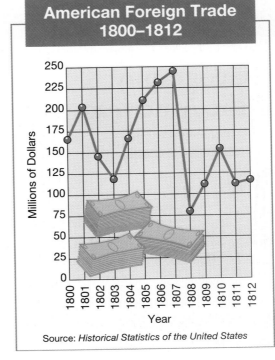

American Foreign Trade 1800–1812

Source: *Historical Statistics of the United States*

The American Nation: Beginnings to 1877 is organized into 5 units and 18 chapters, with Issues for Today sections at the front and back of the book. The Table of Contents lists unit and chapter titles. It also lists Connections and other special features, skill lessons, interdisciplinary activities, maps, charts, graphs, and time lines. In addition, the Table of Contents provides a guide to the Source Readings and Art and to the Reference Section.

Issues for Today

An Introduction   This introduction is a brief visual presentation of five important issues in American history: Multicultural Nation, Spirit of Democracy, Changing Economy, Environment, and Global Interdependence.

Getting Involved   Following the last chapter, this section revisits each of the five issues. Milestones—important events related to each issue—are provided. Case studies show how students took action to make a difference in their communities. Suggested activities help you get involved in your community.

In Each Unit

Unit Opener   Each unit opens with fine art that illustrates a major idea from the unit. The caption explains the connection between the artwork and the unit. In addition, a unit outline presents a brief description of each chapter.

History Through Literature   Each unit concludes with a two-page selection from a well-known work of American literature that relates to the time period. The literary selection provides additional insight into the past.

In Each Chapter

Chapter Opener   Each chapter begins with a Chapter Outline that lists the numbered sections of the chapter. An illustrated time line shows some of the main events that you will read about in the chapter, as well as important world events that occurred during the time period covered in the chapter. The Chapter Setting introduces the chapter. It includes a primary source that sets the tone for the material that follows.

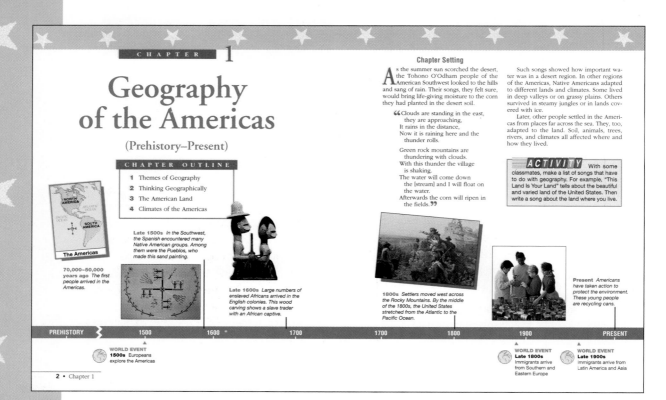

CHAPTER 1

Geography of the Americas

(Prehistory–Present)

CHAPTER OUTLINE

1 Themes of Geography
2 Thinking Geographically
3 The American Land
4 Climates of the Americas

The Americas

70,000–50,000 years ago *The first people arrived in the Americas.*

Late 1500s *In the Southwest, the Spanish encountered many Native American groups. Among them were the Pueblos, who made this sand painting.*

Late 1600s *Large numbers of enslaved Africans arrived in the English colonies. This wood carving shows a slave trader with an African captive.*

Chapter Setting

As the summer sun scorched the desert, the Tohono O'Odham people of the American Southwest looked to the hills and sang of rain. Their songs, they felt sure, would bring life-giving moisture to the corn they had planted in the desert soil.

❝Clouds are standing in the east, they are approaching,
It rains in the distance,
Now it is raining here and the thunder rolls.

Green rock mountains are thundering with clouds.
With this thunder the village is shaking.
The water will come down the [stream] and I will float on the water.
Afterwards the corn will ripen in the fields.❞

Such songs showed how important water was in a desert region. In other regions of the Americas, Native Americans adapted to different lands and climates. Some lived in deep valleys or on grassy plains. Others survived in steamy jungles or in lands covered with ice.

Later, other people settled in the Americas from places far across the sea. They, too, adapted to the land. Soil, animals, trees, rivers, and climates all affected where and how they lived.

ACTIVITY   With some classmates, make a list of songs that have to do with geography. For example, "This Land Is Your Land" tells about the beautiful and varied land of the United States. Then write a song about the land where you live.

1800s *Settlers moved west across the Rocky Mountains. By the middle of the 1800s, the United States stretched from the Atlantic to the Pacific Ocean.*

Present *Americans have taken action to protect the environment. These young people are recycling cans.*

| PREHISTORY | 1500 | 1600 | 1700 | 1700 | 1800 | 1900 | PRESENT |

WORLD EVENT 1500s Europeans explore the Americas

WORLD EVENT Late 1800s Immigrants arrive from Southern and Eastern Europe

WORLD EVENT Late 1900s Immigrants arrive from Latin America and Asia

Activities A wide variety of activities help you understand and respond to the chapter. The activities promote active learning and can be found in every Chapter Setting, Section Review, Connections, Skill Lesson, and History Through Literature.

To Help You Learn Several features help you to read and understand the chapter:

★ *Find Out* Questions at the beginning of each section guide your reading.

★ *Important Terms* Vocabulary words are printed in blue type and are clearly defined the first time they are used. Important historical terms are printed in ***dark slanted type.*** Vocabulary words and many terms also appear in a Glossary.

★ *Section Reviews* Questions at the end of each section test your understanding of what you have read and sharpen your critical thinking skills.

Skill Lesson A step-by-step skill lesson in each chapter helps you to understand and practice important skills.

Illustrations Pictures and other graphics help you to understand major events:

★ *Pictures*—works of fine art, photographs, cartoons, posters, and artifacts—bring history to life. Picture captions include a question that encourages you to explore major ideas of American history.

★ *Maps, Graphs, and Charts* help you to understand major historical developments. Captions provide important background information and also include questions to sharpen your map, graph, and chart skills.

Chapter Review The Chapter Review provides a summary of the chapter and helps you review the main ideas and strengthen geography and critical thinking skills. The Chapter Review also includes the Interdisciplinary Activity:

★ *Interdisciplinary Activity* provides a variety of choices for actively exploring an important idea from the chapter.

Special Features

There are several kinds of special features throughout the book:

★ *Connections* Full-page features connect a main idea from each chapter to one of six subjects: the Arts, the Sciences, Geography, the World, Economics, and Civics.

★ *Up Close* Vivid, in-depth looks at interesting people or events in American history.

★ *Causes and Effects* Charts that trace the causes and effects of a major event in each unit.

★ *Picturing the Past* Photo essays provide a glimpse of the lives of young Americans at different times in our history.

★ *Exploring Technology* Detailed drawings of major advances in technology.

★ *Linking Past and Present* Picture pairs show how ideas and events from the past influence our lives today.

★ *Art Gallery: Our Common Heritage* Major events and people from the American past depicted by present-day artists representing the nation's diverse cultural heritage.

★ *Extended Footnote* Notes that highlight important people, ideas, and events. Footnotes are divided into three categories: Our Common Heritage, Linking Past and Present, and History and You.

Source Readings and Art

This section provides two source readings—one an excerpt from literature, the other a first person account—and a piece of fine art for each chapter.

Reference Section

At the back of the book, you will find a section of reference materials. It includes a Geographic Atlas, charts with information about the 50 states and the Presidents, a Gazetteer of important places, a Glossary, charts that make connections between *The American Nation: Beginnings to 1877* and literature, science, mathematics, fine art, and music, the Declaration of Independence, the Constitution of the United States, and an Index.

An Introduction

"Who cares about the past? I want to live in the present." Many young people would probably agree with this statement. In fact, however, the present reflects the past. The actions of people long ago still affect our lives today. And the actions *we* take will affect the people of the future.

The study of history helps us to understand the relationship between past and present. Only by learning about the past can we truly understand the present. Only by learning about our nation's history can we understand what it means to be an American today—creating history for the Americans of tomorrow.

Threads of History

At first, history may seem like an unconnected mass of names, dates, and places. In truth, several issues serve as threads that tie the facts of American history together: Multicultural Nation, Spirit of Democracy, Changing Economy, Environment, and Global Interdependence.

The many faces of history. The United States was built by people from every part of the globe. In this book, you will read about Native Americans, who first arrived thousands of years ago. You will also learn the stories of the millions of others—Europeans, Africans, Asians, Latin Americans, and peoples from the Caribbean—who helped build our land. In a multicultural nation like ours, all these histories are important.

A democratic political system. Today, some quarter of a *billion* people live in the United States. They include farmers who plow fields and office workers who live in populous cities. Some Americans are recent immigrants to the United States. Others come from families who have been here for hundreds of years.

How can so many different peoples unite in a single nation? An important part of studying American history is learning about the government that holds the nation together. Americans often disagree with one another on important issues.

Issues for Today

Once, we even fought a civil war. Still, our democratic traditions have made this country a model for the rest of the world.

The lessons of economics. Economic history, too, is a part of our past. Blessed with abundant resources and a spirit of invention, Americans have built a thriving economy. At first, this economy revolved around the land and agriculture. In time, however, the focus shifted as Americans moved into "smokestack" industries and later into service and technology. Today, as you will learn, Americans face new challenges as we prepare to move into the global economy of the twenty-first century.

Our land and resources. Environment shapes our history, as well. How have we used our land in the past? What are we doing to ensure that we will preserve our resources for the future? In this book, you will discover how people's attitudes toward the environment have changed over time.

Links across the world. Our history links us with peoples and places all across the world. In both the American Revolution and the Civil War, we looked across the seas for allies. During the 1900s, thousands of Americans fought and died in overseas wars. In the 1970s, decisions made in desert kingdoms of the Middle East forced motorists in the United States to line up for hours at the gas pumps. Events thousands of miles away affect the history of Americans.

Your Role in History

You are about to begin a study of American history. As you read, keep in mind the major issues: Multicultural Nation, Spirit of Democracy, Changing Economy, Environment, and Global Interdependence. Try to discover how these issues helped to shape the lives of earlier Americans. Then make the connection to see how these same issues touch your life today. To help you get started, the picture essays on the following pages offer an overview of each issue.

At the end of the book, Issues for Today: Getting Involved helps you to trace the threads of American history from past to present. It also offers you an opportunity to make a difference for the future. Our history, after all, is far from complete. How Americans deal with the issues in the next hundred years is up to you.

Jim Davidson

Multicultural Nation

Art by Martin Kurzweil, Grade 7

Interlocking hands

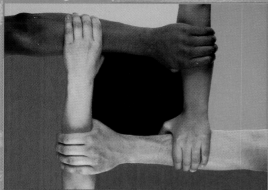

Flag of immigrant faces

Sign in many languages

Multicultural Nation

The United States is unique among nations. The people who make up our country represent hundreds of cultures, languages, and beliefs. This diversity poses a challenge. Americans must find ways to build unity while preserving their separate identities. At the same time, diversity provides the nation with its greatest strength. From food to fashion, from art to politics, American society is enriched by the talents, skills, and ideas of people from all parts of the world.

Welcoming customers of many cultures

Spirit of Democracy

Art by Kathryn DePue, Grade 6

Political convention

Campaign signs

Spirit of Democracy

Two hundred years ago, the United States set up a democratic government based on the ideals of liberty, justice, and equality. Ever since, each new generation of Americans has shaped democracy to reflect its times. Equality, for example, meant something very different to Americans in 1876 than it did to Americans in 1776. The process is never finished. Today, Americans are still struggling to perfect our democracy and to extend our ideals to include all the people in our land.

"Now, you try to get a fire started while I draft a constitution."

Billy Cloud
for
CLASS PRESIDENT

Campaign buttons forming an American flag

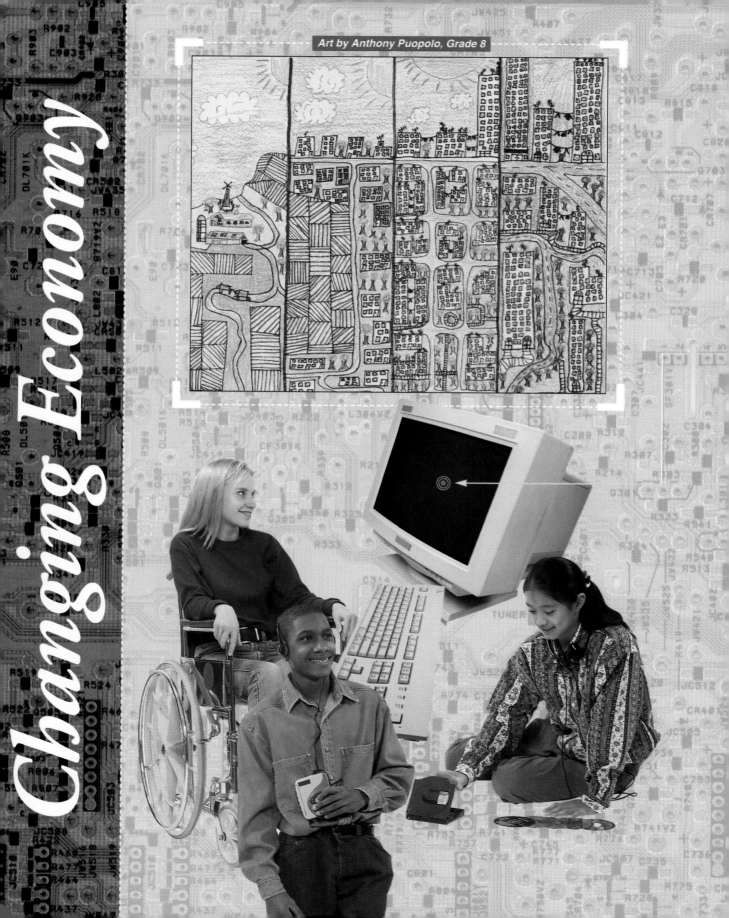

Art by Anthony Puopolo, Grade 8

Changing Economy

Computerized factory

"Oh, too bad, Mrs. Taporek, the computer just ate up all your money."

Changing Economy

When Native Americans first arrived in the Americas thousands of years ago, they lived by hunting and fishing and, in time, by growing crops. Early European settlers also lived off the land. Then in the 1800s, the economy began to change. By 1900, the United States was the leading industrial nation in the world. Today, the American economy has shifted once again. In the Computer Age, workers pursue the American dream not in local farms and factories but in "high tech" global industries that market goods and services around the world.

Computerized tag tracks a cow's diet

Environment

Art by Jennifer Hodgkins, Grade 7

"It's either a global warming trend or merely a fad."

Cleaning up the United States

Rescuing a bird after an oil spill

Environment

For most of our history, Americans have taken for granted the rich resources of our land. As we worked to create opportunity and abundance, we sometimes forgot that the minerals beneath our soil were not limitless. We neglected to take care of our rivers and streams. In recent years, however, Americans have shown a new concern for the environment. Working together, citizens, industries, and government are seeking to balance economic development with the need to preserve and protect the Earth on which we live.

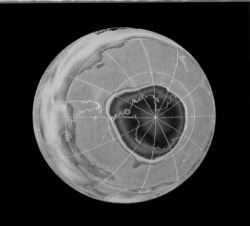

Satellite map showing a hole in the ozone layer

Global Interdependence

Art by Laura Rigolo, Grade 8

GLOBAL INTERDEPENDENCE

USA 29

World University Games Buffalo '93

Stamp honoring the 1993 World University Games

United Nations General Assembly

PAYS / COUNTRY VENTE / SELL

U.S.A.		1.15750
GR. BRITAIN		2.01750
JAPAN		.00871
ITALY		. 0009
FRANCE		. 20310
HOLLAND		6 0 6 2
GERMANY		.6861
SWISS		J 2 390
MEXICO		J 0404
AUSTRALIA		.9 2 46

CHEQUE$ CA$HED

Sign on a bank door

Global Interdependence

In 1796, George Washington, the nation's first President, cautioned Americans not to become involved in the affairs of foreign nations. For nearly 100 years, Americans heeded Washington's advice. Then, the United States began to look overseas. By the mid-1900s, it had become the world's leading political and economic power. Today, the communications revolution has shrunk the world. The United States, like all the world's nations, must learn how to compete—and cooperate—in the new "global village."

Computer image of the "global village"

A Meeting of Different Worlds

NOVA TOTIVS TERRARVM

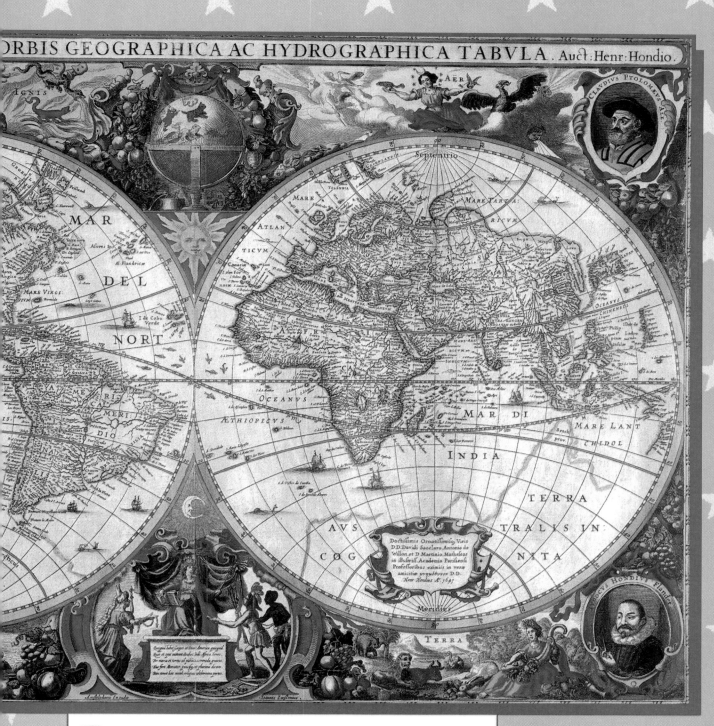

ORBIS GEOGRAPHICA AC HYDROGRAPHICA TABVLA. Auct:Henr:Hondio.

Before 1492, the people of the Americas had no lasting contact with the outside world. Then, Europeans arrived, seeking trade and wealth. The encounter between peoples of different worlds had effects that are still felt today. This map shows a European view of the world in 1630.

Geography of the Americas

(Prehistory–Present)

The Americas

Late 1500s *In the Southwest, the Spanish encountered many Native American groups. Among them were the Pueblos, who made this sand painting.*

30,000–15,000 years ago *The first people arrived in the Americas.*

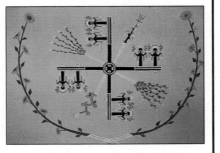

Late 1600s *Large numbers of enslaved Africans arrived in the English colonies. This wood carving shows a slave trader with an African captive.*

PREHISTORY	1500	1600	1700

WORLD EVENT
1500s Europeans explore the Americas

Chapter Setting

As the summer sun scorched the desert, the Tohono O'Odham people of the American Southwest looked to the hills and sang of rain. Their songs, they felt sure, would bring life-giving moisture to the corn they had planted in the desert soil.

> **"**Clouds are standing in the east,
> they are approaching,
> It rains in the distance,
> Now it is raining here and the
> thunder rolls.
>
> Green rock mountains are
> thundering with clouds.
> With this thunder the village
> is shaking.
> The water will come down
> the [stream] and I will float on
> the water.
> Afterwards the corn will ripen in
> the fields. **"**

Such songs showed how important water was in a desert region. In other regions of the Americas, Native Americans adapted to different lands and climates. Some lived in deep valleys or on grassy plains. Others survived in steamy jungles or in lands covered with ice.

Later, other people settled in the Americas from places far across the sea. They, too, adapted to the land. Soil, animals, trees, rivers, and climates all affected where and how they lived.

ACTIVITY
With some classmates, make a list of songs that have to do with geography. For example, "This Land Is Your Land" tells about the beautiful and varied land of the United States. Then write a song about the land where you live.

1800s *Settlers moved west across the Rocky Mountains. By the middle of the 1800s, the United States stretched from the Atlantic to the Pacific Ocean.*

Present *Americans have taken action to protect the environment. These young people are recycling cans.*

1700	1800	1900	PRESENT

WORLD EVENT
Late 1800s
Immigrants arrive from Southern and Eastern Europe

WORLD EVENT
Late 1900s
Immigrants arrive from Latin America and Asia

Themes of Geography

FIND OUT

- How do geographers help historians understand the past?
- What are the five themes of geography?
- How does geography influence the way people live?

VOCABULARY geography, history, latitude, longitude, irrigate

If you read almost any newspaper, you will find stories about the land around you. One story might argue that building a dam will be harmful to a river. Another might announce the discovery of oil. To understand these and other issues, we need to understand geography.

Geography is the study of people, their environments, and their resources. Geographers ask how the natural environment affects the way we live and how we, in turn, affect the environment. By showing how people and the land are related, geography helps to explain both the past and the present.

Geography is closely linked to history. **History** is an account of what has happened in the lives of different peoples. Both historians and geographers want to understand how the characteristics of a place affect people and events. They both ask the question, Why did this happen in this place?

To help show the connection between geography and history, geographers have developed five themes, or topics. The themes are location, place, interaction between people and their environment, movement, and region.

Location

Where did it happen? Both historians and geographers ask this question about an event. Finding out where something happened involves the geographic theme of location.

Exact location. As you study American history, you will sometimes need to know the absolute, or exact, location of a place. For example, where exactly is Washington, D.C., the nation's capital?

To describe the exact location of Washington, D.C., geographers use a grid of numbered lines on a map or globe that measure latitude and longitude. Lines of **latitude** measure distance north and south from the Equator. Lines of **longitude** measure distance east and west from the Prime Meridian, which runs through Greenwich (GREHN ihch), England. (You will read more about latitude and longitude later in this chapter. See page 11.)

The exact location of Washington, D.C., is 39 degrees (°) north latitude and 77 degrees (°) west longitude. In writing, this location is often shortened to 39°N/77°W. The Gazetteer in the Reference Section of this book provides the exact location of many important places in American history.

Relative location. Sometimes you might find it more useful to know the relative location of a place, or where it is located in relation to some other place. Is Washington, D.C., on the east coast or the west coast of the United States? Is it north or south of Richmond, Virginia? These questions involve relative location.

History and You
Geography affects the way people live. Name three ways in which the geography of your area influences your life.

The Maine Coast *The physical and human features of a place are often closely related. The coastline of Maine has thousands of rock-bound bays and inlets. To guide ships through dangerous waters, residents built tall lighthouses.* **Economics** *How might people along the Maine coast earn their living?*

Relative location includes knowing how places are connected to one another. Is a place located near a lake, river, or other source of water and transportation? Is it in the interior or on the coast? Answers to these kinds of questions help explain why cities grew where they did. Chicago, Illinois, for instance, developed at the center of water, road, and railroad transportation in the Midwest.

Place

A second theme that geographers study is place. Geographers generally describe a place in terms of both physical and human features.

The physical features of a place include climate, soil, plant life, animal life, and bodies of water. For example, New England has a hilly terrain, a rock-bound coast, and many deep harbors. Because of these physical features, early Native Americans of the region turned to fishing for a living.

People help to shape the character of a place through their ideas and actions. The human features of a place include the kinds of houses people build as well as their means of transportation, ways of earning a living, languages, and religions.

Think of the human features of the American frontier. In the forests of the frontier, early settlers built log cabins. On the grassy plains, some settlers built their first homes out of sod.

Interaction Between People and Their Environment

A third theme of geography is interaction between people and their environment. Throughout history, people have adapted to and changed their natural environment.

New Mexico Cotton Fields *In much of New Mexico, the average yearly rainfall is less than 10 inches. Yet irrigation has allowed farmers to grow a wide variety of crops. Irrigation canals, like these, bring water from the Rio Grande to desert farms.* **Geography** *What are some negative effects of interaction between people and their environment?*

For example, ancient hunters learned to grow food crops in the Americas. Later, Native Americans in the Southwest found ways to **irrigate,** or bring water to, the desert so that they could farm the land. In the 1860s, workers blasted through mountains and built bridges across rivers for railroads that linked the Atlantic and Pacific coasts.

Today, advanced technology allows people to alter their environment dramatically. People have invented ways to take oil from the ocean floor. They have cut down thick forests to build highways. They have wiped out pests that destroy food crops. Such changes have brought enormous benefits. But they have created new problems, such as air and water pollution.

Movement

A fourth geographic theme involves the movement of people, goods, and ideas. Movement occurs because people and resources are scattered unevenly around the globe. To get what they need or want, people travel from place to place. As they meet other people, they exchange ideas and technology as well as goods.

History provides many examples of the movement of people and ideas. The first

A Street in Chinatown *A region can be as small as a neighborhood. In the 1800s, Chinese immigrants began to form close-knit communities in cities along the Pacific coast. Today, some 30,000 Chinese Americans live in a 16-block area of San Francisco known as Chinatown.* **Multicultural Heritage** *What signs of cultural diversity can you find in your area?*

for example. At the same time, we rely on materials such as oil and rubber from other parts of the world.

Region

Geographers study regions. A region is an area of the world that has similar, unifying characteristics. The characteristics of a region may be physical, such as its climate or landforms. For example, the Great Plains is a region because it has fairly level land, very hot summers, very cold winters, and little rainfall.

A region's characteristics may also be human and cultural. San Francisco's Chinatown is a region because Chinese Americans there have preserved their language and culture.

A region can be any size. It can be as large as the United States or as small as a neighborhood.

people who came to the Americas were hunters following animal herds. Much later, people from all over the world moved to the United States in search of political and religious freedom. These newcomers brought with them customs and beliefs that have helped shape American life.

Today, the movement of goods links the United States with all parts of the globe. American producers ship goods such as grain and computers to Europe and Africa,

SECTION 1 REVIEW

1. **Define:** (a) geography, (b) history, (c) latitude, (d) longitude, (e) irrigate.
2. Why is geography important to the study of history?
3. Briefly describe the five themes of geography.
4. (a) Name two benefits of interaction between people and their environment. (b) Name two problems that can result when people make major changes in their natural environment.
5. CRITICAL THINKING **Synthesizing Information** Why do you think understanding movement is important to the study of history?

ACTIVITY **Writing to Learn** Write a paragraph in which you apply the five themes of geography to a study of your town or city.

2
Thinking Geographically

FIND OUT
- What advantages do flat maps have over globes?
- What are two kinds of map projections?
- Why is the world divided into time zones?

VOCABULARY cartographer, map projection, hemisphere, standard time zone

In a tiny Indian fishing village in the early 1600s, a small group gathered around Samuel de Champlain. They watched closely as the French explorer pointed to the shore and then drew a sweeping line on a deerskin spread out on the ground. The line represented the coastline where they stood. Quickly, the Native American chief drew other lines on the informal map. A young man added piles of rocks to represent the village and nearby settlements.

Champlain and the Native Americans he met on Cape Ann in Massachusetts did not understand one another's languages. Yet they found a way to communicate. Together, they created a map of the local area. Champlain later used the map to aid him in exploring the Massachusetts coast. People today use maps, too, to help them locate places, judge distances, and follow routes.

Maps and Globes

To locate places, geographers use maps and globes. A map is a drawing of the Earth's surface. A globe is a sphere with a map of the Earth's landmasses and bodies of water printed on it. Because a globe is the same shape as the Earth, it shows sizes and shapes accurately.

Even though a globe has this advantage, geographers often use flat maps rather than globes. Unlike a globe, a flat map allows you to see all of the Earth's surface at one time. It also can show more detail. And it is easier to handle. Still, a flat map has the disadvantage that it distorts, or misrepresents, some part of the Earth.

Map Projections

Mapmakers, or **cartographers,** have developed dozens of map projections. **Map projections** are ways of drawing the Earth on a flat surface. Two map projections are shown on page 9.

Any given map projection has benefits and disadvantages. Some projections show the sizes of landmasses correctly but distort their shapes. Others give continents their true shapes but distort their sizes. Still other projections distort direction or distances.

Mercator projection. In 1569, Gerardus Mercator developed the Mercator projection, the best map in its day. For hundreds of years, sailors used the Mercator map. Mercator himself boasted of his map:

66 If you wish to sail from one port to another, here is a chart, and a straight line on it, and if you follow this line carefully you will certainly arrive at your destination. 99

A Mercator map shows the true shapes of landmasses, but it distorts size, especially for places that are far from the Equator. On a Mercator map, for example, Greenland appears as big as all of South America, even though South America is more than eight times larger!

Robinson projection. Today, many geographers use the Robinson projection. It

MAP STUDY

Map projections make it possible for mapmakers to show a round world on a flat map.

1. *Which projection would you use to compare the sizes of North America and Europe?*

2. *Where does the Mercator projection show the least distortion?*

3. **Comparing** *Compare the landmasses on the Mercator and Robinson projections. (a) How are they similar? (b) How are they different?*

Map Projections

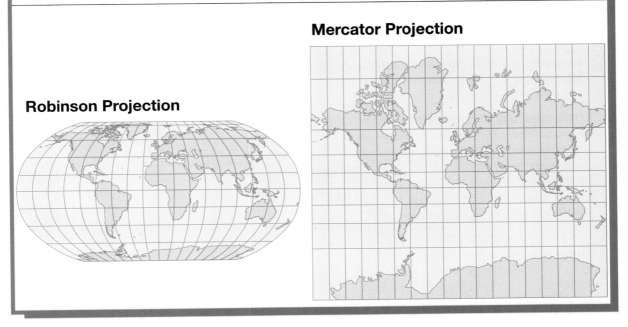

Mercator Projection

Robinson Projection

shows the correct sizes and shapes of landmasses for most parts of the world. The Robinson projection also gives a fairly accurate view of the relationship between landmasses and water.

Kinds of Maps

Maps are part of our everyday lives. You have probably read road or bus maps. As a child, you may have drawn treasure maps. On television, you have seen weather maps and maps of places in the news.

As you study American history, you will use many other kinds of maps. Turn now to the Geographic Atlas in the Reference Section of this book. There, you will find five different kinds of useful maps: political, physical, population, economic, and natural resource.

Each kind of map serves a specific purpose. A political map shows boundaries that people have set up to divide the world into countries and states. A physical map shows natural features, such as mountains and rivers. A population map lets you see how many people live in the various urban and rural areas. An economic map shows how people make a living in a given area. A natural resource map helps you understand the links between the resources of an area and the way people use the land.

MAP, GRAPH, AND CHART SKILLS
The Parts of a Map

Maps are important tools used by historians and geographers. They have many uses. They can show physical features such as lakes, rivers, and mountains. They can show where people live, how people use the land, and where events took place. Some maps, like the one below, show weather patterns for a given area.

To use a map, you need to be able to read its different parts. Most maps in this book have a title, key, scale, and directional arrow.

1. **Look carefully at the map to see what it shows.** The *title* tells you the subject of the map. The *key* explains the meaning of the colors or symbols. (a) What is the title of the map below? (b) What color shows places where the temperature is in the 50s? (c) How is rain shown on the map?

2. **Practice reading distances on the map.** The *scale* helps you read distances on the map in miles or kilometers. On a small-scale map, 1 inch (2.5 cm) might equal 500 miles (800 km). On a large-scale map, 1 inch might equal only 5 miles (8 km). The map below is a small-scale map. (a) What is the distance in miles from Washington, D.C., to Seattle? (b) In kilometers?

3. **Study the map to read directions.** The *directional arrow* shows which way is north, south, east, and west. Generally, north is toward the top of a map, and south is toward the bottom. East is to the right, and west is to the left. (a) In which direction would you travel to get from Miami to Los Angeles? (b) In which direction would you travel from El Paso to reach a place where it is snowing?

ACTIVITY Make a map of your classroom using symbols for doors, windows, desks, chalkboard, and other features. Include a map key, a scale, and a directional arrow. Use your completed map to answer the following questions: (a) How far are the windows from the door? (b) In which direction would you travel to get from the chalkboard to your desk?

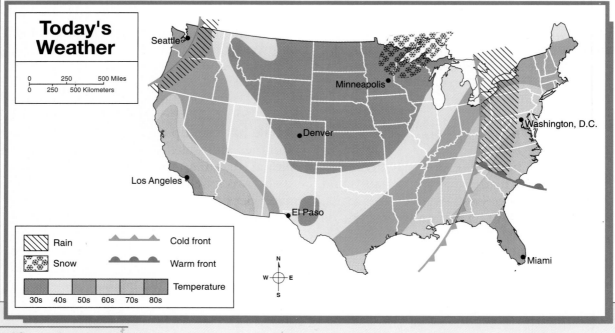

Today's Weather

0 250 500 Miles
0 250 500 Kilometers

Seattle • Minneapolis • Washington, D.C. • Denver • Los Angeles • El Paso • Miami

Rain   Cold front
Snow   Warm front
Temperature
30s 40s 50s 60s 70s 80s

N W E S

Still other kinds of maps you will use this year include election maps, product maps, and battle maps. These maps also let you see the connections between geography and history.

Latitude and Longitude

Most maps and globes include lines of latitude and longitude. The lines form a grid, making it possible to locate places exactly. Each line on the grid is measured in degrees (°).

Latitude. Look at the map of the world, below. Notice that lines of latitude run east and west. As you have read, lines of latitude measure distances north and south from the Equator.

The **Equator** is an imaginary line that lies at 0° latitude. It divides the Earth into two halves, called hemispheres.

The Northern Hemisphere lies north of the Equator. In the Northern Hemisphere, lines of latitude are numbered from 1°N to 90°N, where the North Pole is located.

The Southern Hemisphere lies south of the Equator. There, lines of latitude are numbered from 1°S to 90°S, where the South Pole is located. On the map below, what continent lies mostly between 30°N and 30°S?

Longitude. Lines of longitude on a map or globe run north and south. They measure distances east and west from the **Prime Meridian,** which lies at 0° longitude.

Lines of longitude are numbered from 1° to 179° east or west longitude. The line of longitude at 180° lies directly opposite the Prime Meridian.

The circle formed by the Prime Meridian and 180° divides the Earth into the Eastern and Western hemispheres. The Eastern

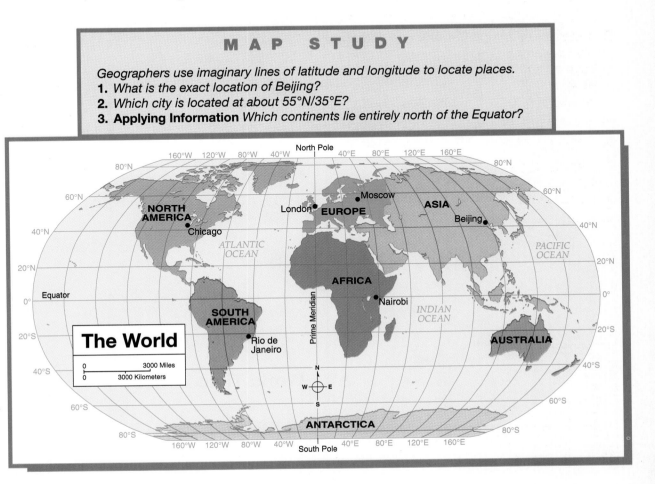

MAP STUDY

Geographers use imaginary lines of latitude and longitude to locate places.
1. *What is the exact location of Beijing?*
2. *Which city is located at about 55°N/35°E?*
3. **Applying Information** *Which continents lie entirely north of the Equator?*

Hemisphere includes most of Europe, Africa, and Asia. The Western Hemisphere includes North America and South America. On the map, through what continent or continents does 90°W run?

Finding locations. To locate places, you need to combine latitude and longitude. Look at the map on page 11. The city of Chicago is located north of the Equator at about 42°N latitude. It lies west of the Prime

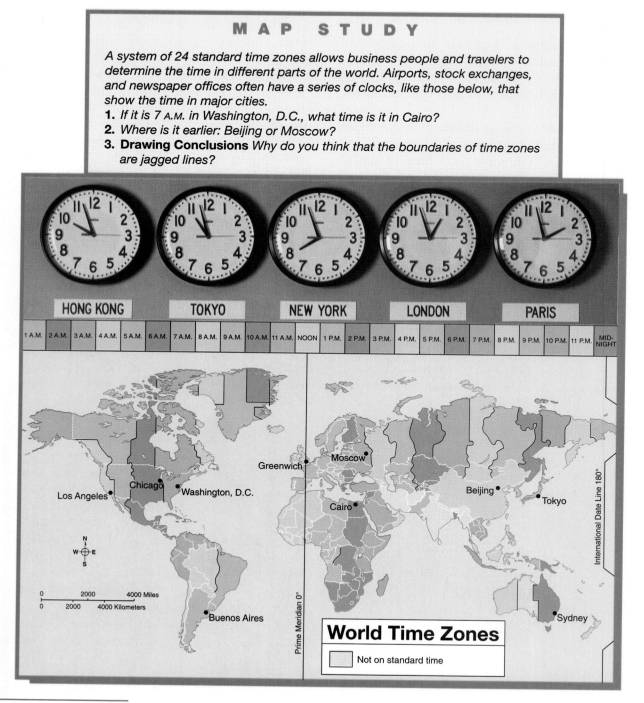

MAP STUDY

A system of 24 standard time zones allows business people and travelers to determine the time in different parts of the world. Airports, stock exchanges, and newspaper offices often have a series of clocks, like those below, that show the time in major cities.

1. If it is 7 A.M. in Washington, D.C., what time is it in Cairo?
2. Where is it earlier: Beijing or Moscow?
3. **Drawing Conclusions** Why do you think that the boundaries of time zones are jagged lines?

HONG KONG   TOKYO   NEW YORK   LONDON   PARIS

| 1 A.M. | 2 A.M. | 3 A.M. | 4 A.M. | 5 A.M. | 6 A.M. | 7 A.M. | 8 A.M. | 9 A.M. | 10 A.M. | 11 A.M. | NOON | 1 P.M. | 2 P.M. | 3 P.M. | 4 P.M. | 5 P.M. | 6 P.M. | 7 P.M. | 8 P.M. | 9 P.M. | 10 P.M. | 11 P.M. | MID-NIGHT |

World Time Zones

☐ Not on standard time

Meridian at about 88°W longitude. In shortened form, its location is 42°N/88°W. Use the United States map in the Reference Section to find the exact location of the capital of your state.

Time Zones

Lines of longitude are also used to help us know what time it is around the world. When it is 11 A.M. in Miami, Florida, it is 8 A.M. in Portland, Oregon. In Lagos, Nigeria, it is 5 P.M.

Why does time differ from place to place? The answer is that the Earth rotates on its axis. As the Earth moves, the sun appears to rise in some places and to set in others. Throughout the world, people determine time by this rising and setting of the sun.

To make it easier to tell time around the world, a system of **standard time zones** was set up in 1884. Under this system, the world was divided into 24 time zones. Standard time is measured from the Prime Meridian, which runs through Greenwich, England.

Find Greenwich, England, on the map of world time zones on page 12. Notice that when it is noon in Greenwich, it is before noon (A.M.) in places west of Greenwich. It is after noon (P.M.) in places east of Greenwich. If you travel east from Greenwich across Europe, Africa, or Asia, you add one hour as you move through each time zone.

History and You

Today, we expect maps to be accurate. Early explorers, however, often used inaccurate maps. Imagine that you are making an automobile trip across the United States. What would happen if you did not have an accurate map?

If you travel west from Greenwich across the Atlantic Ocean and North America, you subtract one hour as you move through each time zone.

Making Accurate Maps

The oldest surviving map in the world today was created by an ancient cartographer on a clay tablet sometime around 2300 B.C. Ever since, geographers have worked to make maps more accurate.

Early mapmakers relied on information from sailors and travelers as well as legends to create maps of the world. As a result, their maps included many errors along with accurate information. Five hundred years ago, cartographers in Europe did not even know that North America and South America existed!

Since the 1500s, mapmaking has improved greatly. Daring sailors gained information about uncharted lands. Explorers studied ocean currents and wind patterns around the world. Scientists learned more about the Earth itself. Today, mapmakers take advantage of high-speed computers and space satellites to create maps that are more accurate than anyone ever believed possible.

Eye in the Sky

One hundred miles above the Earth, Gordon Cooper was living a mapmaker's dream. It was May 1963, and "Gordo" was the sixth American astronaut to ride in space. His Mercury capsule orbited the Earth at 17,000 miles (27,000 km) an hour. Gordo was taking the mission calmly, pointing out the sights as he passed overhead.

An unexpected discovery. "Down there's the Himalayas," he told radio controllers as the world's highest mountain range came into view. With his hand-held camera, Cooper took photographs of the peaks far below. His Oklahoma twang cut right through the static. "Ah-yuh. . . the Himalayas."

Later, passing over Tibet, Cooper reported that he saw individual houses and streets—100 miles (160 km) below! He made even wilder claims as he passed over the desert area of western Texas and Arizona. As he later recalled,

> **"**I saw what I took to be a vehicle along a road. . . .I could first see the dust blowing off the road, then could see the road clearly, and when the light was right, an object that was probably a vehicle.**"**

The ground controllers scratched their heads. Was Gordo joking? True, Cooper had very good eyesight. He could see things from 20 feet away that most people would see only at 12 feet. Still, NASA scientists did not believe that anyone could see a moving vehicle from a distance of 100 miles!

NASA sent investigators to the Texas-Arizona desert. They learned that on the day of Gordo's mission, a large white-topped truck had indeed driven along the little-used desert highway. The truck had been on the highway at exactly the time when Cooper reported seeing a vehicle.

Later, other scientists examined Cooper's photographs. They saw mountains that had never appeared on any map. They found large lakes located miles from where existing maps said they should be.

These discoveries set scientists thinking: Could they use photographs from space to map the Earth? Space satellites had photographed clouds. Those pictures provided information about weather patterns. But no one had studied features on the ground from such a height.

Landsat maps. *Landsat 1,* the first satellite specially designed to study the Earth's surface from space, was launched in 1972. The unmanned butterfly-shaped spacecraft entered an orbit about 570 miles (900 km) above the Earth. It carried television cameras, a scanner that measured light, videotape recorders, and radio receivers and transmitters.

Landsat's orbit gave mapmakers every possible advantage. The spacecraft made a complete circle of the Earth every 103 minutes, 14 times a day. A single Landsat image showed an expanse of land that an airplane

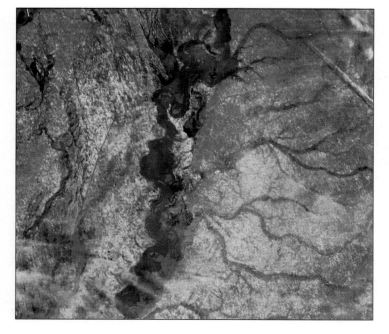

A View From Outer Space *This photograph of the Mississippi River was taken by a Landsat satellite orbiting the Earth. The areas shown in blue are the river and some of its tributaries.* **Science and Technology** *How has Landsat photography changed mapmaking?*

would need 1,000 pictures to depict. Within two years, Landsat had photographed more than 80 percent of the Earth's land areas at least once.

Images from *Landsat 1* and later satellites were remarkable. They revealed uncharted islands and unmapped bends in rivers. They permitted scientists to see entire mountain ranges and drainage basins at a single glance. They allowed surveys of remote areas, such as the polar regions and oceans, that regular aircraft cannot reach. Based on these images, cartographers corrected old maps and mapped some places for the first time.

Landsat has transformed mapmaking. By taking photographs from high in space, Landsat satellites provide clues that no one on the ground can furnish. ■

SECTION 2 REVIEW

1. **Locate:** (a) Equator, (b) Prime Meridian.
2. **Define:** (a) cartographer, (b) map projection, (c) hemisphere, (d) standard time zone.
3. Why does a globe show the Earth more accurately than a flat map?
4. Name one advantage and one disadvantage of the Mercator projection.
5. What is the purpose of lines of latitude and longitude on maps and globes?
6. Why did people set up a system of standard time zones?
7. **CRITICAL THINKING Analyzing Information** Why is it important to have accurate maps?

ACTIVITY Writing to Learn
Write five questions that can be answered by using the time zone map on page 12. For example, If it is 3 P.M. in Los Angeles where you live, what time will it be where your friend lives in Buenos Aires, Argentina? Trade questions with a partner and answer your partner's questions.

3. The American Land

FIND OUT
■ What landforms are found in North America and South America?
■ What are the seven physical regions of North America?
■ What rivers and lakes are important to the United States?

VOCABULARY isthmus, mountain, elevation, relief, hill, plain, plateau, tributary

"**A**merica is so vast," observed the writer James Farrell, "that almost anything said about it is likely to be true, and the opposite is probably equally true." The Americas are truly a land of opposites. For example, one of the world's highest mountains, Mount Aconcagua, is in Argentina. Yet one of the lowest points on the Earth is in Death Valley, California. You will find many examples of contrast as you read more about the American land.

Where Are the Americas?

North America and South America are the world's third and fourth largest continents. These two continents plus the islands in the Caribbean Sea are the major lands in the **Western Hemisphere.**

As the World map in the Reference Section shows, the Atlantic Ocean washes the eastern shores of North America and South America. The Pacific Ocean laps at their western shores. Far to the north lies the ice-choked Arctic Ocean. Far to the south is the Strait of Magellan (muh JEHL uhn), a water passage between the Atlantic and Pacific oceans. Joining the continents of North

Geographic Facts About the United States

Largest state, by area	Alaska	591,004 square miles
Smallest state, by area	Rhode Island	1,212 square miles
Largest state, by population (1990)	California	29,287,000
Smallest state, by population (1990)	Wyoming	468,000
Longest rivers	1. Mississippi 2. Missouri 3. Rio Grande	2,348 miles 2,315 miles 1,885 miles
Highest mountain	Mount McKinley (Alaska)	20,320 feet
Lowest point	Death Valley (California)	282 feet below sea level
Largest lake	Lake Superior*	31,820 square miles
Deepest lake	Crater Lake (Oregon)	1,932 feet
Rainiest spot	Mt. Waialeale (Hawaii)	460 inches rainfall per year
Highest recorded temperature	Death Valley (California)	134° Fahrenheit, on July 10, 1913

*Part of Lake Superior is located in Canada.

Sources: *Statistical Abstract of the United States;* National Geographic Society

CHART SKILLS *Everyone likes to know about extremes. What is the biggest? The smallest? The shortest? The longest? This chart shows some extremes in the geography of the United States.* • *What is the longest river? The highest mountain? What was the highest temperature recorded in the United States?*

America and South America is an **isthmus** (IHS muhs), or narrow strip of land. It is called the ***Isthmus of Panama.***

Types of Landforms

North America and South America have many landforms, or natural features. There are high mountains, rolling hills, and long rivers. There are grassy plains, dense forests, and barren deserts. Within these different landscapes are four basic landforms: mountains, hills, plains, and plateaus (pla TOHZ).

Mountains are high, steep, rugged land. They rise to an **elevation,** or height, of at least 1,000 feet (300 m) above the surrounding land. Few people can live on the steep, rocky sides of high mountains. Yet people often settle in valleys that lie between mountains.

Geographers call the difference in height of land **relief.** In maps in this book, relief is shown by gray shading. For example, see the gray shading indicating mountains and valleys on the map on page 19.

Hills are also areas of raised land, but they are lower, less steep, and more rounded than mountains. More people live in hilly areas than on mountains because farming is possible there.

Plains are broad areas of fairly level land. Very few plains are totally flat. Most are gently rolling. Plains do not usually rise much above sea level. People often settle

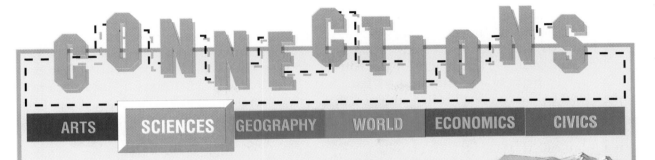

| ARTS | SCIENCES | GEOGRAPHY | WORLD | ECONOMICS | CIVICS |

How the Rocky Mountains Were Formed

When we look at the soaring Rocky Mountains today, it is hard to believe they were not always there. In fact, the Rockies are young mountains. They were first formed only about 63 million years ago — not a very long time in terms of the Earth's 4-billion-year history.

How were the Rockies formed? The answer can be found in a theory scientists call plate tectonics.

Scientists believe that the Earth's outer surface, or crust, is made up of a number of rigid plates. These plates are always moving. Some plates are moving toward each other. Some are moving apart. As they move, major changes occur on the Earth's surface.

About 63 million years ago, moving plates gave birth to the Rocky Mountains. Two huge plates — the North American plate and the Pacific plate — crashed head on into each other. In one great heave, the land rose up in jagged peaks. Over the next million or so years, other collisions caused the crust to crumple and push up more new mountains.

Collision of two plates

Today, the Rockies include some of the highest mountains in North America. But they are still growing and changing. In the next 50 million years, the tectonic plates will continue to move and grind and crash into each other. No one can predict for certain what the future size and shape of the Rocky Mountains will be.

■ How did plate movement form the Rocky Mountains?

ACTIVITY Form clay into two long rectangles and place them on a flat surface. Push the pieces of clay together. What happens to the clay? Use your model to explain how the Rocky Mountains were formed.

Peak in the Colorado Rockies

on plains because it is easy to build farms, roads, and cities on the level land.

Plateaus are large raised areas of flat or gently rolling land. The height of plateaus may range from a few hundred to many thousand feet above sea level. With enough rain, plateaus can be good for farming. Mountains surround some plateaus. Such plateaus are called basins. Basins are often very dry because the mountains cut off rainfall.

Mountains, hills, plains, and plateaus are only a few of the special words that geographers use to describe the Earth. For definitions of these and other geographic terms, you may refer to the Dictionary of Geographic Terms on pages 26–27.

North America From West to East

The mountains, hills, plateaus, and plains of North America form seven major physical regions. The United States also includes an eighth region, the Hawaiian Islands, which lies in the Pacific Ocean. (See the map on page 19.)

The seven physical regions of North America offer great contrasts. There are regions with fertile land where farmers reap rich harvests. Other regions have natural resources such as coal and oil. (☐ See "This Land Is Your Land" on page 538.)

Pacific Coast. Beginning in the West, the first of the seven physical regions is the Pacific Coast. It includes tall mountain ranges that stretch from Alaska to Mexico. In the United States, some of these western ranges hug the Pacific Ocean. The Cascades and Sierra Nevada* stand a bit farther inland. Some important cities of the Pacific Coast are Seattle, Portland, and San Francisco.

Intermountain region. East of the coast ranges is the Intermountain region. It is a rugged region of mountain peaks, plateaus, canyons, and deserts. The Grand Canyon, which is more than 1 mile (1.6 km) deep, and the Great Salt Lake are natural features of this region. Salt Lake City and Phoenix are among its few major cities. (☐ See "Why We Need Wilderness" on page 540.)

Rocky Mountains. The third region, the Rocky Mountains, reaches from Alaska through Canada into the United States. In Mexico, the Rocky Mountains become the Sierra Madre (MAH dray), or mother range.

The Rockies include some of the highest peaks in North America. Many peaks are more than 14,000 feet (4,200 m) high. Throughout history, people have described their grandeur. A gold prospector wrote:

66 No, partner—if you want to see scenery see the Rockies: that's something to look at! Even the sea's afraid of them mountains—ran away from them: you can see 4,000 feet up where the sea tried to climb before it got scared! 99

The Rockies were a serious barrier to European settlement of the United States. When settlers moved west in the 1800s, crossing the Rockies posed great hardships.

Interior Plains. Between the Rockies in the West and the Appalachians in the East is a large lowland area called the Interior Plains. The dry western part of the Interior Plains is called the Great Plains. The eastern part is called the Central Plains.

According to scientists, the Interior Plains were once covered by a great inland sea. Today, some parts are rich in coal and petroleum.* Other parts have fertile soil, making them rich farmlands. Chicago, St. Louis, and Dallas are in the Interior Plains.

Appalachian Mountains. The fifth region, the Appalachian Mountains, runs

---

*Sierra (see EHR uh) is the Spanish word for mountain range. Nevada is Spanish for snowy. Spanish explorers were the first Europeans to see these snow-covered mountains.

---

*The Natural Resources map in the Reference Section shows where natural resources are located.

MAP STUDY

The United States can be divided into eight physical regions.
1. Which region borders the Intermountain region on the west?
2. Through which physical region does the Missouri River flow?
3. **Drawing Conclusions** Based on the map, would you describe the United States as a varied land? Explain.

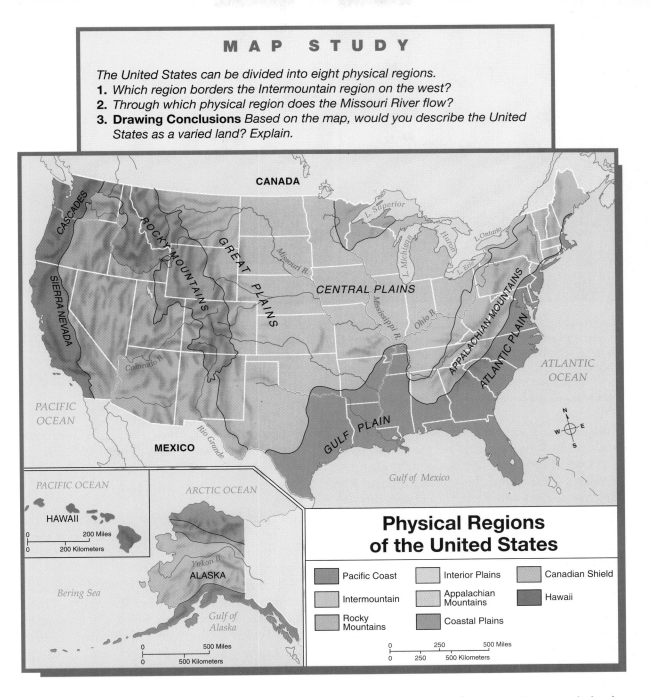

Physical Regions of the United States

■ Pacific Coast	■ Interior Plains	■ Canadian Shield
■ Intermountain	■ Appalachian Mountains	■ Hawaii
■ Rocky Mountains	■ Coastal Plains	

along the eastern part of North America. The Appalachians have different names in different places. For example, the Green Mountains, Alleghenies, Blue Ridge, and Great Smokies are all part of the Appalachian Mountains.

The Appalachians are lower and less rugged than the Rockies. The highest Appalachian peak is Mt. Mitchell in North Car-olina, which is 6,684 feet (2,037 m) high. Still, early European settlers had a hard time crossing these heavily forested mountains.

Canadian Shield. The sixth region is the Canadian Shield. It is a lowland area. Most of it lies in eastern Canada. The southern part extends into the United States. The region was once an area of high mountains. The mountains were worn away to low hills

Contrasting Coastlines *American coastlines offer great contrasts in mood and beauty. At right, the still waters of the Gulf Coast in Florida take on a golden glow in the light of sunset. At left, waves crash against rugged rocks along the Pacific Coast.* **Geography** *What other coastal area is found in mainland United States?*

and plains. The Canadian Shield lacks top-soil for farming, but it is rich in minerals.

Coastal Plains. The seventh region is a lowland area called the Coastal Plains. Part of this region, the Atlantic Plain, lies between the Atlantic Ocean and the foothills of the Appalachians. It was once under water and is now almost flat. The Atlantic Plain is narrow in the North, where Boston and New York City are located. It broadens in the South to include all of Florida.

Another part of the Coastal Plain is the Gulf Plain, which lies along the Gulf of Mexico. The Gulf Plain has large deposits of petroleum. New Orleans and Houston are major cities of the Gulf Plain.

Hawaiian Islands. The eighth physical region of the United States is made up of the Hawaiian Islands. They lie far out in the Pacific, about 2,400 miles (3,860 km) west of California. There are eight large islands and many small islands.

The islands are the tops of volcanoes that erupted through the floor of the Pacific Ocean. Some volcanoes are still active. Mau-na Loa on the island of Hawaii is an active volcano that rises 13,677 feet (4,169 m).

Rivers and Lakes

Great river systems crisscross North America. They collect the runoff from rains and melting snows and carry it into the oceans.

The mighty Mississippi. "What has four eyes and cannot see?" The Mississippi River, of course. You probably knew the answer to this favorite American riddle long before you knew the importance of the Mississippi to American geography and history.

The Mississippi and Missouri rivers make up the longest and most important river system in the United States. This river system flows through the Interior Plains into the Gulf of Mexico.

Many **tributaries,** or streams and smaller rivers, flow into the Mississippi-Missouri river system. Among these tributaries are the Ohio, Tennessee, Arkansas, and Platte rivers.

The Mississippi River carries moisture across the Interior Plains. It also serves as a means of transportation. Today, barges carry freight up and down the river. As in the past, people travel by boat on the river.

The mighty Mississippi has inspired many admiring descriptions. Among them is this one from the 1937 film *The River:*

66From as far west as Idaho,
　　Down from the glacier peaks of
　　　the Rockies—
　　From as far east as New York,
　　Down from the turkey ridges of
　　　the Alleghenies;
　　Down from Minnesota, twenty
　　　five hundred miles,
　　The Mississippi River runs to
　　　the Gulf.
　　Carrying every drop of water,
　　　that flows down two thirds
　　　of the continent,
　　Carrying every brook and rill,
　　　rivulet and creek,
　　Carrying all the rivers that run
　　　down two thirds the continent.
　　The Mississippi runs to the Gulf
　　　of Mexico.99

Borders between nations. The Rio Grande and the St. Lawrence River serve as political boundaries. They form parts of the borders between the United States and its neighbors, Mexico and Canada.

Five large lakes, called the **Great Lakes,** also form part of the border between the United States and Canada. The Great Lakes are Superior, Michigan, Huron, Erie, and Ontario. Today, canals connect the Great Lakes, forming a major inland waterway.

South American Landforms

Like North America, South America has a variety of landscapes. The Andes are a rugged mountain chain. They stretch along the western part of South America.

The tallest peaks of the Andes are much higher than those of the Rockies. The Andes plunge almost directly to the Pacific, leaving only a narrow coastal plain. Many people live in the high plateaus and valleys of the Andes.

To the east of the Andes is an interior plain. The plain is drained by three great river systems: the Orinoco, Amazon, and Paraguay-Paraná. The Amazon is the world's second longest river. It flows about 4,000 miles (6,500 km) from the Andes Mountains to the Atlantic Ocean.

SECTION 3 REVIEW

1. **Locate:** (a) North America, (b) South America, (c) Atlantic Ocean, (d) Pacific Ocean, (e) Sierra Nevada, (f) Rocky Mountains, (g) Interior Plains, (h) Appalachian Mountains, (i) Mississippi River.
2. **Identify:** (a) Western Hemisphere, (b) Isthmus of Panama, (c) Great Lakes.
3. **Define:** (a) isthmus, (b) mountain, (c) elevation, (d) relief, (e) hill, (f) plain, (g) plateau, (h) tributary.
4. (a) What are the eight physical regions of the United States? (b) Describe one feature of each.
5. Why are the Great Lakes important to the United States and Canada?
6. **CRITICAL THINKING Applying Information** What kinds of businesses might be likely to grow up along the Mississippi River?

ACTIVITY Writing to Learn
Write a poem about the American landscape.

Our Common Heritage
Native Americans who live on the slopes of the Andes Mountains have hearts as much as 20 times larger than the average. Their large hearts help them make the most of the limited oxygen at such high altitudes.

4
Climates of the Americas

FIND OUT
- What factors influence climate?
- What are the major climates of North America?
- What is the climate of South America like?

VOCABULARY weather, climate, precipitation, altitude

"**O**h, what a blamed uncertain thing
This pesky weather is;
It blew and snew and then it thew,
And now, by jing, it friz."

Those lines by the humorist Philander Johnson suggest our constant concern with weather. People worry about weather because it affects their lives. It affects jobs, leisure time activities, and the types of homes they build. Throughout history, people have adapted to different kinds of weather.

Factors That Affect Climate

Weather is the condition of the Earth's atmosphere at any given time and place. It may be hot or cold, rainy or dry, or something in between. **Climate** is the average weather of a place over a period of 20 to 30 years. Two main aspects of climate are temperature and **precipitation** (pree sihp uh TAY shuhn), or water that falls from the sky in the form of rain or snow.

Several factors affect climate. One factor is distance north or south from the Equator. Lands close to the Equator, such as Hawaii, usually are hot and wet all year. Lands near the North and South poles are cold all year.

A second factor that affects climate is **altitude,** or height above sea level. In general, highland areas are cooler than lowland areas.

Ocean currents, wind currents, and mountains also influence climate. When winds carrying moisture from the ocean strike the side of a mountain, the air rises and cools rapidly. As the air cools, it cannot hold as much moisture, and the water falls as rain or snow. Plenty of moisture falls on the side of the mountain closest to the body of water. The other side is usually quite dry because the winds have already dumped their moisture. The western sides of the Cascades, for example, get abundant precipitation, while the eastern slopes are dry.

North American Climates

Within North America, climate varies greatly. The United States has 10 major climates. Look at the map on page 23 and at the chart on page 25 to see where these climates are located and to learn about the conditions in each one.

Marine. The strip of land from southern Alaska to northern California is sometimes called the Pacific Northwest. This region has a mild, moist marine climate, with warm summers and cool winters. The Pacific Northwest has many forests that make it the center of a busy lumber industry.

Mediterranean. Most of California has a Mediterranean climate. Winters are mild and wet. Summers are hot and dry. In many areas, the soil is good, but plants need to be watered in the summer. Farmers and fruit growers must irrigate the land there.

Highland. In the Cascades, Sierra Nevada, and Rocky Mountains, a highland climate brings generally cooler temperatures. Exact conditions in a highland climate vary according to altitude. For example, Mount Rainier in the state of Washington, at over 14,000 feet (4,200 m) above sea level, is snow-capped all year.

Steppe. East of the Rockies are the Great Plains. They have a steppe climate with limited rainfall. Summers are hot and winters are cold. Huge herds of buffaloes once grazed on the short grasses of the Great Plains. In the 1800s, settlers brought cattle to graze on the plains. The popular song "Home on the Range" was set on the plains:

66 Oh, give me a home, where the buffalo roam,
Where the deer and the antelope play.
Where seldom is heard a discouraging word
And the skies are not cloudy all day. 99

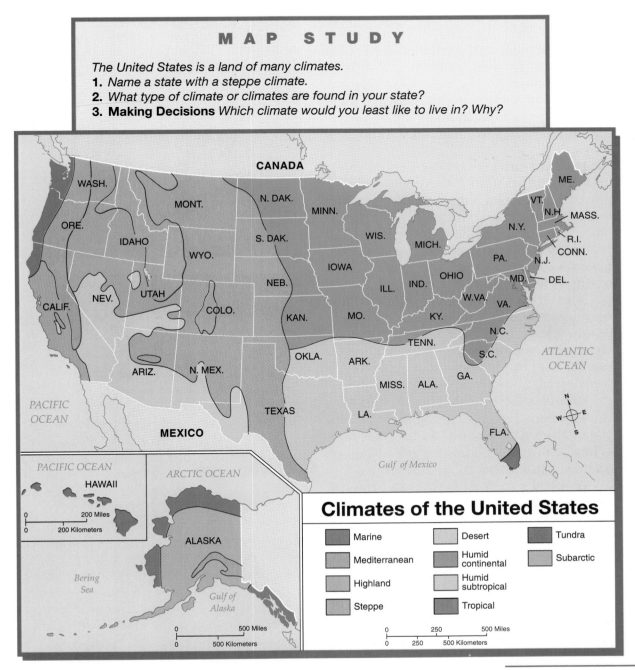

MAP STUDY

The United States is a land of many climates.
1. Name a state with a steppe climate.
2. What type of climate or climates are found in your state?
3. **Making Decisions** Which climate would you least like to live in? Why?

Climates of the United States

Marine
Mediterranean
Highland
Steppe
Desert
Humid continental
Humid subtropical
Tropical
Tundra
Subarctic

CANADA

WASH. · MONT. · N. DAK. · MINN. · ME. · VT. · N.H. · MASS. · N.Y. · ORE. · IDAHO · S. DAK. · WIS. · MICH. · R.I. · CONN. · WYO. · IOWA · PA. · N.J. · NEV. · UTAH · NEB. · ILL. · IND. · OHIO · MD. · DEL. · CALIF. · COLO. · KAN. · MO. · KY. · W.VA. · VA. · N.C. · TENN. · S.C. · ARIZ. · N. MEX. · OKLA. · ARK. · GA. · MISS. · ALA. · TEXAS · LA. · FLA.

ATLANTIC OCEAN

PACIFIC OCEAN

MEXICO

Gulf of Mexico

PACIFIC OCEAN · HAWAII

0 — 200 Miles
0 — 200 Kilometers

ARCTIC OCEAN

ALASKA

Bering Sea

Gulf of Alaska

0 — 500 Miles
0 — 500 Kilometers

0 — 250 — 500 Miles
0 — 250 — 500 Kilometers

Varied Climates *American climates vary a great deal, as these two photographs show. At top, huge sand dunes reflect the desert climate of California's Imperial Valley. At bottom, ice breaks up during the spring thaw in Alaska's tundra climate.* **Daily Life** *How have people adapted to desert and tundra climates?*

Desert. On the eastern side of the Cascades and Sierra Nevada, the land has a desert climate, with hot days and cold nights. This dry region stretches as far east as the Rockies. In the deserts of Nevada, Arizona, and southeastern California, there is almost no rainfall. In many areas, people irrigate the land so that they can grow crops.

Humid continental. The Central Plains and the northeastern United States have a humid continental climate. This climate, with mild summers and cold winters, has more precipitation than the steppe. Tall prairie grasses once covered the Central Plains. Today, American farmers raise much of the world's food in this region.

At one time, forests covered much of the northeastern United States. Early European settlers cleared the forests to build settlements and to grow crops. But many forests remain, and the lumber industry thrives in some areas.

Humid subtropical. The southeastern United States has a humid subtropical climate. Warm temperatures and regular rainfall make this region ideal for growing crops such as cotton, tobacco, and peanuts.

Tropical. Southern Florida and Hawaii, located near the Equator, have tropical climates. The hot, humid conditions make these regions good for growing such crops as pineapples and citrus fruits.

Tundra and subarctic. Northern and western coastal regions of Alaska have a tundra climate. It is cold all year round. The rest of Alaska and northern Canada have a

Climates of the United States

Climate	Weather
Marine	Mild, rainy
Mediterranean	Mild; wet winters; sunny, dry summers
Highland	Seasons and rainfall vary with elevation
Steppe	Very hot summers; very cold winters; little rainfall
Desert	Hot days; cold nights; very little rainfall
Humid continental	Mild summers; cold winters; rainfall varies
Humid subtropical	Humid summers; mild winters
Tropical	Hot, rainy, steamy
Tundra	Very cold winters; very short summers
Subarctic	Very short summers; long, cold winters

CHART SKILLS *This chart shows the weather conditions in each climate of the United States. Compare the chart with the map on page 23.*
● *Describe the weather for your state.*

subarctic climate with long, cold winters and short summers. Few people live in these harsh climates.

South American Climates

South America has many climates. Some of the world's driest deserts and largest rain forests are found in South America.

The huge area drained by the Amazon River is largely tropical rain forest. With warm temperatures and abundant rainfall all year round, the rain forest is rich in a wide variety of vegetation. Today, developers are cutting down the rain forest to make room for farms and to harvest the valuable wood of the forest trees. Destruction of the rain forest is causing concern throughout the world.

A dry climate is found along much of the Pacific coastal plain. Indeed, in the middle of the plain is the Atacama Desert, one of the driest deserts in the world. Winds blowing across the cold currents that flow off western South America drop moisture into the ocean. Only dry winds reach the land, and a desolate wasteland is created.

Large parts of Brazil have a savanna climate. These areas have a short rainy season when huge amounts of rain fall. The rainy season is followed by a long dry season with no precipitation. Other countries in South America—such as Argentina, Uruguay, and Chile—have climates similar to those in the United States.

SECTION 4 REVIEW

1. **Define:** (a) weather, (b) climate, (c) precipitation, (d) altitude.
2. Name two factors that affect climate.
3. (a) List the 10 major climates of the United States. (b) Name two United States climates that are suitable for growing crops.
4. Describe two climates of South America.
5. **CRITICAL THINKING Synthesizing Information** Why do you think climate is important to people's lives?

ACTIVITY **Writing to Learn**
Use the map on page 23 and the chart on page 25 to choose one type of climate. Then write a short story set in that climate. Be sure to show how the climate affects the events of your story.

DICTIONARY OF GEOGRAPHIC TERMS

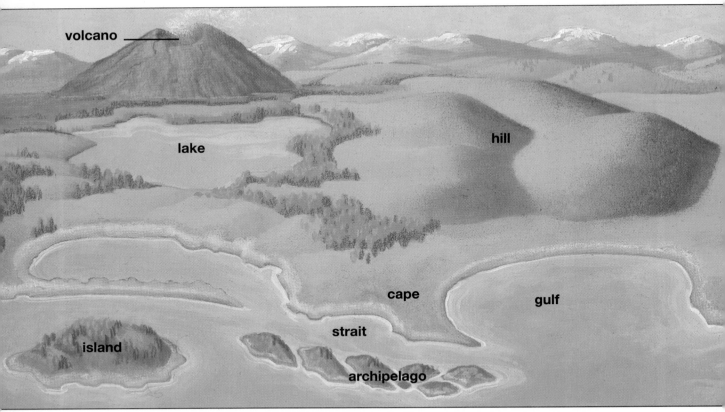

volcano _____

lake

hill

cape

gulf

strait

island

archipelago

The list below includes important geographic terms and their definitions. Sometimes, the definition of a term includes an example in parentheses. An asterisk (*) indicates that the term is illustrated above.

altitude height above sea level.
*archipelago chain of islands. (Hawaiian Islands)
basin low-lying land area that is surrounded by land of higher elevation; land area that is drained by a river system. (Great Basin)
*bay part of a body of water that is partly enclosed by land. (San Francisco Bay)
canal waterway made by people that is used to drain or irrigate land or to connect two bodies of water. (Erie Canal)
*canyon deep, narrow valley with high, steep sides. (Grand Canyon)

*cape narrow point of land that extends into a body of water. (Cape Canaveral)
climate pattern of weather in a particular place over a period of 20 to 30 years.
*coast land that borders the sea. (Pacific Coast)
coastal plain lowland area lying along the ocean. (Gulf Plain)
continent any of seven large landmasses on the Earth's surface. (Africa, Antarctica, Asia, Australia, Europe, North America, South America)
continental divide ridge along the Rocky Mountains that separates rivers that flow east from those that flow west.
*delta land area formed by soil that is deposited at the mouth of a river. (Mississippi Delta)
desert area that has little or no moisture or vegetation. (Painted Desert)

directional arrow arrow on a map that always points north.
downstream in the direction of a river's flow; toward a river's mouth.
elevation the height above sea level.
fall line place where rivers drop from a plateau or foothills to a coastal plain, usually marked by many waterfalls and rapids.
foothills low hills at the base of a mountain range.
*gulf arm of an ocean or sea that is partly enclosed by land, usually larger than a bay. (Gulf of Mexico)
hemisphere half of the Earth. (Western Hemisphere)
*hill area of raised land that is lower and more rounded than a mountain. (San Juan Hill)
*island land area that is surrounded by water. (Puerto Rico)
*isthmus narrow strip of land joining two large land areas or

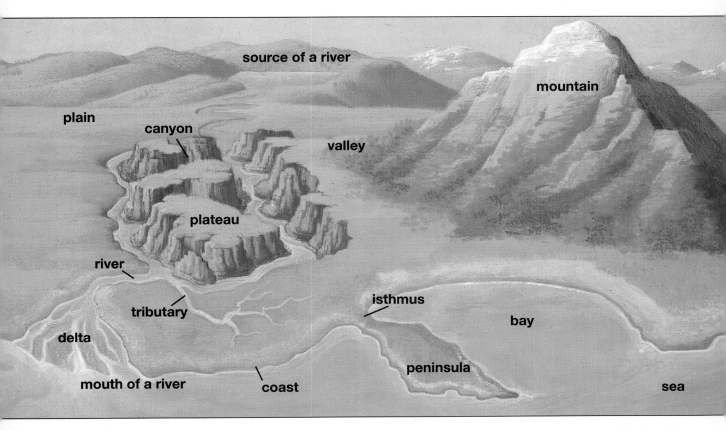

source of a river

mountain

plain

canyon

valley

plateau

river

isthmus

bay

tributary

delta

peninsula

mouth of a river

coast

sea

joining a peninsula to a main-land. (Isthmus of Panama)

lake body of water surrounded by land. (Lake Superior)

latitude the distance in degrees north and south from the Equator.

longitude distance in degrees east or west from the Prime Meridian.

marsh lowland with moist soils and tall grasses.

mountain high, steep, rugged land that rises sharply above the surrounding land. (Mount McKinley)

mountain range chain of connected mountains. (Allegheny Mountains)

mouth of a river place where a river or stream empties into a large body of water.

ocean any of the large bodies of salt water on the Earth's surface. (Arctic, Atlantic, Indian, and Pacific oceans)

peninsula piece of land that is surrounded by water on three sides. (Delmarva Peninsula)

piedmont area of rolling land along the base of a mountain range.

plain broad area of fairly level land that is generally close to sea level.

plateau large area of high, flat, or gently rolling land.

prairie large area of natural grassland with few or no trees or hills.

river large stream of water that empties into an ocean or lake or another river. (Pecos River)

sea large body of salt water that is smaller than an ocean. (Caribbean Sea)

sea level average level of the ocean's surface from which the height of land or depth of the ocean is measured.

source of a river place where a river begins.

steppe flat, treeless land with limited moisture.

strait narrow channel that connects two larger bodies of water. (Straits of Florida)

tributary stream or small river that flows into a larger stream or river.

upstream in the direction that is against a river's flow; toward a river's source.

valley land that lies between hills or mountains. (Shenandoah Valley)

volcano cone-shaped mountain formed by an outpouring of lava—hot, liquid rock—from a crack in the Earth's surface. (Mount St. Helens or Mauna Loa)

weather condition of the air at any given time and place.

Summary

- Five themes help geographers study the Earth and its people: location, place, interaction between people and their environment, movement, and region.
- Maps and globes are among the most useful tools of geography.
- The United States has varied landforms and includes eight physical regions.
- North America has varied climates, depending on factors such as distance from the Equator, altitude, wind and ocean currents, and mountains.

Reviewing the Main Ideas

1. (a) Which theme of geography focuses on where an event happened? (b) What do the human features of a place include?
2. (a) What are the advantages of globes? (b) Of maps?
3. How do people use latitude and longitude?
4. (a) What are the four basic landforms in North and South America? (b) Describe each landform.
5. (a) What are the two parts of the Coastal Plains? (b) Describe one part.
6. (a) What is the most important river system in the United States? (b) Why is this river system important?
7. Describe the weather in the following climates: (a) tropical, (b) tundra.

Thinking Critically

1. **Linking Past and Present** (a) What problems might have arisen before the introduction of standard time zones? (b) How do time zones affect your life today?
2. **Applying Information** (a) How does technology affect both interaction and movement? (b) Give one example of the effect of technology on movement.

3. **Asking Questions** What questions would you ask to learn about your state's physical geography?

Applying Your Skills

1. **Outlining** An outline helps you summarize facts. It includes a list of topics, subtopics, and facts. See the sample below to outline the third section of Chapter 1. To begin, write the main topic—the numbered title on page 15. Below the topic, write the first subtopic—the subsection on page 15. Under the subtopic, write at least two facts. Complete the outline for the third section of Chapter 1.
    I. The American Land (main topic)
        A. Where Are the Americas? (subtopic)
            1. Western Hemisphere
            2. Between Atlantic and Pacific oceans
2. **Comparing** When you compare two or more things, you need to look for ways they are similar and ways they are different. Compare Mercator projections with Robinson projections.

Thinking About Geography

Match the letters on the map with the following places: **1.** North America, **2.** South America, **3.** Atlantic Ocean, **4.** Pacific Ocean, **5.** Isthmus of Panama, **6.** Great Lakes. **Location** What ocean lies to the east of North and South America?

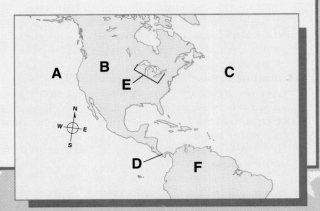

Exploring American Rivers

Form into groups to review rivers in the Americas. Follow the suggestions below to write, draw, sing, or play music to show what you have learned about rivers. You may use the textbook, encyclopedias, atlases, or other materials in your classroom library to complete the tasks. Be able to name your sources of information when you have finished the activity.

CARTOGRAPHERS On a large sheet of paper, create a map of the United States. On the map:
- Draw the 50 states of the United States.
- Draw and label the Mississippi, Missouri, Ohio, Rio Grande, and St. Lawrence rivers.
- Label the states through which each river passes.

MATHEMATICIANS Learn the length of these rivers: Amazon, Orinoco, Mississippi, Missouri, Ohio, Rio Grande, and St. Lawrence. Create a graph comparing their lengths.

ARTISTS Find out about a bridge or a dam located on the Mississippi, Missouri, Ohio, Rio Grande, or St. Lawrence rivers—or on a river near your community. Draw a picture or build a model of the bridge or dam. Be prepared to explain how it makes a difference to people who live in the area.

LANGUAGE EXPERTS Find out how these rivers got their names: Mississippi, Missouri, Ohio, Rio Grande, St. Lawrence. Display the information on a chart.

MUSICIANS Use the information in the chapter to list five facts about American rivers. Then write a song with a river theme, using a familiar tune or one that you have composed. Perform your song for the class.

★ Cut wavy edges along the top and bottom of a sheet of mural paper about 5 feet long. Post the completed activity from each group on the Exploring American Rivers mural.

"Flow Along River Tennessee"

"Across the Wide Missouri"

Missouri River

CHAPTER 2

The First Americans

(Prehistory–1600)

CHAPTER OUTLINE

1 Uncovering the American Past

2 The Peoples of North America

3 Early Civilizations of the Americas

4 After 1492

5000 years ago *People's lives changed when they learned to grow crops. These ears of corn were fashioned from bronze by an Incan metalworker.*

1200s *The peoples known as Mound Builders left records of their culture in large burial mounds. This copper warrior's head was dug up in Oklahoma.*

2000 years ago *The Mayas built a rich civilization in present-day Mexico and Guatemala. This vase shows an athlete playing a traditional Mayan ball game.*

PREHISTORY   1200   1300

WORLD EVENT
30,000–15,000 Years Ago
Hunters from Asia cross land
bridge to the Americas

WORLD EVENT
1200–1400 West
African kingdom of Mali
reaches its height

Chapter Setting

"In the beginning the earth was covered with water, and all living things were below in the underworld. . . . But now the earth was all dry, except for the four oceans and the lake in the center. . . .

All the people came up [from the underworld]. They traveled east until they arrived at the ocean. Then they turned south until they came again to the ocean. Then they went west to the ocean, and then they turned north. And as they went, each tribe stopped where it wanted to.

But the [Apaches] continued to circle around the hole where they had come up from the underworld. Three times they went around it. . . . [Their god] became displeased and asked them where they wished to stop. They said, 'In the middle of the earth.' So he led them to a place [in New Mexico]. . . . There . . . the [Apaches] made their home."

For countless generations, a group of Native Americans known as the Apaches have handed down this story. Some people think that the Apaches were describing the settlement of North America.

Today, we know that the first humans to enter North and South America slowly spread across the land, much as the Apache legend says. We know this because early peoples left behind a trail of evidence, such as earthen burial mounds, stone cities, and pottery. By studying these physical remains, scientists are piecing together the story of the first Americans.

ACTIVITY

Imagine that you arrive in the United States in the year 3000 and find the following items dating from the 1990s: chicken bone, paper with writing on it, TV set, computer, guitar. Discuss what these items would tell you about American life in the 1990s.

1300s *The Aztecs built an empire in Mexico. This drawing celebrates the founding of the Aztec capital.*

1400s *The Incan empire arose in present-day Peru. Skilled artists made ceramic vases such as this one.*

1570s *Peoples of the Eastern Woodlands formed the Iroquois League to promote peace and cooperation.*

1300	1400	1500	1600

WORLD EVENT
1300s Europeans seek trade with Asia

WORLD EVENT
1492 Columbus reaches the Americas

Uncovering the American Past

FIND OUT

- How did people first reach the Americas?
- How do archaeologists learn about the past?
- Who were the Mound Builders?
- How did early peoples in the Southwest adapt to the desert?

VOCABULARY glacier, artifact, archaeology, culture, adobe, pueblo, drought

Crouched low, the small band of hunters crept slowly forward. Ahead, a herd of bison grazed at the edge of a swamp. At a signal, the hunters leaped up, shouting loudly. The startled herd stampeded into the swamp. As the bison struggled in the deep mud, the hunters hurled their spears, bringing down many beasts.

Scenes much like this one took place on the Great Plains more than 10,000 years ago. Skillful hunters were among the first people to settle the Americas. Over many thousands of years, their descendants spread out across two continents. In the process, they developed many different ways of life.

Woolly Mammoth Skeleton *Some 12,000 years ago, hunters of the Clovis culture stalked mammoth across what is now the southwestern United States. Archaeologists have found many Clovis spearheads mixed in with mammoth bones in Arizona.* **Science and Technology** *Why would it be important for early hunters to develop spears and arrows?*

The First Americans

Like other early peoples, the first Americans left no written records to tell us where they came from or exactly when they arrived in the Western Hemisphere. However, scientists have found evidence that suggests the first people reached the Americas sometime during the last ice age.

The land bridge. Between 100,000 and 10,000 years ago, thick sheets of ice, called glaciers, often covered much of the Earth. Because glaciers locked up water from the oceans, sea levels fell. As a result, land appeared that had once been covered by water. In the far north, a land bridge, now known as *Beringia,* joined Siberia in northeastern Asia to Alaska in North America. Today, this land is under the Bering Strait.

Scientists think that the first Americans were probably hunters. Traveling in small bands, they followed herds of woolly mam-

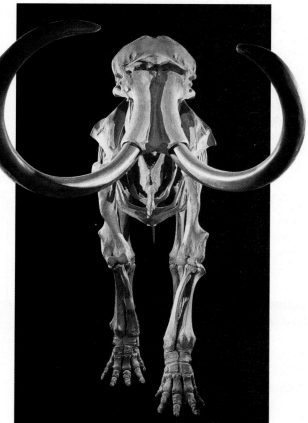

moth, bison, and other game across Beringia from Asia into North America. Some groups may have wandered along the southern coast of Beringia, catching fish and sea mammals.

Experts date the arrival of these first Americans anywhere from 30,000 to 15,000 years ago. Once they reached the Americas, the constant search for better hunting grounds led the newcomers across the land. Over thousands of years, they spread out through North America, Central America, and South America.

Global warming. About 12,000 years ago, temperatures rose around the globe. Glaciers melted, and water once more covered Beringia. At the same time, the woolly mammoths and mastodons died out.

The peoples of the Americas adapted to the new conditions. They hunted smaller game, gathered berries and grains, and caught fish.

Then, about 5,000 years ago, some people learned to grow crops such as corn, beans, and squash. Farming changed those people's lives. People who farmed no longer had to move constantly to find food. They built the first permanent villages in the Americas. As farming methods improved, villagers produced more food that, in turn, allowed populations to grow.

The Study of Early Peoples

Today, experts in many fields are working to develop a clearer picture of the first Americans. Some are studying the remains of ancient peoples of northeast Asia. They hope to learn how these Asian peoples might be related to the first Americans.

Other experts are analyzing the languages of Native Americans living today. *Native Americans* are descendants of the first people to reach the Americas thousands of years ago. Through the study of languages, scholars are trying to trace how these peoples spread out across the Americas.

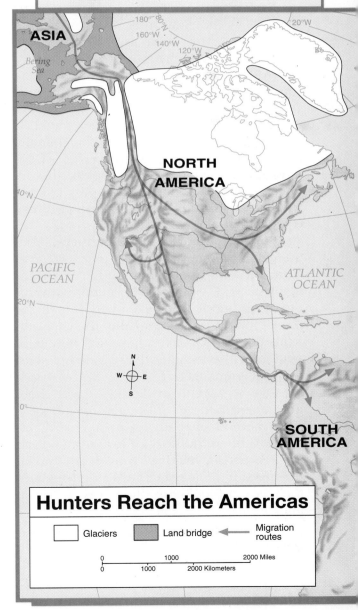

M A P   S T U D Y

The first Americans crossed into Alaska from Asia anywhere from 70,000 to 15,000 years ago. Over thousands of years, these hunters and their descendants populated two huge continents, North America and South America.

1. About how many miles did glaciers stretch from north to south?
2. In which direction did early hunters travel to reach North America?
3. **Drawing Conclusions** Why do you think many of the first Americans continued to travel southward after crossing the land bridge?

Hunters Reach the Americas

☐ Glaciers   ▨ Land bridge   ← Migration routes

0   1000   2000 Miles
0 1000   2000 Kilometers

Still other scholars are examining stone tools, weapons, baskets, and carvings found throughout the Americas. These objects made by humans are called **artifacts** (AHRT uh faktz). They are the building blocks of **archaeology** (ahr kee AHL uh jee), the study of evidence left by early peoples.

Studying the evidence. By studying artifacts, archaeologists can learn much about early people. A finely carved arrowhead suggests that people knew how to make weapons and hunt. Woven plant fibers suggest that they were skilled basket makers.

Each object can provide valuable information. At the same time, each new find raises questions, such as, "When was it made?" and "Who made it?"

In laboratories, experts analyze new finds. By testing the level of carbon in a piece of pottery or bone, they can date it within a few hundred years. They might X-ray a bone to learn more about the animal it came from. They might study kernels of ancient corn through a microscope to discover the climate in which it grew. By piecing together a shattered pot, they can compare it to pots from other areas.

Forming theories about cultures. From artifacts and other evidence, archaeologists form theories about the culture of an ancient people. **Culture** is the entire way of life that a people has developed. It includes the behavior, customs, ideas, beliefs, and skills that a people teaches each new generation. It also includes their homes, clothes, and government.

Often, very little evidence survives about an ancient people. Still, each new find or new method of studying ancient artifacts helps to fill in the story of early Americans.

Protecting Native American burial grounds. In their search for evidence about the past, archaeologists often need to dig up ancient sites. In recent years, however, they have grown more aware of the need to respect Native American landmarks and traditions. Government officials, too, have become more respectful of Native American concerns. Some laws have been passed to protect Native American burial grounds.

The Mound Builders

Archaeologists have found a wealth of artifacts in thousands of earthen mounds in North America. The mounds are scattered across a region stretching from the Appalachian Mountains to the Mississippi Valley and from Wisconsin to Florida. Scholars call the peoples who built these earthworks *Mound Builders.* The Mound Builders belonged to various groups who lived from about 3,000 years ago until the 1700s. Among them were the Hopewell and Mississippian peoples.

Purpose of the mounds. The first mounds were burial grounds, probably for important leaders. Inside the mounds, archaeologists have found carved pipes and stone sculptures as well as copper weapons, tools, and ornaments. They have also found shells from the Gulf of Mexico and turquoise from the Southwest. This evidence shows that the Mound Builders traded with peoples from other parts of North America.

Some mounds were used for religious ceremonies. They are shaped like pyramids with flat tops. On the flat surfaces, the people built temples and homes for the ruling class.

More than 2,000 years ago, Hopewell builders created the twisting Great Serpent Mound. From above, it looks like a snake with a coiled tail. The meaning of this and other animal-shaped mounds remains a mystery.

A sprawling city. Some time between 700 and 1500, the Mississippians built a large city at Cahokia (kah HOH kee ah), in present-day Illinois. As many as 30,000 people may have lived there. Over the years, the people of Cahokia moved tons of soil, basket load by basket load, to build Monk's Mound. This vast platform mound covers

Burial Mounds *The Mound Builders left behind thousands of mounds. The Great Serpent Mound of Ohio, at right, twists across the land for more than 1,200 feet. The painting above shows workers excavating a much smaller, but higher, Mississippian burial mound.* **Linking Past and Present** *Why do you think archaeologists are eager to examine early burial mounds?*

about 16 acres—equal to $14\frac{1}{2}$ football fields! Hundreds of other smaller mounds stand nearby.

The Mississippians built a wooden fence around Cahokia. Beyond it, they placed circles of evenly spaced posts. Some archaeologists think the posts served as a kind of calendar. From the top of Monk's Mound, rulers could see the shadows cast by the posts. Shorter shadows announced the coming of spring. Longer ones showed that autumn was near. To farming people like the Mississippians, knowing when to plant and when to harvest crops was important.

Early Cultures of the Southwest

Through careful study, archaeologists have also learned much about early peoples of the American Southwest. This desert region may seem like a poor place to farm. Annual rainfall is only 5 to 10 inches (13 to 25 cm). Daytime temperatures can soar above 100° Fahrenheit (38°C). Cactus and sagebrush cover the desert floor. Still, at

least 3,000 years ago, people in the Southwest learned to grow crops such as corn. In time, several major farming societies, including the ***Hohokams*** (hoh HOH kahmz) and ***Anasazis*** (ah nuh SAH zeez), made their homes there.

The Hohokams lived in present-day southern Arizona. About 2,000 years ago, they developed ways to turn the desert into farmland. They dug a vast system of irrigation ditches. The ditches channeled water from the Salt and Gila rivers into fields that produced corn, squash, and beans.

In the late 1800s, archaeologists began to study thousands of abandoned stone buildings that dotted the Southwest. Most were built between 750 and 1300.

Who built these structures? When archaeologists asked the Navajos, the Native Americans who live in the region today, they replied, the Anasazis. In the Navajo language, Anasazi means "ancient one."

Anasazi pueblos. Like the Hohokams, the Anasazis farmed the desert by using irrigation. The Anasazis built large, multistoried houses. Walls were made of stone and sun-dried bricks, called adobe. When the Spanish explored the Southwest in the early 1500s, they called these houses that could shelter hundreds of families pueblos (PWEHB lohz), or villages.

At Pueblo Bonito, in New Mexico, a giant house, much like a modern-day apartment complex, was once home to 1,000 people. Its 800 rooms are tiny, but the Anasazis spent much of their time in sunny, outdoor courtyards. The house has no stairways or hallways. To reach rooms on the upper floors, people climbed ladders.

Cliff dwellers. Between 1000 and 1200, some Anasazis sought protection from warlike neighbors. To make their villages harder to attack, they built adobe houses along the faces of cliffs. Toeholds cut into the rock let the Anasazis climb up and down the cliff wall. On top of the cliff, they planted corn and other crops.

A network of roads connected Anasazi villages. Along these roads, traders carried cotton, sandals made from yucca leaves, and blankets woven from turkey feathers. Some Anasazi traders headed into present-day Mexico to trade with people there.

In the late 1200s, the Anasazis abandoned most of their villages. Archaeologists think that a drought, or long dry spell, hit the region. One legend recalls such a disaster:

> "Snow ceased in the north and the west; rain ceased in the south and the east; the mists of the mountains above were drunk up; the waters of the valleys below were dried up. . . . Our ancients who dwelt in the cliffs fled . . . when the rain stopped long, long ago."

Later, some Anasazis may have returned to their homes. Most, however, became part of other cultures. Today, descendants of these early peoples preserve traditions of the ancient Anasazi culture.

Achievements of the Anasazis *Anasazi craftsworkers made fine objects of shell, bone, turquoise, and clay. These highly decorated mugs were found in the ruins of Pueblo Bonito, below.* **Geography** *Why do you think many early peoples made objects of clay?*

SECTION 1 REVIEW

1. **Identify:** (a) Beringia, (b) Native Americans, (c) Mound Builders, (d) Hohokams, (e) Anasazis
2. **Define:** (a) glacier, (b) artifact, (c) archaeology, (d) culture, (e) adobe, (f) pueblo, (g) drought.
3. Describe three kinds of evidence that archaeologists study.
4. What have archaeologists learned about the Mound Builders?
5. How did the Hohokams farm the desert?
6. **CRITICAL THINKING Formulating Questions** Suppose that you are an archaeologist studying an Anasazi ruin. What questions might you ask about Anasazi houses?

ACTIVITY **Writing to Learn**

Imagine that you are a television reporter. Write three questions you would ask the first people who traveled from Asia to the Americas.

2

The Peoples of North America

FIND OUT

- What are 10 major culture areas of North America?
- How did Native Americans adapt to different environments?
- How were religious beliefs important to people's daily lives?

VOCABULARY culture area, igloo, kayak, potlatch, kiva, hogan, tepee, travois, long house, sachem

When Christopher Columbus reached the Americas in 1492, he thought he had reached the East Indies. He called the peo-ple he met "los Indios," or Indians. Soon, all Europeans were calling the people of the Americas Indians. By the time they realized their error, they were used to the term.

The name Indian is misleading for another reason, too. Native Americans do not belong to a single group. In Columbus's time, as now, Native Americans included many different peoples with many distinct cultures. In North America alone, Native Americans spoke hundreds of languages. Their cultures also varied in other ways.

Culture Areas and Tribes

The map on page 42 shows 10 major culture areas of North America, north of Mexico. A **culture area** is a region in which people share a similar way of life.

Within each culture area, there were many different tribes. A tribe was a group of villages or settlements that shared common customs, language, and rituals. Members of a tribe saw themselves as a distinct people who shared the same origin. Throughout their history, tribal organizations have played an important role in Indian life.

Tribe members felt a strong bond with the land, plants, and animals in the region where they lived. As they hunted animals or raised crops or gathered wild plants for food, members of the tribe tried to maintain a balance with the forces of the natural world. Their religious ceremonies and daily customs were designed to help them maintain that balance. (See "'I'm Indian and That's It'" on page 542.)

Peoples of the North

Two culture areas, the Arctic and Subarctic, stretched across the northern part of North America. In both regions, people adapted to harsh climates. In the Arctic, winter temperatures drop to –30° Fahrenheit (–34° C). Snow stays on the ground much of the year.

Arctic. Frozen seas and icy, treeless plains made up the world of the *Inuits,* the people of the Arctic.* The Inuits used all the limited resources of their environment. In summer, they collected driftwood from the ocean shores to make tools and shelters. In winter, they built **igloos,** or houses of snow and ice.

Because food was scarce, the Inuits could not live in the same place all year round. In winter, large bands set up camp at a favorite spot near the sea. There on the thick sea ice, they hunted for seals. In spring, they paddled **kayaks** (KĪ aks), or small skin boats, to spear seal, whale, and walrus. When summer came, they moved inland in smaller bands to hunt caribou or to fish on inland rivers and lakes.

Inuit religious beliefs reflected their close ties to the natural world. Inuits believed that each animal had a spirit. Before the hunt, they offered gifts to the animal they hoped to catch. After a successful hunt, they sang songs of praise and thanks to the animals.

Subarctic. Like their northern neighbors, the peoples of the Subarctic faced a severe environment. They, too, moved from place to place, hunting moose and caribou or fishing in rivers and oceans. They fashioned caribou and rabbit skins into robes and leggings. When Europeans arrived, many Subarctic peoples supplied furs to traders.

Peoples of the Northwest Coast

The peoples of the Northwest Coast enjoyed a favorable climate and abundant food supplies. They gathered rich harvests of fish from the sea. In autumn, the rivers were full of salmon. To show their gratitude, the people returned salmon skeletons to the water. They believed that the Salmon Beings would grow new bodies and continue to provide food.

The fishers of one Northwest Coast group, the Kwakiutls (kwah kee OOT 'lz), chanted this prayer when they caught their first fish of the year:

66We have come to meet alive, Swimmer,
do not feel wrong about what I have done to you,
friend Swimmer,
for that is the reason why you came,
that I may spear you,
that I may eat you,
Supernatural One, you, Long- Life-Giver, you Swimmer.
Now protect us, me and my wife. 99

---

*Inuit, meaning "humans," was the Arctic people's name for themselves. Neighboring people, the Crees, called the Inuits "Eskimos" or "Eaters of Raw Meat."

Basket From the Subarctic *Subarctic hunters moved across the land in search of food and furs. The decorations on this basket show some of the animals they hunted.* **The Arts** *Why do you think that animals such as bear and caribou were a popular subject of Subarctic craftsworkers?*

Mask of a Storyteller *The Kwakiutl people of the Northwest Coast used colorful masks in storytelling ceremonies. This bird's-head mask has a hinged beak. At the climax of the ceremony, the storyteller would throw open the beak to reveal the fiercely decorated human face underneath.* **Geography** *How did favorable geography allow people of the Northwest Coast to develop elaborate arts and ceremonies?*

The Northwest Coast peoples also benefited from the nearby forests. They cut down majestic cedar trees and floated the timber by water to their villages. There, they split the tree trunks into planks for houses and canoes. From the soft inner bark, they made rope, baskets, and clothes. The forests also were home to deer, moose, and bear that the people hunted for meat and hides.

With plenty of food, the peoples of the Pacific Northwest could stay in one place. They built permanent villages and prospered from trade with nearby groups.

Within a village, families gained status according to how much they owned. Families sometimes competed for rank. To improve their standing, they held a potlatch, or ceremonial dinner, to show off their wealth. The family invited many guests and gave everyone presents. The more the family gave away, the more it was respected. At one potlatch, which took years for the family to prepare, gifts included 8 canoes, 54 elk skins, 2,000 silver bracelets, 7,000 brass bracelets, and 33,000 blankets!

Other Peoples of the West

Climates and resources varied in other parts of the West. As people adapted to these environments, they developed very different cultures.

Great Basin. The Great Basin lies in the dry Intermountain region of the United States. With little water, few plants or animals survived. As a result, Great Basin peoples like the Utes (YOOTZ) and Shoshones (shoh SHOH neez) had to spend most of their time looking for food. They hunted rabbits or dug for roots in the desert soil.

Because the land offered so little, only a few related families traveled together in search of food. They had few possessions beyond digging sticks, baskets, and other tools or weapons needed to hunt. When they camped, they built shelters out of willow poles and reeds.

Plateau. The peoples of the Plateau lived between the Rocky Mountains to the east and the Cascades to the west. Their main source of food was fish from rivers like the Columbia and Fraser or from smaller streams. They also hunted and gathered roots, nuts, and berries. In winter, they lived in earth houses that were partly underground. In summer, they set up lodges, placing rush mats over cottonwood frames.

Some groups traded with the Northwest Coast peoples and were influenced by their way of life. Others, like the Nez Percés (NEHZ PER sihz), adopted customs from the peoples of the Great Plains.

California. Differences in climate and resources helped create diverse cultures in California. Coastal peoples fished in the ocean and rivers. In the northern valleys, other groups hunted deer, rabbits, and elk or collected berries and nuts. In the southeast desert, however, small bands lived much like the peoples of the Great Basin.

For many Californians, like the Pomos, acorns were the basic food. Women harvested the nuts in autumn and later pounded them into flour. Both women and men among the Pomos were skilled at weaving baskets, which they decorated with fine designs.

Peoples of the Southwest

The **Pueblos,** the Spanish name for peoples of the Southwest, were descended from the Anasazis. They included groups like the Hopis, Acomas, Zuñis, and Lagunas. By 1500, only the Hopis still farmed on clifftops as the Anasazis had done. Other groups lived in villages along the Rio Grande and its tributaries.

Farming, religion, and family life. Like their ancestors, the Pueblos built adobe houses and grew corn, beans, and squash. Their religious beliefs reflected the importance of farming. Most Pueblo villages had a kiva, or underground chamber where men held religious ceremonies. Through prayers and other rituals, they tried to please the spirits of nature, such as wind, rain, and thunder.

At planting or harvest time, the Hopis and Zuñis held other ceremonies. In the villages, cries rang out: "The kachinas are coming! The kachinas are coming!" The *kachinas* were masked dancers who represented the spirits. The Pueblos believed that the kachina ceremonies would ensure rainfall and good crops.

The Pueblos traced their family lines through the mother. This custom gave women special importance. When a man married, he went to live with his wife's family. Also, Pueblo wives owned most of the family property.

Hunters arrive. About 1500, two new groups reached the Southwest: the Apaches and the Navajos. Both groups lived as hunters but often raided Pueblo fields for food.

In time, the Navajos accepted many Pueblo ways. They began to farm and to build hogans, or houses made of mud plaster over a framework of wooden poles. The Apaches, however, continued to follow herds of buffalo and the other game they hunted. They traded dried buffalo meat and animal skins to the Pueblos for corn and cloth.

Peoples of the Great Plains

Centuries ago, vast grasslands extended across the Great Plains from the Rocky Mountains to the Mississippi River. As artist George Catlin observed in the early 1800s, "The meadows roll on for as far as the eye can see and thought can travel."

ART GALLERY: OUR COMMON HERITAGE

• RAYMOND NAHA *Mixed Kachina Dance, 1964* •

Each June, the Hopi people of the Southwest gathered for the dance of the kachinas. The kachinas, masked dancers representing the spirits, performed the ancient ritual. If the dance was pleasing, the spirits would return as rain for the next season's crops. Raymond Naha, a modern Hopi painter, recreated this part of his Hopi heritage in his painting.
Linking Past and Present *How does Naha's painting help to preserve Hopi culture?*

Because there were few trees, Plains people built their homes of sod, or chunks of thickly matted grass. They also used buffalo hides to make cone-shaped tents called **tepees.**

Some Plains people farmed along riverbanks. In spring, women broke up the soft ground using hoes made from animal bones. They then planted corn, beans, squash, and sunflowers.

Large herds of animals grazed on the Plains, including buffalo, antelope, elk, deer, and bighorn sheep. Plains people hunted the animals on foot. In winter, men hunted near the village. In summer, however, they often traveled for miles in search of buffalo and other animals.

Each village had a ruling council that included the best hunters. The chief was respected by other council members because he spoke well and judged wisely.

Horses Come to the Plains

Until the 1500s, the peoples of North America had no horses. The only species of horse on the North

MAP STUDY

Historians estimate that by 1400, as many as 2 million Native Americans lived in North America north of Mexico. Historians group the Native Americans into major culture areas.

1. Name two groups that lived in the Southeast culture area.
2. About how many miles north to south did the Great Plains culture area extend?
3. **Analyzing Information** In which culture areas could Native Americans probably depend on the sea for food? Explain.

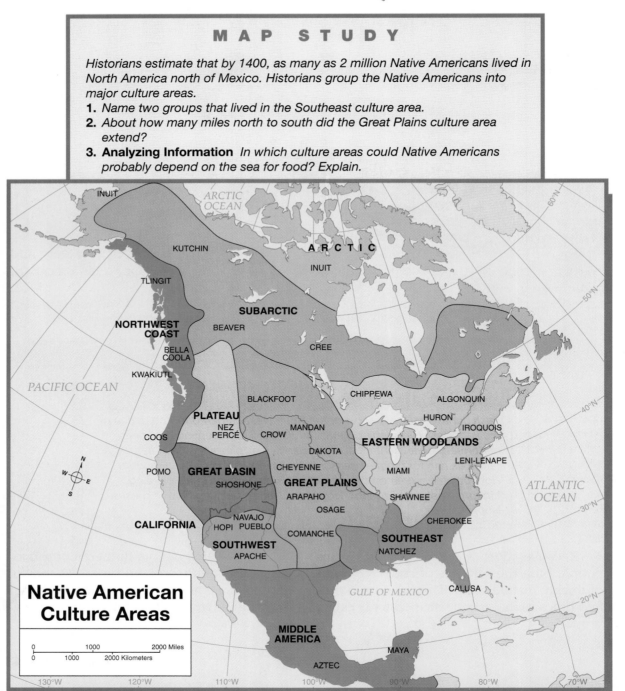

Native American Culture Areas

```
0          1000              2000 Miles
0     1000          2000 Kilometers
```

American continent had died out thousands of years earlier. The Blackfeet, one group of Plains people, tell a story about how horses came to their land.

The Blackfoot story. Shaved Head was leading a band of Blackfeet in search of some Shoshone people. The Shoshones were hunting buffalo in Blackfoot territory. Shaved Head intended to stop them.

Before long, the Blackfeet came upon a Shoshone camp. There, they saw what to them looked like very large dogs. Blackfeet used dogs to haul skin lodges, cooking pots, and other gear on a travois (truh VOI), or sled. These "dogs" were different though. They were as tall as men and as broad as elk.

As the Blackfeet watched in awe, a band of Shoshones rode into camp on yet more of these dogs. With great ease, the riders halted the animals and slid off their backs. They removed pads of buffalo skin from the animals' backs and straps from their heads. Then they tied the animals to a post.

Shaved Head and his men decided to take these creatures to their people. Late at night, they slipped into the Shoshone camp, untied four horses, and led them away.

At a safe distance, a few Blackfeet mounted the animals. When the horses began to move, though, the men became frightened and jumped off. It would be easier, they decided, to lead the animals instead.

The Blackfeet long remembered the return of Shaved Head and his band:

66 When the people heard that Shaved Head had brought back a pack of 'big dogs,' they gathered around the strange animals and looked at them in wonder. They put robes on the horses, but when the animals began to jump, they ran. After a time a woman said, 'Let's put a travois on one of them just like we do on our small dogs.' They made a larger travois and attached it to one of the gentler horses. It didn't kick or jump. They led the horse around with the travois attached. Finally, a woman mounted the horse and rode it. 99

A new way of life. The Blackfeet handed down this story for generations. Although the details may not be exact, historians know that horses reached the northern

Warriors on Horseback *The use of horses transformed the way Plains people lived. They became better hunters and so raised fewer crops. Horses also changed the way Plains people waged war. Here, rival warriors on horseback engage in fierce battle on the Plains.* **Science and Technology** *What advantages would horses give to warriors in battle?*

Plains in the mid-1700s. The Spanish had brought horses to the Southwest 200 years earlier. From there, horses had spread to other areas.

In time, Plains people became skillful riders. Because they could travel farther and faster than before, they raised fewer crops and hunted more. They made larger tepees because horses could pull bigger travois. Slowly, horses transformed the Plains peoples' way of life. ■

Peoples of the Southeast

The Southeast was home to more Native Americans than any other region. A warm climate, fertile soil, and plentiful rain helped Southeast peoples produce good crops.

Most people lived in villages and farmed nearby land. They built houses from saplings, or young trees. They split the trees into strips and wove them to make a frame for walls. Then they plastered the walls with a mixture of clay and dry grass.

Farming and religion. Men and women had clearly defined roles in the community. Men cleared the land and hunted deer and other animals. Women planted, weeded, and harvested the crops. Among rows of corn, they planted beans that climbed up the cornstalks. They also grew squash, pumpkins, and sunflowers.

Most religious ceremonies were linked to farming. The most important, the Green Corn Ceremony, took place in midsummer, when the corn ripened. It marked the end of the year. Celebrations lasted several days. The highlight, on the last day, was the lighting of the sacred fire followed by a dance around its flames. With this event, the new year began.

Natchez society. One Southeast group, the **Natchez** (NACH ihz), hunted, fished, and farmed along the fertile Gulf Coast. They divided the year into 13 months. Each month was named after a food or animal the Natchez harvested or hunted. Names included Strawberry, Little Corn, Mulberry, Deer, Turkey, and Bear.

Natchez religious beliefs centered on worship of the sun. Priests kept a fire going day and night in a temple atop a great mound. The Natchez believed that fire came from the sun.

The Natchez ruler, the Great Sun, was worshipped as a god. He lived atop a giant pyramid mound. The Great Sun's feet never touched the ground. He either rode in a litter or walked on mats. Below the Great Sun were other members of his family, called Little Suns. Next came Nobles, then Honored People, and finally Stinkards, or commoners, who were the majority of the people.

Marriage laws ensured that membership in each class kept changing. By law, noble men and women had to marry Stinkards. Even the Great Sun chose a Stinkard as a wife. In this way, no one family could hold the position of Great Sun forever. In time, even descendants of a Great Sun became Stinkards.

Peoples of the Eastern Woodlands

Many groups lived in the Eastern Woodlands. In the forests and open lands, they hunted deer, moose, and other game. They also planted crops of corn, squash, and pumpkins.

The House Builders. The most powerful people of this region were the **Iroquois**

Our Common Heritage
The peoples of the Southeast played a game called istaboli, an early form of lacrosse. The object of the game was to heave a skin-covered ball into the opposing team's goal. Hitting, kicking, and tackling were permitted. To annoy their opponents, a team would make gobbling sounds like a turkey.

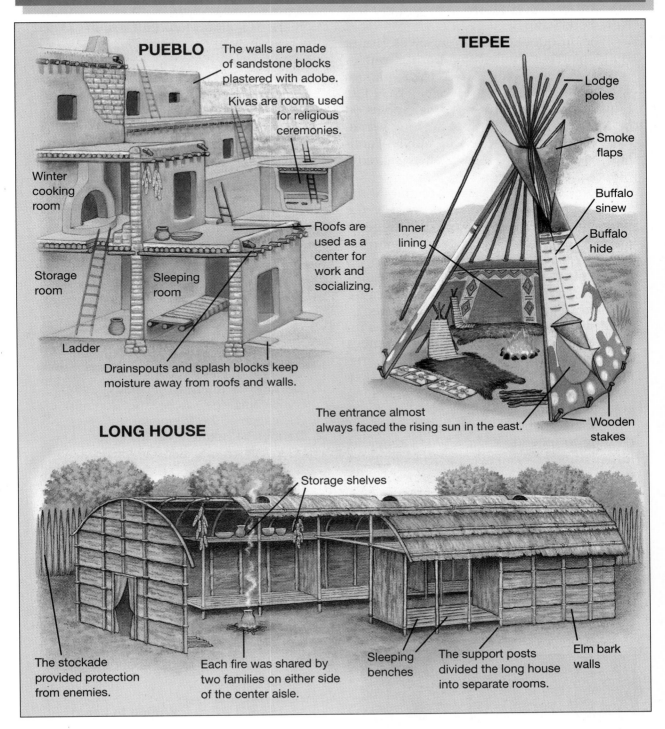

PUEBLO

The walls are made of sandstone blocks plastered with adobe.

Kivas are rooms used for religious ceremonies.

Winter cooking room

Storage room

Sleeping room

Roofs are used as a center for work and socializing.

Ladder

Drainspouts and splash blocks keep moisture away from roofs and walls.

TEPEE

Lodge poles

Smoke flaps

Buffalo sinew

Buffalo hide

Inner lining

The entrance almost always faced the rising sun in the east.

Wooden stakes

LONG HOUSE

Storage shelves

The stockade provided protection from enemies.

Each fire was shared by two families on either side of the center aisle.

Sleeping benches

The support posts divided the long house into separate rooms.

Elm bark walls

Native American Dwellings *Native Americans developed a wide variety of dwellings to suit their different environments. Shown here are a pueblo from the Southwest, a tepee from the Great Plains, and a long house from the Eastern Woodlands.*
Geography *How does each type of dwelling reflect the local environment?*

(IHR uh kwoi). They lived in present-day New York State.

The Iroquois called themselves House Builders. They built **long houses** out of poles sided with bark. A typical long house was about 150 feet (46 m) long and 20 feet (7 m) wide. A hallway, with small rooms on either side, ran the length of the long house. Each room was home to one family. Families living across from each other shared a fireplace in the hallway.

Women had a special place among the Iroquois. They owned all the property in the long house. Also, they were in charge of planting and harvesting crops. Like a Pueblo man, an Iroquois man moved in with his wife's family when he married. Iroquois women also held political power because they chose the **sachems,** or tribal chiefs.

Peace among nations. The Iroquois included five nations: the Mohawk, Seneca (SEHN ih kuh), Onondaga (ahn uhn DAW guh), Oneida (oh NĪ duh), and Cayuga (kay YOO guh). Each nation had its own ruling council.

The five nations fought constantly. According to legend, about 1570, a religious leader named Dekanawida (deh kan ah WEE dah) called for an end to the warfare. He inspired Hiawatha, a Mohawk, to organize a union of the five nations, known as the *League of the Iroquois.* Later, a sixth nation, the Tuscarora (tuhs kuh ROR uh), joined the League. (📖 See "How Fire Came to the Six Nations" on page 543.)

According to legend, the founders of the League of the Iroquois made this promise:

> **66** We bind ourselves together by taking hold of each other's hands. . . . Our strength shall be in union, our way the way of reason, righteousness, and peace. . . . Be of strong mind, O chiefs. Carry no anger and hold no grudges. **99**

A council of 50 members, chosen by women, made decisions for the League. Each nation had one vote. The council could take action only if all nations agreed.

SECTION 2 REVIEW

1. **Identify:** (a) Inuits, (b) Pueblos, (c) kachina, (d) Natchez, (e) Iroquois, (f) League of the Iroquois.
2. **Define:** (a) culture area, (b) igloo, (c) kayak, (d) potlatch, (e) kiva, (f) hogan, (g) tepee, (h) travois, (i) long house, (j) sachem.
3. List 10 major Native American culture areas of North America.
4. Give two examples of how climate and resources affected the kinds of houses Native Americans built.
5. How were farming and religion closely linked among Native American peoples like the Pueblos?
6. **CRITICAL THINKING Evaluating Information** Why do you think many peoples of the Plains developed stories about the arrival of horses?

ACTIVITY Writing to Learn
Imagine you are Hiawatha. Write a speech to convince the ruling councils of the five nations to join the League of the Iroquois.

The Hiawatha Belt *This beaded belt commemorates the founding of the Iroquois League. The four squares linked to the central tree stand for unity among the Iroquois nations.* **Citizenship** *Why was the Iroquois League set up?*

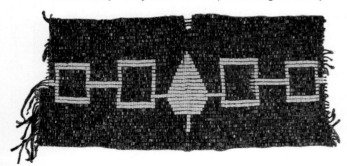

ARTS	SCIENCES	GEOGRAPHY	WORLD	ECONOMICS	CIVICS

How the Iroquois Governed Themselves

Among the Iroquois, the basic unit of society was the "fireside," or family, made up of a woman and all her children. A group of two or more families was known as a clan. Everyone in a clan considered the others in the clan to be relatives. Several clans lived together in a village.

The eldest women from each family chose the man who would serve as leader of the clan. Together, the clan leaders governed the village. If a clan leader did not do his job well, the women could remove him from the position. After the League of the Iroquois was formed in the late 1500s (see page 46), the women also named the 50 sachems, or peace chiefs, who made up the ruling council of the League.

The League council usually met each summer at the main village of the Onondagas. People spoke one at a time. No one was permitted to interrupt or shout, because the purpose of speaking was to persuade, not to argue. Every decision had to be agreed to by all.

Staff used by Iroquois sachem

The Iroquois thought of the League as an "extended lodge"—the long house of the family and clan extended to include all League members. In this way, the close family feelings shared by clan members came to include all the peoples of the six nations.

Decorative comb

■ What role did women play in the League of the Iroquois?

ACTIVITY Plan a student government for your school. Make a chart showing how your government is to be organized.

Women collecting sap to make maple sugar

3

Early Civilizations of the Americas

FIND OUT

- What region did the Mayas, Aztecs, and Incas influence?
- How did each civilization adapt to its environment?
- What were some major achievements of each civilization?

VOCABULARY civilization, hieroglyphics

Large canoes sped along the Caribbean coast of Mexico. Cutting swiftly through the blue waters, they were an impressive sight.

The canoes belonged to the Mayas, whose great cities flourished more than 1,500 years ago. At the height of Mayan culture, more than 4,000 canoes sailed the sea. Mayan traders carried jade statues, turquoise jewelry, parrot feathers, cocoa beans, and other goods across a wide area.

The Mayas were one of several Native American peoples who built great civilizations in the Americas. A civilization is an advanced culture. It usually includes cities, well-organized government, complex religion, social classes, specialized skills and jobs, and some method of keeping records.

The Mayas

Mayan civilization emerged about 3,000 years ago. It grew up in the rain forests of present-day southern Mexico and Guatemala. These rain forests were difficult and dangerous places to live. Poisonous snakes hung from trees. Jaguars prowled the forest floor. Disease-carrying insects infested the swamps.

From earlier peoples, the Mayas learned to grow corn and to build structures of stone. With much work, they cut down the trees and drained the swamps. On the cleared land, they grew corn to feed a growing population.

Large cities. Most Mayas lived in simple homes with mud walls and thatch roofs. Wealthy and powerful Mayas, however, lived in stone palaces in great cities like Tikal and Copán.

Mayan cities rose in many parts of Mexico and Central America. Each city controlled the surrounding area and had its own ruler. Although rival cities sometimes fought, they also enjoyed times of peaceful trade. Roads cut through the jungle, linking inland cities to the coast.

Towering above each city were huge stone pyramids. Atop the pyramid stood a temple. There, priests performed elaborate ceremonies to please the Mayan gods.

Because of their special knowledge, priests were at the top of Mayan society. Nobles, government officials, and warriors also enjoyed high rank. A visitor to a Mayan city could easily spot priests and nobles. They wore gold jewelry, fine headdresses, and colorful cotton garments.

Near the bottom of Mayan society were peasant farmers. Lowest of all were slaves, generally prisoners of war.

Mayan achievements. Mayan priests paid careful attention to time and to the pattern of daily events. By studying the heavens, they tried to predict the future. In that way, they could honor the gods who controlled events, including harvests, trade, and hunts.

Concern with time led the Mayas to learn much about astronomy and mathematics. They created an accurate 365-day calendar. They also developed an advanced number system that included the concept of zero.

To record their findings, Mayan priests invented a system of hieroglyphics, or writing that uses pictures to represent words and ideas. The Mayas carved their records on stone columns or painted them on paper made from bark.

About 850, the Mayas abandoned their cities, and the forests once more took over

Mayan Wall Painting *The Mayan city of Bonampak was noted for its superb frescoes. A fresco is a painting done in watercolor on wet plaster. This fresco shows the elaborate ceremony and carefully crafted headdresses of a Mayan procession.* **Daily Life** *What do you think the purpose of this procession might have been?*

the land. We are unsure why the cities were left to decay. Perhaps peasants rebelled against their rulers. Maybe farming wore out the soil. Even though the cities declined, the Mayan people survived. Today, more than 2 million people speak Mayan languages.

The Aztecs

To the north of the Mayan cities, the Aztecs built a powerful empire. Until the 1300s, the Aztecs were wanderers, moving from place to place in search of food. Then, according to legend, a god told the Aztecs to look for a sign. Search for an eagle perched on a cactus with a snake in its beak, the god said. On that spot, the Aztecs should build their capital. The Aztecs found the eagle in swampy Lake Texcoco (tay SKOH koh), in central Mexico.

A great capital. Following the god's instructions, the Aztecs built their capital, *Tenochtitlán* (tay noch tee TLAHN), on an island in Lake Texcoco. Engineers built causeways, or roads made of packed earth, to connect the island to the mainland.

Farmers dug canals and filled in parts of the lake to create farmland. With long stakes, they attached reed mats to the swampy lake bottom. Then they piled mud onto the mats and planted gardens. Farmers harvested as many as seven crops a year on these floating gardens.

In the 1400s, the Aztecs expanded their power by conquering neighboring peoples. They adopted many beliefs and ideas from these defeated peoples.

Riches from trade and conquest turned Tenochtitlán into a large, bustling city. City marketplaces offered an abundance of goods. "There are daily more than 60,000 people bartering and selling," wrote a Spanish visitor in the 1500s.

Aztec Education *Pictures in an Aztec book show how the Aztecs taught their children. At left, a father teaches his son how to gather firewood, canoe, and fish. The mother, at right, instructs her daughter in grinding grain and weaving cloth.* **Technology** *What items of Aztec technology are shown here?*

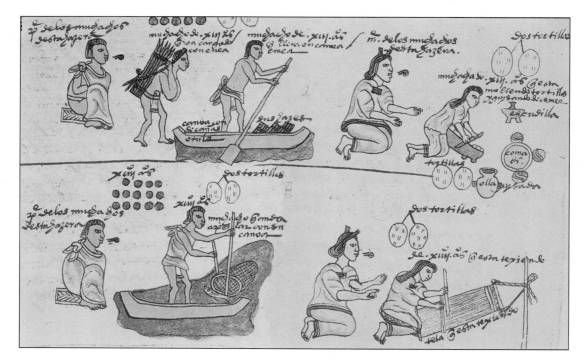

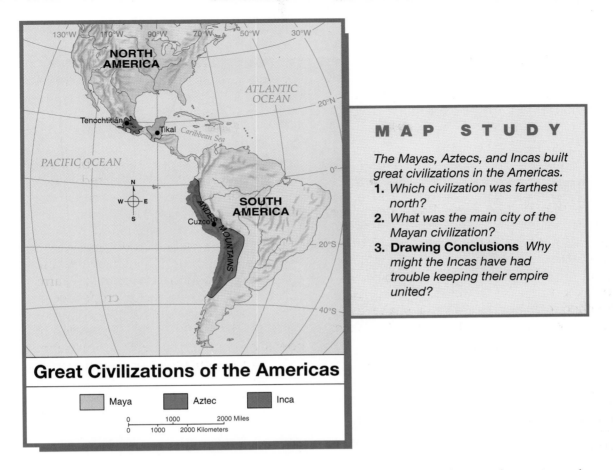

Great Civilizations of the Americas

Maya   Aztec   Inca

| 0 | 1000 | 2000 Miles |
| 0 | 1000 | 2000 Kilometers |

M A P   S T U D Y

The Mayas, Aztecs, and Incas built great civilizations in the Americas.
1. *Which civilization was farthest north?*
2. *What was the main city of the Mayan civilization?*
3. **Drawing Conclusions** *Why might the Incas have had trouble keeping their empire united?*

Canoes darted up the canals that crisscrossed the city. Soldiers and merchants trudged along the causeways between Tenochtitlán and the mainland. Drawbridges on the roads could be raised in case the city was attacked.

Aztec religion. Religion was central to Aztec life. Young men and women attended special schools where they trained to become priests and priestesses. Like the Mayas, Aztec priests studied the heavens and developed advanced calendars. They used these calendars to determine when to plant or harvest and to predict future events. The priests divided the year into 18 months, and each month was governed by its own god. Aztec books contained knowledge about the gods as well as special prayers and hymns.

The sun god was especially important. Each day, the Aztecs believed, the sun battled its way across the heavens. They compared the sun's battles to their own, calling themselves "warriors of the sun." To ensure a successful journey across the sky, the sun required human sacrifices. The Aztecs sacrificed tens of thousands of prisoners of war each year to please their gods.

A powerful empire. By 1500, the Aztecs ruled millions of people from the Gulf of Mexico to the Pacific Ocean. The emperor had absolute power and was treated almost like a god. Servants carried him from place to place on a litter. If the emperor did walk,

Linking Past and Present
During an Aztec wedding ceremony, the priest tied together the clothing of the bride and the groom to symbolize the joining together of their two lives. The practice is still followed in some Mexican villages today.

Machu Picchu *High in the Andes Mountains lie the ruins of the ancient Incan city of Machu Picchu. The city contained a temple, a fortress, and a vast system of terraced gardens. It was abandoned hundreds of years ago, and the ruins remained undiscovered until 1911.* **Geography** *What problems might the Incas have faced in building Machu Picchu?*

nobles scattered flower petals in his path so that his feet never touched the ground. Ordinary people lowered their eyes when he passed.

Heavy taxes and the demand for human sacrifices fueled revolts among the neighboring peoples conquered by the Aztecs. Powerful Aztec armies, however, put down any uprising, taking even more prisoners to be sacrificed to the gods. One Aztec poet boasted, "Who could conquer Tenochtitlán? Who could shake the foundation of heaven?" As you will read in Chapter 3, enemies of the Aztecs would help bring about their defeat in the 1520s.

The Incas

Far to the south of the Aztecs, the Incas united the largest empire in the Americas. By 1492, the Incan empire stretched for almost 3,000 miles (4,800 km) along the western coast of South America. The Incan capital at Cuzco (KYOOS koh) was high in the Andes Mountains. From there, the Incas ruled more than 10 million people living in coastal deserts, lowland jungles, and high mountains.

Expert farmers. Like the Mayas and Aztecs, the Incas adapted customs and ideas from earlier cultures. Among them were the

Moche, who lived along the Pacific coast between about 250 and 700, and the Chimu people, who came after them.

Expanding on farming methods of these early Andean peoples, the Incas carved terraces into the steep mountainsides. Sturdy stone walls kept rains from washing the soil off the terraces. Most gardens produced two crops a year, including more than 100 varieties of potatoes.

The emperor, known as the Sapa Inca, controlled all the land and riches of the empire. Officials kept records of what each family in the empire produced. The government stored surplus, or extra, food in warehouses owned by the Sapa Inca. Famine victims or the sick were given food from these warehouses.

Expert engineers. The Incas perfected highly advanced building techniques. Their huge stone temples and forts showed their expert engineering skills. With only human labor, ropes, and wooden rollers, the Incas moved huge stones weighing as much as 200 tons into place.

Stone masons chiseled each block so that it fit tightly to the next without any kind of cement. Even a knife blade could not fit between blocks. Incan buildings have survived hundreds of earthquakes. Some remain standing today.

Holding the empire together. To unite their sprawling empire, the Incas built a complex network of roads. More than 19,000 miles (30,000 km) of roads linked all parts of the empire. Incan engineers carved roads through rock mountains and stretched rope bridges across deep gorges.

Teams of runners carried royal commands and news quickly across the empire. A runner from Cuzco, for example, would carry a message to a nearby village. From there, another runner would race to the next relay station. Sometimes the runner might bring news of a revolt. Incan armies could move swiftly along the network of roads to crush it.

Achievements in medicine. Besides their success as farmers and engineers, the Incas made several important advances in medicine. They used quinine to treat malaria, performed successful brain surgery, and also discovered medicines to lessen pain.

Religious beliefs. Like the Aztecs, the Incas worshipped the sun. The emperor, they believed, was descended from the sun god. To honor the sun, the Incas lined the walls of palaces and temples with sheets of gold. They called gold "the sweat of the gods." Nobles and priests adorned themselves with gold ornaments.

Very little Incan gold has survived, however. In the 1530s, as you will read, the Spanish rode up Incan highways to the golden city of Cuzco. Weakened by civil war and disease, the Incas were unable to fight off the invaders. The newcomers melted down the riches of the Incan empire to send back to Europe.

SECTION 3 REVIEW

1. **Locate:** (a) Mexico, (b) Guatemala, (c) Tikal, (d) Tenochtitlán, (e) Andes Mountains, (f) Cuzco.
2. **Define:** (a) civilization, (b) hieroglyphics.
3. Where did the Mayas, Aztecs, and Incas build their civilizations?
4. Describe the farming methods of the following: (a) Mayas, (b) Aztecs, (c) Incas.
5. Describe two achievements of each of the following civilizations: (a) Mayas, (b) Aztecs, (c) Incas.
6. CRITICAL THINKING Applying Information A Spanish soldier described the Aztec capital of Tenochtitlán as "something out of a dream." What might he have meant by this description?

ACTIVITY **Writing to Learn**
Imagine that you have visited the Andes. Write a postcard describing the engineering success of the Incas.

4
After 1492

FIND OUT
- How did the 1492 encounter with Europeans affect Native Americans?
- How did Native American cultures influence peoples around the world after 1492?

For thousands of years, many different peoples lived in the vast land we now call the Americas. As you have read, they adapted to their environments and developed a rich variety of cultures. Yet despite great advances, they knew little about the world beyond their shores.

Then, in the late 1400s, strangers began to arrive from lands across the ocean. The first, Christopher Columbus, from a country called Spain, sailed into the Caribbean Sea in 1492. Other Europeans soon followed. At first, the native peoples greeted the newcomers warmly. Before long, however, they came to see these foreigners as invaders and a threat to their way of life.

Early Contacts

Christopher Columbus is the best known of the early voyagers. He and his crew, however, were not the first to land in the Americas. Others had come hundreds of years earlier.

Viking voyages. The *Vikings* were a bold, seafaring people from Scandinavia. In 1001, they settled briefly in North America, in a flat, wooded country they called Vinland. Today, archaeologists believe that the Viking settlement was located in present-day Newfoundland, in Canada.

The Vikings did not stay in Vinland for long. No one is sure why they left. Viking stories, however, describe fierce battles with Skraelings, the Viking name for the Inuits.

Pacific voyages. There are many stories about seafaring peoples from Asia reaching the Americas. Most experts agree that such voyages were very rare, if they occurred at all. Still, some believe that even after the last ice age ended, people continued to cross the Bering Sea from Asia into North America. Others claim that fishing boats from China and Japan blew off course and landed on the western coast of South America.

Encounter in the Caribbean

If these early contacts did in fact take place, they had little impact either on Native Americans or the rest of the world. The encounter in 1492, however, changed history. Columbus's arrival in the Caribbean set off a chain of events whose effects are still felt throughout the world today. (You will read more about Christopher Columbus and other Europeans in Chapter 3.)

A tragic pattern. Columbus first landed in the Americas on a small Caribbean island. Friendly relations with the *Taínos* (TĪ nohz), the Native Americans he met there, did not last. Columbus and the Europeans who followed him had little respect for Native American culture. They claimed Taíno lands for themselves. They forced Taínos to work in gold mines, on ranches, or in Spanish households. Many Taínos died from harsh conditions. Others died from European diseases.

Within 100 years of Columbus's arrival, the Taíno population had been destroyed. The Taínos' experience with Europeans set a pattern that was repeated again and again throughout the Americas.

Cultural Exchange

The 1492 encounter between Native Americans and Europeans had other effects, too. It started an exchange of goods and

MAP, GRAPH, AND CHART SKILLS
Reading a Line Graph

Historians use graphs to present *statistics,* or number facts, in a visual way. The most commonly used graph is a line graph. Other kinds are circle and bar graphs.

A line graph has a grid that is made up of horizontal and vertical lines. A *horizontal axis* runs across the bottom of the grid. A *vertical axis* runs up and down one side of the grid. Information is put on the grid with points, or small dots. The points are then connected to make a *curve.* The curve shows changes that take place over a certain period of time.

Use the steps that follow to read the line graph at right.

1. **Identify the type of information shown on the line graph.** Most graphs have a title, a date, and a source. The title tells you what the subject is. The date tells you what time period is covered. The source tells you where the information was found. (a) What is the title of the graph? (b) What time period does the graph cover? (c) What is the source of the graph?

2. **Study the labels on the graph.** Both the horizontal axis and the vertical axis have labels. (a) What do the numbers on the horizontal axis show? (b) What do the numbers on the vertical axis show?

3. **Practice reading the graph.** The dates on the horizontal axis are spaced evenly. The numbers on the vertical axis are also spaced evenly. The words "in millions" in the label mean that you must add six zeroes to the numbers shown. (a) About how many Native Americans lived in central Mexico in 1520? (b) About how many lived there in 1540? (c) In 1600? (d) During which period did the population fall the most?

4. **Draw conclusions.** Use the graph and your reading in this chapter to answer the following questions: (a) What happened to the population of Native Americans living in central Mexico between 1520 and 1600? (b) Why do you think the Indian population of central Mexico declined so rapidly? (c) What effect do you think the death of so many people might have had on those people who survived? (d) Why do you think the rate of decline slowed down after 1560?

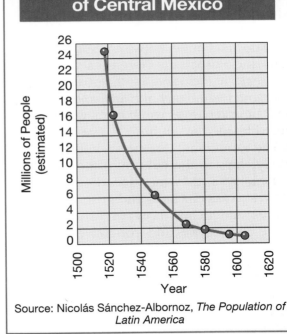

Native American Population of Central Mexico

Source: Nicolás Sánchez-Albornoz, *The Population of Latin America*

ACTIVITY Over a five-day period, keep track of the number of students in your social studies class who are wearing something green each day. Use your statistics to make a line graph.

Riches of the Caribbean *The waters and islands of the Caribbean provided a rich variety of foods. Here, the Caribs, an island people, spread their nets for a harvest of fish.* **Economics** *How did the products of the Caribbean spread throughout the world?*

ideas that transformed people's lives around the globe. In this way, the meeting between two old, very different worlds—the Americas and Europe—led to the creation of one new world.

The exchange between Native Americans and Europeans covered a wide range of areas. It included food, medicine, government, technology, the arts, and language.

The exchange went both ways. Europeans learned much from Native Americans. At the same time, Europeans contributed in many ways to the culture of the Americas. For example, they introduced domestic animals such as chickens and goats and taught Native Americans how to use metals to make copper pots and iron knives. Unfortunately, Europeans also brought disease to the Americas. Millions of Native Americans died of European diseases to which they had no resistance.

Native American Influences

The 1492 encounter introduced Europeans to Native American cultures. Over time, elements of these cultures spread and enriched the entire world.

Food and farming. Over thousands of years, Native Americans had learned to grow a variety of crops. After 1492, Europeans learned of new foods such as corn, potatoes, beans, tomatoes, manioc (a root

vegetable), squash, peanuts, pineapples, and blueberries. Today, almost half the world's food crops come from plants that first grew in the Americas.

Europeans carried the new foods around the world. Everywhere, people's diets changed and populations increased. In South Asia, people used American hot peppers and chilies to spice their curries, or stews. Millions of Chinese peasants began growing sweet potatoes. Italians made sauces from tomatoes. People in West Africa grew manioc and maize.

Language. Native American influences also show up in language. Europeans adopted Native American words for animals they had not known before, including moose, chipmunks, and raccoons. They wore Indian clothing, such as ponchos, moccasins, and parkas. They used Indian inventions like toboggans and hammocks. Europeans also learned about trees with Indian names, such as pecan and hickory.

History and You
English has more than 2,000 words taken from Indian languages. What place names in your area come from Native American words?

In the United States and Canada, most states and provinces have Indian names. Alabama, Texas, Ontario, and Manitoba all are Indian words. Many rivers bear Indian names, including the Mississippi, Potomac, and Monongahela.

Technology. Native Americans helped European settlers survive in North America. Besides showing the newcomers how to grow foods such as corn, Indians taught them hunting skills. They led explorers on foot along Indian trails and paddled them up rivers in Indian canoes.

In the North, they showed Europeans how to use snowshoes and trap fur-bearing animals. Europeans also learned to respect Native American medical knowledge. Indians often treated the newcomers with medicines unknown to Europeans.

Other influences. Native American cultures have influenced the arts, sports, and even government. Today, Indian designs in pottery and leather work are highly prized. Americans play versions of such Indian games as lacrosse. Some early leaders of the United States studied Native American political structures. They saw the League of the Iroquois as a model and urged Americans to unite in a similar way.

In time, all Native Americans felt the effects of European conquest. Still, despite attacks on their cultures, Native Americans survived throughout the Americas. They preserved many traditions, including a respect for nature. Native Americans sought to live in harmony with the natural world. If that harmony was disrupted, they believed, misfortune would result. Today, many people share the same concern for the natural world.

Potato Farming *Andean people first raised potatoes about 2,000 years ago. The Spanish took this vegetable back to Europe. In time, potatoes became an important part of people's diets around the world.* **Geography** *What other food crops first grew in the Americas?*

SECTION 4 REVIEW

1. **Identify:** (a) Vikings, (b) Vinland, (c) Taínos.
2. How were Native Americans affected by the 1492 encounter with Europeans?
3. List three ways in which Native American cultures influenced peoples around the world.
4. **CRITICAL THINKING Analyzing Information** Some experts think that Asians explored the Americas years before Columbus arrived. What kinds of evidence might prove that these experts are correct?

ACTIVITY **Writing to Learn**
List five questions you would like to ask the Taínos about their encounter with Christopher Columbus. Then write a paragraph describing how your life would be different if that encounter had never occurred.

Summary

- By studying physical remains and other evidence, archaeologists are piecing together the story of the first Americans.
- The peoples of North America developed varied ways of life based on their natural environments.
- The Mayas, Aztecs, and Incas developed complex civilizations with important achievements in farming, engineering, medicine, and mathematics.
- The encounter between Native Americans and Europeans that began in 1492 influenced the diet, languages, technology, and ideas of peoples around the world.

Reviewing the Main Ideas

1. How do experts learn about early peoples?
2. Why did the Anasazis build their homes in cliffs?
3. How did the need for food affect the way of life in the following culture areas: (a) Northwest Coast, (b) Great Basin, (c) Southeast?
4. Name three achievements of the Mayas.
5. (a) How did the Aztecs treat captured peoples? (b) Why?
6. What methods of farming did the Incas use?
7. Give one example of Native American influence in each of the following areas: (a) food, (b) language, (c) technology.

Thinking Critically

1. **Evaluating Information** What evidence shows that the Incas had a well-organized empire?
2. **Linking Past and Present** (a) What steps can archaeologists take to show respect for the peoples whose cultures they study? (b) Why is it important that they show respect?

Applying Your Skills

1. **Outlining** Review the outlining steps on page 28. Then outline the section Uncovering the American Past, which begins on page 32.
2. **Understanding Sequence** Place the following events in the correct order. Then write a few sentences explaining why they must have happened in that order. (a) Columbus reaches the Americas. (b) Italians begin to make tomato sauces. (c) Taínos live peacefully on their home island in the Caribbean..
3. **Analyzing a Quotation** "Who could conquer Tenochtitlán? Who could shake the foundation of heaven?" This quotation comes from the work of an Aztec poet. (a) What does it tell you about the Aztecs' view of their empire? (b) Why do you think they viewed their empire this way?

Thinking About Geography

Match the letters on the map with the following places: **1.** Mayan civilization, **2.** Aztec empire, **3.** Incan empire, **4.** Tenochtitlán, **5.** Tikal, **6.** Cuzco. **Interaction** How were the Aztecs able to grow crops on swampland?

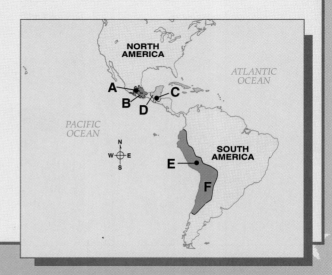

Visiting the Incas

Form into groups to explore the early Incan civilization in South America. Follow the suggestions below to write, draw, or build to show what you have learned about the Incas. You may use the textbook, encyclopedias, atlases, or other materials in your classroom library to complete the tasks. Be able to name your sources of information when you have finished the activity.

Gold Incan hands

CARTOGRAPHERS On a large sheet of paper, create a map of the Americas showing the location of the Incan empire.
On the map:
- Label important cities of the Incan empire.
- Label the Andes Mountains.
- Draw the borders of present-day countries within the Incan empire. Label each country.

SCIENTISTS Draw a diagram of a terrace that the Incas constructed to farm steep hills. Include a paragraph explaining how the Incas used terraced farms to adapt to their environment.

ENGINEERS Make a model or draw a picture of an Incan bridge, road, or building. Be prepared to explain how the Incas carried out these great engineering projects.

GOVERNMENT OFFICIALS Find out how the Incan empire was governed. What was the leader called? Who helped the leader? How were government and religion related? How were royal commands communicated to the people? Make a chart showing the way in which the Incan government was organized.

ARCHAEOLOGISTS Plan a museum exhibit of Incan artifacts. Decide what items will be included, and write a catalog for the exhibit. Illustrate and describe each item.

★ Create a Visiting the Incas brochure that includes an example or summary from each group.

Incan textile

CHAPTER 3

Europeans Reach the Americas

(1000–1650)

CHAPTER OUTLINE

1 Europeans Look Overseas
2 Spain's Empire in the Americas
3 Staking Claims in North America
4 The First English Colonies

1400s *The Incas of Peru built an advanced civilization. These gold ceremonial knives show the riches of their empire.*

1100s *The Anasazis built cliff dwellings in the dry, rugged deserts of the American Southwest.*

1300s *The Aztecs built a powerful empire in Mexico. This feather headdress belonged to the last Aztec ruler.*

1100	1200	1300	1400

WORLD EVENT
1100–1300
Christians go on Crusades to Holy Land

WORLD EVENT
1300s Renaissance begins

Chapter Setting

In 1598, Juan de Oñate (oh NYAH tay) started north up the Rio Grande with about 400 men and several thousand cattle. Oñate's task was to set up the first Spanish colony north of Mexico. The land was rough, and travel was not easy. Along the way, the men stopped at several Pueblo Indian villages. Oñate described such a visit:

> 66On August 3 we went to the great pueblo of the Jemez. . . . [T]he natives came out to meet us, bringing water and bread, at a most difficult hill, and they helped us to take up the cavalry armor and weapons. . . . On the 4th we went down to other Jemez pueblos. . . . The descent was so rough that three horses tumbled down the [cliff], and two of them were killed. Most of us who were on foot also fell.99

After several months, Oñate reached a spot he thought suitable for settlement. Claiming the land for Spain, he set the men to work building a church. On September 8, they held a Roman Catholic service. The Spanish colony of New Mexico was formally founded.

Oñate's travels in the Southwest came at the end of a century of European exploration. Starting in the late 1400s, the nations of Portugal, Spain, England, and France all sent explorers to distant lands. At first, Europeans competed for trade in these new lands. After they reached the Americas, they also became rivals for colonies.

ACTIVITY List three reasons why you might be willing to risk a long, dangerous space journey to explore and settle a distant planet.

1620 *The Pilgrims sailed for the Americas in search of religious freedom. Here, they are signing the Mayflower Compact.*

1500s *After Christopher Columbus reached the West Indies in 1492, Spain set up a vast empire in the Americas. Columbus's ships are shown here.*

Late 1600s *France's colonies grew slowly. This coat of arms was on the gates of Quebec, capital of New France.*

1400   1500   1600   1700

WORLD EVENT
1400s Portuguese slave trade begins

WORLD EVENT
1500s Europeans seek Northwest Passage

FIND OUT

- Why did Europeans look beyond their borders?
- How did attitudes toward learning change during the Renaissance?
- How did Portugal expand its trade?
- What lands did Columbus reach?

VOCABULARY feudalism, manor, serf, magnetic compass, astrolabe, caravel, colony

During the *Middle Ages,* a period from about 500 to 1350, many Europeans thought of the world as a disk floating on a great ocean. The disk was made up of three continents: Europe, Africa, and Asia.

Most Europeans knew little about the lands beyond their small villages. Even mapmakers called the waters bordering Europe the Sea of Darkness. Sailors who strayed into these waters often returned with tales of monsters. "One of these sea monsters," swore one sailor, "has terrible tusks. Another has horns, flames, and huge eyes 16 or 20 feet across."

Were such tales true? The few people who wondered had no way of finding out. Besides, for most Europeans, daily life was hard, and their main concern was survival.

A Changing World

Toward the end of the Middle Ages, Europeans began to look beyond their borders. Religious wars and the lure of new products from faraway lands brought major changes in the way Europeans lived.

The Middle Ages. During the Middle Ages, weak European kings and queens divided their lands among powerful nobles. These nobles, or lords, had their own armies and courts but still owed loyalty to their king. This system of rule by lords who owe loyalty to a king is called feudalism (FYOOD 'l ihz uhm).

Most life in Europe revolved around manors of these powerful lords. The manor included the lord's castle, peasants' huts, and surrounding villages or fields. Most people on the manor were serfs, or peasants bound to the land for life. Serfs worked for

BIOGRAPHY Marco Polo in China *In 1271, at age 17, Marco Polo set out with his father and uncle from Venice, Italy, for lands in the East. He returned 24 years later. His tales of his travels made other Europeans eager to explore the world. This illustration shows the ruler of China receiving the Polo family.* **Geography** *Why did most Europeans in the Middle Ages know little about lands outside Europe?*

the lord and could not leave the manor without the lord's permission.

Under feudalism, there were few merchants and traders. Few roads or towns existed. The manor produced nearly everything people needed. Most manors even provided a place of worship, such as a church or small chapel. Here, serfs and lords heard teachings of the Roman Catholic Church.

Effects of the Crusades. During the Middle Ages, Christians in Western Europe belonged to the Roman Catholic Church. The Church had great influence. In time, Church teachings led Europeans to look beyond their manors.

Christians in Western Europe referred to the Middle East as the Holy Land because Jesus had lived and died there. The region was also sacred to Muslims. Their prophet, Muhammad, had also lived in the Holy Land. From about 1100 to 1300, the Roman Catholic Church fought a series of religious wars to gain control of the Holy Land from Turkish Muslims. The wars were known as the *Crusades.*

Thousands of Christians from all across Europe joined the Crusades. Among them were kings and peasants, adults and children. Many Crusaders sewed a white cross on their shirts and on flags as a symbol of their cause.

The Crusaders did not regain the Holy Land. The Crusades did have lasting effects, however. For the first time, large numbers of Europeans traveled beyond their small towns. In the Middle East, they ate strange foods, such as rice, oranges, and dates. They tasted ginger, pepper, and other spices that both improved the taste of food and helped preserve it. From Arab traders, they bought shimmering silks and tightly woven, colorful rugs from lands to the east, known as Asia.

Italian merchants along the Mediterranean Sea saw that Europeans would pay handsome prices for these foreign goods. They soon began a lively trade with Arab merchants in the Middle East.

Arabs taught Italian sailors how to use new instruments to navigate large bodies of water, such as the Mediterranean Sea. The **magnetic compass,** with a needle that always pointed north, helped ship captains sail a straight course. The **astrolabe** (AS troh layb) made it possible for sailors to measure the positions of stars and figure out latitude at sea. Both the magnetic compass and the astrolabe helped make sailing less frightening.

The Renaissance spirit. Increased trade and travel made Europeans curious about the wider world. Scholars translated the works of ancient Greeks, Romans, and Arabs. They then made discoveries of their own in fields such as medicine, astronomy, and chemistry. This burst of learning was called the *Renaissance* (REHN uh sahns), a French word meaning rebirth. It started in the late 1300s and continued until about 1600.

One invention that helped spread the spirit of the Renaissance was the printing press. It was invented during the mid-1400s by Johannes Gutenberg (GOOT uhn berg) of Germany. Before Gutenberg's invention, monks wrote out books by hand. As a result, only a few copies were available. With the printing press, large numbers of books could be printed at a low cost. As more books became available, more people learned to read. The more people read, the more they learned about the world.

History and You
During the Renaissance, a new ideal person emerged. To meet the ideal, a person had to master every area of learning and be expert in a wide range of skills. Who do you know today who might be considered a "Renaissance person"?

European Explorers

Explorer	Achievements
For Portugal	
Bartolomeu Dias 1487–1488	Sailed around the southern tip of Africa
Vasco da Gama 1497–1498	Sailed around Africa to India
Pedro Álvares Cabral 1500	Reached Brazil
For Spain	
Christopher Columbus 1492–1504	Explored the West Indies and the Caribbean
Vasco Núñez de Balboa 1513	Sighted the Pacific Ocean
Juan Ponce de León 1508–1509, 1513	Explored Puerto Rico Explored Florida
Ferdinand Magellan 1519–1522	Led first expedition to sail around the world
Pánfilo de Narváez/Cabeza de Vaca/ Estevanico 1528–1536	Traveled in the Spanish borderlands
Francisco Coronado 1540–1542	Explored southwestern North America
Hernando De Soto 1516–1520, 1539–1542	Explored Central America Led expedition to the Mississippi River
Juan Cabrillo 1542–1543	Explored west coast of North America
For England	
John Cabot 1497–1501(?)	Explored east coast of North America
Henry Hudson 1610–1611	Explored Hudson Bay
For the Netherlands	
Henry Hudson 1609	Explored east coast of North America and the Hudson River
For France	
Giovanni da Verrazano 1524	Explored east coast of North America, including present-day New York harbor
Jacques Cartier 1534–1542	Explored St. Lawrence River
Samuel de Champlain 1603–1615	Explored St. Lawrence River valley Founded Quebec
Jacques Marquette/Louis Joliet 1673	Explored along the Mississippi River
Robert de La Salle 1679–1682	Explored Great Lakes Reached the mouth of the Mississippi River

CHART SKILLS *Starting in the late 1400s, five major European nations sent out expeditions to explore the world.* ● *Name two explorers who sailed for England. Which areas did they explore?*

Search for New Trade Routes

During the Renaissance, strong rulers slowly gained control over feudal lords. These kings and queens built the foundations of the nations we know today.

European nations seek trade. In England and France, rulers increased their power in a long series of wars. In Portugal and Spain, Christian rulers fought Arab Muslims who had conquered parts of those lands. By 1249, the Portuguese had captured the last Muslim stronghold in Portugal. In Spain, Arabs continued to control territory until 1492.

The new rulers of England, France, Portugal, and Spain all looked for ways to increase their wealth. They could make huge profits by trading with China and other lands in Asia. However, Arab and Italian merchants controlled the trade routes across the Mediterranean Sea. If they wanted a share of the trade, European rulers had to find another route to Asia.

Portugal takes the lead. The Portuguese turned to the Atlantic Ocean. In the early 1400s, Prince Henry, known as the Navigator, encouraged sea captains to sail south along the coast of West Africa. He founded an informal school to help sailors in their explorations.

Using a new type of ship known as a caravel (KAR uh vehl), the Portuguese sailed farther and farther south. The caravel's triangular sails and its steering rudder allowed it to sail against the wind. By 1498, the Portuguese sailor Vasco da Gama passed the southern tip of Africa and continued north and east to India. Later, other Portuguese ships pressed on to the East Indies, the source of trade in spices.

Using their new route, the Portuguese built a successful trading empire in Asia. Along the way, they came into contact with great kingdoms in Africa.

African Trading States

In the 1400s, Europeans knew little about Africa or the many peoples who lived there. A Spanish map, for example, showed an African ruler in the middle of the Sahara, a great desert. The caption read:

66 This Negro lord is called Musa Mali. So abundant is the gold in his country that he is the richest and most noble king in all the land. 99

Advances in Technology
New sailing instruments, such as the astrolabe at left, allowed Europeans to take longer, more hazardous sea voyages. The illustration at right shows Portuguese ships crossing the Atlantic Ocean.
Science and Technology *What other advances in technology encouraged European exploration?*

In fact, Musa Mali's real name was Mansa Musa. He ruled Mali, a kingdom in West Africa. Mali reached its height between 1200 and 1400. In 1324, Mansa Musa traveled from Mali across North Africa to Egypt and the Middle East. He so dazzled the Egyptians with his wealth that news of his visit reached Europe.

West Africa. Mali was only one of several advanced states that rose in West Africa. (See the map below.) In the late 1400s, Songhai (SAWNG hī) became the most powerful kingdom in West Africa. Timbuktu, located on the Niger River, was a thriving center of trade and learning.

Portuguese explorers did not visit these kingdoms inside Africa. They did, however, trade with Africans along the coast. Africans exchanged gold, ivory, and statues of polished teak wood for European weapons and other goods.

East Africa. The Portuguese found well-developed kingdoms along Africa's eastern coast. There, states like Mogadishu and

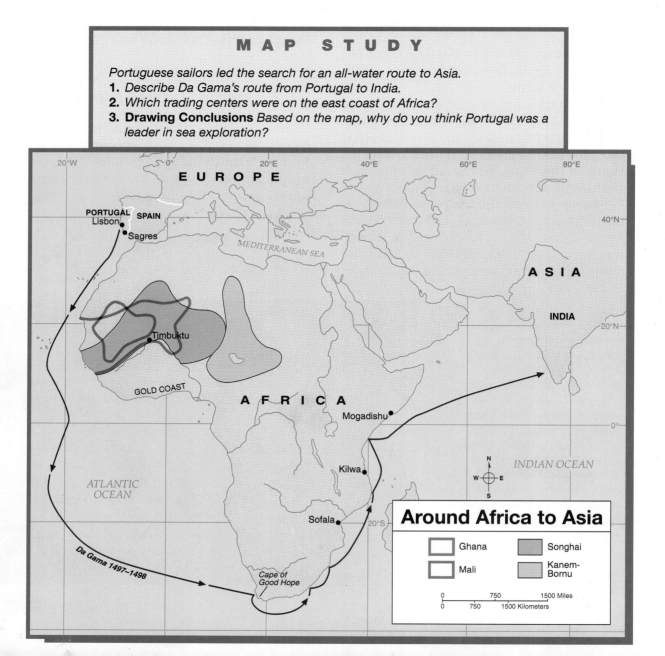

MAP STUDY

Portuguese sailors led the search for an all-water route to Asia.
1. Describe Da Gama's route from Portugal to India.
2. Which trading centers were on the east coast of Africa?
3. **Drawing Conclusions** Based on the map, why do you think Portugal was a leader in sea exploration?

Around Africa to Asia

☐ Ghana	◼ Songhai
☐ Mali	◼ Kanem-Bornu

0   750   1500 Miles
0   750   1500 Kilometers

Kilwa prospered from trade with other ports along the Indian Ocean. Gold from Zimbabwe, a powerful inland state, made its way to the coastal city of Sofala. From there, ships carried the gold up the African coast as well as to India.

Portuguese slave trade. In 1441, the Portuguese raided an African village. They captured about a dozen Africans and sold them as slaves in Europe. By 1460, about 1,000 Africans were sold each year in Portugal. As the trade in slaves increased, Africans from kingdoms along the coast made raids into the interior seeking captives to sell to the Portuguese.

The Portuguese did not introduce slavery. Since ancient times, Europeans, Africans, Arabs, and Asians in many different regions had enslaved and sold people. However, the trade along the West African coast marked a turning point. Over the next 400 years, as many as 11 million Africans would be enslaved and sent across the Atlantic to the Americas.

Voyages of Columbus

As the Portuguese sailed east toward Asia, the Spanish watched with envy. They, too, wanted a share of the rich Asian trade. In 1492, King Ferdinand and Queen Isabella agreed to finance a voyage by Christopher Columbus, a bold Italian sea captain. Columbus planned to reach the East Indies, off the coast of Asia, by sailing west across the Atlantic.

Ivory Carving From West Africa *West African artists produced many fine carvings. This ivory salt cellar was probably carved to order for a European merchant.* **Culture** *What objects did the artist include to show that the man in the carving is European?*

The voyage west. In August 1492, Columbus set sail with three vessels and a crew of 90 sailors. As captain, he commanded the largest ship, the *Santa María*. The other ships were the *Niña* and the *Pinta*.

Fair winds sped the ships along. The crew saw no land for a month. Some of the less experienced sailors began to grumble. They had never been beyond the sight of land for so long. Still, Columbus sailed on.

On October 7, sailors saw flocks of birds flying southwest. Columbus changed course to follow the birds. A few days later, crew members spotted tree branches and flowers floating in the water. On the night of October 11, the moon shone brightly. At 2 A.M. on October 12, the lookout on the *Pinta* spotted white cliffs shining in the moonlight. "Tierra! Tierra!" he shouted. "Land! Land!"

At dawn, Columbus rowed ashore. He planted the banner of Spain in what he believed was the East Indies. In fact, as you have read in Chapter 2, he had reached the island home of the Taínos, in what are now known as the West Indies. Convinced he had reached the East Indies, Columbus called the Taínos Indians.

For three months, Columbus explored the West Indies. To his delight, he found signs of gold on the islands. Eager to report his success, he returned home.

From fame to disgrace. In Spain, Columbus presented King Ferdinand and Queen Isabella with gifts of pink pearls and brilliantly colored parrots. The royal couple listened intently to his descriptions of tobacco leaves, pineapples, and hammocks used for sleeping. Impressed, they agreed to finance future voyages.

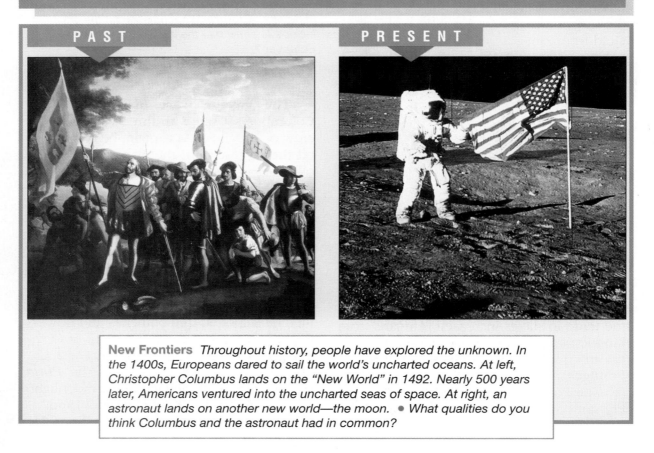

PAST

PRESENT

New Frontiers *Throughout history, people have explored the unknown. In the 1400s, Europeans dared to sail the world's uncharted oceans. At left, Christopher Columbus lands on the "New World" in 1492. Nearly 500 years later, Americans ventured into the uncharted seas of space. At right, an astronaut lands on another new world—the moon.* • *What qualities do you think Columbus and the astronaut had in common?*

Columbus made three more voyages to the West Indies. On his second voyage, in 1493, he founded the first Spanish colony in the Americas, on an island he called Hispaniola. A colony is a group of people who settle in a distant land and are ruled by the government of their native land.

Columbus proved to be a better explorer than a governor. During his third expedition, settlers at Hispaniola complained of his harsh rule. When Isabella sent an official to investigate, the official sent Columbus back to Spain in chains.

In the end, Isabella pardoned Columbus. He died in 1506, still convinced that he had reached Asia.

Columbus: Hero or Villain?

For years, Columbus has been remembered as the bold sea captain who "discovered America." In one sense, he deserves that honor. Europeans knew nothing of the Americas before Columbus brought them news of this "new world." Today, we recognize that other people "discovered" America long before Columbus. Still, his daring journey brought the peoples of Europe, Africa, and the Americas into lasting contact for the first time in history.

Native Americans, however, paid heavily for Columbus's voyage. Columbus and the Europeans who came after him forced

| ARTS | SCIENCES | GEOGRAPHY | **WORLD** | ECONOMICS | CIVICS |

The Columbian Exchange

Before 1492, a typical Aztec meal consisted of corn porridge, tortillas, beans, and tomato or pepper sauce. On the other side of the ocean, Europeans dined on dark bread, cabbage or turnip soup, and cheese. Neither knew the other existed. Neither imagined how their diet—and their entire world—would change after they met.

Then, Christopher Columbus arrived in the West Indies. His visit began an exchange of goods and ideas that transformed the world. Because it began with Columbus, this transfer is called the Columbian Exchange.

The Columbian Exchange involved hundreds of items. Besides foods, these items included peoples, plants, and animals. They also included diseases.

Native Americans taught Europeans to eat corn and potatoes. Easy to grow, these foods became staples in European, African, and Asian diets. At the same time, the introduction of livestock, wheat, bananas, and citrus fruit from Europe, Africa, and Asia changed the way Native Americans ate.

Sugar cane also traveled to the Americas from Europe, carried by Columbus on his second voyage. Soon, sugar was a thriving industry on the Caribbean islands. Europeans brought in millions of Africans to work as slaves in the sugar plantations.

Smallpox victim

Cattle and horses

Perhaps the most terrible item in the Columbian Exchange arrived as an invisible passenger on European ships. Native Americans had no resistance to "European" diseases such as measles, smallpox, or even the common cold. Scholars estimate that between 50 percent and 90 percent of Native Americans died of diseases introduced from Europe.

Potato plant

■ What were three effects of the Columbian Exchange?

ACTIVITY Make a map of the world that illustrates the flow of items in the Columbian Exchange.

native peoples to work in mines or on farms raising sugar cane and cotton. Over the next 50 years, hundreds of thousands of Caribbean Indians died from harsh working conditions and European diseases.

"Discovery" also cost Native Americans their lands. Starting with Columbus, Europeans justified seizing Indian lands. Some believed they had the right to take the lands because Indians were not Christians.

For better or worse, the rise of powerful nations in Europe signaled a new era for the Americas. Curious Europeans wanted to know more about the lands across the Atlantic. They saw the Americas as a place where they could trade and grow rich. Once Columbus reached the Americas, nothing could stop the flood of explorers and settlers who followed him.

SECTION 1 REVIEW

1. **Locate:** (a) Europe, (b) Middle East, (c) Asia, (d) East Indies, (e) Mali, (f) West Indies.
2. **Identify:** (a) Middle Ages, (b) Crusades, (c) Renaissance, (d) Johannes Gutenberg, (e) Mansa Musa, (f) Queen Isabella.
3. **Define:** (a) feudalism, (b) manor, (c) serf, (d) magnetic compass, (e) astrolabe, (f) caravel, (g) colony.
4. What changes did the Crusades bring to Europe?
5. How did exploration help to expand Portugal's trade?
6. (a) Where did Columbus think he landed in 1492? (b) Where did he actually land?
7. **CRITICAL THINKING Analyzing Information** (a) How did Europeans view their arrival in the Americas? (b) How does this compare with the Native American view that you read about in Chapter 2?

ACTIVITY Writing to Learn
Should Americans celebrate Columbus's birthday? Write an editorial expressing your opinion.

2
Spain's Empire in the Americas

FIND OUT
- How did Spain conquer Native American empires?
- How did Spain rule its empire in the Americas?
- Why did the Spanish bring Africans as slaves to the Americas?
- How did Spanish and Indian ways help shape the culture of New Spain?

VOCABULARY conquistador, pueblo, presidio, mission, peninsulare, creole, mestizo, encomienda, plantation

"**W**hat a troublesome thing it is to discover new lands. The risks we took, it is hardly possible to exaggerate." So spoke Bernal Díaz del Castillo, one of the Spanish **conquistadors** (kahn KEES tuh dorz), or conquerors, who marched into the Americas. When asked why conquistadors traveled to the Americas, Díaz responded, "We came here to serve God and the king and also to get rich."

In their search for glory and gold, the conquistadors made Spain one of the richest nations in Europe. Before long, Spanish colonists had created a vast new empire in the Americas. But the arrival of Europeans meant suffering and even death for Aztecs, Incas, and other Native Americans.

Beyond the Caribbean

After Columbus reached the West Indies, the Spanish explored and settled other islands in the Caribbean Sea. By 1511, they had conquered Puerto Rico, Jamaica, and Cuba. They also explored the eastern coast of North America and South America. They were still seeking a western route to Asia, but these lands blocked their way.

Then in 1513, an adventurer named Vasco Núñez de Balboa (bal BOH uh) plunged into the jungles of the Isthmus of Panama. Native Americans had told him that a large body of water lay to the west. With a party of Spanish and Indians, Balboa reached the Pacific Ocean after about 25 days. In full armor, he stood in the crashing surf and claimed the sea for Spain.

The Spanish had no idea how wide the Pacific was until a sea captain named Ferdinand Magellan (muh JEHL uhn) sailed across it. The expedition set out from Spain in 1519. After much hardship, it rounded the stormy southern tip of South America and entered the Pacific Ocean. Crossing the vast Pacific, the sailors were forced to eat rats and sawdust when they ran out of food. Magellan himself was killed in a battle with the local people of the Philippine Islands off the coast of Asia.

Of five ships and about 250 crew members, only one ship and 18 sailors returned to Spain in 1522, three years after they set out. These survivors had found Spain's all-water route to Asia by sailing west. More important, their voyage around the world made Europeans aware of the true size of the Earth.

Conquest of the Aztecs and Incas

Meanwhile, Spanish colonists in the Caribbean began to hear rumors of gold and other riches in nearby Mexico. At the same time, the Aztecs there were hearing about the Spanish.

In 1518, messengers brought strange news to the Aztec emperor, Montezuma (mahn tuh ZYOO muh). They had seen a large house floating on the Gulf of Mexico. It was filled with white men with long, thick beards and clothing of many colors. The next year, Aztecs spotted even more bearded white men.

Were these strangers gods or men? Aztec sacred writings predicted that one day a powerful white-skinned god would return from the east to rule the Aztecs. These white strangers came from the east. And they were certainly powerful. They wore metal armor and had weapons that breathed fire and shattered trees into splinters. Could they be messengers of the Aztec god? Unsure, Montezuma invited them to enter the capital of his empire, Tenochtitlán.

Aztecs Battle the Spanish
Pedro de Alvarado was a conquistador in Mexico. This illustration shows Alvarado and his men retreating from a troop of Aztec soldiers. **Science and Technology** *Based on this picture, what advantages did the Spanish have over the Aztecs?*

MAP STUDY

In the 1500s, Spain built a huge empire in the Americas.
1. Into what two parts was Spain's American empire divided?
2. What other European nation set up colonies in South America?
3. **Forecasting** Why was control of the Caribbean Sea important to Spain?

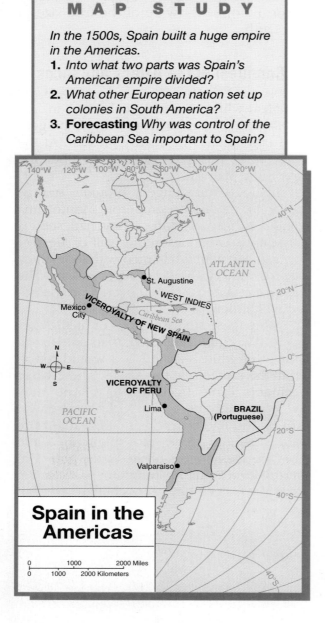

Spain in the Americas

On November 8, 1519, Cortés marched into Tenochtitlán. For six months, he held Montezuma prisoner in his own city. Finally, the Aztecs attacked, driving out the Spanish. But Cortés soon returned. With the help of neighboring peoples the Aztecs had conquered, the Spanish captured and destroyed most of Tenochtitlán. The mighty Aztec empire had fallen. (☐ See "Cortés and Montezuma" on page 546.)

A few years later, a conquistador named Francisco Pizarro (pee ZAR oh) matched Cortés's conquest. Sailing along the Pacific coast of present-day Chile, Pizarro invaded the Incan empire. In a surprise attack, he captured and later killed the Incan ruler, Atahualpa (at ah WAHL pah). By 1535, Pizarro controlled much of the Incan empire.

Reasons for the Spanish conquest. How did the conquistadors, with only a handful of soldiers, manage to conquer these two great empires? First, the Spanish fought with iron swords, guns, and cannons. The Native Americans fought with less powerful bows, arrows, and spears. Second, the Aztecs and Incas had never seen horses. They were frightened by the mounted Spanish knights. Finally, the Indians had no resistance to European diseases. Large numbers of Indians died from chicken pox, measles, and influenza. Some historians believe that disease alone would have ensured Spanish victory over the Indians.

Aztec and Incan treasures made the conquistadors rich. Spain grew rich, too, especially after the discovery of gold and silver in Mexico and Peru. Spanish treasure ships laden with thousands of tons of gold and silver sailed regularly across the Atlantic.

The Spanish Borderlands

The Spanish search for treasure extended beyond Mexico and Peru. Moving north, conquistadors explored the area known as the ***Spanish borderlands.*** The borderlands

Two great empires fall. The Spanish leader, Hernando Cortés (kor TEHZ), accepted Montezuma's invitation. Like other conquistadors, Cortés wanted power and riches. An Indian woman the Spanish called Doña Marina had told Cortés about Aztec gold. With only about 600 soldiers and 16 horses, Cortés set out to defeat the Aztecs.

spanned the present-day United States from Florida to California.

To the east, Juan Ponce de León (PAWN suh day lay AWN) traveled through parts of Florida in 1513, looking for a Fountain of Youth. Indians claimed that anyone who bathed in this magical fountain would remain young forever. But Ponce de León found no fountain.

In 1539, Hernando De Soto arrived in Florida in search of gold and treasure. For the next few years, he explored the borderlands. In 1541, he reached the waters of the broad Mississippi River. De Soto died along the riverbanks, however, without finding the riches he sought.

In the meantime, a conquistador named Francisco Coronado (koh roh NAH doh) heard stories of seven cities of gold. Coronado led an expedition into the southwestern borderlands in 1540. Some of his party went as far as the Grand Canyon. Still, the Zuñi villages he visited had no golden streets.

Adventures in the Spanish Borderlands

One of the most remarkable journeys across the Spanish borderlands began with disaster. In 1528, the conquistador Pánfilo de Narváez (nar VAH ehs) landed in Florida with a few hundred men. Narváez unwisely attacked Native Americans and stole their food. The Indians struck back. The Spanish retreated west along the coast and then across the mouth of the Mississippi River. One stormy night, Narváez, in a small boat, was blown into the Gulf of Mexico, never to be seen again.

Four survivors. In the end, only four men from the expedition survived. Álvar Núñez Cabeza de Vaca became their leader. Estevanico (ehs teh vuh NEE koh), an enslaved African, became the group's transla-

tor and scout. Cabeza de Vaca recalled how desperate they were:

> 66[We] had lost everything. . . . It was November, bitterly cold, and we were in such a state that every bone could be counted. . . . We looked like death itself. 99

The Charucco (chah ROO koh) Indians found the survivors and nursed them back to health. To the surprise of the Spanish, the Indians insisted that the men act as healers. "[The Charuccos] cure illness by breathing on the sick . . . and they ordered us to do the same," Cabeza de Vaca reported.

The survivors resisted at first but finally agreed to cooperate. "Our method," recalled Cabeza de Vaca, "was to bless the sick, breathing on them . . . praying with all earnestness to God our Lord that He would give health." When a number of the sick recovered, the Charuccos were impressed.

Estevanico *Between 1533 and 1536, a tiny band of shipwreck survivors wandered through the Spanish borderlands. Among them was a young African named Estevanico. He is pictured here in his finest clothes, after the journey.* **Daily Life** *What skills did Estevanico have that helped the group survive in the borderlands?*

For nearly five years, the four men lived as slaves of the Charuccos. They ate mainly roots, spiders, worms, caterpillars, lizards, snakes, and ant eggs. Aside from healing the sick, the men were forced to gather and chop firewood. This labor left deep scars on their shoulders and chests.

A long journey. In 1533, the four men escaped their masters and set out in search of Spanish settlements to the west. Walking barefoot from Indian village to Indian village, they crossed the plains of Texas.

Throughout the journey, Estevanico acted as go-between with the Indians. According to Cabeza de Vaca, "He inquired about the road we should follow, the villages—in short, about everything we wished to know." Hundreds of Indians flocked around the four men, running ahead to the next village, bringing news of the great healers.

The journey continued across the Rio Grande and then south through the mountains and desert of Mexico. In 1536, the four men finally reached the Spanish settlement of Compostela (kahm poh STEH lah). It had been an astonishing journey of more than 1,000 miles (1,600 km). (See the map on page 75.) ■

Setting Up a Government

The Spanish expeditions into the borderlands met with little success. Faced with fierce Indian resistance in North America, Spain focused instead on bringing order to its empire to the south.

At first, Spain let the conquistadors govern its lands in the Americas. But the conquistadors proved to be poor rulers. When gold and silver began to flow into Spain from the Americas, the Spanish king decided to set up stronger, more stable governments there.

In 1535, the king divided his lands into New Spain and Peru. (See the map on page 72.) He put a viceroy in charge of each region to rule in his name.

Three kinds of settlements. The viceroy and other royal officials enforced a code of laws called the *Laws of the Indies.* These laws stated in detail how the colonies should be organized and ruled.

The Laws of the Indies provided for three kinds of settlements in New Spain. They were pueblos, presidios (prih SIHD ee ohz), and missions.

Pueblos were towns that were centers of farming and trade. In the middle of the town was a plaza, or public square. Here, townspeople and farmers gathered on important occasions. They also came to worship at the church. Shops and homes lined both sides of the plaza.

Presidios were forts with high adobe walls, where soldiers lived. Inside were

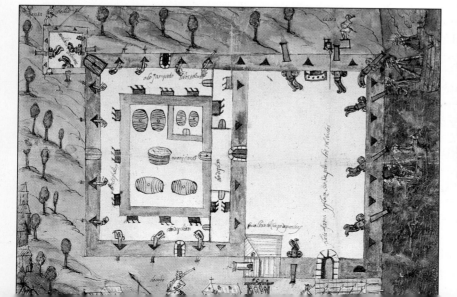

The Presidio at St. Augustine
The Spanish built a string of missions and presidios in the borderlands. This drawing, done in the late 1500s, shows a plan of the first presidio, built at St. Augustine, Florida. **Technology** *Based on this drawing, how did the Spanish defend the presidio?*

MAP STUDY

Conquistadors explored parts of North America in the 1500s. They mapped routes that Spanish missionaries and settlers later followed.
1. **Which explorer was the first to visit Florida?**
2. **Which Spanish settlement was farthest east?**
3. **Linking Past and Present** *Based on the map, in what areas of the present-day United States would you expect to find Spanish influence?*

The Spanish Borderlands

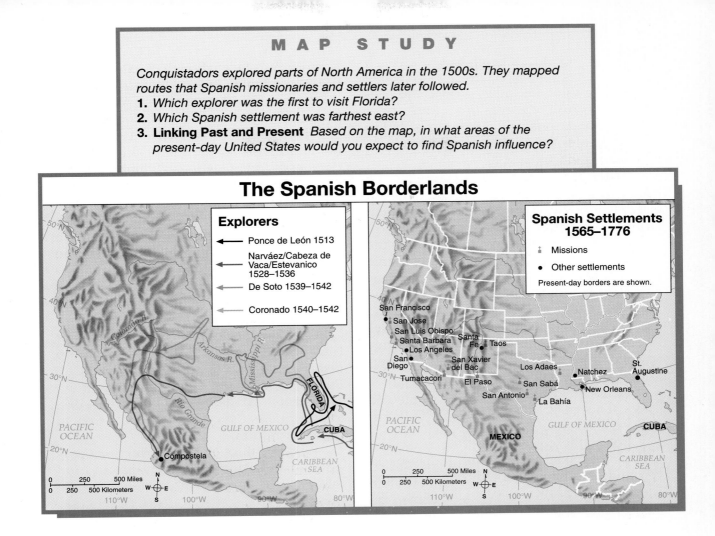

shops, stables for horses, and storehouses for food. Most soldiers lived in large barracks. The farmers who settled around presidios felt safer knowing that military help was close by.

Missions were religious settlements run by Catholic priests and friars. Like other Europeans who settled in the Americas, the Spanish believed that they had a duty to convert Indians to the Christian religion. The missions throughout New Spain forced Indians to live and work on them. By setting up presidios and missions, the Laws of the Indies allowed Spain to rule the conquered Indians.

Missions in the borderlands. During their first hundred years in the Americas, the Spanish did not build settlements in the borderlands. The only exception was at **St. Augustine,** Florida, where a presidio was erected in 1565.

In time, however, Spanish interest in the borderlands grew. As you have read, in 1598, Juan de Oñate founded the colony of New Mexico. Later, Spanish missionaries moved into other areas of the American Southwest. The first mission in Texas was founded at El Paso in 1659.

Father Eusebio Francisco Kino (KEE noh) crossed into present-day Arizona in 1691. During the next 20 years, he set up 24 missions in the area. Missionaries also moved into California. By the late 1700s, a string of missions dotted the California coast from present-day San Diego to San Francisco. (See the map above.)

A Class System

The Laws of the Indies divided the people in Spanish colonies into four social classes: peninsulares (puh nihn suh LAH rayz), creoles (KREE ohlz), mestizos (mehs TEE zohz), and Indians.

At the top of the social scale were the **peninsulares.** Born in Spain, the peninsulares were sent by the Spanish government to rule the colonies. They held the highest jobs in the colonial government and the Catholic Church. They also owned large tracts of land and rich gold and silver mines.

Next below the peninsulares were the **creoles.** Creoles were people born in the Americas to Spanish parents. Many creoles were wealthy and well educated. They owned farms and ranches, taught at universities, and practiced law. However, they could not hold the same jobs as peninsulares. This policy made the creoles resent the peninsulares.

Below the creoles were the **mestizos,** people of mixed Spanish and Indian background. Mestizos worked on farms and ranches owned by creoles. In the cities, they worked as carpenters, shoemakers, tailors, and bakers.

The lowest class in the colonies was the Indians. The Spanish treated them as a conquered people. Under New Spain's strict social system, Indians were kept in poverty for hundreds of years.

Native American and African Workers

The colonists who came to New Spain needed workers for their ranches and farms. The Spanish government helped by giving settlers **encomiendas** (ehn koh mee EHN dahz), or the right to demand labor or taxes from Native Americans living on the land. Indian labor became even more important after the Spanish found large veins of silver and gold in Mexico and Peru.

Indians in mines and on plantations. During the 1500s, Spanish mines in the Americas produced thousands of tons of silver. The mining center at Potosí, Peru, became larger than any city in the Americas or in Spain.

The Spanish forced Native American laborers to work in the mines. In flickering darkness, Indian workers climbed down rickety ladders to narrow tunnels where they hacked out the rich ore. Many died when tunnels caved in.

On the islands of the West Indies, the Spanish imported thousands of Indians to work on **plantations,** or large estates farmed by many workers. They grew sugar cane and tobacco, which plantation owners sold in Spain at a huge profit.

Las Casas seeks reform. Thousands of Native Americans died from overwork on plantations and in mines. As you have read, European diseases killed millions more. These harsh conditions led one priest, Bartolomé de Las Casas (day lahs KAH sahs), to plead for reform.

Traveling through New Spain, Las Casas saw Indians dying of hunger, disease, and mistreatment. In his own words:

66 The Indians were totally deprived of their freedom. . . . Even beasts enjoy more freedom when they are allowed to graze in the field. 99

Horrified, he journeyed to Spain and asked the king to protect the Indians. In the 1540s, the royal government did pass laws stating that Native Americans could not be enslaved. The laws also allowed Indians to own cattle and grow crops. Few officials in New Spain enforced the new laws, however.

Slaves from Africa. As more and more Native Americans died from disease and mistreatment, the Spanish looked for other workers. Bartolomé de Las Casas suggested that Africans be brought as slaves to replace Indian laborers. Unlike Indians, Africans did not catch European diseases, he said. Besides, they were used to doing hard farm work in their homelands.

BIOGRAPHY Sor Juana *Juana Inés de la Cruz was the most talented poet of New Spain. Refused admission to the university in Mexico City because she was a girl, she entered a convent at age 16. There, she devoted herself to studying and to writing poetry. She also wrote a spirited defense of women's right to education.* **Culture** *What obstacles did Sor Juana have to overcome?*

In 1517, colonists began importing Africans to labor as slaves in the Americas. By the time he died, Las Casas came to regret his suggestion. He saw that Africans suffered as much as Indians. By then, though, the plantation system had taken hold. In the years that followed, the African slave trade grew, not only in the Spanish colonies but elsewhere in the Americas.

A Blending of Cultures

By the mid-1500s, a new way of life had begun to take shape in New Spain. It blended Spanish and Indian ways.

Spanish settlers brought their own customs and culture to the colonies. They introduced their language, laws, religion, and learning. In 1539, a printer in Mexico City produced the first European book in the Americas. In 1551, the Spanish founded the University of Mexico.

Native Americans also influenced the culture of New Spain. As you have read in Chapter 2, colonists adopted many items of Indian clothing, such as the poncho, a coat-like blanket with a hole in the middle for the head. The Indians introduced Spanish colonists to new foods, including potatoes, corn, tomatoes, and chocolate. In time, Native American foods spread to Europe, Asia, and Africa, forever changing people's diets there.

Indian labor made it possible for Spanish settlers to build many fine libraries, theaters, and churches. The Indians worked with materials they knew well, such as adobe bricks. Sometimes, Spanish priests allowed Indian artists to decorate the church walls with paintings of harvests and local traditions.

SECTION 2 REVIEW

1. **Locate:** (a) Pacific Ocean, (b) Florida, (c) New Spain, (d) Peru, (e) St. Augustine.
2. **Identify:** (a) Vasco Núñez de Balboa, (b) Ferdinand Magellan, (c) Montezuma, (d) Hernando Cortés, (e) Francisco Pizarro, (f) Spanish borderlands, (g) Laws of the Indies.
3. **Define:** (a) conquistador, (b) pueblo, (c) presidio, (d) mission, (e) peninsulare, (f) creole, (g) mestizo, (h) encomienda, (i) plantation.
4. Why did Las Casas want colonists to bring Africans to labor as slaves in New Spain?
5. (a) How did the Spanish contribute to the culture of New Spain? (b) How did Native Americans contribute?
6. **CRITICAL THINKING** **Synthesizing Information** How did Cabeza de Vaca and his three companions survive for eight years in the Spanish borderlands?

ACTIVITY **Writing to Learn**
Imagine that you are a messenger for Montezuma. Write a report to the emperor describing the arrival of Cortés.

3
Staking Claims in North America

FIND OUT
- What European nations searched for a northwest passage?
- Why did the Protestant Reformation heighten rivalry among nations?
- How were New France and New Netherland founded?
- How did the arrival of Europeans affect Indians in North America?

VOCABULARY northwest passage, coureur de bois

In August 1497, the court of King Henry VII of England buzzed with excitement. Italian sea captain Giovanni Caboto and a crew of sailors from the port of Bristol, England, had just returned from a 79-day Atlantic voyage. Caboto, called John Cabot by the English, reported that he had reached a "new-found" island in Asia where fish were plentiful.

Cabot's voyage was one of many that Europeans made to North America in the late 1400s and early 1500s. England, France, and the Netherlands all envied Spain's new empire. They, too, wanted colonies. Soon, they were sending explorers across the Atlantic Ocean.

GEOGRAPHY AND HISTORY
Search for a Northwest Passage

Throughout the 1500s, European nations looked for a faster way to reach the riches of Asia. Magellan's route around South America took too long, they felt. They searched for a **northwest passage**, or waterway through or around North America. (See the map on page 80.)

Cabot. John Cabot was confident he had found such a passage in 1497. He was mistaken. His "new-found" island off the Asian coast was in fact off North America. Today, it is called Newfoundland and is the most eastern province of Canada.

Verrazano and Cartier. Giovanni da Verrazano (vehr rah TSAH noh), another Italian captain, sailed for the French in 1524. Verrazano journeyed along the coast from the Carolinas to Canada. (□ See "Scouting the Atlantic Coast" on page 548.)

During the 1530s, Jacques Cartier (KAR tee yay), also sailing for the French, spotted the broad opening where the St. Lawrence River flows into the Atlantic. Looking for a route to Asia, he sailed a good distance up the St. Lawrence.

Hudson. In 1609, the English sailor Henry Hudson sailed for the Dutch. His ship, the *Half Moon,* entered what is today New York harbor. Hudson continued some 150 miles (240 km) up the river that now bears his name.

The following year, Hudson made a voyage into the far north—this time for the English. After spending a harsh winter in Hudson Bay, Hudson's crew rebelled. They put Hudson, his son, and seven loyal sailors into a small boat and set it adrift. The boat and its crew were never seen again.

All these explorers failed to find a northwest passage to Asia. But in searching for

Our Common Heritage
Jacques Cartier used the Iroquois word kanata, meaning "settlement," to name the vast land in North America that he claimed for France. Today, our neighbor to the north still bears that Indian name, although its spelling is slightly different: Canada.

one, they did something just as important. They mapped and explored many parts of North America. Now, rulers began thinking about how to profit from the region's rich resources. ∎

Religious and Political Rivalries

As European nations raced to gain riches and trade, differences in religious beliefs heightened their rivalry. Until the 1500s, the Roman Catholic Church was the only church in western Europe. In 1517, however, a new reform movement arose that sharply divided Christians.

Catholics versus Protestants. In that year, a German monk named Martin Luther challenged many practices of the Catholic Church. Luther believed that the Church had become too worldly and greedy. He also objected to the Catholic teaching that believers needed to perform good works in order to gain eternal life. He argued that people could be saved only by their faith in God.

Luther's supporters became known as Protestants because of their protests against the Church. "Faith alone" became their rallying cry. The ***Protestant Reformation,*** as the new movement was known, sharply divided Christians in Europe. Within a short time, the Protestants also split, forming many different Protestant churches.

Rivalries in the Americas. When European states expanded to the Americas, they brought their religious and political rivalries with them. For example, in the late 1500s, Roman Catholic monarchs ruled Spain and France. England had a Protestant queen, Elizabeth. Elizabeth encouraged English adventurers to sail along the coasts of New Spain, raiding Spanish treasure fleets. England and France also were religious rivals. In North America, each tried to claim as much territory as possible.

Not all rivalries were religious, however. The Netherlands, like England, was a Prot-

Elizabeth I *Under Elizabeth I, England engaged in a bitter rivalry with Spain. The rivalry ended in 1588, when England defeated the Spanish Armada, the largest fleet in the world at the time. Here, Elizabeth is being carried by her courtiers.* ***Daily Life*** *How does the painting show the wealth of Elizabeth's court?*

estant nation. Yet Dutch and English merchant ships competed with each other for markets all over the world. Later, the Dutch and the English would be rivals in North America, as well.

Building New France

Early voyages of exploration convinced the French that they could not build an empire of gold in the Americas, as Spain had done. Instead, they profited from riches of the sea. Every year, French fishermen braved winter gales and dangerous icebergs to sail across the Atlantic. Off the coasts of Newfoundland, they pulled codfish from the sea in huge numbers.

French ships brought knives, kettles, cloth, and other items for trade with Native

Americans. In return, the French took home beaver skins. These furs sold for high prices in Europe.

In the early 1600s, the man who promoted French fur trade most was Samuel de Champlain (sham PLAYN). Champlain, an excellent sailor and mapmaker, founded the first permanent settlements in what became known as *New France.* The first colony took root at Port Royal, Nova Scotia, in 1605. Three years later, Champlain led another group of settlers along the route Cartier had pioneered. On a rocky cliff high above the St. Lawrence River, Champlain built a trading post known as Quebec (kwee BEHK).

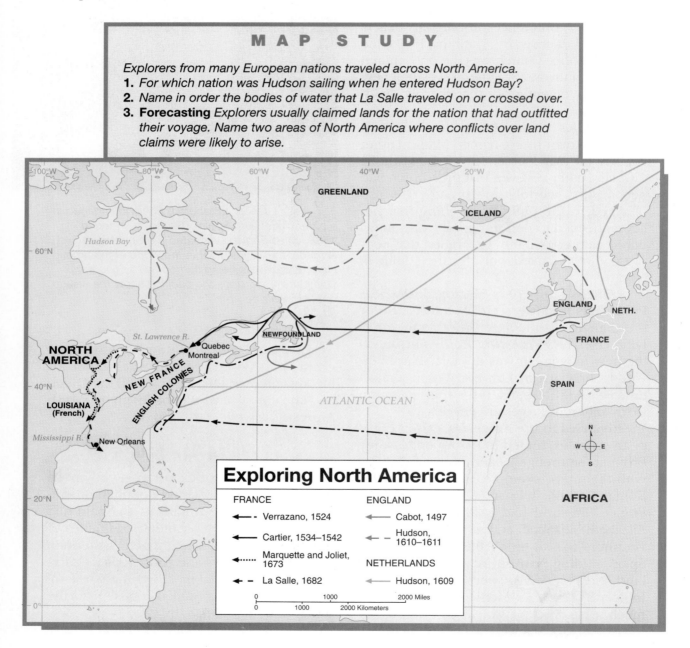

MAP STUDY

Explorers from many European nations traveled across North America.
1. *For which nation was Hudson sailing when he entered Hudson Bay?*
2. *Name in order the bodies of water that La Salle traveled on or crossed over.*
3. **Forecasting** *Explorers usually claimed lands for the nation that had outfitted their voyage. Name two areas of North America where conflicts over land claims were likely to arise.*

Exploring North America

FRANCE	ENGLAND
◄— - Verrazano, 1524	◄— Cabot, 1497
◄— Cartier, 1534–1542	◄— - Hudson, 1610–1611
◄······ Marquette and Joliet, 1673	NETHERLANDS
◄— – La Salle, 1682	◄— Hudson, 1609

Map labels: GREENLAND, ICELAND, Hudson Bay, ENGLAND, NETH., NEWFOUNDLAND, FRANCE, St. Lawrence R., Quebec, Montreal, NORTH AMERICA, NEW FRANCE, ENGLISH COLONIES, SPAIN, LOUISIANA (French), ATLANTIC OCEAN, Mississippi R., New Orleans, AFRICA

Scale: 0 1000 2000 Miles / 0 1000 2000 Kilometers

Claiming the Mississippi Valley *Frenchman Robert de La Salle explored the Mississippi River. In this painting, George Catlin shows the dramatic moment when La Salle claimed the Mississippi Valley for France.* **Multicultural Heritage** *How do you think La Salle's claim affected Native Americans, such as those in the painting?*

Trappers, traders, and missionaries. Most French colonists were trappers and traders. Because they lived in the woods, they became known as coureurs de bois (koo RYOOR duh BWAH), or runners of the woods.

Coureurs de bois learned from Native Americans how to trap and survive in the woods. Many married Indian women. Indians taught the French how to build and use canoes. Each fall, Indians and trappers paddled up the St. Lawrence to winter trapping grounds. In the spring, trappers loaded the furs they had collected into canoes for the trip back down the St. Lawrence.

Catholic missionaries often traveled with the fur traders. The missionaries were determined to convert Native Americans to Christianity. They set up missions, drew maps, and wrote about newly explored lands. Life was difficult, especially in winter.

One priest recalled traveling through deep snow using Indian snowshoes:

> 66If a thaw came, dear Lord, what pain! . . . I was marching on an icy path that broke with every step I took; as the snow softened. . .we often sunk in it up to our knees and a few times up to the waist.99

Reaching the "Father of the Waters." French trappers followed the St. Lawrence deep into the heart of North America. Led by Indian guides, they reached the Great Lakes. Here, Indians spoke of a mighty river, which they called Mississippi, or "Father of the Waters."

In 1673, a French missionary, Father Jacques Marquette (mar KEHT), and a fur trader, Louis Joliet (JOH lee eht), set out with Indian guides to reach the Mississippi. They followed the river for more than 700 miles

(1,100 km) before turning back. In 1682, another explorer, Robert de La Salle (lah SAHL), completed the journey to the Gulf of Mexico. La Salle named the region **Louisiana** in honor of the French king, Louis XIV.

To keep Spain and England out of Louisiana, the French built forts along the Mississippi. One fort, at the mouth of the river, was named New Orleans. New Orleans soon grew into a busy trading center. The French also built forts along the Great Lakes, in the north. Among them was Fort Detroit, built by Antoine Cadillac near Lake Erie.

Government of New France. New France was governed much like New Spain. The French king controlled the government directly, and people in settled areas had little freedom. A council appointed by the king made all decisions.

In the 1660s, to encourage farming, Louis XIV sent about a thousand farmers to the colony. The newcomers included many young women. Some were nobles. Others came from middle-class or peasant families. Most of the women were single, but they soon found husbands. Peasant women were in greatest demand because they were used to hard work.

Despite Louis's efforts, New France grew slowly. By 1680, only about 10,000 settlers lived in the colony. Of those, one third lived on farms along the St. Lawrence. Many more chose the life of the coureurs de bois, who lived largely free of government control.

Building New Netherland

At first, the Dutch paid little attention to Henry Hudson's reports about the river that now bears his name. Finally, in 1626, Peter Minuit (MIHN yoo wiht) led a group of Dutch settlers to North America. There, he bought Manhattan Island from local Indians. Minuit called his settlement New Amsterdam.

Other Dutch colonists settled farther up the Hudson River. The entire colony was known as **New Netherland.** In 1655, the Dutch enlarged New Netherland by taking over New Sweden. The Swedes had set up New Sweden along the Delaware River some 15 years earlier.

New Amsterdam *The Dutch founded New Amsterdam on the Hudson River. From 30 houses, it soon grew into a busy port where ships docked from all around the world. This painting of New Amsterdam was done about 1650.* **Geography** *How did its location on the Hudson River help New Amsterdam to thrive?*

Rivalry over furs. From the beginning, Dutch traders sent furs back to the Netherlands. The packing list for the first shipment included "the skins of 7,246 beaver, 853 otter, 81 mink, 36 cat lynx, and 34 small rats."

In the hunt for furs, the Dutch became fierce rivals of the French and their Indian allies, the Algonquins (al GAHN kwihnz). The Dutch made friends with the Iroquois, longtime enemies of the Algonquins. With Iroquois help, the Dutch brought furs down the Hudson to New Amsterdam. The French and Algonquins tried to block them. For many years, fighting raged among Europeans and their Indian allies.

Dutch ways in North America. By the mid-1600s, New Amsterdam had grown into a bustling port. The Dutch welcomed people of many nations and religions to their colony. One Dutch governor boasted that more than 15 languages could be heard in the streets of New Amsterdam.

The Dutch liked to ice-skate, and in winter the frozen rivers and ponds filled with skaters. Other Dutch customs also became part of American culture. For example, every year on Saint Nicholas's birthday, children put out their shoes to be filled with presents. Later, "Saint Nick" became Santa Claus, bringing gifts on Christmas Eve.

Some Dutch words entered the English language. A Dutch master was a "boss." The people of New Amsterdam sailed in "yachts." Dutch children munched on "cookies" and went for rides through the snow on "sleighs."

Impact on Native Americans

The coming of Europeans to North America brought major changes for Native Americans. As in New Spain, European diseases killed millions of Native Americans. Rivalry over the fur trade brought increased Indian warfare as European settlers encouraged their Indian allies to attack one another. The scramble for furs also led to overtrapping. By 1640, trappers had almost

wiped out the beavers on Iroquois lands in upstate New York.

The arrival of European settlers affected Native Americans in other ways. Missionaries tried to convert Indians to Christianity. Indians eagerly adopted European trade goods, such as copper kettles and knives, as well as muskets and gunpowder for hunting. Alcohol sold by European traders had a harsh effect on Native American life.

The French, Dutch, and English all seized Indian lands. Indian nations that were forced off their lands moved westward onto lands of other Indians. At one time or another, each of these European nations also enslaved Native Americans and sold them to plantations in the West Indies. The conflict between Native Americans and Europeans would continue for many years.

SECTION 3 REVIEW

1. **Locate:** (a) Newfoundland, (b) St. Lawrence River, (c) Hudson Bay, (d) New France, (e) Quebec, (f) Louisiana.
2. **Identify:** (a) Henry Hudson, (b) Protestant Reformation, (c) Samuel de Champlain, (d) Robert de La Salle, (e) New Netherland.
3. **Define:** (a) northwest passage, (b) coureur de bois.
4. Why were Spain and England rivals in the late 1500s?
5. Why did settlers in New France prefer trapping to farming?
6. Name three ways Native Americans were affected by the arrival of Europeans.
7. **CRITICAL THINKING Comparing** (a) Name two ways in which New France differed from New Spain. (b) Name two ways in which they were similar.

ACTIVITY Writing to Learn
Imagine that you are a coureur de bois along the St. Lawrence River. Write a diary entry about a typical day.

4
The First English Colonies

FIND OUT
- How did tobacco help save the Jamestown Colony?
- How did self-government begin in Virginia?
- Why did the Pilgrims start a colony in North America?
- How did Native Americans help the Plymouth colonists?

VOCABULARY charter, burgess, representative government

"**I**f England possesses these places in America, Her Majesty will have good harbors, plenty of excellent trees for masts, good timber to build ships. . . all things needed for a royal navy, and all for no price. "

Richard Hakluyt wrote these words to convince Queen Elizabeth I of England to set up colonies in North America. Hakluyt listed a total of 31 arguments in favor of settlement. "We shall," Hakluyt concluded, "[stop] the Spanish king from flowing over all the face. . . of America."

Hakluyt's pamphlet, written in 1584, appealed to English pride. England's rival, Spain, had built a great empire in the Americas. England was determined to win a place there, too.

Colony at Roanoke

The man who encouraged Hakluyt to write his pamphlet was Sir Walter Raleigh, a favorite of Queen Elizabeth. With the queen's permission, Raleigh raised money to outfit a colony in North America. In 1585, seven ships and about 100 men set sail across the Atlantic.

The expedition landed on Roanoke (ROH uh nohk), an island off the coast of present-day North Carolina. Within a year, colonists had run short of food and quarreled with neighboring Indians. When an English ship stopped in the harbor, the weary settlers climbed aboard and sailed home.

A second attempt. Among the original colonists was an artist, John White. In 1587, Raleigh asked White to return to Roanoke with another group of settlers. To help the settlers set up a farming community, Raleigh sent a number of women. In Roanoke, one woman, Ellinor Dare, gave birth to the first English child born in North America.

When supplies ran low, White returned to England. He left behind 117 colonists. Before sailing, White instructed the settlers carefully. If they moved to another place, they were to carve the name of their new location on a tree. If they were attacked, they were to draw a cross.

American Wildlife *John White made vivid drawings that gave many Europeans their first glimpse of the plants and animals of the Americas. Shown here are a sparrow eating corn, an alligator, and a box turtle.* **Geography** *Why would White's drawings be of value to Europeans who planned to settle in North America?*

Gone without a trace. White planned to return in a few months. In England, however, he found the whole nation preparing for war with Spain. It was three years before he could visit Roanoke again. When he rowed ashore, he found the settlement eerily quiet. Houses stood empty and vines twined through the windows. Pumpkins sprouted from the earthen floors.

Still, White had hope. No cross—the sign for an attack—was found. And the word CROATOAN, the name of a nearby island, was carved on a tree.

White was eager to investigate, but a storm was blowing up and his crew refused to make the trip. The next day, White stood sadly on board as the captain set sail for England. To this day, the fate of Roanoke's settlers remains a mystery.

Settlement at Jamestown

Nearly 20 years passed before England tried again to plant a colony. Then, in 1606, the Virginia Company of London received a charter from King James I. A **charter** is a legal document giving certain rights to a person or company.

The charter gave the Virginia Company the right to settle land to the north of Roanoke, between North Carolina and the Potomac River. The land was called Virginia. The charter guaranteed colonists of Virginia the same rights as English citizens.

Hard times. In the spring of 1607, 105 colonists arrived in Virginia. They sailed into Chesapeake Bay and began building homes along the James River. They named their tiny outpost Jamestown, after their king, James I.

Jamestown was located in a swampy area, however. The water was unhealthy, and mosquitoes spread malaria. Many settlers died from disease.

Governing the colony also proved difficult. The Virginia Company had chosen a council of 13 men to rule the settlement. Members of the council quarreled with each other and did little to plan for the colony's future. By the summer of 1608, the Jamestown colony was near failure.

Captain Smith takes charge. Captain John Smith, a swashbuckling soldier, saved the settlement. Smith had little patience with those who refused to plant crops. "No talk, no hope, nor work," he complained. People only wanted to "dig gold, wash gold, refine gold, load gold." But the colonists found no gold and soon ran out of food.

Smith visited nearby Indian villages to trade for food. Powhatan (pow uh TAN), the most powerful chief in the area, agreed to sell corn to the English. Back in Jamestown, Smith set up stern rules that forced colonists to work if they wished to eat.

Starvation and recovery. Life in the colony might have improved if Smith had remained in charge. In 1609, however, the

BIOGRAPHY Pocahontas *Pocahontas, the daughter of Powhatan, brought food to the starving Jamestown settlers. She later married colonist John Rolfe. With him, she visited England, where an artist painted this portrait of her in English dress.* **Multicultural Heritage** *Why do you think later Americans have honored Pocahontas?*

captain badly injured his leg and had to return to England. For the next few years, the colony suffered terribly. Desperate settlers cooked "dogs, cats, snakes, [and] toadstools" to survive. To keep warm, they broke up houses to burn as firewood.

The economy of Jamestown improved when colonists began to grow tobacco after 1612. Europeans had learned about tobacco and pipe smoking from Native Americans. Although King James I considered smoking "a vile custom," the new fad caught on quickly. By 1620, England was importing more than 30,000 pounds (13,500 kg) of tobacco a year. At last, Virginians had found a way to make money.

The First Africans

In 1619, a Dutch ship landed in Jamestown with about 20 Africans. The Dutch sold the Africans to Virginians who needed laborers for growing tobacco. The colonists valued the farming skills that the Africans brought with them from their homeland.

Two of the Africans, Antoney and Isabella, married after they arrived in Virginia. In 1624, they had a son, William. He was the first child of African descent to be born in the English colonies.

Were the first Africans who came to Virginia treated as servants or as slaves? The records do not say. By 1644, about 300 Africans lived in Virginia. Some of them were slaves for life. Others worked as servants and expected one day to own their own farms. Some Africans were already free planters. In 1651, Anthony Johnson owned 250 acres of land and employed five servants to help him work it.

Later in the 1600s, Virginia would set up a system of laws allowing white colonists to enslave Africans. However, the legal system for slavery was not in place during Virginia's earliest years. For a time, some Africans who came to Virginia owned property, testified in court, and voted in elections.

Important Beginnings

The boom in tobacco saved Virginia's economy. Until 1619, however, the colony lacked a stable government. In that year, the Virginia Company sent a governor with orders to consult settlers on all important matters. Male settlers were allowed to elect **burgesses,** or representatives. The burgesses met in an assembly called the ***House of Burgesses.*** Together with the governor, they made laws for the colony.

Self-government takes root. The House of Burgesses marked the beginning of representative government in the English colonies. A **representative government** is one in which voters elect representatives to make laws for them.

The idea that people had political rights was not new to the English. In 1215, English nobles had forced King John to sign the ***Magna Carta,*** or Great Charter. This document said that the king could not raise taxes without first consulting the Great Council of nobles and church leaders. The Magna Carta showed that the king had to obey the law.

Over time, the rights won by nobles were extended to other English people. The Great Council grew into a representative assembly, called Parliament. By the 1600s, Parliament was divided into the House of Lords, made up of nobles, and an elected House of Commons. Only a few rich men had the right to vote. Still, the English had

Our Common Heritage
The first strike for civil rights may have taken place in Jamestown in 1619. Only English men could vote for the House of Burgesses. Polish settlers who had helped build the colony protested. "No vote, no work," they threatened. In the end, the Virginia Company gave the Poles the right to vote.

established that their king or queen must consult Parliament on money matters and must respect the law.

At first, free Virginians had even greater rights than citizens in England. They did not have to own property in order to vote. In 1670, however, the colony restricted the vote to men who owned property.

As slavery grew, free Africans also lost rights. By 1723, even free African property owners could not vote. Women in Virginia were denied the right to vote throughout the colonial period.

Despite these limits, representative government remained important in Virginia. The idea took root that settlers should have a say in the affairs of the colony.

Women in Virginia. During the early years of the Jamestown Colony, only a few women chose to make the journey from England. The Virginia Company realized that if Jamestown were to last, there had to be more families. In 1619, the investors sent about 100 women to Virginia to help "make the men more settled." This first shipload of women quickly found husbands in Jamestown. Each man who married one of these women had to give the Virginia Company 150 pounds (68 kg) of tobacco.

Women did make the colony more settled. Still, life remained a daily struggle. Women had to make everything from scratch—food, clothing, even medicines. Hard work and childbirth killed many at a young age. Even so, settlers began to have hope that the colony might survive.

Pilgrims Seek Religious Freedom

In 1620, another band of English settlers, the **Pilgrims,** sailed for the Americas. Unlike the Virginians or the Spanish, these colonists sought neither gold nor silver. All they wanted was to practice their religion freely.

In England, the Pilgrims belonged to a religious group known as Separatists. They were called that because they wanted to sep-

arate from the official church, the Church of England. The English government bitterly opposed this. Separatists were fined, jailed, and sometimes even executed.

Leaving England. In the early 1600s, a group of Separatists left England for Leyden, a city in the Netherlands. The Dutch allowed the newcomers to worship freely. Still, the Pilgrims missed their English way

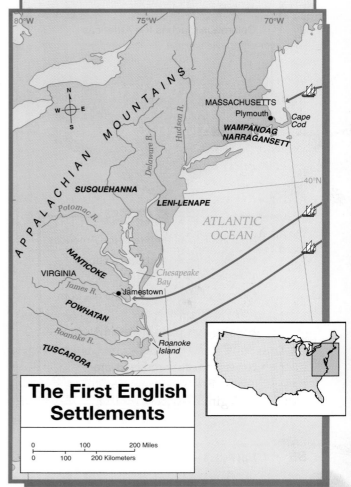

MAP STUDY

In the late 1500s and early 1600s, the English set up colonies in Roanoke, Jamestown, and Plymouth.

1. *Which of these colonies was farthest south?*
2. *The labels in dark capital letters are the names of Indian nations. Which Indians lived near the Plymouth colonists?*
3. **Forecasting** *Based on the map, why do you think the English settlers might come into conflict with Indian nations?*

The First English Settlements

0   100   200 Miles

0   100   200 Kilometers

CRITICAL THINKING SKILLS
Understanding Causes and Effects

Every major event in history has both causes and effects. **Causes** are events or conditions that produced the major event. They explain why the event happened. **Effects** are events or conditions that resulted from the causes.

Causes can be immediate causes or long-range causes. Immediate causes take place shortly before the major event and help trigger it. Long-range causes are underlying causes that build up over time.

Effects can also be immediate or long range. Immediate effects take place shortly after the event. Long-range effects build up over time.

Historians sometimes give word clues for causes and effects. To signal causes, they use words such as *caused, led to,* and *brought about.* To signal effects, they use words such as *therefore, thus,* and *as a result.*

One major event that historians study is European exploration of the Americas. The chart at left lists some causes and effects of European exploration. The arrows show the order of events, from causes of the exploration to its effects.

The following steps will help you understand causes and effects. Use what you have read and the chart to answer the questions.

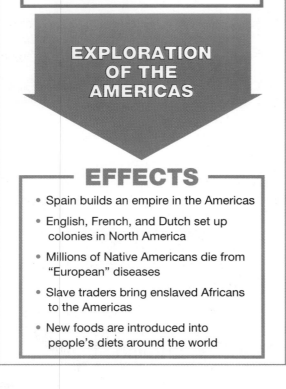

CAUSES

- European trade with the Middle East increases
- Europeans are curious about the world
- Rulers of European nations seek ways to increase their wealth
- European nations look for a new route to Asia
- Columbus reaches the Americas

EXPLORATION OF THE AMERICAS

EFFECTS

- Spain builds an empire in the Americas
- English, French, and Dutch set up colonies in North America
- Millions of Native Americans die from "European" diseases
- Slave traders bring enslaved Africans to the Americas
- New foods are introduced into people's diets around the world

1. **Study events that took place before the major event to find causes.** (a) What were two causes of exploration of the Americas? (b) Which causes of exploration were related to trade? (c) Which cause was most immediate? How do you know?

2. **Study events that took place after the major event to find effects.** (a) What were two effects of exploration of the Americas? (b) What was an effect of exploration on Native Americans? (c) Was the change in people's diets an immediate or a long-range effect? Explain.

3. **Analyze the causes and effects.** (a) Why was increased trade with the Middle East a cause of exploration of the Americas? (b) How was the enslaving of Africans a long-range effect?

ACTIVITY Create a cause-and-effect chart for the Crusades. After you have made your chart, identify immediate causes and effects with an *I* and long-range causes and effects with an *L.*

of life. They also worried that their children were growing up more Dutch than English.

A group of Pilgrims returned to England. Along with some other English people, they won a charter to set up a colony in Virginia. In September 1620, more than 100 men, women, and children set sail aboard a small ship called the *Mayflower.* After a stormy two-month voyage, the Pilgrims landed on the cold, bleak shore of Cape Cod, in present-day Massachusetts. It was November 1620.

Mayflower Compact. Exhausted by the sea voyage, the Pilgrims decided to travel no farther. Their charter, however, was for a colony in Virginia, not Cape Cod. Before going ashore, they needed rules for their new home. Gathering together, the Pilgrims drew up the **Mayflower Compact.** The 41 men who signed it agreed to consult each other about laws for the colony and promised to work together to make the colony succeed:

66 We, whose names are underwritten . . . Having undertaken for the Glory of God, and Advancement of the Christian Faith . . . a voyage to plant the first colony in the northern parts of Virginia . . . do enact, constitute, and frame, such just and equal Laws . . . as shall be thought most [fitting] and convenient for the general Good of the Colony. 99

The Pilgrims named the colony Plymouth. During their first winter there, they had no time to build proper shelters. Most lived in sod houses quickly thrown together. Nearly half the settlers died of disease or starvation. The Pilgrims' religious faith was strong, however. They believed that it was God's will for them to remain in Plymouth.

Help from Native Americans. In the spring, the Pilgrims received help from neighboring Indians. A Pemaquid Indian, Samoset, had learned English from earlier explorers sailing along the coast. He introduced the Pilgrims to Massasoit (MAS uh soit), chief of the local Wampanoag (wahm puh NOH ahg) Indians.

The Wampanoag who helped the Pilgrims most was named Squanto. Squanto brought the Pilgrims seeds of native plants—corn, beans, and pumpkins—and showed them how to plant them. He also taught the settlers to stir up eels from river bottoms and then snatch them with their hands. The grateful Pilgrims called Squanto "a special instrument sent of God."

In the fall, the Pilgrims had a good harvest. Because they believed that God had given them this harvest, they set aside a day for giving thanks. In later years, the Pilgrims celebrated each harvest with a day of thanksgiving. Americans today celebrate **Thanksgiving** as a national holiday.

SECTION 4 REVIEW

1. **Locate:** (a) Roanoke, (b) Jamestown, (c) Cape Cod, (d) Plymouth.
2. **Identify:** (a) Sir Walter Raleigh, (b) John White, (c) Virginia Company, (d) John Smith, (e) House of Burgesses, (f) Magna Carta, (g) Pilgrims, (h) Mayflower Compact, (i) Thanksgiving.
3. **Define:** (a) charter, (b) burgess, (c) representative government.
4. List three things that helped Jamestown to survive.
5. Why did the Pilgrims come to the Americas?
6. List two ways in which Squanto helped the Plymouth colonists.
7. **CRITICAL THINKING Comparing** How were the reasons for founding Jamestown different from the reasons for founding Plymouth?

ACTIVITY Writing to Learn
Imagine that it is 1620. Write an advertising pamphlet to attract settlers to Jamestown.

Summary

- A growing interest in trade led European nations to explore the world beyond their borders.
- Spain built a large and powerful empire in the Americas.
- Throughout the 1500s, the English, French, and Dutch searched for a northwest passage to Asia.
- The first permanent English colonies in the Americas were founded at Jamestown and Plymouth.

Reviewing the Main Ideas

1. What were three results of the Crusades?
2. Why were the Spanish able to conquer the huge Aztec and Incan empires?
3. (a) What four social classes did the Laws of the Indies set up? (b) What did each group do for a living?
4. Why did Europeans send explorers to North America?
5. Name three ways in which the arrival of Europeans affected Native Americans in North America.
6. (a) What was the House of Burgesses? (b) Why was it important?
7. Why did the Pilgrims remain in Plymouth despite terrible hardships?

Thinking Critically

1. **Linking Past and Present** Identify one American tradition or idea that can be traced to each of the following: (a) Native Americans, (b) Spanish, (c) Dutch, (d) English, (e) Africans.
2. **Defending a Position** Do you agree or disagree with the following statement: In trying to help Native Americans, Bartolomé de Las Casas did more harm than good. Defend your position.

3. **Analyzing Information** Review the discussions of government in New Spain and Jamestown on pages 74–77 and 85–87. Which colony gave settlers more say in their government? Explain.

Applying Your Skills

1. **Ranking** Review the explorations of Columbus, Balboa, Magellan, Cartier, and Hudson. Then rank them according to which you think was most important. In a few sentences, explain your ranking.
2. **Making a Generalization** Review the descriptions of relations between Europeans and Native Americans on pages 76, 83, and 89. (a) Make a generalization about how Europeans treated Native Americans. (b) List at least three facts to support your generalization.
3. **Analyzing a Quotation** Review the excerpt from the Mayflower Compact on page 89. (a) Why did the Pilgrims want to set up a colony? (b) What kinds of laws did they plan to enact for the colony?

Thinking About Geography

Match the letters on the map with the following places: **1.** Africa, **2.** Asia, **3.** Europe, **4.** India, **5.** East Indies, **6.** West Indies, **7.** Mediterranean Sea. **Movement** Why did Europeans want to reach Asia?

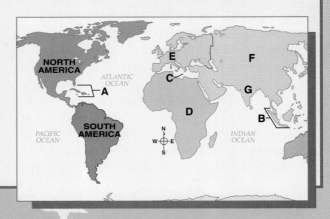

Trading in New France

Form into groups to explore the life of trappers and traders in New France. Follow the suggestions below to write, draw, or dance to show what you have learned about French traders in New France. You may use the textbook, encyclopedias, atlases, or other materials in your classroom library to complete the tasks. Be able to name your sources of information when you have finished the activity.

French trapper

WRITERS AND ARTISTS Make a list of goods that the French traded with Native Americans in the 1600s. Then create a sales catalog of these items. Describe and illustrate each one.

SCIENTISTS Make a list of the animals whose pelts were prized in the fur trade. Then prepare a fact sheet for each animal. Include information such as what the animal eats, where it lives, type of home it builds, and natural enemies. Draw pictures or use pictures from old magazines to illustrate your fact sheets.

POETS AND DANCERS Form into pairs to create a poem and dance about the life of a coureur de bois. Present your poetry-dance recital to the class. Poets can read their poems aloud while dancers perform.

REPORTERS Conduct an interview with Samuel de Champlain. Cover such topics as Champlain's accomplishments as a sailor and mapmaker, his exploration and settlements in North America, and his role in the French fur trade. You might audiotape or videotape your interview to present it to the class as a radio or TV show.

CARTOGRAPHERS Draw a map of North America. On the map, draw the water routes that fur traders might have used to ship their furs to France. Label the waterways.

Powder horn showing route used in fur trade

 Prepare a Trading in New France bulletin board display on which each group presents or describes its completed activity.

Native American fur traders

CHAPTER 4

The 13 English Colonies

(1630–1750)

CHAPTER OUTLINE

1 The New England Colonies

2 The Middle Colonies

3 The Southern Colonies

4 Ruling the Colonies

5 The Colonies in 1750

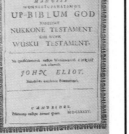

1670s *Relations between colonists and Native Americans ranged from friendly to hostile. This Bible in the Algonquian language was translated by a Puritan missionary.*

1682 *Pennsylvania was founded in 1682. Many settlers who came to Pennsylvania were skilled craftsworkers.*

1630 *Puritans from England set up a colony in Massachusetts Bay. Here, settlers are building a home in Massachusetts.*

| 1630 | 1650 | 1670 | 1690 |

WORLD EVENT
1660s England passes Navigation Acts

WORLD EVENT
1689 William and Mary sign English Bill of Rights

Chapter Setting

On a warm May day in the 1750s, a parade made its way down a main street in Newport, Rhode Island. It was Negro Election Day.

Most of the city's Africans had turned out. Dressed in their finest clothes, they sang and played musical instruments as they marched. One resident later recalled:

❝All the various languages of Africa, mixed with broken . . . English, filled the air, accompanied with the music of the fiddle, tambourine, the banjo, [and] drum.❞

Similar parades took place throughout New England in the mid-1700s. Each year, at about the time white New Englanders voted for their colonial government, Africans held their own elections. In Newport, African residents voted for a "governor." The winner presided over a grand feast. During the year, the governor settled court cases or disputes among black townspeople.

Negro Election Day was a truly American custom, blending traditions from different lands. In part, it was like festivals held by the Ashanti peoples of West Africa. Many Ashanti had been brought to the Americas as slaves. At the same time, it included elements of English election-day celebrations.

As the colonies grew in the 1600s and 1700s, they became home to peoples from many lands. These peoples brought their own customs and traditions. In time, they shaped these old ways into a new American culture.

ACTIVITY Write the following geography terms on a sheet of paper: rocky soil, fertile soil, mild winters, thick forests, long growing season, hilly land, good harbors. Brainstorm to decide how each might affect the way of life settlers developed in a new land.

1700s *Thousands of enslaved Africans arrived each year in the English colonies. This poster advertises a slave auction.*

1750s *New England merchants dominated colonial trade. This painting shows Moses Marcy, a wealthy "Yankee trader."*

1732 *James Oglethorpe founded the colony of Georgia. Here, he presents a group of Native Americans to Georgia's trustees in London.*

1690	1710	1730	1750

 WORLD EVENT
1700s Age of Enlightenment begins

WORLD EVENT
1725 English Quakers speak out against slavery

1

The New England Colonies

FIND OUT

- Why did Puritans set up the Massachusetts Bay Colony?
- Who founded the colonies of Connecticut and Rhode Island?
- How did people in New England make a living?

VOCABULARY toleration

April and May 1630 were cold, stormy months in the North Atlantic. Huddled below deck, colonists aboard the *Arbella* wondered if they had been foolish to sail to a new land. Their leader, John Winthrop, had no doubts. The new colony, he assured them, would set an example to the world:

❝The Lord will make our name a praise and glory, so that men shall say of succeeding [colonies]: 'The Lord make it like that of New England.' For we must consider that we shall be like a City upon a Hill. The eyes of all people are on us. ❞

The passengers on the *Arbella* were among more than 1,000 men, women, and children who left England in 1630 to settle in the Americas. They set up their colony on Massachusetts Bay, north of Plymouth. Over the next 100 years, English settlers would build towns and farms throughout New England.

Puritans in Massachusetts

John Winthrop and his followers were part of a religious group known as *Puritans.* The Puritans wanted to reform the Church of England. They were different from the Pilgrims, who had wanted to separate entirely from the English church. The Puritans called for simpler forms of worship. They wanted to do away with practices borrowed from Roman Catholics, such as organ music and special clothes for priests.

Reasons for leaving England. Puritans were a powerful group in England. Many were well-educated merchants or landowners. Some held seats in the House of Commons. However, Charles I, who became king in 1625, disliked their religious ideas. He took away many Puritan business charters and had Puritans expelled from universities. A few were even jailed.

Some Puritan leaders decided that England had fallen on "evil and declining times." In 1629, they convinced royal officials to grant them a charter to form the Massachusetts Bay Company. The company's bold plan was to build a new society in New England. The new society would be based on the laws of God as they appeared in the Bible. Far from the watchful eye of the king, Puritans would run their colony as they pleased.

Some people joined the colonists for economic rather than religious reasons. They were not Puritans escaping persecution but people looking for land. In England, the oldest son usually inherited his father's estate. Younger sons had little hope of owning land. For these people, Massachusetts Bay offered cheap land or a chance to start their own business.

Settling in. The Puritans sent a small advance party to North America in 1629. John Winthrop and his larger party of colonists arrived the following year. Winthrop was chosen as the first governor of the Massachusetts Bay Colony, as the Puritan settlement was called.

Once ashore, Winthrop set an example for others. Even though he was governor of the colony, he worked as hard as anyone to build a home, clear land, and plant crops. As one colonist wrote, "He so encouraged us that there was not an idle person to be found in the whole colony."

At first, Winthrop tried to govern the colony according to its charter. Only stockholders who had invested money in the Massachusetts Bay Company could vote. However, most settlers were not stockholders. They resented taxes and laws passed by a government in which they had no say.

Voters elect an assembly. Winthrop and other stockholders quickly realized that the colony would run more smoothly if other settlers could take part. On the other hand, the Puritan leaders were determined to keep non-Puritans out of government. As a result, they granted the right to vote for governor to all men who were church members. Later, male church members also elected representatives to an assembly called the *General Court.*

Under the leadership of Winthrop and other Puritans, the Massachusetts Bay Colony grew and prospered. Between 1629 and 1640, more than 20,000 men, women, and children journeyed from England to Massachusetts. This movement of people is known as the *Great Migration.* Many of the newcomers settled in Boston, which grew into the colony's largest town. (📖 See "Forefathers' Song" on page 550.)

Settling Connecticut

In May 1636, about 100 settlers, led by a Puritan minister named Thomas Hooker, left Massachusetts Bay. Pushing west, they drove their cattle, goats, and pigs along Indian trails that cut through the forests. When they reached the Connecticut River, they built a town, which they called Hartford.

Hooker left Massachusetts Bay because he believed that the governor and other officials had too much power. He wanted to set up a colony in Connecticut with laws that set strict limits on government.

In 1639, the settlers wrote a plan of government called the *Fundamental Orders of*

The Puritan *Relying on faith and hard work, the Puritans built a thriving colony at Massachusetts Bay. Augustus Saint-Gaudens, the foremost American sculptor of the 1800s, captured the Puritan spirit in his powerful bronze statue* The Puritan. **American Traditions** *How did their religious beliefs help the Puritans succeed?*

Connecticut. The Fundamental Orders created a government much like that of Massachusetts. There were, however, two important differences. First, the Fundamental Orders gave the vote to all men who were property owners, including men who were not church members. Second, the Fundamental Orders limited the governor's power. In this way, the Fundamental Orders expanded the idea of representative government in the English colonies.

By 1662, 15 towns were thriving along the Connecticut River. In that year, Connecticut became a separate colony, with a new charter granted by the king of England.

MAP STUDY

The New England Colonies were among the first colonies the English set up in North America. Major economic activities in the region included shipbuilding, fishing, and fur trapping.

1. Name the four New England Colonies.
2. What products did Connecticut produce?
3. **Understanding Causes and Effects** How did New England's geography encourage the growth of shipbuilding?

St. Lawrence R.

MAINE
(part of Mass.)

Area claimed by
New York and
New Hampshire

Connecticut R.

Falmouth

NEW
HAMPSHIRE

Portsmouth

Newburyport

NEW
YORK

Salem

MASSACHUSETTS   Boston

Plymouth

CONNECTICUT

ATLANTIC OCEAN

New Haven

Newport

RHODE
ISLAND

N
W   E
S

The New England Colonies

Products

🌾 Grain	🐟 Fish	‡‡ Ships
🐂 Cattle	🐋 Whales	▬ Iron
🌲 Lumber	🦫 Furs	🫙 Rum

0   100   200 Miles

0   100   200 Kilometers

Toleration in Rhode Island

Another Puritan who disagreed with the leaders of Massachusetts Bay was Roger Williams. A young minister in the village of Salem, Williams was gentle and good-natured. Most people, including Governor Winthrop, liked him. In 1635, however, Williams found himself in trouble.

Williams believed strongly that the Puritan church had too much power in Massachusetts. In Williams's view, the business of church and state should be completely separate. The state, said Williams, should maintain order and peace. It should not support a particular church.

Williams also believed in religious toleration. Toleration means a willingness to let others practice their own beliefs. In Puritan Massachusetts, non-Puritans were not permitted to worship freely.

Williams's ideas about these and other matters troubled Puritan leaders. In 1635, the Massachusetts General Court ordered him to leave the colony. Fearing that the court would send him back to England, Williams escaped to Narragansett Bay. He spent the winter with Indians there. In the spring, the Indians sold him land for a settlement. After several years, it became the English colony of Rhode Island.

In Rhode Island, Williams put into practice his ideas about religious toleration. He allowed complete freedom of religion for all Protestants, Jews, and Catholics. He did not set up a state church or require settlers to attend church services. He also gave all white men the right to vote. Before long, settlers who disliked the strict Puritan rule of Massachusetts flocked to Providence and other towns in Rhode Island.

Linking Past and Present
The first synagogue in the United States was built in Newport, Rhode Island, in 1763. The Touro Synagogue, designed by Peter Harrison, still stands today.

The Trial of Anne Hutchinson

One woman who found shelter in Rhode Island was Anne Hutchinson. Hutchinson and her husband, William, had settled in Boston in 1634. She worked as a midwife, helping to deliver babies. Hutchinson herself had 14 children.

Hutchinson was intelligent and God-fearing. Governor Winthrop called her "a woman of a ready wit and bold spirit." In time, however, her bold spirit got her into trouble with Puritan officials.

Forbidden meetings. Hutchinson often held Bible readings in her home. And after church, she and her friends gathered to discuss the minister's sermon. Sometimes, as many as 50 or 60 people flocked to her house to listen.

Anne Hutchinson Preaches at Home *Anne Hutchinson's independent views angered the Puritan leaders of Massachusetts Bay. In 1638, they ordered her to leave the colony. Here, Hutchinson defies Puritan leaders by preaching in her Boston home.* **Citizenship** *Why do you think Hutchinson moved to Rhode Island after leaving Massachusetts Bay?*

At first, Hutchinson merely related what the minister had said. Later, however, she expressed her own views. Often, she seemed to criticize the minister's teachings.

Puritan leaders grew angry. They believed that Hutchinson's opinions were full of religious errors. Even worse, Hutchinson was a woman. A woman did not have the right to explain God's law, they said. That job belonged to ministers. In November 1637, the General Court ordered Hutchinson to appear before it.

On trial. At her trial, Hutchinson answered all the questions put to her by Governor Winthrop and other members of the court. Time after time, she revealed weaknesses in their arguments. They could not prove that she had broken any Puritan laws or challenged any religious teachings. Winthrop was clearly annoyed. "Mrs. Hutchinson can tell when to speak and when to hold her tongue," he concluded sharply.

Then, after two days of questioning, Hutchinson made a serious mistake. She told the court that God spoke directly to her.

66 *Hutchinson:* I bless the Lord. He hath let me see which was the [true] ministry and which [was] wrong. . . .
The court: How do you know that it was God that did reveal these things to you?
Hutchinson: By an immediate revelation.
The court: How! An immediate revelation?
Hutchinson: By the voice of his own spirit to my soul. 99

Members of the court were shocked. The Puritans believed that God spoke only through the Bible, not directly to individuals. The court declared that Hutchinson was "deluded by the Devil" and ordered her out of the colony.

In 1638, Hutchinson, along with her family and some friends, went to Rhode Island. The Puritan leaders had won their case against her. For later Americans, however, Hutchinson became an important symbol of the struggle for religious freedom. ■

Relations With Native Americans

From Massachusetts Bay, settlers fanned out across New England. Some built trading and fishing villages along the coast north of Boston. In 1680, the king of England made these coastal settlements into a separate colony called New Hampshire.

As more colonists settled in New England, they took over lands used by Native Americans for thousands of years. As a result, fighting often broke out between white settlers and Indian nations of the region.

The largest conflict came in 1675, when Wampanoag Indians, led by their chief, Metacom, attacked colonial villages throughout New England. Other Indian groups allied themselves with the Wampanoags. Fighting lasted 15 months. In the end, however, Metacom was captured and killed. The English sold his family and about 1,000 other Indians into slavery in the West Indies. Other Indians were forced from their homes. Many died of starvation.

The pattern of English expansion followed by war between settlers and Indians was repeated throughout the colonies. It would continue for many years to come.

Linking Past and Present
The biggest battle of the war between Metacom and New England settlers took place in a great swamp. Descendants of the Wampanoags have dedicated the spot as a shrine of brotherhood. Each September, they hold a ceremony at the monument that stands there.

BIOGRAPHY Metacom *Native Americans in New England watched with alarm as settlers moved onto Indian lands. More than 10,000 Indians joined the Wampanoag leader Metacom in a war against the New England Colonies.* ***Multicultural Heritage*** *Why do you think many Indians were willing to join Metacom?*

A Life of Hard Work

New England was a difficult land for colonists. But the Puritans believed that daily labor honored God as much as prayer. With hard work, they built a thriving way of life.

Farms, forests, and seas. New England's rocky soil was poor for farming. After a time, however, settlers learned to grow Native American crops, such as Indian corn, beans, squash, and pumpkins.

Although the soil was poor, the forests were full of riches. New Englanders hunted wild turkey and deer, as well as hogs that they let roam free in the woods. In the spring, colonists collected the sweet sap that dripped from gashes cut in sugar maple trees. Settlers also cut down trees and floated them to sawmills near port cities such as Boston, Massachusetts, or Portsmouth, New Hampshire. Here, major shipbuilding centers grew.

Other New Englanders fished the coastal waters for cod and halibut. When the fish were running, fishers worked tirelessly, seldom taking time to eat or sleep. Shellfish in New England were especially large. Oysters sometimes grew to be a foot long. Lobsters stretched up to 6 feet. "Those a foot long," one host recommended, "are better for serving at a table." Larger ones hung off the edge!

In the 1600s, New Englanders also began to hunt whales. Whales supplied them with products such as oil for lamps and ivory. In the 1700s and 1800s, whaling grew into a big business.

Tightly knit towns and villages. Puritans believed that people should worship and take care of local matters as a community. For this reason, New England became a land of tightly knit towns and villages.

At the center of each village was the common, an open field where cattle grazed. Nearby stood the meetinghouse, where Puritans worshipped and held town meetings. Wooden houses with steep roofs lined both sides of the town's narrow streets.

The Puritans took their Sabbath, or holy day of rest, very seriously. On Sundays, no one was allowed to play games or visit taverns to joke, talk, and drink. The law required all citizens to attend church services.

During the 1600s, women sat on one side of the church and men on the other. Blacks and Indians stood in a balcony at the back. Children had separate pews, where an adult watched over them. If they "sported and played" or made "faces [that] caused laughter," they were punished.

At town meetings, settlers discussed and voted on many issues. What roads should be built? What fences needed repair? How much should the schoolmaster be paid? Town meetings gave New Englanders a chance to speak their minds. This early experience encouraged the growth of democratic ideas in New England.

Puritan laws were strict, and lawbreakers faced severe punishment. About 15 crimes carried the death penalty. One crime punishable by death was witchcraft. In 1692, Puritans executed 20 men and women as witches in Salem Village, Massachusetts.

In a New England Home *Most New England homes had no fireplace in the bedroom. Colonists would fill a warming pan (left) with hot coals and slip it between the sheets to warm up the bed. Home furniture was sturdy and practical—like this oak chair that converted into a table. New England craftsworkers also produced fine pewter items, like the teapot at right.* **Daily Life** *How do these items reflect the geography of New England?*

Home and family. The Puritans saw children as a blessing of God. The average family had seven or eight children. The good climate allowed New Englanders to live long lives. Many reached the age of 70. As a result, children often grew up knowing both their parents and their grandparents. This did much to make New England towns closely knit communities.

During the 1700s, the Puritan tradition declined. Fewer families left England for religious reasons. Ministers had less influence on the way colonies were governed. Even so, the Puritans stamped New England with their distinctive customs and their dream of a religious society.

SECTION 1 REVIEW

1. **Locate:** (a) New England Colonies, (b) Massachusetts, (c) Connecticut, (d) Rhode Island, (e) New Hampshire.
2. **Identify:** (a) John Winthrop, (b) Puritans, (c) General Court, (d) Great Migration, (e) Fundamental Orders of Connecticut, (f) Roger Williams, (g) Anne Hutchinson, (h) Metacom.
3. **Define:** toleration.
4. How did the Puritans govern the Massachusetts Bay Colony?
5. (a) Why did Thomas Hooker and Roger Williams leave the Massachusetts Bay Colony? (b) Where did each of them go?
6. How did New Englanders use the resources of the region to make a living?
7. **CRITICAL THINKING Linking Past and Present** (a) Why did the Puritan leaders see Anne Hutchinson as a threat to Massachusetts? (b) Do you think the government would see her as a threat today? Explain.

ACTIVITY Writing to Learn
Write a dialogue between a New England settler and a Wampanoag Indian in which they discuss tensions between their peoples in the mid-1600s.

2 The Middle Colonies

FIND OUT

- What was William Penn's "holy experiment"?
- Why were the Middle Colonies known as the Breadbasket Colonies?
- What peoples settled in the Middle Colonies?
- What was life like in the backcountry?

VOCABULARY patroon, proprietary colony, cash crop, backcountry

In the summer of 1744, a doctor from the colony of Maryland traveled north to Philadelphia. Doctor Hamilton was amazed at the variety of people he met in that city. Describing a meal he had there, he wrote:

&&I dined at a tavern with a very mixed company of different nations and religions. There were Scots, English, Dutch, Germans, and Irish. There were Roman Catholics, Church [of England] men, Presbyterians, Quakers, . . . Moravians, . . . and one Jew.&&

By the mid-1700s, England had four colonies in the region south of New England. Because of their location between New England and the Southern Colonies, they were known as the Middle Colonies. As Doctor Hamilton observed, the Middle Colonies had a much greater mix of peoples than either New England or the Southern Colonies.

New Netherland Becomes New York

As you have read in Chapter 3, the Dutch set up the colony of New Netherland along the Hudson River. In the colony's early years, settlers traded with Indians for furs and built the settlement of New Amsterdam into a thriving port.

Huge land grants. To encourage farming in New Netherland, Dutch officials granted large parcels of land to a few rich families. A single land grant could stretch for miles. Indeed, one grant was as big as Rhode Island! Owners of these huge estates, or manors, were called patroons. In return for the grant, each patroon promised to settle at least 50 European farm families on the land. However, patroons had great power and could charge whatever rents they pleased. Few farmers wanted to work for them.

BIOGRAPHY **Peter Stuyvesant** *As governor of New Netherland in the mid-1600s, Peter Stuyvesant held almost total power. He imposed heavy taxes and punished lawbreakers with public whippings. When colonists demanded a voice in government, he told them his authority came "from God." Stuyvesant had lost a leg fighting in the Caribbean.* **Citizenship** *What are some advantages and disadvantages of having a strong ruler like Stuyvesant?*

Most settlers lived in the trading center of New Amsterdam. They came from all over Europe. Many were attracted by the chance to practice their religion freely.

Freedom of religion. Most Dutch colonists were Protestants who belonged to the Dutch Reformed Church. They did, however, allow people of other religions—including Catholics, French Protestants, and Jews—to buy land. "People do not seem concerned what religion their neighbor is," wrote a shocked visitor from Virginia. "Indeed, they do not seem to care if he has any religion at all."

England takes over. In 1664, the rivalry between England and the Netherlands for trade and colonies led to war in Europe. English warships entered New Amsterdam's harbor and took over the city. King Charles II of England then gave New Netherland to his brother, the Duke of York. He renamed the colony New York in the duke's honor.

Founding New Jersey

At the time, New York stretched as far south as the Delaware River. The Duke of York realized that it was too big to govern easily. He gave some of the land to friends, Lord Berkeley and Sir George Carteret. They set up a proprietary (proh PRĪ uh tuhr ee) colony, which they called New Jersey.

In setting up a proprietary colony, the king gave land to one or more people, called proprietors. Proprietors were free to divide the land and rent it to others. They made laws for the colony but had to respect the rights of colonists under English law.

Like New York, New Jersey attracted people from many lands. English Puritans, French Protestants, Scots, Irish, Swedes, Dutch, and Finns mingled in the colony.

In 1702, New Jersey became a royal colony under control of the English crown. The colony's charter protected religious freedom and the rights of an assembly that voted on local matters.

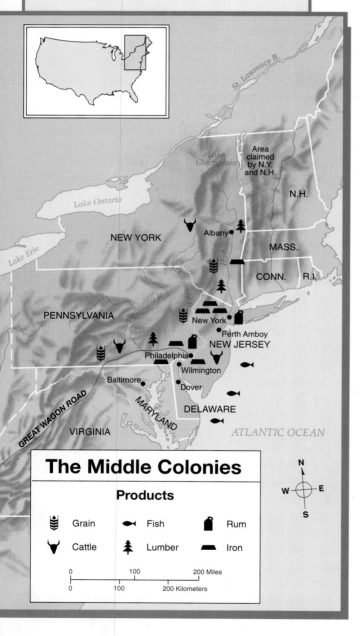

The Middle Colonies

Products

🌾 Grain	🐟 Fish	🍶 Rum
🐂 Cattle	🌲 Lumber	▬ Iron

0   100   200 Miles

0   100   200 Kilometers

Pennsylvania Is Founded

South of New Jersey, another Englishman, William Penn, founded the colony of Pennsylvania. Penn came from a wealthy family. King Charles II was a personal friend. At age 22, however, Penn shocked family and friends by joining the **Quakers,** one of the most despised religious groups in England.

Quaker beliefs. Like Pilgrims and Puritans, Quakers were Protestant reformers. Their beliefs went further than those of other reformers, however. Quakers believed that all people—men and women, nobles and commoners—were equal in God's sight. They refused to bow or remove their hats in the presence of lords and ladies. They spoke out against war and refused to serve in the army.

To most English people, Quaker beliefs seemed wicked. In both England and New England, Quakers were arrested, fined, and even hanged for their beliefs. Penn became convinced that the Quakers must leave England. He turned for help to King Charles.

The king made Penn the proprietor of a large tract of land in North America. The king named the new colony Pennsylvania, or Penn's woodlands.

Penn's "holy experiment." William Penn thought of his colony as a "holy experiment." He wanted it to be a model of religious freedom, peace, and Christian living. Protestants, Catholics, and Jews went to Pennsylvania to escape persecution. Later, English officials forced Penn to turn away Catholic and Jewish settlers.

Penn's Quaker beliefs led him to speak out for fair treatment of Native Americans. Penn believed that the land belonged to the Indians. He said that settlers should pay for the land. Native Americans respected Penn for this policy. As a result, colonists in Pennsylvania enjoyed many years of peace with their Indian neighbors. As one settler remarked:

A Fair and Tolerant Leader *This painting shows William Penn greeting a Native American. Under Penn's leadership, Pennsylvania colonists enjoyed friendly relations with their Indian neighbors. Penn's tolerant policies also attracted settlers like the Pennsylvania Dutch. The pie plate, at right, came from a Pennsylvania Dutch home.* **Culture** *How did Penn's religious beliefs influence his treatment of people of diverse cultures?*

❝And as [Penn] treated the Indians with extraordinary humanity, they became very civil and loving to us. . . . As in other countries, the Indians were [angered] by hard treatment, which hath been the [cause] of much bloodshed, so the [opposite] treatment here hath produced love and affection.❞

Penn sent pamphlets describing his colony all over Europe. Soon, settlers from England, Scotland, Wales, the Netherlands, France, and Germany began to cross the Atlantic Ocean to Pennsylvania. Among the new arrivals were large numbers of German-speaking Protestants. They became known as **Pennsylvania Dutch** because people could not pronounce the word Deutsch (DOICH), which means German.

Most settlers landed at Philadelphia, the colony's capital along the Delaware River. Philadelphia grew quickly. By 1710, an English visitor wrote that it was "the most noble, large, and well-built city I have seen."

Delaware. For a time, Pennsylvania included some lands along the lower Delaware River. The region was known as Pennsylvania's Lower Counties. Settlers in the Lower Counties did not want to send delegates to a far-away assembly in Philadelphia. In 1701, Penn allowed them to elect their own assembly. Later, the Lower Counties broke away to form the colony of Delaware.

Our Common Heritage

The Charter of Liberties that William Penn drew up for his colony specified that Native Americans charged with crimes should be tried by juries containing Native American members. This was a radical idea for the times.

GEOGRAPHY AND HISTORY
A Land of Plenty

Farmers found more favorable conditions in the Middle Colonies than in New England. Unlike New England's thin and rocky soil, the broad Hudson and Delaware river valleys were rich and fertile. Winters were milder than in New England, and the growing season lasted longer.

Food to spare. On such promising land, farmers in the Middle Colonies produced surpluses of wheat, barley, and rye. These were cash crops, or crops that are sold for money on the world market. In fact, the Middle Colonies exported so much grain that they became known as the ***Breadbasket Colonies.***

Farmers of the Middle Colonies also raised herds of cattle and pigs. Every year, they sent tons of beef, pork, and butter to the ports of New York and Philadelphia. From there, the goods went by ship to New England and the South or to the West Indies, England, and other parts of Europe.

A center of manufacturing and crafts. Encouraged by William Penn, skilled German settlers set up shop in Pennsylvania. In time, the colony became a center of manufacturing and crafts. One visitor reported that workshops turned out "most kinds of hardware, clocks, watches, locks, guns, flints, glass, stoneware, nails, [and] paper."

To make household and farm tools, settlers in the Delaware River valley used rich deposits of iron ore. Heating the ore in furnaces, they purified it and then hammered it into nails, tools, and parts for guns. ■

Town and Country

Farms in the Middle Colonies were usually larger than those in New England. Because houses tended to be fairly far apart in the Middle Colonies, towns were less important.

Settling the Middle Colonies *The Middle Colonies attracted a wide variety of European settlers. The painting below shows the farming community of Bethlehem, Pennsylvania. It was founded by a group of Germans seeking religious freedom. The woman on the left is one of the many Irish Catholics who settled in New Jersey.* **Geography** *What attracted settlers to the Middle Colonies?*

The Conestoga Wagon *The Conestoga wagon originated in the Conestoga Creek region of Pennsylvania. Because its wheels did not sink easily into mud, the Conestoga wagon was well suited to the poor roads of the backcountry.* **Daily Life** *Why do you think many new settlers moved westward into the backcountry?*

Building homes. The different groups who settled the Middle Colonies had their own favorite ways of building. Swedish settlers introduced log cabins to the Americas. The Dutch used red bricks to build narrow, high-walled houses. German settlers developed a wood-burning stove that heated a home better than a fireplace, which let blasts of cold air leak down the chimney.

The backcountry. In the 1700s, thousands of German and Scotch-Irish settlers arrived in Philadelphia's booming port. From Philadelphia, they headed west into the backcountry, the area of land along the eastern slopes of the Appalachian Mountains. Settlers followed an old Iroquois trail that became known as the ***Great Wagon Road.***

To farm the backcountry, settlers had to clear thick forests. From Indians, settlers learned how to use knots from pine trees as candles to light their homes. They made wooden dishes from logs, gathered honey from hollows in trees, and hunted wild animals for food. German gunsmiths developed a lightweight rifle for use in forests. Sharpshooters boasted that the "Pennsylvania rifle" could hit a rattlesnake between the eyes at 100 yards.

Many settlers arriving in the backcountry moved onto Indian lands. "The Indians... are alarmed at the swarm of strangers," one Pennsylvania official reported. "We are afraid of a [fight] between them for the [colonists] are very rough to them." On more than one occasion, disputes between settlers and Indians resulted in violence.

SECTION 2 REVIEW

1. **Locate:** (a) Middle Colonies, (b) New York, (c) New Jersey, (d) Pennsylvania, (e) Philadelphia, (f) Delaware.
2. **Identify:** (a) William Penn, (b) Quakers, (c) Pennsylvania Dutch, (d) Breadbasket Colonies, (e) Great Wagon Road.
3. **Define:** (a) patroon, (b) proprietary colony, (c) cash crop, (d) backcountry.
4. How did the land and climate of the Middle Colonies help farmers to prosper?
5. What groups of people settled the Middle Colonies?
6. **CRITICAL THINKING Comparing** (a) How was Penn's "holy experiment" like the Puritan idea of a "City upon a Hill"? (b) How was it different?

ACTIVITY **Writing to Learn**
Imagine that you moved to the backcountry with your family in the 1700s. Write a letter to a friend back in Philadelphia about your new life.

The Southern Colonies

FIND OUT
- Why was each of the Southern Colonies founded?
- What was Bacon's Rebellion?
- How did geography help shape life in the Southern Colonies?
- What was the Middle Passage?

VOCABULARY slave code, racism

In 1763, two English mathematicians, Charles Mason and Jeremiah Dixon, began to survey the 244-mile boundary between Pennsylvania and Maryland. The boundary had been in dispute since 1681. For four years, Mason and Dixon carefully laid stone markers on the border between the two colonies. The sides of the markers facing Pennsylvania were inscribed with the letter P. The sides facing Maryland were inscribed with the letter M. In 1767, the two men completed the *Mason-Dixon Line.*

The Mason-Dixon Line was more than just the boundary between Pennsylvania and Maryland. It also divided the Middle Colonies from the Southern Colonies. Below the Mason-Dixon Line, the Southern Colonies developed a way of life different in many ways from that of the other English colonies.

Lord Baltimore's Maryland

In 1632, Sir George Calvert convinced King Charles I to grant him land for a colony in the Americas. Calvert had ruined his career in Protestant England by becoming a Roman Catholic. Now, he planned to build a colony, Maryland, where Catholics could practice their religion freely. When Sir

George died, his son Cecil, Lord Baltimore, pushed on with the project.

Settling the colony. In the spring of 1634, 200 colonists landed along the upper Chesapeake Bay, across from England's first southern colony, Virginia. The land was rich and beautiful. In the words of one settler:

66 The soil is dark and soft, a foot in thickness, and rests upon a rich and red clay. Every where there are very high trees. . . . An abundance of springs afford water. . . . There is an [endless] number of birds. . . . There is not [anything] wanting to the region. 99

Maryland was truly a land of plenty. Chesapeake Bay was full of fish, oysters,

BIOGRAPHY Lord Baltimore *Cecil Calvert, the second Lord Baltimore, never visited Maryland. However, he influenced the life of the colony by supporting religious toleration for all Christians. This portrait shows Lord Baltimore with his grandson.* **American Traditions** *Why did Lord Baltimore support limited religious toleration?*

and crabs. Across the bay, Virginians were already growing tobacco for profit. Maryland's new settlers hoped to do the same.

Remembering the early problems at Jamestown, the newcomers avoided the swampy lowlands. They built their first town, St. Mary's, in a healthful location.

As proprietor of the colony, Lord Baltimore appointed a governor and a council of advisers. He gave colonists a role in government by creating an elected assembly. To attract settlers, Lord Baltimore made generous land grants to anyone who brought servants, women, and children.

Women set up plantations. A few women took advantage of Lord Baltimore's offer of land. Two sisters, Margaret and Mary Brent, arrived in Maryland in 1638 with nine male servants. In time, they set up two plantations of 1,000 acres each. Later, Margaret Brent helped prevent a rebellion among the governor's soldiers. The Maryland assembly praised her efforts, saying that "the colony's safety at any time [was better] in her hands than in any man's."

Religious toleration. To ensure Maryland's continued growth, Lord Baltimore welcomed Protestants as well as Catholics to the colony. Later, he came to fear that Protestants might try to deprive Catholics of their right to worship freely. In 1649, he asked the assembly to pass an *Act of Toleration.* The act provided religious freedom for all Christians. As in many colonies, this freedom did not extend to Jews.

The Virginia Frontier

Meanwhile, many settlers had gone to Virginia, lured by the promise of profits from tobacco. Wealthy planters took the best lands near the coast. Newcomers had to push inland, onto Indian land. (📖 See "A Complaint From Virginia" on page 551.)

Conflict with Indians. As in New England, conflict over land led to fighting between settlers and Indians. From time to time, Indian and white leaders met to restore peace. Still, new settlers continued to press inland. Indians, in turn, continued to attack these frontier plantations.

After several bloody clashes, settlers called on the governor to take action against Native Americans. The governor refused. He was unwilling to act in part because he profited from his own fur trade with Indians. Frontier settlers were furious.

Bacon's Rebellion. Finally, in 1676, Nathaniel Bacon, a young and ambitious planter, organized angry men and women on the frontier. He raided Native American villages. Then he led his followers to Jamestown and burned the capital.

The uprising, known as *Bacon's Rebellion,* lasted only a short time. When Bacon died suddenly, the revolt fell apart. The governor hanged 23 of Bacon's followers. However, he could not stop English settlers from moving onto Indian lands along the frontier.

The Carolinas

South of Virginia and Maryland, English colonists settled in a region called the Carolinas. Settlement took place in two separate areas.

The settlers. To the north, settlers were mostly poor tobacco farmers who had drifted south from Virginia. They tended to have small farms.

Farther south, a group of eight English nobles set up a larger colony. As proprietors, they received a grant of land from

Our Common Heritage
Groups of escaped slaves, called Maroons, established separate communities in Virginia as early as 1671. In time, there were more than 50 such communities. They were able to survive for years before they were hunted down by white settlers and troops.

King Charles II in 1663. The largest settlement, Charles Town, grew up where the Ashley and Cooper rivers met. Later, Charles Town was shortened to Charleston.

Most early settlers in Charleston were English people who had been living in Barbados, a British colony in the Caribbean. Later, other immigrants arrived, including Germans, Swiss, French Protestants, and Spanish Jews.

Carolina rice. Around 1685, a few planters discovered that rice grew well in the swampy lowlands along the coast. Before long, Carolina rice was a valuable crop traded around the world.

Carolina planters needed large numbers of workers to grow rice. At first, they tried to enslave local Indians. Many Indians died of disease or mistreatment, however. Others escaped into the forests. Planters then turned to slaves from Africa. By 1700, most people coming to Charleston were African men and women brought there against their will.

The northern area of Carolina had fewer slaves. Differences between the two areas led to division of the colony into North Carolina and South Carolina in 1712.

Georgia: A Haven for Debtors

The last of England's 13 colonies was carved out of the southern part of South Carolina. James Oglethorpe, a respected soldier and energetic reformer, founded Georgia in 1732. He wanted the colony to be a place where people jailed for debt in England could make a new start.

Under English law, the government could imprison debtors until they paid what they owed. If they ever got out of jail, debtors often had no money and no place to live. Oglethorpe offered to pay for debtors and other poor people to travel to Georgia. "In America," he said, "there are enough fertile lands to feed all the poor of England."

Early years. In 1733, Oglethorpe and 120 colonists built the colony's first settlement at Savannah, above the Savannah River. Oglethorpe set strict rules for the colony. Farms could be no bigger than 50 acres, and slavery was forbidden.

At first, Georgia grew slowly. Later, however, Oglethorpe changed the rules to allow large plantations and slave labor. After that, the colony grew more quickly.

Spanish and Indian neighbors. Spain and England both claimed the land between South Carolina and Florida. Spain, aided by Creek allies, tried to force the English out. But Oglethorpe and the Georgians held their ground.

A woman named Mary Musgrove greatly helped Oglethorpe during this time. The daughter of a Creek mother and an English father, Mary spoke both Creek and English. She helped to keep peace between the Creeks and the settlers in Georgia. Mus-

Founding the Colony of Georgia
James Oglethorpe was eager to attract settlers to his new colony. This illustration advertising the colony shows Georgia as a green, thriving land of fertile soil and ideal weather.
Economics *Why would a picture like this appeal to the kind of settlers Oglethorpe was trying to attract?*

grove's efforts did much to allow the colony of Georgia to develop in peace.

Plantation Life

The Southern Colonies enjoyed warmer weather and a longer growing season than the colonies to the north. Virginia, Maryland, and parts of North Carolina all became major tobacco-growing areas. Settlers in South Carolina and Georgia raised rice and indigo, a plant used to make a blue dye.

Colonists soon found that it was most profitable to raise tobacco and rice on large plantations. Anywhere from 20 to 100 slaves did most of the work. Most slaves worked in the fields. Some were skilled workers, such as carpenters, barrelmakers, or blacksmiths. Still other slaves worked as cooks, servants, or housekeepers.

Location. Geography affected where southerners built plantations. Along the coastal plain, an area of low land stretched like fingers among broad rivers and creeks. Because the land was washed by ocean tides, the region was known as the *Tidewater.* The Tidewater's gentle slopes and rivers offered rich farmland for plantations.

Inland, planters settled along rivers. Rivers provided an easy way to move goods to market. Along the riverbanks, planters loaded their crops on ships bound for the West Indies and Europe. On the return trip, the ships carried English manufactured goods and other luxuries for planters and their families.

Most Tidewater plantations had their own docks, and merchant ships picked up crops and delivered goods directly to them. For this reason, few large seaport cities developed in the Southern Colonies.

Planters set the style. Only a small percentage of white southerners owned large plantations. Yet, planters set the style of life in the South. Life centered around the Great House, where the planter and his family lived. The grandest of these homes had

M A P   S T U D Y

The Southern Colonies stretched from Maryland to Georgia. Farm products and lumber were important to the economy of the region.
1. Name the Southern Colonies.
2. What were the major products of the backcountry?
3. **Comparing** Compare this map with the map on page 102. (a) How were the products of the Southern Colonies similar to those of the Middle Colonies? (b) How were they different?

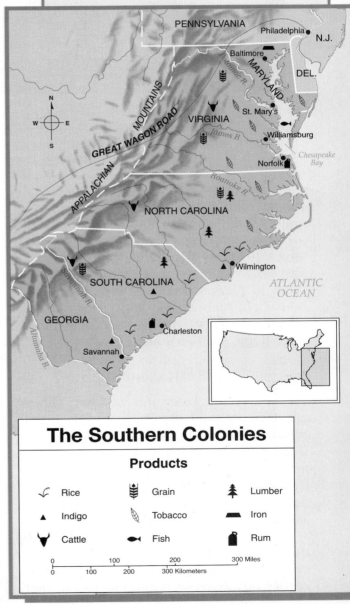

The Southern Colonies

Products

◡ Rice	🌾 Grain	🌲 Lumber
▲ Indigo	🍃 Tobacco	▬ Iron
Ⴤ Cattle	🐟 Fish	🍶 Rum

0   100   200   300 Miles
0   100   200   300 Kilometers

A Tidewater Plantation *This painting shows a typical Tidewater plantation. The Great House of the planter and his family dominates the scene. Slave cabins, barns, and warehouses dot the hillside.* **Geography** *Why do you think the painting shows all roads leading to the river?*

elegant quarters for the family, a parlor for visitors, a dining room, and guest bedrooms.

In the growing season, planters decided which fields to plant, what crops to grow, and when to harvest the crops and take them to market. Planters' wives kept the household running smoothly. They directed house slaves and made sure daily tasks were done, such as milking cows.

The Backcountry

West of the Tidewater was very different. Here, at the base of the Appalachians, rolling hills and thick forests covered the land. As in the Middle Colonies, this inland area was called the backcountry. Attracted by rich soil, settlers followed the Great Wagon Road into the backcountry of Maryland, Virginia, and the Carolinas.

The backcountry was more democratic than the Tidewater. Settlers treated one another as equals. Men worked in their tobacco or corn fields or hunted game. Women cooked meals and fashioned simple clothing out of wool or deerskins.

Life in the backcountry was not easy. Hardship, however, brought families closer. Families gathered to husk corn or help one another raise barns. Spread out along the edge of the Appalachians, these hardy families felled trees, grew crops, and changed the face of the land.

Growth of Slavery

The first Africans in the English colonies included free people and servants as well as slaves. In the early years, however, even those who were enslaved enjoyed some freedom. In South Carolina, for example, some enslaved Africans worked as cowboys, herding cattle to market.

African farming skills. On plantations throughout the Southern Colonies, enslaved Africans used farming skills they had brought from West Africa. They showed English settlers how to grow rice. They also knew how to use wild plants unfamiliar to the English. They made water buckets out of gourds, and they used palmetto leaves to make fans, brooms, and baskets.

By 1700, plantations in the Southern Colonies relied on slave labor. Slaves cleared the land, worked the crops, and tended the livestock.

To control the large number of slaves, colonists passed slave codes. These laws set out rules for slaves' behavior and denied slaves their basic rights. Slaves were seen not as humans but as property.

Attitudes toward slavery. Most English colonists did not question the justice of owning slaves. They believed that black Africans were inferior to white Europeans. The belief that one race is superior to another is called racism. Some colonists claimed that they were helping slaves by introducing them to Christianity.

A handful of colonists saw the evils of slavery. In 1688, Quakers in Germantown, Pennsylvania, became the first group of colonists to call for an end to slavery.

The Slave Trade

As demand for slaves grew, European slave traders set up posts along the African coast. They offered guns and other goods to African rulers who brought them slaves. They loaded the captives aboard Spanish, Portuguese, Dutch, English, and French ships headed for the Americas.

Most slave ships went to Brazil and the Caribbean. However, by the 1720s, between 2,000 and 3,000 Africans were arriving each year in North American English colonies.

The trip from Africa to the Americas was called the *Middle Passage.* Slaves were crammed into small spaces below deck. "Each had scarcely room to turn himself, [and the heat] almost suffocated us," recalled Olaudah Equiano (oh LAW dah ehk wee AH noh), an African who made the voyage.

The Middle Passage *Conditions on ships that carried enslaved Africans to the Americas were brutal. As the diagram shows, slave traders squeezed their human cargo into every available space. The painting was done by an English officer on a slave ship.* **Multicultural Heritage** *What qualities did Africans need to survive on slave ships?*

Once or twice a day, the crew allowed the captives up on deck to eat and exercise.

Some Africans fought for their freedom during the trip. Others refused to eat. Equiano recalled:

66 One day...two of my wearied countrymen who were chained together...jumped into the sea; immediately another...followed their example.... Two of the wretches were drowned, but [the ship's crew] got the other, and afterwards flogged him unmercifully for thus attempting to prefer death to slavery. 99

Records of slave voyages show that about 10 percent of all Africans shipped to North America in the 1700s did not survive the Middle Passage. On some tragic voyages, the number of deaths was much higher.

SECTION 3 REVIEW

1. **Locate:** (a) Southern Colonies, (b) Maryland, (c) Virginia, (d) North Carolina, (e) South Carolina, (f) Georgia.
2. **Identify:** (a) Mason-Dixon Line, (b) Margaret Brent, (c) Act of Toleration, (d) Bacon's Rebellion, (e) James Oglethorpe, (f) Mary Musgrove, (g) Tidewater, (h) Middle Passage.
3. **Define:** (a) slave code, (b) racism.
4. Why did Lord Baltimore ask the assembly to pass the Act of Toleration?
5. What caused Bacon's Rebellion?
6. How did climate affect development of the Southern Colonies?
7. CRITICAL THINKING **Forecasting** Why do you think tensions might have developed between the backcountry and the Tidewater?

ACTIVITY Writing to Learn
Study the painting of the Middle Passage on page 111. Based on the painting, list five adjectives that describe conditions during the Middle Passage.

4
Ruling the Colonies

FIND OUT
- Why did colonists resent the Navigation Acts?
- What items did the colonies trade?
- What rights did colonists gain as a result of the Glorious Revolution?
- How was self-rule strengthened in the colonies?

VOCABULARY mercantilism, import, export, triangular trade, legislature

Philadelphia bustled with activity in 1750. Young men drove cattle, pigs, and sheep to market along narrow cobblestone streets. On the docks, sailors unloaded barrels of molasses from the West Indies, wines from Spain and Portugal, Dutch and English cloth, as well as spices, leather goods, tea, and coffee. "There is actually everything to be had in Pennsylvania that may be obtained in Europe," commented one German visitor.

Philadelphia was the largest and busiest seaport in the colonies. But by the 1700s, trade flourished all along the Atlantic coast. As trade increased, England began to take a new interest in its colonies.

England Regulates Trade

Like other European nations at the time, England believed that the purpose of colonies was to benefit the home country. This belief was part of an economic theory known as mercantilism (MER kuhn tihl ihz uhm). According to this theory, a nation became strong by building up its gold supply and expanding trade.

Founding of the Colonies

Colony/Date Founded	Leader	Reasons Founded
New England Colonies		
Massachusetts Plymouth/1620 Massachusetts Bay/1630	William Bradford John Winthrop	Religious freedom Religious freedom
New Hampshire/1622	Ferdinando Gorges John Mason	Profit from trade and fishing
Connecticut Hartford/1636 New Haven/1639	Thomas Hooker	Expand trade; religious and political freedom
Rhode Island/1636	Roger Williams	Religious freedom
Middle Colonies		
New York/1624	Peter Minuit	Expand trade
Delaware/1638	Swedish settlers	Expand trade
New Jersey/1664	John Berkeley George Carteret	Expand trade; religious and political freedom
Pennsylvania/1682	William Penn	Profit from land sales; religious and political freedom
Southern Colonies		
Virginia/1607	John Smith	Trade and farming
Maryland/1632	Lord Baltimore	Profit from land sales; religious and political freedom
The Carolinas/1663 North Carolina/1712 South Carolina/1712	Group of eight proprietors	Trade and farming; religious freedom
Georgia/1732	James Oglethorpe	Profit; home for debtors; buffer against Spanish Florida

CHART SKILLS *The 13 English colonies were founded for many different reasons.* ● *Which colonies were founded by people seeking religious freedom? Which were founded by people seeking to expand trade?*

Trade takes place when goods are exchanged. **Imports** are goods brought into a country. **Exports** are goods sent to markets outside a country. Because exports help a country earn money, mercantilists thought that a country should export more than it imports.

New laws. Beginning in the 1650s, Parliament passed a series of laws to regulate trade between England and its colonies. The laws were known as the **Navigation Acts.** Parliament passed the laws to ensure that only England benefited from trade with the colonies.

For example, under the new laws, only colonial or English ships could carry goods to and from the colonies. The Navigation Acts also listed certain products, such as tobacco and cotton, that colonial merchants could ship only to England. In this way, Parliament created jobs for English workers who cut and rolled tobacco or spun cotton into cloth.

Colonists react. In many ways, the Navigation Acts helped the colonies as well as England. The law that required the use of English or colonial ships encouraged colonists to build their own ships. New England became a prosperous center for shipbuilding. Moreover, because of the acts, colonial merchants did not have to compete with foreign merchants.

Still, many colonists resented the Navigation Acts. In their view, the laws favored English merchants. Colonial merchants often ignored the Navigation Acts or found ways to get around them.

Molasses, Rum, and Slaves

The colonies produced a wide variety of goods. Ships moved up and down the Atlantic coast in an active trade. Merchants from New England dominated colonial trade. They were known as **Yankees,** a nickname that implied they were clever and hard-working. Yankee traders earned a reputation for getting a good buy and profiting from any deal.

Trade routes. Colonial merchants developed many trade routes. One route was known as the triangular trade because the three legs of the route formed a triangle. On the first leg of the journey, ships from New England carried fish, lumber, and other goods to the West Indies. There, they bought sugar and molasses, a dark-brown syrup made from sugar cane. They then car-

A Flourishing City *Almost from its founding in 1682, Philadelphia was a thriving port. This painting shows the busy Philadelphia waterfront in 1720.* **Economics** *Why did ports become the major cities of the colonies?*

ried the sugar and molasses back to New England, where colonists used them to make rum.

On the second leg, ships carried rum, guns, gunpowder, cloth, and tools from New England to West Africa. In Africa, merchants traded these goods for slaves. On the final leg, ships carried enslaved Africans to the West Indies. With the profits from selling the enslaved Africans, traders bought more molasses.

Breaking the law. Many New England merchants grew wealthy from the triangular trade. In doing so, they often disobeyed the Navigation Acts. Traders were supposed to buy sugar and molasses only from English colonies in the West Indies. However, the demand for molasses was so high that New Englanders bought from the Dutch, French, and Spanish West Indies, too. Although this trade was illegal, bribes made customs officials look the other way.

Travel and Communication

In the 1600s and early 1700s, travel in the colonies was slow and difficult. Roads were rough and muddy, and there were few bridges over streams and rivers. Most colonists stayed close to home.

Colonists set up a postal system, but it was slow. In 1717, it took one month for a letter to get from Boston to Williamsburg, Virginia. In winter, it took two months.

History and You
Settlers kept up a busy exchange of letters. Writing was a chore, however, done with goose quill pens that had to be dipped in ink every few moments. Why do you think people in colonial times went to so much trouble to write letters? Why do most people today write few personal letters?

Slowly, roads and mail service improved. Families built taverns along main roads and in towns and cities. Colorful signs attracted customers, who stopped to rest and to exchange news and gossip with local people.

Colonial printers spread news and ideas by publishing pamphlets and books. By 1750, most colonies published at least one weekly newspaper.

Rights of English Citizens

By the late 1600s, each colony had developed its own form of government. Still, the governments had much in common. In each colony, a governor directed the colony's affairs and enforced the laws. Usually, the governor was appointed by the king or the colony's proprietor. Rhode Island and Connecticut, though, elected their own governor.

Colonial assemblies. Each colony also had a legislature. A legislature is a group of people who have the power to make laws. In most colonies, the legislature had an upper house and a lower house. The upper house was also known as the governor's council. The council was made up of advisers appointed by the governor.

The lower house was an elected assembly. It approved laws and protected the rights of citizens. Just as important, it had the right to approve or disapprove any taxes the governor asked for. This "power of the purse," or right to raise or spend money, was an important check on the governor's power. Any governor who ignored the assembly risked losing his salary.

The right to vote. Each colony had its own rules about who could vote. By the 1720s, however, all the colonies had laws that restricted the right to vote to white Christian men over the age of 21. In some colonies, only Protestants or members of a particular church could vote. All voters had to own property. Colonial leaders believed that only property owners knew what was best for a colony.

On election day, voters and their families gathered in towns and villages. A buzz of excitement filled the air as people exchanged news and gossip. Smiling candidates shook hands with voters and slapped them heartily on the back. In some areas, they offered to buy them drinks. When things quieted down, the sheriff called the voters together. One by one, he read out their names. Everyone listened as each man announced his vote aloud:

> **66** *Sheriff:* Mr. Blair, whom do you vote for?
> *Mr. Blair:* John Marshall.
> *Mr. Marshall:* Your vote is appreciated, Mr. Blair. **99**

Rights from the Glorious Revolution. Colonists took great pride in their elected assemblies. They also valued the rights the Magna Carta gave them as English subjects. (See page 86.) In 1689, colonists won still more rights as a result of the *Glorious Revolution* in England.

The Glorious Revolution began in 1688. Parliament removed King James from the throne and asked William and Mary of the Netherlands to rule. In return for Parliament's support, William and Mary signed the *English Bill of Rights* in 1689. It protected the rights of individuals and gave anyone accused of a crime the right to a trial by jury. Just as important, the English Bill

Our Common Heritage
In early Carolina, many people enjoyed the right to vote. In 1706, a citizen observed, "For this last election, Jews, Strangers, Sailors, Servants, Negroes, & almost every French Man in Craven & Berkly county came down to elect, & their votes were taken."

of Rights said that a ruler could not raise taxes or an army without the approval of Parliament.

Limited rights. The rights of English citizens did not extend to everyone in the colonies. Africans and Indians had almost no rights. Neither did women or servants.

Like women in Europe, colonial women had few legal rights. A woman's father or husband was supposed to protect her. A married woman could not start her own business or sign a contract unless her husband approved it. In most colonies, unmarried women and widows had more rights than married women. They could make contracts and sue in court. In Maryland and the Carolinas, women settlers who headed families could buy land on the same terms as men.

SECTION 4 REVIEW

1. **Identify:** (a) Navigation Acts, (b) Yankees, (c) Glorious Revolution, (d) English Bill of Rights.
2. **Define:** (a) mercantilism, (b) import, (c) export, (d) triangular trade, (e) legislature.
3. (a) List three ways the Navigation Acts helped England. (b) Why did colonists resent them?
4. What goods were included in the triangular trade?
5. How were colonial governments organized?
6. **CRITICAL THINKING Linking Past and Present** (a) Which rights granted by the English Bill of Rights are similar to rights Americans have today? (b) Why is each important?

ACTIVITY **Writing to Learn**
Write a dialogue between Yankee merchants in which they discuss their feelings about the Navigation Acts.

MAP, GRAPH, AND CHART SKILLS
Using a Time Line

Historians study events that happened in the past. They often look at these events in **chronological order,** or the order in which they occurred. In this way, they can judge whether or not events might be related.

A **time line** is one way to show the order in which events took place. A time line also shows the dates when events happened.

A time line appears at the beginning of each chapter in this book. These time lines are called horizontal time lines because they set out dates and events on a line from left to right.

Study the time line below. Then, use these steps to read the time line.

1. **Identify the time period covered in the time line.** (a) What is the earliest event shown on the time line below? (b) What is the latest event? (c) What is the period covered by this time line?

2. **Decide how the time line is divided.** Time lines are always divided into equal parts or time periods. Some time lines are divided into 10-year periods. A 10-year period is called a **decade**.

Some time lines are divided into 100-year periods, called **centuries.** The period from 1701 to 1800, for example, is called the eighteenth century. (a) List the dates that are marked off on the time line below. (b) How many years are there between each date? (c) What events occurred during the decade of the 1670s? (d) What century is shown on this time line?

3. **Study the time line to discover how events might be related.** Use your reading in this chapter and the time line to answer these questions. (a) When did the Glorious Revolution take place? (b) Was the English Bill of Rights passed before or after the Glorious Revolution? (c) Was there a relationship between these two events? Explain your answer.

4. **Draw conclusions.** Use your reading in the chapter and the time line to draw conclusions about the events taking place during this period. (a) What events took place in 1630, 1639, and 1689? (b) What do these events tell you about the growth of self-government in the colonies? Explain. (c) What events took place in 1675 and 1676? (d) Based on these events, what generalization can you make about relations between Native Americans and English settlers in the late 1600s?

ACTIVITY Make a time line of important events in your life.

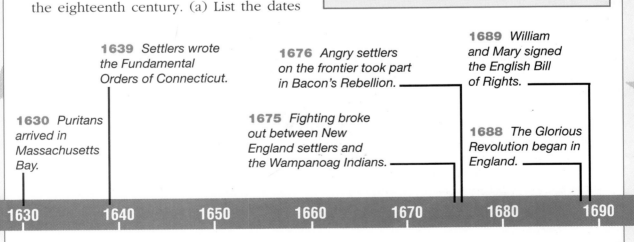

1639 Settlers wrote the Fundamental Orders of Connecticut.

1676 Angry settlers on the frontier took part in Bacon's Rebellion.

1689 William and Mary signed the English Bill of Rights.

1630 Puritans arrived in Massachusetts Bay.

1675 Fighting broke out between New England settlers and the Wampanoag Indians.

1688 The Glorious Revolution began in England.

1630 1640 1650 1660 1670 1680 1690

5

The Colonies in 1750

FIND OUT

- How did the Great Awakening increase religious tolerance?
- What was life like for women in the backcountry and in cities?
- How did colonists educate their children?
- What was the Enlightenment?

VOCABULARY gentry, indentured servant, public school, apprentice

In 1743, Benjamin Franklin, a leading citizen of Philadelphia, made a proposal to the English colonists. It began:

66 The first drudgery of settling new colonies. . . is now pretty well over, and there are many in every province. . . [who have time] to cultivate the finer arts, and improve the common stock of knowledge. 99

Franklin wanted colonists to put their spare time to good use. He invited them to join a society to promote "USEFUL KNOWLEDGE among British [colonies] in America." Thanks to Franklin's efforts, the American Philosophical Society was born.

Franklin's new society was only one sign that the English colonies were coming of age. By the mid-1700s, they had developed a culture quite different from that of England. Blending the traditions of Native Americans, Europeans, and Africans, this culture was truly new and American.

Social Classes

Colonists enjoyed more social equality than people in England did. Still, class differences existed.

At the top of society stood the **gentry.** The gentry included wealthy planters, merchants, ministers, successful lawyers, and royal officials. They could afford to dress in elegant clothes and follow the latest fashions from London.

Below the gentry was the middle class. The middle class included farmers who worked their own land, skilled craftsworkers, and some tradespeople. Nearly three quarters of all white colonists belonged to the middle class. They prospered because land in the colonies was plentiful and easy to buy. Also, laborers were in demand, and skilled workers received good wages.

The lowest social class included hired farmhands, indentured servants, and slaves. **Indentured servants** promised to work without wages for four to seven years for whomever would pay their ocean passage to the Americas. When their term of service was completed, indentured servants received "freedom dues": a set of clothes, tools, and 50 acres of land.

Women in the Colonies

Women throughout the colonies did many of the same tasks—whether they lived in Connecticut or Delaware or South Carolina. A woman took care of her household, husband, and family. By the kitchen fire, she baked squash or a kind of boiled corn known as hominy grits. She milked cows, watched the children, and made clothing.

Backcountry women often worked with their husbands in the fields at harvest time. There was too much to be done to worry about whether it was proper "woman's work." A visitor from the East was amazed by a backcountry woman's activities:

66 She will carry a gunn in the woods and kill deer, turkeys &c., shoot down wild cattle, catch and tye hoggs, knock down [cattle] with an ax, and perform the most manfull Exercises as well as most men. 99

Colonial Women at Work *Women played a major role in the economic life of the colonies. The woman at left is spinning thread into cloth. The woman at right is making pins.* **Daily Life** *How did the lives of these women differ from those of women in the backcountry?*

In cities, women sometimes worked outside the home. A young single woman from a poorer family might work as a maid, a cook, or a nurse for one of the gentry. Other women were midwives, like Anne Hutchinson, delivering babies. Still others sewed fine hats, dresses, or cloaks to be sold to women who could afford them. Learning these skills required many years of practice and training.

Women sometimes learned trades from their fathers, brothers, or husbands. They worked as shoemakers, silversmiths, and butchers. Quite a few women became print-

ers. Then, too, a woman might take over her husband's business when he died.

African Cultural Influences

By the mid-1700s, the culture of Africans in the colonies varied greatly. On rice plantations in South Carolina, slaves saw few white colonists. As a result, African customs remained strong. For example, parents often chose African names for their children, such as Quosh or Juba or Cuff. In some coastal areas, slaves spoke a distinctive combination of English and West African languages, known as Gullah.

The Southern Colonies. In Charleston and other South Carolina port towns, more than half the population was African. Many of them worked along the docks, making rope or barrels or helping to build ships. Skilled craftsworkers made fine wood cabinets or silver plates and utensils. Although most Africans in these towns were enslaved, many opened their own shops or stalls in the market.

Our Common Heritage
Elizabeth Timothy was the first woman publisher in the English colonies. She took over her husband's newspaper, the South Carolina Gazette, *after he died. In all, it is estimated that 30 colonial women published newspapers.*

MAP STUDY

New immigrants from Europe, as well as enslaved Africans, carried their own cultures to the American colonies.
1. Where did most enslaved Africans live?
2. Which group settled the farthest inland?
3. **Drawing Conclusions** (a) Which group settled in all the colonies? (b) How would you explain this?

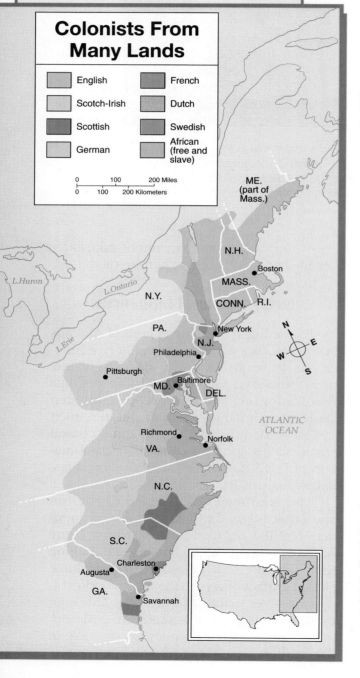

Colonists From Many Lands

- English
- Scotch-Irish
- Scottish
- German
- French
- Dutch
- Swedish
- African (free and slave)

0   100   200 Miles
0   100   200 Kilometers

ME. (part of Mass.)

N.H.

Boston

MASS.

L.Huron

L.Ontario

N.Y.

CONN.   R.I.

PA.   New York

N.J.

Philadelphia

L.Erie

Pittsburgh

MD.   Baltimore

DEL.

ATLANTIC OCEAN

Richmond   Norfolk

VA.

N.C.

S.C.

Charleston

Augusta

GA.

Savannah

In Virginia and Maryland, African traditions were weaker. Africans in the Chesapeake region were less isolated from white farmers and planters. Also, by the 1750s, the number of new slaves arriving in the region each year had begun to decline. Even so, many old customs survived. One traveler observed an African-style funeral. Mourners took part in a ceremony to speed the dead to his home, which they believed was in Africa.

The Middle and New England colonies. Fewer Africans lived in the Middle Colonies and New England. Still, Africans arrived there in greater numbers after the 1740s. Most lived in such cities as Philadelphia, New York, and Newport. Often, the men outnumbered the women. As a result, the number of African families remained small.

A Renewal of Faith

In the 1730s and 1740s, a religious movement known as the ***Great Awakening*** swept through the colonies. Its drama and emotion touched people of all backgrounds.

A New England preacher, Jonathan Edwards, set off the Great Awakening in the colonies. Edwards called on colonists to examine their lives. In powerful sermons, he warned listeners that unless they heeded the Bible's teachings, they would be "sinners in the hands of an angry God," headed for the fiery torments of hell.

In 1739, when an English minister named George Whitefield arrived in the colonies, the movement spread like wildfire. Whitefield drew huge crowds to outdoor meetings from Massachusetts to Georgia. His voice rang with feeling as he called on sinners to reform. Jonathan Edwards's wife described the impact Whitefield had on his listeners:

66[Whitefield] casts a spell over an audience. . . . I have seen upwards of a thousand people hang on his

African Crafts *African craftsworkers created much fine wooden furniture. Many of these works, such as this detail from a fireplace mantel, often had African-inspired designs.* **The Arts** *Compare this carving to the African carving shown on page 67. How are they similar?*

words with breathless silence, broken only by an occasional half-suppressed sob. **"**

The Great Awakening aroused bitter debate. People who supported it often split away from their old churches to form new ones. Opponents warned that the movement was too emotional. Still, the growth of so many new churches forced colonists to become more tolerant of people with different beliefs.

Concern With Education

Among the colonists, New Englanders were most concerned about education. Puritans believed that all people had a duty to study the Bible. If settlers did not learn to read, how would they fulfill this duty?

Public schools in New England. In 1647, the Massachusetts assembly passed a law ordering all parents to teach their children "to read and understand the principles of religion." Beyond that, they required all towns with 50 families to hire a schoolteacher. Towns with 100 families or more had to set up a grammar school that prepared boys for college.

In this way, Massachusetts set up the first public schools, or schools supported by taxes. Public schools were important because they allowed both rich and poor children to get an education.

The first New England schools had only one room for students of all ages. Parents paid the schoolteacher with corn, peas, or other foods. Each child was expected to bring a share of wood to burn in the stove. Students who forgot would find themselves seated in the coldest corner of the room!

Middle and Southern colonies. In the Middle Colonies, churches and individual families set up private schools. Pupils paid to attend. As a result, only wealthy families could afford to educate their children.

In the Southern Colonies, people lived too far apart to bring children together in one building. Some planters hired tutors, or private teachers. The wealthiest planters sent their sons to school in England. As a rule, slaves were denied education of any kind.

Learning by doing. Some children served as apprentices (uh PREHN tihs ehz). An apprentice worked for a master to learn a trade or a craft. For example, when a boy reached age 12 or 13, his parents might apprentice him to a master glassmaker. The young apprentice lived in the glassmaker's home for six or seven years. The glassmaker gave him food and clothing and treated him like a member of the family. He was also supposed to teach the boy how to read and write and provide him with religious training.

In return, the apprentice worked without pay in the glassmaker's shop and learned the skills he needed to become a

Ben Franklin: Practical Inventor

Ben Franklin was always asking questions. To his restless mind, there was nothing that could not be learned; nothing that could not be improved.

One of Franklin's nagging concerns was fireplaces. The fireplace was the heart of the colonial home. But fireplaces of the day worked poorly. They spewed black smoke throughout the house and sent most of the heat up the chimney.

To solve these problems, Franklin invented the "Pennsylvania Fireplace." Set in the middle of the room, the fireplace gave off heat from three sides. Once cold air entered the fireplace, it was heated in an "air box." The heated air then rushed into the room through vents in the fireplace sides. As for smoke, a wall at the back of the fireplace forced smoke up a pipe, into the chimney, and out of the house.

The new fireplace saved money, too. As Franklin proudly pointed out, the "Franklin stove" made the room "twice as warm with a quarter of the wood."

The Pennsylvania Fireplace was only the first of Franklin's many inventions. During his long life, he designed a chair that turned into a step stool, a pole with "fingers" to reach books on high shelves, and a windmill to turn his meat roaster.

In his old age, Franklin grew tired of removing his reading glasses so that he could see things far away. To remedy this problem, he designed his own bifocal glasses. The top half of the lens was for distance vision, and the bottom half was for reading.

Ben Franklin

Franklin's inventions offered practical solutions to everyday problems. He probably could have become wealthy from them. He refused to patent his creations, however. "As we enjoy great advantages from the inventions of others," he wrote, "we should be glad of an opportunity to serve others by an invention of ours."

■ What were some of Franklin's inventions?

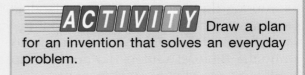
Scientific models for an experiment with lightning

Franklin stove

ACTIVITY Draw a plan for an invention that solves an everyday problem.

master glassmaker. He was then ready to start his own shop. Boys were apprenticed in many trades, including papermaking, printing, and leather tanning.

Education for girls. In New England, some girls attended dame schools, or private schools run by women in their own homes. Most schools in the colonies accepted only boys, however. Girls learned skills from their mothers, who taught them to spin wool, weave, and embroider. A few were also taught to read and write.

An Age of Reason

During the 1600s, European scientists tried to use reason and logic to understand the world. They developed theories and then performed experiments to test them. In doing so, they discovered many laws of nature. Isaac Newton, for example, explained how the force of gravity kept planets from flying out of their orbits.

European thinkers of the late 1600s and 1700s believed that the same methods could be applied to the study of society. They tried to discover the natural laws that governed human behavior. Because these thinkers believed in the light of human reason, the movement that they started is known as the *Enlightenment.*

Benjamin Franklin. The best example of the Enlightenment spirit in the colonies was Benjamin Franklin. Franklin was born in 1706, the son of a poor Boston soap and candle maker. A strong believer in self-improvement, Franklin worked his way from poverty to become an important colonial leader. Although he had only two years of formal schooling, he used his spare time to read and to study literature, mathematics, and foreign languages.

At age 17, Franklin ran away from Boston and made his way to Philadelphia. There, he built up a successful printing business. His most popular publication was *Poor Richard's Almanac.* Published yearly, it contained clever quotes, calendars, and other useful information.

Science and change. Franklin's many interests included science. In 1752, he proved that lightning was a form of electricity. To do this, he flew a kite during a thunderstorm. A bolt of lightning struck a wire fastened to the kite and caused an electric spark.

Like other Enlightenment thinkers, Franklin wanted to use reason to improve the world around him. Using what he learned about electricity, he invented the lightning rod to protect buildings from fire during thunderstorms.

Franklin convinced city officials to pave Philadelphia's streets and to organize a fire company. With his help, local leaders also set up the first lending library in the Americas. Ben Franklin's practical inventions and his public service earned him worldwide fame.

SECTION 5 REVIEW

1. **Identify:** (a) Great Awakening, (b) Jonathan Edwards, (c) George Whitefield, (d) Enlightenment, (e) Benjamin Franklin.
2. **Define:** (a) gentry, (b) indentured servant, (c) public school, (d) apprentice.
3. What were the results of the Great Awakening?
4. Why did the Puritans support public education?
5. List three contributions of Benjamin Franklin.
6. **CRITICAL THINKING Comparing** Compare the lives of women in the backcountry with those of women in cities.

ACTIVITY Writing to Learn
Imagine that you are an apprentice to a master craftsworker. Write a short story about life with your master.

Summary

- New England colonists were farmers, fishers, and merchants who lived in close-knit communities centered around the church.
- Blessed by rich land and mild climate, people from many lands enjoyed a prosperous way of life in the Middle Colonies.
- Two ways of life grew up in the South: plantation life, which relied on enslaved Africans, and the rougher life of the backcountry.
- Colonial governments included a governor and an elected assembly, which passed laws and protected citizens' rights.
- Despite differences, colonists developed a uniquely American culture by the mid-1700s.

Reviewing the Main Ideas

1. (a) Why did the Puritans start the Massachusetts Bay Colony? (b) Why was Maryland founded?
2. How did Quaker beliefs influence William Penn when he set up Pennsylvania?
3. Describe settlers' relations with Native Americans on the frontier in the late 1600s.
4. How was life in the Tidewater different from life in the backcountry?
5. What contributions did Africans make to the economies of the colonies?
6. Describe the triangular trade.
7. In what ways was Benjamin Franklin an example of the Enlightenment spirit?

Thinking Critically

1. **Evaluating Information** Do you think racism was a major or a minor factor in the growth of slavery? Explain.
2. **Applying Information** Why do you think there was greater social equality in the colonies than there was in England?

3. **Linking Past and Present** Review the description of early New England public schools on page 121. How do they compare with public schools today?

Applying Your Skills

1. **Analyzing a Quotation** James Oglethorpe believed that once debtors reached Georgia, they could work "in a land of liberty and plenty, where...they are unfortunate indeed if they can't forget their sorrows." What do you think he meant?
2. **Constructing a Time Line** Make a time line showing events related to religious toleration in the English colonies. Then draw at least one conclusion based on the time line you have made.
3. **Using a Painting as a Primary Source** Study the painting on page 110. (a) Which building do you think was the Great House? Why? (b) Which building or buildings were the slaves' houses? Why? (c) How do the hill and the houses on it show the different classes in the South?

Thinking About Geography

Match the letters on the map with the following places: **1.** New England Colonies, **2.** Middle Colonies, **3.** Southern Colonies, **4.** Massachusetts, **5.** Pennsylvania, **6.** Virginia. **Region** Name the five Southern Colonies.

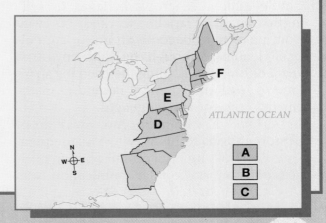

ATLANTIC OCEAN

Living in the English Colonies

Form into groups to review life in the English colonies. Follow the suggestions below to write, draw, build, or present a broadcast to show what you have learned about colonial life. You may use the textbook, encyclopedias, atlases, or other materials in your classroom library to complete the tasks. Be able to name your sources of information when you have finished the activity.

A colonial wedding

GOVERNMENT OFFICIALS Find out about government in the Massachusetts Bay Colony, Connecticut, Rhode Island, Pennsylvania, Maryland, and Georgia. Make a large wall chart comparing government in these colonies. Include information about the role of leaders, the legislature, voting, freedom of religion, and slavery.

ECONOMISTS Make a chart showing the contributions slaves made to the economy of the Southern Colonies.

WRITERS Review the life of women in the backcountry and in cities. Write a story, dialogue, or play in which a city woman and a backcountry woman meet and compare their lives.

ARCHITECTS Find out about one type of house design in the English colonies, including materials used and special features. Make a diagram or build a model of the house. Be prepared to explain why colonists built houses in that way. For example, did available materials or climate conditions affect the design?

Farmer in the Middle Colonies

REPORTERS Prepare a newscast about election day in the colonies. Provide background information about who voted and what government offices the candidates were running for. Also include "person on the street" interviews with candidates, voters, other citizens, and visitors from other countries. Present your newscast to the class.

★ Create a Living in the English Colonies corner in your classroom. Display or describe your completed activity there.

Iron garden tools made by enslaved Africans in the Southern Colonies

LITERATURE

The Double Life of Pocahontas
Jean Fritz

Introduction   Pocahontas was the daughter of Powhatan, leader of a powerful alliance of Indians in present-day Virginia. After the English established a colony at Jamestown, Pocahontas acted as a link between the Native Americans and the English. She befriended Captain John Smith and later married another English colonist. This excerpt is from a biography of Pocahontas written for young adults. It describes her life just before the arrival of the Jamestown colonists.

Vocabulary   Before you read the selection, find the meaning of this word in a dictionary: **drought**

Pocahontas had every reason to be happy. It was the budding time of the year; who would not be happy? The world was new-green, cherry trees were afroth, and strawberries, like sweet red secrets, fattened on the ground. At first birdcall, Pocahontas would run splashing into the river, and along with the others in the village she would wait to greet the Sun as it rose.

Together they would watch the sky turn from gray to pink, to gold. Then suddenly they would shout. There it came! And was it not a wonder that always it returned again and yet again? All the people welcomed it, scattering sacred tobacco into a circle, lifting up their hands and singing to please their god, Okee, in the way their priests had taught them. One must not forget Okee, for it was He who held danger in his hands—lightning, floods, drought, sickness, war.

Indeed, Pocahontas could hardly help but be happy. At eleven, she was the right age for happiness. Still young enough to romp with the children, yet old enough to join the dance of unmarried girls. And how she danced—whirling and stamping and shouting until her breath was whisked into the wind, until she had grown wings like a bird, until she had become sister to the trees, until she was at one with everything that lived and grew. With the world itself, round like a plate under the sky. And in the center of the plate, there was her father, the great Chief Powhatan, seated high, twelve mats under him, raccoon robe around him with tails dangling. And beside him, there was Pocahontas herself, for was she not her father's favorite? Did he not say that Pocahontas was as dear to him as his own life? So of course Pocahontas was happy.

Around the edges of the world plate, Pocahontas knew, were unfriendly tribes. And somewhere on the far, far rim beyond the waters there were strangers from a land she could not picture at all.

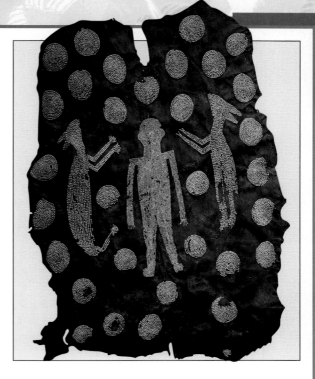

Powhatan's Cloak *This cloak belonged to Pocahontas's father, Powhatan. Made of buckskin and decorated with shells, it is one of the oldest surviving examples of Native American art.* **Culture** *How do the cloak and the excerpt reveal a close connection between Pocahontas's people and nature?*

Sometimes these strangers came to her father's kingdom, coat-wearing men with hair on their faces. The last time, these men had kidnapped a chief's son and killed a chief, but since then the geese had flown north three times and they had not come back. Perhaps they would not come again.

There was no way, of course, for Pocahontas to know that at that very moment three English ships with one hundred and four such coat-wearing men were approaching Chesapeake Bay. No one told these men that the land was taken, that this was Powhatan's kingdom, but even if they had, the English would not have cared. Naked savages, they would have said—they were like herds of deer. How could they legally own land? The world was made for civilized people, for people who wouldn't let the land go to waste, for people who knew the right way to live. In other words, for Christians.

The year, according to the Christian calendar, was 1607, and these Christians were here to stay. They had already named this place Virginia, and they meant to make it theirs.

Source: Jean Fritz, from *The Double Life of Pocahontas* (Grey Castle Press, Lakeville, Connecticut, 1983).

THINKING ABOUT LITERATURE

1. Why did Pocahontas and her people greet the sun each morning?
2. Why did Pocahontas have "every reason to be happy"?
3. **CRITICAL THINKING Recognizing Points of View** (a) Based on this excerpt, how did Pocahontas and her people view the English? (b) How did the English view Pocahontas's people?

ACTIVITY Imagine that you are Pocahontas. Based on this excerpt and what you have read in Chapter 3, create a picture book for a younger sister or brother about your life before and after the arrival of the English in Jamestown.

From Revolution to Republic

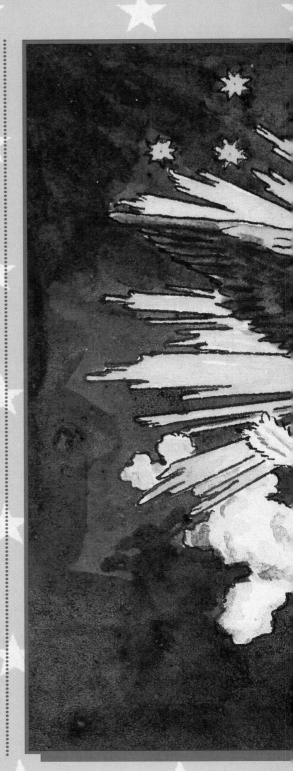

After years of protesting British rule, the colonists won independence in the American Revolution. The eagle became a symbol of the freedom and power of the new nation.

CHAPTER 5

The Road to Revolution

(1745–1775)

CHAPTER OUTLINE

1 Rivalry in North America
2 The French and Indian War
3 A Storm Over Taxes
4 To Arms!

1740s *English settlers moved westward into the Ohio Valley. Here settlers clear the land.*

1754 *As a young major, George Washington played an important role when fighting began in the French and Indian War.*

1759 *The battle for Quebec, shown here, was a turning point in the French and Indian War.*

1745	1750	1755	1760

WORLD EVENT
1748 Britain and France fight for control of trade in India

WORLD EVENT
1756–1763 Seven Years' War is fought in Europe

Chapter Setting

"Yesterday Morning at break of day was discovered hanging upon a tree in the street of the town a [likeness]. . . of Mr. Andrew Oliver. . . . That night a mob carried the effigy to. . . Mr. Oliver's house where they burnt the effigy in a bonfire. . . . The mob finding the doors of the house [blocked]. . . beat in all the doors and windows. . . . As soon as they got possession they searched about for Mr. Oliver, declaring that they would kill him."

In this letter, Massachusetts Governor Francis Bernard described an attack on Andrew Oliver by an angry Boston mob in 1765. Who was Andrew Oliver? What had stirred the mob's anger?

The mob unleashed its fury on Oliver because he was a tax collector for the English government. A series of wars had left England deeply in debt. To raise money to repay the debt, Parliament decided to tax the colonies. Colonists were outraged. They saw Parliament's action as an attack on their basic liberties.

As time went by, the colonists' anger grew. By early 1775, it became clear to many that only war could settle the quarrel with England.

ACTIVITY Brainstorm to identify a government policy that Americans today might consider unjust. Make a poster protesting that policy.

1763 Conflict with Native Americans, led by Chief Pontiac, convinced Britain to issue the Proclamation of 1763. It closed western lands to further settlement.

1765 To raise money from the colonies, Britain passed the Stamp Act. All items listed in the act had to carry a stamp, such as this one.

1775 The war for American independence began with shots fired in Lexington and Concord. This bronze statue honors the colonial minutemen.

1760   1765   1770   1775

WORLD EVENT
1763 Treaty of Paris ends French power in North America

WORLD EVENT
1774 Quebec Act guarantees religious freedom in Canada

Rivalry in North America

FIND OUT

■ What nations were rivals for North America?

■ How did the French prevent expansion of the English colonies?

■ Why did Native Americans become involved in the struggle between France and England?

In June 1749, the governor of New France sent a group of men to the Ohio Valley. The men traveled down the Ohio River. From time to time, they stopped to nail an engraved lead plate to a tree or to set one in the ground. These plates proclaimed that the land belonged to France.

About the same time, Christopher Gist, a Virginia fur trader working for the Ohio Company, roamed the Ohio Valley. King George II of England had given the Ohio Company a huge tract of land in the valley. The company sent Gist to find a good spot for settlement. He chose a site where the Ohio and Allegheny rivers meet. On a rock beside the water, he carved these words:

> The Ohio Company
> FEBy 1751
> By Christopher Gist

The stage was set for a battle between France and England. At stake was more than control of the Ohio River valley. Each nation hoped to drive the other out of North America altogether.

Competing Claims

By the mid-1700s, the nations of Europe were locked in a worldwide struggle for empire. England, France, Spain, and the Netherlands were competing for trade and colonies in far-flung corners of the globe. The English colonies in North America soon became caught up in the contest.

Spanish claims. By the late 1600s, England had two rivals in North America: Spain and France. The major threat from Spain

Trading With North Americans *French traders exchanged a variety of goods with Native Americans in return for furs. In this painting, Native Americans inspect a blanket being offered in trade. Copper pots and pans, such as those shown below, were also popular trading items.* **Economics** *How did both sides benefit from this trade?*

was in the West Indies and along the border between Georgia and Spanish Florida. England and Spain clashed often in these areas.

Spain also had settlements in present-day New Mexico, Texas, and Arizona. However, these settlements lay far away from England's colonies on the Atlantic coast. As a result, the English paid little attention to them.

French claims. The threat from France was much more serious. France claimed a vast area in North America. French land claims stretched west from the St. Lawrence River all the way to the Great Lakes and south to the Gulf of Mexico. To protect their lands, the French built a system of forts. (See the map at right.)

Conflict in the Ohio Valley. At first, most English settlers were content to remain along the Atlantic coast. By the 1740s, however, traders from New York and Pennsylvania were crossing the Appalachian Mountains in search of furs. Pushing into the Ohio Valley, they tried to take over the profitable French trade with the Indians.

The French were determined to stop the English from intruding on their territory. The Ohio River was especially important to them because it provided a vital link between their lands in Canada and the Mississippi River. In 1751, the French government sent the following orders to its officials in New France:

> 66 Drive from the Ohio River any European foreigners, and do it in a way that will make them lose all taste for trying to return. 99

Native Americans Choose Sides

Native Americans had hunted animals and grown crops in the Ohio Valley for centuries. They did not want to give up the land to European settlers, French *or* English. One Native American protested to an English trader:

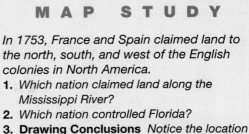

MAP STUDY

In 1753, France and Spain claimed land to the north, south, and west of the English colonies in North America.
1. Which nation claimed land along the Mississippi River?
2. Which nation controlled Florida?
3. **Drawing Conclusions** Notice the location of French forts in North America. Why do you think the French built forts at these places?

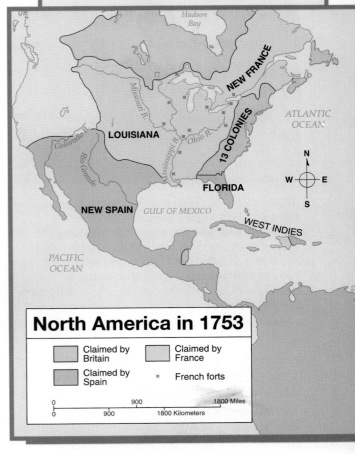

North America in 1753

- Claimed by Britain
- Claimed by Spain
- Claimed by France
- ✕ French forts

0   900   1800 Miles
0   900   1800 Kilometers

> 66 You and the French are like the two edges of a pair of shears. And we are the cloth which is to be cut to pieces between them. 99

Some Native Americans decided that the only way to protect their way of life was to take sides in the struggle.

Competing for allies. Both France and England tried to make Indian allies because

BIOGRAPHY Joseph Brant *Joseph Brant, a Mohawk chief, helped persuade the Iroquois nations to side with the English in their struggle against the French. In later years, Joseph Brant became a Christian and helped translate the Bible into the Mohawk language.* **Multicultural Heritage** *How does the painting show that Brant combined Native American and English cultures?*

Indians controlled the fur trade in the heart of North America. The French expected the Indians to side with them. Most French in North America were trappers and traders, not farmers. They did not destroy hunting grounds by clearing forests for farms. Also, many French trappers married Native American women and adopted their ways.

In contrast, English settlers were mostly farm families. They ignored Indian rights when they cleared land for crops, and they did not respect Indian ways. Indians fought back as the English moved onto their lands.

Algonquins, Hurons, and Iroquois. In the end, both France and England found allies among Native Americans. The French gained the support of the Algonquins and Hurons. In time, the English won over the powerful Iroquois nations, who were old enemies of the Algonquins.

An English trader and official, William Johnson, helped gain Iroquois support for England. Johnson was one of the few English settlers who had an Indian wife. He was married to Molly Brant, sister of Joseph Brant, a Mohawk chief. The Iroquois respected Johnson, and they listened carefully when he urged them to side with the English.

Some Indians supported the English because they charged lower prices for trade goods than the French did. Many Indians began to buy goods from English rather than French traders. The loss of Indian trade angered the French, who were determined to defend their claims in the Ohio Valley.

SECTION 1 REVIEW

1. **Locate:** (a) Ohio River, (b) St. Lawrence River, (c) Great Lakes, (d) Gulf of Mexico, (e) Canada, (f) Mississippi River.
2. (a) Name three European nations that claimed lands in North America. (b) Where did conflict between these nations occur?
3. How did France protect its lands in North America?
4. (a) Which Indians sided with the English? (b) Why?
5. **CRITICAL THINKING Synthesizing Information** How did the rivalry between Spain, France, and England in North America relate to their worldwide struggle?

ACTIVITY Writing to Learn
Imagine that you are a Native American leader in the Ohio Valley in the 1750s. Would you support the French or the English? Write a speech urging other Native Americans to adopt your position.

CRITICAL THINKING SKILLS
Using a Primary Source

Historians use primary sources to learn about the past. A *primary source* is firsthand information about people or events. Letters, diaries, maps, drawings, and artifacts are all primary sources. The primary sources below are from speeches by Native Americans about English actions in the Ohio Valley in the 1760s.

1. **Identify the source.** (a) Who made these statements? (b) What are they about? (c) When were they made?

2. **Recognize the author's point of view.** Many eyewitnesses have a special reason for writing or speaking about an event. Often, they want to persuade the listener to share their views. When you read a primary source, you need to recognize the author's point of view. (a) What opinion did these Native Americans have of the English?

(b) What words or phrases show you how strongly they felt?

3. **Decide whether the source is reliable.** (a) Do you think these Native Americans gave an accurate view of the situation in the Ohio Valley in the 1760s? Why? (b) Have they left out any important information? (c) Would you say that these are reliable sources for learning about relations between the English and Native Americans in the mid-1700s? Explain.

ACTIVITY

Prepare a document that would provide useful information to a future historian studying the 1990s. Your document can be a letter, a diary entry, a petition, or a speech describing the concerns of young Americans today. Trade documents with a classmate and determine whether each document is a reliable primary source.

A Seneca Chief, July 1761

❝The English treat us with much disrespect, and we have the greatest reason to believe, by their behavior, they intend to cut us off entirely. They have possessed themselves of our country. It is now in our power to dispossess them and recover it, if we will but embrace the opportunity before they have time to assemble together and [strengthen] themselves. There is no time to be lost, let us strike immediately.❞

An Iroquois, August 1761

❝We, your brethren of the several nations, are penned up like hogs. There are forts all around us, and therefore we are [fearful] that Death is coming upon us.❞

Pontiac, 1763

❝The Great Spirit [told a Delaware Indian to] be seated, and thus addressed him:

'I am the Maker of heaven and earth, the trees, lakes, rivers, and all things else. I am the Maker of mankind; and because I love you, you must do my will. The land on which you live I have made for you, and not for others. Why do you suffer the white men to dwell among you? My children, you have forgotten the customs and traditions of your forefathers. Why do you not clothe yourselves in skins, as they did, and use the bows and arrows, and the stone-pointed lances, which they used. You have bought guns, knives, kettles, and blankets, from the white men, until you can no longer do without them; and what is worse, you have drunk the poison fire-water, which turns you into fools. Fling all these things away; live as your wise forefathers lived before you. And as for these English—these dogs dressed in red, who have come to rob you of your hunting-grounds, and drive away the game,—you must lift the hatchet against them.'❞

2

The French and Indian War

FIND OUT

- What were the causes of the French and Indian War?
- What advantages did each side have in the war?
- How did the Treaty of Paris affect North America?

Captain Joncaire had just sat down to dinner on December 4, 1753, when a tall young man strode into the room. He introduced himself as Major George Washington. He said he had a letter from the English lieutenant governor of Virginia, Robert Dinwiddie, to the commander of the French forces in the Ohio Valley.

Joncaire told Washington where the commander could be found and then invited him to dine. As they ate, Joncaire boasted, "It is our absolute design to take possession of the Ohio, and by God, we will do it!" The remark made Washington pause. Dinwiddie's letter, he knew, warned the French to get out of the Ohio Valley. A conflict between England and France seemed certain.

Opening Shots

Three times between 1689 and 1748, France and Great Britain* had fought for power in Europe and North America. Each war ended with an uneasy peace. In 1754,

---

*In 1707, England and Scotland were officially joined into the united kingdom of Great Britain. After that date, the terms Great Britain and British were used to describe the country and its people. However, the terms England and English were still used throughout much of the 1700s.

fighting broke out again. The long conflict that followed was called the *French and Indian War.*

Major Washington. Scuffles between France and Britain in the Ohio River valley triggered the opening shots of the French and Indian War. Young Major Washington played an important part as fighting began.

George Washington had grown up on a plantation in Virginia, the son of wealthy parents. At age 15, he began work as a surveyor. His job took him to frontier lands in western Virginia. When Lieutenant Governor Dinwiddie wanted to warn the French in Ohio in 1753, Washington offered to deliver the message.

After Washington returned, Dinwiddie promoted him. He also sent the young man west again. This time, Dinwiddie ordered Washington to take 150 men and build a fort where the Monongahela and Allegheny rivers meet. (See the map on page 139.) The fort was to protect Virginia's land claims in the upper Ohio River valley.

Trapped at Fort Necessity. In April 1754, Washington and his party headed for Ohio country. Along the way, they heard disturbing news. The French had just completed Fort Duquesne (doo KAYN) at the fork of the Monongahela and Allegheny rivers. The fork was the precise spot where Washington was to build a British fort.

Determined to carry out his orders, Washington continued on. Indian allies revealed that a French scouting party was camped in the woods ahead. Marching quietly through the night, Washington surprised and scattered the French.

Washington's success was short-lived, however. Hearing that the French were planning to counterattack, he and his men quickly built a makeshift stockade. They named it *Fort Necessity.* A huge force of French and Indians surrounded the fort. Trapped and heavily outnumbered, the Virginians were forced to surrender. Soon after,

Washington Meets With Iroquois Chiefs *Young George Washington played an important role in the opening skirmishes of the French and Indian War. Here, Washington confers with chiefs of the Iroquois nations.* **Geography** *What region was at the heart of the conflict that triggered the French and Indian War?*

the French released Washington, and he returned home to Virginia.

The British quickly saw the importance of the skirmish. "The volley fired by this young Virginian in the forests of America," a British writer noted, "has set the world in flames."

The Albany Congress

While Washington was defending Fort Necessity, delegates from seven colonies gathered in Albany, New York. The delegates met for two reasons. They wanted to persuade the Iroquois to help them against the French. They also wanted to plan a united defense.

Iroquois leaders listened patiently to the delegates, but they were wary of the request for help. The British and French "are quarreling about lands which belong to us," pointed out Hendrik, a Mohawk chief. "And such a quarrel as this may end in our destruction." The Iroquois left without agreeing to help the British. But they did not join the French either.

The delegates in Albany knew that the colonists needed to work together if they were to defeat the French. Benjamin Franklin, the delegate from Pennsylvania, proposed the *Albany Plan of Union.* The plan called for a Grand Council with representatives from each colony. The council would make laws, raise taxes, and set up the defense of the colonies.

The delegates voted to accept the Plan of Union. When the plan was submitted to the colonial assemblies, however, not one approved it. None of the colonies wanted to give up any of its powers to a central council. In the words of the disappointed Franklin:

> ❝Everyone cries a union is necessary. But when they come to the manner and form of the union, their weak noodles are perfectly distracted.❞

Early Years of the War

At the start of the French and Indian War, the French enjoyed several advantages over the British. Because the English colonies could not agree on a united defense, 13 separate colonial assemblies had to approve all decisions. New France, on the other hand, had a single government that could act quickly when necessary. Also, the French had the support of many more Indian allies than the British did.

Britain, however, also had strengths. The English colonies were clustered along the coast, so they were easier to defend than the widely scattered French settlements. At the same time, the population of the English colonies was about 15 times greater than that of New France. And although most Indians sided with the French, the British did have some Indian allies. Finally, the British navy ruled the seas.

"Bulldog" Braddock. In 1755, General Edward Braddock led British and colonial troops in an attack against Fort Duquesne. The general boasted that he would sweep the French from the Ohio Valley.

Braddock was a stubborn man, called "Bulldog" behind his back. He knew how to fight a war in the open fields of Europe. However, he knew little about how to fight in the wilderness of North America.

Braddock's men moved slowly because they had to clear a road through thick forests for their cannons and other heavy gear. George Washington, who went with Braddock, was upset by the slow pace. Indian scouts warned Braddock that he was headed for trouble. He ignored them.

Disaster for the British. As the British neared Fort Duquesne, the French and their Indian allies launched a surprise attack.

Sharpshooters hid in the forest and picked off British soldiers, whose bright-red uniforms made them easy targets. Braddock had five horses shot out from under him before he fell, fatally wounded. Washington was luckier. As he later reported, he "escaped without a wound, although I had four bullets through my coat."

Almost half the British were killed or wounded. Washington and other survivors returned to Virginia with news of Braddock's defeat. Washington was now put in command of a small force of men. For the rest of the war, he had the almost impossible task of guarding the long Virginia frontier against Indian attack.

During the next two years, the war continued to go badly for the British. British attacks against several French forts ended in failure. Meanwhile, the French won important victories, capturing Fort Oswego on Lake Ontario and Fort William Henry on Lake George. (See the map on page 139.) To English colonists, the situation looked grim. In the words of Massachusetts minister Jonathan Edwards:

> ❝God indeed is remarkably frowning upon us every where; our enemies get up above us very high, and we are brought down very low: They are the Head, and we are the Tail. . . . What will become of us God only knows.❞

A Bold Leader Takes Charge

In 1757, William Pitt became head of the British government. Pitt was a bold leader. "I believe that I can save this nation and that no one else can," he declared with great confidence.

Pitt set out to win the war in North America. Once that was done, he argued, the British could focus on victory in other parts of the world. Pitt sent Britain's best generals to North America. To encourage

MAP STUDY

During the French and Indian War, Britain and France battled for control of North America.

1. *Which French forts were located on Lake Ontario?*
2. *About how many miles did advancing British troops travel from Louisbourg to Quebec?*
3. **Analyzing Information** *Based on the map, do you think naval power was important in fighting the French and Indian War? Explain.*

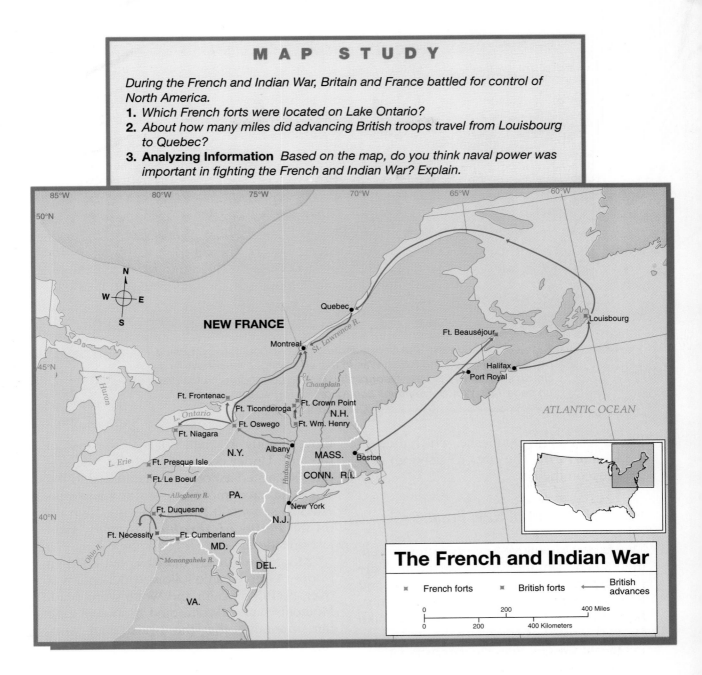

The French and Indian War

French forts · British forts · British advances

0   200   400 Miles
0   200   400 Kilometers

colonists to support the war, he promised large payments for military services and supplies.*

---

*By 1756, fighting between the French and the British had broken out in Europe. There, it became known as the Seven Years' War. The British and the French also fought in India. In the early years of the war, the British suffered setbacks on every front.

Under Pitt's leadership, the tide of battle turned. In 1758, Major General Jeffrey Amherst captured *Louisbourg,* the most important fort in French Canada. That year, the British also won more Iroquois support.

The Iroquois persuaded the Delawares at Fort Duquesne to abandon the French. Without the Delawares, the French could no longer hold the fort. Acting quickly, the

Battle of Louisbourg *The British capture of Louisbourg was a turning point in the French and Indian War. In this engraving, cannonballs fly as British ships shell the fort.* **Geography** *Locate Louisbourg on the map on page 139. Why do you think control of this fort was important?*

British seized Fort Duquesne, which they renamed *Fort Pitt.* The city of Pittsburgh later grew up on the site.

The Fall of New France

The British enjoyed even greater success in 1759. By summer, they had pushed the French from Fort Niagara, Crown Point, and Fort Ticonderoga (tī kahn duh ROH guh). Now, Pitt sent General James Wolfe to take *Quebec,* capital of New France.

Battle for Quebec. Quebec was vital to the defense of New France. Without Quebec, the French would be unable to supply their forts farther up the St. Lawrence River. But Quebec was well defended. The city sat atop a steep cliff above the St. Lawrence. An able French general, the Marquis de Montcalm, was prepared to fight off any British attack.

General Wolfe devised a bold plan. Late one night, he ordered British troops to move quietly in small boats to the foot of the cliff. Under cover of darkness, the soldiers swarmed ashore and scrambled to the top. The next morning, Montcalm awakened to see 4,000 British troops drawn up on the *Plains of Abraham,* a grassy field just outside the city.

Montcalm quickly marched out his own troops. A fierce battle followed. When it was over, both Montcalm and Wolfe were dead. Moments before Wolfe died, a soldier gave him the news that the British had won.

Linking Past and Present
The British commander who seized Fort Duquesne and rebuilt it as Pittsburgh was a Scotsman. He used the Scottish spelling "burgh" for the name, rather than the more common English "burg" or "boro." Later Pittsburghers resisted government efforts to make them drop the "h."

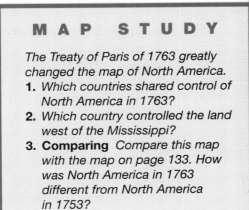

MAP STUDY

The Treaty of Paris of 1763 greatly changed the map of North America.
1. *Which countries shared control of North America in 1763?*
2. *Which country controlled the land west of the Mississippi?*
3. **Comparing** *Compare this map with the map on page 133. How was North America in 1763 different from North America in 1753?*

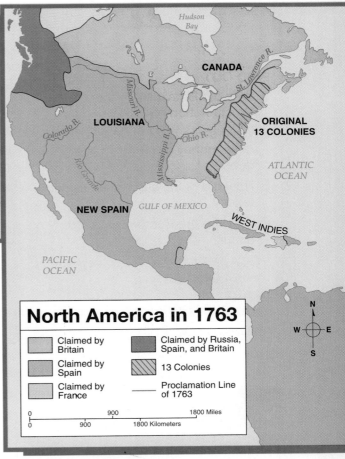

North America in 1763

Claimed by Britain	Claimed by Russia, Spain, and Britain
Claimed by Spain	13 Colonies
Claimed by France	Proclamation Line of 1763

0   900   1800 Miles
0   900   1800 Kilometers

Wolfe reportedly whispered, "Now, God be praised, I will die in peace."

Treaty of Paris. The fall of Quebec sealed the fate of New France. In 1760, the British took Montreal, and the war in North America ended. Fighting dragged on in Europe until Britain and France signed the *Treaty of Paris* in 1763.

The Treaty of Paris marked the end of French power in North America. Under the treaty, Britain gained Canada and all French lands east of the Mississippi River. France was allowed to keep a few sugar-growing islands in the West Indies. Spain, which had entered the war on the French side in 1762, gave up Florida to Britain. In return, Spain received all French land west of the Mississippi, as well as the city of New Orleans.

After years of fighting, peace returned to North America. But in a few short years, a new struggle would break out. This struggle would pit Britain against its own colonies.

SECTION 2 REVIEW

1. **Locate:** (a) Fort Necessity, (b) Louisbourg, (c) Fort Pitt, (d) Quebec.
2. **Identify:** (a) French and Indian War, (b) George Washington, (c) Albany Plan of Union, (d) Edward Braddock, (e) James Wolfe, (f) Marquis de Montcalm, (g) Plains of Abraham, (h) Treaty of Paris.
3. Why did the British and French go to war in North America in 1754?
4. List two strengths of the British in the French and Indian War.
5. What lands did Britain gain under the Treaty of Paris?
6. **CRITICAL THINKING Evaluating Information** Under the Albany Plan of Union, the Grand Council could "draw on the fund in the Treasury of any Colony" during war. Why might colonial assemblies object?

ACTIVITY **Writing to Learn**
Write a short scene for a TV movie depicting the battle for Quebec.

A Storm Over Taxes

FIND OUT

- Why did Britain issue the Proclamation of 1763?

- What steps did Britain take to raise money to repay its war debts?

- How did colonists protest British taxes?

- Why did the Boston Massacre occur?

VOCABULARY boycott, repeal, writ of assistance, nonimportation agreement, committee of correspondence

As Britain celebrated the victory over France, a few officials in London expressed some of their concerns. Now that the French were no longer a threat, they wondered, would the 13 colonies become too independent? Might the colonies even unite one day against Great Britain? Benjamin Franklin, who was visiting London at the time, gave his opinion:

> **"**If [the colonies] could not agree to unite for their defense against the French and Indians, . . . can it reasonably be supposed there is any danger of their uniting against their own nation? . . . I will venture to say, a union amongst them for such a purpose is not merely improbable, it is impossible.**"**

But Franklin misjudged the situation. After the French and Indian War, new British policies toward the colonies aroused angry cries from Massachusetts to Georgia. Despite their differences, colonists were moving toward unity.

New Troubles on the Frontier

By 1760, the British had driven France from the Ohio Valley. Their troubles in the region, however, were not over. For many years, fur traders had sent back glowing reports of the land beyond the Appalachian Mountains. With the French gone, English colonists eagerly headed west to farm the former French lands.

Relations with Indians worsen. Many Native American nations lived in the Ohio Valley. They included the Senecas, Delawares, Shawnees, Ottawas, Miamis, and Hurons. As British settlers moved into the valley, they often clashed with these Native Americans.

In 1762, the British sent Lord Jeffrey Amherst to the frontier to keep order. French traders had always treated Native Americans as friends, holding feasts for them and giving them presents. Amherst refused to do this. He raised the price of British goods traded to Indians. He also allowed English settlers to build forts on Indian lands.

Discontented Native Americans found a leader in Pontiac, an Ottawa chief who had fought with the French. An English trader remarked that Pontiac "commands more respect amongst these nations than any Indian I ever saw." In April 1763, Pontiac spoke out against the British, calling them "dogs dressed in red, who have come to rob [us] of [our] hunting grounds and drive away the game."

Fighting on the frontier. Soon after, Pontiac led an attack on British troops at Fort Detroit. Other Indians joined the fight, and in a few months they captured most British forts on the frontier. British and colonial troops struck back and regained much of what they had lost.

Pontiac's War, as it came to be called, did not last long. In October 1763, the French informed Pontiac that they had signed the Treaty of Paris. As you have read,

Ottawa War Council *Chief Pontiac led Native Americans against the British in the Ohio Valley. Here, Pontiac addresses a war council in 1763.* **Economics** *For what uses did the British want Indian lands?*

the treaty marked the end of French power in North America. As a result, the Indians could no longer hope for French aid against the British. One by one, the Indian nations stopped fighting and returned home. "All my young men have buried their hatchets," Pontiac sadly observed.

Proclamation of 1763

Pontiac's War convinced the British to close western lands to settlers. To do this, the government issued the ***Proclamation of 1763.*** The proclamation drew an imaginary line along the crest of the Appalachian Mountains. Colonists were forbidden to settle west of the line. The proclamation ordered all settlers already west of the line "to remove themselves" at once. To enforce the law, Britain sent 10,000 troops to the colonies. Few troops went to the frontier, however. Most stayed in cities along the Atlantic coast.

The proclamation angered colonists. Some colonies, including New York, Pennsylvania, and Virginia, claimed lands in the West. Also, colonists had to pay for the additional British troops that had been sent to enforce the law. In the end, many settlers simply ignored the proclamation and moved west anyway.

Stamp Act Crisis

The French and Indian War had plunged Britain deeply into debt. As a result, the tax bill for citizens in Britain rose sharply. The British prime minister, George Grenville, decided that colonists in North America should help share the burden. After all, he reasoned, it was the colonists who had gained most from the war.

New taxes. Grenville persuaded Parliament to pass two new laws. The Sugar Act of 1764 placed a new tax on molasses. The ***Stamp Act*** of 1765 put a tax on legal documents such as wills, diplomas, and marriage papers. It also taxed newspapers, almanacs, playing cards, and even dice. All items named in the law had to carry a stamp showing that the tax had been paid. Stamp taxes were used in Britain and other countries to raise money. However, Britain had never used such a tax in its colonies.

When British officials tried to enforce the Stamp Act, they met with stormy protests. Riots broke out in New York City, Newport, and Charleston. Angry colonists threw rocks at agents trying to collect the unpopular tax. Some tarred and feathered the agents. In Boston, as you read, a mob burned an effigy, or likeness, of Andrew Oliver and then destroyed his home. As John Adams, a Massachusetts lawyer, wrote:

66 Our presses have groaned, our pulpits have thundered, our legislatures have resolved, our towns have voted, the crown officers everywhere trembled. 99

No taxation without representation!
The fury of the colonists shocked the British. After all, Britain had spent a great deal of money to protect the colonies against the French. Why, the British asked, were colonists so angry about the Stamp Act?

Colonists replied that the taxes imposed by the Stamp Act were unjust. The taxes, they claimed, went against the principle that there should be no taxation without representation. That principle was rooted in English traditions dating back to the Magna Carta. (See page 86.)

Colonists insisted that only they or their elected representatives had the right to pass taxes. Since the colonists did not elect representatives to Parliament, Parliament had no right to tax them. The colonists were willing to pay taxes—but only if the taxes were passed by their own colonial legislatures.

A call for unity. The Stamp Act crisis brought a sense of unity to the colonies. Critics of the law called for delegates from every colony to meet in New York City. There, the delegates would consider actions against the hated Stamp Act.

In October 1765, nine colonies sent delegates to what became known as the Stamp Act Congress. The delegates drew up petitions, or letters, to King George III and to Parliament. In these petitions, they rejected the Stamp Act and asserted that Parliament had no right to tax the colonies. Parliament paid little attention.

The colonists took other steps to change the law. They joined together to **boycott** British goods. To boycott means to refuse to buy certain goods and services. The boycott of British goods took its toll. Trade fell off by 14 percent. British merchants suffered.

LINKING PAST AND PRESENT

PAST	PRESENT

Protesting Taxes *From colonial times, Americans exercised the right to protest unfair treatment. One issue that has stirred strong emotions is taxation. In the painting at left, colonists are protesting the hated Stamp Act of 1765. They have strung up one British tax collector from a Liberty Pole and are preparing to tar and feather another. Today, tax protests are more orderly but just as intense. In the picture at right, a demonstrator tries to gain the support of passing motorists. • What other issues have Americans protested in recent years?*

So, too, did British workers who made goods for the colonies. Finally, in 1766, Parliament repealed, or canceled, the Stamp Act.

More Taxes

In May 1767, Parliament continued the debate over taxing the colonies. George Grenville, now a member of Parliament, clashed with Charles Townshend, who was in charge of the British treasury:

> **❝** *Grenville:* You are cowards, you are afraid of the Americans, you dare not tax America!
> *Townshend:* Fear? Cowards? I dare tax America!
> *Grenville:* Dare you tax America? I wish I could see it!
> *Townshend:* I will, I will!**❞**

The next month, Parliament passed the **Townshend Acts,** which taxed goods such as glass, paper, paint, lead, and tea. The taxes were low, but colonists still objected. The principle, they felt, was the same: Parliament did not have the right to tax them without their consent. (📖 See "What Should Colonists Do?" on page 554.)

The Townshend Acts set up new ways to collect taxes. Using legal documents known as writs of assistance, customs officers could inspect a ship's cargo without giving a reason. Colonists protested that the writs violated their rights as British citizens. Under British law, an official could not search a person's property without a good reason for suspecting the owner of a crime.

Colonists Fight Back

The colonists' response to the Townshend Acts was loud and clear. From north to south, merchants and planters signed nonimportation agreements. In these agreements, they promised to stop importing goods taxed by the Townshend Acts. The colonists hoped that the new boycott would win repeal of the Townshend Acts.

Colonists supported the boycott in various ways. Men and women refused to buy cloth made in Britain. Instead, they wore clothes made of fabric spun at home, or homespun. A popular Boston ballad encouraged women to avoid British cloth and "show clothes of your own make and spinning." Harvard College printed its graduation program on coarse paper made in the colonies instead of buying British paper.

Some angry colonists joined the **Sons of Liberty.** This group was first formed during the Stamp Act crisis to protest British policies. Women set up their own group, known as **Daughters of Liberty.**

In cities from Boston to Charleston, Sons and Daughters of Liberty placed lanterns in large trees. Gathering around these Liberty Trees, as they were called, they staged mock hangings of cloth or straw figures dressed like British officials. The hangings were meant to show tax collectors what might happen to them if they tried to collect the unpopular taxes.

Sons and Daughters of Liberty also used other methods to strengthen their cause. Some visited merchants to urge them to sign the nonimportation agreements. A few even threatened people who continued to buy British goods.

Leaders in the Struggle

During the struggle over taxes, leaders emerged in all the colonies. Men and women in the New England colonies and Virginia were especially active in the colonial cause.

History and You
Young colonial women considered it a great sacrifice to give up fine British cloth for rough "homespun." Would you be willing to give up wearing blue jeans to protest an injustice?

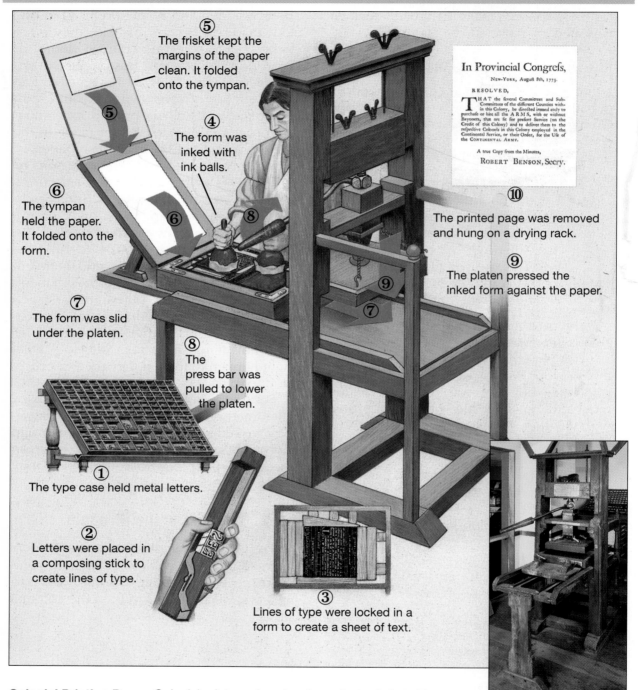

⑤ The frisket kept the margins of the paper clean. It folded onto the tympan.

④ The form was inked with ink balls.

⑥ The tympan held the paper. It folded onto the form.

⑥

In Provincial Congrefs,
New-York, August 8th, 1775.
RESOLVED,
THAT the feveral Committees and Sub-Committees of the different Counties within this Colony, be directed immediately to purchafe or hire all the A R M S, with or without Bayonets, that are fit for prefent Service (on the Credit of this Colony) and to deliver them to the refpective Colonels in this Colony employed in the Continental Service, or their Order, for the Ufe of the CONTINENTAL ARMY.

A true Copy from the Minutes,
ROBERT BENSON, Secry.

⑩ The printed page was removed and hung on a drying rack.

⑨ The platen pressed the inked form against the paper.

⑦ The form was slid under the platen.

⑧ The press bar was pulled to lower the platen.

① The type case held metal letters.

② Letters were placed in a composing stick to create lines of type.

③ Lines of type were locked in a form to create a sheet of text.

Colonial Printing Press *Colonial printers played an important role in uniting colonists against the British. Besides publishing newspapers and magazines, they also printed letters and pamphlets that kept colonists informed of anti-British activities. The drawing and photograph above are of a typical colonial printing press.*
Science and Technology *Why would printing a document with this printing press be very time consuming?*

The Mighty Pen *Colonial writers supported the cause of liberty. Samuel Adams (left) and Mercy Otis Warren (right) used their pens to stir feelings against the British—Adams with his letters, Warren with her plays. Both of these portraits were painted by John Singleton Copley, a leading artist of the period.* **Linking Past and Present** *How do writers influence public opinion today?*

In Massachusetts. Samuel Adams of Boston stood firmly against Britain. Sam Adams seemed an unlikely leader. He was a failure in business and a poor public speaker. But he loved politics. He was always present at Boston town meetings and Sons of Liberty rallies.

Adams worked day and night to unite colonists against Britain. He organized a **committee of correspondence,** which wrote letters and pamphlets reporting on events in Massachusetts. The idea worked well, and soon there were committees of correspondence in every colony. Adams's greatest talent was organizing people. He knew how to work behind the scenes, arranging protests and stirring public support.

Sam's cousin John was another important leader in Massachusetts. John Adams was a skilled lawyer. More cautious than Sam, he weighed evidence carefully before acting. His knowledge of British law earned him much respect.

Mercy Otis Warren also aided the colonial cause. Warren published plays that made fun of British officials. She formed a close friendship with Abigail Adams, who was married to John Adams. The two women used their pens to spur the colonists to action.

In Virginia. Virginia contributed many leaders to the struggle against taxes. In the House of Burgesses, George Washington joined other Virginians to protest the Townshend Acts.

A young firebrand, Patrick Henry, gave speeches that moved listeners to both tears and anger. In one speech, Henry attacked Britain with such fury that some listeners cried out, "Treason!" Henry boldly replied, "If this be treason, make the most of it!"

Centers of Protest

Port cities such as Boston and New York were centers of protest. In New York, a dispute arose over the **Quartering Act.** Under

CONNECTIONS

ARTS · SCIENCES · GEOGRAPHY · WORLD · ECONOMICS · CIVICS

Paul Revere and the Boston Massacre

Coffins of massacre victims

Could a picture change history? Paul Revere's engraving of the Boston Massacre, below, may not have caused the American Revolution. But it played a major role in whipping up colonial fury against the British.

In the engraving, Revere purposely distorted events. At right, for example, is a British officer, Captain Thomas Preston. Sword raised, he orders his men to fire. At left, unarmed and orderly citizens look on helplessly. A few distressed Patriots pick up their dead.

This scene, however, did not really take place. According to eyewitnesses, Captain Preston never gave an order to shoot. The redcoats, faced by an unruly and threatening mob, acted on their own and opened fire. Revere altered other details, too. He set the bloody scene in front of a building labeled Butcher's Hall. In fact, the building was the Boston customs house. Finally, at the bottom of the engraving, Revere lists seven dead. In truth, five Patriots, not seven, were killed. Revere wrote a poem to go with the engraving. It, too, sought to stir anti-British sentiment. One stanza is reprinted below.

Within days, copies of Revere's engraving appeared on walls all over Massachusetts. The "Bloody Massacre," as the engraving was titled, aroused cries of rage. Revere's vivid but distorted portrayal created a rallying point for colonists who resented British rule.

■ Name three ways that Revere's engraving distorted events to stir up anti-British feeling.

ACTIVITY Create a poster to support a cause. Use words, pictures, or a combination of both.

"Unhappy Boston. See thy sons deplore,
Thy hallow'd Walks besmear'd with guiltless Gore:
While faithless Preston and his savage Bands,
With murd'rous Rancour stretch their bloody hands,
Like fierce Barbarians grinning o'er their Prey,
Approve the Carnage and enjoy the Day."

Revere's poem

Paul Revere's engraving of the Boston Massacre

that law, colonists had to provide housing, candles, bedding, and beverages to British soldiers stationed in the colonies. New Yorkers saw the law as another way to tax them without their consent. The New York assembly refused to obey the law. As a result, in 1767, Britain dismissed the assembly.

Britain also sent two regiments of British soldiers to Boston to protect customs officers from local citizens. To many Bostonians, the soldiers' tents set up on Boston Common were a daily reminder that Britain was trying to bully them into paying unjust taxes. When British soldiers walked along the streets of Boston, they risked insults or even beatings. The time was ripe for disaster.

The Boston Massacre

On the night of March 5, 1770, a crowd gathered outside the Boston customs house. Colonists shouted insults at the "lobsterbacks," as they called the redcoated British who guarded the building. Then they began to throw snowballs, oyster shells, and chunks of ice at the soldiers.

The crowd grew larger and rowdier. Suddenly, the soldiers panicked. They fired into the crowd. When the smoke from the musket volley cleared, five people lay dead or dying. Among them was Crispus Attucks, a black sailor who was active in the Sons of Liberty.

Sam Adams quickly wrote to other colonists about the shooting, which he called the *Boston Massacre.* As news of the Boston Massacre spread, colonists' outrage grew.

The soldiers were arrested and tried in court. John Adams agreed to defend them, saying that they deserved a fair trial. He wanted to show the world that the colonists believed in justice, even if the British government did not. At the trial, Adams argued that the crowd had provoked the soldiers. His arguments convinced the jury. In the end, the British soldiers received very light sentences.

Repeal of the Townshend Acts

By chance, on the day of the Boston Massacre, Parliament voted to repeal most of the Townshend Acts. British merchants, hurt by the nonimportation agreements, had pressured Parliament to end the Townshend taxes. But King George III asked Parliament to keep the tax on tea. "There must always be one tax to keep up the right [to tax]," argued the king. Parliament agreed.

News of the repeal delighted the colonists. Most people dismissed the remaining tax on tea as not important and ended their boycott of British goods. For a few years, calm returned.

SECTION 3 REVIEW

1. **Locate:** Appalachian Mountains.
2. **Identify:** (a) Pontiac's War, (b) Proclamation of 1763, (c) Stamp Act, (d) Townshend Acts, (e) Sons of Liberty, (f) Daughters of Liberty, (g) Sam Adams, (h) Mercy Otis Warren, (i) Quartering Act, (j) Crispus Attucks, (k) Boston Massacre.
3. **Define:** (a) boycott, (b) repeal, (c) writ of assistance, (d) nonimportation agreement, (e) committee of correspondence.
4. What event convinced Britain to issue the Proclamation of 1763?
5. How did Britain try to raise money to repay its war debt?
6. (a) Why did colonists object to the Stamp Act? (b) What actions did colonists take to protest the Townshend Acts?
7. **CRITICAL THINKING Drawing Conclusions** Why do you think Pontiac felt he had to fight the British?

ACTIVITY Writing to Learn
Write an article for a colonial newspaper reporting the events of the Boston Massacre.

To Arms!

FIND OUT
- Why did Britain pass the Tea Act?
- What was the Boston Tea Party?
- How did colonists respond to the Intolerable Acts?
- What was the shot heard 'round the world?

VOCABULARY militia, minuteman

One night in July 1774, John Adams stopped at a tavern in eastern Massachusetts. After riding more than 30 miles (48 km), he was hot and dusty, and his body ached with fatigue. Adams asked the innkeeper for a cup of tea. He would have to drink coffee, she said. She did not serve tea. In a letter to his wife, Adams later praised the innkeeper's conduct. "Tea," he wrote, "must be... [given up]" by all colonists. He promised to break himself of the habit as soon as possible.

Why did colonists like John Adams give up tea? The answer was taxes. When Parliament decided to enforce a tea tax in 1773, a new crisis exploded. This time, colonists began to think the unthinkable. Perhaps the time had come to reject British rule and declare independence.

Uproar Over Tea

Tea became popular after it was brought to the colonies in the early 1700s. By 1770, at least one million Americans brewed tea twice a day. People "would rather go without their dinners than without a dish of tea," a visitor to the colonies noted.

Parliament passes the Tea Act. Most tea was brought to the colonies by the British East India Company. The company sold its tea to colonial tea merchants. The merchants then sold the tea to the colonists.

In the 1770s, however, the British East India Company found itself in deep financial trouble. More than 15 million pounds of its tea sat unsold in British warehouses. Britain had kept a tax on tea as a symbol of its right to tax the colonies. The tax was a small one, but colonists resented it. They refused to buy English tea.

Parliament tried to help the East India Company by passing the ***Tea Act*** of 1773. The act let the company bypass the tea merchants and sell directly to colonists. Although colonists would still have to pay the tea tax, the tea itself would cost less than ever before.

To the surprise of Parliament, colonists protested the Tea Act. Colonial tea merchants were angry because they had been cut out of the tea trade. If Parliament ruined tea merchants today, they warned, what would prevent it from turning on other businesses tomorrow? Even tea drinkers, who would have benefited from the law, scorned the Tea Act. They believed that it was a British trick to make them accept Parliament's right to tax the colonies.

Boycott the "accursed STUFF"! Once again, colonists responded with a boycott. One colonial newspaper warned:

> 66Do not suffer yourself to sip the accursed, dutied STUFF. For if you do, the devil will immediately enter into you, and you will instantly become a traitor to your country.99

Daughters of Liberty and other women led the boycott. They served coffee or made "liberty tea" from raspberry leaves. Sons of Liberty enforced the boycott by keeping the British East India Company from unloading cargoes of tea.

Much early protest against the British occurred in the city of Boston. This map shows Boston in the 1770s.

1. *(a) At which building did colonists gather before the Boston Tea Party? (b) On which street was it located?*
2. *In what part of Boston did the Boston Tea Party take place?*
3. **Drawing Conclusions** *Why would taxes on trade be especially unpopular in cities like Boston?*

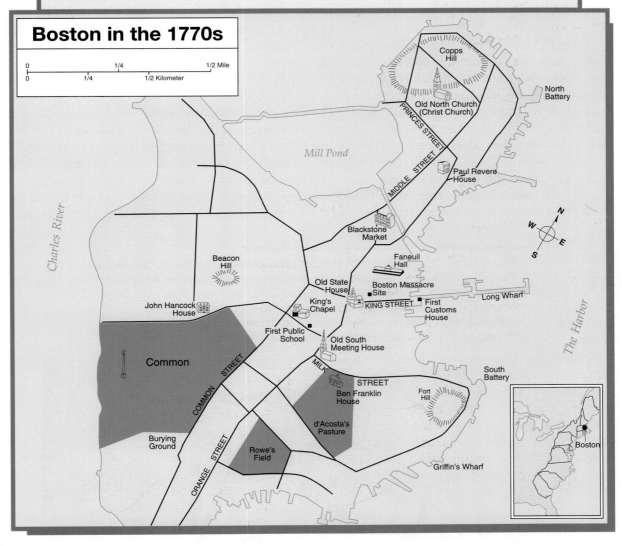

Boston in the 1770s

The Boston Tea Party

In late November 1773, three ships carrying tea arrived in Boston harbor. Governor Thomas Hutch- inson ordered the captain to pay the required taxes, unload, and sell the tea as usual. If the taxes were not paid within 20 days, he would seize the cargo and have it sold. The deadline was Thursday, December 16.

A demand that the tea ships leave. All that day, Boston seethed with excitement. Townspeople roamed the streets, wondering what the Sons of Liberty would do. Farmers and workers from nearby towns joined the crowds. "Committee Men & Mob Men were buzzing about in Swarms, like Bees," reported a nephew of Governor Hutchinson.

By 10 A.M., thousands of people had made their way along Milk Street to the Old South Meetinghouse. Sam Adams was there, directing affairs. The wealthy merchant John Hancock was also present. At the meeting, colonists voted that the tea ships should leave Boston that afternoon—without unloading. Runners were sent to the customs house to voice the colonists' demand.

By afternoon, word came back. Customs officers would not act without the governor. Messengers then set off to see Governor Hutchinson.

Nervously, Sam Adams waited. So did the 5,000 people who had gathered in and around the meetinghouse. Finally, the messengers returned. The governor would not let the ships sail. The crowd's angry roar echoed far down the streets of Boston.

"Boston harbor a teapot tonight!" Adams waved for silence. "This meeting can do nothing further to save the country," he announced. Suddenly, as if on cue, a group of men burst into the meetinghouse. Dressed like Mohawk Indians, they waved hatchets in the air. The crowd stirred. What was this? From the gallery above, voices cried, "Boston harbor a teapot tonight! The Mohawks are come!"

George Hewes was one of the "Mohawks" poised for action. He later reported:

The Boston Tea Party *British officials were outraged by the Boston Tea Party, shown here. One called it "the most wanton and unprovoked insult offered to the civil power that is recorded in history." John Adams, however, believed that many colonists wished that "as many dead Carcasses were floating in the Harbour, as there are Chests of Tea."* ***Economics*** *Why were colonial tea merchants angered by the Tea Act?*

"I [had] dressed myself in the costume of an Indian, equipped with a small hatchet after having painted my face and hands with coal dust in the shop of a blacksmith. . . . When I first appeared in the street after being thus disguised, I fell in with many who were dressed, equipped and painted as I was, and . . . marched in order to the place of our destination."

That place was Griffin's Wharf, where the tea ships lay at anchor. About 50 or 60 people disguised as Indians were there. Some were carpenters and barbers. Others were doctors and merchants. In the cold, crisp night, under a nearly full moon, the men worked quickly. They boarded the ships, split open the tea chests, and dumped the tea into the harbor. On shore, the crowd watched silently. The only sounds were the chink of hatchets and the splash of tea landing in the water.

By 10 P.M., the job was done. The **Boston Tea Party,** as it was later called, had ended. However, the effects would be felt for a long time to come. ■

Britain Strikes Back

Did Sam Adams organize the Boston Tea Party? Although he never said so publicly, he very likely knew that it was planned. Whoever led the tea party, however, made sure that the protest was orderly. Only tea was destroyed. No other cargo was touched. The Boston Tea Party was meant to show Britain that the colonists would act firmly.

Colonists had mixed reactions to the event. Some cheered the action. Others worried that it would encourage lawlessness in the colonies. Even those who condemned the Boston Tea Party were shocked at Britain's response to it.

Punishment for Massachusetts. The British were outraged by what they saw as Boston's lawless behavior. In 1774, Parliament, encouraged by King George III, acted to punish Massachusetts. First, Parliament shut down the port of Boston. No ship could enter or leave the harbor—not even a small boat. The harbor would remain closed until the colonists paid for the tea.

Second, Parliament said colonists could call no more than one town meeting a year without the governor's permission. In the past, colonists had had frequent meetings. (📖 See "Early Thunder" on page 556.)

Third, Parliament provided for customs officers and other officials charged with major crimes to be tried in Britain instead of in Massachusetts. Colonists protested. They said that a dishonest official could break the law in the colonies and avoid punishment "by being tried, where no evidence can pursue him."

Fourth, Parliament passed a new Quartering Act. No longer would redcoats camp in tents on Boston Common. Instead, British commanders could force citizens to house troops in their homes. The colonists called these laws the **Intolerable Acts** because they were so harsh.

Colonists support Boston. The committees of correspondence spread news of the Intolerable Acts. People from other colonies responded quickly to help the people of Boston, who faced hunger while their port was closed.

British Grenadier *The Intolerable Acts forced Bostonians to open their homes to British soldiers, such as the one shown here.* **Citizenship** *What were the other provisions of the Intolerable Acts?*

Carts rolled into the city with rice from South Carolina, corn from Virginia, and flour from Pennsylvania.

In the Virginia assembly, a young lawyer named Thomas Jefferson suggested that a day be set aside to mark the shame of the Intolerable Acts. The royal governor of Virginia rejected the idea and dismissed the assembly. But the colonists went ahead anyway. On June 1, 1774, church bells tolled slowly. Merchants closed their shops. Many colonists prayed and fasted all day.

The First Continental Congress

In response to the Intolerable Acts, colonial leaders called a meeting in Philadelphia. In September 1774, delegates from 12 colonies gathered in what became known as the *First Continental Congress.* Only Georgia did not send delegates.

After much debate, the delegates passed a resolution backing Massachusetts in its struggle against the Intolerable Acts. They agreed to boycott all British goods and to stop exporting goods to Britain until the harsh laws were repealed. The delegates also urged each colony to set up and train its own militia (muh LIHSH uh). A militia is an army of citizens who serve as soldiers during an emergency.

Before leaving Philadelphia, the delegates agreed to meet again the following May. Little did they know that by May 1775 an incident in Massachusetts would have changed the fate of the colonies forever.

The Shot Heard 'Round the World

In Massachusetts, newspapers called on citizens to prevent what they called "the Massacre of American Liberty." Volunteers

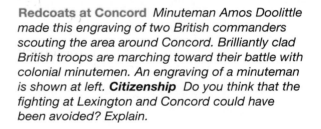

Redcoats at Concord *Minuteman Amos Doolittle made this engraving of two British commanders scouting the area around Concord. Brilliantly clad British troops are marching toward their battle with colonial minutemen. An engraving of a minuteman is shown at left.* **Citizenship** *Do you think that the fighting at Lexington and Concord could have been avoided? Explain.*

known as minutemen trained regularly. Minutemen got their name because they kept their muskets at hand, prepared to fight at a minute's notice. Meanwhile, Britain built up its forces. More troops arrived in Boston, bringing the total number in that city to 4,000.

Early in 1775, General Thomas Gage, the British commander, learned that minutemen had a large store of arms in Concord, a village about 18 miles (29 km) from Boston. General Gage planned a surprise march to Concord to seize the arms.

On April 18, about 700 British troops quietly left Boston under cover of darkness. The Sons of Liberty were watching. As soon as the British set out, they hung two lamps from the Old North Church in Boston as a signal that the redcoats were on the move.

Sounding the alarm. Colonists who were waiting across the Charles River saw the signal. Messengers mounted their horses and galloped through the night toward Concord. One midnight rider was Paul Revere. "The British are coming! The British are coming!" shouted Revere as he passed through each sleepy village along the way.

At daybreak on April 19, the redcoats reached Lexington, a town near Concord. There, waiting for them on the village green, were 70 minutemen commanded by Captain John Parker. The British ordered the minutemen to go home. Outnumbered, the colonists began to leave. A shot suddenly rang out through the chill morning air. No one knows who fired it. In the brief struggle that followed, eight colonists were killed and one British soldier was wounded.

The British pushed on to Concord. Finding no arms in the village, they turned back to Boston. On a bridge outside Concord, they met 300 minutemen. Again, fighting broke out. This time, the British were forced to retreat. As they withdrew, colonial sharpshooters took deadly aim at them from the woods and fields. By the time they reached Boston, the redcoats had lost 73 men. Another 200 were wounded or missing.

A turning point. News of the battles at Lexington and Concord spread swiftly. To many colonists, the fighting ended all hope of reaching an agreement with Britain. Only war would decide the future of the 13 colonies.

More than 60 years after the battles, a well-known New England poet, Ralph Waldo Emerson, wrote a poem about them. It begins:

> By the rude bridge that arched the flood,
> Their flag to April's breeze unfurled,
> Here once the embattled farmers stood,
> And fired the shot heard round the world.

The "embattled farmers" faced long years of war. At the war's end, though, the 13 colonies would stand firm as a new, independent nation.

SECTION 4 REVIEW

1. **Locate:** (a) Boston, (b) Concord, (c) Lexington.
2. **Identify:** (a) Tea Act, (b) Boston Tea Party, (c) Intolerable Acts, (d) First Continental Congress, (e) Paul Revere.
3. **Define:** (a) militia, (b) minuteman.
4. (a) Why did Britain pass the Tea Act? (b) Why did the act anger colonists?
5. How did the Intolerable Acts help unite the colonies?
6. Describe the events that led to fighting at Lexington.
7. CRITICAL THINKING **Analyzing Information** Do you think that the organizers of the Boston Tea Party would have ended their protests against Britain if Parliament had repealed the tax on tea? Explain.

ACTIVITY Writing to Learn
Imagine that you are a writer for the Massachusetts committee of correspondence. Write a letter informing colonists about the Intolerable Acts.

Our Common Heritage

One colonist who heeded Paul Revere's call to action was a minuteman named Peter Salem. A former slave, Salem marched with his company to face the British at Concord. Armed with a flintlock musket, he kept firing until the redcoats retreated.

Summary

- In the mid-1700s, rivalry between France and England in the Ohio Valley led to the French and Indian War.
- By 1763, Britain had driven France out of most of North America.
- Tensions between colonists and Britain grew when Parliament imposed new taxes to help repay Britain's huge war debts.
- The first armed clashes between minutemen and British troops took place at Lexington and Concord in April 1775.

Reviewing the Main Ideas

1. Why did Native Americans take sides in the struggle between France and Britain?
2. (a) Why did George Washington lead troops into the Ohio Valley in 1754? (b) Why was his clash with the French at Fort Necessity important?
3. (a) Why did Pontiac fight the British? (b) How did Pontiac's War affect British policy in the colonies?
4. What were the main results of the Treaty of Paris of 1763?
5. (a) List three ways Parliament tried to tax the colonies. (b) How did colonists respond to each?
6. (a) How did colonists protest the Tea Act? (b) What did Britain do in response?
7. (a) Why did General Gage send troops to Concord? (b) What happened when they reached Lexington?

Thinking Critically

1. **Linking Past and Present** How might your life be different if France, not England, had won the French and Indian War?
2. **Understanding Causes and Effects** Make a cause-and-effect chart about the Stamp Act. Use at least two causes and two effects.

3. **Evaluating Information** The dictionary defines a massacre as the cruel and violent killing of large numbers of people. Why do you think Sam Adams called the incident in Boston a massacre when only five people were killed?

Applying Your Skills

1. **Analyzing a Quotation** Review the following statement made by a Native American to an English trader in the mid-1700s: "You and the French are like the two edges of a pair of shears. And we are the cloth which is to be cut to pieces between them." (a) What did the speaker mean by these words? (b) Do you think he felt that Native Americans could hold out against the British and French? Explain.
2. **Ranking** List the events discussed in Sections 3 and 4. Then rank them in the order of their importance in bringing about war between the colonists and Britain.

Thinking About Geography

Match the letters on the map with the following places: **1.** Spanish lands in 1763, **2.** British lands in 1763, **3.** Original 13 English colonies, **4.** Mississippi River, **5.** Ohio River. **Location** What body of water formed the western boundary of British lands in North America in 1763?

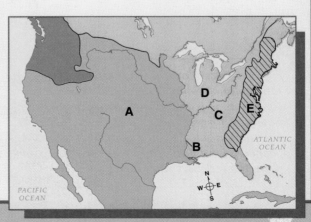

Protesting British Policies

Form into groups to review British policies toward the colonies after 1763. Follow the suggestions to write, draw, or perform to show what you have learned about the colonists' reaction to these policies. You may use the textbook, encyclopedias, atlases, or other materials in your classroom library to complete the tasks. Be able to name your sources of information when you have finished the activity.

Stamp Act riot

ECONOMISTS Review the taxes Britain imposed on the 13 English colonies in the 1760s and 1770s. Then create a Taxation Time Line showing the British tax acts. Illustrate your time line with drawings of your own or pictures cut from newspapers or old magazines.

ARTISTS Imagine that you live in one of the 13 English colonies after the French and Indian War. Draw a political cartoon expressing your reaction to British taxes.

Teapot protesting the Stamp Act

MUSICIANS List five reasons for the colonists' anger with Britain. Based on your list, write a song of protest against British treatment. You can make up your own melody or write new words to an existing tune. Sing or play your song for the class.

WRITERS In the 1760s and 1770s, colonists staged acts of protest against the British. Imagine that you are a movie director. Write a scene dramatizing the Boston Massacre for a movie titled "The Road to Revolution."

CITIZENS Review the events of the Boston Tea Party. Make a chart with two columns. In one column, list reasons for colonists' support of the Boston Tea Party. In the other column, list reasons for condemning the event.

Tax stamp

★ Publish a pamphlet titled "The Road to Revolution." Include the completed activity of each group.

"Song of Liberty"

The MASSACHUSETTS Song of LIBERTY.

Come swallow your bumpers, ye Tories, and roar, That the Sons of fair Freedom are hamper'd once more; But know that no Cut-throats our

The American Revolution

(1775–1783)

1776 *The Declaration of Independence marked the colonists' formal break from Britain. Delegates used the pen and ink set shown here to sign the Declaration.*

1777 *American victory at the Battle of Saratoga convinced France to help the Patriot cause. The young Frenchman, the Marquis de Lafayette, fought with Washington's army.*

1779 *The Americans enjoyed their greatest naval victory when the* Bonhomme Richard *defeated the British warship* Serapis.

1775   1776   1777   1778   1779

WORLD EVENT
1778 France recognizes
American independence

Chapter Setting

"Gentlemen may cry, 'Peace! peace!'—but there is no peace. The war is actually begun! . . . Our brethren are already in the field! Why stand we here idle? . . . Is life so dear, or peace so sweet, as to be purchased at the price of chains and slavery? Forbid it, Almighty God! I know not what course others may take; but as for me, give me liberty or give me death!"

Patrick Henry's words echoed through St. John's Church in Richmond, Virginia. By March 1775, the 13 colonies stood on the brink of war.

Delegates from across Virginia had gathered at the church to debate what action to take. Some wanted to give Britain one last chance to change its conduct toward the colonies. Others, like Henry, were ready to fight to protect their rights. "There is no longer any room for hope," cried Henry. "We have done everything that could be done to [prevent] the storm which is coming on us now."

Similar debates raged in other colonies. As the British sent more and more troops to Boston, colonists faced a hard decision: Should they accept British actions? Or should they fight for their liberties? In July 1776, colonial leaders took a fateful step. One by one, they voted to form a new nation, the United States of America. To make that nation free and independent, however, colonists had to fight a long, hard war.

ACTIVITY Stage a debate between English colonists in 1775 on the following question: Should the 13 English colonies fight to win independence from Britain?

1781 The American Revolution ended with the Patriot victory at the Battle of Yorktown. This painting shows the surrender of the British.

1783 Britain signed the Treaty of Paris, recognizing the United States as an independent nation. This medal celebrated the coming of peace.

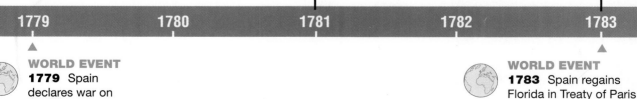

| 1779 | 1780 | 1781 | 1782 | 1783 |

WORLD EVENT
1779 Spain declares war on Great Britain

WORLD EVENT
1783 Spain regains Florida in Treaty of Paris

FIND OUT

- What actions did the Second Continental Congress take in 1776?
- What were the strengths and weaknesses of each side in the Revolution?
- How did colonists force the British to leave Boston?

VOCABULARY blockade

As darkness fell, the redcoats limped into Boston from Lexington and Concord. All along the route, rebels had fired on them. The events of April 19, 1775, left the British stunned. How had a handful of rebels forced 700 redcoats to retreat? That night, British soldiers grew even more uneasy as they watched rebels set up campfires all around Boston.

In the weeks and months ahead, the campfires remained. They were a clear sign that the quarrel between Britain and its colonies had blazed into war. Many colonists clung to hopes for a peaceful solution to the crisis. The rebels outside Boston, however, were ready to fight.

The Green Mountain Boys

In 1775, the colonies did not have a united army—or even a united government. In each colony, rebels took daring action. Ethan Allen, a Vermont blacksmith known for his strength and fierce temper, flew into a rage when he learned of events in Massachusetts. "I read with horror," he later wrote, of the "bloody attempt at Lexington to enslave America."

Allen led a band of Vermonters, known as the *Green Mountain Boys,* in a surprise attack on Fort Ticonderoga. The fort was located at the southern tip of Lake Champlain. (See the map on page 163.) Allen knew that it had many cannons, which the colonists badly needed.

In early May, the Green Mountain Boys slipped through the morning mists at Fort Ticonderoga. They quickly overpowered the guard on duty and entered the fort. Allen rushed to the room where the British commander slept. "Come out, you old rat!" he shouted.

The commander demanded to know on whose authority Allen acted. "In the name

Ethan Allen Captures Ticonderoga *In May 1775, Ethan Allen and the Green Mountain Boys made a bold attack on Fort Ticonderoga. Here, Allen demands that the British commander surrender.* **Geography** *Why was Fort Ticonderoga important?*

of the Great Jehovah and the Continental Congress!" Allen replied. The commander had no choice but to surrender the fort with its cannons and valuable supply of gunpowder. Allen's success gave the Americans control of a key route into Canada.

Last Efforts for Peace

While the Green Mountain Boys celebrated their victory, delegates from the colonies met at the Second Continental Congress in Philadelphia. Although fighting had begun, most delegates did not want to break with Britain. A few, however, including Sam and John Adams, secretly wanted the colonies to declare independence.

After much debate, the Continental Congress voted to patch up the quarrel with Britain. Delegates sent King George III the **Olive Branch Petition.** In it, they declared their loyalty and asked the king to repeal the Intolerable Acts.

At the same time, the Congress took a bold step. It set up the **Continental Army.** John Adams proposed George Washington of Virginia as commander:

&&I [have] in my mind for that important command...a gentleman whose skill and experience as an officer, whose independent fortune, great talents, and excellent universal character would command the [approval] of all America.&&

Washington heard Adams's words. Embarrassed by the praise, he quietly slipped out of the room. In a vote, all delegates approved Washington as commander.

Strengths and Weaknesses

Without wasting any time, Washington left Philadelphia to take charge of the forces around Boston. He faced an uphill struggle. Colonial forces were untrained. They had few cannons, little gunpowder, and no navy.

The British, on the other hand, had highly trained, experienced troops. Britain's navy was the most powerful in the world. Its ships could move soldiers quickly up and down the Atlantic coast.

Still, Britain faced serious problems. Its armies were 3,000 miles (4,800 km) from home. News and supplies took months to travel from Britain to North America. Also, British soldiers risked attacks by colonists once they marched out of the cities into the countryside.

The Americans had certain advantages. They were fighting to defend their homes, farms, lands, and shops. Reuben Stebbins of Williamstown, Massachusetts, was typical of many farmers. When he heard that the British were nearby, he rode off to battle. "We'll see who's goin' t' own this farm!" he cried.

Although few Americans had military training, many owned rifles and were good shots. Also, the colonists had a brilliant leader in George Washington. He demanded—and received—respect from his troops.

Taking a Stand at Bunker Hill

While Washington was riding toward Boston, rebels tightened their circle around the city. The Americans wanted to keep the British from marching out of the city.

At sunset on June 16, 1775, Colonel William Prescott led 1,200 minutemen to take up a position on Bunker Hill in Charlestown, across the river from Boston.

History and You
Patriots used many different flags during the Revolution. Besides the familiar stars and stripes, flags featured a variety of symbols, including a pine cone and an eagle. What symbols would you use to represent the United States today?

Battle of Bunker Hill *American forces fought fiercely but could not prevent the British from taking Bunker Hill. This painting by Winthrop Chandler gives a bird's-eye view of this first major battle of the Revolution.* **Geography** *Why did the Americans take up a position on a hill?*

From there, they could fire on British ships in Boston harbor.

"Dig, men, dig." Prescott soon saw that nearby Breed's Hill was a better position. He had his men dig trenches there. "Dig, men, dig," he urged. Prescott knew that the trenches must be ready before dawn. Otherwise, the British could force him off the hill.

At sunrise, the British general, William Howe, spotted the Americans. He ferried about 2,400 redcoats across the harbor to Charlestown. The British then had to cross rough fields and climb Breed's Hill. Each soldier carried a heavy pack that weighed about 125 pounds. It was hot, exhausting work, and the soldiers moved slowly.

From their trenches, the Americans watched the British approach. Because the colonists had very little gunpowder, their commanders warned, "Don't shoot until you see the whites of their eyes!"

The deadly attack. As the enemy advanced, "We gave them such a hot fire that they were obliged to retire nearly 150 yards before they could rally," recalled Colonel Prescott. Twice, the British advanced up the hill. Twice, they had to retreat under deadly fire.

On the third try, the British pushed over the top. By then, the colonists had run out of gunpowder. The British took both Bunker Hill and Breed's Hill. They paid a high price for their victory, however. "The day ended in glory," noted a British officer, "but the loss was uncommon in officers for the number engaged." More than 1,000 redcoats lay dead or wounded. American losses numbered 400.

The ***Battle of Bunker Hill*** was the first major battle of the Revolution. It proved that the Americans could fight bravely. It also showed that the British would not be easy to defeat.

Redcoats Leave Boston

Washington finally reached Boston in midsummer. There, he found about 16,000 troops camped in huts and tents at the edge of the city. Their weapons ranged from rifles to swords made by local blacksmiths.

General Washington quickly began to turn raw recruits into a trained army. His job was especially difficult because soldiers from different colonies mistrusted one another. "Connecticut wants no Massachusetts men in her corps," he wrote. And "Massachusetts thinks there is no necessity for a Rhode Islander to be introduced into her [ranks]." Slowly, Washington won the loyalty of his troops. They, in turn, learned to take orders and work together.

By January 1776, the Continental Army had a firm grip around Boston. From Ticonderoga, soldiers had dragged cannons on sleds across the mountains. Washington had the cannons placed on Dorchester Heights, overlooking Boston and its harbor. General Howe realized that he could not overpower the Americans. In March 1776, he and his troops sailed from Boston to Halifax, Canada.

Although the British left New England, they had not given up. King George III ordered a blockade of all colonial ports. A **blockade** is the shutting off of a port to keep people or supplies from moving in or out. The king also hired Hessian troops from Germany to help fight the colonists.

March on Canada

Some Americans wanted to attack the British in Canada. They hoped to win support from French Canadians, who were not happy under British rule.

In the fall of 1775, two American armies moved north into Canada. (See the map at right.) Richard Montgomery led one army from Fort Ticonderoga to Montreal. He seized that city in November 1775. He then moved toward the city of Quebec.

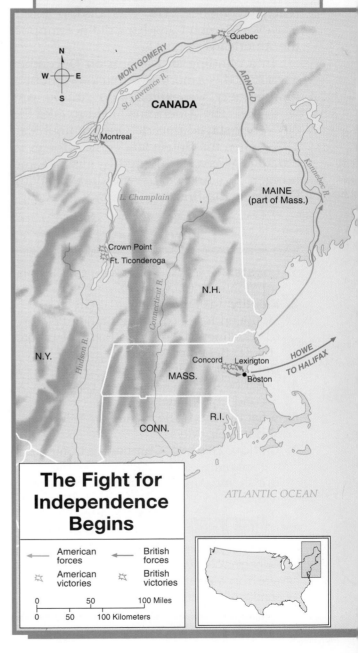

MAP STUDY

The first clashes of the Revolution took place in the northern colonies and in Canada.
1. *In which direction did Benedict Arnold march to reach Quebec?*
2. *About how far did Montgomery have to travel from Fort Ticonderoga to Quebec?*
3. **Analyzing Information** *Based on the map, which American commander would have had a harder time reaching Quebec? Explain.*

The Fight for Independence Begins

← American forces
← British forces
☆ American victories
☆ British victories

0   50   100 Miles
0   50   100 Kilometers

Benedict Arnold led the second army north through Maine. He was supposed to join forces with Montgomery in Quebec.

Arnold and his troops had a terrible journey through the Maine woods in winter. Rainstorms followed by freezing nights coated their clothes with ice. Supplies ran so low that soldiers survived only by eating boiled bark and shoe leather. Finally, Arnold reached Quebec. He was disappointed, however. French Canadians did not support the Americans.

In a blinding snowstorm on December 31, 1775, the Americans attacked Quebec. Montgomery was killed, and Arnold was wounded. The Americans failed to take the city. They stayed outside Quebec until May 1776, when the British landed new forces in Canada. At last, weakened by disease and hunger, the Americans withdrew, leaving Canada to the British.

SECTION 1 REVIEW

1. **Locate:** (a) Fort Ticonderoga, (b) Boston, (c) Montreal, (d) Quebec.
2. **Identify:** (a) Ethan Allen, (b) Green Mountain Boys, (c) Olive Branch Petition, (d) Continental Army, (e) Battle of Bunker Hill, (f) Benedict Arnold.
3. **Define:** blockade.
4. Describe three actions taken by the Second Continental Congress.
5. What did the Battle of Bunker Hill reveal about each side?
6. **CRITICAL THINKING Comparing** Compare the strengths and weaknesses of the British and Americans at the start of the war.

ACTIVITY Writing to Learn

Imagine that you have George Washington's job at the beginning of the American Revolution. Write several diary entries describing the task you face as commander of the Continental Army.

2
Independence Declared

FIND OUT
- How did *Common Sense* influence the colonists?
- What are the main ideas of the Declaration of Independence?
- How did Americans respond to the Declaration of Independence?

VOCABULARY traitor

George III was furious when he heard about the Olive Branch Petition. The colonies, he raged, are in a "desperate [plot] to establish an independent empire!" He vowed to bring the rebels to justice.

Colonists learned of the king's response in November 1775. At first, most still hoped to patch up the quarrel with Britain. As the months passed, however, attitudes changed. More and more colonists spoke openly of breaking away from Britain.

Common Sense

In January 1776, a pamphlet appeared on the streets of Philadelphia. "I offer nothing more than simple facts, plain arguments, and common sense," said its author, Thomas Paine. The pamphlet, *Common Sense,* created a great stir. Paine's "plain arguments" boldly urged the colonies to declare their independence.

Paine had only recently arrived from England. Still, he shared the colonists' desire for liberty. In *Common Sense,* he showed how colonists had nothing to gain from staying under British rule. He pointed out that there were many disadvantages in their current situation:

“[It is foolish]. . . to be always running three or four thousand miles with a tale or petition, waiting four or five months for an answer, which when obtained requires five or six more to explain it in.”

Since King George had just rejected the Olive Branch Petition, that argument made sense to many colonists.

Paine also attacked the idea of having kings and queens as rulers. One honest man, he insisted, was worth more "in the sight of God than all the crowned ruffians that ever lived."

In *Common Sense,* Paine's reasoning was so clear that he won many colonists to the idea of independence. In six months, more than 500,000 copies were printed and sold. "*Common Sense* is working a powerful change in the minds of men," George Washington observed. It even changed the general's own habits. Until 1776, Washington followed the custom of toasting the king at official dinners. After reading Paine's pamphlet, he ended this practice.

The Fateful Step

Common Sense affected members of the Continental Congress, too. In June 1776, Richard Henry Lee of Virginia offered a resolution saying that "these United Colonies are, and of right ought to be, free and independent States."

Delegates faced a difficult decision. There could be no turning back if they declared independence. If they fell into British hands, they would be hanged as traitors. A **traitor** is a person who betrays his or her country.

Writing the Declaration. The delegates took a fateful step. They chose a committee to draw up a declaration of independence. The committee included John Adams, Benjamin Franklin, Thomas Jefferson, Robert Livingston, and Roger Sherman. Their job was to tell the world why the colonies were

Down With the King! *In July 1776, angry New Yorkers tore down a statue of King George III. Patriots, like Laura Wolcott (at right), used lead from the statue to make cartridges for Washington's army.* **American Traditions** *How did Thomas Paine's writings inflame American opinion against the king?*

Declaring Independence *Thomas Jefferson labored many hours perfecting the Declaration of Independence. Here, Jefferson and other committee members present the Declaration to the Continental Congress. The delegates' signatures on the document appear at right.* **American Traditions** *What was the purpose of the Declaration of Independence?*

breaking away from Britain. The committee asked Jefferson to write the document.

Jefferson was one of the youngest delegates. A quiet man, he spoke little at formal meetings. But among friends, he liked to sprawl in a chair with his long legs stretched out and talk for hours. In late June, Jefferson completed the declaration, and it was read to the Congress.

The vote. On July 2, the Continental Congress voted that the 13 colonies were "free and independent States." Two days later, on July 4, 1776, the delegates accepted the ***Declaration of Independence.*** Since then, Americans have celebrated July 4th as Independence Day.

John Hancock, president of the Continental Congress, signed the Declaration first. He penned his signature boldly, in large,

clear letters. "There," he said, "I guess King George will be able to read that."

The Declaration

Across the colonies, people read the Declaration of Independence. The document has three main parts. (The complete Declaration

Linking Past and Present

The Declaration of Independence gained new meaning over time. Americans now accept that the words "all men are created equal" mean "all people are created equal." This includes women and African Americans, as well as minorities of all kinds.

of Independence is printed in the Reference Section.)

Basic rights. The first part of the Declaration describes the basic rights on which the nation was founded. In bold, ringing words, Jefferson wrote:

66 We hold these truths to be self-evident, that all men are created equal, that they are endowed by their Creator with certain unalienable rights, that among these are life, liberty, and the pursuit of happiness. 99

How do people protect these rights? By forming governments, the Declaration says. Governments can exist only if they have the "consent of the governed." If a government takes away its citizens' rights, then it is the people's "right [and] duty, to throw off such government, and provide new guards for their future security."

British wrongs. The second part of the Declaration lists the wrongs committed by Britain. Jefferson carefully showed how George III had abused his power. He condemned the king for disbanding colonial legislatures and for sending troops to the colonies in times of peace. He listed other wrongs to show why the colonists had the right to rebel.

An independent nation. The last part of the Declaration announces that the colonies had become "the United States of America." All ties with Britain were cut. As a free and independent nation, the United States could make alliances and trade with other countries.

Choosing Sides

John Dunlap of Philadelphia printed the Declaration of Independence on July 4, 1776. Later, Mary Katherine Goddard, a Baltimore printer, produced the first copies that included the names of all the signers. As colonists studied the document, they had to decide what course to take.

Opinion was divided. Some colonists were **Patriots,** people who supported independence. Others were **Loyalists,** people who remained loyal to Britain. Many families were split. Ben Franklin, for example, was a Patriot. His son, the royal governor of New Jersey, supported King George.

During the American Revolution, tens of thousands of people supported the British. Loyalists included wealthy merchants and former officials of the royal government. However, many farmers and craftsworkers were Loyalists, too. There were more Loyalists in the Middle States and the South than in New England.

Life was difficult for Loyalists everywhere. Patriots tarred and feathered people known to favor the British. Many Loyalists fled to England or Canada. Others found shelter in cities controlled by the British. Those who fled lost their homes, stores, and farms.

SECTION 2 REVIEW

1. **Identify:** (a) Thomas Paine, (b) Richard Henry Lee, (c) Thomas Jefferson, (d) Declaration of Independence, (e) Mary Katherine Goddard, (f) Patriot, (g) Loyalist.
2. **Define:** traitor.
3. What arguments did Thomas Paine offer in favor of independence?
4. Describe the three main parts of the Declaration of Independence.
5. Why was life difficult for Loyalists during the Revolution?
6. CRITICAL THINKING **Comparing** Compare the viewpoints of Patriots and Loyalists at the outbreak of the Revolution.

ACTIVITY **Writing to Learn** Imagine that you are one of the delegates to the Continental Congress. Write a letter to a friend describing your feelings about signing the Declaration of Independence.

CRITICAL THINKING SKILLS
Comparing Points of View

A primary source, or firsthand account, reflects the author's point of view. Two people writing about the same subject can have different points of view.

The letters below were written by Abigail and John Adams. During the Revolution, John Adams was away from home for long periods. His wife, Abigail, wrote to him often. When the Continental Congress was preparing the Declaration of Independence, she wrote her husband the first letter reprinted below. The second letter is John Adams's reply.

1. **Study the contents of each source.** (a) What does Abigail Adams want her husband to do? (b) What is John Adams's response to her request? (c) Who is John Adams referring to with the words "another tribe, more numerous and powerful than all the rest"?

2. **Compare the points of view.** (a) What does Abigail Adams think men are like? (b) Does John Adams agree with his wife's view? Explain.

3. **Evaluate the usefulness of the sources.** (a) What do these letters tell you about American society in 1776? (b) Do you think these letters are a reliable source of information? Explain.

ACTIVITY Write a letter expressing your views about whether women in the armed forces should be allowed to take part in combat. Would your letter be a reliable primary source 100 years from now? Explain.

Abigail Adams wrote:

"I long to hear that you have declared independence. And by the way, in the new code of laws that I suppose you will make, I wish you would remember the ladies and be more generous and favorable to them than your ancestors. Do not put such unlimited power in the hands of husbands. Remember, all men would be tyrants if they could. If particular care and attention is not paid to the ladies, we are determined to stir up a rebellion and will not regard ourselves as bound by any laws in which we have had no voice or representation."

John Adams replied:

"As to your extraordinary code of laws, I can't help laughing. We have been told that our struggle has loosened the bonds of government everywhere, that children and apprentices were disobedient, that schools and colleges had grown turbulent, that Indians slighted their guardians and negroes grow insolent to their masters. But your letter was the first hint that another tribe, more numerous and powerful than all the rest, had grown discontented.

Depend upon it, we know better than to repeal our masculine systems. Although they are in full force, you know they are little more than theory. . . . In practice, you know, we are the subjects. We have only the title of masters, and rather than give this up, which would subject us completely to the power of the petticoat, I hope General Washington and all our brave heroes would fight."

Desperate Days

FIND OUT

■ What battles were fought in the Middle States?

■ Why was the Battle of Saratoga important?

■ How did volunteers from other lands help the Americans?

VOCABULARY cavalry, neutral

One morning in late June 1776, rifleman Daniel McCurtin glanced out his window at New York harbor. A startling sight met his eyes. He saw "something resembling a wood of pine trees trimmed." As he watched, the forest moved across the water. Suddenly, he realized that the trees were the masts of ships!

66 I could not believe my eyes... when in about ten minutes, the whole bay was full of shipping as ever it could be. I declare that I thought all London was afloat. 99

By noon, a British fleet was anchored offshore. General Howe and his redcoats had arrived in force.

The arrival of the British fleet in New York marked a new stage in the war. Most early battles of the American Revolution were fought in New England. In mid-1776, the heavy fighting shifted to the Middle States. There, the Continental Army suffered through the worst days of the war.

Campaign in New York

Washington had expected Howe's attack and had led his forces south from Boston. His army, however, was no match for the British. Howe had 34,000 troops, 10,000 sailors, and ships to ferry them ashore. Washington had fewer than 20,000 poorly trained troops. Worse, he had no navy.

Washington did not know exactly where Howe would land. He sent some forces to Long Island. Others he sent to Manhattan.

On the run. In August, Howe's army pushed ashore on Long Island. In the *Battle of Long Island,* more than 1,400 Americans were killed, wounded, or captured. The rest retreated to Manhattan. The British followed. To avoid capture, Washington hurried north. (See "A Teenage Prisoner of War" on page 559.)

Pursuing General Washington
*In November 1776, the Continental Army retreated from New York into New Jersey. The British followed closely behind. This sketch shows British troops landing at Fort Lee, New Jersey. **Geography** What river did the two armies have to cross to reach New Jersey?*

In 1776 and 1777, American and British forces fought many battles over a large land area. An American victory at the Battle of Saratoga in October 1777 marked a major turning point of the war.

1. What route did St. Leger's army take after leaving Montreal?
2. Who won the Battle of Brandywine?
3. **Understanding Causes and Effects** Based on the map, why do you think many Patriots left Philadelphia in 1777?

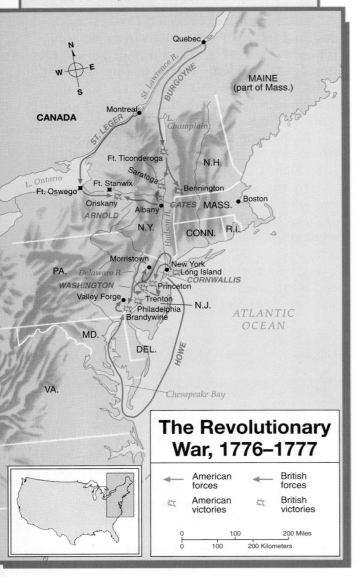

The Revolutionary War, 1776–1777

← American forces   ← British forces

☆ American victories   ☆ British victories

0   100   200 Miles

0   100   200 Kilometers

Throughout the autumn, Washington fought a series of battles with Howe's army. In November, he crossed the Hudson River into New Jersey. Pursued by the British, the Americans retreated across the Delaware River into Pennsylvania. (See the map at left.)

Nathan Hale. During the campaign for New York, Washington needed information about Howe's forces. Nathan Hale, a young Connecticut officer, slipped behind British lines and returned with the details. Soon after, the British captured Hale. They tried and condemned him to death. As Hale walked to the gallows, he is said to have declared: "I only regret that I have but one life to lose for my country."

New Hope for Americans

Months of campaigning took a toll on the Continental Army. In December 1776, Washington described his troops as sick, dirty, and "so thinly clad as to be unfit for service." Every day, soldiers fled camp to return home. Washington wrote to his brother: "I am wearied to death. I think the game is pretty near up."

The Crisis. Thomas Paine had retreated with the army through New Jersey. Once again, he took up his pen. This time, he wrote *The Crisis*, urging Americans to support the army.

    "These are the times that try men's souls. The summer soldier and the sunshine patriot will, in this crisis, shrink from the service of his country; but he that stands it *now* deserves the love and thanks of man and woman. **"**

Grateful for Paine's inspiring words, Washington had *The Crisis* read aloud to his troops.

A bold move. The Americans needed more than words to help their cause, however. General Washington decided on a bold move—a surprise attack on Trenton.

On Christmas night, Washington secretly led his troops across the icy Delaware River. Soldiers shivered as spray from the river froze on their faces. Once ashore, they marched through swirling snow. "Soldiers, keep by your officers," Washington urged.

Early on December 26, the Americans surprised the Hessian troops guarding Trenton and took most of them prisoner. An American summed up the **Battle of Trenton:** "Hessian population of Trenton at 8 A.M.— 1,408 men and 39 officers; Hessian population at 9 A.M.— 0."

Cheered by victory. British General Charles Cornwallis set out at once to retake Trenton and capture Washington. Late on January 2, 1777, he saw the lights of Washington's campfires. "At last we have run down the old fox," he said, "and we will bag him in the morning."

Washington fooled Cornwallis. He left the fires burning and slipped behind British lines to attack Princeton. There, the Continental Army won another victory. From Princeton, Washington moved to Morristown, where the army spent the winter. The victories at Trenton and Princeton gave the Americans new hope.

A New British Strategy

In London, British officials were dismayed by the army's failure to crush the rebels. Early in 1777, General John Burgoyne (buhr GOIN) presented George III with a new plan for victory. If British troops cut off New England from the other colonies, he argued, the war would soon be over.

Burgoyne wanted three British armies to march on Albany from different directions. They would crush American forces there. Then, in control of the Hudson River, the British could stop the flow of soldiers and supplies from New England to Washington.

ART GALLERY
OUR COMMON HERITAGE

OSCAR DE MEJO
Crossing the Delaware, 1986

On Christmas Eve 1776, Washington led his troops across the icy Delaware River to surprise Hessian troops dug in at Trenton, New Jersey. In this striking painting, Oscar de Mejo, an Italian-born American artist, captures the drama of Washington's crossing. De Mejo has a deep interest in American history and has painted many scenes from the nation's past. **The Arts** What impression does this painting give of George Washington?

Brandywine and Germantown. Burgoyne's plan called for General Howe to march on Albany from New York City. George III, however, wanted Howe to capture Philadelphia first.

In July 1777, Howe sailed from New York to the Chesapeake Bay. (See the map on page 170.) Despite Washington's efforts to stop him, Howe captured Philadelphia. He then went on to defeat the Americans at the battles of Brandywine and Germantown. Howe now retired to comfortable quarters in Philadelphia for the winter. Washington retreated to Valley Forge, where he set up his own makeshift camp.

Meanwhile, two other British armies under Barry St. Leger (lay ZHAIR) and Burgoyne marched from Canada toward Albany. St. Leger tried to take Fort Stanwix. However, Benedict Arnold drove him back with a strong American army.

Success at Saratoga. Only Burgoyne was left to march on Albany. His army moved slowly because it had many heavy baggage carts to drag through the woods. To slow Burgoyne further, Patriots cut down trees to block the route and dammed up streams to create swampy bogs.

Burgoyne retook Fort Ticonderoga. He then sent troops into Vermont to find food and horses. Patriots attacked the redcoats. At the Battle of Bennington, they wounded or captured nearly 1,000 British.

Burgoyne's troubles grew. The Green Mountain Boys hurried into New York to help the American forces. At the village of Saratoga, the Americans surrounded the British. When Burgoyne tried to break free, the Americans beat him back. Realizing he was trapped, Burgoyne surrendered his army to the Americans on October 17, 1777.

A Powerful Ally

The American victory at the **Battle of Saratoga** was a turning point in the war. It ended the British threat to New England. It also boosted American spirits at a time when Washington's army was suffering defeats in Pennsylvania. Most important, it convinced France to become an ally of the United States.

In 1776, the Continental Congress had sent Benjamin Franklin to Paris. His job was to persuade the French king, Louis XVI, to help the Americans with weapons and other badly needed supplies. The Congress also wanted France to declare war on Britain. France had a strong navy that could stand up to the British.

The French were still angry about their defeat by the British in the French and Indian War. But Louis XVI did not want to help the colonists openly unless he was sure they could win. Saratoga provided that proof.

In February 1778, France became the first nation to sign a treaty with the United States. In it, Louis XVI recognized the new nation and agreed to provide military aid.

Cold Winter at Valley Forge

French aid arrived too late to help Washington's ragged army at Valley Forge. During the long, cold winter of 1777–1778, the Continental Army suffered severe hardships in Pennsylvania.

American soldiers shivered in damp, drafty huts. Many slept on the frozen ground. They had little or no warm clothing. Some soldiers stood on guard wrapped only in blankets. Many had no shoes, and they wrapped bits of cloth around their feet. As the bitter winter wore on, soldiers suffered from frostbite and disease. An army surgeon from Connecticut wrote about the suffering:

66 There comes a Soldier, his bare feet are seen thro his worn-out stockings, his Breeches not sufficient to cover his nakedness. . .his whole appearance pictures a person forsaken & discouraged. 99

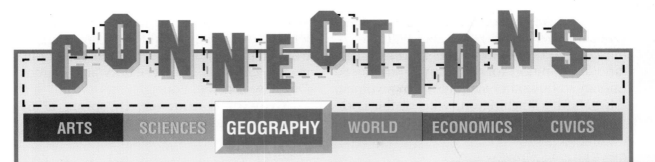

Through the Wilderness to Saratoga

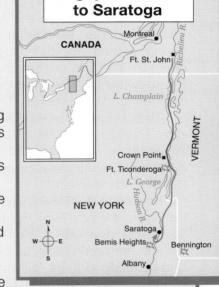

Burgoyne's March to Saratoga

The plan seemed simple. All General Burgoyne had to do was lead his men from Canada to Albany. There, they would meet up with two other British forces. They would take control of the Hudson River and drive a wedge between New England and the rest of the colonies. The rebellion, Burgoyne assured his superiors, would soon be over.

Burgoyne set out down Lake Champlain with 9,500 men in June 1777. He was sure he would be in Albany by the end of summer. He did not realize that his planned route of attack crossed lakes, swamps, mountains, and trackless forests. His splendidly equipped army was ill suited to fighting a war in a wilderness.

At first, things went well for the British. They captured Fort Ticonderoga with little opposition. Burgoyne was now supposed to continue southward by way of Lake George to the Hudson River. Instead, he chose to turn east and march overland to the Hudson. That proved a serious mistake.

Burgoyne's advance slowed to a crawl. The army took 24 days to cover 23 miles. Soldiers clothed in wool worked up to their chests in mud to build bridges across streams.

Mosquitoes and "punkies," tiny insects with needle-sharp bites, rose from the swamps to attack the men. The Americans slowed British progress even more by felling trees and rolling boulders across trails.

Burgoyne's forces finally broke out of the forests in late July. Weakened and short of supplies, they clashed with the Americans several times.

Burgoyne met the main body of the American forces in the area of Bemis Heights, near Saratoga. Outnumbered by more than three to one, Burgoyne surrendered on October 17, 1777. All that remained of his force—5,700 men—became prisoners of war.

■ How did Burgoyne's lack of knowledge about the American land help cause his defeat?

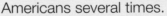

ACTIVITY Imagine that you are General Burgoyne. Write a series of telegrams to your superiors in London describing your trek through the wilderness.

British cannon

When Americans learned about conditions at Valley Forge, they sent help. Women collected food, medicine, warm clothes, and ammunition for the army. They raised money to buy other supplies. Some women, like Martha Washington, wife of the commander, went to Valley Forge to help the sick and wounded.

Help From Abroad

Throughout the war, volunteers from Europe arrived to join the American cause. The Marquis de Lafayette (lah fee YEHT), a young French noble, brought trained soldiers to the United States. He fought at Brandywine and became one of Washington's most trusted friends.

Two Polish officers joined the Americans. Thaddeus Kosciusko (kahs ee UHS koh), an engineer, helped build forts and other defenses. Casimir Pulaski trained cavalry, or troops on horseback.

Bernardo de Gálvez. Help for the Americans came from New Spain, too. At first, Spain was neutral—it did not take sides in the war between Britain and its colonies. But Bernardo de Gálvez, governor of Spanish Louisiana, favored the Patriots. He secretly supplied medicine, cloth, muskets, and gunpowder to the Americans. He also sent cattle from Texas to feed the Continental Army.

Spain entered the war against Britain in 1779. Gálvez then seized British forts along the Mississippi and Gulf of Mexico. He also drove the British out of West Florida.

A Prussian officer. Friedrich von Steuben (STOO buhn) from Prussia helped train Continental troops. Von Steuben had served in the Prussian army, considered the best in Europe. A lively man, Von Steuben kept everybody in good spirits. At the same time, he taught American soldiers skills, such as how to use bayonets. Until then, many soldiers had used their bayonets to roast meat over a fire!

Although Von Steuben spoke little English, he drilled troops and taught them to march. He ordered each soldier to put his left hand on the shoulder of the man in front of him. Then, Von Steuben called out in his German accent: "Forward march! One, Two, Three, Four!"

Growing confidence. By spring 1778, the army at Valley Forge was more hopeful. A New Jersey soldier observed:

66The army grows stronger every day. The troops are instructed in a new and so happy a method of marching that they will soon be able to advance with the utmost regularity, even without music and on the roughest grounds.99

While soldiers drilled, Washington and his staff planned new campaigns against the British.

SECTION 3 REVIEW

1. **Locate:** (a) New York, (b) Delaware River, (c) Princeton, (d) Albany, (e) Saratoga, (f) Valley Forge.
2. **Identity:** (a) Battle of Long Island, (b) Nathan Hale, (c) Battle of Trenton, (d) John Burgoyne, (e) Battle of Saratoga, (f) Marquis de Lafayette, (g) Thaddeus Kosciusko, (h) Friedrich von Steuben.
3. **Define:** (a) cavalry, (b) neutral.
4. Why did many Patriots feel discouraged from late 1776 to early 1778?
5. Describe three results of the Battle of Saratoga.
6. Why was an alliance with France important to Americans?
7. **CRITICAL THINKING Analyzing Ideas** Why do you think that people from other lands—such as Lafayette, Pulaski, and Gálvez—were willing to risk their lives for the American cause?

ACTIVITY **Writing to Learn**
Write a newspaper article about a battle of the American Revolution.

4

Other Battlefronts

FIND OUT
- What role did Native Americans play in the Revolution?
- What battles did Americans win in the West and at sea?
- How did African Americans and women contribute to the war?

Flying Crow, a Seneca chief, looked sternly at the British officers who were seated before him. "If you are so strong, Brother, and they but a weak boy, why ask our assistance?"

Like many Native American leaders, Flying Crow did not want to become involved in a war between the "weak boy"—the United States—and Britain. Yet Native Americans could not avoid the struggle. Fighting took place not only in the East but also on or near Indian lands in the West. The war was also fought at sea.

Fighting on the Frontier

During the war, white settlers continued to push west of the Appalachians. In Kentucky, newcomers named a settlement Lexington, after the first battle of the Revolution. They called another wilderness settlement Louisville, in honor of the new American ally, Louis XVI of France. In the West, settlers clashed with Native Americans, whose lands they were invading.

Native Americans choose sides. When the Revolution began, most Indians tried to stay neutral. "It is a family affair," said an Iroquois chief. He told whites that he preferred "to sit still and see you fight it out."

As the war spread, some Indians did take sides. The Six Nations of the Iroquois were divided, although most helped the British. In Massachusetts, the Algonquins supported the Patriots. In the West, many Indians joined the British to protect their lands from American settlers.

In Tennessee, most Cherokees were at first neutral or even favored the Patriots. Nancy Ward, a Cherokee leader, warned American settlers of a raid planned by a small group of Cherokees. Settlers responded by attacking all the Cherokees. This betrayal of trust led the Cherokees to join the British.

Victory at Vincennes. In 1778, George Rogers Clark led Virginia frontier fighters against the British in the Ohio Valley. With

MAP STUDY

In 1778 and 1779, American and British forces fought for control of lands west of the Appalachian Mountains.
1. Along which river did Clark's men travel after setting out from Fort Pitt?
2. Which British forts did Clark capture?
3. **Applying Information** Why was control of lands west of the Appalachians important to Americans?

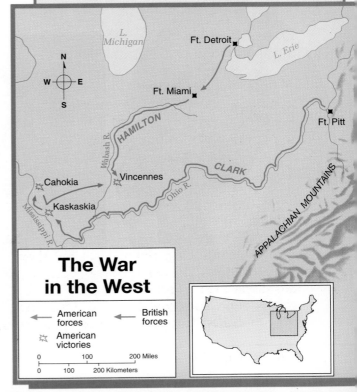

L. Michigan
Ft. Detroit
L. Erie
Ft. Miami
Ft. Pitt
Wabash R.
HAMILTON
CLARK
APPALACHIAN MOUNTAINS
Cahokia
Vincennes
Ohio R.
Mississippi R.
Kaskaskia

The War in the West

← American forces
← British forces
☆ American victories

0   100   200 Miles
0   100   200 Kilometers

help from Miami Indians, Clark captured the British forts at Kaskaskia and Cahokia. (See the map on page 175.)

Clark then plotted a surprise winter attack on the British fort at Vincennes. He led a small band 150 miles (240 km) through heavy rains, swamps, and icy rivers. When they reached the fort, they spread out through the woods to make their numbers appear greater than they really were. The strategy worked. The British commander thought it was useless to fight so many Americans. He surrendered Vincennes in February 1779.

A Victory at Sea

The Americans could do little against the powerful British navy. British ships blockaded American ports. From time to time, however, a bold American captain captured a British ship.

The most daring American captain was John Paul Jones, who raided the English coast. In his most famous battle, in September 1779, Jones commanded the *Bonhomme*

Richard. He was sailing in the North Sea near Britain when he spotted 39 enemy merchant ships. They were guarded by a single warship, the *Serapis.* The *Serapis* was larger than the *Bonhomme Richard,* but Jones attacked it.

In a furious battle, cannonballs ripped through the *Bonhomme Richard,* setting it on fire. The British commander called on Jones to surrender. "I have not yet begun to fight!" Jones replied.

Jones sailed close to the *Serapis* so that his sailors could board the enemy ship. In hand-to-hand combat, the Americans defeated the British. Jones earned a hero's welcome on his return home.

African Americans in the Battle for Freedom

At the outset of the Revolution, more than a half million African Americans lived in the colonies. At first, the Continental Congress refused to let African Americans, whether free or enslaved, join the army. The British, however, offered freedom to any

African Americans in the Revolution *Many African Americans contributed to the Revolution. Peter Williams, at right, risked his life to save an outspoken Patriot clergyman from British officers. Agrippa Hull, at left, served for four years under the Polish war hero Thaddeus Kosciusko.* **Citizenship** *Why did Washington decide to allow free African Americans to serve in the Continental Army?*

The Home Front *Americans on the home front played an important role. This printed handkerchief shows three sisters who took charge of the family farm when their husbands joined the fighting.* **American Traditions** *In what other ways did women on the home front aid the Continental Army?*

male slave who served the king. In response, Washington changed his policy and allowed free African Americans to enlist.

Comrades in arms. About 5,000 African Americans fought against the British. At least nine black minutemen saw action at Lexington and Concord. One of them, Prince Estabrook, was wounded. Two others, Peter Salem and Salem Poor, went on to fight bravely at Bunker Hill.

Some African Americans formed special regiments. Others served in white regiments as drummers, fifers, spies, and guides. Thousands of black sailors also served on American ships. Whites recognized the courage of their African American comrades, as this eyewitness account shows:

> 66 Three times in succession, [African American soldiers] were attacked. . . by well-disciplined and veteran [British] troops, and three times did they successfully repel the assault, and thus preserve our army from capture. 99

"All men are created equal." Black Patriots hoped that the Revolution would bring an end to slavery. After all, the Declaration of Independence proclaimed that "all men are created equal." In Massachusetts and elsewhere, enslaved African Americans sent petitions to lawmakers asking for freedom.

Some white leaders also hoped the war would end slavery. James Otis wrote that "the colonists are by the law of nature free born, as indeed all men are, white or black."

By the 1770s, slavery was declining in the North, where a number of free African Americans lived. During the Revolution, several states moved to outlaw slavery, including Vermont, Massachusetts, New Hampshire, and Pennsylvania. Other states debated the issue.

Women in the War

Women also helped in the struggle for independence. When men went off to war, women took on added work. They planted and harvested the crops that fed the Continental Army. They made guns and other weapons. One woman, known as "Handy Betsy the Blacksmith," was famous for supplying cannons and guns to the army.

Women made shoes and wove cloth for blankets and uniforms. Betsy Ross of Philadelphia sewed flags for Washington's army. Legend claims that Washington asked her to make the first American flag of stars and stripes. But the story cannot be proved.

Many women also joined their soldier-husbands at the front. There, they washed clothes, cooked, and cared for the wounded. Martha Washington joined her husband whenever she could.

A few women took part in battle. During the Battle of Monmouth in 1778, Mary Ludwig Hays carried water to her husband and other soldiers. The soldiers called her Moll of the Pitcher or Molly Pitcher. When her husband was wounded, she took his place, loading and firing a cannon. Deborah Sampson of Massachusetts dressed as a man and fought in several battles. Later, she wrote about her life in the army.

A Young Girl's War

Most colonists saw little actual fighting. For them, daily life went on much as usual. But when armies marched through an area, no one escaped the effects of war.

For 16-year-old Sally Wister of Philadelphia, the war brought both excitement and fear. In 1777, Sally and her family fled when the British approached Philadelphia. The Wisters were Quakers and opposed fighting. Still, they favored the Patriot cause. They settled behind American lines, in a country house outside Philadelphia.

A house full of officers. One autumn day, two Patriot officers rode up to the house to warn the Wisters of British troops nearby. "About seven o'clock we heard a great noise," Sally reported in her diary.

> **❝**To the door we all went. A large number of waggons, with about three hundred of the Philadelphia Militia [were outside]. They begged for drink, and several pushed into the house.**❞**

Even though the men were Patriots, Sally rushed out the back door, "all in a shake with fear; but after a while, seeing the officers appear gentlemanly . . . my fears were in some measure dispelled, tho' my teeth rattled, and my hand shook like an aspen leaf."

For a time, Patriot General William Smallwood and his officers made the Wister home their headquarters. "How new is our situation!" Sally wrote. "I feel in good spirits, though surrounded by an Army, the house

A Quaker Aids the Patriots *Even though they did not take part in the fighting, many Quakers helped the Patriot cause. Here, a young Quaker woman gives news of British troop movements to one of General Washington's aides.* **Multicultural Heritage** *Review page 102. Why did Quakers refuse to serve in the army?*

full of officers, the yard alive with soldiers—very peaceable sort of men, tho'."

Many Patriot officers came from other colonies. Sally "took great delight in teasing" two Virginians about their accents. They, in turn, told her about life at home and "how good turkey hash and fryed hominy is."

Handsome Major Stoddert. Sally's favorite soldier was 26-year-old Major Benjamin Stoddert. But the handsome young man from Maryland was "vastly bashful" at first. He said little to her except "Good morning," and "Your servant, madam."

One night, Major Stoddert stood by the dining room table, holding a candle so that General Smallwood could read his newspaper. Sally managed to strike up a conversation. "We talked and laughed for an hour. He is very clever, amiable, and polite. He has the softest voice, never pronounces the *R* at all."

Before long, the militia—and Major Stoddert—had to move on. "Good-bye, Miss Sally," he said, in a voice so "very low" that Sally guessed he was sorry to leave her.

A month later, Major Stoddert returned. He could "scarcely walk," reported Sally, and "looked pale, thin, and dejected." He had caught a fever. The Wisters looked after him until he recovered. Then he was off to war once more. Sally never saw him again.

Back home. Sally Wister's experience of war was like that of many Americans. At times, armies marched and drilled nearby while musket and cannon fire sounded in the distance. Then life returned to normal.

In mid-1778, the British left Philadelphia. Sally Wister returned to the city and "the rattling of carriages over the streets." By then, the fighting had shifted from the Middle States to the South. ■

SECTION 4 REVIEW

1. **Locate:** (a) Kaskaskia, (b) Cahokia, (c) Vincennes.
2. **Identify:** (a) Nancy Ward, (b) George Rogers Clark, (c) John Paul Jones, (d) Peter Salem, (e) Mary Ludwig Hays, (f) Deborah Sampson.
3. Why did Native Americans in the West help the British?
4. Why was John Paul Jones a hero to Americans?
5. How did women help in the struggle for independence?
6. **CRITICAL THINKING Linking Past and Present** Suppose that you were living in a country at war today. Would your experience be similar to that of Sally Wister during the American Revolution? Explain.

ACTIVITY Writing to Learn
Imagine that you are a free African American man in New England during the Revolution. Write a paragraph explaining why you either will or will not join the Continental Army.

5
The World Turned Upside Down

FIND OUT
- Why did fighting shift to the South in 1778?
- How did Washington force the British to surrender at Yorktown?
- What were the terms of the Treaty of Paris?

VOCABULARY ratify

Thomas Young was only 16 years old when he set out with 900 other Patriots to capture King's Mountain in South Carolina. Although most of the Patriots were barefoot, they moved quickly up the wooded hillside, shouldering their old muskets. The Patriots were determined to take the mountain from the Loyalists dug in at the top.

Whooping and shouting, Young and his comrades dashed from tree to tree, dodging bullets as they fired their own weapons. Suddenly, Thomas heard the cry "Colonel Williams is shot!"

❝I ran to his assistance for I loved him as a father. He had ever been kind to me and almost always carried a cake in his pocket for me and his little son Joseph. They...sprinkled some water in his face. He revived, and his first words were, 'For God's sake boys, don't give up the hill!'...I left him in the arms of his son Daniel, and returned to the field to avenge his fate.❞

The Patriots captured King's Mountain on October 7, 1780. The victory boosted morale after a string of Patriot defeats in the South.

War in the South

Scattered fighting had taken place in the South from the start of the Revolution. In February 1776, North Carolina Patriots defeated a Loyalist army at the **Battle of Moore's Creek Bridge.** This battle is sometimes called the Lexington and Concord of the South.

After France entered the war, the British focused their efforts on the South. They counted on the support of Loyalists there. Greatly outnumbered, the Patriots suffered many setbacks. In December 1778, the British seized Savannah, Georgia. They later took Charleston, South Carolina. "I have almost ceased to hope," wrote Washington when he learned of the losses.

An American traitor. In September 1780, Washington received more bad news. Benedict Arnold, one of his best generals, had joined the British. Arnold had fought bravely in many battles. One soldier recalled that Arnold always led—never followed—his men into battle. "It was 'Come on, boys!' not 'Go on, boys!' He didn't care for nothin'. He'd ride right in."

Washington had put Arnold in command of the key fort at West Point. But Arnold was angry. He felt he had not received enough credit for his victories. He also needed money. He secretly offered to turn over West Point to the British. By chance, a Patriot patrol captured the messenger carrying Arnold's offer. Although Arnold escaped to join the British, West Point was saved.

The Patriots rally. The victory at King's Mountain in October 1780 helped rally Patriots. Slowly, the tide turned in their favor.

Several Patriots made hit-and-run attacks on the British. Francis Marion of South Carolina led a small band of men who slept by day and traveled by night. Marion was known as the Swamp Fox. He would ap-

The **"Swamp Fox" and His Men** *Francis Marion, known as the "Swamp Fox," kept the British off guard in South Carolina. This painting by William Ranney shows Marion and his rough band of men setting out on a raid.* **Geography** *How did Marion use the geography of South Carolina to surprise the British and avoid capture?*

pear suddenly out of the swamps, attack the British, and then retreat into the swamps. His attacks kept the British off balance. (☐ See "Marion's Men" on page 560.)

Two American generals, Daniel Morgan and Nathanael Greene, won victories in the South. Morgan was a big, bull-necked man. His company of Virginia Riflemen had served well in the Battle of Saratoga. In January 1781, he defeated the British at the Battle of Cowpens in South Carolina.

Like Marion, General Greene used hit-and-run tactics. His attacks wore down the British. Raids by bands of fierce backcountry Patriots, who struck often and without warning, also took their toll. The harassed British general, Charles Cornwallis, decided to move his army north into Virginia in the spring of 1781.

Victory at Last

Cornwallis set up camp at Yorktown, on a strip of land that juts into the Chesapeake Bay. He felt safe there, knowing that British ships could supply his troops from the sea.

Washington knew the area well. He realized that he could trap Cornwallis at Yorktown. While a French fleet under Admiral de Grasse sailed toward the Chesapeake, Washington prepared to march south from New York. French troops under the Comte de Rochambeau (roh shahm BOH) had landed in Rhode Island the previous year. Now, they joined Washington, and the combined forces rushed toward Virginia.

Meanwhile, De Grasse's fleet kept British ships out of the Chesapeake. Cornwallis was cut off. He could not get supplies. And he could not escape by sea.

Cornwallis held out for three weeks before he surrendered his army on October 17, 1781. Two days later, the defeated British turned their weapons over to the Americans. A British army band played the tune "The World Turned Upside Down."

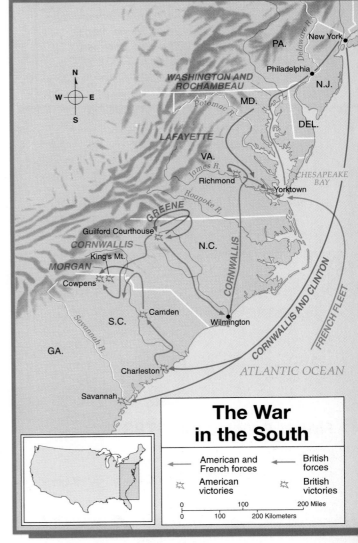

MAP STUDY

The final battles of the Revolution were fought in the South. The Americans suffered a string of defeats between 1778 and 1780, but the tide slowly turned. Finally, trapped at Yorktown in 1781, the British surrendered.
1. Name three British victories in the South.
2. (a) Who commanded American troops at Yorktown? (b) Who commanded British troops?
3. **Analyzing Information** How did the French fleet contribute to the American victory at Yorktown?

The War in the South

| American and French forces | British forces |
| American victories | British victories |

0   100   200 Miles
0   100   200 Kilometers

Making Peace

Americans rejoiced when they heard the news from Yorktown. In London, however, the defeat shocked the British. "It is all over," cried the British prime minister, Lord North. Left with no other choice, he agreed to peace talks.

The talks began in Paris in 1782. Congress sent Benjamin Franklin and John Adams, along with John Jay of New York and Henry Laurens of South Carolina, to work out a treaty. Because Britain was eager to end the war, the Americans got most of what they wanted.

Under the **Treaty of Paris,** the British recognized the United States as an independent nation. The borders of the new nation extended from the Atlantic Ocean to the Mississippi River. The southern border stopped at Florida, which was returned to Spain.

On their part, the Americans agreed to ask state legislatures to pay Loyalists for property they lost in the war. In the end, however, most states ignored the Loyalist claims.

On April 15, 1783, Congress ratified, or approved, the Treaty of Paris. It was almost eight years to the day since the battles of Lexington and Concord.

Washington's Farewell

The Revolution had been a long and difficult struggle for the Americans. They fought a much more powerful nation that had better-armed and better-trained soldiers.

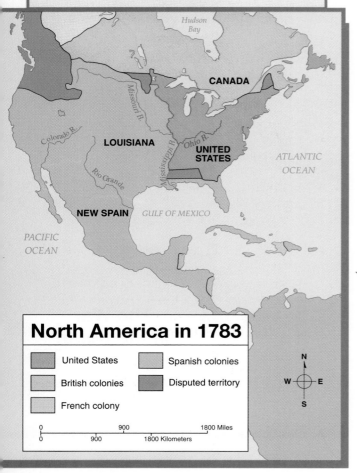

MAP STUDY

Under the Treaty of Paris of 1783, Britain recognized the United States as an independent nation.
1. *Which nation held land west of the new United States?*
2. *What natural feature formed the western border of the United States?*
3. **Comparing** *Compare this map with the map on page 141. (a) According to the maps, what was the major difference between North America in 1783 and in 1763? (b) Name one way in which North America was the same in 1783 and in 1763.*

North America in 1783

- United States
- British colonies
- French colony
- Spanish colonies
- Disputed territory

0   900   1800 Miles
0   900   1800 Kilometers

Our Common Heritage
Almost 100,000 Loyalists fled the United States after the Revolution. Among them were more than 10,000 African Americans who had supported Britain in hopes of winning freedom. They moved to Canada, England, Spanish Florida, Jamaica in the West Indies, and Sierra Leone in Africa. There, they lived as free men and women.

In the end, money, arms, and soldiers from France helped the Americans win the war. But the strength and courage of leaders like Washington played a major role in the American victory.

In December 1783, General Washington bid farewell to his officers at Fraunces' Tavern in New York City. Colonel Benjamin Tallmadge recalled the event:

66Such a scene of sorrow and weeping I had never before witnessed. . . . The simple thought that we were then about to part from the man who had conducted us through a long and bloody war, and under whose conduct the glory and independence of our country had been achieved, and that we should see his face no more in this world, seemed to me utterly [unbearable].99

All along Washington's route home to Mount Vernon, Virginia, crowds cheered the hero of American independence. The new nation faced difficult days ahead. Before long, Americans would again call on Washington to lead them.

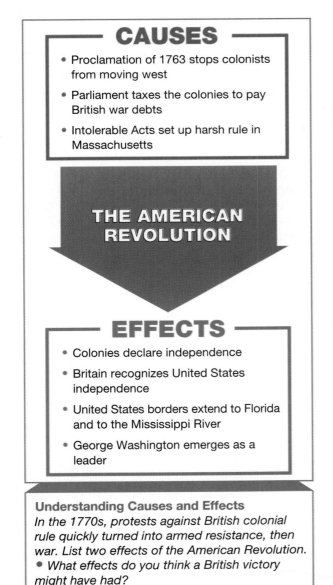

CAUSES

- Proclamation of 1763 stops colonists from moving west
- Parliament taxes the colonies to pay British war debts
- Intolerable Acts set up harsh rule in Massachusetts

THE AMERICAN REVOLUTION

EFFECTS

- Colonies declare independence
- Britain recognizes United States independence
- United States borders extend to Florida and to the Mississippi River
- George Washington emerges as a leader

Understanding Causes and Effects
In the 1770s, protests against British colonial rule quickly turned into armed resistance, then war. List two effects of the American Revolution.
• *What effects do you think a British victory might have had?*

SECTION 5 REVIEW

1. **Locate:** (a) King's Mountain, (b) Savannah, (c) Charleston, (d) Cowpens, (e) Yorktown.
2. **Identify:** (a) Battle of Moore's Creek Bridge, (b) Benedict Arnold, (c) Francis Marion, (d) Daniel Morgan, (e) Nathanael Greene, (f) Admiral de Grasse, (g) Comte de Rochambeau, (h) Treaty of Paris.
3. **Define:** ratify.
4. Why did Britain focus its efforts on the South after 1778?
5. Why was Cornwallis forced to surrender at Yorktown?
6. What were the boundaries of the United States in 1783?
7. **CRITICAL THINKING Analyzing Ideas** Why do you think the British played "The World Turned Upside Down" when they surrendered at Yorktown?

ACTIVITY **Writing to Learn**
Imagine that you are General Cornwallis. In a letter to George III, describe the events at Yorktown.

Summary

- When the American Revolution began in 1775, Americans faced an uphill struggle.
- The Declaration of Independence set out the basic ideas on which the United States was founded and explained why the colonies were breaking away from Britain.
- The American victory at Saratoga marked a turning point in the war.
- Native Americans, African Americans, and women made important contributions to the war effort.
- After Cornwallis surrendered at Yorktown in 1781, Britain recognized the United States as an independent nation.

Reviewing the Main Ideas

1. (a) Why did John Adams think George Washington was a good choice for commander of the Continental Army? (b) What problems did Washington face in 1775?
2. How did the pamphlet *Common Sense* influence colonists?
3. Why was the Battle of Saratoga a turning point in the American Revolution?
4. (a) Why was the winter of 1777–1778 a bad time for the Americans? (b) Describe conditions at Valley Forge.
5. How did each of the following people help the Patriot cause: (a) Bernardo de Gálvez, (b) Nancy Ward, (c) George Rogers Clark, (d) Peter Salem, (e) Mary Ludwig Hays?
6. How did France help the Americans win the Battle of Yorktown?
7. Describe the major points of the Treaty of Paris of 1783.

Thinking Critically

1. **Linking Past and Present** Review the Declaration of Independence in the Reference Section. (a) What basic rights does the Declaration guarantee? (b) Do Americans today enjoy these rights? Explain.
2. **Defending a Position** After the Declaration of Independence was issued, enslaved Africans sent petitions to state legislatures asking for freedom. How might they have used the Declaration of Independence to support their position?

Applying Your Skills

1. **Comparing Points of View** Read about the Olive Branch Petition on pages 161 and 164. (a) What was the subject of the Olive Branch Petition? (b) How do you think colonists viewed the petition? (c) How did King George III respond to the petition? (d) What arguments might each side have used to defend its point of view?
2. **Analyzing a Quotation** Reread the quotation from *The Crisis* on page 170. (a) What did Paine mean by the words, "These are the times that try men's souls"? (b) What are "sunshine patriots"? (c) What do you think Washington's soldiers thought about Paine's words?

Thinking About Geography

Match the letters on the map with the following places: **1.** Bunker Hill, **2.** Trenton, **3.** Saratoga, **4.** Vincennes, **5.** Cowpens, **6.** Savannah, **7.** Yorktown. **Movement** Why was British control of the Chesapeake Bay important to Cornwallis at Yorktown?

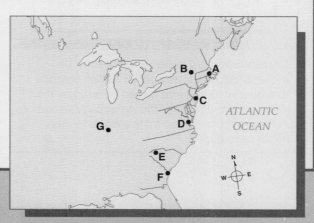

INTERDISCIPLINARY ACTIVITY

Fighting With the Continental Army

Form into groups to learn more about the American Revolution. Follow the suggestions below to write, dance, draw, or talk to show what you have learned about the Continental Army during the Revolution. You may use the textbook, encyclopedias, atlases, or other materials in your classroom library to complete the tasks. Be able to name your sources of information when you have finished the activity.

Flag of a Pennsylvania regiment

CARTOGRAPHERS On a large sheet of paper, about 3 feet by 5 feet, draw a map of North America. On the map, show the major battles of the American Revolution. Mark each battle with a symbol to show which side won. Create a map key explaining the symbols you used. Leave space on the map for a battle chart created by class mathematicians.

MATHEMATICIANS Compile statistics on the major battles of the American Revolution. Include the dates on which the battles were fought, the number of soldiers who fought in each, the number of soldiers killed, and how long the battle lasted. Put your information in chart form, and display it on the battle map created by class cartographers.

Flag of a Massachusetts regiment

DANCERS Review what you learned about Molly Pitcher. Then create a dance portraying her actions at the Battle of Monmouth.

WRITERS Imagine that you are a soldier with Washington's army at Valley Forge. Write a letter to your family describing conditions in the camp. What are your feelings about the chances of winning the war?

ARTISTS Locate a painting in your textbook or in another book showing a scene from the American Revolution. Plan a brief talk describing the picture and giving background information about the scene depicted.

★ Hold a Fighting With the Continental Army press conference at which each group presents or describes its completed activity.

Continental Army medicine chest

Continental Army musket

Creating a Republic

(1776–1790)

1778 *The winter at Valley Forge was a low point for Washington's army, but by spring 1778 Americans became more hopeful.*

1783 *The Treaty of Paris formally ended the American Revolution. John Adams used this seal at the signing of the treaty.*

1777 *While Americans fought for independence, the Continental Congress completed the Articles of Confederation.*

1776	1780	1784

WORLD EVENT
1778 British Captain Cook becomes first European to reach Hawaii

Chapter Setting

"The American war is over: but this is far from being the case with the American revolution. On the contrary, nothing but the first act of the great drama is closed. It remains yet to establish and perfect our new forms of government."

Those words, spoken by Dr. Benjamin Rush in January 1787, reflected the feelings of many Americans after the Revolution. They knew that winning the war against Britain had been only a beginning.

Rush was a respected doctor. In Philadelphia, he set up the nation's first free medical clinic. At the University of Pennsylvania, he taught the latest medical theories.

Rush had been an outspoken Patriot. In 1775, he urged Thomas Paine to write a pamphlet in favor of independence and suggested the title *Common Sense*. As a member of the Continental Congress, Rush signed the Declaration of Independence.

With his fellow Patriots, he celebrated the signing of the Treaty of Paris in 1783.

Now, however, Rush was worried about the health of the nation. Could the United States succeed in its bold experiment at self-government? During the war, Americans had set up their first government. Rush believed that the government was too weak to hold the 13 states together. Others agreed. In May 1787, a special convention met in Philadelphia. There, the curtain rose on the next act of the American Revolution.

ACTIVITY

Imagine that you live in the United States after the Revolution. Design a coat of arms for your new nation. Include elements that make the nation special. Under the coat of arms, list three problems that you think a new nation might face.

1787 *The Northwest Ordinance set up a way to admit new states to the United States. This map shows the Northwest Territory.*

1788 *The Constitution united the country under a strong central government.*

1791 *The Bill of Rights guaranteed individual rights and freedoms.*

1784   1788   1792

WORLD EVENT
1787 Sierra Leone founded as settlement for free slaves

WORLD EVENT
1789 French Revolution begins

A Confederation of States

FIND OUT

■ What kinds of government did the states set up?

■ What problems did the nation face in the early years?

■ How did the Northwest Ordinance provide for growth of the United States?

■ What were the causes and results of Shays' Rebellion?

VOCABULARY constitution, execute, bill of rights, economic depression

One afternoon in January 1776, a Patriot mob aimed a cannon at the home of John Wentworth, governor of New Hampshire. Wentworth, a Loyalist, did not wait to find out what the mob would do. He scurried to safety in a nearby British fort.

When the war broke out, royal officials throughout the colonies fled. "The sudden and abrupt departure of our late Governor," announced the New Hampshire assembly, "creates the necessity of establishing a [new] form of government."

In May 1776, the Continental Congress asked each colony to set up a government to protect "the lives, liberties, and properties" of its citizens. In July, the Congress set about the more difficult task of organizing a new national government.

State Constitutions

During the Revolution, most states wrote their own constitutions. A **constitution** is a document that sets out the laws and principles of a government. States wanted written constitutions for two reasons. First, a written constitution would spell out the rights of all citizens. Second, it would set limits on the power of government.

In writing their constitutions, states often followed the basic form of their old colonial charters. These, in turn, were based on English law. Some states simply kept the charters but struck out all mention of the king. Others wrote new constitutions, which voters approved.

Dividing power. Colonists were concerned about putting too much power in the hands of a few people. To avoid this, they divided the power of state governments between a legislature and an executive.

Every state had a legislature that passed laws. Lawmakers were elected by voters. Power within the legislature was divided between an upper house, called a senate, and a lower house. All states except Pennsylva-

A New England Town *Exeter, New Hampshire, shown here in the late 1700s, had its own way of doing things. Few Americans wanted to give control to a national government.* **Linking Past and Present** *Do you think towns like Exeter could manage today without help from the national government? Explain.*

nia had a governor, who **executed,** or carried out, the laws.

Protecting freedoms. Virginia further limited the power of government by including a bill of rights in its constitution. A **bill of rights** lists freedoms that the government promises to protect. In Virginia, the bill of rights protected freedom of religion and freedom of the press. Citizens also had the right to a trial by jury. Other states followed Virginia's example and included bills of rights in their own constitutions.

Expanding the right to vote. Under state constitutions, more people had the right to vote than in colonial times. To vote, a citizen had to be a white male and be over age 21. He had to own a certain amount of property or pay a certain amount of taxes. For a time, some women in New Jersey could vote. In a few states, free black men could vote. Enslaved African Americans could not vote in any state.

Forming a National Government

Although the states had formed 13 separate governments, the Continental Congress drafted a plan for the nation as a whole. Delegates believed that the colonies could not succeed in their struggle for independence unless they were united by a national government.

The first national constitution. Writing a constitution that all the states would approve was difficult. In 1776, few Americans thought of themselves as citizens of one nation. Instead, they felt loyal to their own states. "Virginia, Sir, is my country," said Thomas Jefferson. "Massachusetts is our country," John Adams told a friend.

The states were unwilling to turn over power to the national government. They did not want to replace the "tyranny" of British rule with another strong government. In 1777, after much debate, the Continental Congress completed the first American constitution, the *Articles of Confederation.*

Women at the Polls *For a brief time, from 1790 to 1807, the state of New Jersey let women vote. This picture shows New Jersey women at the polls.* **Citizenship** *What other people were denied the right to vote after the Revolution?*

The Articles of Confederation created a "firm league of friendship" among the 13 states. The states agreed to send delegates to a Confederation Congress. Each state had one vote in Congress.

Congress could pass laws, but at least 9 of the 13 states had to approve a law before it would go into effect. Congress could not regulate trade between states or even between states and foreign countries. Nor could it pass any laws regarding taxes. To raise money, Congress had to ask the states for it. No state, however, could be forced to contribute.

Under the Articles, Congress could declare war, appoint military officers, and coin money. Congress was also responsible for foreign affairs. However, these powers were few compared with those of the states.

A loose alliance. The Articles created a loose alliance among the 13 states. The national government was weak. The Articles did not provide for a president to carry out laws. It was up to the states to enforce laws passed by Congress

.Despite these weaknesses, the Articles might have worked if the states could have agreed about what needed to be done. Many disputes arose, however. And there was no way of settling them because the Articles did not set up a system of courts. As

MAP STUDY

By 1783, a number of states claimed lands west of the Appalachians.

1. *Which state claimed land directly south of Lake Superior?*
2. *Which states had no claims to western lands?*
3. **Solving Problems** *Why did Thomas Jefferson, a Virginian, persuade Virginia to give up its claims to western lands?*

Claims to Western Lands

| | Original 13 states | **1784** | Date ceded to the United States |
| | Areas claimed | | |

0   50   100 Miles

0   50   100 Kilometers

Noah Webster, a teacher from New England, warned:

> 66So long as any individual state has power to defeat the measures of the other twelve, our pretended union is but a name, and our confederation, a cobweb.99

Disputes Over Western Lands

The first dispute between the states arose even before the Articles of Confederation went into effect. Most states quickly ratified the Articles. Maryland, however, refused to ratify. It would not sign, it said, until all lands between the Appalachian Mountains and the Mississippi River were turned over to Congress.

Virginia and several other states claimed lands in the West. (See the map at left.) As a small state, Maryland worried that states such as Virginia would become too powerful if they were allowed to keep the western lands. Also, what if Virginia sold its western lands to gain income? Then, Virginia would not need to tax its citizens. What would prevent people and businesses in Maryland from flocking to Virginia to escape taxes?

At first, the "landed" states rejected Maryland's demand. One by one, however, all the states except Virginia agreed to give up their claims. In Virginia, Thomas Jefferson and other leaders strongly believed that a national government was needed. Finally, they convinced state lawmakers to give up Virginia's claims to western lands. In 1781, Maryland ratified the Articles of Confederation, and the first American government went into effect.

Serious Challenges for the Articles of Confederation

By 1783, the United States had won independence. The new nation faced many problems, however. From 1783 to 1787,

State Bank Notes *After the Revolution, each state issued its own money. The bills pictured here were issued by Rhode Island and South Carolina.* **Economics** *Give an example of how your life would be affected if each state issued its own money today.*

Americans had reason to doubt whether their country could survive.

Troubles with money and trade. Perhaps the biggest problem the nation faced was money. As a result of borrowing during the Revolution, the United States owed millions of dollars. But it had no way to repay its debts. Under the Articles of Confederation, Congress could ask the states for money. The states, however, had the right to turn down the request. Often, they did.

During the Revolution, the Continental Congress solved the problem of raising funds by printing paper money. With the crank of a printing press, plain paper was turned into Continental dollars. Without gold or silver to back up the paper money, however, it had little value. Soon, Americans were describing any useless thing as "not worth a Continental." (📖 See "Comments From a German Visitor" on page 562.)

As Continental dollars became worthless, states printed their own paper money. This caused confusion. How much was a North Carolina dollar worth? Was a Virginia dollar as valuable as a Maryland dollar? Most states refused to accept the money of other states. As a result, trade between states became difficult.

Other troubles. The new nation faced other troubles. New Hampshire and New York both claimed Vermont. Under the Articles of Confederation, these states had no way to settle their dispute.

Foreign countries took advantage of the new government's weakness. Britain, for example, refused to withdraw its troops from the Ohio Valley, as it had agreed to do under the Treaty of Paris. Spain, too, challenged the United States. It closed its port in New Orleans to American farmers in the western lands. This was a serious blow to the farmers, who needed the port to ship their products to markets in the East.

GEOGRAPHY AND HISTORY

A Farsighted Policy for Western Lands

Settlers in the western lands posed still another problem. The Articles of Confederation said nothing about admitting new states to the United States. Some settlers in the West took matters into their own hands. For example, in eastern Tennessee, people set up a government called the State of Franklin and applied for admission to the United States.

Congress realized it needed to provide for local governments in the western lands. Thousands of settlers lived in these lands, and every year many more headed west.

To meet the challenge, Congress passed two laws. Both concerned the Northwest Territory, the name used for lands lying north of the Ohio River and east of the Mississippi. (See the map on page 192.) The principles set out in the two laws were later applied to other areas of settlement.

Townships and sections. The first law, the ***Land Ordinance of 1785,*** set up a system for settling the Northwest Territory. The law called for the territory to be surveyed and then divided into townships.

Each township would have 36 sections. A section was 1 square mile and contained 640 acres. (See the diagram below.) Congress planned to sell sections to settlers for $640 each. One section in every township was set aside to support public schools.

A plan for new states. The second law, passed in 1787, was the ***Northwest Ordinance.*** It set up a government for the Northwest Territory, outlawed slavery there, and provided for the region to be divided into three to five separate territories in the future. (📖 See "The Trees" on page 564.)

When the settlers of a territory numbered 60,000 free settlers, they could ask Congress to admit the territory as a new state. The newly admitted state would be

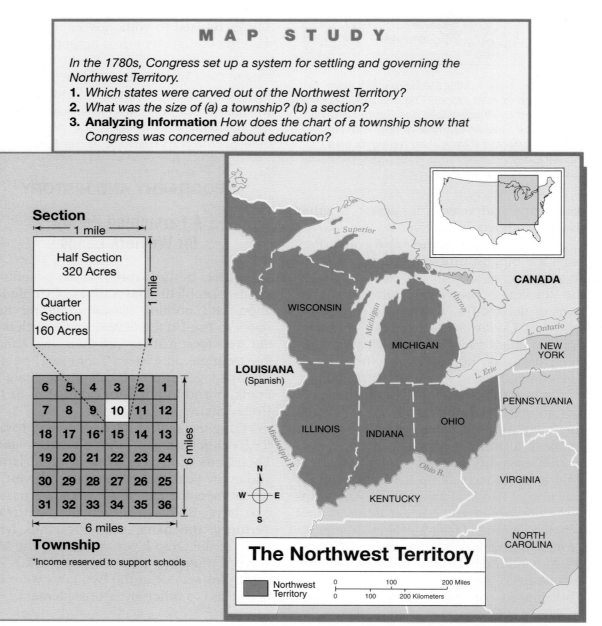

MAP STUDY

In the 1780s, Congress set up a system for settling and governing the Northwest Territory.
1. Which states were carved out of the Northwest Territory?
2. What was the size of (a) a township? (b) a section?
3. **Analyzing Information** How does the chart of a township show that Congress was concerned about education?

Section

1 mile
Half Section 320 Acres
Quarter Section 160 Acres	

1 mile

6	5	4	3	2	1
7	8	9	10	11	12
18	17	16*	15	14	13
19	20	21	22	23	24
30	29	28	27	26	25
31	32	33	34	35	36

6 miles

6 miles

Township
*Income reserved to support schools

The Northwest Territory

CANADA

WISCONSIN

MICHIGAN

L. Superior

L. Michigan

L. Huron

L. Erie

L. Ontario

NEW YORK

LOUISIANA (Spanish)

Mississippi R.

ILLINOIS

INDIANA

OHIO

PENNSYLVANIA

Ohio R.

KENTUCKY

VIRGINIA

NORTH CAROLINA

N W E S

	Northwest Territory

0 100 200 Miles
0 100 200 Kilometers

CONNECTIONS

| ARTS | SCIENCES | GEOGRAPHY | WORLD | **ECONOMICS** | CIVICS |

Barter on the Western Frontier

Few people had money on the American frontier. Pioneers traveled west with the clothes on their backs, a wagon, perhaps a horse and a cow, and a little seed corn. If they needed anything else once they reached their new home, they got it through barter. That is, they exchanged something they could do or shoot or grow or make for the items they needed.

Skins and furs were among the most common barter items. As one pioneer noted, "Furs and [pelts] were the people's money. They had nothing else to give in exchange for rifles, salt, and iron."

Making cloth

Milling grain into flour was strictly a barter business on the frontier. The young man of the family carted the grain to the local mill. There, he waited his turn, often overnight, to have the grain ground into flour. For this service, he paid the miller a portion of the flour, usually one eighth of it.

Women on the frontier produced a variety of goods for barter. A woman might raise a few pounds of cotton each year, spin it, and then weave it into cloth. Seven yards of cotton cloth could be traded for a pig. Nine yards might bring a calf in exchange.

Device for broiling meat

As frontier communities became more settled, their economies changed. After a few years, families produced more than they needed for themselves. They entrusted the surplus to merchants, who shipped it to markets to be sold for cash. In this way, a cash economy slowly replaced the barter system on the frontier.

■ How did the barter system work on the frontier?

> **ACTIVITY** Draw a picture of two items you might offer for barter if you were a pioneer on the frontier. Then hold a barter session to trade for items that you need.

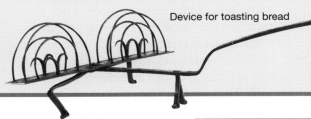

Device for toasting bread

"on an equal footing with the original states in all respects whatsoever."

The Northwest Ordinance was the finest achievement of the national government under the Articles of Confederation. It provided a way to admit new states to the United States. It guaranteed that new states would be treated the same as the original 13 states. In time, five states were carved from the Northwest Territory: Ohio, Indiana, Illinois, Michigan, and Wisconsin. ■

A Farmers' Revolt

After the Revolution, the nation suffered an **economic depression.** An economic depression is a period when business activity slows, prices and wages fall, and unemployment rises.

Hard times for farmers. The depression hit farmers especially hard. During the Revolution, the demand for farm products had been high. Eager to produce more food, farmers borrowed money for land, seed, animals, and tools. Now, as soldiers returned to their home states, demand for farm goods fell. Many farmers could not repay their loans.

In Massachusetts, matters were made even worse when the state raised farmers' taxes. The courts seized the farms of people who could not pay their taxes or loans. Angry farmers protested what they considered unfair treatment.

Rebellion in Massachusetts. In 1786, discontent flared into rebellion. Daniel Shays, a Massachusetts farmer who had fought at Bunker Hill and Saratoga, was determined to save his debt-ridden farm.

Shays gathered a force of nearly 2,000 farmers. The ragged band traveled around the state, attacking courthouses and preventing the sale of property as payment for debts. When they tried to raid a warehouse full of rifles and gunpowder, the Massachusetts legislature sent the militia to drive them off. This ended *Shays' Rebellion.*

Time for action. Shays' Rebellion worried many Americans. They saw it as a sign that the Articles of Confederation did not work. George Washington shared their concern. He felt that a desperate crisis was in store for the nation:

66 No day was ever more clouded than the present. . . . I predict the worst consequences from a half-starved, limping government, always moving upon crutches and tottering at every step. 99

Leaders from several states called for a convention to discuss ways to revise the Articles of Confederation. They decided to gather in Philadelphia in May 1787. The action they took when they met, however, went far beyond what many had imagined.

SECTION 1 REVIEW

1. **Locate:** Northwest Territory.
2. **Identify:** (a) Articles of Confederation, (b) Land Ordinance of 1785, (c) Northwest Ordinance, (d) Shays' Rebellion.
3. **Define:** (a) constitution, (b) execute, (c) bill of rights, (d) economic depression.
4. Why did states want written constitutions?
5. (a) What were the terms of the Northwest Ordinance? (b) Why was it important?
6. **CRITICAL THINKING Analyzing Ideas** "I like a little rebellion now and then," wrote Thomas Jefferson when he heard about Shays' Rebellion. "The spirit of resistance to government is so valuable on occasion that I wish it to be always kept alive." Do you think Shays' Rebellion was good for the United States? Explain.

ACTIVITY **Writing to Learn**
Imagine that you live in the United States under the Articles of Confederation. Write a letter to a friend explaining why the Articles should be revised.

2

A Grand Convention

FIND OUT
- Why did the Constitutional Convention meet in secret?
- How did the delegates settle the question of representation?
- What other issues did the Convention resolve?

VOCABULARY legislative branch, executive branch, judicial branch, compromise

An air of mystery hung over the Pennsylvania State House in Philadelphia during the summer of 1787. Philadelphians watched as the nation's greatest leaders passed in and out of the building. Eleven years earlier, some of the same men had signed the Declaration of Independence there. What was going on now? Susannah Dillwyn wrote her father about the excitement:

> 66 There is now sitting in this city a grand convention, who are to form some new system of government or mend the old one. I suppose it is a body of great consequence, as they say it depends entirely upon their pleasure whether we shall in the future have a congress. 99

What would this "grand convention" decide? No one knew. For almost four months, Americans waited for an answer.

The Priceless Notebook

The *Philadelphia Flier* came to a halt in the center of town. The coach's passengers climbed slowly down, stiff and weary. Jammed together on hard, backless benches, they had endured a long, bruising ride to Philadelphia.

Among the passengers was a short, thin young man. Picking up his bags, he headed to a nearby boarding house. His mind was not on the journey, however. He was thinking of the convention set to begin on May 14, only 11 days away.

Madison the delegate. At age 36, James Madison was one of the youngest delegates to the *Constitutional Convention.* He also was the best prepared.

For months, Madison had secluded himself on his father's plantation in Virginia. There, he read stacks of books on history, politics, and commerce. During the night, he would rise at odd hours to read more or to write notes. He arrived in Philadelphia with a case bulging with research.

BIOGRAPHY James Madison *James Madison's careful notes at the Constitutional Convention provided a valuable record for future generations of Americans.* **Citizenship** *Why was it important for later Americans to know how the framers of the Constitution made their decisions?*

On May 14, Madison eagerly walked the few blocks to the State House. Only the delegates from Virginia and Pennsylvania were there, however. Madison was deeply disappointed. Without representatives from at least seven states, the work of the Convention could not start.

Madison waited impatiently for more than a week. One by one, delegates braved the spring rains, flooded streams, and muddy roads to reach Philadelphia. At last, on May 25, there were enough delegates for the Convention to begin.

Madison the historian. Madison watched as delegates greeted one another and began taking their seats. He did not want to miss a thing.

> **66**I chose a seat in front of the presiding member, with the other members on my right and left hand. . . . I was not absent a single day nor more than a fraction of an hour in any day so that I could not have lost a single speech, unless a very short one.**99**

Each night, by candlelight, he filled in from memory any gaps in his notes. Surely, he reasoned, future Americans would want to know how the delegates arrived at their decisions.

During the weeks that followed, Madison kept a full and clear record of the proceedings. Madison was a wise man, however. He knew that the delegates needed to speak freely. Often, they made statements or took positions that some people might not understand. He decided that his account should not become public so long as a single delegate was still alive.

The notes are published. As it turned out, Madison himself was the last surviving delegate. But even then, he turned down requests to publish his notes. Only in 1840, four years after his death, was Madison's record of the Constitutional Convention printed. At last, Americans learned how, during the hot summer of 1787, the framers of the Constitution created a strong and enduring government. ■

The Delegates Begin

The 55 delegates who gathered in Philadelphia were a remarkable group. Every state except Rhode Island sent representatives. At age 81, Benjamin Franklin was the oldest. He was wise in the ways of government and human nature. George Washington, like Madison, was a delegate from Virginia. Washington was so well respected that the delegates at once elected him president of the Convention.

Other delegates were young men in their twenties and thirties. Among them was Alexander Hamilton of New York. During the Revolution, Hamilton had served for a time as Washington's private secretary. Hamilton made no secret of his dislike for the Articles of Confederation. "The nation," he wrote, "is sick and wants powerful remedies." The powerful remedy he prescribed was a strong national government.

Delegates decided to keep their talks secret so that they could speak their minds freely. To ensure secrecy, guards stood at the door. The windows were left closed to keep passersby from overhearing the debates. The closed windows made the room very hot, however. The summer of 1787 was the hottest in many years.

History and You
The delegates to the Constitutional Convention believed that they had two loyalties: to their state and to a national government. Do you consider yourself more a citizen of your town, your state, or the whole country? Explain your answer.

Hopelessly Divided

Soon after the meeting began, delegates decided to do more than revise the Articles of Confederation. They chose instead to write an entirely new constitution for the nation. They disagreed, however, about what form that government should take.

Virginia makes a proposal. Early on, Edmund Randolph and James Madison, both from Virginia, put forward a plan for the new government. It became known as the *Virginia Plan.* In the end, much of the plan was included in the new constitution.

The Virginia Plan called for a strong national government with three branches: the legislative, the executive, and the judicial. In general, the legislative branch of government passes the laws. The executive branch carries out the laws. The judicial branch, or system of courts, decides if laws are carried out fairly.

The Virginia Plan also called for a two-house legislature. Seats in both houses would be awarded to each state on the basis of population. Thus, in both houses, larger states would have more representatives than smaller ones. This differed from the Articles of Confederation, which gave every state, regardless of population, one vote in Congress.

Small states object. Small states objected strongly to the Virginia Plan. They feared that the large states could easily outvote them. Supporters of the Virginia Plan responded that it was only fair for a state with more people to have more representatives.

After two weeks of debate, William Paterson of New Jersey presented a plan that had the support of the small states. The *New Jersey Plan* also called for three branches of government. However, it provided for a legislature that had only one house. Each state, no matter what the size of its population, would have one vote in the legislature.

African Americans in the New Nation *The Constitutional Convention made many decisions affecting African Americans. African Americans, however, had no representation at the Convention. Leaders such as Absalom Jones formed the Free African Society to work for their rights.* **Citizenship** *What other groups would not have been represented at the Convention?*

Breaking the Deadlock

The two sides deadlocked. With tempers flaring, it seemed that the Convention would fall apart without adopting any plan. Finally, Roger Sherman of Connecticut worked out a compromise between the large and small states. A compromise is a settlement in which each side agrees to give up some of its demands.

Sherman's compromise called for a legislature with a lower and an upper house. Members of the lower house, known as the House of Representatives, would be chosen by all men who could vote. Seats in the lower house would be awarded to each state according to its population. This idea, which resembled the Virginia Plan, was popular with the larger states.

Members of the upper house, called the Senate, would be chosen by state legislatures. Each state, no matter what its size, would have two senators. This part of Sherman's compromise appealed to the smaller states.

On July 16, the delegates narrowly approved Sherman's plan. It became known as the *Great Compromise.* Each side gave up some demands to preserve the nation as a whole.

Compromises Between North and South

The Great Compromise raised another thorny issue. Would slaves be counted as part of a state's population? The answer to this question was important because it affected the number of votes a state would have in the House of Representatives.

Should slaves be counted? The question of slavery led to bitter arguments between the North and the South. Southerners wanted to include slaves in the population count even though they would not let slaves vote. Northerners protested. If slaves were counted, southern states would have more representatives than northern states. Northerners argued that since slaves could not vote, they should not be counted.

Once again, the delegates compromised. They agreed that three fifths of the slaves in any state would be counted. In other words, if a state had 5,000 slaves, 3,000 of them would be included in the state's population count. This agreement became known as the *Three-Fifths Compromise.*

The slave trade. Northerners and southerners also disagreed over another issue related to slavery. By 1787, some northern states had banned the slave trade within their borders. They wanted the new Congress to ban the slave trade in the entire nation. Southerners warned that such a ban would ruin their economy.

In the end, the two sides compromised. Northerners agreed that Congress could not outlaw the slave trade for at least 20 years. After that, Congress could regulate the trade if it wished. Northerners also agreed that no state could stop a fugitive slave from being returned to an owner who claimed him.

Signing the Constitution *On September 17, 1787, the work of the Constitutional Convention was done. Here, George Washington looks on as delegates sign the new Constitution of the United States.* **Citizenship** *Why was it important that delegates to the Constitutional Convention were willing to compromise?*

Signing the Constitution

As summer drew to a close, the weary delegates struggled with other difficult questions. How many years should the President, head of the executive branch, serve? How should the courts be organized? Would members of Congress be paid?

Finally, on September 17, 1787, the Constitution was ready. Gathering for the last time in the State House, delegates listened quietly as the final document was read aloud. Then, one by one, delegates came forward to sign the document. They had done something truly remarkable. In just a few months, they had set up the framework for a lasting government.

SECTION 2 REVIEW

1. **Identify:** (a) James Madison,
   (b) Constitutional Convention, (c) Virginia Plan, (d) New Jersey Plan, (e) Roger Sherman, (f) Great Compromise,
   (g) Three-Fifths Compromise.
2. **Define:** (a) legislative branch,
   (b) executive branch, (c) judicial branch,
   (d) compromise.
3. (a) How did the Virginia Plan arrange for seats to be awarded in the legislature?
   (b) Why did small states object to this arrangement?
4. (a) What compromises did the North and South reach? (b) Why were these compromises necessary?
5. **CRITICAL THINKING Defending a Position** James Madison said that "no Constitution would ever have been adopted by the Convention if the debates had been made public." Do you agree or disagree? Explain.

ACTIVITY Writing to Learn
Write a dialogue between a delegate from a large state and a delegate from a small state about the best plan for allotting seats in the legislature.

3
A More Perfect Union

FIND OUT
- How did Enlightenment ideas influence the Constitution?
- How was power divided between the federal government and the states?
- How did the framers of the Constitution limit the power of government?

VOCABULARY republic, separation of powers, federalism, electoral college, checks and balances, bill, veto, override, impeach

As the Constitutional Convention ended, a woman rushed up to Benjamin Franklin. "Well, Doctor," she asked, "what have we got, a republic or a monarchy?" "A republic," he replied. "If you can keep it."

A republic is a nation in which voters elect representatives to govern them. "We the people of the United States," the preamble, or introduction, to the Constitution begins. Those words make clear that the power of government comes from the people. As Franklin pointed out, it was up to the people to make their new government work.

Ideas That Shaped the Constitution

Americans were the first people to write a constitution setting up a government. Yet many ideas in the Constitution had come from other sources.

League of the Iroquois. Many early American leaders admired the Iroquois system of government. They considered the League of the Iroquois as a model for the idea of unity. In the League, member nations governed their own affairs but joined together for defense. When Benjamin Franklin urged a similar union of colonies in 1754, he pointed to the League's success:

> **"**The strength of the League . . . has bound our Friends the Iroquois together in a common tie which no crisis, however grave, since its foundation, has managed to disrupt. **"**

John Rutledge also admired the Iroquois union. At the Constitutional Convention, Rutledge read to delegates from an Iroquois treaty, which began, "We, the people, to form a union, to establish peace, equity and order." The framers used similar language when they wrote the preamble of the United States Constitution.

Ideas from Europe. Ideas in the Constitution also came to the United States from Europe. The idea of limiting the power of the ruler, for example, was included in England's Magna Carta. (See page 86.) From England, too, came the idea of representative government. Since the mid-1200s, representatives in Parliament had made laws for the country. Since 1689, the English Bill of Rights had protected the rights of individuals. (See page 116.)

The Constitution reflects ideas from the Enlightenment, too. During the Enlightenment, thinkers believed that people could improve society through the use of reason. Many of the Constitution's framers had read the works of Enlightenment thinkers, such as John Locke and the Baron de Montesquieu (MOHN tehs kyoo).

John Locke. In 1690, John Locke published *Two Treatises on Government*. In it, he stated two important ideas.

First, Locke declared that all people had natural rights to life, liberty, and property. Second, he suggested that government is an agreement between the ruler and the ruled. The ruler must enforce the laws and protect the people. If a ruler violates the people's

The Scales of Justice *In this tavern sign of the late 1700s, a woman holds the scales of justice. Americans valued the idea of justice, and they made establishing justice a goal of the Constitution.* **Linking Past and Present** *In what ways does the government establish justice today?*

natural rights, the people have a right to rebel.

Locke's ideas were popular among Americans. The framers of the Constitution wanted to protect the natural rights of the people and limit the power of government. They drew up the Constitution as a contract between the people and their government.

Montesquieu. In 1748, the French thinker Montesquieu published *The Spirit of Laws*. In it, he urged that the power of government be divided among three separate branches: the legislative, executive, and judicial. Such a division was designed to keep any person or group from gaining too much power. This idea became known as the **separation of powers.**

Montesquieu stressed the importance of the rule of law. The powers of government, he said, should be clearly defined. This would prevent individuals or groups from using government power for their own purposes. In the Constitution of the United States, the framers set out the basic laws of the nation, defining and limiting the powers of the government.

A Federal System

The need to limit government power was only one of the issues Americans debated in 1787. Just as important, they had to decide how to divide power between the national government and the states.

Under the Articles of Confederation, the states had more power than Congress. The new Constitution changed that. Under the Constitution, the states delegated, or gave up, some of their powers to the national government. At the same time, the states reserved, or kept, other powers. This division of power between the states and the national government is called **federalism.** (See the chart on page 221 in the Civics Overview.)

Federalism has given Americans a flexible system of government. The people elect both national and state officials. The federal, or national, government has the power to act for the nation as a whole. At the same time, the states have power over many local matters.

History and You
Is there a division of powers in the running of events at your school? Which activities are planned and controlled by leaders of the student council or various clubs? What powers are reserved by the school administration?

What powers does the federal government have? The Constitution spells out the powers of the federal government. For example, only the federal government can coin money or declare war. The federal government can also regulate trade between the states and with other countries.

What powers do states have? Under the Constitution, states have the power to regulate trade within their borders. They decide who can vote in state elections. They also have power to establish schools and local governments.

In addition, the Constitution says that powers not given to the federal government belong to the states or the people. This point pleased people in small states, who were afraid that the federal government might become too powerful.

What powers are shared? The Constitution lists some powers that are to be shared by federal and state governments. Both governments, for example, can build roads and raise taxes.

"The supreme law of the land." The framers of the Constitution had to decide how the states and the federal government would settle disagreements. They did so by making the Constitution "the supreme law of the land." In other words, in any dispute, the Constitution is the final authority.

Separation of Powers

The Constitution set up a strong federal government. To keep the government from becoming too powerful, the framers relied on Montesquieu's idea of separation of powers. In the Constitution, they created three branches of government and then defined the powers of each. (See the chart on page 202.)

The legislative branch. Congress is the legislative branch of government. It is made up of the House of Representatives and the Senate. Members of the House are elected for two-year terms. Senators are elected for

Separation of Powers

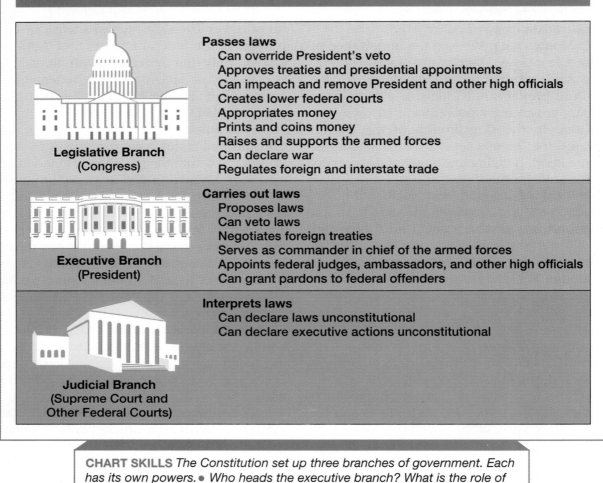

Legislative Branch
(Congress)

Passes laws
- Can override President's veto
- Approves treaties and presidential appointments
- Can impeach and remove President and other high officials
- Creates lower federal courts
- Appropriates money
- Prints and coins money
- Raises and supports the armed forces
- Can declare war
- Regulates foreign and interstate trade

Executive Branch
(President)

Carries out laws
- Proposes laws
- Can veto laws
- Negotiates foreign treaties
- Serves as commander in chief of the armed forces
- Appoints federal judges, ambassadors, and other high officials
- Can grant pardons to federal offenders

Judicial Branch
(Supreme Court and Other Federal Courts)

Interprets laws
- Can declare laws unconstitutional
- Can declare executive actions unconstitutional

CHART SKILLS *The Constitution set up three branches of government. Each has its own powers.* ● *Who heads the executive branch? What is the role of the legislative branch?*

six-year terms. The main function of Congress is to make laws.

Under the Constitution, voters in each state elect members of the House of Representatives. Delegates to the Constitutional Convention wanted the House to represent the interests of ordinary people. At first, the Constitution provided for senators to be chosen by state legislatures. In 1913, this was changed. Today, senators are elected in the same way as House members.

Article 1 of the Constitution sets out the powers of Congress. These include the power to collect taxes and to regulate foreign and interstate trade. In foreign affairs, Congress has the power to declare war and to "raise and support armies."

The executive branch. Some delegates in Philadelphia objected to the idea of a strong executive branch. They remembered the power that King George III had exercised over the colonies. Madison argued, however, that a strong executive was needed to balance the legislature. Otherwise, a headstrong Congress might pass "tyrannical laws" and then execute them "in a tyrannical way." His arguments prevailed.

Article 2 of the Constitution sets up the executive branch of government. It is headed by the President. The executive branch also includes the Vice President and any advisers appointed by the President. The President and Vice President serve four-year terms.

The President is responsible for carrying out all laws passed by Congress. The President is also commander in chief of the armed forces and is responsible for foreign relations.

The judicial branch. Article 3 of the Constitution calls for a Supreme Court. This article also allowed Congress to set up other federal courts. The Supreme Court and other federal courts hear cases that involve the Constitution or any laws passed by Congress. They also hear cases arising between two or more states.

Electing the President

Delegates took great pains to ensure that the President would not become too strong. Some delegates feared that if the President were elected directly by the people, he might become too independent of Congress and the states.

The delegates had another worry. In the late 1700s, news traveled slowly. How would voters get to know a candidate who lived outside their area? New Englanders would probably know little about a candidate from the South. A candidate from Pennsylvania might be unknown to voters in Massachusetts or South Carolina.

To solve these problems, delegates set up the electoral college. The electoral college would be made up of electors from every state. Every four years, the electors would meet as a group and vote for the President and Vice President of the United States.

The framers of the Constitution expected that the electors would be well-informed citizens who were familiar with the national government. They believed that such men would choose a President and Vice President wisely.

A System of Checks and Balances

The Constitution set up a system of checks and balances. Under this system, each branch of the federal government has some way to check, or control, the other two branches. The system of checks and balances is another way in which the Constitution limits the power of government. (See the chart on page 223.)

Checks on Congress. The system of checks and balances works in many ways. For example, to do its work, Congress passes bills, or proposed laws. A bill then goes to the President to be signed into law. (See the chart on page 223.)

The President can check the power of Congress by vetoing, or rejecting, a bill. Congress can then check the President by overriding, or overruling, the President's veto. To override a veto, two thirds of both houses of Congress must vote for the bill again. In this way, a bill can become law without the President's signature.

Checks on the President. Congress has other checks on the President. The President appoints officials such as ambassadors to foreign countries and federal judges. However, the Senate must approve these appointments. The President can negotiate treaties with other nations. But a treaty becomes law only if two thirds of the Senate approves it.

Congress also has the power to remove a President from office if it finds the President guilty of a crime or serious misbehavior. First, the House of Representatives must impeach, or bring charges against, the President. A trial is then held in the Senate. If two thirds of the senators vote for conviction, the President must leave office.

Checks on the courts. Congress and the President have checks on the power of the courts. The President appoints judges, who must be approved by the Senate. If judges misbehave, Congress may remove them from office.

The Articles of Confederation and the Constitution

The Articles	The Constitution
1. Legislative branch: Congress is made up of one house	1. Legislative branch: Congress is made up of two houses—Senate and House of Representatives
2. Each state has one vote in Congress	2. Each state has two votes in Senate; each state has one or more votes in House of Representatives, depending on population
3. At least 9 of 13 states must approve a law	3. A majority of each house must appprove a law
4. No executive branch	4. Executive branch, headed by President, carries out laws
5. No judicial branch	5. Judicial branch, headed by Supreme Court, interprets laws
6. Only states can tax	6. Congress can tax
7. Each state can coin its own money	7. Only Congress can coin money
8. Each state can regulate trade with other states	8. Only Congress can regulate trade between states
9. Each state can act independently	9. States accept Constitution as supreme law of land

CHART SKILLS *The Constitutional Convention met to revise the Articles of Confederation. Instead, the delegates wrote a completely new document—the United States Constitution.* • *Compare the way the two documents treat each of the following: (a) the legislative branch, (b) the executive branch, (c) the power to tax.*

A Living Document

The Constitution carefully balances power among three branches of the federal government and between the states and the federal government. This system has been working for more than 200 years, longer than any other written constitution in the world. The Constitution has lasted because it is a living document. As you will read in this and later chapters, it can be changed to meet new conditions in the United States.

SECTION 3 REVIEW

1. **Identify:** (a) John Locke, (b) Baron de Montesquieu.

2. **Define:** (a) republic, (b) separation of powers, (c) federalism, (d) electoral college, (e) checks and balances, (f) bill, (g) veto, (h) override, (i) impeach.
3. Name two Enlightenment ideas that influenced the Constitution.
4. Why did the framers of the Constitution set up a system of federalism?
5. **CRITICAL THINKING Applying Information** How did the following ideas limit government: (a) separation of powers, (b) checks and balances?

ACTIVITY **Writing to Learn**
Write the text for a picture book describing the main features of the Constitution.

Ratifying the Constitution

FIND OUT

■ How did the views of Federalists and Antifederalists differ?

■ How can the Constitution be amended?

■ What rights does the Bill of Rights protect?

VOCABULARY amend, due process

At home and in town squares, Americans discussed the new Constitution. Many supported it. Many others did not. Its critics especially worried that the Constitution had no bill of rights. In Virginia, Patrick Henry sounded the alarm:

❝Show me an age and country where the rights and liberties of the people were placed on the sole chance of their rulers being good men, without a consequent loss of liberty!❞

Was a bill of rights needed? Did the Constitution give too much power to the federal government? In the fall of 1787, citizens debated the document sentence by sentence. The Convention had done its work. Now the states had to decide whether or not to ratify the new frame of government.

A Vigorous Battle

The framers of the Constitution sent the document to Congress along with a letter from George Washington. "In our deliberations," wrote Washington, "we kept steadily in view. . . the greatest interests of every true American." He then called on Congress to support the plan.

The framers had set up a process for the states to decide on the new government. At least 9 of the 13 states had to ratify the Constitution before it could go into effect. In 1787 and 1788, voters in each state elected delegates to special state conventions. These delegates then met to decide whether or not to ratify the Constitution.

Heated debate. In every state, heated debates took place. Supporters of the Constitution called themselves *Federalists.* They called people who opposed the Constitution *Antifederalists.*

Federalists favored a strong national government. Among the best-known Federalists were James Madison, Alexander Hamilton, and John Jay. They wrote a series of essays, called *The Federalist Papers,* defending the Constitution. They used pen names, but most people knew who they were.

Antifederalists opposed the Constitution for many reasons. They felt that it made the national government too strong and left the states too weak. They thought that the Constitution gave the President too much power. Most people expected George Washington to be elected President. Antifederalists admired him. They worried, however, about future Presidents who might lack Washington's honor and skill.

Need for a bill of rights. The chief argument used by Antifederalists against the Constitution was that it had no bill of rights. Americans had just fought a revolution to protect their freedoms. They wanted a bill of rights in the Constitution that spelled out those basic freedoms.

Federalists replied that the Constitution protected citizens very well without a bill of rights. Anyway, they argued, it was impossible to list all the natural rights of people. Antifederalists responded that if rights were not written into the Constitution, it would be easy to ignore them. Several state conventions refused to ratify the Constitution unless they received a firm promise that a bill of rights would be added.

The states vote to ratify. One by one, states voted to ratify. In June 1788, New Hampshire became the ninth state to ratify the Constitution. Now the new government could go into effect.

Still, the future of the United States remained in doubt. New York and Virginia, two of the largest states, had not yet ratified the plan. In both states, Federalists and Antifederalists were closely matched.

In Virginia, Patrick Henry strongly opposed the Constitution. "There will be no checks, no real balances in this government," he cried. In the end, however, Washington, Madison, and other Virginia Federalists prevailed. In late June, Virginia approved the Constitution.

In New York, the struggle went on for another month. At last, in July 1788, the state convention voted to ratify. North Carolina ratified in November 1789. Rhode Island was the last state to approve the Constitution, finally doing so in May 1790.

"We Have Become a Nation"

Throughout the land, Americans celebrated the news that the Constitution was ratified. Philadelphia set its festival for July 4, 1788. At sunrise, church bells rang. In the harbor, the ship *Rising Sun* boomed a salute from its cannons.

A festive parade filed along Market Street, led by soldiers who had fought in the Revolution. Thousands cheered as six colorfully outfitted horses pulled a blue carriage shaped like an eagle. Thirteen stars and stripes were painted on the front, and the Constitution was raised proudly above it.

That night, even the skies seemed to celebrate. The northern lights, vivid bands of

Americans Celebrate the Constitution   *When the Constitution was ratified, celebrations and huge parades, such as this one in New York City, were held across the nation.* **United States and the World**   *Why do you think many newly formed nations have used the United States Constitution as a model for their own?*

color, lit up the sky above the city. Benjamin Rush wrote to a friend: "'Tis done. We have become a nation."

Americans voted in the first election under the Constitution in January 1789. As expected, George Washington was elected President. John Adams was chosen Vice President. The first Congress was made up of 59 representatives and 22 senators. It met in New York City, the nation's first capital.

Adding a Bill of Rights

The first Congress quickly turned its attention to adding a bill of rights to the Constitution. The framers had set up a way to amend, or change, the Constitution. They wanted the Constitution to be able to change as times changed. They did not want people to make changes lightly, however. So they made the process of amending the Constitution fairly difficult.

The amendment process. To start the amendment process, an amendment must be proposed. This can be done in two ways. Two thirds of both houses of Congress can vote to propose an amendment. Or two thirds of the states can request special conventions to propose amendments.

Next, the amendment must be ratified. Three fourths of the states must vote for the amendment before it becomes part of the Constitution.

In the more than 200 years since the Constitution was adopted, only 27 amendments have been approved. Ten of these amendments were added in the first years after the Constitution was ratified.

Columbia *Americans felt great pride in their new Constitution.* Columbia, *shown here, became a symbol of the new nation.* **Citizenship** *What symbols represent the United States today?*

Ten amendments. The first Congress proposed a series of amendments to the Constitution in 1789. By December 1791, three fourths of the states had ratified ten amendments. Those ten amendments became known as the *Bill of Rights.*

James Madison, who wrote the amendments, insisted that the Bill of Rights does not *give* Americans any rights. People already have the rights listed in the amendments. They are natural rights, said Madison, that belong to all human beings. The Bill of Rights simply prevents the government from taking away these rights.

Protecting individual rights. The First Amendment guarantees freedom of religion, freedom of speech, freedom of the press, freedom of petition, and freedom of assembly, or the right to meet in groups. The next three amendments came out of the colonists' struggle with Britain. For example, the Third Amendment prevents Congress from forcing citizens to quarter, or house, troops in their homes. Before the Revolution, you will remember, Parliament tried to make colonists house and feed British soldiers.

Linking Past and Present
Over the years, many constitutional amendments have been proposed but few were ratified. In the 1970s, for example, Congress proposed the Equal Rights Amendment, designed to promote equal opportunity for women and men. After 10 years of debate, the amendment failed to receive the support of enough states to be ratified.

Freedom of Religion *The Bill of Rights guaranteed Americans the right to worship as they choose. Richard Allen, at right, founded the Bethel Church, shown here, one of the nation's first African American churches.* **Multicultural Heritage** *Why might Allen have felt that African Americans needed their own church?*

Amendments 5 through 8 protect citizens accused of crimes and brought to trial. Every citizen has the right to due process of law. **Due process** means that the government must follow the same fair rules in all cases brought to trial. Among these rules are the right to trial by jury, the right to be defended by a lawyer, and the right to a speedy trial. The last two amendments limit the powers of the federal government to those that are specifically granted in the Constitution.

With the Bill of Rights in place, the new framework of government was complete. Over time, the Constitution became a living document that grew and changed along with the nation.

SECTION 4 REVIEW

1. **Identify:** (a) Federalist, (b) Antifederalist, (c) Bill of Rights.
2. **Define:** (a) amend, (b) due process.
3. Why were Antifederalists opposed to the Constitution?
4. How can the Constitution be amended?
5. **CRITICAL THINKING Making Decisions** (a) List five rights protected by the Bill of Rights. (b) Which do you think is most important? Explain.

ACTIVITY Writing to Learn
Write a newspaper editorial taking a stand for or against ratifying the Constitution.

CRITICAL THINKING SKILLS
Finding Main Ideas

Each paragraph or group of paragraphs in this book has a main idea and supporting details. Finding the main idea is an important skill. It helps you to understand what you have read.

The main idea usually appears in a topic sentence. The topic sentence is often the first sentence of the paragraph. However, a topic sentence may also be at the beginning or at the end of the paragraph.

Read the essay below, and follow the steps to find the main ideas.

1. **Identify the main idea of each paragraph.** (a) What is the main idea of the first paragraph? (b) Which sentence best expresses the main idea? (c) Which sentence in the second paragraph states the main idea?

2. **Identify supporting details.** (a) What is the main idea of the third paragraph? (b) What two details support this main idea? (c) What are the supporting details in the fourth paragraph?

3. **Determine the main idea of the essay.** The main idea or ideas of the essay is the sum of the main ideas of the paragraphs. The main ideas of the paragraphs serve as supporting details for the main idea of the essay. (a) What is the main idea of "Religion and the Bill of Rights"? (b) What details support this main idea?

ACTIVITY Select a subsection of this chapter. Find the main ideas and supporting details. Present them in a concept map.

Religion and the Bill of Rights

Many Americans in 1789 worried that the new Constitution contained no protection of religious freedom. Without such written protection, they feared, their freedom to worship would not be secure. They called on the new government to adopt a bill of rights that would guarantee freedom of religion.

Religious leaders joined the battle for a bill of rights. Among them was Moses Brown, a Quaker leader from Rhode Island. Brown refused to support ratification of the Constitution until he received a promise that a bill of rights would be added. Baptist minister John Leland of Virginia and Bishop John Carroll of Maryland made similar stands in their states.

President Washington supported the efforts of these leaders. He wrote, "Every man . . . ought to be protected in worshiping the Deity according to the dictates of his own conscience." He promised that the new government would support religious freedom.

Religious freedom became law in 1791. In that year, the Bill of Rights was added to the Constitution. The First Amendment guaranteed religious freedom by stating, "Congress shall make no law respecting an establishment of religion, or prohibiting the free exercise thereof."

Summary

- Under the Articles of Confederation, the nation faced serious problems involving money, trade, and disputes between states.
- At the Constitutional Convention, leaders wrote a new Constitution.
- The Constitution divides power between the states and the federal government. It limits the government through separation of powers and through a system of checks and balances.
- After much debate, the states ratified the Constitution. Soon after, a Bill of Rights was added.

Reviewing the Main Ideas

1. How was the power of Congress limited under the Articles of Confederation?
2. Compare the Virginia Plan with the New Jersey Plan.
3. What is federalism?
4. (a) List the three branches of government under the Constitution. (b) What is the main job of each?
5. Give one example of how the legislative and executive branches of the federal government can check each other's power.
6. What process did the framers set up for ratifying the Constitution?
7. How does the Bill of Rights protect citizens who are accused of crimes?

Thinking Critically

1. **Linking Past and Present** (a) Name two issues on which the Constitutional Convention compromised. (b) Why were those compromises important? (c) Describe one local or national issue today that you think requires compromise.
2. **Synthesizing Information** How did the system of federalism help to solve some of the problems the government faced under the Articles of Confederation?
3. **Understanding Causes and Effects** How do you think the experience of many Americans under British rule influenced the kind of government they set up under the Constitution?

Applying Your Skills

1. **Reading a Diagram** Study the diagram on page 192 that shows a township and section in the Northwest Territory. (a) How large is a township? (b) How many sections are there in a township? (c) How large is a section? (d) Can a section be subdivided? Explain.
2. **Exploring Local History** The Pennsylvania State House, where the Constitutional Convention took place, is a national historic landmark today. What historic buildings are located in your community or state?
3. **Analyzing a Quotation** Reread the exchange between Benjamin Franklin and an unidentified woman on page 199. What do you think Franklin was trying to say with his remark?

Thinking About Geography

Match the letters on the map with the following places: **1.** Original 13 states, **2.** Northwest Territory, **3.** Spanish Louisiana, **4.** Spanish Florida, **5.** Canada. **Movement** Why did settlers travel to the Northwest Territory?

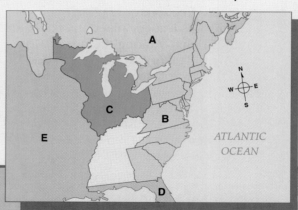

Covering the Constitutional Convention

Form into groups to explore the Constitutional Convention. Follow the suggestions below to write, draw, or perform to show what you have learned about the Convention. You may use the textbook, encyclopedias, atlases, or other materials in your classroom library to complete your task. Be able to name your sources of information when you have completed the activity.

Pennsylvania State House

LANGUAGE EXPERTS Use your textbook to draw up a list of constitutional terms, such as legislative, executive, judicial, separation of powers, checks and balances, ratify, and amend. Define the terms, using a separate sheet of paper for each. Illustrate the definitions with pictures from newspapers or old magazines. Finally, compile definitions and illustrations in a Constitution Dictionary.

ACTORS What was it like to be an ordinary citizen in Philadelphia at the time of the Constitutional Convention? With your group, prepare a skit in which citizens discuss what could be going on behind the closed doors of the Convention. Perform your skit for the class.

ARTISTS Express a point of view about the Constitutional Convention in one of the following ways:
- Draw a political cartoon.
- Design a stamp to commemorate the event.
- Create a button or badge that a street vendor might sell outside the State House where delegates are meeting.

Symbols of the United States

CITIZENS Select one of the compromises made by Convention delegates. Write a letter to a newspaper explaining why this compromise is important to the success of the Convention.

HISTORIANS Create a TV program explaining the ideas that helped shape the Constitution. Use a large wall chart showing the main ideas to illustrate your talk. Interview a Convention delegate to explore how these ideas influenced the form of government the framers set up.

★ Design a bulletin board display on which each group presents or describes its coverage of the Constitutional Convention.

Preamble to the Constitution

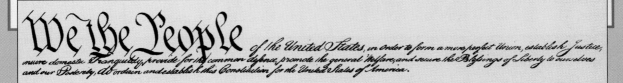

History Through LITERATURE

Johnny Tremain

Esther Forbes

Introduction   *Johnny Tremain* is a historical novel about a teenage boy in Boston just before the American Revolution. As a member of the Sons of Liberty, Johnny comes in contact with Patriot leaders such as John Hancock and Paul Revere. He also takes part in important events such as the Boston Tea Party. As this excerpt begins, Johnny rushes to warn Paul Revere of British plans to march on Lexington and Concord.

Vocabulary   Before you read the selection, find the meaning of these words in a dictionary: stealthily, billeted, spire, sufficient, piteous

"It is tonight all right," Johnny said to Doctor Warren, "and Colonel Smith will command." He went on to tell what he had found out from Dove. That the expedition would start tonight and that Lexington and Concord were the likely objects, the men sitting about in Warren's surgery had already guessed. . . .

Outside the closed window on Tremont Street a small group of soldiers were marching stealthily toward the Common. These were the first they heard. But soon another group marched past, then another. A man whose duty it was to watch the British boats at the foot of the Common came in to say he had actually seen the men getting into the boats, heading for Cambridge.

Doctor Warren turned to Johnny. . . . "Go to North Square. I've got to talk to Paul Revere before he starts. . . . "

Johnny ran toward North Square. This he found crowded with light infantry and grenadier companies, all in full battle dress. They got in his way and he in theirs.

One of the men swore and struck at him with his gun butt. The regulars were getting ugly. He could not get to the Reveres' front door, but by climbing a few fences he reached their kitchen door, and knocked softly. Paul Revere was instantly outside in the dark with him.

"Johnny," he whispered, "the *Somerset* has been moved into the mouth of the Charles. Will you run to Copp's Hill and tell me if they have moved in any of the other warships? I think I can row around one, but three or four might make me trouble."

"I'll go look."

"Wait. Then go to Robert Newman—you know, the Christ's Church sexton. He lives with his mother opposite the church."

"I know."

"They have British officers billeted on them. *Don't rap at that door.* Take this stick. Walk by the house slowly, limping, tapping with the stick until the light in an upper window goes out. Then go 'round to the alley behind the house. Tell Newman the lanterns are to be hung now. Two of them. He knows what to do."

As Johnny stood among the graves of lonely Copp's Hill looking across the broad mouth of the Charles, he could see lights

Paul Revere's Ride *In April 1775, Paul Revere, as shown in this painting by Grant Wood, galloped across the countryside, alerting Patriots of the British advance.*
American Traditions
What do you think would have happened if Revere had been unable to make his ride?

in the houses of Charlestown. And over there he knew men were watching Boston, watching Christ's lofty spire—waiting for the signal. And as soon as they saw it, the best and fastest horse in Charlestown would be saddled and made ready for Paul Revere, who had himself promised to get over—if possible. Ride and spread the alarm. Summon the Minute Men. He watched the riding lights on the powerful sixty-four-gun *Somerset*. The British had evidently thought her sufficient to prevent boats crossing the river that night. She was alone. . . .

Salem Street, where the Newmans lived, like North Square, was filled with soldiers. The redcoats were assembling here, getting ready to march down to the Common—and they would be a little late. Their orders were to be ready by moonrise. A sergeant yelled at Johnny as he started to limp past them, but when he explained in a piteous whine that his foot had been squashed by a blow from a soldier's musket and all he wanted was to get home to his mama, an officer said the men were to let "the child" pass. Johnny was sixteen, but he could pull himself together and play at being a little boy still.

Downstairs in the Newman house he could look in and see a group of officers as usual, almost as always, playing at cards. Their jackets were unbuttoned, their faces flushed. They were laughing and drinking. There was on the second floor one light. Johnny couldn't believe anyone up there could hear him tapping in the street below. Instantly the light went out. He had been heard.

Newman, a sad-faced young man, got out at a second-story window in back, ran across a shed roof, and was in the alley waiting for Johnny.

"One or two?" he whispered.

"Two."

That was all. Robert Newman seemed to melt away in the dark. Johnny guessed what the little tinkle was he heard. Newman had the keys to Christ's Church in his hand.

THINKING ABOUT LITERATURE

1. What did Revere ask Johnny to do?
2. How did Johnny fool the sergeant on the street where Newman lived?
3. **CRITICAL THINKING Analyzing Information** Why did the British want to leave Boston secretly?

ACTIVITY Imagine that you are a news reporter assigned to interview Paul Revere just after he returns from warning Patriots at Lexington and Concord. Based on this excerpt and the information in Chapter 5, write 10 questions that you would ask Revere.

The Constitution at Work

1788 *Americans ratified the Constitution. Here, crowds in Washington, D.C., celebrate the 200th anniversary.*

1791 *The Bill of Rights was ratified. These first 10 amendments to the Constitution guaranteed Americans certain basic rights.*

1700	1750	1800	1850

WORLD EVENT
1700s Age of Enlightenment

WORLD EVENT
1789 French Revolution begins

Overview Setting

Imagine what your life might be like if there were no Constitution. For example, suppose you wanted to visit a neighboring state. Without the Constitution, you might need a passport. Or the state might deny you entry because of your religion or race.

Now suppose that you were to send a letter to the local newspaper criticizing the governor. Without the Constitution, the newspaper might ignore your letter because it must print only what the state government approves. Perhaps the governor might even order your arrest and imprisonment without a trial.

As you can see, the Constitution affects you personally. Under its protection, you are free to express your opinions. It also guarantees you equal opportunity under the law—whatever your religion, sex, race, or national origin. Most important, the Constitution allows you to make your own choices about how to live your life.

The Constitution has remained as the framework of our government for more than 200 years. It endures in part because it guarantees people their rights. At the same time, it has allowed the people to further define and extend those rights.

ACTIVITY Imagine that you and your classmates are stranded on a desert island. Write five laws for governing the group.

1920 *The Nineteenth Amendment gave women the right to vote. Here, a woman registers to vote in Florida.*

1870 *The Fifteenth Amendment extended the right to vote to African American men. Here, a voter in New York signs in on election day.*

1971 *The Twenty-sixth Amendment extended the vote to Americans 18 years or older. This change gave millions of young Americans a voice in government.*

1850	1900	1950	Present

WORLD EVENT
1893 New Zealand is first nation to give vote to women

WORLD EVENT
1994 First time people of all races vote in South Africa

1
The Goals of the Constitution

FIND OUT

- How does the national government help to unify the nation?
- Why is a national system of courts necessary?
- How does the Constitution protect the rights of the people?

VOCABULARY justice, domestic tranquillity, general welfare, liberty

"We the people of the United States, in order to form a more perfect Union, establish justice, ensure domestic tranquillity, provide for the common defense, promote the general welfare, and secure the blessings of liberty to ourselves and our posterity, do ordain and establish this Constitution for the United States of America."

Those words make up the **Preamble,** or opening statement, of the Constitution. In the Preamble, the people proudly announce that they have established the Constitution. They have done so, they declare, to achieve certain goals. As you read about these goals, think about their importance to you.

Form a More Perfect Union

What do the words "my country" mean to you? You probably will say the United States. If you lived in the 1780s, however, you probably would have answered Virginia, Massachusetts, or whatever state you came from.

Indeed, under the Articles of Confederation, the United States was a loose alliance of independent, quarreling states. Many states acted like separate nations. The framers of the Constitution, however, saw the need for states to work together as part of a single, united nation.

How does the Constitution attempt to achieve "a more perfect union"? It provides the national government with the powers needed to unify and strengthen the nation.

For example, Congress—one part of the national government—has powers important to a healthy national economy. It can raise taxes and regulate trade between the states. It also has the sole power to coin and print money.

Other parts of the national government also have powers that help to unify the nation. The President is responsible for carrying out all the laws of the nation. National courts ensure fair treatment of all people under one system of law.

Establish Justice

A second goal of the Constitution is to establish justice, or fairness. The Constitution gives this task to a national system of courts.

The national courts deal with a broad range of cases. They hear cases involving the Constitution, national laws, treaties, foreign ambassadors, and ships at sea. They also decide disputes between individuals, between individuals and the national government, and between the states.

When the national courts decide cases, they often interpret, or explain, the law. The Supreme Court, the highest court in the land, can rule that a law is not permitted by the Constitution.

Why is a national system of courts necessary? Without it, the state or local courts would interpret national laws. Judges in some states might refuse to act on laws they did not like. Disputes about the meaning of certain laws would remain unsettled. The result would be confusion and injustice.

Ensure Domestic Tranquillity

In 1786, Daniel Shays marched on a Massachusetts courthouse with nearly 1,200 other protesters. Upon hearing about Shays' Rebellion, George Washington warned, "We are fast verging to [absence of government] and confusion!" The uprising made it clear that the national government must have the means to ensure domestic tranquillity, or peace at home.

The Constitution allows for means to keep the peace. State and local governments have the power to use their own police to enforce national laws. When crime crosses state borders, however, national police agencies can step in to help protect life and property.

Have you ever watched a news broadcast about a civil emergency, such as a riot or a flood? If so, you probably saw members of the National Guard keeping the peace. The President can summon such aid if a state or local community cannot or will not respond to the emergency.

Provide for the Common Defense

After the American Revolution, the United States could not defend its new borders. Without a national army, it could not force British troops to leave the frontier. Lacking a navy, it was unable to prevent Spain from closing part of the Mississippi River to American trade.

The framers of the Constitution realized that strong armed forces are important to a nation's foreign policy. Military power helps not only to prevent attack by other nations but also to protect economic and political interests.

The Constitution gives Congress the power to "raise and support Armies" and to "provide and maintain a Navy." Today, the

Contents of the Constitution

CHART SKILLS *The Constitution includes a preamble, 7 articles, and 27 amendments. To find where they appear in this book, see the page numbers in the chart. ● On what pages will you find the Bill of Rights?*

armed forces include the army, navy, air force, marine corps, and coast guard.

Promote the General Welfare

The Constitution gives the national government the means to promote the **general welfare,** or well-being of all the people. The national government has the power to collect taxes. It also has the power to set aside money for programs that will benefit the people.

In the workplace. The workplace provides many examples of how the national government—often in cooperation with state governments—has acted to promote the general welfare. Factory owners are required to meet safety standards for work areas. Workers who are disabled or unemployed receive financial support. Thanks to the Social Security system, all workers are entitled to income upon retirement.

In the school. Another area in which the national government helps to promote the general welfare is education. Education helps to prepare people to become responsible citizens. It also provides tools and training for employment.

Support for education takes many forms. The national government pays for school nutrition programs in local school districts. Many students receive money to help pay the costs of a college education.

In the laboratory. The national government supports scientific research and development to improve the quality of life. For example, researchers at the National Institutes of Health lead the fight against many diseases. Scientists at the Department of Agriculture help farmers to improve their crops and develop better livestock.

Secure the Blessings of Liberty

Protection of liberty was a major reason that colonists fought the American Revolution. It is no wonder, then, that the framers of the Constitution made securing liberty a major goal. **Liberty** is the freedom to live as you please, as long as you obey the laws and respect the rights of others.

One way that the Constitution ensures liberty is to limit the powers of government. For example, the **_Bill of Rights,_** the first 10 amendments to the Constitution, lists the liberties that Americans have. The amendments present these liberties as basic rights and freedoms that the government may not take away.

The Constitution provides yet another safeguard of liberty—the right to vote. The people can select the leaders who make the laws. At the same time, they can remove from office those leaders who have done a poor job.

The "blessings of liberty" have been extended to more Americans since the Constitution was written. Changes in the Constitution have been made to ensure that all

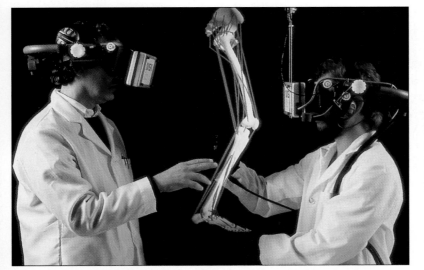

Government-Sponsored Research *The government supports a variety of scientific research. Here, two scientists use advanced equipment to study the human leg.* **Science and Technology** *Do you think the government should spend tax money on scientific research? Explain.*

Voting to Protect Liberty *The ballot box has long been a symbol of liberty. Through the vote, Americans have a say in government decisions and are able to safeguard their rights.* **Citizenship** *How does the Bill of Rights protect the "blessings of liberty" for Americans?*

Americans—no matter what sex or race—have the same rights regarding voting, education, housing, employment, and other choices in life.

SECTION 1 REVIEW

1. **Identify:** (a) Preamble, (b) Bill of Rights.
2. **Define:** (a) justice, (b) domestic tranquillity, (c) general welfare, (d) liberty.
3. List two powers of the national government that help to form a more perfect union.
4. Why would confusion and injustice result without a national court system?
5. List two ways in which the national government helps workers.
6. **CRITICAL THINKING Evaluating Information** Which goal of the Constitution do you think is most important? Explain.

ACTIVITY **Writing to Learn**
Create a crossword puzzle using the vocabulary words listed at the beginning of this section.

2 Five Principles of the Constitution

FIND OUT
- What is popular sovereignty?
- What is limited government?
- How does federalism divide power?
- How does the separation of powers limit government?
- How does the system of checks and balances prevent abuse of power?

VOCABULARY representative government, ratify, tyranny, federal, veto, override, bill, unconstitutional

The Constitution sets up a strong national government. At the same time, it safeguards the liberty of the people. Five basic principles, or rules, support this delicate balance. They are popular sovereignty, limited government, federalism, separation of powers, and checks and balances. In large part, the framers drew on European ideas for these principles. (See Chapter 7, pages 200 to 201.) As you read about the basic principles of the Constitution, think about how they help to protect you.

Popular Sovereignty Means the People Rule

The first three words of the Constitution, "We the people," express the principle of popular sovereignty. According to this principle, the people rule. They hold the final authority, or ruling power, in government.

A contract with the government. The Constitution is a contract, or formal, written agreement, between the people and their government. In it, the people grant the government the powers it needs to achieve its goals. At the same time, they limit the power of government by spelling out what the government may not do.

The people vote. How does popular sovereignty work? In a large society, people cannot always take part directly in government. Instead, they exercise their ruling power indirectly. The people elect public officials to make laws and other government decisions for them. This practice is called representative government.

The people elect public officials by voting in free and frequent elections. Americans today have the constitutional right to vote for members of the House of Representatives (Article 1, Section 2) and for members of the Senate (Amendment 17). The people also elect the members of the electoral college, who, in turn, choose the President (Article 2, Section 1).

The right to vote has been gradually expanded over time. When the Constitution was ratified, or approved, only white men over age 21 who owned property could vote. As the chart at right shows, other Americans have won the right to vote since then. Today, if you are a citizen, you are eligible to vote at age 18.

The Government's Power Should Be Limited

The framers of the Constitution remembered well the harsh rule of the British king. Like most Americans, they feared tyranny, or cruel and unjust government. However, the failures of the Articles of Confederation made it clear that the national government had to be strong.

How could the framers strike a balance between too much government and too little government? The answer was limited government, or a government by law. According to this principle, the government

The Right to Vote

Year	People Allowed to Vote
1789	White men over age 21 who met property requirements (state laws)
Early 1800s–1850s	All white men over age 21 (state laws)
1870	Black men (Amendment 15)
1920	Women (Amendment 19)
1961	People in the District of Columbia in presidential elections (Amendment 23)
1971	People over age 18 (Amendment 26)

CHART SKILLS *The right to vote has expanded since the Constitution first went into effect.*
● *Who could vote in 1789? In 1971? Which amendment granted women the right to vote?*

does not have complete power. It has only the powers that the people grant it.

Limits on power. The Constitution states the powers of the national government. You and every other citizen can tell what powers Congress, the President, and the courts have. The Constitution also states what powers the government does not have. This list of denied powers puts still more limits on the government.

Guarantees to the people. The most important limits on government are set out in the Bill of Rights. In these amendments, the Constitution guarantees the individual freedoms of the people. One of the 10 amendments states that the people have other rights in addition to those listed in the Constitution (Amendment 9). In other words, the rights of the people cannot be limited to those in the Constitution. Still another amendment gives the states or the people any powers not granted to the national government (Amendment 10).

Limited government is also known as the "rule of law." The Constitution is the law of the land. No person—not you, not the highest government official—is above it.

Federalism Results in a Sharing of Power

The framers of the Constitution faced a difficult conflict. They saw the need for a strong national government. At the same time, they did not want to take away all power from the states. Like most Americans, they believed that state governments would better understand the special needs and concerns of their citizens.

The framers choose federalism. The framers solved this conflict by basing the government on the principle of federalism.

Under federalism, power is divided between the **federal,** or national, government and the state governments. The national government has the power to deal with national issues. The states have the power to meet local needs.

A division of power. The Constitution delegates, or assigns, certain powers to the national government. Other powers are reserved, or left, to the states. Still other powers, sometimes called concurrent powers, are shared by the national and state governments. The chart below shows how powers are divided under federalism.

The powers of the states. The Constitution does not clearly list the powers of the states. Instead, it says that all powers not specifically granted to the national government are reserved to the states (Amendment 10). At the same time, it makes clear exactly what powers are denied to the states (Article 1, Section 10).

Besides reserved powers, the Constitution makes other guarantees to the states.

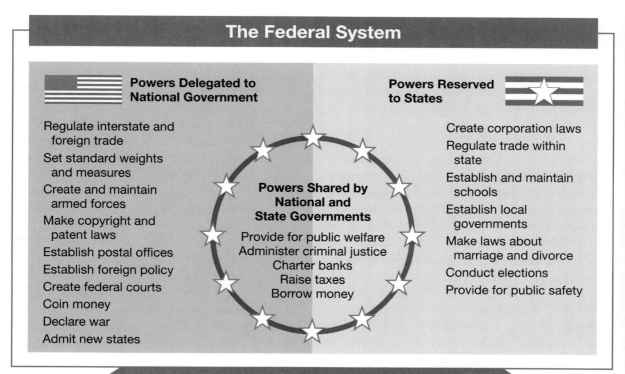

The Federal System

Powers Delegated to National Government

Regulate interstate and foreign trade

Set standard weights and measures

Create and maintain armed forces

Make copyright and patent laws

Establish postal offices

Establish foreign policy

Create federal courts

Coin money

Declare war

Admit new states

Powers Shared by National and State Governments

Provide for public welfare
Administer criminal justice
Charter banks
Raise taxes
Borrow money

Powers Reserved to States

Create corporation laws

Regulate trade within state

Establish and maintain schools

Establish local governments

Make laws about marriage and divorce

Conduct elections

Provide for public safety

CHART SKILLS *The system of federalism divides power between the national government and the state governments. • Name two powers reserved to the states. Who has the power to raise taxes?*

Public Schools *The power to establish and maintain schools is reserved to the states. Although the federal government provides funds, Americans exercise local control over schools.* **Citizenship** *Why do you think Americans want to keep local control over education?*

All states must be treated equally in matters of trade (Article 1, Section 9). Each state must respect the laws of the others (Article 4, Section 1). Perhaps most important of all, states are given representation in the national government.

National supremacy. Federalism creates a working partnership between the national government and the state governments. However, when a dispute arises between them, there is no doubt where the final authority lies. The Constitution is the "supreme law of the land" (Article 6, Section 2). Only national courts can settle the dispute.

Separation of Powers Further Limits the Government

In 1787, nearly every government in Europe was a monarchy. The king or queen made and enforced the laws and appointed judges to interpret the laws. This system was dangerous. It put all political power in the hands of a few people.

Three branches of government. In the United States, the Constitution prevents one person or group from having all the power. It separates the national government into three branches: the legislative, the executive, and the judicial. Each branch has its own powers and responsibilities. This division of the national government is known as separation of powers. (See the chart in Chapter 7 on page 202.)

The legislative branch. Article 1 of the Constitution sets up the legislative branch. This branch, called Congress, makes the laws. It has two houses: the House of Representatives and the Senate. Its many powers include the power to tax, to coin money, and to declare war.

The executive branch. Article 2 describes the executive branch, which carries out the laws. The President heads the executive branch and appoints advisers and other officials to assist him.

The executive branch plays an important role in foreign affairs. As commander in chief, the President has broad military powers. The President also can make treaties.

The judicial branch. Article 3 creates the Supreme Court to head the judicial branch. This branch interprets and explains the laws. Congress may set up lower courts as necessary.

Checks and Balances Prevent Abuse of Power

The Constitution divides the powers of government among the three branches. But how does it prevent one branch of government from having too much power? The answer lies in a system of checks and bal-

System of Checks and Balances

Executive Branch (President carries out laws)	Checks on the Legislative Branch	Checks on the Judicial Branch
	Can propose laws Can veto laws Can call special sessions of Congress Makes appointments Negotiates foreign treaties	Appoints federal judges Can grant pardons to federal offenders
Legislative Branch (Congress makes laws)	**Checks on the Executive Branch**	**Checks on the Judicial Branch**
	Can override President's veto Confirms executive appointments Ratifies treaties Can declare war Appropriates money Can impeach and remove President	Creates lower federal courts Can impeach and remove judges Can propose amendments to overrule judicial decisions Approves appointments of federal judges
Judicial Branch (Supreme Court interprets laws)	**Check on the Executive Branch**	**Check on the Legislative Branch**
	Can declare executive actions unconstitutional	Can declare acts of Congress unconstitutional

CHART SKILLS *Through the system of checks and balances, each branch of government has checks, or controls, on the power of the other branches.* • *Name one check that the President has on Congress. How can the Supreme Court check Congress?*

ances. Each branch can check, or control, the power of the other two branches.

How does the system of checks and balances work? The chart above shows some of the checks that Congress, the President, and the Supreme Court have on each other.

Checks on Congress. Congress has the power to pass laws. However, the President can check Congress by **vetoing,** or rejecting, a proposed law. Congress, in turn, can check the President by **overriding,** or setting aside, a presidential veto. In this way, a **bill,** or proposed law, can become a law without the signature of the President.

The Supreme Court also can have a say in lawmaking. It can declare a law passed by Congress **unconstitutional,** or not permitted by the Constitution. That law then cannot take effect.

Checks on the President. The President has broad powers, especially in matters of foreign policy. As the chart shows, however, Congress has several checks on these powers.

For example, the President has the power to make treaties with foreign nations. However, the Senate must ratify treaties. Also, the President is commander in chief of the

Principles of the Constitution

Principle	Definition
Popular sovereignty	Principle of government in which the people hold the final authority or power
Limited government	Principle that the government is not all powerful but can do only what the people say it can do
Federalism	Division of power between the national government and the state governments
Separation of powers	Division of the operations of the national government into three branches, each with its own powers and responsibilities
Checks and balances	Means by which each branch of the national government is able to check, or control, the power of the other two branches

CHART SKILLS *The Constitution is based on five principles.*
● According to the principle of limited government, what can the government do? Which principle calls for dividing power between the national government and the state governments?

armed forces. However, Congress, not the President, holds the power to declare war.

The President also faces possible checks by the Supreme Court. The Court has the power to declare that an act of the President is unconstitutional.

Checks on the courts. Both the President and Congress have several checks on the power of the judiciary. The President appoints all federal judges. However, the Senate must approve the President's appointments. In addition, Congress can remove federal judges from office if they are found guilty of wrongdoing. Congress may also propose a constitutional amendment to overrule a judicial decision.

SECTION 2 REVIEW

1. **Define:** (a) representative government, (b) ratify, (c) tyranny, (d) federal, (e) veto, (f) override, (g) bill, (h) unconstitutional.

2. According to the principle of popular sovereignty, who holds the final ruling power?
3. Why is limited government known as the "rule of law"?
4. How does the system of federalism divide power?
5. (a) List the three branches of government. (b) Name one power of each.
6. How can Congress check the President's power to make treaties?
7. **CRITICAL THINKING Analyzing Ideas** Explain the following statement: The Constitution sets up a government of law, not of people.

ACTIVITY Writing to Learn
Imagine that your local radio station is broadcasting public service announcements about the Constitution. Write a brief announcement describing the system of checks and balances and explaining its importance.

A Living Constitution

FIND OUT

- How can the Constitution be formally changed?
- What is the purpose of the Bill of Rights?
- What informal changes have been made in the Constitution?

VOCABULARY amendment, precedent, Cabinet, judicial review

"I do not think we are more inspired, have more wisdom, or possess more virtue than those who will come after us," said George Washington. The framers of the Constitution agreed with Washington. Like him, they realized that the nation would grow and change. As a result, they provided future Americans with a living Constitution—one that could be adapted and altered to meet new conditions and challenges.

The Constitution Provides for Formal Changes

The Constitution allows amendments, or formal written changes, to the Constitution. Amending the Constitution is not easy, however. The process requires two difficult steps: proposal and ratification. (See the chart below.)

Proposing an amendment. Article 5 describes two methods for proposing amendments. Two thirds of each house of Congress can vote to propose an amendment. Or, two thirds of the state legislatures can demand that Congress summon a national "convention for proposing amendments."

So far, only the first method—a vote by Congress—has been used. As experts have pointed out, the Constitution does not give

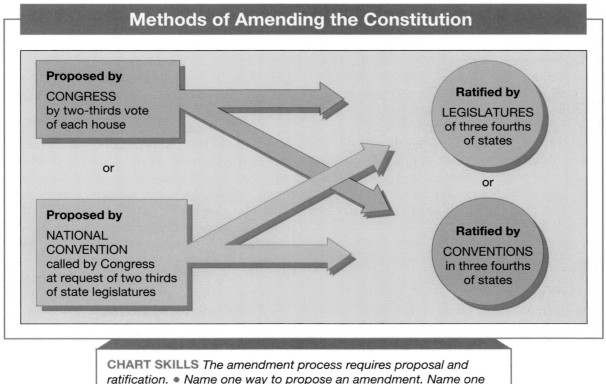

Methods of Amending the Constitution

Proposed by
CONGRESS
by two-thirds vote
of each house

or

Proposed by
NATIONAL
CONVENTION
called by Congress
at request of two thirds
of state legislatures

Ratified by
LEGISLATURES
of three fourths
of states

or

Ratified by
CONVENTIONS
in three fourths
of states

CHART SKILLS *The amendment process requires proposal and ratification. ● Name one way to propose an amendment. Name one way to ratify an amendment.*

Citizens Exercise Their Rights *Constitutional amendments protect many individual rights. At left, members of the Gray Panthers, a group that promotes the needs of older citizens, exercise their right to assemble in a peaceful protest. At right, an 18-year-old exercises his right to vote.* **Citizenship** *Which amendments protect the rights shown in these pictures? Explain.*

guidelines for a national convention. Who should set the agenda? How should delegates be selected? Those and other questions probably would cause much delay and confusion.

Ratifying an amendment. Article 5 also outlines two methods of ratifying a proposed amendment. Either three fourths of the state legislatures, or three fourths of the states meeting in special conventions, must approve the amendment.

Congress decides which method of ratification to use. Until now, only the Twenty-first Amendment was ratified by special state conventions. All other amendments have been ratified by state legislatures.

In recent years, Congress has set a time limit for ratification of amendments. The time limit today is seven years, but it may be extended.

The Constitution Has 27 Amendments

As you can see, the amendment process is a difficult one. Since 1789, more than 9,000 amendments have been introduced in Congress. Yet only 27 amendments have been ratified.

Bill of Rights. The original Constitution did not list basic freedoms of the people. In fact, several states refused to approve the Constitution until they were promised that a bill of rights would be added. Those states wanted to ensure that the national government would not be able to take away basic freedoms.

The Bill of Rights includes the first 10 amendments to the Constitution. It was ratified in 1791. See the chart on page 217 for a list of the 10 amendments in the Bill of Rights.

You will easily recognize many of the freedoms in the Bill of Rights. For example, the First Amendment protects your right to worship freely, to speak freely, to write freely, to hold peaceful meetings, and to ask the government to correct wrongs. The Fourth Amendment protects you from "unreasonable" search and seizure of your home and property. The Sixth Amendment guarantees you the right to a trial by jury and to a lawyer.

Amendments 11 through 27. Only 17 amendments have been ratified since 1791. Several of these amendments reflect changing ideas about equality.

Amendments 13 through 15—the so-called Civil War amendments—were passed to protect the rights of former slaves. The Thirteenth Amendment ended slavery. The Fourteenth Amendment guaranteed citizenship and constitutional rights to African Americans. The Fifteenth Amendment guaranteed African Americans the right to vote.

Equality was also the goal of two later amendments. The Nineteenth Amendment gave women the right to vote. The Twenty-sixth Amendment set age 18 as the minimum voting age.

The chart on page 217 lists Amendments 11 through 27. For more information about the amendments, refer to the Constitution printed in the Reference Section.

Language and Tradition Allow Informal Changes

The language of the Constitution provides a general outline rather than specific details about the national government. Over time, this flexible language has allowed each branch of government to fulfill its role and meet the changing needs of the nation.

"Necessary and proper." The framers knew that they could not foresee the future. To deal with this problem, Article 1, Section 8, Clause 18, gives Congress the power to make all laws that shall be "necessary and proper" to carry out the powers of the national government. This so-called **Elastic Clause** has allowed Congress to stretch its power to pass laws.

"Regulate commerce." Still another clause of the Constitution has allowed Congress to extend its powers. Article 1, Section 8, Clause 3, gives Congress the power to "regulate" trade with other nations and between the states.

Armed with the **Commerce Clause** and the Elastic Clause, Congress has been able to keep pace with change. For example, it has passed laws that regulate the airline industry, television, nuclear energy, and genetic engineering.

A more powerful executive branch. The Constitution does not describe in detail the powers of the President. Some Presidents, however, have taken actions or made decisions that set a **precedent,** or example, for later Presidents.

George Washington set one such precedent. The Constitution does not state that the President may appoint a **Cabinet,** or group of close advisers. President Washington assumed the power to do so on his own. Every President since then has followed his lead.

In national emergencies, Presidents have expanded their constitutional role. During the Great Depression, President Franklin

Controlling Pollution *The flexible language of the Constitution has allowed the government to keep up with changing needs. It set up the Environmental Protection Agency to deal with hazards such as automobile emissions.* **Citizenship** *What clauses of the Constitution have allowed Congress to expand its powers?*

Roosevelt expanded the size and power of the executive branch to propose and carry out programs that would restore the national economy.

A broader role for the judiciary. The Supreme Court can decide whether acts of a President or laws passed by Congress are unconstitutional. This power is known as judicial review.

The Constitution does not list judicial review as a power of the judicial branch. Like the unstated powers of the President, judicial review is implied in the words and structure of the Constitution. In the case of *Marbury* v. *Madison,* an early Supreme Court decision interpreted Article 3, Section 2, to mean that the Supreme Court has the right to decide whether a law violates the Constitution.

SECTION 3 REVIEW

1. **Identify:** (a) First Amendment, (b) Sixth Amendment, (c) Thirteenth Amendment, (d) Fourteenth Amendment, (e) Fifteenth Amendment, (f) Nineteenth Amendment, (g) Twenty-sixth Amendment, (h) Elastic Clause, (i) Commerce Clause, (j) *Marbury* v. *Madison.*
2. **Define:** (a) amendment, (b) precedent, (c) Cabinet, (d) judicial review.
3. Describe the amendment process.
4. List four rights protected by the Bill of Rights.
5. (a) How did George Washington expand the powers of the President? (b) How did Franklin Roosevelt expand the role of the President during the Great Depression?
6. **CRITICAL THINKING Drawing Conclusions** Why have there been more informal changes than formal changes in the Constitution?

ACTIVITY **Writing to Learn**
Which amendment is most important in your life? Write a paragraph explaining your choice.

4
The National Government at Work

FIND OUT
- Why has Congress set up committees?
- What roles does the President play?
- How is the federal court system organized?

VOCABULARY appropriate, standing committee, joint committee, impeach, constituent, executive agreement, jury, appeal

The Constitution sets up three branches of government, each with its own clearly defined powers. The three branches work together to accomplish the same goal: a government of laws. Together, they make, carry out, and interpret the laws of the United States.

The Legislative Branch Makes the Laws

Congress, the legislative branch of government, is made up of two houses: the House of Representatives and the Senate. Together, the two houses have the power to make the laws that govern all 50 states. At the same time, the states have a say in making those laws.

House of Representatives. The larger house, the House of Representatives, seats 435 members. Representatives serve two-year terms and are elected on the basis of a state's current population. The more people that live in a state, the greater its number of representatives. Each state, however, is guaranteed at least one representative.

MAP, GRAPH, AND CHART SKILLS
Reading a Flowchart

A flowchart gives a lot of information in a simple, easy-to-understand way. It shows a process or development step by step. For example, under the Constitution, Congress can pass a bill and the President can sign it into law. Over the years, a complicated process has developed whereby a bill actually becomes a law.

1. **Identify the parts of the flowchart.** (a) What is the title of the flowchart? (b) What does each of the four columns show? (c) What do the red arrows show? (d) What color shows House action? Senate action?

2. **Practice reading the flowchart.** (a) Where is a bill usually introduced? (b) What happens to a bill after it has been introduced?

(c) What happens after the House and Senate have both passed their own forms of a bill? (d) What is the last step a bill goes through before it becomes a law?

3. **Evaluate the information shown on the flowchart.** During every two-year term, about 10,000 bills are introduced in Congress. Only about 1,000 ever make it through the many steps to become a law. (a) Why do you think House and Senate committees hold hearings on bills that have been introduced? (b) Using the flowchart, why do you think only a few bills actually become laws?

ACTIVITY Construct a flowchart that shows the step-by-step process you follow to get to school.

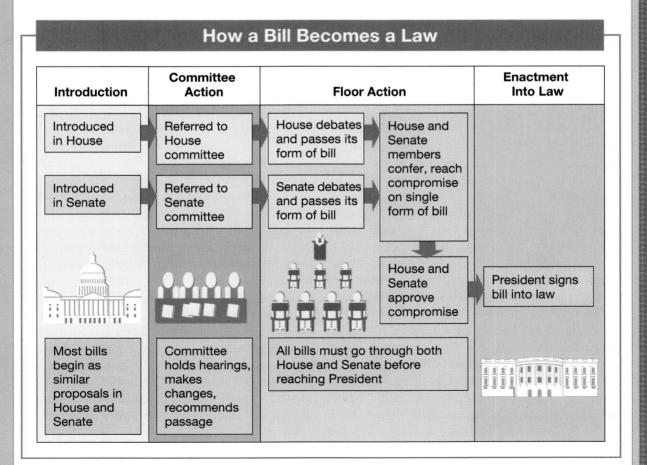

How a Bill Becomes a Law

Introduction	Committee Action	Floor Action		Enactment Into Law
Introduced in House	Referred to House committee	House debates and passes its form of bill	House and Senate members confer, reach compromise on single form of bill	
Introduced in Senate	Referred to Senate committee	Senate debates and passes its form of bill		
			House and Senate approve compromise	President signs bill into law
Most bills begin as similar proposals in House and Senate	Committee holds hearings, makes changes, recommends passage	All bills must go through both House and Senate before reaching President		

A Vote in the House *An electronic voting board keeps track of the votes cast by members of the House of Representatives. A bill passes if the majority of the representatives vote yes.* **Citizenship** *Who else must approve the bill before it becomes a law?*

Senate. In contrast to the House, the Senate has only 100 members. Each state has two senators, no matter how large or small the population of the state. Senators serve for six-year terms. The terms are staggered, however. As a result, one third of the Senate is up for election every two years.

Power to spend money. The chief purpose of Congress is to make the nation's laws. Congress has another important power. It decides what laws or programs will receive funds.

The federal government cannot spend money unless Congress has **appropriated** it, or set aside the money for a special purpose. In this way, Congress controls how much money the government spends on military aircraft, school lunches, national highways, and other programs.

How a bill becomes a law. A bill is a proposal for a new law. It must be passed by both houses of Congress and signed by the President to become law. The chart on page 229 shows the steps a bill must pass through before becoming a law.

Congress Relies on Committees

During the first session of Congress, 31 bills were proposed by both houses. Today, thousands of bills are introduced every year in Congress.

It would be impossible for each of the 535 members of Congress to study and make recommendations about every bill. This job is reserved for committees, or special groups, that work on legislation.

Committees in each house. The House of Representatives and the Senate each have **standing committees,** or permanent committees. These committees study special issues such as agriculture, labor, and energy. They are often broken up into subcommittees that study certain problems in depth.

Committees of both houses. Congress sometimes creates **joint committees,** or groups made up of both House and Senate members. One of the most important kinds of joint committee is the conference committee. Its task is to settle differences between the House and the Senate versions of

The Federal Deficit

The federal government spends more money each year than it earns in taxes and other revenue. To pay all its expenses, the government must borrow money. The amount that the government owes is called the deficit. Most Americans believe that the deficit should

be reduced. Deciding how to reduce the deficit, however, often stirs fierce debate.

One way that the federal government can reduce the deficit is to cut spending. For example, some Americans want to cut spending for defense. Others protest that the government spends too much on programs for the general welfare. They want the government to cut back on housing, medical, and other programs.

Another way that the government can reduce the deficit is by raising taxes. Americans argue over how much taxes should be raised and who should pay more taxes. Some people believe that raising taxes will hurt the economy.

The government faces difficult choices in trying to lower the deficit. Although solving the problem will not be easy, most Americans agree that a solution must be found.

■ What can the federal government do to reduce the deficit?

ACTIVITY Conduct a poll about the deficit among five adults you know. Ask them what steps they think the government should take to reduce the deficit. Organize the responses in a chart.

the same bill. Members of a conference committee try to find a middle ground and to agree on the language of the bill. Very often, compromise is difficult.

Passing a bill requires the cooperation of many individuals. For example, a recent trade bill was 1,000 pages long. It required the efforts of 200 members of Congress, working in 17 subcommittees, to get it passed. Most bills introduced in Congress do not meet with such success. In fact, more

than 90 percent of all the bills introduced are defeated in committees.

Congress Plays Other Roles

Members of Congress have duties other than serving on committees and making laws. They also guard the public trust and respond to the special needs of their states.

A "watchdog." For example, the House of Representatives can **impeach,** or bring a

Federal Officeholders

Office	Number	Term	Selection	Requirements
Representative	At least 1 per state; based on population	2 years	Elected by voters of congressional district	Age 25 or over Citizen for 7 years Resident of state in which elected
Senator	2 per state	6 years	Original Constitution— elected by state legislature Amendment 17— elected by voters	Age 30 or over Citizen for 9 years Resident of state in which elected
President and Vice President	1	4 years	Elected by electoral college	Age 35 or over Natural-born citizen Resident of U.S. for 14 years
Supreme Court Justice	9	Life	Appointed by President	No requirements in Constitution

CHART SKILLS *The Constitution details the number, length of term, methods of selection, and requirements for officeholders in the three branches of government.* • *What are the requirements for the President? For a senator?*

formal charge of wrongdoing, against the President or another federal official. The Senate acts as a court to try the accused. Congress also acts as a "watchdog" by supervising the way the executive branch carries out the laws.

The people "back home." Responsible representatives and senators must remember their constituents, or the people who elected them. Therefore, members of Congress actively support bills that have a direct impact on the people "back home." Such bills might include promoting new post offices, improving highways, and helping pay for local education programs.

The President Has Several Roles

The framers created an executive branch to carry out the laws. However, they left out details about the President's powers. Over the years, the powers of the President have been increased or decreased, depending on the needs of the time. Still, Americans expect the President to fill certain roles.

Chief executive. The main role of the President is to carry out the nation's laws. As chief executive, the President oversees the many departments, agencies, and commissions that help to accomplish this task.

Chief of state. The President is the living symbol of the nation. In this role, the President represents all American citizens at many occasions. For example, the President greets visiting foreign leaders and gives medals to national heroes.

Chief diplomat. The President directs the nation's foreign policy. Three important powers allow the President to influence relations with other countries. They are the powers to appoint ambassadors, make treaties, and enter into executive agreements. Executive agreements are informal agreements with other heads of state, usually dealing with trade. Unlike treaties, they do not require Senate approval.

Commander in chief. The President is the highest-ranking officer in the armed forces. As commander in chief, the President can appoint and remove top military commanders. The President may also use the armed forces to deal with crises both at home and abroad.

Chief legislator. The President suggests new laws and works for their passage. In this role, the President often meets with members of Congress to win their support. Sometimes, the President campaigns for public support through television or radio speeches and press conferences.

The President also can use persuasion to oppose a bill. In this case, however, the President's most powerful weapon is the power to veto a bill.

The President Carries Out the Laws

The nation's laws cover a broad range of concerns—defense, housing, crime, and pollution, to name a few. To carry out these laws and to perform other duties, the President needs the help of millions of government workers. These workers make up five major groups.

Executive Office. One group of assistants, the Executive Office, includes many agencies and individuals. They range from the Vice President to the Office of Management and Budget, which prepares the total budget of the United States. In all, the Executive Office has about 1,600 workers.

Executive departments. The President's Cabinet, called secretaries, are the heads of executive departments. President Washington had only four departments. Today, the President relies on 14 executive departments—among them, the Departments of Defense, Commerce, Justice, Labor, and Energy. Each department has many concerns. For example, the Department of Agriculture deals with food quality, crop improvement, and nutrition.

Independent executive agencies. More than 30 independent executive agencies also help the President carry out duties. For example, the Central Intelligence Agency

Presidents at Work *The President serves as both chief diplomat and commander in chief. At left, President Bill Clinton meets with Prime Minister Benazir Bhutto of Pakistan at the White House. At right, President George Bush greets American troops in the Middle East.* **Citizenship** *Describe two other roles of the President.*

(CIA) provides the President with secret information about the world's trouble spots. The National Aeronautics and Space Administration (NASA) is in charge of the nation's space program.

Independent regulatory commissions. The fourth group of workers, 11 independent regulatory commissions, enforce national laws. They set down specific rules, rates, and standards for trade, business, science, and transportation. For example, a law of Congress forbids "false or misleading advertising." It was the Federal Trade Commission (FTC), however, that ruled that cigarettes may not be advertised as "kind" to your throat.

Government corporations. There are at least 60 government corporations today. They include the United States Postal Service, the Tennessee Valley Authority, and Amtrak.

The Judicial Branch Interprets the Laws

Article 3 of the Constitution gives the judicial power of the United States to the Supreme Court and to lower courts that Congress may set up. Under the Judiciary Act of 1789, Congress created the system of federal courts that still operates today.

District courts. Most federal cases begin in the district courts. These courts are placed in more than 90 districts around the country. Cases brought to these courts may involve matters of criminal law, such as kidnapping and murder, or matters of civil law, such as bankruptcy and divorce. In district courts, decisions are made by either a judge or a jury, which is a panel of citizens.

Circuit courts. Every citizen has the right to appeal a decision, or ask that it be reviewed by a higher court. These higher courts of appeal are called circuit, or appellate, courts. The United States has 13 circuit courts of appeal.

Circuit courts operate differently from district courts. A panel of three judges reviews each case. The judges decide if rules of trial procedure were followed in the original trial. If errors did occur, the circuit court may reverse, or overturn, the original decision. Or it may send back the case to the district court for a new trial.

Supreme Court. The Supreme Court is the highest court in the United States. It is made up of a Chief Justice and eight Associate Justices.

Only two kinds of cases can begin in the Supreme Court. The first kind involves disputes between states. The second involves foreign ambassadors.

The Supreme Court *The Chief Justice and eight Associate Justices of the Supreme Court interpret the laws according to the Constitution. A majority of five Justices can determine a Supreme Court decision.* **Citizenship** *What kinds of cases does the Supreme Court hear?*

Otherwise, the Supreme Court serves as a final court of appeals. It hears cases that have been tried and appealed as far as law permits in federal and state courts.

The Supreme Court hears only issues about the Constitution, federal law, or treaties. It selects only about 120 cases from the 4,000 or more requests it receives each year. Most of the cases involve laws written in unclear language. The Court must decide what each law means, whom it affects, and whether it is constitutional.

A Supreme Court decision rests on a simple majority vote of at least five Justices. It is a final decision. There are no other courts of appeal. If Congress strongly disagrees with a Supreme Court decision, however, it can take other action. It can pass a modified version of the law, or it can propose an amendment to the Constitution.

SECTION 4 REVIEW

1. **Identify:** (a) House of Representatives, (b) Senate, (c) Supreme Court.
2. **Define:** (a) appropriate, (b) standing committee, (c) joint committee, (d) impeach, (e) constituent, (f) executive agreement, (g) jury, (h) appeal.
3. Name three programs for which Congress might appropriate money.
4. (a) What duties does the President perform as chief executive? (b) As chief legislator?
5. (a) What is the role of circuit courts? (b) What is the role of the Supreme Court?
6. **CRITICAL THINKING Analyzing Ideas** Why is it important for Congress to approve the President's choices for Supreme Court Justices?

ACTIVITY Writing to Learn
Imagine that you are the President of the United States. Write a diary entry that describes your activities for the past week.

5
Citizenship at Work

FIND OUT
- How did the Fourteenth Amendment help to expand rights?
- What responsibilities do citizens have?

VOCABULARY due process of law

The Constitution and its amendments guarantee rights to you and every other American citizen. Along with these rights of citizenship, however, come responsibilities.

Citizens Have Rights

Americans first proclaimed their rights in the Declaration of Independence. "All men are created equal," the Declaration states, and they have "certain unalienable rights," including "life, liberty, and the pursuit of happiness." Since the birth of the nation, Americans have struggled to reach this ideal of basic rights for all citizens.

The first step. The original Constitution protected some individual rights by limiting government actions. For example, Article 6, Section 3, prevents government from making religion a requirement for public service. Also, Article 1, Section 9, forbids passing any law that makes someone guilty of a crime without a trial.

Bill of Rights. As you have read, many Americans demanded a more specific list of rights. The first 10 amendments to the Constitution further spell out rights. For example, the First Amendment forbids government actions that limit freedom of religion, speech, press, assembly, and petition. (See the chart on page 236.)

The Bill of Rights, however, applied only to the national government. It did not affect

Liberties Protected by the First Amendment

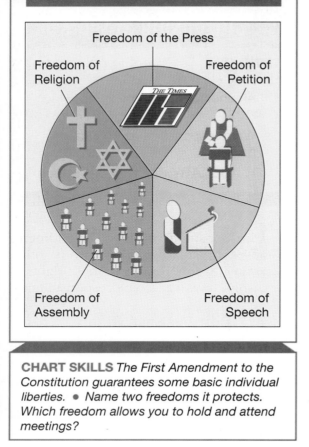

Freedom of the Press

Freedom of Religion

Freedom of Petition

Freedom of Assembly

Freedom of Speech

CHART SKILLS *The First Amendment to the Constitution guarantees some basic individual liberties. • Name two freedoms it protects. Which freedom allows you to hold and attend meetings?*

the actions of state governments. As a result, states were able to limit or deny basic rights of many Americans, including African Americans, Asian Americans, and women. The federal government sometimes restricted basic rights, too, through laws and in court decisions.

Fourteenth Amendment. An amendment passed in 1868 paved the way for a major expansion of rights. The Fourteenth Amendment states that persons born or naturalized in the United States are citizens of both the nation and their state. No state, the amendment says, may limit the rights of citizens or deny citizens **due process of law,** or a fair hearing or trial. States are also forbidden to deny citizens "equal protection of the laws."

Court decisions. Over the years, the Supreme Court has decided that the Four-

teenth Amendment's guarantee of due process and equal protection includes rights listed in the Bill of Rights. For example, in the 1960s, the Court ruled that due process of law includes the Sixth Amendment rights to a speedy trial by jury and to a lawyer. States cannot deny citizens the protections of the Bill of Rights.

Ideas of liberty grow. As the Ninth Amendment states, the people have rights beyond those described in the Constitution. Americans still strive to define and guarantee those rights. Many believe that their rights include the opportunity to pursue a good education, to find a job, and to live in decent housing.

Citizens Have Responsibilities

You and every other citizen must do your part to safeguard your rights. That role includes responsibilities.

Learn about your rights. You cannot protect your rights unless you know what they are. Books, government pamphlets, and groups such as the League of Women Voters, the National Association for the Advancement of Colored People (NAACP), and the Legal Aid Society can give you information about your rights and the law.

Respect the rights of others. Your rights are only as safe as your neighbor's. If you abuse or allow abuse of another citizen's rights, your rights may be at risk someday.

Express your views. The First Amendment guarantees you the freedom to speak, write, sign petitions, and meet with others freely. You can use those freedoms not only to defend your rights but also to take a stand on political and community issues. It is important to remember that such expressions should be truthful and peaceful.

Learn about community and national issues. As a responsible citizen, keep informed about issues critical to the nation and to your community. Besides reading newspapers and magazines, attend local meetings. At a town council meeting, for example, you might learn about proposed solutions to pollution problems. Or the League of Women Voters might offer a debate by candidates for political office.

Vote. Good government depends on good leaders. Therefore, citizens have the responsibility to exercise their right to vote and to select the best candidate. If citizens have studied the candidates and the issues in an election, they will be able to make responsible decisions.

Obey laws. Citizens enter into a contract with the government. They give the government the power to make certain laws. In return, they expect government to protect the health and well-being of society. As part of this contract, the government has the power to set penalties if laws are broken.

Like other citizens, you have a responsibility to obey the laws that safeguard your rights and the rights of others. For example, you should not steal, damage the property of others, or harm someone physically.

Serve on juries. The Bill of Rights guarantees citizens the right to a trial by jury. Every citizen, in turn, has the responsibility to serve on juries when called.

Serving on a jury is a serious duty. Jurors must take time out from their work and personal life. Deciding the guilt or innocence of the accused can be difficult.

Volunteer. Responsible citizens offer their time and talents to help others and to improve the community. For example, you can join or start a group to clean up parks or to serve food to senior citizens. You can also take part in a walk-a-thon or bike-a-thon to raise money for a worthy cause.

Defend the nation. At age 18, all young men must report their name, age, and address to the government. In time of war, the government may draft, or choose, them to serve in the armed forces. Some young citizens feel the duty to enlist in, or join, the military on their own.

Biking for the March of Dimes *Responsibilities of citizens include helping others. Here, volunteers take part in a bike-a-thon to raise money for medical research.* **Citizenship** *What can you do to help others in your community?*

SECTION 5 REVIEW

1. **Define:** due process of law.
2. What are the five basic freedoms guaranteed by the First Amendment?
3. What does the Fourteenth Amendment guarantee?
4. List three responsibilities of citizenship.
5. **CRITICAL THINKING Applying Information** Why has the Fourteenth Amendment been called the "nationalization" of the Bill of Rights?

ACTIVITY **Writing to Learn**
Select an issue in the news today. Write a newspaper editorial taking a position on that issue.

Summary

- The people have established the Constitution to achieve five major goals: form a more perfect union, establish justice, ensure domestic tranquillity, provide for the common defense, and promote the general welfare.
- The Constitution is based on five important principles that support a strong but limited national government.
- The Constitution is a living document that has been adapted to changes in the nation through formal and informal methods.
- The three branches of the national government work together to achieve a government of laws.
- The Constitution extends basic rights to all citizens, but citizens must assume responsibilities to safeguard their rights.

Reviewing the Main Ideas

1. List two goals of the Constitution. Describe one way that the national government helps to achieve each goal.
2. List the branches of the national government. Describe the role of each branch.
3. How can the President and the Supreme Court check the power of Congress to pass laws?
4. Describe two methods of proposing an amendment to the Constitution.
5. Describe two ways that the nonspecific language of the Constitution has allowed informal changes.
6. (a) Describe standing committees and joint committees. (b) What task does a conference committee have?
7. What three powers enable the President to direct foreign policy?
8. How did the Fourteenth and Fifteenth amendments pave the way for a major expansion of individual rights?

Thinking About the Constitution

1. **Linking Past and Present** Are the goals of the nation today the same as those set out in the Preamble? Explain.
2. **Synthesizing Information** How are the principles of popular sovereignty and limited government related?
3. **Defending a Position** Do you think the amendment process should be made simpler? Explain your answer.
4. **Analyzing Information** Former Chief Justice Hughes said, "We are under a Constitution, but the Constitution is what the judges say it is." What do you think Hughes meant?
5. **Comparing** Describe the differences between district courts and circuit courts. Which are the higher courts?
6. **Evaluating Information** What are the advantages and disadvantages of the process that a bill must go through to become a law?

Applying Your Skills

1. **Outlining** Review the outlining steps you learned on page 28. Then outline the section Five Principles of the Constitution, which begins on page 219.
2. **Reading a Chart** Review the chart on page 221. (a) Name three powers delegated to the national government. (b) Name three powers shared by the national government and state governments.
3. **Reading a Chart** Review the chart on page 232. Write a paragraph about Supreme Court Justices based on information in the chart.
4. **Ranking** Review the subsection The President Has Several Roles, beginning on page 232. List the roles of the President. Then rank the roles in order of importance. Explain your ranking.

Participating in Democracy

Form into groups to review the Constitution. Follow the suggestions below to write, draw, or perform to show what you have learned about the government that the Constitution set up. You may use the textbook, encyclopedias, atlases, or other materials in your classroom library to complete the tasks. Be able to name your sources of information when you have finished the activity.

ARTISTS Review the discussion of the national government in the Civics Overview. Then create a comic book for younger students explaining the three branches of government set up by the Constitution. Be sure to include information about the separation of powers and the system of checks and balances.

GOVERNMENT LEADERS Organize a debate on a proposal for a new constitutional amendment. You might examine the idea of limiting the President to a single six-year term, or you may choose a proposal of your own.

ACTORS Find out more about what happens in a federal court trial. Then conduct a mock trial. Assign students to play the parts of attorneys, judge, members of the jury, witnesses, and so on.

WRITERS Write a short story about what might happen if people had no political rights. You might set the story in an imaginary place or in the United States in the future.

Voting

CITIZENS Exercise your rights and responsibilities by writing a letter to a representative in Congress about a national issue on which you have strong feelings.

★ Hold a class Participating in Democracy workshop. Use your completed projects as the focus of the event.

Celebrating the Constitution

The New Republic

T he new republic faced many challenges. However,
economic and political growth and a good
showing in the War of 1812 gave Americans a
sense of national pride. Here, boats move along the new
Erie Canal.

The New Government Begins

(1789–1800)

1789 *George Washington, hero of the Revolution, was inaugurated as the first President of the United States.*

1791 *The Bank of the United States was set up to handle the finances of the new nation.*

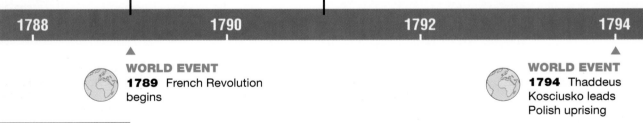

1788   1790   1792   1794

WORLD EVENT
1789 French Revolution begins

WORLD EVENT
1794 Thaddeus Kosciusko leads Polish uprising

Chapter Setting

To most Americans, George Washington was a great hero. After all, he had led the nation to independence. Americans welcomed his election as their first President. In a biography of Washington, Mason Weems describes the excited crowds that greeted Washington as he rode to New York City to take the oath of office:

66 As soon as it was officially notified to him, in the spring of 1789, that he was unanimously elected President of the United States...he set out for [New York]. Then all along the roads where he passed ...it was only said, 'General Washington is coming.'...The inhabitants all hastened from their houses to the highways, to get a sight of their great countryman; while the people of the towns, hearing of his approach, sallied out...to meet him. In eager throngs, men, women and children pressed upon his steps. 99

As President, Washington faced difficult tasks both at home and abroad. In all recorded history, no republican form of government had survived for long. Washington and other American leaders knew that the odds of creating a successful republic were against them. Washington was the first President of a new nation that many people—especially the British—thought would fail.

The decisions made by the country's first two Presidents, George Washington and John Adams, set the young nation on a firm foundation. Thanks in part to their actions, the United States would become a strong republic and a model for nations around the world.

ACTIVITY Imagine that George Washington was planning to visit the United States today. Prepare a short skit to show him some major differences between life in his time and life today.

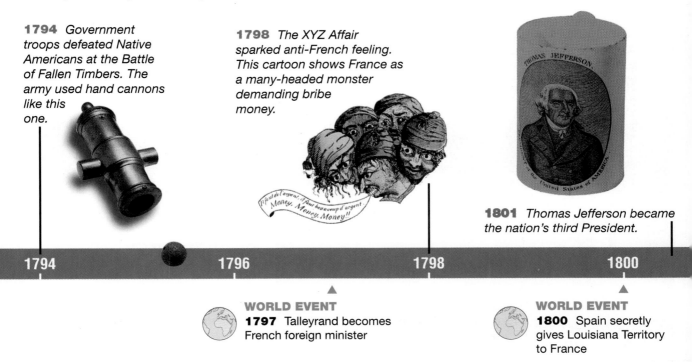

1794 *Government troops defeated Native Americans at the Battle of Fallen Timbers. The army used hand cannons like this one.*

1798 *The XYZ Affair sparked anti-French feeling. This cartoon shows France as a many-headed monster demanding bribe money.*

1801 *Thomas Jefferson became the nation's third President.*

1794   1796   1798   1800

WORLD EVENT
1797 Talleyrand becomes French foreign minister

WORLD EVENT
1800 Spain secretly gives Louisiana Territory to France

Organizing the New Government

FIND OUT

- Why were Washington's actions as President so important to the future of the United States?
- How did Hamilton propose to pay government debts and strengthen the economy?
- Why did some groups oppose Hamilton's economic plans?

VOCABULARY precedent, Cabinet, bond, national debt, speculator, tariff, protective tariff

When Congress met for the first time in the spring of 1789, Vice President John Adams brought up a curious question. How should people address the President of the United States?

For weeks, members of Congress debated the issue. Some felt the title "President Washington" was just fine. Others thought it lacked dignity. They tried out titles like "His Elective Highness" or "His Highness the President of the United States and Protector of the Rights of the Same."

The debate ended when Washington let Congress know he was content with "President of the United States." The lawmakers had taken three weeks to settle this small issue. They intended to carefully examine each of their actions as the new government took shape.

President Washington

George Washington took the oath of office on April 30, 1789. He looked "grave, almost to sadness," reported one witness. Washington no doubt was feeling the awesome weight of office. Americans looked to him to make the new government work.

Setting an example. As the first President, Washington knew he was setting an example for future generations. "There is scarcely any part of my conduct," he said, "which may not hereafter be drawn into precedent." A precedent (PREHS uh dehnt) is an act or decision that sets an example for others to follow. (☐ See "Jefferson Describes Washington" on page 566.)

During his two terms in office, Washington set many precedents. In 1796, he decided not to run for a third term. His refusal to seek a third term set a precedent that later Presidents followed until 1940.

The First President *Crowds cheered George Washington as he arrived in New York City to be inaugurated as the nation's first President. The button above was issued to celebrate the inauguration.* **Citizenship** *Why did Americans have confidence in President Washington?*

The first Cabinet. The Constitution said little about how the executive branch should be organized. It was clear, however, that the President needed people to help him carry out his duties. When the first Congress met in 1789, it created five executive departments. They were the departments of State, Treasury, and War and the offices of Attorney General and Postmaster General.

Washington chose well-known leaders to head these departments. He appointed Thomas Jefferson as Secretary of State and Alexander Hamilton as Secretary of the Treasury. Henry Knox served as Secretary of War. The Attorney General was Edmund Randolph, and Samuel Osgood became Postmaster General. These department heads made up the President's Cabinet. Members of the Cabinet gave Washington advice and directed their departments.

The federal court system. The Constitution called for a Supreme Court. Congress, however, had to organize the federal court system. In 1789, Congress passed the *Judiciary Act.* It called for the Supreme Court to have one Chief Justice and five Associate Justices.* Washington named John Jay as the first Chief Justice of the Supreme Court.

The Judiciary Act also set up district courts and circuit courts across the nation. Decisions made in these lower courts could be appealed to the Supreme Court, the highest court in the land.

Hamilton and the National Debt

As Secretary of the Treasury, Alexander Hamilton wanted to build a strong economy. He faced many major problems, however. Among the most pressing was the large government debt.

Government bonds. During the Revolution, both the national government and the individual states needed money to pay

soldiers and buy supplies. They borrowed money from foreign countries and ordinary citizens.

Then, as now, governments borrowed money by issuing bonds. A bond is a certificate that promises to repay the money loaned plus interest on a certain date. For example, if a person buys a bond for $100, the government agrees to pay back $100 plus interest in five or ten years. The total sum of money a government owes is called the national debt.

By 1789, most southern states had paid off their debts from the Revolution. Other states and the federal government had not. Hamilton insisted that all these debts be repaid. After all, he said, who would lend money to the United States in the future if the country did not pay its old debts?

Plan for repayment. Hamilton developed a plan to repay both the national and state debts. He wanted to buy up all bonds issued by the national and state governments before 1789. He planned to sell new bonds to pay off those old debts. When the economy improved, the government would be able to pay off the new bonds.

Opposition to Hamilton's Plan

Many people, including bankers and investors, welcomed Hamilton's plan. Others attacked it.

Linking Past and Present
Early in his first term, Washington went to the Senate to gain approval of a treaty with the Creek Indians. After a brief debate, the senators set up a committee to study the issue. Washington returned in a few days, and the senators debated again. Disgusted, Washington never returned to the Senate chamber. Instead, he sent written messages—a precedent that still guides Presidents today.

---

*Today, the Supreme Court has eight Associate Justices.

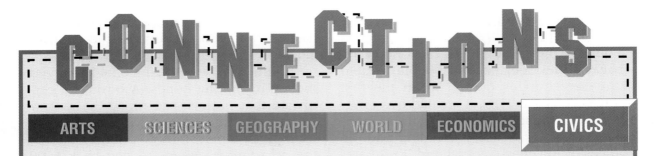

First Lady of the Land

The people do not elect them. The Constitution does not define their job. Yet more than 30 women have served the United States in this crucial position. They are the First Ladies.

When Martha Washington became the first First Lady, no one knew exactly what she should do. There had never been a First Lady before. What should she be called, Americans wondered. "The Presidentress"? "Lady President"? "Lady Washington"? All of these were tried. It was not until nearly a century later that "First Lady" came into common use.

Martha Washington decided that her main job as First Lady was to serve as hostess for the President. She regularly entertained guests at dinners and afternoon gatherings. She kept these affairs formal. She wanted guests, especially Europeans, to take the new country and its President seriously. Entertaining foreign leaders and other important people remains an important task of the First Lady today.

Martha Washington also believed that the First Lady should serve the public in some way. She took up the cause of needy veterans of the Revolution. In later years, First Ladies continued to work for causes, such as the environment, education, or health care.

Each First Lady has brought her own interests and personality to the job. Some enjoyed the excitement of the position. Others became important advisers to their husbands in office. All of them helped to define the position that has been called "the most demanding unpaid, unelected job in America."

Martha Washington

■ How did Martha Washington view her responsibility as First Lady?

Martha Washington's slippers

Greeting guests at a reception

Madison leads the opposition. James Madison led the opposition to Hamilton's plan. Madison argued that the plan was unfair because it would reward speculators. A *speculator* is someone willing to invest in a risky venture in the hope of making a large profit.

During the Revolution, the government had paid soldiers and citizens who supplied goods with bonds. Many of these bondholders needed cash to survive. They sold their bonds to speculators. Speculators paid only 10 or 15 cents for bonds that had an original, or face, value of one dollar.

If the government repaid the bonds at face value, speculators stood to make great fortunes. Madison thought that speculators did not deserve to make such profits.

Hamilton disagreed. The country must repay its bonds in full, he said, to gain the trust and help of investors. The support of investors, he argued, was crucial for building the new nation's economy. After much debate, Hamilton convinced Congress to accept his plan of repaying the national debt.

As a southerner, Madison also led the fight against another part of Hamilton's plan. It called for repaying state debts. But many southern states had already paid their debts. They thought other states should also pay for their own debts. So they bitterly opposed Hamilton's proposal.

Hamilton's compromise. To win support, Hamilton suggested a compromise. He knew that many southerners wanted to move the nation's capital to the South. He offered to persuade his northern friends to vote for a capital in the South if the southerners supported the repayment of state debts.

Madison and other southerners accepted this compromise. In July 1790, Congress passed bills taking over state debts and providing for a new capital city. (See "Great Little Madison" on page 568.)

The capital would not be part of any state. Instead, it would be on land along the Potomac River between Maryland and Virginia. Congress called the area the District of Columbia. Today, it is known as Washington, D.C. Congress hoped the new capital

BIOGRAPHY **Benjamin Banneker** *Benjamin Banneker was an astronomer, farmer, mathematician, and surveyor. As a boy, he taught himself mathematics and astronomy. Years later, George Washington appointed him to help lay out the boundaries of the new capital city, shown in the map below.* **Multicultural Heritage** *How did Banneker make a lasting contribution to the United States?*

would be ready by 1800. Meanwhile, the nation's capital was moved to Philadelphia.

Strengthening the Economy

Hamilton had resolved the problem of the national debt. Now he took steps to build up the new nation's economy.

A national bank. Hamilton called on Congress to set up a national bank. In 1791, Congress passed a bill setting up the *Bank of the United States.* The government deposited the money it collected in taxes in the Bank. The Bank, in turn, issued paper money. The government used the paper money to pay its bills. The Bank also made loans to farmers and businesses, helping them to expand.

Protecting the nation's industries. Hamilton also wanted to give American manufacturing a boost. He proposed that Congress pass a tariff, or tax, on all foreign goods brought into the country. Hamilton called for a very high tariff. He wanted to make imported goods more expensive to buy than goods made in the United States. Because such a tariff would protect American industry from foreign competition, it was called a protective tariff.

In the North, where factories were growing, many people supported Hamilton's plan. Southern farmers, however, bought more imported goods than northerners did. They did not want a tariff that would make these goods more expensive.

In the end, Congress did pass a tariff bill. However, it was meant to raise money for operating the government, not to protect American industries. For this reason, it was much lower than the protective tariff called for by Hamilton.

The Whiskey Tax

New taxes also created tensions in the backcountry. In 1791, Congress taxed all liquor made and sold in the United States. Settlers in the backcountry exploded in anger.

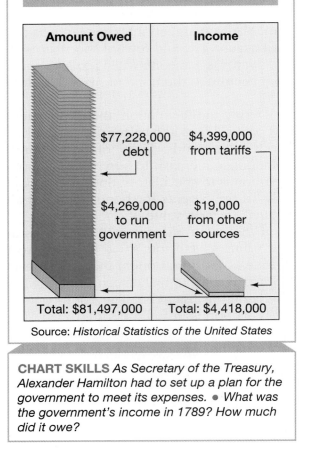

Money Problems of the New Nation, 1789–1791

Amount Owed	Income
$77,228,000 debt	$4,399,000 from tariffs
$4,269,000 to run government	$19,000 from other sources
Total: $81,497,000	Total: $4,418,000

Source: *Historical Statistics of the United States*

CHART SKILLS *As Secretary of the Treasury, Alexander Hamilton had to set up a plan for the government to meet its expenses.* ● *What was the government's income in 1789? How much did it owe?*

Like many Americans, backcountry farmers grew corn. Corn was bulky to haul over rough backcountry roads. Instead, farmers turned their corn into whiskey, which they could easily ship in barrels to markets in the East.

Backcountry farmers loudly protested the whiskey tax. They compared it to the hated taxes Britain had forced on the colonies in the 1760s. Many refused to pay the tax. A backcountry poet wrote:

66Some chaps whom freedom's
  spirit warms
Are threatening hard to take up
  arms. . . .
Their liberty they will maintain,
They fought for't, and they'll fight
  again. 99

The Whiskey Rebellion

When tax collectors appeared in western Pennsylvania to enforce the new law, they faced angry farmers. Some tax collectors, like John Neville, were treated harshly.

One spring morning, Neville and his wife were heading home from Pittsburgh. Mrs. Neville's saddle began to slip off her horse. Neville stopped to adjust it. Behind him, he heard the clip-clop of an approaching horse. A voice called out:

"Are you Neville, the tax collector?"

Still busy with his wife's saddle, Neville replied without turning round. "Yes, I'm Neville," he said.

"Then I must give you a whipping!" shouted the stranger. He grabbed Neville by the throat. The two men struggled. Finally, Neville threw his attacker to the ground and frightened him into running off. The incident showed Neville just how unpopular he was.

William Miller receives a summons. If the farmers refused to pay the whiskey tax, they were required to appear in distant federal courts. William Miller, a farmer who distilled whiskey, learned the hard way about the heavy hand of the law.

One hot July day in 1794, a stranger appeared at William Miller's door. The man said he was a sheriff from Philadelphia. He had come to serve legal papers on Miller. Next to the sheriff stood the hated tax collector, John Neville.

Miller read the summons. It ordered him to set aside "all manner of business and excuses" and appear before the court in little more than a month. To obey, Miller would have to make a long journey east. Even worse, the court papers seemed to say that he owed the government a tax of $250, a huge sum in those days. Later, Miller recalled his anger:

66 I felt myself mad with passion. I thought $250 would ruin me; and to have to go [to] the federal court at Philadelphia would keep me from going to Kentucky this fall [as I had planned]. . . . I felt my blood boil at seeing General Neville along to pilot the sheriff to my very door. 99

Farmers rebel. News quickly spread that a sheriff had come to take Miller to Philadelphia. Before long, angry farmers set out to find Neville and the sheriff. Some had muskets. Others had pitchforks. The sheriff and Neville fled.

Washington Reviews the Troops *When Pennsylvania farmers rioted against the whiskey tax, President Washington called out the state militias to restore order.* **Citizenship** *What role of the President does this painting illustrate?*

Next day, farmers and Neville met head-on. This time, Neville fired, killing a man. Several others were wounded.

Mobs formed elsewhere. Thousands of farmers marched through Pittsburgh. They set up Liberty Trees, sang Revolutionary songs, and tarred and feathered tax officials.

Government response. News of the **Whiskey Rebellion** spread quickly. Alexander Hamilton called the revolt "treason against society, against liberty, against everything that ought to be dear to a free, enlightened, and prudent people." President Washington quickly responded to this challenge to authority. He called up the militia in several states.

When the rebels heard that troops were coming, they scattered. The government's show of strength worked. The President's quick response to the Whiskey Rebellion proved to Americans that their new government would act firmly in times of crisis. ■

SECTION 1 REVIEW

1. **Identify:** (a) Judiciary Act, (b) Bank of the United States, (c) Whiskey Rebellion.
2. **Define:** (a) precedent, (b) Cabinet, (c) bond, (d) national debt, (e) speculator, (f) tariff, (g) protective tariff.
3. Describe a precedent set by Washington.
4. Why did Hamilton want to repay the national and state debts?
5. Describe two of Hamilton's ideas for strengthening the economy.
6. Why did some Americans oppose a protective tariff?
7. **CRITICAL THINKING Analyzing Ideas** Why do you think some Americans who had fought in the Revolution looked on the Whiskey Rebellion as "treason"?

ACTIVITY Writing to Learn
Imagine that you attended Washington's inauguration. Write a description of the event.

2
War Clouds

FIND OUT
- How did Americans respond to the French Revolution?
- What was the purpose of the Neutrality Proclamation?
- Why did fighting erupt in the Northwest Territory?
- What were the main ideas of Washington's Farewell Address?

Late in 1789, French ships arriving at American ports brought startling news. On July 14, a mob in Paris, France, had destroyed the Bastille (bahs TEEL), a huge fort that was used as a prison. The attack on the Bastille marked the beginning of the **French Revolution.**

The French Revolution broke out a few years after Americans won independence. Like the Americans, the French fought for liberty and equality. As the French Revolution grew more violent, however, it ignited political quarrels that had been smoldering in the United States.

Upheaval in France

The French had many reasons to rebel against their king, Louis XVI. Peasants and the middle class paid heavy taxes, while nobles paid none. Reformers called for a constitution to limit the power of the king. They also wanted a guarantee of rights like that in the American Constitution.

Americans support the revolution. At first, most Americans welcomed the French Revolution. They knew what it meant to struggle for liberty. Then, too, France had been America's first ally in the war against

The French Revolution *At first, Americans supported the French Revolution, but the violence split public opinion. Here, a group of French women march toward the palace of the king.* **United States and the World** *Why would the French expect Americans to support their revolution?*

Great Britain. Many Americans felt that they should rally behind the Marquis de Lafayette, a leading French reformer. After all, Lafayette had fought with them in the American Revolution.

In the 1790s, however, the French Revolution entered a very violent stage. A radical group gained power. In 1793, they beheaded Louis XVI and his family. During a "reign of terror" that swept the country, tens of thousands of French citizens were executed.

Violence divides opinion. The violence in France divided Americans. Thomas Jefferson and others condemned the killings. Still, they felt that the French people had the right to use violence to win freedom. Later, Jefferson even said that he was willing to see "half the earth devastated" in order to win the "liberty of the whole."

Alexander Hamilton, John Adams, and others disagreed. They thought the French Revolution was doomed to fail. The French could no more create a democracy in that way, claimed Adams, "than a snowball can exist in the streets of Philadelphia under a burning sun."

A Policy of Neutrality

The French Revolution shocked rulers and nobles across Europe. They feared the spread of revolutionary ideas to their own lands. With this in mind, Britain, Austria, Prussia, the Netherlands, and Spain sent armies to overpower the revolutionaries in France. Europe was soon plunged into a war that continued on and off from 1792 to 1815.

The war in Europe threatened to involve the United States. In 1778, the United States and France signed a treaty that allowed French ships to use American ports. Now, the French wanted to use American ports to supply their ships and attack British ships.

Washington faced a difficult decision. He wanted to remain neutral. "It is the sincere wish of United America," said the President, "to have nothing to do with...the squabbles of European nations." How could the United States honor its treaty with France and still avoid war?

That question deepened divisions within Washington's Cabinet. Both Hamilton and

Jefferson wanted to avoid war. They disagreed, however, about how to do this.

After much debate, Washington issued the **Neutrality Proclamation** in April 1793. It stated that the United States would not support either side in the war. It also forbade Americans to aid either Britain or France in any way.

An Unpopular Treaty

Declaring neutrality was easier than enforcing it. American merchants wanted to trade with both Britain and France. However, those warring nations ignored the rights of neutral ships. They seized American cargoes headed for each other's ports.

In 1793, the British captured more than 250 American ships trading in the French West Indies. Americans clamored for war. Washington, however, knew that the United States was too weak to fight. He sent Chief Justice John Jay to Britain for talks.

Jay worked out a treaty. It called for Britain to pay damages for American ships seized in 1793. At the same time, Americans had to pay debts to British merchants, owed from before the Revolution. Britain agreed to give up forts it still held in the Ohio Valley. The treaty did not, however, protect the rights of neutral American ships to trade where they wanted.

Jay's Treaty sparked a storm of protest. Many Americans felt they were giving up more than Britain was. After a furious debate, the Senate finally approved the treaty in 1795. Washington accepted the treaty because he wanted to avoid war. "Such is the popularity of the President," noted Jefferson, "that the people will support him in whatever he will do."

War in the West

On the western frontier, the President faced another crisis. Thousands of white settlers moved into the Northwest Territory in the 1790s. The newcomers ignored treaties the United States had signed with the Indian nations of that region. They simply took over Indian lands.

Spreading conflict. Native Americans responded to the invasion by attacking settlers and traders. White settlers took revenge. Often, they killed Indians who had not taken part in the attacks. The violence soon spread.

In 1791, the Miamis in Ohio joined with other Indian nations. Little Turtle, a skilled fighter, led the Miami nation. Armed with muskets and gunpowder supplied by the British, the Miamis drove white settlers from the area.

President Washington sent an army under General Arthur St. Clair to Ohio. Little Turtle and the Miamis defeated St. Clair's army. Frustrated, Washington replaced St. Clair with General Anthony Wayne.

Battle of Fallen Timbers. In 1794, Wayne marched a well-trained army into Miami territory. Blue Jacket, a Shawnee leader who served under Little Turtle, gathered the Native American forces at Fallen Timbers. Blue Jacket thought that Wayne would have trouble fighting there because the land was covered with fallen trees. But Wayne's forces pushed through the tangle of logs and defeated the Indians.

In 1795, the Miamis and 11 other Indian nations signed the **Treaty of Greenville** with the United States. In it, they gave up land that would later become the southern half of Ohio. In return, the Indian nations received $20,000 and the promise of more money if they kept the peace.

Our Common Heritage
Although they were defeated at Fallen Timbers, the Miami Indians are honored in southwestern Ohio. Miami County, the city of Miamisburg, the town of New Miami, and Miami University were named for them.

Treaty of Greenville *In the Treaty of Greenville, Native Americans agreed to give up the southern half of present-day Ohio for about ⅛ cent per acre. Here, Indian leaders meet with General Wayne to discuss the terms of the treaty, shown at right.* **Linking Past and Present** *How do you think future generations of Indians viewed the terms of the treaty?*

Washington Retires

By 1796, Washington had weathered many crises. He had kept the nation out of war and set it on a path of growth. That year, he published his *Farewell Address.* In it, he announced he would retire. He urged that the United States remain neutral in its relations with other countries:

> ❝Observe good faith and justice toward all nations. Cultivate peace and harmony with all. . . . Nothing is more essential than that permanent, [habitual hatred] against particular nations and passionate attachments for others should be excluded.❞

Washington warned Americans to avoid becoming involved in European affairs. " 'Tis our true policy to steer clear of permanent alliances with any portion of the foreign world," said the retiring President. Such alliances, he felt, would pull the United States into war. That advice guided American foreign policy for many years.

Washington further called on Americans to avoid political parties. During his years in office, rival groups had grown up around Hamilton and Jefferson. Americans in different regions had diverse interests. Once Washington left office, those differences began to grow.

SECTION 2 REVIEW

1. **Identify:** (a) French Revolution, (b) Neutrality Proclamation, (c) Jay's Treaty, (d) Treaty of Greenville, (e) Farewell Address.
2. Why were Americans divided in their reaction to the French Revolution?
3. Why did Washington issue the Neutrality Proclamation?
4. How did Britain and France respond to the Neutrality Proclamation?
5. What events led to the Battle of Fallen Timbers?
6. **CRITICAL THINKING Analyzing Information** How did location help the United States to "steer clear of permanent alliances" with European nations for many years?

ACTIVITY **Writing to Learn**
Write a series of five headlines that highlight the crises Washington faced in the 1790s.

3

Rise of Political Parties

FIND OUT

- Why did political parties form in the United States?
- How did Hamilton and Jefferson differ on major issues?
- How did newspapers influence the growth of political parties?
- Why did the election of 1796 increase political tensions?

VOCABULARY unconstitutional

Divisions in Congress worried Thomas Jefferson in the 1790s. Backers of Hamilton argued with supporters of Jefferson and James Madison. Jefferson described the unpleasant mood:

66Men who have been [friends] all their lives cross streets to avoid meeting, and turn their heads another way, lest they should be obliged to touch their hats.99

The split had occurred gradually since 1789. When Washington first took office, the country had no political parties. By the time he retired, there were two parties competing for power.

A Distrust of Political Parties

Most Americans distrusted political parties. They had seen how political parties worked in Britain. There, party members were more interested in personal gain than in the public good.

Americans also saw parties as a threat to unity. They agreed with George Washington, who warned that parties would lead to "jealousies and false alarms."

Despite the President's warning, parties grew up around two of his advisers: Alexander Hamilton and Thomas Jefferson. The two men differed in looks and personality as well as in politics. Hamilton was of medium height and slender. He dressed in fine clothes and spoke forcefully. Energetic, brilliant, and restless, Hamilton enjoyed political debate.

Jefferson was tall and a bit gawky. Although he was a wealthy Virginia planter, he dressed and spoke informally. As one senator recalled:

66His clothes seem too small for him. He sits in a lounging manner, on one hip commonly, and with one of his shoulders elevated much above the other. His face has a sunny aspect. His whole figure has a loose, shackling air. . . . He spoke almost without ceasing. [His conversation] was loose and rambling; and yet he scattered information wherever he went.99

Differing Views

Hamilton and Jefferson did not agree on many issues. At the root of their quarrels were different views about what was best for the country.

Manufacturing or farming? Hamilton thought the United States should model itself on Britain. He wanted the government

---

History and You

During recent elections, candidates for President and Vice President have tried to win the support of young voters by appearing for interviews on a music video television network. What are some other ways in which political parties could capture your support for their candidates?

A Nation of Farmers *Thomas Jefferson believed the nation's strength rested with small, independent farmers, such as those in this painting by Edward Hicks.* **Citizenship** *How did this differ from Hamilton's vision of the nation?*

to encourage trade and manufacturing. He also favored the growth of cities.

Jefferson believed that farmers were the backbone of the new nation. "Cultivators of the earth," he wrote, "are the most valuable citizens." He feared that a manufacturing economy would corrupt the United States. "Let our workshops remain in Europe," Jefferson urged. "The mobs of the great cities add just so much to the support of pure government, as sores do to the strength of the human body."

Federal or state governments? Hamilton and Jefferson disagreed about the power of the federal government. Hamilton wanted the federal government to have more power than state governments. Jefferson thought the opposite. He feared that the federal government might take over powers that the Constitution gave to the states.

Strict or loose interpretation? The two leaders also clashed over the Bank of the United States. Jefferson opposed Hamilton's

plan for the Bank. He said it gave too much power to the federal government and the wealthy investors who helped run it. Jefferson said that the law creating the Bank was unconstitutional, that is, not permitted by the Constitution.

Jefferson objected to the Bank because he interpreted the Constitution very strictly. Nowhere did the Constitution give Congress the power to create a Bank, he argued. He thought that any power not specifically given to the federal government belonged to the states.

Hamilton interpreted the Constitution more loosely. The Constitution gave Congress the power to make all laws "necessary and proper" to carry out its duties. Hamilton argued that the Bank was necessary for the government to collect taxes and pay its bills.

Britain or France? Finally, Hamilton and Jefferson had different ideas about foreign policy. Hamilton wanted to form close ties with Britain, an important trading partner.

CRITICAL THINKING SKILLS
Distinguishing Fact From Opinion

Primary sources—such as letters, diaries, and speeches—often express the opinions of the people who wrote them. Therefore, when historians study primary sources, they have to distinguish fact from opinion. A *fact* is something that can be proved or observed. An *opinion* is a judgment that reflects a person's beliefs or feelings. It may not always be true.

In the letter below, Alexander Hamilton writes about political differences between himself and the party led by James Madison and Thomas Jefferson. Like many writers, Hamilton combines fact and opinion. Read the letter, and distinguish fact from opinion.

1. **Determine which statements are facts.** Remember that facts can be proved. Use your reading in this chapter to help answer these questions. (a) Find two statements of fact in Hamilton's letter. (b) How can you prove that each statement is a fact?

2. **Determine which statements are opinions.** Writers often show that they are expressing an opinion by saying "in my view" or "I think" or "I believe." (a) Find two statements in which Hamilton gives his opinion. (b) How can you tell that each is an opinion?

3. **Determine how a writer mixes fact and opinion.** Reread the last sentence of the letter. (a) What did Hamilton mean by a "womanish attachment to France and a womanish resentment against Great Britain"? (b) Is it true that Jefferson supported France and opposed Britain? (c) What country did Hamilton want the United States to support? (d) Why do you think Hamilton mixed fact and opinion in the statement?

ACTIVITY Select an editorial from a recent newspaper. List the opinions expressed in the editorial. Underline the words that tell you these are opinions. Then, under each opinion list the facts the writers used to support it.

Alexander Hamilton wrote:

❝It was not until the last session of Congress that I became completely convinced that Mr. Madison and Mr. Jefferson are at the head of a faction that is hostile toward me. They are motivated by views that, in my judgment, will undermine the principles of good government and are dangerous to the peace and happiness of the country.

Freneau, the present publisher of the *National Gazette,* was a known Antifederalist. It is certain that he was brought to Philadelphia by Mr. Jefferson to be the publisher of a newspaper. At the same time as he was starting his paper, he was also a clerk in the Department of State. His paper is devoted to opposing me and the measures that I have supported. And the paper has a general unfriendly attitude toward the government of the United States.

On almost all questions, great and small, which have come up since the first session of Congress, Mr. Jefferson and Mr. Madison have been found among those who want to limit federal power. In respect to foreign policy, the views of these gentlemen are, in my judgment, equally unsound and dangerous. They have a womanish attachment to France and a womanish resentment against Great Britain.❞

Jefferson favored France, the first ally of the United States and a nation struggling for its own liberty.

Party Rivalry

At first, Hamilton and Jefferson clashed in private. When Congress began to pass Hamilton's programs, Jefferson and James Madison decided to organize public support for their views. They turned first to important New York leaders, including Governor George Clinton and Aaron Burr.

Republicans and Federalists. Soon, leaders in other states began to side with either Hamilton or Jefferson. Jefferson's supporters called themselves *Democratic Republicans.* They often shortened the name to Republicans.* Republicans included small farmers, craftsworkers, and some wealthy planters.

Hamilton and his supporters were called *Federalists* because they wanted a strong federal government. Federalists drew support from merchants and manufacturers in cities such as Boston and New York as well as from some southern planters. See the chart at right.

Newspapers begin to take sides. In the late 1700s, the number of American newspapers more than doubled—from about 100 to more than 230. They grew to meet the demand for information. A visitor from Europe noted with surprise that so many Americans could read.

66 The common people [there] are on a footing, in point of literature with the middle ranks of Europe. They all read and write, and understand arithmetic; almost every little town now furnishes a circulating library. 99

---

*Jefferson's Republican party was not the same as today's Republican party. In fact, his party later grew into the Democratic party.

The First Political Parties

Federalists	Republicans
1. Led by A. Hamilton	1. Led by T. Jefferson
2. Wealthy and well educated should lead nation	2. People should have political power
3. Strong central government	3. Strong state governments
4. Emphasis on manufacturing, shipping, and trade	4. Emphasis on agriculture
5. Loose interpretation of Constitution	5. Strict interpretation of Constitution
6. Pro-British	6. Pro-French
7. Favored national bank	7. Opposed national bank
8. Favored protective tariff	8. Opposed protective tariff

CHART SKILLS *By the 1790s, two political parties had formed—the Federalist party and the Republican party. • Who led each party? What were two ways in which the parties differed on economic issues?*

Newspaper publishers lined up behind the parties. In the *Gazette of the United States,* publisher John Fenno backed Alexander Hamilton. Thomas Jefferson's friend Philip Freneau (frih NOH) started a rival paper, the *National Gazette.* He vigorously supported Republicans.

Newspapers had great influence on public opinion. In stinging language, they raged against opponents. Often, articles mixed rumor and opinion with facts. Emotional attacks and counterattacks fanned the flames of party rivalry. Yet, they also kept people informed and helped shape public opinion.

A Slim Victory

Political parties played an important part in choosing George Washington's successor. In 1796, Republicans backed Thomas Jefferson for President and Aaron Burr for Vice President. Federalists supported John Adams for President and Thomas Pinckney for Vice President.

The election had an unexpected outcome, which created new tensions. Under the Constitution, the person with the most electoral votes became President. The person with the next highest total was made Vice President. John Adams, a Federalist, won office as President. The leader of the Republicans, Thomas Jefferson, came in second and became Vice President.

With the President and Vice President from different parties, political tensions remained high. Events would fuel the distrust between the two men. Meanwhile, Adams took office in March 1797 as the second President of the United States.

SECTION 3 REVIEW

1. **Identify:** (a) Democratic Republicans, (b) Federalists.
2. **Define:** unconstitutional.
3. Why did many Americans distrust political parties?
4. On what four issues did Hamilton and Jefferson disagree?
5. How did newspapers contribute to rivalry between the two parties?
6. What role did political parties play in the election of 1796?
7. **CRITICAL THINKING** **Drawing Conclusions** Why do you think political parties emerged even though many Americans opposed them?

ACTIVITY Writing to Learn

Write a campaign slogan for each of the candidates in the 1796 election.

4
John Adams as President

FIND OUT
- Why did many Americans want to declare war on France?
- Why did Adams lose the support of Federalists?
- What were the Alien and Sedition acts?

VOCABULARY alien, sedition, nullify

Late in life, John Adams wrote his autobiography. He knew that Washington, Franklin, and Jefferson were more widely admired than he was. To counter this, he wrote proudly of his work:

66 I have done more labor, run through more and greater dangers, and made greater sacrifices than any man. . .living or dead, in the service of my country. 99

Still, Adams found it hard to boast of his achievements. In the end, he concluded: "I am not, never was, and never shall be a great man."

Neither statement was completely true. Although he was not a popular hero, Adams was an honest, able leader. As President, he tried to act in the best interests of the nation, even if it hurt him politically.

The XYZ Affair

No sooner did Adams take office than he faced a crisis with France. The French objected to Jay's Treaty between the United States and Britain. In 1797, French ships began to seize American ships in the West Indies, as the British had done.

The XYZ Affair *The French demand for tribute outraged Americans. In the cartoon above, grinning French agents rob "Madame Amerique" and even pluck the feathers from her hat. Despite the furor over the XYZ Affair, President John Adams, at right, resisted demands to go to war with France.* **United States and the World** *What events led to the XYZ Affair?*

Once again, Americans called for war—this time against France. Adams tried to avoid war by sending diplomats to Paris to discuss the rights of neutrals.

"Not a sixpence!" The French foreign minister, Charles Maurice de Talleyrand, would not deal directly with the Americans. Instead, he sent three secret agents to offer the Americans a deal.

"You must pay money," the agents said. "You must pay a great deal of money." Before Talleyrand would begin talks, he wanted $250,000 for himself and a loan to France of $10 million. "Not a sixpence!" replied one of the American diplomats.

The diplomats informed the President about the bribe. Adams, in turn, told Congress. He did not reveal the names of the French agents, referring to them only as X, Y, and Z.

When Americans heard about the ***XYZ Affair*** in 1798, they were outraged. They took up the slogan, "Millions for defense, but not one cent for tribute!" They were willing to spend money to defend their country, but they refused to pay a bribe to another nation.

Adams avoids war. Despite growing pressure, Adams refused to ask Congress to declare war on France. He did, however, strengthen the American navy. Shipyards built frigates—fast-sailing ships with many guns. This show of strength convinced France to stop attacking American ships. Talleyrand also assured Adams that he would treat American diplomats with respect.

The Federalist Party Splits

Many Federalists, led by Alexander Hamilton, criticized Adams's peace policy. They hoped a war would weaken Jefferson and the Republicans, longtime friends of France. War would also force the United States to build up its army and navy. A stronger military would mean increased federal power, which was a major Federalist goal.

Although John Adams was a Federalist, he would not give in to Hamilton. Their disagreement created a split in the Federalist party. Hamilton and his supporters were called *High Federalists.*

Over Hamilton's opposition, Adams again sent diplomats to France. When they arrived, they found a young army officer, Napoleon Bonaparte, in charge. Napoleon was eager to expand French power in Europe. He did not have time for a war with the United States. Napoleon signed the *Convention of 1800.* In this agreement, he promised to stop seizing American ships in the West Indies.

Like Washington, Adams kept the nation out of war. His success, however, cost him the support of many Federalists.

Alien and Sedition Acts

During the crisis with France, High Federalists pushed through several laws in Congress. Passed in 1798, the laws were known as the Alien and Sedition acts.

The *Alien Act* allowed the President to expel any alien, or foreigner, thought to be dangerous to the country. Another law made it harder for people to become citizens. Before, white people could become citizens after living in the United States for 5 years. Now, they had to wait 14 years. This law was meant to keep new arrivals from voting—often for Republicans.

Republican anger grew when Congress passed the *Sedition Act.* Sedition means stirring up rebellion against a government. Under this law, citizens could be fined or jailed if they criticized the government or its officials.

Republicans protested that the Sedition Act violated the Constitution. After all, the First Amendment protected freedom of speech and the press. The new law would make it a crime "to laugh at the cut of a congressman's coat, [or] to give dinner to a Frenchman," said one Republican.

Under the new law, several Republican newspaper editors, and even members of Congress, were fined and jailed for their opinions. Jefferson warned that the new laws threatened American liberties:

> 66 If this goes down, we shall immediately see attempted another act of Congress, declaring that the President shall continue in office during life, and after that other laws giving both the President and the Congress life terms in office. 99

The Rights of States

Republicans believed that the Alien and Sedition acts were unconstitutional. They did not turn to the Supreme Court, however, because most justices were Federalists.

Instead, Jefferson urged the states to act. He argued that the states had the right to nullify, or cancel, a law passed by the federal government. In this way, states could resist the power of the federal government.

Helped by Jefferson and Madison, Kentucky and Virginia passed resolutions in 1798 and 1799. The *Kentucky and Virginia resolutions* claimed that each state "has an equal right to judge for itself" whether a law is constitutional. If a state decides a law is unconstitutional, it can nullify that law within its borders.

The Kentucky and Virginia resolutions raised a difficult question. Did a state have the right to decide on its own that a law was unconstitutional?

The question remained unanswered in Jefferson's lifetime. Before long, the Alien and Sedition acts were changed or dropped. But the issue of a state's right to nullify federal laws would come up again.

Linking Past and Present
In 1800, the United States took its second census. The total population numbered 5,308,483—less than the population of New York City today.

Election of 1800

By 1800, the fear of war with France had faded. As the election approached, Republicans hoped to sweep the Federalists from office. They focused on two issues. First, they attacked the Federalists for raising taxes to prepare for war. Second, they opposed the unpopular Alien and Sedition acts.

Republicans chose Jefferson to run for President and Aaron Burr for Vice President. Adams was the Federalist candidate.

A deadlock. In the race for President, the Republicans won. But when the electoral college voted, Jefferson and Burr each received 73 votes.

Under the Constitution, the House of Representatives decides an election in case of a tie vote. The House was evenly split. It voted 35 times. Each time, the vote was a tie.

The voting went on for four days. As an observer noted:

66The scene was ludicrous. Many had sent home for nightcaps and pillows, and wrapped in shawls and great-coats, lay about the floor of the committee-rooms, or sat sleeping in their seats. 99

Finally, the tie was broken. The House chose Jefferson as President. Burr became Vice President.

Congress then passed the Twelfth Amendment. It required electors to vote separately for President and Vice President. The states ratified the amendment in 1804.

Federalists lose favor. Jefferson's election marked the end of the Federalist era. After 1800, Federalists won fewer seats in Congress. In 1804, the Federalist leader, Alexander Hamilton, was killed in a duel with Aaron Burr.

Although it declined, the Federalist party had helped shape the new nation. President Adams kept the country out of war. Also, over time, Republican Presidents kept most of Hamilton's economic programs.

Victory Flag for Jefferson *The election of Thomas Jefferson in 1800 marked the end of the Federalist era. This hand-painted flag celebrates Jefferson's victory.* **Citizenship** *Why did American voters reject the Federalists in 1800?*

SECTION 4 REVIEW

1. **Identify:** (a) XYZ Affair, (b) High Federalists, (c) Convention of 1800, (d) Alien Act, (e) Sedition Act, (f) Kentucky and Virginia resolutions.
2. **Define:** (a) alien, (b) sedition, (c) nullify.
3. Why did many Americans want war with France in 1797?
4. What caused the split between Adams and High Federalists?
5. Why did Republicans oppose the Sedition Act?
6. **CRITICAL THINKING Applying Information** How did the Kentucky and Virginia resolutions reflect Jefferson's views on government?

ACTIVITY **Writing to Learn**
Choose new titles for Section 4 and its subsections. Write a sentence explaining each of your choices.

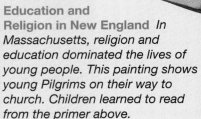

Education and Religion in New England *In Massachusetts, religion and education dominated the lives of young people. This painting shows young Pilgrims on their way to church. Children learned to read from the primer above.*

A Pause in the Day's Work *For enslaved African Americans, free time was rare. Here, a group of slaves enjoy a pause in the day's labor.*

Be My Valentine *Young people found some time for courtship. Many of the symbols on this valentine, such as hearts and Cupids, are still popular today.*

Apprentices at Work *Being an apprentice was hard work. For many boys, however, it was the only way to learn a craft or trade.*

Games of the Eastern Woodlands
Young Native Americans amused themselves with a variety of games. At right, two young Indians play "cat's cradle." The bowl and peach pits below were used for another game of skill, played by the Iroquois.

Sewing Sampler *Girls began learning skills such as needlecraft at a very early age. Young Abigail Purintunn spent many hours embroidering this finely detailed sampler.*

A Doll *It is hard to tell whether this doll was meant to be a child or an adult. Generally, the clothing worn by colonial children was just a smaller version of what their parents wore.*

Picturing the Past

Young Americans Before 1800

For people of all ages, life before 1800 tended to be a daily round of hard work. Like adults, young Americans did a variety of chores, such as churning butter, planting crops, and hunting wildlife. As for leisure, young Americans relied on their imagination for amusement, along with a variety of simple, often homemade, games and toys.

■ *Describe two ways your life would be different if you were growing up before 1800.*

Summary

- As the nation's first President, George Washington worked with Congress to organize the new government.
- The French Revolution divided public opinion, but Washington kept the United States out of war.
- Two political parties formed in the 1790s, representing opposing views on the economy, foreign policy, and the role of the federal government.
- The Federalist party split because President John Adams refused to declare war against France.

Reviewing the Main Ideas

1. Why did Alexander Hamilton support each of the following: (a) repayment of national and state debts, (b) national bank, (c) protective tariff?
2. What caused the Whiskey Rebellion?
3. What was the Neutrality Proclamation?
4. (a) What was one cause of the war in the Northwest Territory in the 1790s? (b) What was one result?
5. (a) How did political parties develop? (b) Who supported the Federalists? (c) Who supported the Republicans?
6. Describe two results of the XYZ Affair.
7. What important issue was raised by the Kentucky and Virginia resolutions?

Thinking Critically

1. **Linking Past and Present** (a) What advice did Washington give in his Farewell Address? (b) Do you think Americans today would agree with Washington? Explain your answer.
2. **Defending a Position** Do you think the Alien and Sedition acts were necessary to protect the nation? Explain.

3. **Synthesizing Information** What problems did the first Presidents face?

Applying Your Skills

1. **Skimming a Chapter** Skimming is reading quickly for the general idea. To skim a chapter in this book, first look at the list of section titles in the Chapter Outline. Next, look at the blue and boldface headings that show the main topics in each section. Finally, quickly read the first and last sentence of each paragraph.

   Skim the first half of Chapter 8 (pages 242–253). (a) What does the Chapter Outline tell you about chapter content? (b) List the main topics in the section War Clouds. (c) What do you think is the main idea of this section? Explain.
2. **Analyzing a Quotation** After George Washington became President, he said, "There is scarcely any part of my conduct which may not hereafter be drawn into precedent." What do you think Washington meant by this statement?

Thinking About Geography

Match the letters on the map with the following places: **1.** New York City, **2.** Philadelphia, **3.** Washington, D.C., **4.** Virginia, **5.** Kentucky. **Location** On what river is Washington, D.C., located?

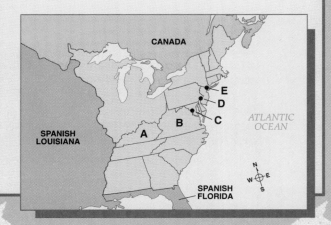

Election of 1800

Form into groups to review the election of 1800. Follow the suggestions below to write, draw, sing, or act to show what you have learned about this election. You may use the textbook, encyclopedias, atlases, or other materials in your classroom library to complete the tasks. Be able to name your sources of information when you have finished the activity.

WRITERS Form into two groups— *National Gazette* (Republicans) and *Gazette of the United States* (Federalists). Work with your group to prepare an issue of your newspaper. Your issue should include news articles, editorials, cartoons, and advertisements related to the election of 1800.

Newspaper mastheads

ECONOMISTS Make a chart comparing Federalist and Republican views about the nation's economy. Then make a list of questions you would ask each candidate about his economic views and how they would affect the nation.

ACTORS Review how the election of 1800 was finally decided after four days and 35 tie votes. Then prepare a skit about the voting in the House of Representatives. Representatives should present arguments to persuade other House members to support the candidate of their choice.

John Adams on a ceramic jar

ARTISTS Study the pictures on pages 244 and 261 to get an idea of how artists showed support for a political figure in the late 1700s and early 1800s. Then design a poster or a flag to support one of the candidates for President in the 1800 election.

MUSICIANS List the important issues in the election of 1800. Then make up a campaign song based on these issues. You may use a familiar tune or one you have composed. Perform your song for the class.

★ Plan an election rally in which each group presents or describes its completed activity.

Thomas Jefferson

CHAPTER **9**

The Jefferson Era

(1801–1816)

1804 *Lewis and Clark set out to explore the Louisiana Purchase. Clark used this compass to guide him during the journey.*

1805–1807 *The British navy seized thousands of American sailors and forced them to serve on British ships. Americans were enraged by this violation of their rights.*

1800	1802	1804	1806	1808

 WORLD EVENT
1800 France regains Louisiana Territory in treaty with Spain

WORLD EVENT
1803 France and Britain go to war

Chapter Setting

"Educate and inform the whole mass of the people. Enable them to see that it is their interest to preserve peace and order, and they will preserve them. . . . They are the only [ones to rely on] for the preservation of our liberty. . . . This reliance cannot deceive us, as long as we remain [good]; and I think we shall . . . as long as agriculture is our principal object. . . . When we get piled up on one another in large cities, as in Europe, we shall become corrupt as in Europe, and go to eating one another as they do there."

In this letter to James Madison, Thomas Jefferson expressed his faith in the American people. At that time, nearly nine out of ten Americans were farmers. This fact gave Jefferson confidence in the nation's future.

Jefferson, himself, came from a wealthy family. But he was convinced that ordinary people, especially farmers, would best preserve the nation's peace, order, and liberty.

As President, Jefferson sought to protect and expand the rights of these ordinary citizens. The Federalists, he believed, had worried too much about the wealthy few. Jefferson wanted to represent the farmers who formed the backbone of the nation. As he pursued this goal, Jefferson turned the nation in a new direction.

> **ACTIVITY** List the ways in which power might pass from one government to another. Then discuss why the peaceful passing of power from the Federalists to the Republicans was important to the future of the nation.

1810 *Shawnee leader Tecumseh, at right, warned settlers against taking over Indian lands.*

1815 *Andrew Jackson led the Americans to victory in the Battle of New Orleans.*

1812 *The Leni-Lenape, who fought on the American side in the War of 1812, received this pipe in recognition of their support.*

1808	1810	1812	1814	1816

WORLD EVENT
1814 Britain defeats France

Republicans in Power

FIND OUT
- What steps did Jefferson take to limit government power?
- Why did Federalists control the federal courts?
- Why was *Marbury* v. *Madison* important?

VOCABULARY democratic, laissez faire, judicial review

In 1801, Thomas Jefferson became the first President to be inaugurated in Washington, D.C., the nation's new capital. The city was located on swampy land near the Potomac River. Dense forests surrounded the area, and travel there was difficult.

Many visitors to Washington complained about its muddy streets and unfinished buildings. President Jefferson, however, was happy with the new capital. He believed that the success of the American republic signaled the dawning of a new age. It was only fitting, he thought, that the young nation should carve its new capital out of the wilderness.

A New Style of President

Jefferson brought new ideas to the capital. He strongly believed in the good sense of ordinary people, and he promised to make the government more democratic. Democratic means ensuring that all people have the same rights.

An informal air. Jefferson's personal style matched his democratic beliefs. The new President preferred quiet dinners to the formal parties that had been given by Washington and Adams. He wore casual clothes and greeted people by shaking hands instead of bowing. With his informal manner, Jefferson showed that the President was an ordinary citizen.

Easing Federalist fears. Some Federalists worried about how Jefferson would govern. In his inaugural address, he tried to quiet their fears. As a minority, Federalists "possess their equal rights, which equal laws must protect," he told the nation. He called for an end to the bitter political quarrels of past years. "We are all Republicans, we are all Federalists," the President said.

Republican changes. Jefferson had no plan to punish Federalists. He did, however, want to change their policies. In his view, the Federalists had made the national

BIOGRAPHY **Thomas Jefferson** *Thomas Jefferson, third President of the United States, was a man of wide-ranging talents and interests. An avid reader, Jefferson designed the revolving book stand, below, to hold as many as five books at once.* **Citizenship** *What were Jefferson's goals for the government?*

government too large and too powerful. To reduce government power, Jefferson wanted to cut the federal budget and lower taxes.

Jefferson believed in an idea known as laissez faire (lehs ay FAYR), from the French term for "let alone." According to laissez faire, government should play as small a role as possible in economic affairs. Laissez faire was very different from the Federalist idea of government. Alexander Hamilton, you recall, wanted government to promote trade, commerce, and manufacturing.

A Small and Simple Government

Jefferson chose a Cabinet that would help him reach his goals. He appointed Albert Gallatin as Secretary of the Treasury. A wizard at finances, Gallatin helped Jefferson cut government expenses.

For Secretary of State, Jefferson chose James Madison, his friend and Virginia neighbor. Madison had helped Jefferson build the Republican party. Like Jefferson, he believed that under the Federalists the national government had taken on powers that belonged to the states.

Limiting federal power. As President, Jefferson tried to reduce the role of government in people's lives. He decreased the size of government departments and cut the federal budget. With the approval of Congress, he reduced the size of the army and navy and halted construction of new naval ships. He also asked Congress to repeal the unpopular whiskey tax.

Linking Past and Present
When Thomas Jefferson became President in 1801, there were fewer than 1,000 federal employees. Today, the United States government employs more than 2 million people— not counting those in the armed services.

The Sedition Act had expired the day before Jefferson took office. Jefferson had hated the law, and he quickly pardoned those few men who were still in jail as a result of it. He also asked Congress to restore the five-year waiting period for foreign-born people who wanted to become citizens of the United States.

Some Federalist policies remain. Jefferson did not discard all Federalist programs, however. Secretary of the Treasury Gallatin convinced the President to keep the Bank of the United States. The federal government also continued to pay off state debts that it had taken over when Washington was President.

A Stronger Supreme Court

The election of 1800 had given Republicans control of Congress. Federalists, however, remained powerful in the courts.

Three months passed between election day and Jefferson's inauguration on March 4, 1801. During that time, Federalists in the old Congress passed a law increasing the number of federal judges. President Adams then appointed Federalists to fill these new positions.

John Marshall. Among the judges that Adams had appointed was John Marshall, Chief Justice of the Supreme Court. In some ways, Marshall was like Thomas Jefferson. He was a rich Virginia planter with a brilliant mind. Unlike Jefferson, however, Marshall was a staunch Federalist. He wanted to make the federal government stronger.

The framers of the Constitution expected the federal courts to balance the powers of the President and Congress. Yet John Marshall found the courts to be the weakest branch of government. In his view, it was not clear what powers the federal courts had. In 1803, Marshall decided a case that increased the power of the Supreme Court.

BIOGRAPHY John Marshall *John Marshall grew up in frontier Virginia and served in the American Revolution. Under his strong leadership as Chief Justice, the Supreme Court gained prestige and power.* **Citizenship** *How did Marshall's decision in* Marbury v. Madison *strengthen the power of the Supreme Court?*

A "midnight judge." Another judge appointed by Adams was William Marbury. Adams made the appointment on his last night as President. But before Marbury could take office, Adams's term ended.

The Republicans refused to accept this "midnight judge." They accused Federalists of using unfair tactics to keep control of the courts. Jefferson ordered Secretary of State Madison not to deliver the official papers confirming Marbury's appointment.

Marbury* v. *Madison. Marbury sued Madison. According to the Judiciary Act of 1789, only the Supreme Court could decide a case brought against a federal official. The case, therefore, was tried before the Supreme Court.

In the case of ***Marbury* v. *Madison,*** the Supreme Court ruled against Marbury. Chief Justice Marshall wrote the decision. He stated that the Judiciary Act was unconstitutional. Nowhere, he continued, did the Constitution give the Supreme Court the right to decide cases brought against federal officials. Therefore, Congress could not give the Court that power by passing the Judiciary Act.

The Supreme Court's decision in *Marbury* v. *Madison* set an important precedent. It gave the Supreme Court the power to decide whether laws passed by Congress were constitutional. This power of the Court is called **judicial review.**

Jefferson was displeased with the decision. It gave more power to the Supreme Court, where Federalists were still strong. Even so, the President and Congress accepted the right of the Supreme Court to overturn laws. Today, judicial review is one of the most important powers of the Supreme Court.

SECTION 1 REVIEW

1. **Identify:** (a) Albert Gallatin, (b) John Marshall, (c) *Marbury* v. *Madison.*
2. **Define:** (a) democratic, (b) laissez faire, (c) judicial review.
3. (a) Name two Federalist policies that Jefferson changed. (b) Name two Federalist policies he allowed to continue.
4. How did Federalists keep control of the courts?
5. What precedent did *Marbury* v. *Madison* set?
6. **CRITICAL THINKING Analyzing a Quotation** "We are all Republicans, we are all Federalists." What did Jefferson mean by this statement?

ACTIVITY Writing to Learn

Imagine that you are an adviser to President Adams. Write a letter to a friend describing your reactions to Jefferson as President.

The Louisiana Purchase

FIND OUT

- Why was the Mississippi River important to western farmers?
- How did the United States gain Louisiana?
- What was the purpose of the Lewis and Clark expedition?

VOCABULARY continental divide

One day during his second term of office, President Jefferson received several packages. Inside, he found hides and skeletons of various animals, horns of a mountain ram, and a tin box full of insects. There were also cages of live birds and squirrels, as well as gifts from the Mandan and Sioux Indians.

The packages were from Meriwether Lewis and William Clark. Jefferson had sent the two men to explore the vast lands west of the Mississippi. Almost two years before, Jefferson had boldly purchased the territory for the United States. The packages confirmed his belief that the new lands were a valuable addition to the nation.

New Orleans and the Mississippi River

By 1800, almost one million Americans lived between the Appalachians and the Mississippi River. Most were farmers.

There were only a few roads west of the Appalachians. Western farmers relied on the Mississippi River to ship their wheat and corn to markets in the East. First, they shipped their goods down the Mississippi to New Orleans. There, the goods were stored in warehouses. Finally, the goods were loaded onto ships and carried to the Atlantic coast.

From time to time, Spain threatened to close the port of New Orleans to Americans. In 1795, President Washington sent Thomas Pinckney to find a way to keep the port open. In the **_Pinckney Treaty,_** Spain agreed to let Americans ship their goods down the Mississippi and store them in New Orleans.

Shortly afterward, Spain signed a secret treaty with Napoleon Bonaparte, the ruler of France. The treaty gave Louisiana back to France. President Jefferson was alarmed. Napoleon had already set out to conquer Europe. Jefferson feared that Napoleon might now attempt to build an empire in North America.

Market Day in New Orleans *In the bustling port of New Orleans, people from a wide variety of cultures met to do business. The traders shown here included African Americans from the South and the Caribbean, as well as many creoles—descendants of French and Spanish settlers.* **Geography** *Why was New Orleans important to the United States?*

Revolt in Haiti

Jefferson had good reason to worry. Napoleon wanted to grow food in Louisiana and ship it to the French islands in the West Indies. However, events in Haiti thwarted his plan.

Haiti was the richest French colony in the Caribbean. There, enslaved Africans worked sugar plantations that made French planters wealthy. During the French Revolution, slaves in Haiti were inspired to fight for their liberty. Toussaint L'Ouverture (too SAN loo vehr TYOOR) led the revolt. By 1801, Toussaint and his followers had nearly forced the French out of Haiti.

Napoleon sent troops to recapture Haiti. He expected his army to win easily, but the Haitians fought back fiercely. Although the French captured Toussaint, they did not regain control of the island. In 1804, Haitians declared their independence. Haiti became the second republic in the Americas, after the United States.

Toussaint L'Ouverture *A self-educated former slave, Toussaint L'Ouverture led slaves in Haiti in a revolt against French rule. For enslaved African Americans, Toussaint became a symbol of the struggle for liberty.* **United States and the World** *Why would President Jefferson be concerned about the revolt in Haiti?*

The Nation Doubles in Size

About the time that Haiti forced out the French, President Jefferson decided to try to buy New Orleans from Napoleon. Jefferson wanted to be sure that American farmers would always be able to ship their goods through the port of New Orleans. The President appointed Robert Livingston and James Monroe to negotiate with the French. He instructed then to buy New Orleans and West Florida for $2 million—a sum that Congress had set aside for that purpose. If necessary, Jefferson said, they could offer as much as $10 million.

A surprising proposal. Livingston and Monroe talked to Talleyrand, the French foreign minister. At first, Talleyrand showed little interest in the offer. Then, events quickly changed.

Napoleon's dream of an empire in the Americas ended when the French lost con-

trol of Haiti. Also, Napoleon needed money to finance his wars in Europe. Talleyrand now asked Livingston an unexpected question: "What will you give for the *whole* of Louisiana?"

Livingston was shocked and delighted. France was willing to sell all of Louisiana, not just New Orleans. Livingston offered $4 million.

"Too low!" said Talleyrand. "Reflect, and see me tomorrow."

Livingston and Monroe debated the matter. They had no authority to buy all of Louisiana. They knew, however, that Jefferson wanted control of the Mississippi. They agreed to pay the French $15 million. Neither the French nor the Americans consulted the various Indian nations in Louisiana about the purchase.

Was the purchase constitutional? Jefferson was pleased by the news from France. But did the Constitution give him

MAP STUDY

After buying Louisiana in 1803, Thomas Jefferson was eager to have it explored and mapped. Eventually, many new states were carved from the Louisiana Purchase.

1. What rivers flowed across the Louisiana Territory?
2. What are the longitude and latitude of Pikes Peak?
3. **Forecasting** Judging from this map, in what territory would you expect the United States to become involved in future disputes with another country? Explain.

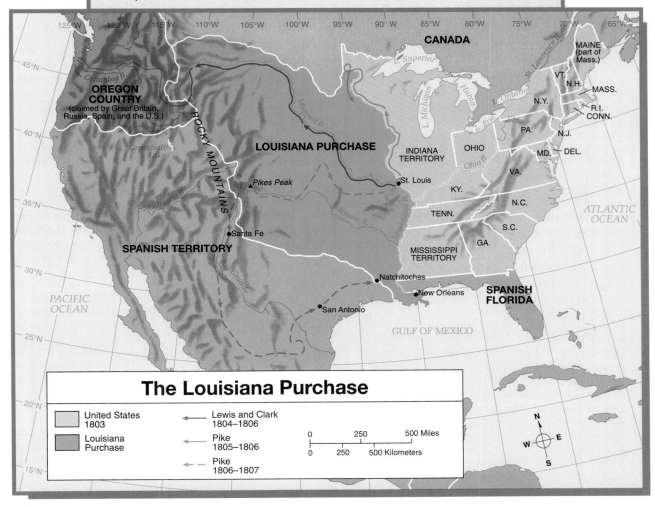

The Louisiana Purchase

the power to buy land? Jefferson had always insisted that the federal government had only those powers spelled out in the Constitution. The document said nothing about a President's power to purchase territory.

After much thought, Jefferson decided that he could buy Louisiana. The Constitution allowed the President to make treaties. At his request, the Senate quickly approved a treaty making the **Louisiana Purchase.** In 1803, the United States took control of the vast lands west of the Mississippi. (📖 See "The Man Without a Country" on page 570.)

Lewis and Clark's Assignment

The United States now owned Louisiana. However, few Americans knew anything about the territory. In 1803, Congress provided money for a team of explorers to study the new lands. Jefferson chose Meriwether Lewis, his private secretary, to head the expedition. Lewis asked William Clark, another Virginian, to join him. About 50 men made up their band.

Detailed instructions. Jefferson gave Lewis and Clark careful instructions. "Your observations are to be taken with great pains and accuracy," the President said. He even reminded them to write neatly so that others could read their notes. Jefferson asked the men to map a route to the Pacific Ocean.

Jefferson instructed the explorers to study the climate, wildlife, soil, and mineral resources of the new lands. The President requested a report on the following:

> 66 Climate as characterized by the thermometer, by the proportion of rainy, cloudy, and clear days, by lightning, hail, snow, ice...by the winds prevailing at different seasons, the dates at which particular plants put forth or lose their flower, or leaf, times of appearance of particular birds, reptiles or insects. 99

Friendship with Native Americans. Jefferson also wanted Lewis and Clark to learn about the many Indian nations who lived in the Louisiana Purchase. For decades, these Native Americans had carried on a busy trade with English, French, and Spanish merchants. Jefferson hoped that the Indians

could be convinced to trade with Americans instead. For this reason, he urged Lewis and Clark to tell the Indians of "our wish to be neighborly, friendly, and useful to them."

GEOGRAPHY AND HISTORY
The Expedition Begins

In May 1804, Lewis and Clark started up the Missouri River from St. Louis. In time, their trip would take them to the Pacific Ocean. (Follow their route on the map on page 273.)

At first, their progress was slow as they traveled against the Missouri's swift current. One night, the current tore away the riverbank where they were camping. The party scrambled into boats to avoid being washed downstream.

As they traveled, the expedition met people from various Indian nations. Lewis and Clark had brought many presents for Native Americans. They carried medals stamped with the United States seal, mirrors, beads, knives, and blankets, as well as more than 4,000 sewing needles and some 3,000 fishhooks.

As winter approached, the explorers arranged to stay with the Mandans near present-day Bismarck, North Dakota. The Mandan villages had been major trading centers for hundreds of years. (See Connections at right.)

Over the Rockies

Lewis and Clark planned to continue up the Missouri in the spring. But they worried about how they would cross the steep Rocky Mountains.

Luckily, a Shoshone woman, Sacajawea (sahk uh juh WEE uh), was also staying with the Mandans that winter. The Shoshones (shoh SHOH neez) lived in the Rockies, and Sacajawea knew the region well. She offered to guide the explorers across the mountains. She would also translate for

History and You

Among the supplies that Lewis and Clark took on their journey were 15 guns, a chronometer for calculating longitude, and 193 pounds of soup concentrate. Imagine that you are planning a cross-country camping trip today. What items would you take along?

Mandan Traders

Lewis and Clark were lucky to meet up with the Mandans during the winter of 1804. The Mandans were a prosperous people, with a rich and ancient culture. Living in neatly laid out villages high above the Knife River, they grew corn and other crops. They also hunted the game that roamed the surrounding hills. Most important, however, they engaged in trade.

Since prehistoric times, the Mandans had been at the center of a vast trading network. They controlled the trade in Knife River flint, a hard, glassy stone prized for making strong tools and weapons. Native Americans from far and wide gave the Mandans exotic items such as shells and copper in return for the precious flint. As their farming prospered, the Mandans also traded surplus crops to wandering peoples for buffalo skins, dried meat, and other items.

In the 1600s, European goods entered the trading network. The Mandans proved themselves shrewd traders in these products as well. They acted as agents for exchanges between Europeans and other Native Americans. By the mid-1700s, Crows, Assiniboines, Cheyennes, Arapahoes, and Kiowas all traveled to the Mandans' Knife River villages to exchange horses

Mandan battle scene

for European guns, metal pots, hatchets, and knives.

■ What was the most important part of the Mandan economy?

ACTIVITY Create an advertisement for Mandan goods and services. Use words, pictures, or a combination of both.

A Mandan village

them with different Native American groups. Sacajawea's French Canadian husband would travel with them, too.

In early spring, the party set out. In the foothills of the Rockies, the landscape and wildlife changed. Bighorn sheep ran along the high hills. The thorns of prickly pear cactus jabbed the explorers' moccasins. One day, a grizzly bear chased Lewis while he was exploring alone.

Sacajawea contributed greatly to the success of the expedition. She gathered wild vegetables and advised the men where to fish and hunt game. She knew about the healing qualities of different herbs, so the expedition relied on her for medical help.

When the party reached the mountains, Sacajawea recognized the lands of her people. One day, Lewis met several Shoshone leaders and invited them back to camp. Sacajawea began "to dance and show every mark of the most extravagant joy." One of the men, she explained, was her brother. Sacajawea persuaded her Shoshone relatives to supply the expedition with the food and horses it needed to continue. The Shoshones advised Lewis and Clark about the best route to take over the Rockies.

Reaching the Pacific

As they crossed the Rockies, the explorers noted that the rivers flowed west,

Peace Medals *During their journey through the West, the Lewis and Clark expedition gave out peace medals as a token of friendly relations between Native Americans and the United States government.* **Multicultural Heritage** *How did Sacajawea help create good relations between Native Americans and the Lewis and Clark expedition?*

toward the Pacific Ocean. They had crossed the continental divide. A continental divide is a mountain ridge that separates river systems. In North America, the continental divide is located in the Rocky Mountains. Rivers east of the divide flow into the Mississippi, which drains into the Gulf of Mexico. West of the divide, rivers flow into the Pacific Ocean.

Entering the Pacific Northwest. After building canoes, Lewis and Clark's party floated down the Columbia River. It carried them into the Pacific Northwest. There, they met the Nez Percé Indians.

Lewis and Clark wanted to learn about the Nez Percés. However, every question had to be translated four times. First, their English words were translated into French for Sacajawea's husband. He then translated the French into Mandan. Sacajawea translated the Mandan into Shoshone. Then, a Shoshone who lived with the Nez Percés translated the question into Nez Percé. Each answer went through the same process in reverse.

A view of the west coast. On November 7, 1805, Lewis and Clark finally reached their goal. Lewis wrote in his journal: "Great joy in camp. We are in view of the ocean, this great Pacific Ocean which we have been so long anxious to see." On a nearby tree, Clark carved, "By Land from the U. States in 1804 & 5."

The return trip to St. Louis took another year. In 1806, Americans celebrated the return of Lewis and Clark. The explorers brought back much useful information about the Louisiana Purchase. Except for one small battle, their relations with Native Americans had been peaceful.

Pike Explores the West

Before Lewis and Clark returned, another explorer set out from St. Louis. From 1805 to 1807, Zebulon Pike explored the upper

MAP, GRAPH, AND CHART SKILLS
Following Routes on a Map

Every map tells a story. Some maps in this book tell the story of explorers moving across the land and the seas. Other maps show the movements of troops or ships during a war. The map below shows the route that Lewis and Clark followed as they crossed the Continental Divide.

1. **Study the map to see what it shows.** (a) What is the subject of the map? (b) What symbol shows their route? (c) What symbol shows Lewis and Clark campsites? (d) How does the map show Indian nations? (e) What types of landforms did Lewis and Clark travel through?

2. **Practice reading directions on the map.** To follow a route on a map, you need to determine in which direction or directions the route goes. Find the directional arrow that shows N, S, E, and W. Sometimes you need to combine directions. For example, when explorers travel in a direction be-

tween north and east, they are said to be traveling northeast (NE). They could also travel northwest (NW), southeast (SE), or southwest (SW). (a) In which direction did Lewis and Clark travel after they crossed the Continental Divide? (b) In which direction did they travel after they left the campsite at Traveller's Rest?

3. **Describe movements on a map in terms of direction.** Maps like this one show movement. (a) Describe the movements of Lewis and Clark as they traveled from Great Falls to the Continental Divide. (b) Why do you think they took this route to cross the Continental Divide?

ACTIVITY Make a map that shows the route you take to get to school from your home. Give your map a title and a key that explains the symbols and colors you used. Include a scale and a directional arrow. In which directions do you travel on your way to school?

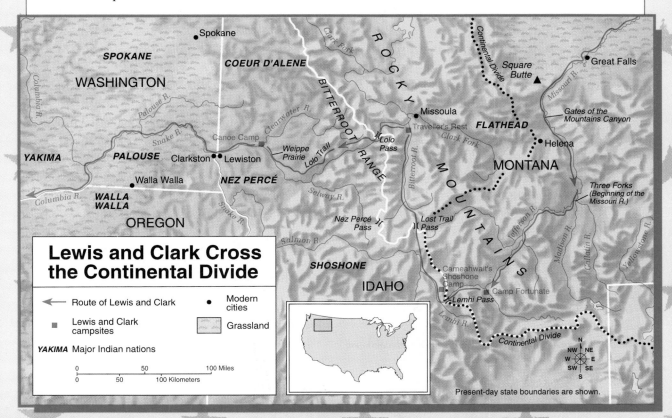

Lewis and Clark Cross the Continental Divide

Mississippi River, the Arkansas River, and parts of present-day Colorado and New Mexico. On Thanksgiving Day in 1806, Pike saw a mountain peak rising above the Colorado plains. Today, this mountain is known as Pikes Peak. (See the map on page 273.)

The journeys of Lewis and Clark and Zebulon Pike excited Americans. It was a number of years, however, before settlers moved into the rugged western lands. As you will read, they first settled the region closest to the Mississippi River. Within a short time, the area around New Orleans had a large enough white population for the settlers to apply for statehood. In 1812, this area entered the Union as the state of Louisiana. ■

SECTION 2 REVIEW

1. **Locate:** (a) Mississippi River, (b) New Orleans, (c) Haiti, (d) St. Louis, (e) Missouri River, (f) Rocky Mountains, (g) Pikes Peak.
2. **Identify:** (a) Pinckney Treaty, (b) Toussaint L'Ouverture, (c) Louisiana Purchase, (d) Lewis and Clark, (e) Sacajawea, (f) Zebulon Pike.
3. **Define:** continental divide.
4. Why was New Orleans important to many American farmers?
5. Why did France offer to sell Louisiana to the United States?
6. (a) What did Jefferson instruct Lewis and Clark to do on their expedition? (b) What did Lewis and Clark accomplish?
7. **CRITICAL THINKING Analyzing Information** Was Jefferson's decision to purchase Louisiana based on a strict or a loose interpretation of the Constitution? Explain.

ACTIVITY **Writing to Learn**
Imagine that you are Sacajawea. Write a diary entry about the problems of translating for Lewis and Clark.

3 Protecting American Neutrality

FIND OUT
■ How did overseas trade grow in the early 1800s?
■ Why did British warships seize American sailors?
■ Why was the Embargo Act unpopular?

VOCABULARY impressment, embargo

The letter had been smuggled off a British ship and carried to the United States. The handwritten message described the desperate situation of a young American sailor, James Brown:

66Being on shore one day in Lisbon, Portugal, I was [seized] by a gang and brought on board the [British ship] *Conqueror,* where I am still confined. Never have I been allowed to put my foot on shore since I was brought on board, which is now three years. 99

Brown's situation was not unusual. The British forced thousands of American sailors to serve on their ships in the early 1800s. This was only one of many dangers that Americans faced as their sea trade began to thrive.

Trading Around the World

After the Revolution, American overseas trade grew rapidly. Ships sailed from New England ports on voyages that sometimes lasted three years. Everywhere they went, Yankee captains kept a sharp lookout for

PAST

PRESENT

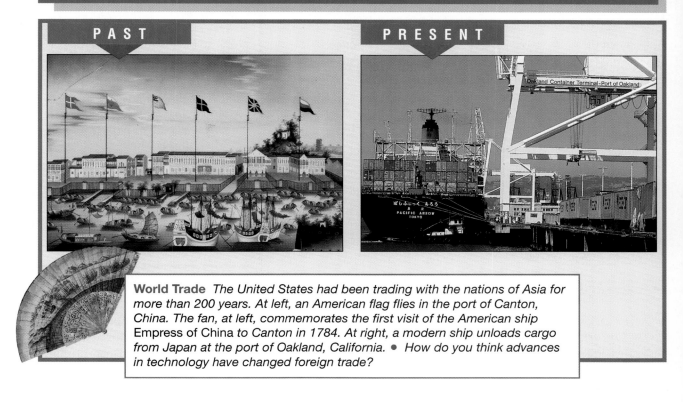

World Trade *The United States had been trading with the nations of Asia for more than 200 years. At left, an American flag flies in the port of Canton, China. The fan, at left, commemorates the first visit of the American ship* Empress of China *to Canton in 1784. At right, a modern ship unloads cargo from Japan at the port of Oakland, California.* • *How do you think advances in technology have changed foreign trade?*

new goods to trade and new markets in which to sell. One clever trader cut up winter ice from New England ponds, packed the slabs deep in sawdust, and transported them to India. There, he traded the ice for silks and spices.

Yankee merchants. Yankee merchants sailed up the Pacific coast of North America in the 1790s. In fact, Yankee traders visited the Columbia River more than 10 years before Lewis and Clark. Indeed, so many traders from Boston visited the Pacific

Linking Past and Present
Yankee ships carried on a profitable trade in ginseng—a plant that grew wild in New England and that was used by the Chinese to make medicine. Ginseng is still used today as a medicine and as a tonic to maintain shiny hair and a clear complexion.

Northwest that Native Americans called every white man "Boston." Traders bought furs from Native Americans. Then they sold the furs for large profits in China.

To make a good profit, American traders ran great risks, especially in the Mediterranean Sea. For many years, pirates from nations along the coast of North Africa attacked vessels from Europe and the United States. The North African nations were called the **Barbary States.** To protect American ships, the United States paid a yearly tribute, or bribe, to the rulers of the Barbary States.

War with Tripoli. In the early 1800s, the ruler of Tripoli, one of the Barbary States, demanded a larger bribe than usual. When President Jefferson refused to pay, Tripoli declared war on the United States. In response, Jefferson ordered the navy to blockade the port of Tripoli.

During the blockade, the American ship *Philadelphia* ran aground near Tripoli. Pirates boarded the ship and hauled the crew

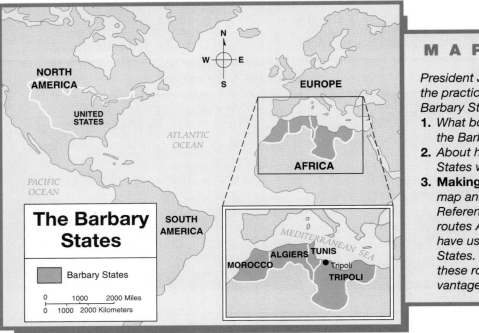

MAP STUDY

President Jefferson wanted to end the practice of paying tribute to the Barbary States.
1. What bodies of water bordered the Barbary States?
2. About how far from the United States were the Barbary States?
3. **Making Decisions** Use this map and the World map in the Reference Section to describe routes American traders might have used to avoid the Barbary States. What advantage would these routes have? What disadvantage?

to prison. The pirates planned to use the *Philadelphia* to attack other ships.

Stephen Decatur, an officer in the United States Navy, took action. Very late one night, Decatur and his crew quietly sailed a small ship into Tripoli harbor. When they reached the captured ship, they set it on fire so that the pirates could not use it.

In the meantime, a force of American marines landed in North Africa. The marines marched 500 miles (805 km) to launch a surprise attack on Tripoli. The war with Tripoli lasted until 1805. In the end, the ruler of Tripoli signed a treaty promising not to interfere with American ships.

Attacks on American Ships

In 1803, Britain and France went to war again. As in the 1790s, the European war gave a boost to American trade. British and French ships were so busy fighting that they could not carry trade goods. American merchants made profits trading with both sides.

Violating American neutrality. Of course, neither Britain nor France wanted the United States to sell supplies to its enemy. As in the 1790s, they ignored American claims of neutrality. Each tried to cut off American trade with the other. Napoleon seized American ships bound for England, and the British stopped Yankee traders on their way to France. Between 1805 and 1807, hundreds of American ships were captured.

Seizing American sailors. Britain did more than take American ships. The British navy also kidnapped American sailors and forced them to serve on British ships. This practice of forcing people into service, called **impressment,** was common in Britain. For centuries, impressment gangs had raided villages and forced young men to serve in the navy.

To fight France, the British navy needed more men than ever before. British warships even stopped and searched American vessels. If a British officer found British sailors on an American ship, he forced them off the ship. Even worse, the British impressed thousands of American sailors.

A Ban on Trade

Americans were furious with the British for attacking their ships and impressing their sailors. Many wanted to go to war with

Britain. But Jefferson, like Washington and Adams, hoped to avoid war. He knew that the small American fleet was no match for the powerful British navy. Also, budget cuts had weakened the American navy.

A total ban. Jefferson convinced Congress to pass the Embargo Act in 1807. An embargo is a ban on trade with another country. The ***Embargo Act*** forbade Americans to export or import goods. Jefferson hoped that the embargo would hurt France and Britain by cutting off needed supplies. "Our trade is the most powerful weapon we can use in our defense," one Republican newspaper wrote.

The embargo hurt Britain and France. Americans, however, suffered even more.

Exports dropped from $108 million in 1807 to $22 million in 1808. American sailors had no work. Farmers lost money because they could not ship wheat overseas. Docks in the South were piled high with cotton and tobacco. The Embargo Act hurt New England merchants most of all, and they protested loudly.

A limited ban. After more than a year, Jefferson admitted that the Embargo Act had failed. In 1809, Congress voted to end the embargo. They passed the ***Nonintercourse Act*** in its place. Less severe than the embargo, this act allowed Americans to trade with all nations except Britain and France.

The Embargo Act was the most unpopular measure of Jefferson's years in office. Still, the Republicans remained strong. In 1808, Jefferson followed the precedent set by Washington and refused to run for a third term. James Madison, his fellow Republican, ran and easily won. When Madison took office in 1809, he hoped that Britain and France would soon agree to stop violating American neutrality.

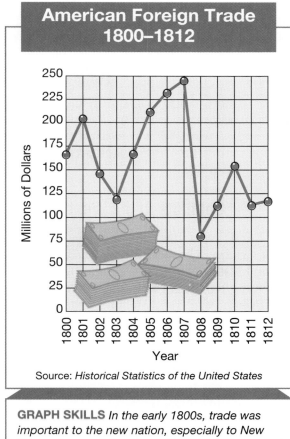

American Foreign Trade 1800–1812

Source: *Historical Statistics of the United States*

GRAPH SKILLS *In the early 1800s, trade was important to the new nation, especially to New Englanders.* ● *Why do you think trade decreased sharply between 1807 and 1808?*

SECTION 3 REVIEW

1. **Locate:** Tripoli.
2. **Identify:** (a) Barbary States, (b) Embargo Act, (c) Nonintercourse Act.
3. **Define:** (a) impressment, (b) embargo.
4. Why did the United States and Tripoli go to war?
5. How did renewed war in Europe affect American overseas trade?
6. (a) What was the purpose of the Embargo Act? (b) Why did it fail?
7. **CRITICAL THINKING Linking Past and Present** How would an embargo affect the economy of the United States today?

ACTIVITY **Writing to Learn**

Imagine that it is 1807 and you are a Yankee trader. Write a letter to President Jefferson protesting the Embargo Act.

The Road to War

FIND OUT

- Why did the South and the West want war with Britain?
- How did the Prophet and Tecumseh try to stop white settlement?
- Why did President Madison agree to war with Britain?

VOCABULARY nationalism

James Madison was a quiet, scholarly man. Like Presidents who came before him, he wanted to avoid war.

Many Americans, however, felt that Madison's approach was too timid. They argued that the United States must stand up to foreign countries. How could the nation win respect if it allowed Britain and France to seize American ships? The cost of war might be great, said one member of Congress. But, he continued, who would count in money "the slavery of our impressed seamen"?

In time, this kind of talk aroused the nation. By 1812, Americans were clamoring for war.

War Hawks

In 1810, President Madison tried a new plan. If either Britain or France would stop seizing American ships, he said, the United States would halt trade with the other nation. Seizing the chance, Napoleon quickly announced that France would respect American neutrality. As promised, Madison declared that the United States would continue to trade with France but stop all shipments to Britain.

The President did not want war. Other Americans were less cautious, however. Except in New England, where merchants wanted to restore trade with Britain, anti-British feeling ran strong. Members of Congress from the South and the West clamored for war with Britain. They were known as *War Hawks.*

War Hawks had a strong sense of nationalism. Nationalism is pride in or devotion to one's country. War Hawks felt that Britain was treating the United States as if it were still a British colony. "If we submit [to Britain]," warned one War Hawk, "the independence of this nation is lost."

Henry Clay of Kentucky was the most outspoken War Hawk. Clay wanted war for two reasons. He wanted revenge on Britain for seizing American ships. He also wanted an excuse to conquer Canada. "The militia of Kentucky are alone [able] to place Montreal and Upper Canada at your feet," Clay boasted to Congress. Canadians, Clay believed, would be happy to leave the British empire and join the United States.

War Hawks saw other advantages of war with Britain. South of the United States, Florida belonged to Spain, Britain's ally. If Americans went to war with Britain, War Hawks said, the United States could seize Florida from Spain.

Conflicts in the West

War Hawks had yet another reason to fight Britain. They claimed that Britain was arming Native Americans on the frontier and encouraging them to attack settlers. In fact, the British, who held military forts in Canada, tried to take advantage of troubles along the frontier.

Settlers push west. An important reason for frontier troubles was increasing settlement. As you have read, in 1795 the Treaty of Greenville forced Native Americans to sell much of their land in Ohio. (See page 252.) Ohio joined the Union in 1803. By then, thousands of settlers were pushing beyond Ohio into Indiana Territory.

MAP STUDY

As settlers moved west, they took over Native American lands.
1. Which Indian groups lost their lands between 1784 and 1810?
2. When did the Natchez lose their land?
3. **Forecasting** Notice the areas of the map shaded tan. Based on what you have learned, what do you think happened to Indian lands in these areas after 1810? Explain.

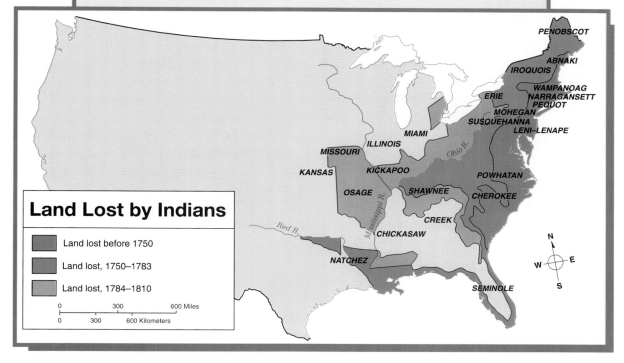

Land Lost by Indians

Land lost before 1750
Land lost, 1750–1783
Land lost, 1784–1810

0   300   600 Miles
0   300   600 Kilometers

The flood of settlers created big problems for Native Americans. Settlers built farms on land reserved for Indians. They hunted deer and birds that Indians depended on for food. "Stop your people from killing our game," Shawnee chiefs told the federal government. "They would be angry if we were to kill a cow or hog of theirs. The little game that remains is very dear to us."

Native Americans resist. Sometimes, Indian nations protested to the federal government about the new settlements. Other times, small bands attacked settlers to drive them off the land. Native Americans found it difficult to unite to oppose settlement, however. Indians who had once been enemies did not easily become allies.

During the same years that Americans considered war with Britain, many Native Americans determined to halt the flow of settlers. They were led by two Shawnee brothers, the Prophet and Tecumseh.

Two Shawnee Brothers Seek Unity

One winter evening in 1804, a 30-year-old Shawnee sat before a blazing campfire. Lifting a burning stick, he lit his long pipe. Suddenly, he gasped and fell to his side as if dead.

A journey to the spirit world. Families from the other lodges came running. They wanted to know what had happened to Tenskwatawa (ten SKWAH tah wah), as the dead man was called. Imagine their amazement when the dead man sat up.

Shawnee Leaders *Tecumseh, left, and the Prophet, right, believed that the land belonged to all Indians. No nation had the right to sell any part of it unless all agreed.* **Multicultural Heritage** *What message did the Prophet include in his teachings?*

At last, Tenskwatawa was able to speak. He reported that he had had a strange vision. His soul, he said, had taken a journey to the spirit world. There, he learned the path that all Indians must take if they were to live happily.

In the weeks that followed, Tenskwatawa repeated his experiences to all who came to listen. They began to call him the Prophet.

The Prophet's message. According to the Prophet, Native Americans must give up white ways. From settlers, Indians learned about the white people's way of life. Many Native Americans had come to depend on trade goods from the East, such as muskets, cloth, iron cooking pots, and whiskey. The Prophet said Native Americans must no longer trade for white goods. If Indians returned to the old ways, he believed, they would gain power to resist the settlers.

In 1808, the Prophet built a village for his followers along Tippecanoe Creek in In-

diana Territory. From as far away as Missouri, Iowa, and Minnesota, Indians traveled to hear his message. His teachings brought hope to many.

Tecumseh (tih KUHM suh), the Prophet's older brother, visited other Indian nations. Tall, handsome, and energetic, Tecumseh organized many Native Americans into a confederation, or league. Although the Prophet was the spiritual leader of the confederation, Tecumseh became its spokesperson. He said all Indians must unite "in claiming a common right in the land."

In 1809, William Henry Harrison, governor of the Indiana Territory, signed a treaty with several Indian leaders. The leaders gave up 3 million acres of Indian land for less than half a cent an acre. Tecumseh was enraged. He said that the chiefs who signed the treaties had no right to sell the land. The land belonged to all Native Americans, he said.

Tecumseh's message. In the summer of 1810, Tecumseh decided to deliver a firm message to Governor Harrison. He and 75 warriors marched to Vincennes, in Indiana Territory. Awaiting their arrival, Governor Harrison arranged chairs on his front porch for the meeting. Tecumseh objected. He insisted that they meet on the grass of the forest—on Indian ground.

Tecumseh impressed Harrison. "He is one of those uncommon geniuses which spring up occasionally to produce revolutions and overturn the established order of things," Harrison commented.

As Tecumseh addressed the governor, he warned of the need for change:

66 You are continually driving the red people [from their land], when at last you will drive them into the [ocean] where they can't either stand or work. Brother, you ought to know what you are doing with the Indians. . . . It is a very bad thing and we do not like it. 99

Tecumseh insisted that Harrison give his message to President Madison. The governor agreed, but he warned that it was not likely to change Madison's mind. Tecumseh stared grimly. He knew that if whites did not stop moving onto Indian land, war would surely come. ■

Showdown at Tippecanoe

Old rivalries among Indian nations kept Tecumseh from uniting Native Americans east of the Mississippi River. Still, white settlers were alarmed at his success. "I am inclined to believe that a crisis is fast approaching," said Governor Harrison.

In 1811, Harrison decided to march with 1,000 soldiers to Prophetstown, on Tippecanoe Creek. He knew that Tecumseh was organizing Indians in the South. While he was away, the Prophet was in charge.

The Prophet learned of Harrison's approach. He decided to meet the danger with a surprise night attack on Harrison's troops.

In the battle that followed, neither side won a clear victory. Still, whites in the East celebrated the **Battle of Tippecanoe** as a major victory.

Congress Declares War

The Battle of Tippecanoe marked the beginning of a long and deadly war on the frontier. Fighting between Native Americans and settlers spurred the War Hawks to call even louder for war with Britain. Convinced that the British were arming the Indians, one newspaper called the war "purely BRITISH."

President Madison at last gave in to war fever. In June 1812, he asked Congress to declare war on Britain. The House voted 79 to 49 in favor of war. The Senate vote was 19 to 13. Americans soon discovered, however, that winning the war would not be as easy as declaring it.

SECTION 4 REVIEW

1. **Locate:** (a) Canada, (b) Spanish Florida, (c) Ohio, (d) Indiana Territory.
2. **Identify:** (a) War Hawks, (b) Henry Clay, (c) the Prophet, (d) Tecumseh, (e) Battle of Tippecanoe.
3. **Define:** nationalism.
4. Why did Henry Clay and other War Hawks want to fight the British?
5. How did the increased number of settlers affect Native Americans?
6. Why did President Madison ask Congress to declare war on Britain?
7. CRITICAL THINKING **Comparing** How was the Prophet's message different from Tecumseh's?

ACTIVITY **Writing to Learn**
Imagine that you are publishing a newspaper about the events discussed in this section. Write four headlines for the front page.

5
The War of 1812

FIND OUT

■ How did Americans prepare for the War of 1812?

■ What part did Native Americans play in the fighting?

■ What was the outcome of the war?

Many Republicans welcomed the news of war with Britain. In some cities, they fired cannons and guns and danced in the streets. One New Jersey man wrote a song calling for a swift attack on Canada:

> **❝**On to Quebec's embattled halls!
> Who will pause, when glory calls?
> Charge, soldiers, charge, its lofty walls.
> And storm its strong artillery.**❞**

Other Americans were less enthusiastic. New Englanders, especially, talked scornfully of "Mr. Madison's war." In fact, before the war ended, some New Englanders would plot to leave the Union and make a separate peace with Britain.

Preparing for War

The United States was not ready for war. The navy had only 16 ships to fight against the huge British fleet. The army was small and ill equipped. Moreover, many of the officers knew little about the military. "The state of the Army," commented a member of Congress, "is enough to make any man who has the smallest love of country wish to get rid of it."

Since there were few regular troops, the government relied on volunteers to fight the war. Congress voted to give them $124 and 360 acres of land for their service. The mon-

ey was high pay at the time—equal to a year's salary for most workers.

Lured by money and the chance to own their own farm, young men eagerly enlisted. They were not trained, however, and did not know how to be good soldiers. Many deserted after a few months. Others would not fight unless they were paid. One officer complained that his men "absolutely refused to march until they had [received] their pay."

Fighting at Sea

The American declaration of war took Britain by surprise. The British were locked in a bitter struggle with Napoleon. They could not spare troops to fight the United States. The powerful British navy, however, blockaded American ports.

The American navy was too small to break the blockade. Yet several sea captains won stunning victories. One famous battle took place early in the war, in August 1812. Sailing near Newfoundland, Isaac Hull, captain of the *Constitution,* spotted the British frigate *Guerrière* (gai ree AIR). For close to an hour, the two ships jockeyed for position. The *Guerrière* fired on the *Constitution* several times. Captain Hull ordered his cannons to hold their fire.

At last, Hull felt he was close enough to the enemy. Bending over, he shouted to the sailors on the deck below: "Now, boys, you may fire!" The cannons on the *Constitution* roared. They tore holes in the sides of the *Guerrière* and shot off both masts.

When the smoke cleared, Hull asked the British captain if he had "struck" his flag— that is, lowered his flag in surrender. "Well, I don't know," replied the stunned British captain. "Our mizzenmast is gone, our mainmast is gone. And, upon the whole, you may say we *have* struck our flag."

American sea captains won other victories at sea. But although these victories cheered Americans, they did little to win the war.

"Old Ironsides" *In this painting by famed marine artist Thomas Birch, the U.S.S.* Constitution *levels a broadside blast at the British frigate* Guerrière. *After its remarkable victory against the* Guerrière, *the* Constitution *won the nickname "Old Ironsides."* **Geography** *What was the goal of the British navy during the War of 1812?*

War in the West

As you have read, one goal of the War Hawks was to conquer Canada. They were sure that Canadians would welcome the chance to throw off British rule.

Americans invade Canada. William Hull led American troops into Canada from Detroit. The Canadians had only a few untrained troops to fight the invasion. But General Isaac Brock tricked the Americans.

First, Brock paraded his soldiers in red cloaks to make it appear that well-trained British redcoats were helping the Canadians. Brock also let a false "secret" message fall into Hull's hands. It said that more than 5,000 Indians were fighting on Brock's side. The real number was much smaller. Brock's

ally, Tecumseh, staged raids on the Americans that seemed to confirm the message.

Brock's strategy worked. Hull retreated from Canada. The invasion of Canada had failed.

Tecumseh's last battle. In September 1813, the tide turned when the Americans gained control of Lake Erie. William Henry Harrison, veteran of Tippecanoe and now a general in the army, invaded Canada in search of Tecumseh and the British. The Americans won a decisive victory at the ***Battle of the Thames.***

Tecumseh died in the fighting. For Native Americans, his death was a great loss. Without Tecumseh's leadership, the Indian confederation he had worked so hard to form fell apart.

The War of 1812 was fought on several fronts.
1. What battles took place in or near Canada?
2. (a) Name two American victories shown on the maps. (b) Name two British victories.
3. **Comparing** Compare the American invasion of Canada in the Revolution with the invasion of Canada in the War of 1812. (See pages 163–164.) Were they similar or different? Explain.

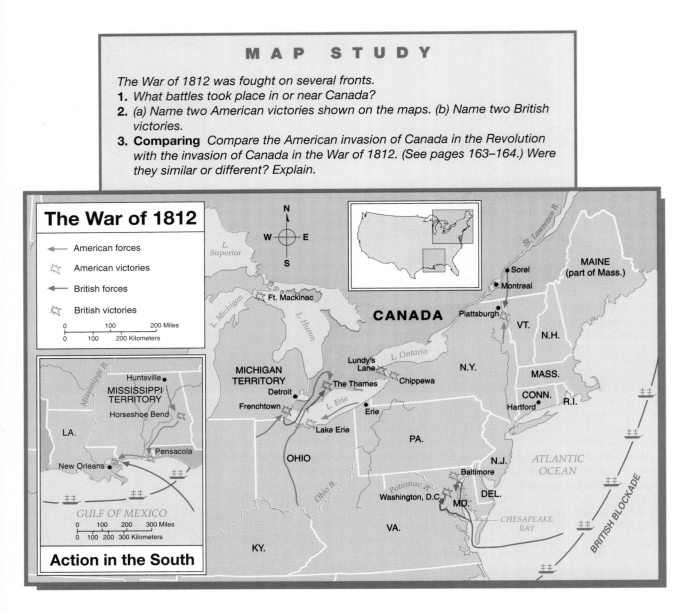

The War of 1812

- American forces
- ☆ American victories
- British forces
- ☆ British victories

0   100   200 Miles
0   100   200 Kilometers

Action in the South

0 100 200 300 Miles
0 100 200 300 Kilometers

MISSISSIPPI TERRITORY
Huntsville
Horseshoe Bend
LA.
Pensacola
New Orleans
GULF OF MEXICO

MICHIGAN TERRITORY
Detroit
Frenchtown
Ft. Mackinac
Lundy's Lane
The Thames
Chippewa
Lake Erie
Erie
L. Erie
L. Ontario
L. Superior
L. Michigan
L. Huron
CANADA
St. Lawrence R.
Sorel
Montreal
Plattsburgh
MAINE (part of Mass.)
VT.
N.H.
N.Y.
MASS.
CONN.
Hartford
R.I.
PA.
OHIO
Ohio R.
KY.
VA.
Washington, D.C.
Baltimore
MD.
DEL.
N.J.
Potomac R.
CHESAPEAKE BAY
ATLANTIC OCEAN
BRITISH BLOCKADE

The Creeks surrender. The Creeks, Tecumseh's allies in the South, were divided over what to do. Some wanted to keep fighting the bloody war against the settlers. Andrew Jackson, a Tennessee officer, took command of the American troops in the Creek War.

In 1814, Jackson led American troops into battle. With the help of the Cherokees, Jackson won a decisive victory at the **Battle of Horseshoe Bend.** The leader of the Creeks walked alone into Jackson's camp to surrender:

❝I am in your power. Do unto me as you please. . . . If I had an army I would yet fight, and contend to the last. . . . But your people have destroyed my nation.❞

For the time being, the fighting ended. Once again, Native Americans were forced to give up land to whites.

The British Burn Washington

In 1814, Britain and its allies defeated France. Now, Britain could send its troops and ships to the United States.

March on the capital. That summer, British ships sailed into Chesapeake Bay. Soldiers came ashore about 30 miles (48 km) from Washington, D.C. Americans tried to stop the British at Bladensburg, Maryland. President Madison himself rode out to watch the battle. To Madison's dismay, the battle-hardened British quickly scattered the untrained Americans and continued their march to the capital.

In the President's mansion, Dolley Madison waited for her husband to return. Hastily, she scrawled a note to her sister:

> **❝**Will you believe it, my sister? We have had a battle or skirmish near Bladensburg and here I am still within sound of the cannon! Mr. Madison comes not. May God protect us. Two messengers covered with dust come bid me fly. But here I mean to wait for him.**❞**

Soon after, British troops marched into the capital. Dolley Madison gathered up important papers of the President's and a portrait of George Washington. Then, she fled south. She was not there to see the British burn the President's mansion and other buildings.

Bombardment of Baltimore. From Washington, D.C., the British marched north to-

BIOGRAPHY Dolley Madison *As First Lady, Dolley Madison was best known for her skill at smoothing over quarrels between politicians. But when British troops burned Washington, D.C., Madison showed that she was also a woman of determination and courage.* **American Traditions** *How did Dolley Madison help to preserve the nation's heritage?*

ward Baltimore. The key to Baltimore's defense was Fort McHenry. From evening on September 13 until dawn on September 14, British rockets bombarded the harbor. When the early morning fog lifted, the "broad stripes and bright stars" of the American flag still waved over Fort McHenry. The British gave up the attack. Soon after, Francis Scott Key wrote a poem about the bombardment. Years later, "The Star-Spangled Banner" was set to music and adopted as the national anthem of the United States.

Linking Past and Present

When Americans rebuilt Washington, D.C., after the War of 1812, they gave the President's mansion a coat of whitewash to cover the charred wood. Ever since, it has been called the White House.

Jackson Defends New Orleans

Meanwhile, the British prepared to attack New Orleans. From there, they hoped to sail up the Mississippi.

Andrew Jackson was waiting for the British. His forces included thousands of frontiersmen, many of them expert riflemen. Hundreds of African Americans from New Orleans and a group of Filipino Americans also volunteered to defend their city.

Jackson's troops dug trenches to defend themselves. On January 8, 1815, the British tried to overrun Jackson's line. Again and again, British soldiers charged the American trenches. More than 2,000 British fell. Only seven Americans died.

All over the country, Americans celebrated the victory at the ***Battle of New Orleans.*** Overnight, Andrew Jackson became a national hero, second only to George Washington. (📖 See "At the Battle of New Orleans" on page 573.)

Jackson's fame did not dim even when Americans later learned that the long and bloody battle could have been avoided. The Battle of New Orleans took place two weeks after the United States and Britain had signed a peace treaty in Europe ending the war.

Peace at Last

News took weeks to cross the Atlantic Ocean in the early 1800s. By late 1814, Americans knew that peace talks had begun. But they did not know how they were progressing or how long they would last. While Jackson was preparing to fight the British at New Orleans, New Englanders were meeting to protest "Mr. Madison's war."

New Englanders protest. Delegates from around New England met in Hartford, Connecticut, in December 1814. Most were Federalists. They disliked the Republican President and the war.

The British blockade had hurt New England's sea trade. Also, many New Englanders felt that the South and the West had more to gain if the United States won land in Florida and Canada. If new states were carved out of these lands, New England would lose influence.

Delegates to the ***Hartford Convention*** threatened to leave the Union if the war continued. However, while the delegates debated what to do, news of the peace treaty arrived. The Hartford Convention ended quickly. With the war over, the protest was meaningless. The Federalist party died out completely with the end of the war.

The Battle of New Orleans
In this engraving, Andrew Jackson, at right, spurs the Americans on to victory in the Battle of New Orleans. Neither side, however, knew that the war was already over. **Geography** *Why did the British want to gain control of New Orleans?*

"Our Flag Was Still There" *Rockets lit up the night sky as the British bombarded Fort McHenry. But when dawn came, the American flag, right, still flew over the fort. The event inspired Francis Scott Key to write "The Star-Spangled Banner."* **American Traditions** *Why is a national anthem important to citizens?*

"Nothing was settled." Peace talks had been held in Ghent, Belgium. The ***Treaty of Ghent*** was signed on December 24, 1814. John Quincy Adams, one of the Americans at Ghent, summed up the treaty in one sentence: "Nothing was adjusted, nothing was settled."

Both sides agreed to return matters to the way they had been before the war. The treaty said nothing about impressment or American neutrality. Since Britain was no longer at war with France, these conflicts had faded. Other issues were settled later. In 1818, the two countries agreed to set much of the border between Canada and the United States at 49°N latitude.

Looking back, some Americans believed that the War of 1812 had been a mistake. Others argued that Europe would now treat the young republic with more respect. The victories of Isaac Hull and Andrew Jackson had given Americans new pride in their country. In the words of one Republican, "The people are now more American. They feel and act more as a nation."

SECTION 5 REVIEW

1. **Locate:** (a) Detroit, (b) Chesapeake Bay, (c) Washington, D.C., (d) Baltimore.
2. **Identify:** (a) Battle of the Thames, (b) Battle of Horseshoe Bend, (c) Dolley Madison, (d) Andrew Jackson, (e) Battle of New Orleans, (f) Hartford Convention, (g) Treaty of Ghent.
3. What problems did Americans face in preparing for war?
4. What part did Tecumseh play in the War of 1812?
5. What were the terms of the Treaty of Ghent?
6. **CRITICAL THINKING Analyzing Information** Why do you think the War of 1812 has been called the Second War of American Independence?

ACTIVITY **Writing to Learn**

List the reasons why the delegates to the Hartford Convention opposed the War of 1812. Use the list to write a petition to Congress calling for an end to the war.

Summary

- President Jefferson worked to limit the power of the federal government and to make the nation more democratic.
- The Louisiana Purchase doubled the size of the United States.
- To protect American neutrality, Congress passed the Embargo Act, banning all foreign trade.
- Giving in to the War Hawks, in 1812 the United States declared war on Britain.
- Neither the United States nor Britain won the War of 1812, but Americans gained a new sense of national pride.

Reviewing the Main Ideas

1. How did Jefferson's economic policies differ from those of the Federalists?
2. (a) What did the Supreme Court decide in *Marbury* v. *Madison*? (b) Why was the decision important?
3. (a) Why did Americans want to control the Mississippi River? (b) How did the revolt in Haiti influence Napoleon's decision to sell Louisiana?
4. (a) How did American overseas trade grow after the Revolution? (b) Why did Jefferson blockade Tripoli?
5. Why did the War Hawks want war?
6. Why was Tecumseh unable to unite all Native Americans east of the Mississippi River?
7. How did the War of 1812 affect Americans?

Thinking Critically

1. **Synthesizing Information** (a) How did the Louisiana Purchase affect the size of the United States? (b) What did the journey of Lewis and Clark prove? (c) How might these two events have affected the view Americans had of their country?

2. **Linking Past and Present** Reread the paragraphs on page 290 about the Hartford Convention. (a) What did the delegates threaten to do if the war continued? (b) How do state representatives today protest government actions?

Applying Your Skills

1. **Skimming a Chapter** Review the steps on skimming a chapter on page 264. Then skim Chapter 9. (a) What are the main topics? (b) What is the main idea of the section Republicans in Power?
2. **Following Routes on a Map** Study the map on page 273. (a) How does the map show Pike's route during 1805 and 1806? (b) During 1806 and 1807? (c) In which directions did Pike travel in 1805 and 1806? (d) In which direction was Pike headed when he crossed the Rio Grande?
3. **Analyzing a Quotation** What did Tecumseh mean when he said that Native Americans must unite in "claiming a common right to the land"?

Thinking About Geography

Match the letters on the map with the following places: **1.** Canada, **2.** Battle of the Thames, **3.** Battle of Horseshoe Bend, **4.** Battle of New Orleans, **5.** Baltimore, **6.** British blockade. **Movement** How did the British blockade hurt the United States?

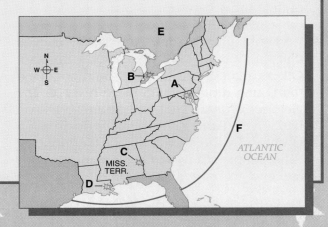

Exploring With Lewis and Clark

Form into groups to think about the Lewis and Clark expedition. Follow the suggestions below to write, draw, or perform to show what you have learned about the expedition. You may use the textbook, encyclopedias, atlases, or other materials in your classroom library to complete the tasks. Be able to name your sources of information when you have finished the activity.

GEOGRAPHERS On a large sheet of paper, create a map of the United States in 1803. On the map:
- Draw the route of the Lewis and Clark expedition.
- Show the climate in the areas visited by the expedition.
- Show at least five plants and animals found in the areas visited by Lewis and Clark.

MATHEMATICIANS Create a bar graph comparing the land area of the United States before and after the Louisiana Purchase.

ACTORS Find out the details of an interesting incident during the Lewis and Clark expedition. Prepare a skit about the incident. Assign roles to group members, and perform the skit for the class.

ARTISTS, POETS, AND MUSICIANS Find out about the Native Americans who lived in the territory of the Louisiana Purchase. How did they feel about the arrival of the explorers on their land? Share your findings in a drawing, poem, or song.

REPORTERS Review President Jefferson's instructions to Lewis and Clark. Then write a letter or videotape a message to the explorers explaining why the task they are about to perform is important for the country.

★ Create an Exploring With Lewis and Clark corner in the classroom, and display your completed activity there.

Clark's sketch of a salmon

Clark's sketch of a bird

Lewis and Clark and Sacajawea greet a group of Indians

CHAPTER **10**

Years of Growth and Expansion

(1790–1825)

CHAPTER OUTLINE

1 The Industrial Revolution

2 From Workshops to Factories

3 Americans on the Move

4 Building National Unity

5 Neighboring Nations Gain Independence

1700s *Many enslaved African Americans fled to Spanish Florida. Some, like this young man, joined the Seminole Indians.*

1790 *Samuel Slater opened the first water-powered spinning mill in the United States.*

1790s *The Lancaster Turnpike was built in Pennsylvania. Better roads made stagecoach travel faster.*

1785	1790	1795	1800	1805

▲
WORLD EVENT
1700s The Industrial Revolution begins in Britain

▲
WORLD EVENT
1802 Child labor law enacted in Britain

Chapter Setting

Clang-clang-clang-clang! At dawn each day, the factory bell woke 11-year-old Lucy Larcom. Rising quickly, she ate breakfast and hurried off to work. Lucy worked in a factory in Lowell, Massachusetts. The factory turned raw cotton into cloth. Years later, Lucy described her workplace:

❝I never cared much for machinery. The buzzing and hissing and whizzing of pulleys and rollers and spindles and flyers around me often grew tiresome. . . .

The last window in the row behind me was filled with flourishing houseplants. . . . Standing before that window, I could look across the room and see girls moving backwards and forwards among the spinning frames, sometimes stooping, sometimes reaching up their arms, as their work required. . . .

On the whole, it was far from being a disagreeable place to stay in. . . . [But] in the sweet June weather I would lean far out of the window, and try not to hear the unceasing clash of sound inside. Looking away to the hills, my whole stifled being would cry out, 'Oh, that I had wings!'❞

A growing number of Americans, like Lucy Larcom, took jobs in the factories that were built in the early 1800s. As factories sprang up, cities grew up around them. Most Americans still lived in rural areas. Yet changes were underway that would transform life in the United States.

 **ACTIVITY** Imagine that you are a worker in the mill at Lowell, Massachusetts. Write a song about your average workday.

1807 *The launching of the* Clermont *ushered in the steamboat era. This riverboat is on the Mississippi River near St. Louis.*

1821 *The Boston Associates built a factory town in Massachusetts. The women who worked in the mills published their own magazine.*

1825 *This plate celebrates the opening of the Erie Canal, which linked the Great Lakes with the Hudson River.*

1805   1810   1815   1820   1825

 WORLD EVENT
1810 Mexico and South America begin struggles for independence

 WORLD EVENT
1821 Mexico, Guatemala, and Peru win independence from Spain

The Industrial Revolution

FIND OUT

- How did the early Industrial Revolution change people's lives?
- What inventions led to the Industrial Revolution?
- How did the Industrial Revolution reach the United States?

VOCABULARY spinning jenny, cotton gin, capitalist, factory system

Shortly before his death in 1790, Benjamin Franklin wrote to a friend:

❝I wished it had been my destiny to have been born two or three centuries [later]. For invention and improvement are everywhere. The present progress is nothing less than astounding.❞

Franklin died just before a new revolution swept the United States. Unlike the revolution against British rule, this one had no battles and no fixed dates. Instead, it was a long, slow process that completely changed the way goods were produced.

New Ways to Produce Goods

The revolution in the way goods were produced is known as the *Industrial Revolution.* Before the Industrial Revolution, most goods were produced by hand at home or in workshops. Most people were farmers and lived in rural areas. As the Industrial Revolution got underway, machines replaced hand tools. At the same time, new sources of power, such as steam and electricity, replaced human and animal power.

The Industrial Revolution generated widespread changes. The economy shifted from farming to manufacturing. As a result, people moved from farms to cities.

New technology. The Industrial Revolution began in Britain in the mid-1700s. There, inventors developed new technologies that transformed the textile industry.

In 1764, James Hargreaves developed a machine he called the spinning jenny. With a spinning jenny, a worker could spin several threads at once—not just one thread as on a spinning wheel. Richard Arkwright took the process a step further. In 1769, he invented a machine that could hold 100 spindles of thread. Because the machine was too heavy to be operated by hand, it required water power to turn its wheels. As a result, it became known as the water frame.

Other inventions speeded up the process of weaving thread into cloth. In the 1780s, Edmund Cartwright built a loom powered by water. Using this power loom, a worker could produce 200 times more cloth in a day than was possible before.

In 1793, Eli Whitney, an American, gave a further boost to the textile industry. Whitney invented the cotton gin, a machine that speeded up the process of cleaning cotton fibers. (You will read more about effects of the cotton gin in Chapter 13.)

Birth of the factory. Machines like the water frame had to be set up near rivers. Water flowing rapidly downstream or over a waterfall turned a water wheel that produced the power to run the machines.

Our Common Heritage
One byproduct of the Industrial Revolution was a rise in immigration to the United States. Between 1815 and 1818, for example, more than 15,000 Irish immigrants came to the United States. Many were skilled weavers and artisans who found work in American mills and factories.

A Changing Landscape *The Industrial Revolution changed the face of the nation. This painting shows an early factory set among the church spires and green fields of a New England town.* **Daily Life** *How do you think the factory affected the life of the townspeople?*

The new machines were expensive and had to be housed in large buildings. Most were owned by capitalists, people with capital, or money, to invest in business to make a profit. Early capitalists built spinning mills and hired hundreds of workers to run the machines.

The spinning mills led to a new system of production in Britain. Instead of spinning and weaving in their homes, people went to work in factories. The new factory system brought workers and machines together in one place to produce goods. In factories, everyone had to work a certain number of hours each day. Workers were paid daily or weekly wages.

A Secret Crosses the Atlantic

Britain tried to keep its inventions secret. It did not want rival nations to copy the new machines. To protect national interests, the British Parliament passed a law forbidding anyone to take plans of Arkwright's water frame out of the country. It also forbade factory workers to leave Britain.

Samuel Slater's memory. Samuel Slater soon showed that the law could not be enforced. Slater was a skillful mechanic in one of Arkwright's mills. When he heard that Americans were offering large rewards for plans of British factories, he decided to leave England.

In 1789, Slater boarded a ship bound for New York. He knew that British officials often searched the baggage of passengers sailing to the United States. To avoid getting caught, he memorized the design of the machines in Arkwright's mill. He even used a false name when he traveled.

In New York, Slater learned that Moses Brown, a Quaker merchant, wanted to build a spinning mill in Rhode Island. Slater wrote confidently to Brown:

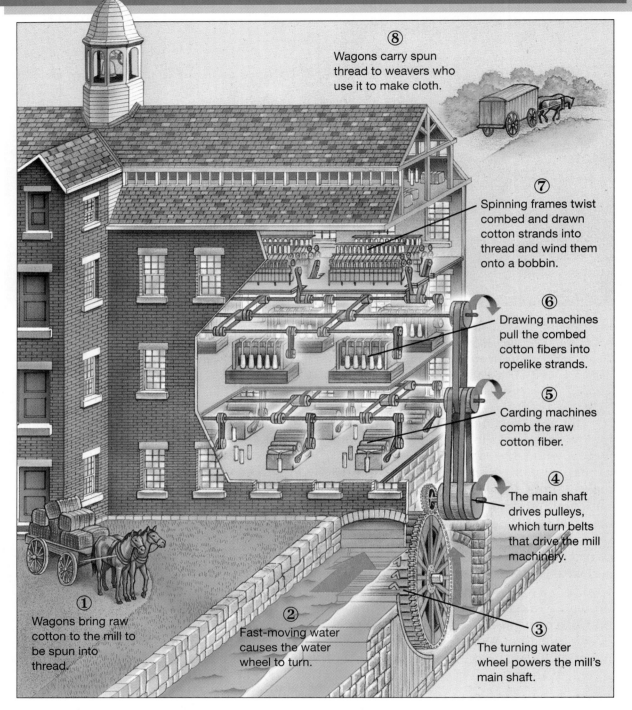

⑧ Wagons carry spun thread to weavers who use it to make cloth.

⑦ Spinning frames twist combed and drawn cotton strands into thread and wind them onto a bobbin.

⑥ Drawing machines pull the combed cotton fibers into ropelike strands.

⑤ Carding machines comb the raw cotton fiber.

④ The main shaft drives pulleys, which turn belts that drive the mill machinery.

① Wagons bring raw cotton to the mill to be spun into thread.

② Fast-moving water causes the water wheel to turn.

③ The turning water wheel powers the mill's main shaft.

Spinning Mill *The swift-moving streams of New England provided power for the nation's first factories. As shown here, rapidly moving water turned a water wheel that produced the power to run the machines.* **Local History** *Would your town or community have been a suitable place for a water-powered spinning mill? Why or why not?*

"If I do not make as good yarn as they do in England, I will have nothing for my services, but will throw the whole of what I have attempted over the bridge."

Brown replied at once: "If thou canst do what thou sayest, I invite thee to come to Rhode Island."

The first American mill. By December 1790, Slater and Brown were ready to start production in their spinning mill. On a bitter cold morning, Slater chopped ice off the water wheel. As Brown looked on, the machinery cranked into motion. Soon the 2 water frames and 72 spindles were turning out cotton thread.

In 1793, the two men built an improved mill. Hannah Slater, wife of Samuel, discovered how to make thread stronger so that it would not snap on the spindles. Before long, other American manufacturers began to build mills using Slater's ideas.

SECTION 1 REVIEW

1. **Identify:** (a) Industrial Revolution, (b) Samuel Slater, (c) Moses Brown.
2. **Define:** (a) spinning jenny, (b) cotton gin, (c) capitalist, (d) factory system.
3. What are four ways in which the Industrial Revolution changed daily life?
4. (a) Name two inventions of the Industrial Revolution. (b) How did each change the way goods were produced?
5. How did Samuel Slater bring Arkwright's ideas to the United States?
6. **CRITICAL THINKING Linking Past and Present** What present-day inventions do you think would astonish Benjamin Franklin most?

ACTIVITY **Writing to Learn**
Write an article for a Rhode Island newspaper about the opening of the mill built by Slater and Brown.

2
From Workshops to Factories

FIND OUT
- How did the War of 1812 help American manufacturers?
- How was Lowell a model community?
- What were working conditions like in early factories?
- What were the advantages and disadvantages of city life in the early 1800s?

VOCABULARY interchangeable parts

The Constitution gave Congress the authority "to promote science and useful arts." To achieve that goal, Congress passed the Patent Act in 1790. The new law protected the rights of inventors.

Mary Kies of Connecticut was the first woman to take out a patent. In 1809, she patented a new weaving process for straw hats. Kies's invention gave a major boost to the New England hat industry.

Mary Kies was just one of many inventors working in the United States in the early 1800s. Inventors and other bold thinkers transformed American manufacturing.

The Lowell Experiment

Before the Revolution, colonists imported most manufactured goods from Britain. After independence, Americans were eager to build their own industries. For many years, however, progress was slow.

Britain's blockade of the United States during the War of 1812 provided a boost to American industries. Cut off from foreign

Textile Workers *In the 1820s, the town of Lowell, Massachusetts, became a leading center of the American textile industry. Many of the machines in the Lowell mills were operated by women, as shown above.* **Economics** *How did the factory system benefit capitalists?*

suppliers, Americans had to produce more goods themselves.

Francis Cabot Lowell. As in Britain, early advances occurred in the textile industry. A Boston merchant, Francis Cabot Lowell, had toured British textile mills. There, he saw how one factory spun thread while another wove it into cloth. Lowell had a better idea. Why not combine spinning and weaving under one roof?

To finance his project, Lowell joined with several partners to form the ***Boston Associates*** in 1813. They built a textile mill in Waltham, Massachusetts. The factory had all the machines needed to turn raw cotton into finished cloth. The machines were powered by water from the nearby Charles River.

A model community. Lowell died in 1817, but the Boston Associates continued. In time, they took on a more ambitious project. They built an entire factory town on the Merrimack River. They named the new town after Francis Lowell.

In 1821, Lowell, Massachusetts, was a village of five farm families. By 1836, it boasted more than 10,000 people along with factories, banks, schools, stores, a library, and a church. Visitors flocked to this showplace of American industry. One left this description:

> 66There are huge factories, five, six or seven stories high, each capped with a little white belfry... which stands out sharply against the dark hills on the horizon. There are small wooden houses, painted white, with green blinds, very neat, very snug, very nicely carpeted, and with a few small trees around them. 99

"Lowell girls." The Boston Associates hired young women from nearby farms to work in the mills. Usually, the "Lowell girls," as they were called, worked for a few years in the mills. Then they returned home to marry. Most sent their wages home to their families. Some saved part of their wages to help set up their own homes.

At first, parents hesitated to let their daughters work in the mills. To reassure parents, the Boston Associates built boarding houses for their workers. They hired housemothers to manage the houses. The company also built a church and made rules to protect the young women.

At Work in the Mills

In Lowell and elsewhere, mill owners mostly hired women and children. They did this because they could pay women and

---

History and You

It is hard to go to school and work at the same time. Massachusetts passed a law in 1837 prohibiting children from being employed more than nine months a year so that they could attend school for at least three months. Have you ever held a job during the school year? What type of work did you do and for how many hours each day?

children half of what they would have had to pay men.

Child labor. Children as young as 7 years of age worked in the mills. Because they were quick and small, they could squeeze around large machines to change spindles. Such children were called "doffers." They doffed, or took off, full spindles of thread and replaced them with empty ones. "I can see myself now," recalled a woman who had worked in a mill as a child, "carrying in front of me a [spindle] bigger than I was."

For many years, Americans have looked on child labor as cruel. Yet in the 1800s, farm boys and girls also worked long hours. Most people did not see much difference between children working in a factory or on a farm. Often, a child's wages were needed to help support the family.

Long hours. Working hours in the mills were long—12 hours a day, 6 days a week. True, farmers also put in long hours. But farmers worked shorter hours in winter. Mill workers, by contrast, worked the same hours all year round.

At first, conditions in American mills were better than in most European factories at the time. As industries grew, however, competition increased. As a result, employers took less interest in the welfare of their workers. Conditions worsened and wages fell.

Eli Whitney

Manufacturers benefited from the pioneering work of Eli Whitney. In the early 1800s, skilled workers made goods by hand. A gunsmith, for example, spent days making the stock, barrel, and trigger for a musket. Each musket differed a bit from the next because the parts were handmade. If a part broke, a gunsmith had to fashion a new part to fit that gun.

Whitney wanted to speed up the making of guns by having machines manufacture each part. Machine-made parts would all be

CAUSES

- British ideas of a spinning mill and power loom reach the United States
- Eli Whitney invents the cotton gin
- War of 1812 prompts Americans to make their own goods
- Eli Whitney introduces the idea of interchangeable parts

THE INDUSTRIAL REVOLUTION IN THE UNITED STATES

EFFECTS

- Factory system spreads
- Young women and children from nearby farms work in mills
- Growing cities face problems of fire, sewage, garbage, and disease

CHART SKILLS *The Industrial Revolution was a period of great change.* • *What inventions and ideas helped to produce the Industrial Revolution? Do you think the effects of the Industrial Revolution were positive or negative? Explain.*

alike. Stocks would be the same size and shape. Barrels would be the same length. Whitney's idea of **interchangeable parts** would save time and money.

Because the government bought many guns, Whitney took his idea to Washington. At first, officials laughed at his plan. Whitney paid them no attention. Carefully, he sorted parts for 10 muskets into separate piles. He then asked an official to choose one part from each pile. In minutes, the first musket was assembled. Whitney repeated the process until 10 muskets were complete.

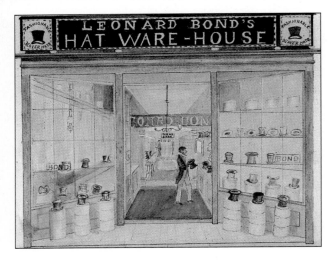

Shopping *In the early 1800s, most Americans depended on door-to-door peddlers for ready-made goods. In the growing cities, however, people could do their shopping in stores, like the one shown here.* **Daily Life** *What advantages can you see in each form of shopping?*

Onlookers, reported one observer, responded with "sheer amazement."

The idea of interchangeable parts spread rapidly. Inventors designed machines to produce parts for locks, knives, and many other goods. With such machines, small workshops grew into factories.

Growing Cities

As factories grew, so did the towns and cities where they were located. By today's standards, these cities were small. A person could walk from one end of any American city to the other end in 30 minutes.

Hazards. Cities had many problems. Dirt and gravel streets turned into mudholes when it rained. Cities had no sewers, and people threw garbage into the streets. An English visitor to New York reported:

66 The streets are filthy, and the stranger is not a little surprised to meet the hogs walking about in them, for the purpose of devouring the vegetables and trash thrown into the gutter. 99

In these dirty, crowded conditions, disease spread easily. Yellow fever and cholera (KAHL er uh) epidemics raged through cities, killing hundreds.

Fire posed another threat. If a sooty chimney caught fire, the flames quickly spread from one wooden house to the next. Many cities had volunteer fire companies. Often, rival companies competed to get to a blaze first. Sometimes, companies fought each other instead of the fire!

Attractions. Cities had attractions, too. Circuses, racetracks, plays, and museums created an air of excitement. In New York, P. T. Barnum made a fortune exhibiting rare animals at his American Museum.

Cities also had fine stores that sold the latest fashions. Some offered modern "ready-to-wear" clothing. A New York store boasted that "gentlemen can rely upon being as well fitted from the shelves as if their measures were taken." Women still sewed most of their own clothes, but they enjoyed visiting china shops, "fancy-goods" stores, and shoe stores.

SECTION 2 REVIEW

1. **Identify:** (a) Francis Cabot Lowell, (b) Boston Associates, (c) Eli Whitney.
2. **Define:** interchangeable parts.
3. How did the War of 1812 help the growth of American industry?
4. How did the Boston Associates make the Lowell mills attractive to workers?
5. Why did mill owners hire women and children?
6. **CRITICAL THINKING Understanding Causes and Effects** How did industrial development help to bring about social change in the United States in the 1800s?

ACTIVITY Writing to Learn
Write a help-wanted ad to attract young women to work at the Lowell mills.

CRITICAL THINKING SKILLS
Using a Concept Map

A concept map is a way to organize ideas visually. Using a concept map is similar to taking notes. It helps you to keep track of the main ideas and supporting details as you read.

A concept map is made up of connected circles. In the center is the general topic. The general topic is often the same as the heading or title. The main ideas and supporting details are arranged around the general topic. Lines connect main ideas with their supporting details.

Study the concept map below. It shows the ideas in the subsection Growing Cities, on page 302.

1. **Identify the general topic.** (a) What is the general topic of the subsection? (b) How do you know that it is the general topic?

2. **Identify the main ideas.** The main ideas are connected with lines to the general topic. (a) How many main ideas are there in the subsection? (b) What are the main ideas of the subsection?

3. **Find the supporting details.** Two of the main ideas have one or more supporting details. (a) What are the supporting details for the main idea "Hazards"? (b) How do you know that these are supporting details? (c) What supporting details are connected to the main idea "Attractions"?

4. **Use the concept map to see how events and ideas are related.** (a) Why were people attracted to city life? (b) What were the hazards of city life?

ACTIVITY Locate a brief newspaper or magazine article about the economy or city life today. Circle the main idea or ideas in the article. Draw a square box around the supporting details. Then make a concept map using the information you have highlighted in the article.

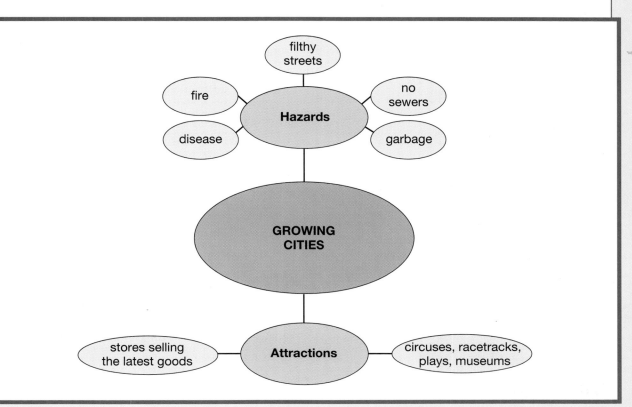

3

Americans on the Move

FIND OUT

- How did settlers travel west?
- What steps did Americans take to improve roads?
- How did steamboats and canals change transportation?

VOCABULARY turnpike, corduroy road, canal

An Irish visitor described a stagecoach trip through Maryland:

66 The driver frequently had to call to the passengers in the stage, to lean out of the carriage first at one side, then at the other, to prevent it from oversetting in the deep ruts with which the road abounds: 'Now gentlemen, to the right,'. . . 'Now gentlemen, to the left,' and so on. 99

In the 1790s, travel was as difficult as it had been in colonial times. Most roads were mud tracks. River travel could be difficult, too, when boats had to push upstream against the current. As the young nation grew, Americans saw the need to improve transportation.

GEOGRAPHY AND HISTORY
Heading West

In the early 1800s, thousands of settlers headed west, to the land between the Appalachians and the Mississippi. "Old America seems to be breaking up and moving westward," noted a visitor. By 1820, so many people had moved west that the population in some of the original 13 states had actually declined.

Western routes. Settlers took a number of routes west. One well-traveled path was the Great Wagon Road across Pennsylvania. Colonists had pioneered it years before. (See page 105.) Some settlers continued south and west along the trail opened by Daniel Boone before the Revolution. Called the Wilderness Road, it led through the Cumberland Gap into Kentucky.

Other settlers pushed west to Pittsburgh. There, they loaded their animals and wagons onto flatboats and journeyed down the Ohio River into Indiana, Kentucky, and Illinois. Flatboats were well suited to the shallow waters of the Ohio. Even with heavy loads, these raftlike barges rode high in the water.

Pioneers from Georgia and South Carolina followed other trails west. Enslaved African Americans helped to carve plantations in the rich, fertile soil of Alabama and Mississippi.

New Englanders, "Yorkers," and Pennsylvanians pushed into the Northwest Territory. Some traveled west from Albany, New York, along the Mohawk River and across the Appalachians. Some settlers then followed Indian trails around Lake Erie. Others sailed across the lake into Ohio.

New states. With the flood of settlers, there were enough people in some western lands to apply for statehood. Between 1792 and 1819, eight states joined the Union: Kentucky (1792), Tennessee (1796), Ohio (1803), Louisiana (1812), Indiana (1816), Mississippi (1817), Illinois (1818), and Alabama (1819).

Better Roads

Settlers faced a rough journey. Many roads were narrow trails that were barely wide enough for a single wagon. One pioneer wrote of "rotten banks down which horses plunged" and streams that "almost drowned them." The nation badly needed better roads.

ART GALLERY: OUR COMMON HERITAGE

JOAN LANDIS BAHM
My Ancestors Coming to America, 1990

In this quilt, Joan Landis Bahm records the journeys of her ancestors from Switzerland to the United States in the 1700s and 1800s. The symbols that border the quilt—steamships, canal barges and mules, covered wagons—indicate the many types of transportation that the settlers used in their new land. **Geography** *Locate the Erie Canal on the quilt. What form of transportation does Bahm show there?*

Turnpikes and covered bridges. Probably the best road in the United States was the *Lancaster Turnpike.* It was built in the 1790s by a private company. The road linked Philadelphia and Lancaster, Pennsyl-vania. Because the road was set on a bed of gravel, water drained off quickly. It was topped with smooth, flat stones.

Private companies built other gravel and stone roads. To pay for these roads, the companies collected tolls. At various points along the road, a pike, or pole, blocked the road. After a wagon driver paid a toll, the pike keeper turned the pole aside. These toll roads became known as **turnpikes.**

In swampy areas, roads were made of logs. These roads were called **corduroy roads** because the lines of logs looked like corduroy cloth. Corduroy roads kept wagons from sinking into the mud, but they made for a bumpy ride.

Bridges carried travelers across streams and rivers. Stone bridges were costly to build, but wooden ones rotted quickly. A clever Massachusetts carpenter designed a wooden bridge with a roof to protect it from the weather. Covered bridges lasted much longer than open ones.

The National Road. In 1806, Congress approved spending for the ***National Road,*** from Cumberland, Maryland, to Wheeling, in western Virginia. Work began in 1811 and was completed in 1818. Later, the road was extended into Illinois. (📖 See "Traveling Westward" on page 575.)

Increased traffic. Better roads helped not only travelers but also freight haulers. Heavy wagons pulled by eight or ten hors-

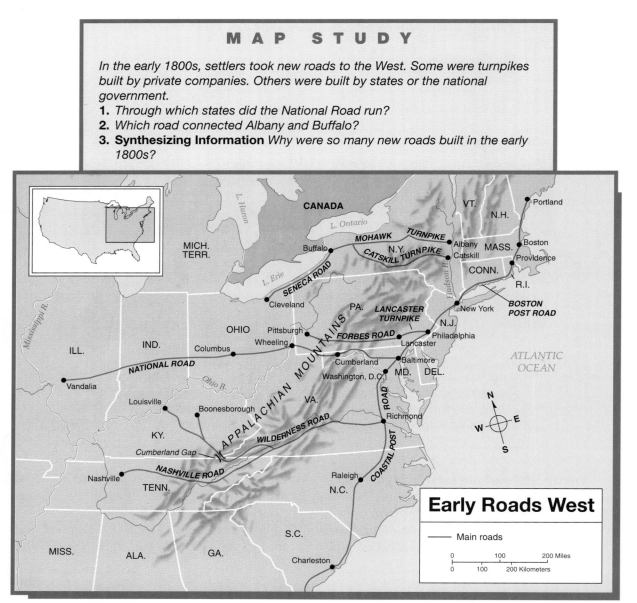

MAP STUDY

In the early 1800s, settlers took new roads to the West. Some were turnpikes built by private companies. Others were built by states or the national government.

1. Through which states did the National Road run?
2. Which road connected Albany and Buffalo?
3. **Synthesizing Information** Why were so many new roads built in the early 1800s?

Early Roads West

— Main roads

0   100   200 Miles

0   100   200 Kilometers

es rumbled along the roads. Small farm wagons drawn by one or two horses also plodded along. All wagons moved aside when stagecoaches sped recklessly past.

From October to December, roads were filled with animals being driven to market. Herders, called drovers, used dogs to keep hogs, cattle, sheep, and even turkeys moving along. ∎

Steam Transport

When possible, travelers and freight wagons used river transportation. Floating downstream on a flatboat was faster, cheaper, and more comfortable than bumping along rutted roads.

River travel had its problems, too. Moving upstream was difficult. To travel upstream, people used paddles or long poles to push boats against the current. Sometimes, they hauled boats from the shore with ropes. Both methods were slow. A boat could travel downstream from Pittsburgh to New Orleans in six weeks. The return trip upstream took at least 17 weeks!

Fitch and Fulton. Progress in river travel came from a new invention—the steam engine. In 1787, John Fitch showed members of the Constitutional Convention how a steam engine could propel a boat. Soon after, Fitch opened a ferry service on the Delaware River. Few people used his ferry, however, and Fitch went out of business.

Robert Fulton succeeded where Fitch had failed. Fulton had probably seen Fitch's steamboat in Philadelphia. In 1807, Fulton launched his own steamboat, the *Clermont,* on the Hudson River. On its first run, the *Clermont* carried passengers from New York City to Albany and back. The 300-mile (480-km) round trip took just 62 hours—a record at the time. Within three months, Fulton was making a profit on this run.

The age of steamboats. Fulton's success ushered in the age of steamboats. Soon, steamboats were ferrying passengers up and down the Atlantic coast. More important, they revolutionized travel in the West. Besides carrying people, steamboats on the Mississippi, Ohio, and Missouri rivers gave farmers and merchants a cheap means of moving goods. Because western rivers were shallow, Henry Shreve designed a flat-bottomed steamboat. It could carry heavy loads without getting stuck on sandbars.

"Floating palaces." By the 1850s, some western steamboats had become "floating palaces." Wealthy passengers strolled on vessels that had three decks and a saloon for eating. Along the walls of the saloon were double-decker berths, where men slept. Women had a separate "ladies' parlor." They entered the saloon only for meals. The poor traveled in less comfort on boats with leaky roofs. They slept on pillows stuffed with corn husks.

Steamboat travel could be dangerous. Sparks from smokestacks could kindle fires. Steamboats used high-pressure boilers to make steam. As steamboat captains raced each other along the river, boilers sometimes exploded. Between 1811 and 1851, 44 steamboats collided, 166 burned, and more than 200 exploded. (📖 See "Life on the Mississippi" on page 576.)

The Canal Boom

Steamboats and better roads brought some improvements. But they did not help western farmers get their goods directly to markets in the East. To meet this need, Americans built canals. A **canal** is a channel dug by people, then filled with water to allow boats to cross a stretch of land.

The first canals were only a few miles long. Often, they were dug to get around waterfalls. Others linked a river to a nearby lake. By the early 1800s, Americans were building longer canals.

"Little short of madness." Some New Yorkers had a bold idea. They wanted to build a canal linking the Great Lakes with

The success of the Erie Canal, completed in 1825, set off an age of canal building.
1. *About how long was the Erie Canal?*
2. *What two bodies of water were linked by the Ohio and Erie Canal?*
3. **Synthesizing Information** *Use the map to describe an all-water route from Evansville, Indiana, to New York City.*

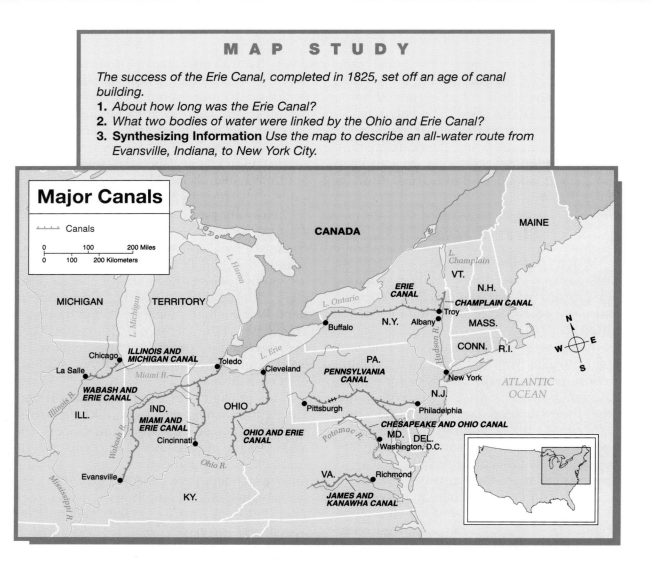

Major Canals

the Mohawk and Hudson rivers. The canal would let western farmers ship their goods to the port of New York. It would also bring business to towns along the route.

To many people, such a canal seemed farfetched. When President Jefferson heard about it, he exclaimed:

66 Why, sir, you talk of making a canal 350 miles through the wilderness—it is little short of madness to think of it at this day! 99

Digging the waterway. Governor De Witt Clinton of New York disagreed. He convinced state lawmakers to provide money for the project.

Work on the ***Erie Canal*** began in 1817. At first, workers dug the waterway by hand. To speed up progress, inventors developed new equipment. One machine, a stump-puller, could pull out nearly 40 tree stumps a day. In two places, the canal had to cross over rivers. Workers built stone bridges to carry the canal over the rivers.

By 1825, the immense job was finished. On opening day, a cannon fired a volley in Buffalo, New York. When the sound got to the next town along the route, it, too, fired a cannon. Town after town fired their cannons—all the way to New York City. The thunderous salute took 80 minutes to complete.

| ARTS | SCIENCES | GEOGRAPHY | WORLD | ECONOMICS | CIVICS |

Along the Erie Canal

"Low Bridge!" rang out the cry. What canal boat passenger would dare ignore the warning? A low bridge could bring a mighty crack in the head. Unheeding passengers might even be swept overboard.

"Low bridge, everybody down" begins the refrain of just one of the many songs that celebrate life along the Erie Canal. Each verse reveals more about the work of the mule drivers on the canal. Plodding slowly along the tow path, these "canal boys" led the animals that pulled the canal boats and barges. Like laborers everywhere, they eased the monotony of their work with songs about their jobs.

    ❝I've got a mule and her name
      is Sal,
    Fifteen miles on the Erie Canal.
    We've hauled some barges in
      our day
    Filled with lumber, coal, and hay,
    And we know every inch of
      the way
    From Albany to Buffalo.**❞**

Refrain:

    ❝Low bridge, everybody down!
    Low bridge! We're a-coming to
      a town.
    You'll always know your
      neighbor,
    You'll always know your pal
    If you've ever navigated on the
      Erie Canal.**❞**

There are many versions of "The Erie Canal." Although they began along the canal, they soon passed by word of mouth far beyond its banks. In time, many were written down. Today, we treasure folk songs such as "The Erie Canal" for the glimpses they give us of the past.

■ What can you learn about the Erie Canal from the song?

Sheet music

Erie Canal

ACTIVITY Based on the song, create a comic strip in which you show events that might happen during a canal boy's 15-mile stretch along the Erie Canal.

An instant success. The Erie Canal was an instant success. In a single day, more than 50 canal boats might be seen moving along its length. Standing on a bridge above the canal, one eyewitness described the scene:

66It is an impressive sight to gaze up and down the canal. In either direction, as far as the eye can see, long lines of boats can be observed. By night, their flickering head lamps give the impression of swarms of fireflies.**99**

The Erie Canal brought many benefits. It reduced travel time and lowered the cost of shipping goods. Goods sent from Buffalo to New York by canal now took less than 20 days. The canal also helped to make New York City a center of commerce.

The success of the Erie Canal led other states to build canals. These canals created vital economic links between western farms and eastern cities.

SECTION 3 REVIEW

1. **Locate:** (a) National Road, (b) Erie Canal.
2. **Identify:** (a) Lancaster Turnpike, (b) Robert Fulton, (c) *Clermont,* (d) Henry Shreve, (e) De Witt Clinton.
3. **Define:** (a) turnpike, (b) corduroy road, (c) canal.
4. What different means of transportation did settlers use to move west?
5. (a) How did road travel improve in the early 1800s? (b) How did river travel change?
6. CRITICAL THINKING **Understanding Causes and Effects** (a) Describe two immediate effects of the Erie Canal. (b) Describe two long-range effects.

ACTIVITY Writing to Learn
Write a newspaper report about opening day on the Erie Canal.

4
Building National Unity

FIND OUT
- What was the Era of Good Feelings?
- How did Congress try to strengthen the national economy?
- What was Henry Clay's American System?

VOCABULARY dumping

The Marquis de Lafayette made a triumphal tour of the United States in 1824. Everywhere, crowds cheered the hero who had helped Americans win independence more than 40 years earlier. Lafayette visited New Orleans. He traveled up the Mississippi by steamboat. He saw Cincinnati, a city that had not existed a few years before.

At the end of his trip, Lafayette spoke to Congress. He admired the "immense improvements" he saw everywhere. Lafayette praised "all the grandeur and prosperity of these happy United States, which. . . reflect on every part of the world the light of a far superior political civilization."

By the 1820s, Americans were feeling confident. After the War of 1812, the country grew and expanded. New lands opened to settlers with improved transportation. New industries appeared. In Congress, political leaders sought to direct this growth and expansion.

An Era of Good Feelings

In 1816, the Republican candidate for President, James Monroe, easily defeated the Federalist, Rufus King. Once in office, Monroe spoke of a new sense of national unity.

In 1817, Monroe made a goodwill tour of the country. Not since George Washington had a President made such a tour. In Boston, crowds welcomed this tall, dignified man in his old-fashioned clothes and three-cornered hat.

Boston newspapers expressed surprise at the warm welcome. After all, Boston had been a Federalist stronghold. Monroe was a Republican from Virginia. One newspaper wrote that the United States was entering an "Era of Good Feelings." The bitter disputes between Republicans and Federalists had begun to fade.

When Monroe ran for a second term in 1820, no one opposed him. By then, the Federalist party had disappeared.

Three Political Giants

Although conflict between political parties declined, disputes between different sections of the nation sharpened. In Congress, three ambitious young men took center stage. They were John C. Calhoun of South Carolina, Daniel Webster of Massachusetts, and Henry Clay of Kentucky.

All three played key roles in Congress for more than 30 years. Each represented a different section of the country.

John C. Calhoun. Calhoun spoke for the South. He had grown up on a farm on the South Carolina frontier. Later, he went to Yale College in Connecticut. Slim and handsome, Calhoun had deep-set eyes, a high forehead, and immense energy. His way of speaking was so intense that some people felt uncomfortable in his presence.

Daniel Webster. Webster spoke for the North. With dark hair and flashing eyes, Webster was an impressive sight in Congress. When he spoke, he stood straight as a ramrod, with shoulders thrown back. The hall would fall silent. "He will not be outdone by any man, if it is within his power to avoid it," observed a friend. Webster served first in the House and later as a senator from Massachusetts.

A New Generation of Leaders *Three young politicians rose to prominence in the early 1800s. Both Daniel Webster, left, and Henry Clay, right, urged the government to take a larger role in developing the nation's economy. John C. Calhoun, center, had fears of making the central government too powerful.* **Citizenship** *How did sectional politics play a role in the rise of Calhoun, Webster, and Clay?*

Henry Clay. From the West came Henry Clay. He had grown up on a backcountry farm. He was a man of action who had been a War Hawk in 1812. (See page 282.) As a young lawyer, Clay was once fined for brawling with an opposing lawyer. Usually, however, Clay charmed both friends and rivals. He enjoyed staying up late to discuss politics or to play cards. Like Calhoun and Webster, Clay could move people to laughter or tears with his speeches.

A New National Bank

After the War of 1812, a major problem facing leaders like Calhoun, Webster, and Clay was the nation's economic weakness. The problem was due in part to the lack of a national bank.

The charter for the first Bank of the United States ran out in 1811. Without the Bank to lend money and regulate the nation's money supply, the economy suffered. State banks made loans and issued money. Often, they put too much money into circulation, causing prices to rise rapidly.

In the nation's early years, Republicans, like Jefferson and Madison, had opposed a national bank. By 1816, however, many Republicans saw that a bank was needed. They supported a law to charter the second Bank of the United States. By lending money to individuals and restoring order to the money supply, the Bank helped American businesses grow.

Competition From Abroad

Another problem the nation faced after the War of 1812 was foreign competition, especially from Britain. In the early 1800s, the Embargo Act and then the War of 1812 kept most British goods out of the United States. In response, ambitious Americans, like Samuel Slater and Francis Cabot Lowell, set up mills and factories.

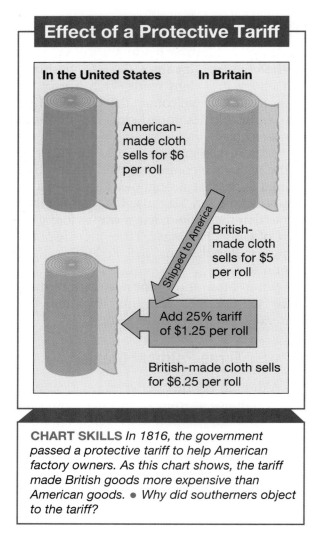

Effect of a Protective Tariff

In the United States

In Britain

American-made cloth sells for $6 per roll

British-made cloth sells for $5 per roll

Shipped to America

Add 25% tariff of $1.25 per roll

British-made cloth sells for $6.25 per roll

CHART SKILLS *In 1816, the government passed a protective tariff to help American factory owners. As this chart shows, the tariff made British goods more expensive than American goods. ● Why did southerners object to the tariff?*

A flood of British goods. In 1815, British goods again poured into the United States. The British could make and sell goods more cheaply than Americans, who had to pay for building their new factories.

Sometimes, British manufacturers sold cloth for less than it cost to make. The practice of selling goods in another country at very low prices is called **dumping.** Through dumping, British manufacturers hoped to put American rivals out of business.

Congress acts. Dumping caused dozens of New England businesses to fail. Angry factory owners asked Congress for a protective tariff on all goods imported from Europe. As you recall, a protective tariff is meant to protect a country's industries from foreign competition. (See the diagram at left.)

Congress responded by passing the Tariff of 1816. It greatly raised tariffs on imports. This increase made imported goods far more expensive than American-made goods.

Southerners protest. Higher tariffs led to angry protests, especially from southerners. The South had few factories to benefit from the tariff. Also, southerners had long been buying British goods. The new tariff forced them to buy costly American-made goods. Southerners saw the tariff as a law that made northern manufacturers rich at the expense of the South.

Henry Clay's American System

The bitter dispute over tariffs reflected the growing importance of sectional interests. Americans identified themselves as southerners, northerners, and westerners. In Congress, clashes occurred between representatives from different sections.

Henry Clay wanted to promote economic growth for all sections. He set out a program that became known as the ***American System.*** It called for high tariffs on imports, which would help northern factories. With wealth from industry, northerners would buy farm products from the West and the South. High tariffs would also reduce American dependence on foreign goods.

Clay also hoped to boost the national economy by calling for internal improvements—the building of roads, bridges, and canals. He urged Congress to use money from tariffs on such improvements. A better transportation system, he believed, would make it easier—and cheaper—for farmers in the West and the South to ship goods to city markets.

Clay's American System never went into effect. Tariffs remained high, but Congress spent little on internal improvements. Southerners especially disliked Clay's plan. The South had many fine rivers to transport goods. Many southerners opposed paying for roads and canals that brought them no direct benefits.

Improving Travel *Many Americans argued that improved transportation was vital to the growth of the nation. Here, the* Paragon, *one of Robert Fulton's boats, steams up the Hudson River.* ***Geography*** *Why did many southerners oppose spending money for internal improvements?*

SECTION 4 REVIEW

1. **Identify:** (a) John C. Calhoun, (b) Daniel Webster, (c) Henry Clay, (d) American System.
2. **Define:** dumping.
3. Why were the years after Monroe became President known as the Era of Good Feelings?
4. Explain how Congress tried to solve each of the following problems: (a) the money supply, (b) dumping.
5. How did the tariff debate reflect sectional differences?
6. **CRITICAL THINKING Defending a Position** Do you think that Clay's American System was a good plan for the nation? Explain.

ACTIVITY Writing to Learn

Write a dialogue between two of the "political giants" in this section. Topics can include the tariff, national bank, and American System.

5

Neighboring Nations Gain Independence

FIND OUT

- How did Canada achieve self rule?
- How did revolutions change Latin America?
- Why did the United States issue the Monroe Doctrine?

In 1812, a rebel army gathered in Caracas, in present-day Venezuela. For two years, they had been fighting to free their land from Spanish rule. Victory seemed near.

Then, on Thursday, March 26, the earth trembled and rolled. Buildings housing the rebel troops collapsed, killing thousands.

Only a few miles away, the Spanish Army was untouched. Simón Bolívar (see MOHN boh LEE vahr), a young rebel officer, leaped onto the rubble, crying: "If Nature thwarts us and our plans, we shall fight against her, and make her obey."

Throughout Latin America,* Spanish-ruled colonies fought long wars for independence in the early 1800s. Elsewhere in the hemisphere, Canada won self-rule largely through peaceful means.

Self-Government for Canada

In the early 1800s, Canada had a diverse population. Canadians included French and English settlers as well as Native Americans. Indian nations controlled much of what is today northern and western Canada.

Two cultures. In 1763, the British had won control of Canada. (See page 141.) The British conquest left Canada a troubled land. French Canadians and English Canadians distrusted one another. The two groups spoke different languages and practiced different religions. Most English settlers were Protestants. Most French settlers were Roman Catholics.

During and after the American Revolution, more than 40,000 Loyalists fled north to Canada. Many settled in Nova Scotia, New Brunswick, Prince Edward Island, and the area north of the Great Lakes. Among the newcomers were more than 3,000 enslaved African Americans who sought freedom in Canada.

Two Canadas. As Canada's population grew, Britain decided to rule the two groups separately. In 1791, it divided Canada into Upper and Lower Canada. Upper Canada included the area around the Great Lakes settled by English-speaking people. Lower

---

*Latin America refers to the parts of the Western Hemisphere where Latin-based languages such as Spanish, French, and Portuguese are spoken. It includes Mexico, Central and South America, and the West Indies.

Canada included lands along the lower St. Lawrence River settled by the French. Each province had its own government, but Britain made all important decisions.

By the early 1800s, most Canadians were pressing for change. They called for self-rule. They also wanted to reduce the power of a few wealthy families who controlled the government.

In 1837, uprisings occurred in both Upper and Lower Canada. The British had learned from their experience in the American Revolution. Faced with bands of armed patriots, they looked for peaceful solutions.

Britain sent Lord Durham to Canada to decide "the form and future government" of the provinces. Durham urged Britain to give Canadians control over local affairs. He also called for Upper and Lower Canada to be united. The Durham Report became the basis for Canadian self-rule.

The Dominion of Canada. Canadians slowly moved toward self-government. In 1867, the provinces of Nova Scotia, New Brunswick, Ontario, and Quebec joined to form the ***Dominion of Canada.*** Later on, Prince Edward Island, Manitoba, Alberta, Saskatchewan, and British Columbia also joined the Dominion.

By slow and generally peaceful means, Canada gained self-rule. Its government was similar to Britain's. Canada had an elected parliament and a prime minister. A governor general represented the British ruler but had little power.

Upheavals in Latin America

In the early 1800s, revolutions broke out in Spain's colonies in Latin America. Discontent was widespread. Most people had no say in government. Some were inspired by the French and American revolutions to seek self-rule. The poor hoped to end the harsh laws that ruled their lives.

Since the 1500s, Spain had put down many revolts. In Mexico and Peru, Indians

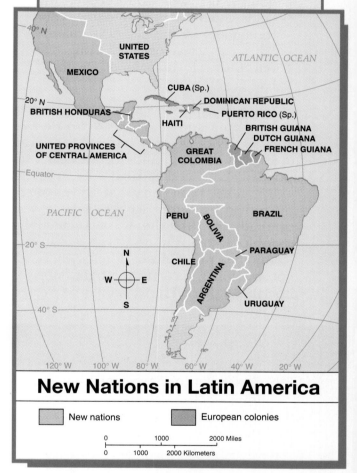

MAP STUDY

The wars of independence in Latin America led to the creation of many new nations.
1. Which new nation was farthest north?
2. Which places remained European colonies?
3. **Linking Past and Present** Use the world map in the Reference Section to name the nations that were eventually carved out of the United Provinces of Central America.

New Nations in Latin America

New nations

European colonies

0   1000   2000 Miles

0   1000   2000 Kilometers

had resisted Spanish control. In the late 1700s, unrest among Spanish settlers also grew.

The early rebellions mostly involved Indians and mestizos. Creoles took no part in the uprisings. Without support from the creoles, the rebels could not succeed.

Independence for Mexico

One Sunday in September 1810, the church bell of the village of Dolores rang longer than usual. Hurrying to the square, people found their priest, Father Miguel Hidalgo (mee GEHL ee DAHL goh), making a stirring speech. No one knows the exact words, but Mexicans remembered his message:

66My children.... Will you free yourselves? Will you recover the lands stolen 300 years ago from your forefathers by the hated Spaniards? We must act at once.... Long live our Lady of Guadalupe! Death to bad government!99

Grito de Dolores. Father Hidalgo's message became known as the *Grito de Dolores,* or Cry of Dolores. It sounded the call to revolution. Thousands of Mexicans responded and joined Hidalgo.

The rebels won control of several Mexican provinces before Father Hidalgo was captured. In 1811, he was executed by troops loyal to Spain.

Another priest, José Morelos (hoh ZAY moh RAY lohs), took up the fight. Morelos proclaimed that all races should be treated equally. He called for a program to give land to peasants. Wealthy creoles opposed him. Before long, he, too, was captured and killed by the Spanish.

Success at last. Slowly, creoles began to support the revolution. In 1821, an army led by a creole officer, Agustín de Iturbide (ah goos TEEN day ee toor BEE day), won control of Mexico. After 300 years of Spanish rule, Mexicans won independence. A few years later, Mexico became a republic with its own constitution.

The Liberator

While Mexicans fought for freedom, people elsewhere in Latin America sought independence. Among the heroes of the wars of independence was Simón Bolívar. Because he fought so long and hard, Bolívar became known as the Liberator.

Bolívar came from a wealthy creole family in Venezuela. As a young man, he took up the cause of independence, vowing:

66I will never allow my hands to be idle, nor my soul to rest until I have broken the shackles which chain us to Spain.99

The Triumph of Mexico *This painting uses symbols to tell the story of Mexico's struggle for independence. Father Miguel Hidalgo, at left, places a victory wreath on the head of a woman representing Mexico. The feathers in her crown symbolize the nation's Indian heritage.* **The Arts** *Who do you think the man in the lower left represents?*

Bolívar visited France and the United States. He admired the military genius of the French leader Napoleon Bonaparte. He also admired the republican form of government of the United States.

Back in Venezuela, Bolívar headed the struggle against Spain. In a bold move, he led an army from Venezuela over the ice-capped Andes Mountains into Colombia. There, he took Spanish forces by surprise and defeated them in 1819.

Soon after, Bolívar became president of the independent Republic of Great Colombia. It included the present-day nations of Venezuela, Colombia, Ecuador, and Panama.

Other New Nations

Other independent nations emerged in Latin America. José de San Martín (san mahr TEEN) led Argentina to freedom in 1816. Like Bolívar in the north, San Martín also led an army on a dangerous march across the Andes. He then helped the peoples of Chile, Peru, and Ecuador to win their freedom.

In 1821, the peoples of Central America declared independence from Spain. Two years later, they formed the United Provinces of Central America. It included the present-day nations of Nicaragua, Costa Rica, El Salvador, Honduras, and Guatemala. By 1825, Spain had lost all its colonies in Latin America except Puerto Rico and Cuba.

The Portuguese colony of Brazil won independence without a battle. Prince Pedro, son of the Portuguese king, ruled the colony. The king had advised his son, "If Brazil

Our Common Heritage

George Washington and Simón Bolívar each helped their nations win independence. Their nations honored them in similar ways. Each man has a state, a tall mountain, and many towns, streets, squares, and buildings in his country named for him.

demands independence, proclaim it yourself and put the crown on your own head." In 1822, Brazilian patriots demanded freedom. Pedro agreed and had himself crowned emperor of the new nation.

The New Republics

The new republics modeled their constitutions on that of the United States. Yet their experience after independence was very different from that of their neighbor to the north.

Unlike the people of the 13 British colonies, the peoples of Latin America did not unite into a single country. Instead, they set up many different nations. In part, geography made unity difficult. Spain's American lands had covered a huge area. Mountains like the high, rugged Andes were a serious barrier to travel and communication.

The new nations had a hard time setting up stable governments. Under Spanish rule, the colonists had little experience in self-government. Deep divisions between social classes and economic problems increased discontent. Powerful leaders took advantage of the turmoil to seize control. As a result, the new republics were often unable to achieve their goal of democratic rule.

Showdown in Spanish Florida

Change was also taking place in Spanish Florida. For more than 100 years, Florida had been a refuge for many enslaved African Americans. During the 1700s, Spanish officials protected slaves who fled from plantations in Georgia and South Carolina. Seminole Indians allowed African Americans to live near their villages. In return, these "black Seminoles" gave the Indians a share of the crops they raised every year.

The black Seminoles adopted many Indian customs. They lived in houses with roofs thatched of palmetto leaves. They wore moccasins, colorful hunting shirts, and brightly colored turbans around their heads.

The Negro Fort. After the War of 1812, about 300 African Americans occupied a fort built by the British on the Apalachicola River. They invited runaway slaves from all across Florida to settle nearby. Runaways from the United States also found a welcome in the Florida fort.

Soon, some 1,000 African Americans lived on the banks of the Apalachicola. For 50 miles (80 km) along the river, they set up farms and began planting corn, sweet potatoes, melons, and beans. The Negro Fort, as it became known, provided them with protection.

American gunboats attack. General Andrew Jackson, himself a slave owner, demanded that Spain demolish the Negro Fort. When the Spanish governor refused, Jackson sent in American troops. They were to destroy the fort, Jackson insisted, "regardless of the ground it stands on."

Jackson's gunboats invaded Spanish territory in 1816, sailing up the muddy Apalachicola River. On a bluff above the river, they spotted the Negro Fort. Above the fort, a red flag fluttered.

Inside the fort, a force of about 300 free African Americans waited, their muskets loaded and cannons aimed. The red flag was a symbol of their defiance. Many of the fort's defenders had once been slaves–or their parents had. They knew that the Americans had come to return them to slavery. "Most of them determined never to be taken alive," commented one soldier.

Fighting for freedom. A seasoned fighter named Garcia commanded the Negro Fort. When the Americans demanded his surrender, he replied that he would sink any gunboat that tried to pass. Garcia's followers

"Black Seminoles" *This drawing shows an African American with Seminole Indians in Florida. Many "black Seminoles" spoke English, Spanish, and Indian languages. This gave them great influence as advisers and interpreters for the Seminoles.* **Multicultural Heritage** *Why did many African Americans go to Florida?*

cheered loudly and then fired their cannons at the ships.

The Americans returned fire. Even the ship's heaviest cannonballs thudded harmlessly into the fort's thick earthen walls. Then the sailing-master had an idea. He ordered a cannonball to be heated red-hot in the cook's galley. Sailors loaded the cannon, aimed carefully, and fired.

The heated ball screamed over the fort's wall. The ball landed in the magazine where the fort's gunpowder was stored. With a deafening roar and a huge orange flash, the magazine exploded. Within seconds, the entire fort was destroyed. The few defenders who remained alive surrendered.

With the fort destroyed, black settlers along the Apalachicola were forced to flee. Many joined Seminole Indians along the nearby Suwanee River. But the showdown at the Negro Fort had demonstrated how strongly African Americans were willing to fight for their freedom. Along with the Seminoles, they continued to resist American raids into Florida. ■

Spain Cedes Florida to the United States

In 1818, Jackson was determined once and for all to destroy the Seminole and African American forces in Florida. Commanding an army of over 3,000, he headed south again. President Monroe did not give Jackson formal permission to invade Spanish territory. He did not stop Jackson, either.

Jackson captured several Spanish towns. Although Spain protested, it was busy fighting rebels in Latin America. It could not risk war with the United States.

In the end, Spain agreed to peace talks. John Quincy Adams, the Secretary of State, worked out a treaty with Spain. The **Adams-Onís Treaty** took effect in 1821. In it, Spain gave Florida to the United States and received $5 million in exchange.

The Monroe Doctrine

Americans welcomed the Adams-Onís Treaty. They also cheered the success of Latin American nations in winning independence. The actions of European powers, however, worried American officials.

In 1815, Russia, Prussia, Austria, and France seemed ready to help Spain regain its colonies in Latin America. In addition, Russia claimed lands on the Pacific coast of North America.

The British, too, were concerned about other European nations meddling in the Western Hemisphere. They spoke of issuing a joint statement with the United States. It would guarantee the freedom of the new nations of Latin America.

President Monroe decided to act without the British. In 1823, he made a statement on foreign policy that is known as the **Monroe Doctrine.** The United States, he said, would not interfere in the affairs of European nations or European colonies in the Americas. At the same time, he warned European nations not to interfere with the newly independent nations of Latin America. He stated:

> **❝**The American continents...are henceforth not to be considered as subjects for future colonization by any European powers....We should consider any attempt on their part to extend their system to any portion of this hemisphere as dangerous to our peace and safety.**❞**

The Monroe Doctrine showed that the United States was determined to keep European nations from recolonizing the Americas. The United States did not have the power to enforce the Monroe Doctrine. Britain, however, supported the statement. With its strong navy, it could stop Europeans from interfering in the Americas.

SECTION 5 REVIEW

1. **Locate:** (a) Mexico, (b) Great Colombia, (c) Argentina, (d) United Provinces of Central America, (e) Brazil.
2. **Identify:** (a) Dominion of Canada, (b) Miguel Hidalgo, (c) *Grito de Dolores,* (d) Simón Bolívar, (e) José de San Martín, (f) Adams-Onís Treaty, (g) Monroe Doctrine.
3. (a) Why did rebellions break out in Canada in 1837? (b) What recommendations did Lord Durham make?
4. What Latin American nations won independence from Spain in the early 1800s?
5. Why did the United States issue the Monroe Doctrine?
6. **CRITICAL THINKING Drawing Conclusions** How would the defenders of the Negro Fort inspire enslaved Africans in the United States?

ACTIVITY **Writing to Learn**
Write a series of headlines that newspapers in the United States might have run before, during, and after General Jackson's invasion of Florida.

Summary

- By the early 1800s, the Industrial Revolution that had started in Britain was spreading to the United States.
- The War of 1812 spurred the growth of industry in the United States.
- New roads, canals, and steamboats helped improve transportation.
- During the Era of Good Feelings, conflict between political parties declined, but sectional differences emerged.
- Canada and the nations of Latin America achieved independence.

Reviewing the Main Ideas

1. How did the Industrial Revolution come to the United States?
2. What new idea did Francis Cabot Lowell introduce to the textile industry?
3. Describe how interchangeable parts improved the way goods were produced.
4. Describe three ways that transportation improved in the early 1800s.
5. (a) Why did northern manufacturers want a protective tariff? (b) Why did southerners oppose the tariff?
6. How did Florida become part of the United States?
7. (a) Why did the United States fear that European nations might interfere in the Western Hemisphere? (b) Why was British support of the Monroe Doctrine important?

Thinking Critically

1. **Linking Past and Present** (a) What were the problems of city life in the early 1800s? (b) What advantages did cities offer? (c) Do cities today still have the same problems and advantages? Explain.
2. **Analyzing Information** (a) How did geography make travel to the West difficult? (b) How did Americans overcome these travel problems?
3. **Comparing** (a) Compare the way Canada won its independence with the way the Spanish colonies won theirs. (b) Suggest two reasons why their experiences were different.

Applying Your Skills

1. **Analyzing a Quotation** Reread the quotation on page 295. (a) What did Lucy Larcom dislike about factory life? (b) Why did Lucy Larcom enjoy looking out the window? (c) Did Lucy think factory life was completely bad? Explain.
2. **Making a Review Chart** Make a review chart with three vertical columns. Label the columns Inventor, Invention, and Importance. Then use the information in the chapter to complete the chart.
3. **Identifying the Main Idea** Reread "The New Republics" on page 317. (a) What is the main idea of the subsection? (b) What facts support the main idea?

Thinking About Geography

Match the letters on the map with the following places: **1.** Wheeling, Virginia, **2.** New York City, **3.** Cumberland Gap, **4.** Lancaster Turnpike, **5.** National Road, **6.** Erie Canal. **Interaction** What obstacles did Americans overcome in building the Erie Canal?

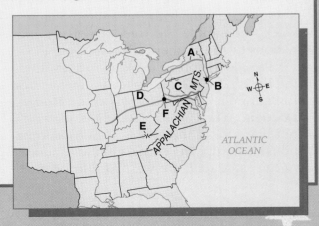

Investigating the Industrial Revolution

Form into groups to review inventions and industry in the early 1800s. Follow the suggestions below to write, draw, interview, or perform to show what you have learned. You may use the textbook, encyclopedias, atlases, or other materials in your classroom library to complete the tasks. Be able to name your sources of information when you have finished the activity.

HISTORIANS Create a time line of inventions for the period 1790–1825. Be prepared to explain the importance of each item on the time line.

CITIZENS Make a chart showing the positive effects and the negative effects of the inventions in the historians' time line.

SCIENTISTS Draw a diagram or prepare a demonstration to show how early factories harnessed the force of water to create power to run machines.

Fulton's design for a steamboat engine

REPORTERS Conduct an interview with a traveler on a Mississippi River steamboat. Ask questions to find out about the kinds of cargo on board, the hazards and thrills of steamboat travel, and the traveler's purpose and destination.

DANCERS AND POETS Review the descriptions of working conditions in mills and factories. Form into pairs to create a dance and poem that portray a day in the life of a worker. Poets might read their poems aloud while dancers perform in a recital for the class.

★ Set up an Industrial Revolution display in your classroom. Have each group present or describe its completed activity.

Interchangeable parts for a revolver

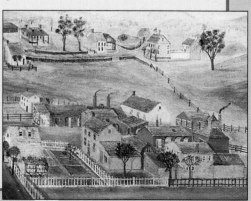

Factory town in New England

History Through LITERATURE

Who Is Carrie?

James Lincoln Collier and *Christopher Collier*

Introduction The new United States government faced a difficult problem. It had to find a way to repay bonds, or notes, used to pay soldiers and purchase supplies during the Revolution. *Who Is Carrie?* is a historical novel about an enslaved teenage girl in New York City. Her friend Dan, also a slave, owns hundreds of dollars worth of the notes. In this excerpt, Carrie and Dan wonder how and if the government will repay the bonds.

Dan's notes were pretty confusing, and as frequent as he'd explained it to me, I never did understand the ins and outs of it all. What happened was Dan's father, who was Jack Arabus, fought in the Revolution right next to General Washington. He got free for fighting and a whole lot of money, too. Only it wasn't real money. It was just pieces of paper called notes that said the government owed you some money.

Well, of course Dan's daddy got drowned, and after that the notes belonged to Dan. . . .

The thing was, nobody knew if the notes would be worth real money. It was up to the government to decide if they would pay them off or not. And on top of it, the states had put out their own notes, too, which people had taken instead of real money, and nobody knew if they'd be worth anything, either.

So naturally, while everybody was waiting to see if the states could get together and make themselves into one big country, some people was going around buying other people's notes for a cheap price. Say, if your notes was worth a hundred dollars, somebody might give you a dollar, or ten dollars or something for them on the gamble that the states would be able to get themselves together. And finally they did get themselves together and made the United States of America; and people who owned these notes was mighty cheered up, because they figured that the government would pay them off. Maybe they wouldn't pay them off a hundred percent, but they might declare that your hundred-dollar note was worth fifty dollars or some such.

But then it come out that *maybe* the government would pay off the notes and *maybe* they wouldn't. And it also come out that *maybe* they would pay off the states' notes for them, too, and *maybe* they wouldn't. The whole thing was as full of maybes as a bushel of potatoes, and it was making people like Dan, who'd got notes, just wild crazy. . . .

And for Dan it wasn't just the money. It was freedom, because if they paid off the notes a hundred percent, he'd have six hundred dollars, and maybe more, which

Under My Wings, Everything Prospers
Americans faced many challenges as they built their new nation. Despite problems, however, they looked forward to the future with hope and confidence. **Citizenship** *What problem did the new government face in repaying its debts from the Revolution?*

would be enough to buy his freedom, and his Ma's, too. But if they decided the other way, the notes wouldn't be worth nothing, and Dan and his Ma would have to stay slaves and work for Captain Ivers the rest of their lives.

"What are they worth now, Dan?" I said.

"Right now about half," Dan said. "People are buying them for half, because now that there's a government and a president and all, they figure there's a good chance that Congress will vote to pay them off. My notes is worth three hundred dollars, I reckon."

"That's a powerful lot of money," I said. "I'd sell them. I wouldn't risk waiting around. I'd sell them quick."

"It's a powerful lot," he said, "but it ain't enough to buy both me and Ma off. Captain Ivers, he said, if I gave him the notes he'd set me free, but that would leave Ma stuck."

"You know what I'd do," I said. "I'd grab the money and buy myself free and then work and save up money until I had enough to get my Ma free."

Dan shook his head. "I thought about that. I reckoned it up. It would take me near ten years to save up three hundred dollars. That's a powerful lot of money for anyone to save, and worse for a black man who don't get paid the same as whites.". . .

"What are you going to do?"

"Chance it," he said. "Chance it that the new government will pay off the notes a hundred percent."

THINKING ABOUT LITERATURE

1. How did Dan get the notes?
2. What did Dan hope to do with the money he received for his notes?
3. **CRITICAL THINKING Analyzing Information** How would the American people and other governments view the United States government if it decided *not* to repay the notes?

ACTIVITY Imagine that you are a writer for a television series based on *Who Is Carrie?* Write the dialogue for a scene in which Captain Ivers tries to convince Dan to give him the notes in exchange for Dan's freedom.

An Expanding Nation

Americans worked to build a more democratic society. At the same time, they moved steadily westward—often onto Indian lands. Here, Native Americans are shown in their Rocky Mountain home.

CHAPTER 11

The Jackson Era

(1824–1840)

CHAPTER OUTLINE

1 Champion of the People
2 Jackson in the White House
3 A Strong President
4 Jackson's Successors

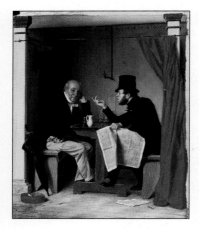

1820s *The right to vote was extended to almost all white men. Here, two voters discuss the issues of the day.*

1828 *Andrew Jackson was elected President. Many Americans considered his election a victory for the common people.*

1830 *Congress passed the Indian Removal Act, which forced Native Americans to move west of the Mississippi River. This painting shows Indians on the "Trail of Tears."*

| 1824 | 1826 | 1828 | 1830 | 1832 |

WORLD EVENT
1824 Simón Bolívar becomes President of Peru

WORLD EVENT
1829 Swiss adopt universal male suffrage, freedom of the press, and equality before the law

Chapter Setting

"Yesterday the President's house was open at noon. . . . The old man stood in the center of a little circle . . . and shook hands with anybody that offered. . . . There was a throng of apprentices, boys of all ages, men not civilized enough to walk about the rooms with their hats off; the vilest . . . [group] that ever [gathered] in a decent house; many of the lowest gathering around the doors, pouncing . . . upon the wine and refreshments, tearing the cake . . . all fellows with dirty faces and dirty manners; all the [trash] that Washington could turn forth from its workshops and stables."

George Bancroft described this scene at the White House in 1831. Bancroft, who came from an old, wealthy family, did not like what he saw. In his opinion, the President should not welcome roughnecks to the White House. To Andrew Jackson, however, these workers and simple frontier folk were the backbone of America.

Jackson reflected the democratic spirit sweeping the country. In the early 1800s, more and more white men gained the right to vote. In 1828, the new voters helped send Jackson, a popular frontier hero, to Washington. Both supporters and critics knew that Jackson would usher in a new era.

ACTIVITY

Based on George Bancroft's description, draw a picture showing the scene at the White House in 1831. Then hold a discussion about whether or not the President should welcome ordinary people to the White House.

1832 *President Jackson vetoed the charter of the Bank of the United States. A cartoon of the time shows Jackson boxing with the Bank's president.*

1835–1842 *Seminole forces battled the United States Army in the Seminole War. Chief Osceola, shown here, led the Seminoles in their fight.*

1840 *William Henry Harrison was elected President. The log cabin used as a symbol of Harrison's campaign was meant to show that he was a "man of the people."*

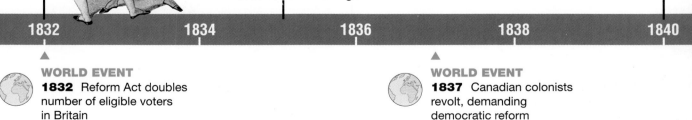

| 1832 | 1834 | 1836 | 1838 | 1840 |

WORLD EVENT
1832 Reform Act doubles number of eligible voters in Britain

WORLD EVENT
1837 Canadian colonists revolt, demanding democratic reform

Champion of the People

FIND OUT

- Why was the election of 1824 disputed?
- What policies did John Quincy Adams support?
- How did the country become more democratic in the 1820s?

VOCABULARY suffrage, caucus, nominating convention

Harry Ward, a New England schoolteacher, visited Cincinnati, Ohio, during the 1824 election campaign. Writing to a friend, he described how Ohioans felt about Andrew Jackson, who was running for President. "Strange! Wild! Infatuated! All for Jackson!" he observed.

On election day, more people voted for Andrew Jackson than for the other candidates. Oddly enough, Jackson did not become President that year.

A Disputed Election

There were four candidates for President in 1824. Each had support in different parts of the country. John Quincy Adams was strong in New England. Henry Clay and Andrew Jackson had support in the West. William Crawford was favored in the South but became too ill to campaign.

The candidates. John Quincy Adams came from a famous New England family. As the son of Abigail and John Adams, he had been close to national affairs since birth. He was a talented diplomat, and he served as Secretary of State under President Monroe. People admired Adams for his intelligence and high morals. Yet to many, he seemed hard and cold.

Henry Clay, by contrast, was charming. A Kentuckian, Clay was a shrewd politician who had become Speaker of the House of Representatives. In Congress, Clay proved to be a skillful negotiator. He worked out several key compromises. Despite his abilities, Clay was less popular than the other candidate from the West, Andrew Jackson.

To most Americans, Andrew Jackson was the "Hero of New Orleans." (See page 290.) They also saw him as a man of the people. Although Jackson owned land and slaves, he had started life poor.

The "corrupt bargain." In the election, Jackson won a majority of the popular vote. But no candidate won a majority of electoral votes. As a result, the House of Representatives had to choose the President from among the top three candidates. Clay, who finished fourth, was out of the running. As

BIOGRAPHY John Quincy Adams *President John Quincy Adams had great plans for improving the nation. He lacked the political skill, however, to win support for his programs.* **Citizenship** *Why did Americans oppose Adams's projects?*

Speaker of the House, though, he could influence the results.

Clay urged his supporters in the House to vote for Adams. After Adams won, he made Clay his Secretary of State. Jackson and his backers were furious. They accused Adams and Clay of making a "corrupt bargain" to steal the election. (☐ See "The President's Lady" on page 578.)

An Unpopular President

Adams knew that the election had angered many Americans. To "bring the whole people together," he pushed for a program of internal improvements. His plan backfired, however, and opposition to him grew.

Promoting economic growth. Like Alexander Hamilton, Adams thought that the federal government should promote economic growth. He called for the government to pay for new roads and canals. These internal improvements would help farmers to transport goods to market.

Adams wanted the United States to back national projects like governments in Europe did. He suggested building a national university and an observatory for astronomers. He backed projects to promote farming, manufacturing, science, and arts.

As Adams discovered, most Americans objected to spending money on such programs. In part, they feared that the federal government would become too powerful. In the end, Congress approved money for a national road and some canals. It turned down most of Adams's other programs.

A bitter campaign. In 1828, Adams was facing an uphill battle for reelection. This

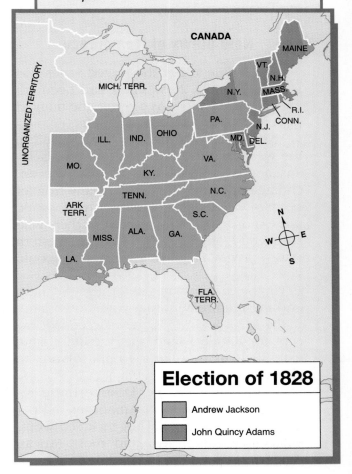

MAP STUDY

In the election of 1828, Andrew Jackson ran against President John Quincy Adams.
1. Who won the election?
2. (a) In which three states was the vote split between Jackson and Adams? (b) How did the mapmaker show this information?
3. **Analyzing Information** Judging from this map, do you think regional differences played a role in the election of 1828? Explain.

Election of 1828

▢ Andrew Jackson
▢ John Quincy Adams

★★★ *Linking Past and Present*
Politicians today often complain that reporters will do anything to get a story. Determined reporters, however, are nothing new. In the summer of 1828, for example, a reporter, Anne Royall, spied John Quincy Adams swimming in the Potomac River. Royall set herself down on Adams's clothes on the riverbank and refused to budge until, neck deep in water, he gave her an interview.

time, Andrew Jackson was Adams's only opponent.

The campaign turned into a bitter contest. Jackson supporters renewed charges of a "corrupt bargain" following the 1824 election. They attacked Adams as an aristocrat, or member of the upper class. Adams supporters replied with similar attacks. They dubbed Jackson a "military chieftain." If Jackson were to be elected, they warned, he could become a dictator like Napoleon Bonaparte.

Jackson won the election easily. His supporters cheered this victory for the common people. By common people, they meant farmers in the West and South and urban workers in the East. A disappointed Adams supporter warned that Jackson had been swept into office by "the howl of raving Democracy."

New Views of Democracy

During the 1820s, the United States was growing rapidly. New states had been admitted to the Union. As a result, the number of voters increased.

New voters. Many new voters lived in the western states between the Appalachians and the Mississippi. Frontier life encouraged a democratic spirit. Many frontier people were poor. Through hard work, some prospered. They respected others who succeeded on their own. In the western states, any white man over age 21 could vote.

In the eastern states, reformers fought to end the requirement that voters own land. In the 1820s and 1830s, they succeeded. Except for Rhode Island, every eastern state extended **suffrage,** or the right to vote, to all white men.

Limits on suffrage. Despite these reforms, large numbers of Americans did not have the right to vote. They included women, Native Americans, and most African Americans. Slaves had no political rights.

In fact, while more white men were winning suffrage, free African Americans were losing this right. Most northern states had allowed free African Americans to vote in the early 1800s. In the 1820s, many of these states took away that right. By 1830, only a few New England states allowed African Americans to vote.

New Political Practices

In the 1830s, new political parties were taking shape. They grew out of the conflict between John Quincy Adams and Andrew Jackson.

Two new parties. People who supported Adams and his programs for national growth called themselves National Republicans. In 1834, they became known as **Whigs.** Whigs wanted the federal government to spur the economy. Whigs included most eastern business people, some southern planters, and former Federalists.

Jackson and his supporters called themselves **Democrats.** Today's Democratic party traces its roots to Andrew Jackson's time. Democrats included frontier farmers as well as factory workers in the East.

New ways to choose candidates. Political parties developed new ways to choose candidates for President. In the past, powerful members of each party held a **caucus,** or private meeting. There, they chose their candidate. Critics called the caucus system undemocratic because so few people took part in it.

In the 1830s, both parties began to hold **nominating conventions.** At a convention, delegates from the states chose the party's candidate for President. Nominating conventions gave people a more direct voice in choosing future leaders. Today's political parties still hold nominating conventions.

As parties took shape, a new figure emerged—the professional politician. These people organized campaigns and worked to get out the vote.

| ARTS | SCIENCES | GEOGRAPHY | WORLD | ECONOMICS | CIVICS |

No Democracy for African Americans

There were 320,000 free African Americans living in the United States in the early 1830s. Some saved money to buy their freedom. Some had earned freedom as a reward, such as the slave who saved the Georgia capital from burning down. Others ran away or were freed on their master's death.

What did freedom mean for an African American at that time? It was not the same as the freedom enjoyed by whites. During the Jackson era, white men made important democratic gains. African Americans, meanwhile, lost ground. As one northerner commented, "The policy and power of the national and state governments are against them. . . .Their prospects. . .are dreary."

Northerners capture a freedman

From a high point at the time of the American Revolution, the rights of African Americans steadily declined. By the mid-1830s, every southern state had laws that barred African Americans—slave or free—from voting. In the North, African Americans could vote on equal terms with white males only in five New England states. In New York, African American males had to own property in order to vote. White males did not.

Wherever they lived, African Americans lacked basic civil rights. By 1835, most southern states and several northern states restricted or forbade the entry of free African Americans. In Pennsylvania, for example, African Americans had to post a $500 bond for "good behavior" to stay in the state. This sum was beyond the means of most Americans of any race at that time.

A barber at work

The 1830s also was a time of increased violence against free African Americans. White mobs attacked African Americans and burned their property in New York City, Philadelphia, Cincinnati, and Pittsburgh. Whether they were in the South or the North, free African Americans were not really free. Instead, they might more accurately have been called "slaves without masters."

■ How were the rights of free African Americans limited in the 1830s?

ACTIVITY Draw a political cartoon showing how the rights of free African Americans were limited in the 1830s.

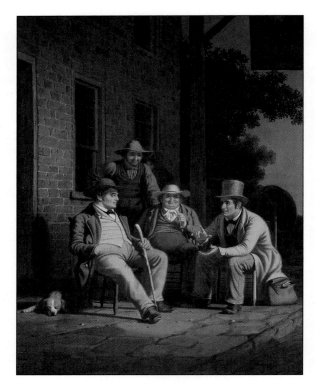

On the Campaign Trail *A democratic spirit swept the nation during the Jackson era. This painting by popular artist George Caleb Bingham shows a political candidate campaigning for votes on the frontier.* **Linking Past and Present** *How do candidates campaign for votes today?*

Growing Spirit of Equality

The spirit of democracy affected American attitudes toward one another. Americans no longer felt that the rich deserved special respect. "Does a man become wiser, stronger or more virtuous and patriotic because he has a fine house?" asked a Democrat.

European visitors were surprised that servants expected to be treated as equals. Butlers and maids refused to be summoned with bells, as in Europe. A coach driver complained that his employer "had had private meals every day and not asked him to the table."

Andrew Jackson's inauguration in 1829 reflected this spirit of equality. For the first time, thousands of ordinary people flooded the capital to watch the President take the oath of office. They then followed Jackson to a reception at the White House. The behavior of the "common people" shocked an onlooker:

>❝A rabble, a mob, of boys, negros, women, children, scrambling, fighting, romping. What a pity, what a pity! No arrangements had been made, no police officers on duty, and the whole house had been [filled] by the rabble mob.❞

The President, he continued, was "almost suffocated and torn to pieces by the people in their eagerness to shake hands." Critics said the scene showed that "King Mob" was ruling the nation. Amos Kendall, a Jackson supporter, disagreed: "It was a proud day for the people. General Jackson is *their own* President."

SECTION 1 REVIEW

1. **Identify:** (a) John Quincy Adams, (b) Henry Clay, (c) Whigs, (d) Democrats.
2. **Define:** (a) suffrage, (b) caucus, (c) nominating convention.
3. Why was the outcome of the election of 1824 a bitter blow to Andrew Jackson?
4. Why did most Americans reject Adams's programs for national growth?
5. (a) How did the United States become more democratic in the 1820s and 1830s? (b) Which groups did not benefit from increased suffrage?
6. **CRITICAL THINKING Applying Information** "Does a man become wiser, stronger or more virtuous and patriotic because he has a fine house?" How might a Jackson supporter have responded to this question?

ACTIVITY **Writing to Learn**
Write a dialogue in which John Quincy Adams and Andrew Jackson discuss the election of 1824.

Jackson in the White House

FIND OUT

■ What qualities helped Jackson succeed?

■ Why did Jackson replace many officeholders?

■ Why did Jackson make war on the Bank of the United States?

VOCABULARY spoils system, pet bank

Dozens of stories about Andrew Jackson made the rounds during the 1828 election. Like the one that follows, they often showed Jackson's courage and grit.

Years before he ran for President, Jackson was a judge in Tennessee. One day, a disorderly lawbreaker, Russell Bean, refused to appear before the court. Bean scared off the sheriff, but not Andrew Jackson. The story tells how Jackson strode out of the courthouse. "Surrender, you infernal villain," he roared, "or I'll blow you through." Bean looked into Jackson's blazing eyes and quietly surrendered. The iron will that made Bean surrender also made Jackson a powerful President.

Tough as Hickory

Like many of the people who admired him, Jackson was born in a log cabin on the frontier. His parents had left Ireland to settle on the Carolina frontier. Both had died before Jackson was 15. Young Andrew had to grow up quickly.

"He would never stay throwed." By his teens, Jackson could defend himself. Even though he had a slight build, he was strong and determined. A friend who wrestled with him recalled, "I could throw him three times out of four, but he would never stay throwed."

Jackson showed his toughness during the American Revolution. At age 13, he joined the Patriots but was captured by the British. When a British officer ordered the young prisoner to clean his boots, Jackson refused. The officer slashed the boy's hand and face with a sword. Jackson bore the scars of that attack all his life.

A self-made man. As a young man, Jackson studied law in North Carolina. Later, he moved to Tennessee, where he set up a law practice. He became wealthy by buying and selling land. While still in his twenties, he was elected to Congress.

Jackson won national fame during the War of 1812. As you have read, he commanded American forces at New Orleans. To settlers on the frontier, Jackson was already well known. He had defeated the Creek Indians at Horseshoe Bend and forced them to give up vast amounts of land in Georgia and Alabama.

BIOGRAPHY Andrew Jackson *Andrew Jackson was a strong, self-confident man, as the portrait shows. As President, he greatly increased the prestige and power of the national government. The white beaver hat became one of Jackson's trademarks.* **American Traditions** *How did Jackson earn national fame during the War of 1812?*

Jackson's nicknames told something about his character. The Creeks called him Sharp Knife. His own men gave him another name—**Old Hickory.** To them, he was hard and tough as the wood of a hickory tree. The name stuck even after he became President.

The Spoils System

In 1828, President Jackson knew that Americans wanted change. "The people expected reform," he said. "This was the cry from Maine to Louisiana."

Reward for victory. After taking office, Jackson fired many federal employees. He replaced them with his own supporters. Although most other Presidents had done the same, Jackson did it on a larger scale.

Critics complained that Jackson was rewarding Democrats who had helped elect him. He was not choosing qualified and ex-

---

A Meeting of the Kitchen Cabinet *President Jackson relied for advice on an informal group of advisers known as the kitchen cabinet. This cartoon gives one artist's view of Jackson's kitchen cabinet.* **Citizenship** *What do you think was the cartoonist's opinion of Jackson's kitchen cabinet? Explain.*

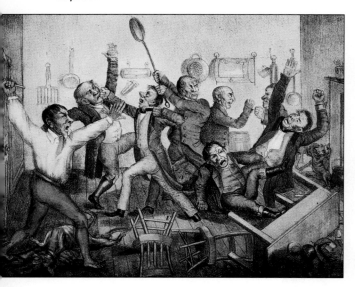

perienced men, they said. Jackson replied that he was fulfilling a goal of democracy by letting more citizens take part in government. He felt that ordinary Americans could fill government jobs. "The duties of all public officers are...so plain and simple that men of intelligence may readily qualify themselves for their performance," he said.

A Jackson supporter explained the system another way. "To the victor belong the spoils," he declared. Spoils are profits or benefits. From then on, the practice of rewarding supporters with government jobs became known as the spoils system. In the years ahead, the spoils system grew.

An unofficial Cabinet. Jackson rewarded some supporters with Cabinet jobs. Only Secretary of State Martin Van Buren was truly qualified for his position.

Jackson seldom met with his official Cabinet. Instead, he relied on advice from Democratic leaders and newspaper editors. These men had a good sense of the nation's mood. Because Jackson met with them in the White House kitchen, the group became known as the ***kitchen cabinet.***

The Bank War

President Jackson waged war on the Bank of the United States. Like many westerners, he disliked the Bank. He thought that it was too powerful.

Mr. Biddle's bank. From the first, the Bank of the United States had been a subject of dispute. (See page 255.) The Bank had great power because it controlled loans made by state banks. When the Bank's directors thought that state banks were making too many loans, they limited the amount these banks could lend. The cutbacks angered farmers and merchants who borrowed money to buy land or finance new businesses.

Jackson and other Democrats saw the Bank as undemocratic. Although Congress had created the Bank, it was run by private bankers. Jackson especially disliked Nicholas Biddle, president of the Bank since 1823.

Biddle came from a wealthy Philadelphia family. He was well qualified to run the bank, but he was also an arrogant, vain man. Jackson believed that Biddle used the Bank to benefit only the rich. He also resented Biddle's influence over certain members of Congress.

The war begins. Biddle and other Whigs worried that the President might try to destroy the Bank. Two Whig senators, Henry Clay and Daniel Webster, thought of a way to save the Bank and defeat Jackson at the same time.

The Bank's charter was not due for renewal by Congress until 1836. But Clay and Webster wanted to make the Bank an issue in the 1832 election. They convinced Biddle to apply for renewal early.

The Whigs believed that most Americans supported the Bank. If Jackson vetoed the bill to renew the charter, they felt sure that he would anger voters and lose the election.

Clay pushed the charter renewal bill through Congress in 1832. Jackson was sick in bed when he heard that Congress had renewed the Bank's charter. "The Bank . . . is trying to kill me," he fumed, "but I will kill it!"

Jackson's veto. In an angry message to Congress, Jackson vetoed the Bank bill. Nicholas Biddle compared the President's veto message to "the fury of a chained panther biting the bars of his cage."

King Andrew the First *To his opponents, Andrew Jackson's veto of the Bank bill was an abuse of presidential power. This Whig cartoon from the 1830s shows Jackson as a tyrant trampling on the Constitution.* **Citizenship** *Did Jackson as President have the right to go against the will of Congress?*

Jackson gave two reasons for his veto. First, he declared the Bank unconstitutional, even though the Supreme Court had ruled in the Bank's favor. Jackson believed that only states, not the federal government, had the right to charter banks. Second, Jackson felt that the Bank was a monster that helped the rich at the expense of the common people. He warned:

66 When the laws undertake . . . to make the rich richer and the potent more powerful, the humble members of society—the farmers, mechanics, and laborers—who have

Linking Past and Present
A supporter of Andrew Jackson started a tradition when he handed his baby to the President for a kiss. Unlike most modern politicians, however, Jackson declined to kiss the child. Instead, he handed him to Secretary of War John Eaton to do the honors.

neither the time nor the means of securing like favors to themselves, have a right to complain of the injustice of their government. **99**

As planned, the Whigs made the Bank a major issue in the election of 1832. They chose Henry Clay to run against Andrew Jackson. When the votes were counted, Jackson won a stunning victory. The common people had supported Jackson and rejected the Bank.

The Bank closes. Without a new charter, the Bank would have to close in 1836. Jackson did not want to wait. He ordered Secretary of the Treasury Roger Taney to stop putting government money in the Bank. Instead, Taney deposited federal money in state banks. They became known as **pet banks** because Taney and his friends controlled many of them.

The loss of federal money crippled the Bank of the United States. Its closing in 1836 would contribute to an economic crisis, as you will read.

SECTION 2 REVIEW

1. **Identify:** (a) Old Hickory, (b) kitchen cabinet, (c) Nicholas Biddle, (d) Roger Taney.
2. **Define:** (a) spoils system, (b) pet bank.
3. List three qualities that helped make Andrew Jackson a powerful national figure.
4. Why did critics object to the spoils system?
5. Why did Jackson dislike the Bank of the United States?
6. **CRITICAL THINKING Defending a Position** Do you think that the spoils system furthers democracy? Why or why not?

ACTIVITY **Writing to Learn**
Write the script for a television talk show in which Andrew Jackson and Nicholas Biddle discuss the Bank of the United States.

3
A Strong President

FIND OUT
- How did tariffs lead to the Nullification Crisis?
- Why did South Carolina threaten to withdraw from the Union?
- Why were Native Americans forced off their lands?

VOCABULARY nullification, states' rights, secede

The war on the Bank made Jackson more popular than ever among certain Americans. "The Jackson cause is the cause of democracy," boasted one Democrat. Another praised the President's strong stand:

66Who but General Jackson would have had the courage to veto the bill rechartering the Bank of the United States, and who but General Jackson could have withstood the overwhelming influence of that corrupt Aristocracy? **99**

In his second term of office, Jackson would face new tests of strength. To achieve his goals, he would extend the powers of the Chief Executive.

The Tariff of Abominations

Early in Jackson's second term, a crisis over tariffs threatened to split the nation. In 1828, Congress passed the highest tariff in the nation's history. Southerners called it the *Tariff of Abominations.* An abomination is something that is hated.

Like earlier tariffs, the new law benefited northern manufacturers by protecting them from foreign competition. Southern planters, however, were hurt by the tariff.

They sold their cotton in Europe and bought European goods in return. The high tariff meant that southerners had to pay more for these imported goods.

Calhoun for states' rights. Vice President John C. Calhoun led the South's fight against the tariff. He used an argument that Thomas Jefferson had made in the Kentucky and Virginia resolutions. (See page 260.) Like Jefferson, Calhoun claimed that a state had the right to nullify, or cancel, a federal law that it considered unconstitutional. The idea of a state declaring a federal law illegal is called **nullification.**

Calhoun raised a serious issue. Did states have the right to limit the power of the federal government? Or did the federal government have final power? Calhoun supported **states' rights,** the right of states to limit the power of the federal government. As he pointed out, the states had created the national government. Therefore, the states had final authority.

Webster for the Union. Daniel Webster disagreed. In 1830, he made a speech in the Senate attacking the idea of nullification. The Constitution, he said, united the American people, not just the states. If states had the right to nullify federal laws, the nation would fall apart. Webster ended his speech with stirring words: "Liberty and Union, now and forever, one and inseparable."

The Vice President Resigns

Calhoun and other southerners expected Jackson to support their view. After all, Jackson had been born in the South and had lived in the West. Both sections supported states' rights.

The President's stand soon became clear. In 1830, a group of states' rights supporters invited both Jackson and Vice President Calhoun to dinner. Several guests made toasts in favor of states' rights. Finally, Jackson rose. The room fell silent. Old Hickory raised his glass, looked straight at the

The Tariff of Abominations *The 1828 tariff divided the nation, as this cartoon shows. The figure on the left represents the South, carrying the burden of the tariff. The well-fed figure on the right represents the prosperous North.* ***Economics*** *Why did the tariff have different effects on the North and the South?*

Vice President, and declared, "Our Federal Union—it must be preserved!"

The drama continued. Calhoun raised his glass and answered the President's challenge with his own: "The Union—next to our liberty, most dear." To him, the liberty of a state was more important than the Union.

The debate over states' rights would rage for years. Because Calhoun disagreed with Jackson, he resigned from the office of Vice President. He was then elected senator from South Carolina. Martin Van Buren became Jackson's Vice President in 1833.

Challenge From South Carolina

As anger against the tariff grew in the South, Congress took action. In 1832, it passed a new tariff that lowered the rate slightly. South Carolina was not satisfied. It passed the Nullification Act, declaring the new tariff illegal. At the same time, it threatened to **secede,** or withdraw, from the Union if challenged.

Jackson was furious when he heard the news. He knew that nullification could destroy the nation. "It leads directly to civil war and bloodshed," he declared. In private, he raged:

> **"** If one drop of blood be shed there in defiance of the laws of the United States, I will hang the first man of them I can get my hands on to the first tree I can find. **"**

Publicly, the President was more practical. He supported a compromise tariff proposed by Henry Clay. The bill would lower tariffs. At the same time, Jackson asked Congress to pass the Force Bill. It allowed him to use the army, if necessary, to enforce the tariff in South Carolina.

Faced with Jackson's firm stand, no other state supported South Carolina. Calhoun gave in and agreed to Clay's compromise tariff. South Carolina repealed the Nullification Act.

The ***Nullification Crisis*** passed. However, sectional tensions between the North and South would increase.

New Threats to Native Americans

Jackson took a firm stand on another key issue. It affected the fate of Native Americans. For more than 300 years, Europeans had been pushing Native Americans off their land. In the United States, white settlers had forced Indians to move west. Indian leaders like Pontiac and Tecumseh had tried to stop the invasion. But their efforts had ended in defeat.

Indian nations in the Southeast. By the 1820s, only about 125,000 Indians still lived east of the Mississippi. Many belonged to the Creek, Chickasaw, Cherokee, Choctaw, and Seminole nations. They lived on the fertile lands of the Southeast.

The Indians wanted to live in peace with their white neighbors. Their land, however, was ideal for growing cotton. To the land-hungry settlers, the Indians stood in the way of progress.

Like earlier Presidents, Jackson sided with the white settlers. At his urging, the government set aside lands beyond the Mississippi and then persuaded or forced Indians to move there. Jackson believed that such a policy would open up land to white settlers. It would also protect Native Americans from destruction.

The Cherokee nation. Few Indians wanted to move. Some, like the Cherokee nation, had adapted to the customs of white settlers. The Cherokees lived in farming villages. They had a constitution that set up a republican form of government.

Sequoyah (sih KWOI uh), a Cherokee, created a written alphabet for his people. Using Sequoyah's letters, Cherokee children

BIOGRAPHY Sequoyah *Sequoyah adapted Greek, Hebrew, and English letters to create the 86 symbols of his Cherokee alphabet. The Cherokee nation used Sequoyah's alphabet to write its constitution.* ***Multicultural Heritage*** *Why do you think Sequoyah wanted to create a written alphabet for the Cherokee language?*

learned to read and write. The Cherokees used their alphabet to publish a newspaper.

A legal battle. In 1828, Georgia claimed the right to make laws for the Cherokee nation. The Cherokees went to court to defend their rights. They pointed to their treaties with the federal government that protected their rights and property. Led by Chief Justice John Marshall, the Supreme Court ruled in favor of the Cherokees. It declared Georgia's action unconstitutional.

Jackson then stepped in. In the Nullification Crisis, he defended the power of the federal government. In this case, he backed states' rights. Georgia had the right to extend its authority over Cherokee lands, he said. The federal government could not stop this action.

The President refused to enforce the Court's decision. "John Marshall has made his decision," Jackson reportedly said. "Now let him enforce it."

A Tragic March

In 1830, Jackson supporters in Congress pushed through the **Indian Removal Act.** Under it, Native Americans were forced to sign treaties agreeing to move west of the Mississippi. Whites thought the region was a vast desert. They did not mind turning it over to Indians.

Forced to leave. The Cherokees held out longest. Then in 1838, the United States Army forced them to leave at gunpoint.

Our Common Heritage
Like the United States Constitution, the Cherokee constitution established a legislature with two houses; an executive branch, consisting of a principal chief and vice principal chief; and a judicial branch. It also denied the vote to women and descendants of enslaved African Americans.

ART GALLERY
OUR COMMON HERITAGE

CHRIS WOLF EDMONDS
Cherokee Trail of Tears, 1979

In 1838, soldiers drove more than 15,000 Cherokees on a westward march to Oklahoma. On the 116-day journey, more than one out of every four Indians died from illness or exhaustion. The Cherokees called the westward route Nuna-da-ut-sun'y—"The Trail Where They Cried." Some 140 years later, Chris Wolf Edmonds created this quilt as a memorial to the Cherokee Trail of Tears.
Linking Past and Present *Why do you think artists portray events from the past?*

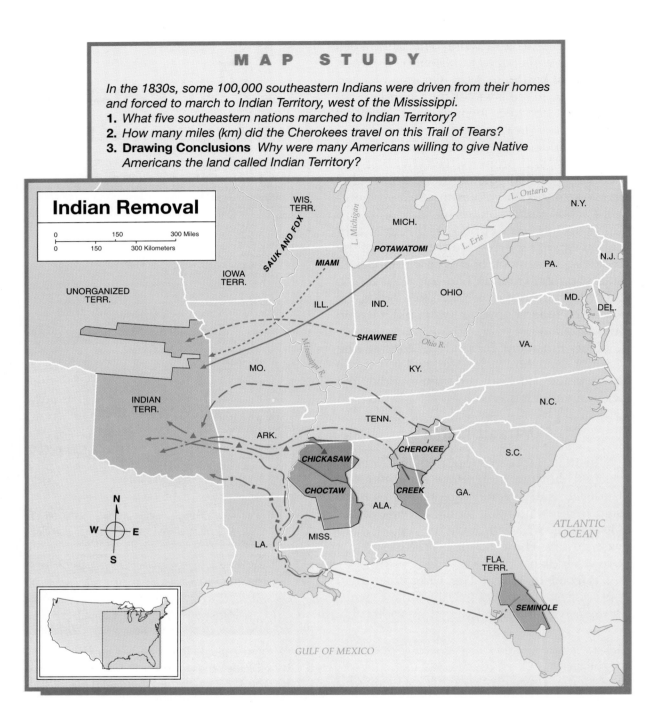

MAP STUDY

In the 1830s, some 100,000 southeastern Indians were driven from their homes and forced to march to Indian Territory, west of the Mississippi.

1. What five southeastern nations marched to Indian Territory?
2. How many miles (km) did the Cherokees travel on this Trail of Tears?
3. **Drawing Conclusions** Why were many Americans willing to give Native Americans the land called Indian Territory?

Indian Removal

0   150   300 Miles
0   150   300 Kilometers

WIS. TERR.

MICH.

L. Michigan

L. Ontario

L. Erie

N.Y.

POTAWATOMI

PA.

N.J.

SAUK AND FOX

MIAMI

IOWA TERR.

UNORGANIZED TERR.

ILL.

IND.

OHIO

MD.

DEL.

SHAWNEE

Ohio R.

VA.

MO.

KY.

Mississippi R.

INDIAN TERR.

N.C.

TENN.

ARK.

CHEROKEE

S.C.

CHICKASAW

CHOCTAW

CREEK

GA.

ALA.

N
W   E
S

MISS.

LA.

FLA. TERR.

ATLANTIC OCEAN

SEMINOLE

GULF OF MEXICO

The Cherokees trekked hundreds of miles into lands they had never seen before. (See the map above.) They had little food or shelter. Thousands perished during the march, mostly children and the elderly. In all, about one fourth of the Indians died.

The Cherokees' long, sorrowful journey west became known as the *Trail of Tears.* An eyewitness described the suffering:

66The Cherokees are nearly all prisoners. They had been dragged from their homes and encamped at the forts and military places, all over the nation. In Georgia especially, multitudes were allowed no time to take anything with them except the clothes they had on. . . . The property of many has been taken and sold before their eyes for almost nothing. **"**

The Seminoles resist. In Florida, the Seminole Indians resisted removal. Led by Chief Osceola (ahs ee OH luh), they fought the United States Army. The **Seminole War** lasted from 1835 to 1842. It was the costliest war waged by the government to gain Indian lands. In the end, the Seminoles were defeated. By 1844, only a few thousand Native Americans remained east of the Mississippi River.

SECTION 3 REVIEW

1. **Locate:** (a) South Carolina, (b) Georgia, (c) Mississippi River.
2. **Identify:** (a) Tariff of Abominations, (b) Nullification Crisis, (c) Sequoyah, (d) Indian Removal Act, (e) Trail of Tears, (f) Seminole War.
3. **Define:** (a) nullification, (b) states' rights, (c) secede.
4. (a) How did northerners benefit from tariffs? (b) Why did southerners oppose tariffs?
5. How did Jackson respond to the Nullification Crisis?
6. (a) How did the Cherokees try to protect their lands? (b) Why did they fail?
7. **CRITICAL THINKING Analyzing Information** Why do you think Andrew Jackson supported states' rights in the Cherokee case but not in the Nullification Crisis?

ACTIVITY Writing to Learn
Imagine that you are a Cherokee on the Trail of Tears. Write a brief story about your experiences.

4
Jackson's Successors

FIND OUT
- What economic problems did Martin Van Buren face?
- How did William Henry Harrison campaign for President?
- Why did Tyler have little success as President?

A weary Andrew Jackson retired from office after two terms. Americans then sent Martin Van Buren, Jackson's friend and Vice President, to the White House.

As Van Buren took the oath of office in March 1837, Jackson stood at his side. Onlookers watched the retiring President, not Van Buren. As Old Hickory left the platform, the crowd cheered. They had nothing but respect for the outgoing leader.

An Economic Crisis

Martin Van Buren was very different from Jackson. He was a politician, not a war hero. Davy Crockett, a member of Congress from Tennessee, once described Van Buren as "an artful, cunning, intriguing, selfish, speculating lawyer." As President, Van Buren needed more than sharp political instincts. Two months after taking office, he faced the worst economic crisis the nation had known. It was called the **Panic of 1837.**

The panic begins. The panic had several causes. During the 1830s, the government sold millions of acres of public land in the West. Farmers bought some land, but speculators bought even more. To pay for the land, speculators borrowed money from state banks, especially western banks. After the Bank of the United States closed, state banks could lend money without limit.

To meet the demand for loans, state banks printed more and more paper money. Often, the paper money was not backed by gold or silver. Paper money had value only if people had trust in the banks that issued it.

Before leaving office, Jackson had become alarmed at the wild speculation in land. To slow it down, he ordered that anyone buying public land had to pay for it with gold or silver. Speculators and others rushed to state banks to exchange their paper money for gold and silver. Many banks did not have enough gold and silver and had to close.

Banks fail. The panic spread. More and more people hurried to banks to trade in their paper money. In New York, one bank "was jammed with depositors crying 'Pay, pay!'" reported a witness. Hundreds of banks failed, leaving depositors empty-handed.

The panic worsened when cotton prices went down because of an oversupply. Cotton planters often borrowed money, which they repaid when they sold their crop. With cotton prices low, planters could not repay the loans. As a result, more banks failed. Business slowed, and the nation plunged into a deep economic depression.

Tough Times

In the worst days of the depression, 90 percent of the nation's factories were closed. Thousands of people were out of work. In

History and You

One of the causes of the Panic of 1837 was that banks allowed people to borrow more money than they could repay. Today, many people use credit cards when they shop. If you had a credit card, what limits would you put on your spending to make sure that you are able to pay for what you buy?

The Long Bill *Ordinary people suffered greatly in the Panic of 1837. People had bought on credit, sure that they could pay later. Now, many people, like the customer shown here, faced a "long bill" that they could not pay.* **Economics** *How did the sale of western lands contribute to the Panic of 1837?*

some cities, hungry crowds broke into warehouses and stole food.

Van Buren's response. The panic was not Van Buren's fault, but he was blamed for it. Once it began, he took little action. "The less the government interferes with private pursuits," he said, "the better for the general prosperity."

Van Buren did try to set up a more stable banking system, but with limited success. He also cut back on expenses at the White House. Guests, for example, were served simple dinners. As the depression dragged on, support for the President fell. Even so, the Democrats chose Van Buren to run for reelection.

The hero of Tippecanoe. In 1840, the Whigs saw a chance to win the White House. Learning from the Democrats, they chose a candidate who would appeal to the common people. He was William Henry

Harrison of Ohio. Harrison was known as the hero of the Battle of Tippecanoe. (See page 285.) To run for Vice President, the Whigs chose John Tyler.

The Log Cabin Campaign

Harrison's campaign reflected a new sort of politics that was emerging. Politicians made speeches, and candidates campaigned at rallies and banquets. Political parties competed for votes by offering exciting entertainment.

A war hero and man of the people. Most Americans knew little about William Henry Harrison's stand on the issues. To appeal to voters, the Whigs focused on his war record. "Tippecanoe and Tyler too" became their campaign slogan.

They also created an image for Harrison as a "man of the people." They presented him as a humble Ohio farmer who had been born in a log cabin. In fact, Harrison was a wealthy, educated man from Virginia whose family had owned a large estate.

Still, the Whigs made the log cabin their campaign symbol. In a typical Whig cartoon, Harrison stands outside a log cabin, greeting Van Buren and his aides:

66 Gentlemen, . . . If you will accept the [simple food] of a log cabin, with a western farmer's cheer, you are welcome. I have no champagne but can give you a mug of good cider, with some ham and eggs, and good clean beds. I am a plain backwoodsman. I have cleared some land, killed some Indians, and made the Red Coats fly in my time. 99

Attacks on Van Buren. The Whigs also attacked Van Buren. They blamed "Martin Van Ruin" for the economic depression. "King Mat," they sneered, was a "democratic peacock, plumed, perfumed, and strutting around the White House." Daniel Webster charged that the Democrats had replaced "Old Hickory" Jackson with "Slippery Elm" Van Buren.

Both parties used name-calling, half-truths, and lies. A Whig newspaper falsely reported that Van Buren spent "thousands of the people's dollars" to install a bathtub in the White House.

On the campaign trail. Harrison campaigned across the land, making speeches and greeting voters. Along the campaign trail, Whigs built log cabins to use as their headquarters. They even set up log cabins in large cities such as New York. Parades

Log Cabin Politics
The log cabin was the symbol of William Henry Harrison's campaign. Whigs sang the "Log Cabin March" and drank cider out of log cabin bottles. **Linking Past and Present** *Could the techniques of the Harrison campaign be used today? Explain.*

featured log cabins carried on wagons. And at every stop, Whigs served free cider.

Ordinary citizens joined in the rallies. They gave speeches, marched in parades, and sang campaign songs like this one:

> "The times are bad, and want
>   curing;
> They are getting past all
>   enduring;
> So let's turn out Martin Van
>   Buren
> And put in old Tippecanoe!"

"Keep the ball rolling." In towns across the United States, Harrison supporters rolled huge balls down the streets. The balls were 12 feet in diameter, made of twine, and covered with slogans. "Keep the ball rolling," people chanted as they marched.

Enterprising merchants sold campaign souvenirs. They offered badges, handkerchiefs, and even containers of shaving cream with the Tippecanoe slogan. A popular item was a bottle shaped like a log cabin.

Although women could not vote, they campaigned for Harrison. Women wrote pamphlets, sewed banners, rode on floats, and paraded with brooms to "sweep" the Democrats out of office. Young women's sashes proclaimed, "Whig husbands or none."

A Whig victory at last. The Democrats responded to Whig attacks with their own name-calling. "Granny Harrison, the Petticoat General," they revealed, had resigned from the army before the War of 1812 ended. They accused "General Mum" of not speaking out on the issues.

"Should Harrison be elected?" they asked voters. "Read his name spelled backwards," they advised. "No sirrah."

Harrison won the election easily, forcing the Democrats out of the White House for the first time in 12 years. "We have taught them how to conquer us!" lamented one Democrat. "We've been sung down," another complained. (📖 See "Campaign Hoopla" on page 580.) ∎

Whigs in the White House

The Whigs had a clear-cut program. They wanted to create a new Bank of the United States and improve roads and canals. Also, they wanted a high tariff.

Whig hopes were soon dashed. Just weeks after taking office, President Harrison died of pneumonia. John Tyler became the first Vice President to succeed a President who died in office.

President Tyler disappointed the Whigs. He had once been a Democrat and opposed the Whig plan to develop the economy. When the Whigs in Congress passed a bill to recharter the Bank of the United States, Tyler vetoed it.

In response, Tyler's entire Cabinet resigned, except for Daniel Webster. The Whigs then threw Tyler out of their party. Democrats welcomed the squabbling. "Tyler is heartily despised by everyone," reported an observer. "He has no influence at all." With few friends in either party, Tyler could do little during his term in office.

SECTION 4 REVIEW

1. **Identify:** Panic of 1837.
2. How did Jackson's policies contribute to the Panic of 1837?
3. How did the oversupply of cotton deepen the depression?
4. Why did the Whigs back William Henry Harrison for President in 1840?
5. How did John Tyler disappoint the Whigs?
6. **CRITICAL THINKING Synthesizing Information** Why was the log cabin a successful campaign symbol for Harrison in 1840?

ACTIVITY Writing to Learn

Write the words for a song that one of the candidates might have used in the election campaign of 1840.

MAP, GRAPH, AND CHART SKILLS
Reading a Circle Graph

Circle graphs are one method of showing statistics in a visual way. (See Skill Lesson 2 on page 55 to review what you have learned about reading a line graph.) A circle graph is sometimes called a pie graph because it is divided into wedges, like a pie. Each wedge, or part, can be compared to every other wedge, or part.

A circle graph shows the relationship between each of the parts and the whole. To compare information over a period of time, two circle graphs can be used.

1. **Identify the information shown on the graphs.** (a) What year does the circle graph on the left show? (b) What year does the circle graph on the right show? (c) What do the colors on the circle graphs represent?

2. **Practice reading the graphs.** In a circle graph, you can compare any part with every other part or with the whole graph. The graph shows each part as a percentage of the whole. The whole graph is 100 percent. (a) What percentage of the electoral vote did the Whigs get in 1836? In 1840? (b) What percentage of the electoral vote did the Democrats get in 1836? In 1840? (c) Which party got a greater percentage of the electoral vote in 1840? (d) Did the independent party affect the outcome of the election in 1836? Explain.

3. **Interpret the information shown on the graphs.** Compare the two graphs. (a) How did the Whig electoral vote in 1836 compare with the Democratic electoral vote in 1836? (b) Based on the graphs, draw a conclusion about the popularity of the two political parties. (c) Based on your reading in the chapter, what reasons might you give to explain the changes in each party's popularity?

ACTIVITY Construct a circle graph that shows the percentage of students in your class whose last names begin with a letter in the following groups: A–H, I–P, Q–Z. What percentage of names falls in each group?

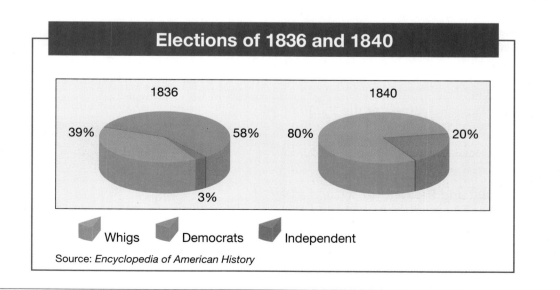

Elections of 1836 and 1840

1836

39%   58%

3%

1840

80%   20%

Whigs   Democrats   Independent

Source: *Encyclopedia of American History*

Summary

- By the late 1820s, the growing spirit of democracy resulted in more and more white men getting the right to vote.
- As President, Andrew Jackson rewarded supporters with government jobs and fought against the national Bank.
- Jackson was a strong President who supported states' rights in the policy of Indian removal but not in the Nullification Crisis.
- President Van Buren did little to end the economic depression that started with the Panic of 1837, and William Henry Harrison defeated his bid for reelection in 1840.

Reviewing the Main Ideas

1. (a) What were President John Quincy Adams's programs for national growth? (b) Why did Americans reject his programs?
2. (a) What were the major political parties in the 1830s? (b) Who supported each party?
3. How did Jackson defend the spoils system?
4. Identify the role each of the following men played in the battle over the Bank of the United States: (a) Henry Clay, (b) Nicholas Biddle, (c) Andrew Jackson.
5. (a) What was the Nullification Crisis? (b) How was it resolved?
6. (a) Why did the Cherokee nation go to court? (b) How did President Jackson respond to the Supreme Court's decision in the Cherokee case?
7. (a) What were the causes of the Panic of 1837? (b) What was its effect?

Thinking Critically

1. **Linking Past and Present** (a) What group of Americans gained more rights in the 1820s? (b) What groups have gained more rights since then? (c) What groups are seeking more rights today?

2. **Synthesizing Information** Why was Andrew Jackson considered the people's President? Explain.

Applying Your Skills

1. **Reading a Political Cartoon** Study the cartoon on page 335. (a) Who is pictured in the cartoon? (b) What symbols does the cartoonist use? (c) What do you think the cartoonist thought of President Jackson? Explain.
2. **Making a Review Chart** Prepare a chart with two columns and three rows. Label the columns John Quincy Adams and Andrew Jackson. Label the rows Family, Education, Experience in Public Life. Fill out the chart. (a) What were the differences between Adams and Jackson? (b) How do the differences reflect the changes in American politics in the 1820s?
3. **Understanding Sequence** (a) When was the Tariff of Abominations passed? (b) When did South Carolina pass the Nullification Act? (c) What is the relationship between the two events?

Thinking About Geography

Match the letters on the map with the following places: **1.** Indian Territory, **2.** Chickasaw, **3.** Choctaw, **4.** Creek, **5.** Cherokee, **6.** Seminole. **Place** Why did settlers want Cherokee lands in the Southeast?

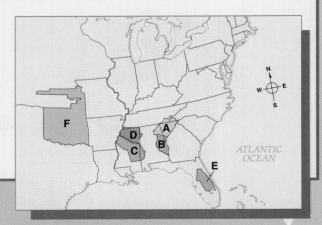

Painting a Portrait of Andrew Jackson

Form into groups to explore the life of Andrew Jackson. Follow the suggestions below to write or draw to show what you have learned about Jackson. You may use the textbook, encyclopedias, atlases, or other materials in your classroom library to complete the tasks. Be able to name your sources of information when you have finished the activity.

HISTORIANS Research the major events and issues related to Andrew Jackson's life and career. Then create an Andrew Jackson board game. The game should trace Jackson's rise from poor beginnings on the western frontier to popular military hero and President. You might ask the class artists to help you design and construct your game.

ARTISTS Select an issue or incident related to Andrew Jackson's presidency. Then create a political cartoon based on your selection. Remember that political cartoonists represent a point of view in their work.

Andrew Jackson

ECONOMISTS Review what you have read about Andrew Jackson and the Bank of the United States. Also review the cause-and-effect charts in this book. Then create a chart showing the causes and effects of the dispute over the Bank.

ACTORS AND DANCERS Review what you have read about the Indian Removal Act, and study the quilt portraying the Trail of Tears on page 339. Then prepare a presentation dramatizing this event.

CITIZENS List the events in which states clashed with the federal government during Jackson's years in office. Then make a chart showing these issues and explaining why they were important.

Comb with
Jackson image

★ Create an Andrew Jackson bulletin board display. Include the completed works in the display.

Political cartoon

TO THE VICTORS SPOILS.

CHAPTER 12

From Sea to Shining Sea

(1820–1860)

TEXAS!!

Emigrants who are desirous of assist-ing Texas at this important crisis of her affairs may have a free passage and equip-ments, by applying at the
NEW-YORK and PHILADELPHIA HOTEL,
On the Old Levee, near the Blue Stores.

Now is the time to ensure a fortune in Land: To all who remain in Texas during the War will be allowed 1280 Acres.
To all who remain Six Months, 640 Acres.
To all who remain Three Months, 320 Acres.
And as Colonists, 4600 Acres for a family and 1470 Acres for a Single Man.
New Orleans, April 23d, 1836.

1836 *The Republic of Texas was formed. An advertisement offered free land to anyone who would help Texans fight for independence.*

1821 *The first American traders arrived in Santa Fe, New Mexico. Goods were loaded on mules and transported along the Santa Fe Trail.*

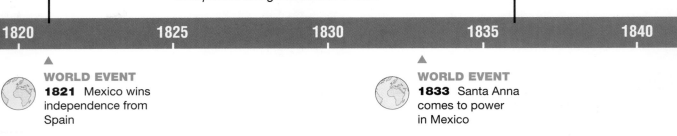

| 1820 | 1825 | 1830 | 1835 | 1840 |

WORLD EVENT
1821 Mexico wins independence from Spain

WORLD EVENT
1833 Santa Anna comes to power in Mexico

Chapter Setting

"Last spring, 1846, was a busy season in the city of St. Louis. Not only were emigrants from every part of the country preparing for the journey to Oregon and California, but an unusual number of traders were making ready their wagons and outfits for Santa Fe. The hotels were crowded, and the gunsmiths and saddlers were kept constantly at work in providing arms and equipments for the different parties of travellers. Steamboats were leaving the [dock] and passing up the Missouri, crowded with passengers on their way to the frontier."

As American historian Francis Parkman noted in this passage from *The Oregon Trail,* St. Louis bustled with activity in the spring of 1846. Like Parkman, thousands of Americans had gathered in the city, ready to head west.

Moving west was not new to the people of the United States. The nation had begun as a string of colonies dotting the Atlantic coast. As the nation grew, pioneers moved inland, across the Appalachians to the Mississippi River.

By the 1830s, Americans were looking for new frontiers. Hardy settlers pushed west once more, into Texas, New Mexico, California, and Oregon. By 1850, the United States had expanded its borders until they reached "from sea to shining sea."

ACTIVITY Use your five senses to imagine what moving west in the mid-1800's must have been like. Then complete the following sentences: Moving west looks like _____. Moving west feels like _____. Moving west smells like _____. Moving west tastes like _____. Moving west sounds like _____.

1843 *Wagon trains began taking thousands of Americans to Oregon Country. Space was limited, and settlers crammed whatever they could into trunks.*

CALIFORNIA REPUBLIC

1846 *Americans in northern California declared independence from Mexico. Their new nation was known as the Bear Flag Republic.*

1860 *A mix of peoples contributed to California's rich culture. Here, Mexican American settlers enjoy a celebration known as a fiesta.*

1840	1845	1850	1855	1860

WORLD EVENT
1840 Britain recognizes Texas as an independent nation

1

Oregon Fever

FIND OUT
- Why did the United States and Britain agree to share Oregon Country?
- Why did Mountain Men go to the Far West?
- What hardships did travelers face on the Oregon Trail?

VOCABULARY rendezvous

In 1846, Horace Greeley, a New York newspaper editor, published an article titled "To Aspiring Young Men." In it, Greeley offered the following advice:

> 66If you have no family or friends to aid you, . . . turn your face to the great West and there build up your home and fortune.99

Greeley's advice exactly suited the spirit of the times. Before long, his statement was shortened to four simple words: "Go West, young man." Thousands of Americans rallied to the cry "Westward Ho!"

GEOGRAPHY AND HISTORY
Oregon Country: A Varied Land

By the 1820s, white settlers occupied much of the land between the Appalachians and the Mississippi River. Families in search of good farmland continued to move west. Few, however, settled on the Great Plains between the Mississippi and the Rockies. Instead, they were drawn to lands in the Far West.

Americans first heard about Oregon Country in the early 1800s. *Oregon Country* was the huge area beyond the Rockies. To-day, this land includes Oregon, Washington, Idaho, and parts of Wyoming, Montana, and Canada. (See the map on page 353.)

The land that early settlers called Oregon Country has a varied geography. Along the Pacific coast, the soil is fertile and rainfall is plentiful. Temperatures are mild all year round. Early white settlers found fine farmland in the Willamette River valley and the lowlands around Puget Sound. Trappers were lured by beaver that filled the dense forests of coastal mountains farther inland.

Between the coastal mountains and the Rockies is a high plateau. This Intermountain region is much drier than the coast and has some desert areas. Temperatures are also more extreme here.

The Rocky Mountains formed the eastern boundary of Oregon Country. As in the coastal range, beaver and other fur-bearing animals roamed the Rockies. As a result, trappers flocked to the area. ■

Competing Claims

In the early 1800s, four countries had competing claims to Oregon. They were the United States, Great Britain, Spain, and Russia. Of course, Native Americans had lived in Oregon for thousands of years. The land rightfully belonged to them. But the United States and competing European nations gave little thought to Indian rights.

The United States based its claim to Oregon on several expeditions to the area. For example, Lewis and Clark had journeyed through the area in 1805 and 1806.

The British claim to Oregon dated back to a visit by Sir Francis Drake in 1579. Also, Fort Vancouver, built by the British, was the only permanent outpost in Oregon Country.

In 1818, the United States and Britain reached an agreement. The two countries would occupy Oregon jointly. Citizens of each nation would have equal rights in Oregon. Spain and Russia had few settlers in the area and agreed to drop their claims.

Fur Trappers in the Far West

At first, the only Europeans or Americans who settled in Oregon Country were a few hardy trappers. These adventurous men hiked through Oregon's vast forests, trapping animals and living off the land. They were known as *Mountain Men.*

Lives filled with danger. Mountain Men could make a small fortune trapping beaver in Rocky Mountain streams. They led dangerous lives, however. Bears, wildcats, and other wild animals lurked in the thick forests where they hunted. And the long, cold mountain winters demanded special survival skills.

Mountain Men wore shirts and trousers made of animal hides and decorated with porcupine quills. Their hair reached to their shoulders. Pistols and tomahawks hung from their belts. Around their necks dangled a "possibles sack," filled with a pipe, some tobacco, a mold to make bullets, and other items of "possible" use.

Living off the land. In warm weather, when game was plentiful, Mountain Men gorged themselves with food. During lean times, however, trappers ate almost anything. "I have held my hands in an anthill until they were covered with ants, then greedily licked them off," one Mountain Man recalled.

Trappers often spent winters in Native American villages. In fact, they learned many of their trapping skills and survival methods from Indians. Relations with Native Americans were not always friendly, how-

BIOGRAPHY James Beckwourth *One of the most daring Mountain Men was James Beckwourth. The son of an enslaved Virginian, Beckwourth went west as a young man. He discovered a pass in the Sierra Nevada that became a major route to California.* **Linking Past and Present** *Why are mountain passes less important to travelers today than in the 1800s?*

ever. Indians sometimes attacked Mountain Men who trapped on Indian hunting grounds without permission.

Trading furs. During the fall and spring, Mountain Men tended their traps. Then in July, they tramped out of the wilderness, ready to meet the fur traders. They headed to a place chosen the year before, called the **rendezvous** (RAHN day voo). Rendezvous is a French word meaning get-together.

For trappers, the first day of the rendezvous was a time to have fun. A visitor to one rendezvous captured the excitement:

66[The trappers] engaged in contests of skill at running, jumping, wrestling, shooting with the rifle, and running horses.... They sang, they laughed, they whooped; they tried to out-brag and out-lie each other in stories of their adventures and achievements. Here the...trappers were in all their glory. 99

After the "laughing and whooping" were done, trappers and traders settled down to bargain. Because beaver hats were in great demand in the East and in Europe, Mountain Men got a good price for their furs. "With their hairy bank notes, the beaver skins, they can obtain all the luxuries of the mountains, and live for a few days like lords," one visitor said of the trappers.

By the late 1830s, the fur trade was dying out. Trappers had killed so many beavers that the animals had grown scarce. Also, beaver hats went out of style. Even so, the Mountain Men's skills were still in demand.

Heading for the Rendezvous *The yearly rendezvous was a chance both to have fun and to make a profit. This painting shows Mountain Men and Native Americans on their way to a rendezvous.* **United States and the World** *How did European fashions affect the American fur trade?*

Some took on a new job—leading settlers across the rugged trails into Oregon.

Mountain Men Explore New Lands

In their search for furs, Mountain Men explored new territory in the West. They followed Indian trails across the Rockies and through mountain passes. Later, they showed these trails to settlers moving west.

One Mountain Man, Jedediah Smith, led white settlers across the Rockies through South Pass, in present-day Wyoming. Manuel Lisa, a Spanish American fur trader, led a trip up the Missouri River in 1807. He founded Fort Manuel, the first outpost on the upper Missouri.

At least one Mountain "Man" was a woman. Marie Dorion, an Iowa Indian, first went to Oregon with fur traders in 1811. She won fame for her survival skills.

Missionaries in Oregon

The first white Americans to build permanent homes in Oregon Country were missionaries. Among them were Marcus and Narcissa Whitman. The couple married in 1836 and set out for Oregon, where they planned to convert local Native Americans to Christianity.

Arriving in Oregon, the Whitmans built their mission near the Columbia River. They set out to work with the Cayuse (KĪ yoos) Indians. Soon, other settlers joined the Whitmans. They took over Indian lands for their houses and farms.

Missionaries like the Whitmans helped stir up interest in Oregon Country. Eager to have others join them, the missionaries sent back glowing reports about the land. People throughout the nation read these reports. By 1840, more and more Americans were ready to make the long and difficult journey to Oregon.

Wagon Trains West

Throughout the 1840s, the settlement in Oregon grew. Back in the United States, farmers marveled at stories of wheat that grew taller than a man and Oregon turnips 5 feet around. "Oregon Fever" broke out. Soon, pioneers clogged the trails west. Beginning in 1843, wagon trains left every spring for Oregon following the **Oregon Trail.** (See the map at right.)

Leaving from Independence. Families planning to go west met at Independence, Missouri, in the early spring. When enough families had gathered, they formed a wagon train. Each group elected leaders to make decisions along the way.

The Oregon-bound pioneers hurried to leave Independence in May. Timing was important. Travelers had to reach Oregon by early October, before snow began to fall in the mountains. This meant that pioneers had to cover 2,000 miles (3,200 km) on foot in five months!

Life on the trail. Once on the trail, pioneer families woke to a bugle blast at dawn. Each person had a job to do. Young girls helped their mothers prepare breakfast. Men and boys harnessed the horses and oxen. By 6 A.M., the cry of "Wagons Ho!" rang out across the plains.

Wagon trains stopped for a brief meal at noon. Then it was back on the trail until 6 or 7 P.M. At night, wagons were drawn up in a circle to keep the cattle from wandering.

Most pioneer families set out on the journey west with a lot of heavy gear. When it came time to cross rivers and scale mountains, however, many possessions were left behind to lighten the load. Soon, the Oregon Trail was littered with junk. One traveler found the trail strewn with "black-smiths' anvils, ploughs, large grind-stones, baking ovens, kegs, barrels, harness [and] clothing."

Rain, snow, and disease. The long trek west held many dangers. During spring rains, travelers risked their lives floating wagons across swollen rivers. In summer, they faced blistering heat on the treeless plains. Early snowstorms often blocked passes through the mountains.

The biggest threat was sickness. Cholera and other diseases could wipe out whole wagon trains. Because the travelers lived so close together, germs spread quickly.

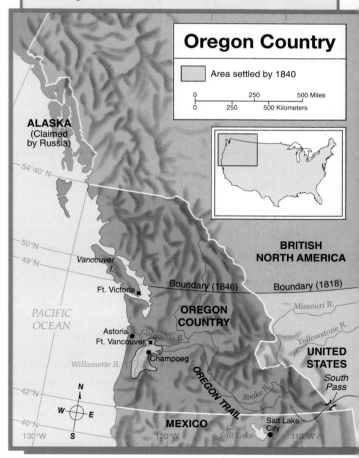

MAP STUDY

Oregon Country was the first area in the Far West to draw settlers from the United States.

1. *What two rivers did the Oregon Trail follow as it wound into Oregon Country?*
2. *What line of latitude marked the northern boundary of Oregon Country?*
3. **Analyzing Information** *Why do you think the Oregon Trail often followed the course of a river?*

Oregon Country

Area settled by 1840

| 0 | 250 | 500 Miles |
| 0 | 250 | 500 Kilometers |

ALASKA
(Claimed by Russia)

54°40' N

50°N
49°N   Vancouver I.

PACIFIC
OCEAN

Ft. Victoria

Astoria
Ft. Vancouver   Columbia R.

Willamette R.   Champoeg

42°N

N
W   E
S

40°N
130°W

120°W

BRITISH
NORTH AMERICA

Boundary (1846)   Boundary (1818)

OREGON
COUNTRY

Missouri R.

Yellowstone R.

UNITED
STATES

South
Pass

OREGON TRAIL

Snake R.

MEXICO   Great
Salt Lake

Salt Lake
City

110°W

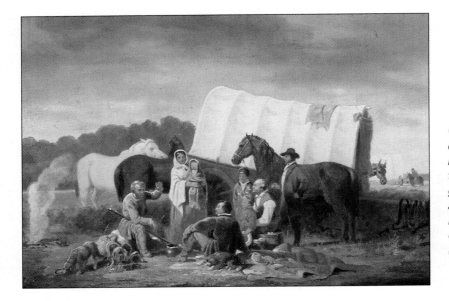

On the Trail *Wagon trains crowded the trails to the West in the mid-1800s. Here, travelers listen closely as a guide tells them what lies ahead.* **Geography** *What hardships did travelers face on the trail?*

Trading with Native Americans. As they moved west toward the Rockies, pioneers often saw Indians. The Indians seldom attacked the whites trespassing on their land. A guidebook published in 1845 warned that pioneers had more to fear from their own guns than from Indians: "We very frequently hear of emigrants' being killed from the accidental discharge of firearms; but we very seldom hear of their being killed by Indians."

Many Native Americans traded with the wagon trains. Hungry pioneers were grateful for food the Indians sold. "Whenever we camp near any Indian village," a traveler said, "we are no sooner stopped than a whole crowd may be seen coming galloping into our camp. The [women] do all the swapping."

Oregon at last! Despite the many hardships, more than 50,000 people reached Oregon between 1840 and 1860. Their wagon wheels cut so deeply into the plains that the ruts can still be seen today.

By the 1840s, Americans greatly outnumbered the British in parts of Oregon. As you have read, the two nations agreed to occupy Oregon jointly in 1818. Now, many Americans began to feel that Oregon should belong to the United States alone.

SECTION 1 REVIEW

1. **Locate:** (a) Oregon Country, (b) South Pass, (c) Oregon Trail, (d) Independence.
2. **Identify:** (a) Mountain Man, (b) Jedediah Smith, (c) Manuel Lisa, (d) Marie Dorion, (e) Marcus and Narcissa Whitman.
3. **Define:** rendezvous.
4. What agreement did the United States and Britain reach about Oregon Country?
5. How did Mountain Men help open the Far West?
6. Why did settlers pour into Oregon Country?
7. **CRITICAL THINKING Analyzing Information** What qualities do you think Mountain Men needed to survive in the wilderness?

ACTIVITY Writing to Learn
Write lyrics to a song that Mountain Men might have sung during a rendezvous.

Our Common Heritage
Pioneer women on the Oregon Trail had to be resourceful to feed their families. One trick that many learned was to use the rocking of the wagons on the rough trail to churn their butter.

CRITICAL THINKING SKILLS
Using a Diary as a Primary Source

A diary is a useful primary source because it tells what the writer saw, heard, said, thought, and felt. It gives firsthand information about people, places, and events. Because diaries are private, writers often say what they honestly think.

The excerpts below are taken from a diary that was kept by Amelia Stewart Knight. With her husband and children, Knight traveled west along the Oregon Trail in 1853. Her diary tells about the hardships the family faced on their way to a new life in Oregon Country.

1. **Identify the primary source.** (a) Who wrote the diary? (b) In what year was the diary written? (c) Under what conditions was it written? (d) Why do you think the writer wrote it?

2. **Analyze the information in the primary source.** Study the diary for information about how the writer lived. (a) What evidence supports the claim that life on the Oregon Trail was hard? (b) Describe the geography of the area the Knight family traveled through. (c) What chores did Amelia Knight do? (d) What chores did the children do?

3. **Draw conclusions about the writer's point of view.** Decide how the writer felt about making the journey west. (a) How do you think Knight felt about the hardships of the journey? (b) How might keeping the diary have helped her face these hardships? (c) What personal qualities did a person need to make the journey to Oregon County?

ACTIVITY
Keep a diary for a week. Then study your entries. Will your diary serve as a reliable primary source for someone trying to find out about life in the 1990s? Why or why not?

Amelia Stewart Knight's Diary

Monday, April 18th Cold; breaking fast the first thing; very disagreeable weather; wind east cold and rainy, no fire. We are on a very large prairie, no timber to be seen as far as the eye can reach. Evening—Have crossed several bad streams today, and more than once have been stuck in the mud.

Saturday, April 23rd Still in camp, it rained hard all night, and blew a hurricane almost. All the tents were blown down, and some wagons capsized. Evening—It has been raining hard all day; everything is wet and muddy. One of the oxen missing; the boys have been hunting him all day. (Dreary times, wet and muddy, and crowded in the tent, cold and wet and uncomfortable in the wagon. No place for the poor children.)

I have been busy cooking, roasting coffee, etc. today, and have come into the wagon to write this and make our bed.

Friday, May 6th We passed a train of wagons on their way back, the head man had drowned a few days before, in a river called the Elkhorn, while getting some cattle across. With sadness and pity I passed those who a few days before had been well and happy as ourselves.

Friday, August 19th After looking in vain for water, we were about to give up, when husband came across a company of friendly Cayuse Indians, who showed him where to find water. The men and boys have driven the cattle down to water and I am waiting to get supper. We bought a few potatoes from an Indian, which will be a treat for our supper.

2

A Country Called Texas

FIND OUT

■ Why did Mexico want Americans to settle in Texas?

■ How was the Republic of Texas set up?

■ Why did the United States refuse to annex Texas?

VOCABULARY annex

In late 1835, the word spread: Americans in Texas had rebelled against Mexico! Joseph Barnard, a young doctor, recalled:

❝I was at Chicago, Illinois, practicing medicine, when the news of the Texan revolt from Mexico reached our ears, in the early part of December, 1835. They were in arms for a cause that I had always been taught to consider sacred, [that is,] Republican principles and popular institutions.❞

Dr. Barnard took a steamship down the Mississippi and made his way to Texas. Like hundreds of other Americans, he wanted to help Texans fight for independence.

Americans in Mexican Texas

Since the early 1800s, American farmers had looked eagerly at the vast region called Texas. At the time, Texas was part of the Spanish colony of Mexico.

At first, Spain refused to let Americans move into the region. Then in 1821, Spain gave Moses Austin a land grant in Texas. Austin died before he could set up a colony. His son Stephen took over the project.

Meanwhile, Mexico had won its independence from Spain. (See page 316.) The new nation agreed to let Stephen Austin lead settlers into Texas. Only about 4,000 Mexicans lived there. Mexico hoped that the Americans would help develop the area and control Indian attacks.

Mexico gave Stephen Austin and each settler a large grant of land. In return, the settlers agreed to become citizens of Mexico, obey its laws, and worship in the Roman Catholic Church. In 1821, Austin and 300 families moved to Texas. The colony grew under Austin's leadership. By 1830, about 20,000 Americans had resettled in Texas.

Mexico Tightens Its Laws

Stephen Austin and his settlers had agreed to become Mexican citizens and Catholics. However, Americans who later flooded into Texas felt no loyalty to Mexico. They spoke only a few words of Spanish,

A Texan Ranch *In the 1820s, thousands of Americans poured into Texas. They built prosperous farms and ranches, such as the one shown here.* **United States and the World** *Why do you think Mexicans might have been concerned about the arrival of so many Americans in Texas?*

the official language of Mexico. Also, most of the Americans were Protestants. Conflict soon erupted between the newcomers and the Mexican government.

In 1830, Mexico passed a law forbidding any more Americans to move to Texas. Mexico feared that the Americans wanted to make Texas part of the United States. This fear had some basis. The United States had already tried to buy Texas, once in 1826 and again in 1829.

Mexico also decided to make Texans obey Mexican laws that they had ignored for years. One law banned slavery in Texas. Another required Texans to worship in the Catholic Church. Texans resented the laws and the Mexican troops who came north to enforce them.

In 1833, General Antonio López de Santa Anna came to power in Mexico. Two years later, Santa Anna threw out the Mexican constitution. Rumors spread wildly. Santa Anna, some said, intended to drive all Americans out of Texas.

Texans Take Action

Americans in Texas felt that the time had come for action. In this, they had the support of many *Tejanos* (teh HAH nohs), Mexicans who lived in Texas. The Tejanos did not necessarily want independence from Mexico. But they hated General Santa Anna, who ruled as a military dictator. They wanted to be rid of him.

Fighting begins. In October 1835, Texans in the town of Gonzales (gahn ZAH lehs) clashed with Mexican troops. (See the map at right.) The Texans defeated the Mexicans, forcing them to withdraw. Inspired by the victory, Stephen Austin and other Texans aimed to "see Texas forever free from Mexican domination."

Two months later, Texans stormed and took San Antonio. Santa Anna was furious. Determined to stamp out the rebellion, he marched north with a large army.

Declaring independence. While Santa Anna massed his troops, Texans declared their independence from Mexico on March 2, 1836. They set themselves up as a new nation called the ***Republic of Texas*** and appointed Sam Houston as commander of their army. The army drew volunteers of all

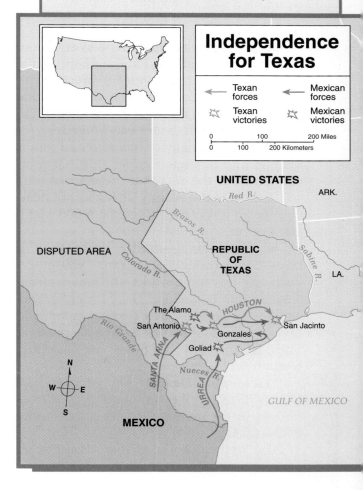

MAP STUDY

The Texan war for independence was brief but bloody.
1. Where did Santa Anna's army first fight the Texans?
2. Who won the battle at Gonzales?
3. **Comparing** Refer to the map of the United States in the Reference Section. How do the boundaries of the Republic of Texas compare with the boundaries of Texas today?

Independence for Texas

← Texan forces		← Mexican forces
☆ Texan victories		☆ Mexican victories

0   100   200 Miles
0   100   200 Kilometers

UNITED STATES

Red R.

ARK.

Brazos R.

DISPUTED AREA

Colorado R.

REPUBLIC OF TEXAS

Sabine R.

LA.

The Alamo

Rio Grande

San Antonio

HOUSTON

Gonzales

San Jacinto

Goliad

SANTA ANNA

Nueces R.

URREA

GULF OF MEXICO

N W E S

MEXICO

races and nationalities. Free blacks, slaves, and Tejanos, as well as other people of many nationalities, joined to fight for Texan independence.

By the time Santa Anna arrived in San Antonio, many of the Texans who had taken the city had drifted away. Fewer than 200 Texans remained as defenders. Despite the odds against them, the Texans refused to give up. Instead, they retired to an old Spanish mission called the ***Alamo.***

Remember the Alamo!

The Spanish had built the Alamo in the mid-1700s. It was like a small fort, surrounded by walls 12 feet high and 3 feet thick. The Alamo, said an observer, was "a strong place."

Ill prepared to fight. However, Texan defenders who gathered in the Alamo in the winter of 1835–1836 were ill prepared to fight. Supplies of ammunition and medicine were low. Food consisted of some beef and corn, and access to water was limited. As for warm clothing, many of the men had only a blanket and a single flannel shirt! Of most concern was the fact that there were only 187 Texans in the Alamo. This was not nearly enough to defend it against 6,000 Mexican troops.

William Travis—hardly more than a boy—commanded the Texans. Volunteers inside the mission included the famous frontiersmen Jim Bowie and Davy Crockett. Several Tejano families, two Texan women, and two young male slaves were also present. They later helped to nurse the sick and wounded.

"Victory or Death!" On February 23, 1836, a Texan lookout spotted the gleam of swords in the sunlight. Santa Anna's army had arrived!

The first shots from the Alamo were rapid and deadly and took the Mexicans by surprise. Commander Travis had three or four rifles placed by each man's side. In that way, a Texan could fire three or four shots in the time it took a Mexican to fire one.

Still, Travis knew that unless he received help, he and his men were doomed. On February 24, he sent a Texan through the Mexican lines with a message. It was addressed "to the People of Texas and all the Americans in the World":

> **"**Fellow Citizens and Compatriots— I am besieged by a thousand or more of the Mexicans under Santa Anna. I have sustained a continual bombardment for 24 hours and have not lost a man. The enemy have demanded a surrender. . . . I have answered the demand with a cannon shot and our flag still waves proudly from the walls.
>
> *I shall never surrender or retreat.*
>
> I call on you in the name of Liberty, of patriotism, and of everything dear to the American character to come to our aid with all dispatch. The enemy are receiving reinforcements daily. . . . If this call is neglected, I am determined to sustain myself as long as possible & die like a soldier who never forgets what is due to his own honor or that of his country. *Victory or Death!*
>
> W. Barret Travis**"**

Travis also sent scouts to seek additional soldiers and provisions. About 60 men were able to sneak through enemy lines and join the fighters in the Alamo. However, no large force ever arrived.

The final siege. Daily, the Mexicans bombarded the Alamo. For 12 days, the defenders bravely held them off. Then, at dawn on March 6, 1836, Mexican cannon fire broke through the Alamo walls. Thousands of Mexican soldiers poured into the mission. When the bodies were counted,

Siege at the Alamo *For 12 days, a small band of Texans held off Mexican troops at the Alamo. Most of the Texans were killed. Their heroic stand, however, inspired others to fight for the Republic of Texas, whose flag is shown above.* **Multicultural Heritage** *Why did many Tejanos support the revolt against Mexican rule?*

183 Texans and almost 1,500 Mexicans lay dead. The five Texan survivors, including Davy Crockett, were promptly executed at Santa Anna's order.

The slaughter at the Alamo angered Texans and set off cries for revenge. The fury of the Texans grew even stronger three weeks later, when Mexicans killed several hundred Texan soldiers at Goliad after they had surrendered. Volunteers flooded into Sam Houston's army. Men from the United States also raced south to help the Texan cause. ■

Texan Independence

While the Mexicans were busy at the Alamo, Sam Houston organized his army. Six weeks later, on April 21, 1836, Houston decided that the moment had come to attack.

Santa Anna was camped with his army near the San Jacinto (jah SEEN toh) River. With cries of "Remember the Alamo!" the Texans charged the surprised Mexicans. The Battle of San Jacinto lasted only 18 minutes. Although they were outnumbered, Texans killed 630 Mexicans and captured 700 more.

The next day, Texans captured Santa Anna himself. They forced the general to sign a treaty granting Texas its independence.

The Lone Star Republic

In battle, Texans had carried a flag with a single white star. After winning independence, they nicknamed their nation the **Lone Star Republic.** They drew up a constitution based on the Constitution of the United States and elected Sam Houston as their president.

History and You

Have you ever been fooled by false advertising? Many Americans in 1837 were persuaded by newspaper ads to buy land in a "booming new metropolis" in Texas called Houston. On arrival, they discovered just a small, rough settlement. Most stayed, however, and helped to build the city. Today, Houston is the fourth largest city in the United States.

The new country faced huge problems. First, Mexico refused to accept the treaty signed by Santa Anna. Mexicans still claimed Texas as part of their country. Second, Texas was nearly bankrupt. Most Texans thought that the best way to solve both problems was for Texas to become part of the United States.

In the United States, Americans were divided about whether to annex Texas. To annex means to add on. Most white southerners favored the idea. Many northerners, however, were against it. At issue was slavery.

Antislavery feelings were growing in the North in the 1830s. Knowing that many Texans owned slaves, northerners did not want to allow Texas to join the Union. President Andrew Jackson also worried that annexing Texas would lead to war with Mexico. As a result, the United States refused to annex Texas.

SECTION 2 REVIEW

1. **Locate:** (a) Mexico, (b) Gonzales, (c) San Antonio, (d) Republic of Texas.
2. **Identify:** (a) Stephen Austin, (b) Antonio López de Santa Anna, (c) Tejano, (d) Sam Houston, (e) Alamo, (f) Lone Star Republic.
3. **Define:** annex.
4. (a) Who were the first settlers from the United States to move into Texas? (b) Why did Mexico encourage Americans to settle in Texas?
5. Why did northerners and southerners disagree about annexing Texas?
6. CRITICAL THINKING **Analyzing Information** How was the defeat at the Alamo also a victory for Texans?

ACTIVITY **Writing to Learn**
Imagine you are a Texan in the 1830s. Write a letter to Americans stating your views on independence from Mexico.

3
Manifest Destiny

FIND OUT
- Who were the first white settlers in New Mexico and California?
- What was mission life like for Native Americans?
- What did Americans mean by Manifest Destiny?

In 1819, John Quincy Adams expressed the belief that the United States had the right to all of North America. He wrote:

66[The world has to accept] the idea of . . . the continent of North America as our proper dominion. From the time we became an independent nation, it was as much a law of nature that this would become our claim as that the Mississippi should flow to the sea. 99

By the 1840s, many Americans agreed. They looked with interest toward California and New Mexico. Like Adams, they felt it was the "destiny" of the United States to expand all the way to the Pacific Ocean.

New Mexico Territory

The entire Southwest belonged to Mexico in the 1840s. This huge region was called *New Mexico Territory.* It included most of the present-day states of Arizona and New Mexico, all of Nevada and Utah, and parts of Colorado. The capital of New Mexico Territory was Santa Fe.

Much of the Southwest is hot and dry. In some areas, thick grasses grow. There are also desert and mountain areas. Before the arrival of the Spanish, Pueblo and Zuñi Indians irrigated and farmed the land. Other

M A P   S T U D Y

Americans followed a number of trails to the West.
1. Which trails ended in cities in California?
2. About how long was the Mormon Trail?
3. **Analyzing Information** (a) What would be the best route for a pioneer family to take from Independence, Missouri, to Sutter's Fort, California? (b) What mountains would they cross? (c) In which town might they seek shelter along the way?

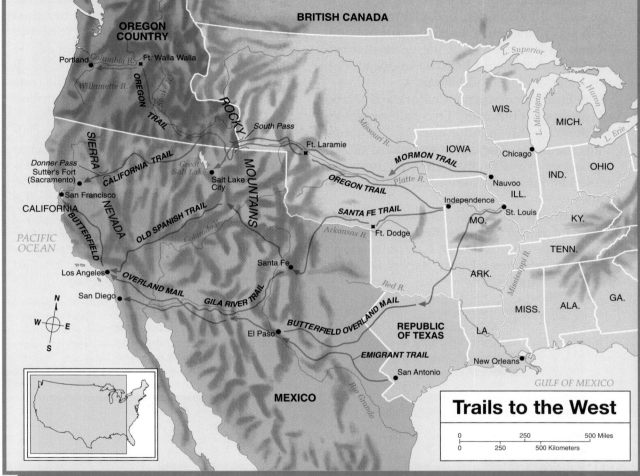

Trails to the West

Native Americans, such as the Apaches, lived by hunting.

Santa Fe. As you have read, the explorer Juan de Oñate claimed the territory of New Mexico for Spain in 1598. In the early 1600s, the Spanish built Santa Fe as the capital of the territory.

Under the Spanish, Santa Fe grew into a busy trading town. But Spain refused to let

Americans settle in New Mexico. Only after Mexico won its independence in 1821 were Americans welcome in Santa Fe.

The first Americans arrive. William Becknell, a merchant and adventurer, was the first American to head for Santa Fe. In 1821, Becknell led a group of traders on the long trip from Franklin, Missouri, across the plains. When they reached Santa Fe, they found Mexicans eager to buy their goods. Other Americans soon followed Becknell's route. It became known as the *Santa Fe Trail.* (See the map on page 361.)

Early Years in California

California, too, belonged to Mexico in the early 1840s. Spain had claimed the region 100 years before English colonists built homes in Jamestown. In the years that followed, Spanish and Native American cultures shaped life in California.

A land of contrasts. California is a land of dramatic contrasts. Two tall mountain ranges slice through the region. One range hugs the coast. The other sits inland on the border of Nevada and Arizona. Between these two ranges is California's fertile Central Valley.

Northern California receives plenty of rain. But in the south, water is scarce and much of the land is desert. California enjoys mild temperatures all year, except for areas high in the mountains.

A string of missions. As you have read, Spanish soldiers and priests built the first European settlements in California. In 1769, Captain Gaspar de Portolá led a group of soldiers and missionaries up the Pacific coast. The chief missionary was Father Junípero Serra (hoo NEE peh roh SEHR rah).

Father Serra built his first mission at San Diego. He went on to build 20 other missions along the California coast. (See the map on page 75.) Each mission claimed the surrounding land and soon took care of all its own needs. Spanish soldiers built forts near the missions. The missions supplied meat, grain, and other foods to the forts.

Mission life for Native Americans. California Indians lived in small, scattered groups. They were generally peaceful people. They did not offer much resistance to soldiers who forced them to work for the missions.

Native Americans herded sheep and cattle and raised crops for the missions. In return, they lived at the missions and learned about the Catholic religion. But mission life

A California Mission *The Spanish forced many West Coast Indians into missions. This picture shows Native Americans at a mission in northern California.* **Daily Life** *Study the picture. What seems to be the main building? Where on the mission grounds did Native Americans live?*

was hard for Native Americans. Thousands died from overwork and diseases.

After Mexico won its independence, conditions for Native Americans grew even worse. The new Mexican government offered mission land to ranchers. Some of the ranchers cruelly mistreated the Indians. One American reported:

66 The natives [in California]...are in a state of absolute [slavery], even more degrading, and more oppressive than that of our slaves in the South. 99

These harsh conditions had a deadly effect. Between 1770 and 1850, the Native American population of California declined from 310,000 to 100,000.

Expansion: A Right and a Duty

As late as the mid-1840s, only about 700 people from the United States lived in California. Every year, however, more and more Americans looked toward the West.

The nation's destiny. Many Americans saw the culture and the democratic government of the United States as the best in the world. They believed that the United States had the right and the duty to spread its rule all the way to the Pacific Ocean.

In the 1840s, a New York newspaper coined a phrase for this belief. The phrase was *Manifest Destiny.* Manifest means clear or obvious. Destiny means something that is sure to happen. Americans who believed in

★ ★
Our Common Heritage
When Spanish missionaries arrived in California, Native Americans there spoke more than 100 different languages. Within a few generations, however, most of those languages died out. The Indian children were taught only Spanish in the missions.

Manifest Destiny thought that the United States was clearly meant to expand to the Pacific.

Manifest Destiny had another side, too. Many Americans believed that they were better than Native Americans and Mexicans. For these Americans, racism justified taking over lands belonging to Indians and Mexicans whom they considered inferior.

Election of 1844. Manifest Destiny played an important part in the election of 1844. The Whigs nominated Henry Clay for President. Clay was a respected national leader. The Democrats chose a little-known man named James K. Polk.

Voters soon came to know Polk as the candidate who favored expansion. Polk demanded that Texas and Oregon be added to the United States. He made Oregon a special campaign issue. Polk insisted on the whole region for the United States—all the way to its northern border at latitude 54°40'N. "Fifty-four forty or fight!" cried the Democrats. On election day, Americans showed that they favored expansion by electing Polk President.

SECTION 3 REVIEW

1. **Locate:** (a) Santa Fe, (b) Santa Fe Trail, (c) San Diego.
2. **Identify:** (a) New Mexico Territory, (b) William Becknell, (c) Junípero Serra, (d) Manifest Destiny, (e) James K. Polk.
3. How did mission life affect Native Americans in California?
4. Why did Americans elect James Polk President in 1844?
5. CRITICAL THINKING Analyzing Information How do you think missionaries justified forcing Indians to live and work in missions?

ACTIVITY Writing to Learn
Write a dialogue between a Mexican and an American about Manifest Destiny.

4
The Mexican War

FIND OUT

- How did the United States gain Oregon?
- What events led to war with Mexico?
- What lands did the United States gain from the Mexican War?
- How did Spanish and Indian traditions blend in the new lands?

VOCABULARY cede

In 1845, President Polk rode into the White House on a wave of popular support. Americans eagerly endorsed his promise to expand the United States from sea to sea.

Fulfilling that promise was a difficult task. First, the new President faced a showdown with Britain over the issue of Oregon. Happily for the nation, he resolved this issue peacefully. However, Polk also was determined to add Texas to the United States. To fulfill this dream, he led the United States into a bloody war with Mexico.

Annexing Texas

The United States refused to annex Texas in 1836. By 1844, many Americans had changed their minds. As Polk's election showed, expansionist feelings were strong in the United States.

In 1844, Sam Houston, the president of Texas, signed a treaty of annexation with the United States. The Senate refused to ratify the treaty. Senators feared that annexing Texas would cause a war with Mexico.

Sam Houston did not give up. To persuade Americans to annex Texas, he pretended that Texas might become an ally of Britain. The trick worked. Americans did not want Europe's greatest power to gain a foothold on their western border. In 1845, Congress passed a joint resolution admitting Texas to the Union.

Annexing Texas led at once to a dispute with Mexico. Texas claimed that its southern border was the Rio Grande. Mexico argued that it was the Nueces (noo AY says) River. The Nueces was some 200 miles (320 km) north of the Rio Grande. (See the map on page 365.) The United States supported Texan claims. Trouble with Mexico seemed likely.

Dividing Oregon

The quarrel over Texas was not the only problem Polk faced when he took office in March 1845. Acting on a campaign promise, he moved to gain control of Oregon. It seemed that Britain and the United States would go to war.

Despite his expansionist beliefs, President Polk did not really want a war with Britain. In 1846, he agreed to a compromise. Oregon was divided at latitude 49°N. Britain got the lands north of the line, and the United States got the lands south of the line. The

BIOGRAPHY Sam Houston *While a teenager, Sam Houston lived for three years among the Cherokee Indians. Later, he helped protect the Cherokees against fraud by government agents.* **Citizenship** *What role did Houston play in getting the United States to annex Texas?*

United States named its portion the Oregon Territory. The states of Oregon (1859), Washington (1889), and Idaho (1890) were later carved out of the Oregon Territory.

War With Mexico

Meanwhile, the United States and Mexico stood on the brink of war. Mexico had never accepted the independence of Texas. Now, the annexation of Texas made Mexicans furious. They also were concerned that the example set by Texas would encourage Americans in California and New Mexico to rebel.

Americans, in turn, were angry with Mexico. President Polk offered to pay Mexico $30 million for California and New Mexico. However, Mexico strongly opposed any further loss of territory and refused the offer. Many Americans felt that Mexico stood in the way of Manifest Destiny.

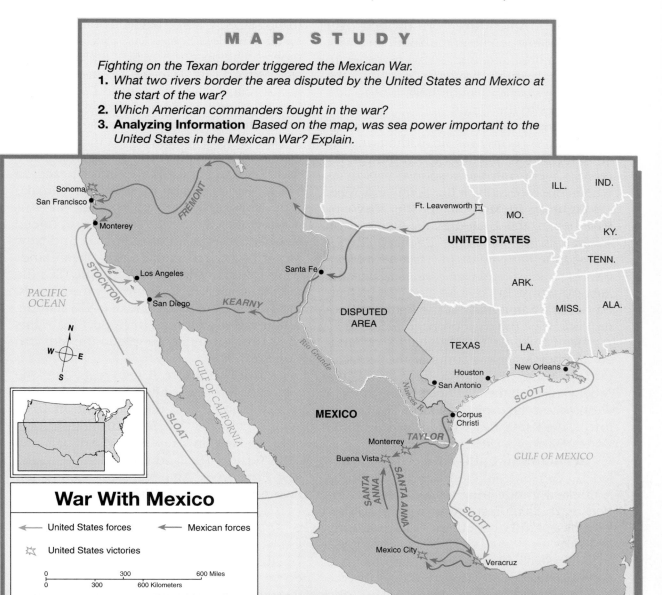

MAP STUDY

Fighting on the Texan border triggered the Mexican War.
1. *What two rivers border the area disputed by the United States and Mexico at the start of the war?*
2. *Which American commanders fought in the war?*
3. **Analyzing Information** *Based on the map, was sea power important to the United States in the Mexican War? Explain.*

War With Mexico

← United States forces ← Mexican forces

☆ United States victories

0   300   600 Miles
0   300   600 Kilometers

Sparking the war. In January 1846, Polk ordered General Zachary Taylor to cross the Nueces River and set up posts along the Rio Grande. Polk knew that Mexico claimed this land and that the move might spark a war. In April 1846, Mexican troops crossed the Rio Grande and fought briefly with the Americans. Soldiers on both sides were killed.

President Polk claimed that Mexico had "shed American blood upon the American soil." At his urging, Congress declared war on Mexico. Americans were divided over the war. Many people in the South and West wanted more land and so were eager to fight. Northerners, however, opposed the war. They saw it as a southern plot to add slave states to the Union.

Still, many Americans joined the war effort. Since the army was small, thousands of volunteers were needed. When the call for recruits went out, the response was overwhelming, especially in the South and West.

Fighting in Mexico. As the *Mexican War* began, the United States attacked on several fronts. General Zachary Taylor crossed the Rio Grande into northern Mexico. There, he won several battles against the Mexican army. In February 1847, he defeated General Santa Anna at the Battle of Buena Vista. (See the map on page 365.)

Meanwhile, General Winfield Scott landed another American army at the Mexican port of Veracruz. After a long battle, the Americans took the city. Scott then marched west toward the capital, Mexico City. He followed the same route taken by Hernando Cortés 300 years earlier.

Rebellion in California. A third army, led by General Stephen Kearny, captured Santa Fe without firing a shot. Kearny hurried on to San Diego. After several battles, he took control of southern California early in 1847.

Americans in northern California had risen up against Mexican rule even before hearing of the Mexican War. Led by John Frémont, the rebels declared California an independent republic on June 14, 1846. They called their new nation the *Bear Flag Republic.* Later in the war, Frémont joined forces with the United States Army.

A Nation's Dream Comes True

By 1847, the United States controlled all of New Mexico and California. Meanwhile, General Scott had reached the outskirts of the Mexican capital, Mexico City. There his troops faced a fierce battle. Young Mexican soldiers made a heroic last stand at Chapultepec (chah POOL tuh pehk), a fort just outside Mexico City. Like the Texans who died at the Alamo, the Mexicans at Chapultepec fought to the last man. Today, Mexicans honor these young men as heroes.

Peace with Mexico. With the American army in Mexico City, the Mexican government had no choice but to make peace. In 1848, Mexico signed the Treaty of Guadalupe Hidalgo (gwah duh LOOP ay ih DAHL goh). Under the treaty, Mexico was forced to cede, or give, all of California and New Mexico to the United States. These lands were called the *Mexican Cession.* (See the map on page 367.) In return for these lands, the United States paid Mexico $15 million. Americans also agreed to respect the rights of Spanish-speaking people in the Mexican Cession.

A final addition. A few years after the Mexican War, the United States completed its expansion across the continent. In 1853, it agreed to pay Mexico $10 million for a strip of land in present-day Arizona and New Mexico. The land was called the *Gadsden Purchase.* Americans rejoiced. Their dream of Manifest Destiny had come true.

A Rich Heritage

Texas, New Mexico, and California added vast new lands to the United States. In these lands, Americans found a rich culture

By 1848, the United States stretched all the way from the Atlantic Ocean to the Pacific Ocean.

1. *What area on this map was the last to be added to the United States?*
2. *How did Oregon Country become part of the United States?*
3. **Analyzing Information** *Refer to the United States map in the Reference Section. When and in what way did your state become part of the United States?*

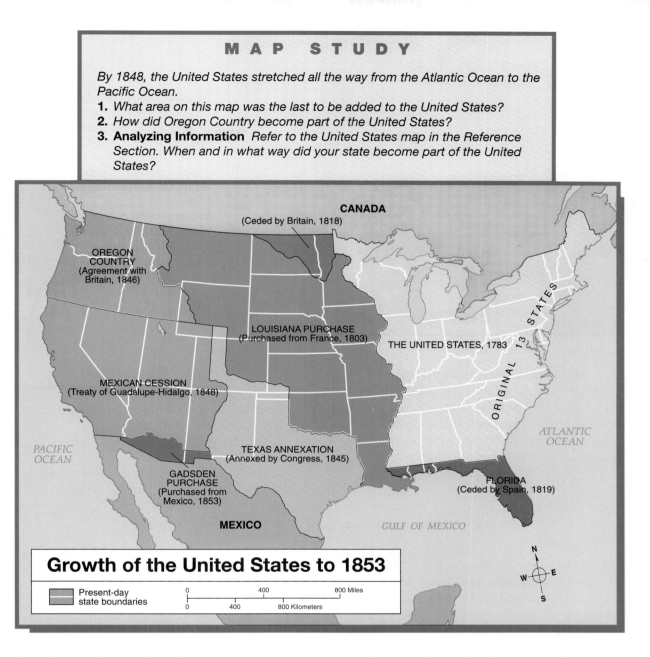

CANADA
(Ceded by Britain, 1818)

OREGON COUNTRY
(Agreement with Britain, 1846)

LOUISIANA PURCHASE
(Purchased from France, 1803)

THE UNITED STATES, 1783

ORIGINAL 13 STATES

MEXICAN CESSION
(Treaty of Guadalupe-Hidalgo, 1848)

ATLANTIC OCEAN

PACIFIC OCEAN

TEXAS ANNEXATION
(Annexed by Congress, 1845)

GADSDEN PURCHASE
(Purchased from Mexico, 1853)

FLORIDA
(Ceded by Spain, 1819)

MEXICO

GULF OF MEXICO

Growth of the United States to 1853

Present-day state boundaries

0   400   800 Miles

0   400   800 Kilometers

that blended Spanish and Native American traditions. (□ See "Death Comes for the Archbishop" on page 582.)

A mix of cultures. English-speaking settlers poured into the Southwest bringing their own culture with them, including their ideas about democratic government. At the same time, they learned a great deal from the older residents of the region. Mexican Americans taught the newcomers how to irrigate the soil and how to mine silver and other

minerals. Spanish and Indian words became part of the English language. They included stampede, buffalo, soda, and tornado.

Americans kept some Mexican laws. One law said that a husband and wife owned property together. In the rest of the United States, married women could not own property. Another Mexican law said that landowners could not cut off water to their neighbors. This law was important in the Southwest, where water was scarce.

Fandango in Texas *Spanish traditions were strong in the Southwest. In this painting, couples enjoy a traditional Spanish dance. The brooch, right, also shows Spanish influence.* **Multicultural Heritage** *What other groups influenced the culture of the Southwest?*

Mexican Americans and Indians. Newcomers often treated Mexican Americans and Indians poorly. The earlier residents struggled to protect their traditions and rights. When Mexican Americans went to court to defend their property, they found that judges rarely upheld their claims. The family of Guadalupe Vallejo (vah YAY hoh) had lived in California for decades before the English-speaking settlers arrived. Vallejo noted bitterly:

❝In their dealings with the rancheros, [Americans] took advantage of laws which they understood, but which were new to the Spaniards, and so robbed the latter of their lands.❞

Our Common Heritage
Southwestern cooking reflects many of the cultures that have merged in the region. Popular foods include corn meal and chili peppers of Native American origin, cinnamon brought from Spain, and combinations of tortillas and ground beef developed by Mexicans.

SECTION 4 REVIEW

1. **Locate:** (a) Rio Grande, (b) Nueces River, (c) Buena Vista, (d) Mexico City, (e) Mexican Cession, (f) Gadsden Purchase.
2. **Identify:** (a) Sam Houston, (b) Zachary Taylor, (c) Mexican War, (d) Stephen Kearny, (e) John Frémont, (f) Bear Flag Republic, (g) Chapultepec.
3. **Define:** cede.
4. What event sparked the beginning of the Mexican War?
5. What were the terms of the Treaty of Guadalupe Hidalgo?
6. (a) Name two things that English-speaking settlers learned from Mexican Americans in the Southwest. (b) Name one tradition that English-speaking settlers brought to the Southwest.
7. **CRITICAL THINKING Drawing Conclusions** Why do you think the United States was willing to make a boundary compromise with Britain but not with Mexico?

ACTIVITY **Writing to Learn**
Write an editorial defending the right of the United States to expand to the Pacific Ocean.

Surge to the Pacific

FIND OUT

- How did the Mormons set up a successful community in Utah?
- How did the discovery of gold affect life in California?
- What mix of peoples helped California to grow and prosper?

VOCABULARY forty-niner, vigilante

In 1848, James Marshall was helping John Sutter build a sawmill on the American River, north of Sacramento, California. On the morning of January 24, Marshall set out to inspect a ditch his crew was digging. He later told a friend what he saw that day:

> It was a clear, cold morning; I shall never forget that morning. As I was taking my usual walk, . . . my eye was caught with the glimpse of something shining in the bottom of the ditch. There was about a foot of water running then. I reached my hand down and picked it up; it made my heart thump, for I was certain it was gold.

Word of Marshall's find spread like wildfire. From all over the nation, thousands of prospectors flocked to California to seek their fortunes. The California Gold Rush had begun!

Gold was not the only thing that attracted settlers to the West in the mid-1800s. California, New Mexico, Oregon, Texas—all were now part of the United States. Restless pioneers, always eager to try something new, headed into these lands to build homes and a new way of life.

Mormons Seek Refuge in Utah

The largest group of settlers to move into the Mexican Cession were the **Mormons.** Mormons belonged to the Church of Jesus Christ of Latter-day Saints. The church was founded by Joseph Smith in 1830. Smith, a farmer who lived in upstate New York, attracted many followers.

Troubles with neighbors. Smith was an energetic and popular man. His teachings, however, angered many non-Mormons. For example, Mormons at first believed that property should be owned in common. Smith also said that a man could have more than one wife. Angry neighbors forced the Mormons to leave New York for Ohio. From Ohio, they were forced to move to Missouri, and from there to Illinois. In the 1840s, the Mormons built a community called Nauvoo in Illinois.

Before long, the Mormons again clashed with their neighbors. In 1844, an angry mob killed Joseph Smith. The Mormons chose Brigham Young as their new leader.

Brigham Young realized that the Mormons needed a home where they would be safe. He had read about a valley between the Rocky Mountains and the Great Salt Lake in Utah. Young decided that the isolated valley would make a good home for the Mormons.

A difficult journey. To move 15,000 men, women, and children from Illinois to Utah in the 1840s was an awesome challenge. Relying on faith and careful planning, Brigham Young achieved his goal.

In 1847, Young led an advance party into the Great Salt Lake valley. Wave after wave of Mormons followed. For the next few years, Mormon wagon trains struggled across the plains and over the Rockies to Utah. When they ran short of wagons and oxen, thousands made the long trip pulling their gear in handcarts.

The Mormons prosper in the desert. In Utah, the Mormons had to survive in a harsh

Traveling to Utah *"This is the place," said Brigham Young when he and a small band of Mormons reached the Great Salt Lake in Utah. Other groups of Mormons, like the ones shown here, soon followed.*
American Traditions *What other states were settled by people seeking religious freedom?*

desert climate. Once again, Young proved to be a gifted leader. He planned an irrigation system to bring water to farms. He also drew up plans for a large city, called *Salt Lake City,* to be built in the desert.

The Mormon settlement in Utah grew quickly. Like other whites, Mormons took over thousands of acres of Native American land, usually paying nothing for it.

Congress recognized Brigham Young as governor of the Utah Territory in 1850. Trouble later broke out when non-Mormons moved to the area. In the end, peace was restored, and Utah became a state in 1896.

Gold in California!

While the Mormons trekked to Utah, thousands of other Americans were racing to California. They all had a single objective: Gold!

Sutter's Mill. As you have read, James Marshall found gold at Sutter's Mill in California in January 1848. In a few days, word of the gold strike spread to San Francisco. Carpenters threw down their saws. Bakers left bread in their ovens. Schools emptied as teachers and students joined the rush to the gold fields.

The news spread outward from San Francisco. Thousands of Americans caught gold fever. People in Europe and South America joined the rush as well. More than 80,000 people made the long journey to California in 1849. They became known as **forty-niners.**

In the gold fields. The first miners needed little skill. Because the gold was near the surface of the Earth, they could dig it out with knives. Later, the miners found a better way. They loaded sand and gravel from the riverbed into a washing pan. Then, they held the pan under water and swirled it gently. The water washed away lighter gravel, leaving the heavier gold in the pan. This process was known as "panning for gold."

Only a few miners struck it rich. Most went broke trying to make their fortunes. Although many miners left the gold fields, they stayed in California. (📖 See "In the Gold Fields of California" on page 584.)

A new state. The Gold Rush brought big changes to life in California. Almost overnight, San Francisco grew from a sleepy town to a bustling city.

Greed turned some forty-niners into criminals. Murders and robberies plagued mining camps. To fight crime, **vigilantes** (vihj uh LAN teez), self-appointed law enforcers, dealt out punishment even though they had no legal power to do so. Sometimes an accused criminal was lynched, or hanged without a legal trial.

Californians realized they needed a government to stop the lawlessness. In 1849, they drafted a state constitution. They then asked to be admitted to the Union. Their request caused an uproar in the United States. Americans wondered whether or not the new state would allow slavery. As you will read in Chapter 15, after a heated debate, California was admitted to the Union in 1850 as a free state.

California's Unique Culture

Most mining camps included a mix of peoples. One visitor to a mining town met runaway slaves from the South, Native Americans, and New Englanders. There were also people from Hawaii, China, Peru, Chile, France, Germany, Italy, Ireland, and Australia.

Most of the miners, however, were white Americans. During the wild days of the Gold Rush, they often ignored the rights of other Californians.

Native Americans. Indians fared worst of all. Many Native Americans were driven

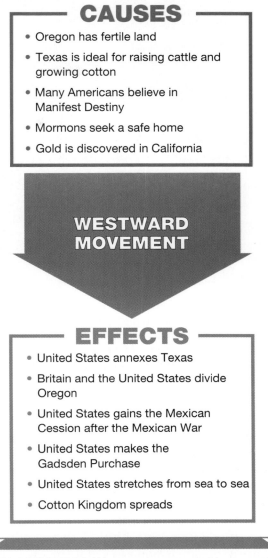

CAUSES

- Oregon has fertile land
- Texas is ideal for raising cattle and growing cotton
- Many Americans believe in Manifest Destiny
- Mormons seek a safe home
- Gold is discovered in California

WESTWARD MOVEMENT

EFFECTS

- United States annexes Texas
- Britain and the United States divide Oregon
- United States gains the Mexican Cession after the Mexican War
- United States makes the Gadsden Purchase
- United States stretches from sea to sea
- Cotton Kingdom spreads

CHART SKILLS *Westward movement increased in the mid-1800s.* ● *List two attractions that drew Americans west. According to this chart, was Manifest Destiny successful? Explain.*

off their lands and later died of starvation or diseases. Others were murdered. In 1850, about 100,000 Indians lived in California. By the 1870s, there were only 17,000 Indians left in the state.

Mexican Americans. In many instances, Mexican Americans lost land they had owned for generations. Still, they fought to

Prospecting for Gold *The lure of gold drew thousands of prospectors to California. These miners are using a wooden sluice to wash the lighter gravel away from the heavier gold.* **Multicultural Heritage** *How did the Gold Rush contribute to California's unique culture?*

preserve the customs of their people. José Carrillo (cah REE yoh) was from one of the oldest families in California. In part through his efforts, the state's constitution was written in both Spanish and English.

Chinese Americans. Attracted by the tales of a "mountain of gold," thousands of Chinese began arriving in California in 1848. Since California needed workers, the Chinese were welcomed at first. When the Chinese staked claims in the gold fields, how-

Linking Past and Present
California continues to attract newcomers in record numbers. In fact, in 1990, more than 30 percent of the immigrants coming to the United States settled in California. The largest group were those from Asia.

ever, white miners often drove them off. Still, many Chinese Americans stayed in California and helped the state to grow. They farmed, irrigated, and reclaimed vast stretches of land.

African Americans. Free blacks, like other forty-niners, rushed to the California gold fields hoping to strike it rich. Some did become wealthy. By the 1850s, in fact, California had the richest African American population of any state. Yet African Americans were also denied certain rights. For example, California law denied blacks and other minorities the right to testify against whites in court. After a long struggle, blacks gained this right in 1863.

In spite of these problems, California thrived and grew. Settlers continued to arrive in the state. By 1860, it had 100,000 citizens. The mix of peoples in California gave it a unique culture.

SECTION 5 REVIEW

1. **Locate:** (a) Sacramento, (b) Nauvoo, (c) Salt Lake City, (d) San Francisco.
2. **Identify:** (a) Mormons, (b) Joseph Smith, (c) Brigham Young.
3. **Define:** (a) forty-niner, (b) vigilante.
4. Why did Brigham Young lead the Mormons to Utah?
5. What problems did Californians face because of the Gold Rush?
6. Explain the problems that each of the following faced in California: (a) Native Americans, (b) Mexican Americans, (c) Chinese Americans, (d) African Americans.
7. **CRITICAL THINKING Comparing** Compare the settling of Utah with the settling of California.

ACTIVITY **Writing to Learn**
Imagine that you are a gold prospector in California in 1850. Write a journal entry describing a typical day.

CONNECTIONS

ARTS | SCIENCES | GEOGRAPHY | **WORLD** | ECONOMICS | CIVICS

A Mountain of Gold

The penalty for trying to leave China in the 1800s was harsh and sure—a swift beheading. Yet, between 1848 and 1851, 25,000 Chinese risked the executioner's ax to sail 7,000 miles (11,265 km) to California. Oddly, almost all of these people came from the Toishan district of southern China.

Why did the people of Toishan risk death to leave China? The answer: hunger and poverty. Located in the mountains, Toishan was rocky and barren. Even with hard work, its people could grow only enough to feed themselves four months of the year. Life was a daily struggle for survival.

In 1848, exciting news reached Toishan. Mountains of gold had been discovered in a place called California. It was there just for the digging!

Wooden rocker for washing away gravel

Leaving their families behind, the men of Toishan rushed to the nearby port of Hong Kong. There, they crowded into ships for the three-month journey east to California.

Few of the Toishanese got rich in the California gold fields. Most found jobs, however, and many sent money back home. In fact, the money they sent to Toishan helped transform it into a prosperous, well-fed community. In this small way, California had fulfilled its promise as a "mountain of gold."

■ Why did many Chinese travel to California after 1848?

Mining tools

Chinese immigrant

ACTIVITY Create a storybook for younger children about the people of Toishan and the "mountain of gold." Illustrate your book with colorful pictures and a map showing the journey to California.

Summary

- Thousands of settlers traveled to Oregon Country along the Oregon Trail.
- Americans in Texas declared their independence from Mexico in 1836.
- Americans believed it was their Manifest Destiny to expand to the Pacific.
- The United States gained California and New Mexico after the Mexican War.
- The Mormons set up a successful community in Utah, while thousands of people rushed to California in search of gold.

Reviewing the Main Ideas

1. (a) What attracted settlers to Oregon Country in the mid-1800s? (b) How did they travel there?
2. Describe how each of the following groups helped to open the West: (a) Mountain Men, (b) missionaries, (c) forty-niners.
3. What action by Santa Anna convinced Texans to fight for independence?
4. Describe the life of Native Americans on missions in California.
5. What role did the idea of Manifest Destiny play in the election of 1844?
6. (a) What problem did the Mormons face in Utah? (b) How did Brigham Young help the Mormons to solve this problem?
7. How did the discovery of gold change life in California?

Thinking Critically

1. **Understanding Causes and Effects** Review the events leading up to the Mexican War. (a) What was the immediate cause of war with Mexico? (b) What were the long-range causes?
2. **Solving Problems** Do you think that the United States could have avoided war with Mexico in 1846? Explain.

3. **Linking Past and Present** (a) Why do you think forty-niners risked their savings and lives looking for gold in California? (b) Can you think of people today who take risks to earn great wealth? Explain.

Applying Your Skills

1. **Making a Review Chart** Make a chart with four columns and two rows. Title the chart American Expansion. Label the columns Oregon, Texas, Mexican Cession, Gadsden Purchase. Label the rows Date Added, How Added. Use the material in the chapter to complete the chart.
2. **Using a Primary Source** This excerpt is from the diary of a Mormon woman traveling to Utah: "To start out on such a journey in the winter and in our state of poverty, it would seem like walking into the jaws of death. But we put our trust in [our heavenly father], feeling that we were his chosen people." (a) What does the writer think the trip will be like? Explain. (b) Why is she willing to face the hardships of the trip?

Thinking About Geography

Match the letters on the map with the following places: **1.** Louisiana Purchase, **2.** Gadsden Purchase, **3.** Oregon Country, **4.** Florida, **5.** The United States, 1783, **6.** Texas Annexation, **7.** Mexican Cession. **Location** At what latitude did the United States and Britain agree to divide Oregon?

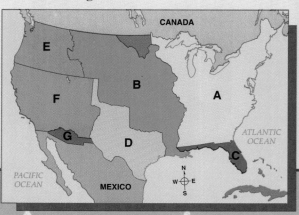

Traveling Along the Oregon Trail

Form into groups to review life along the Oregon Trail. Follow the suggestions below to research, write, sing, or act to show what you have learned about this subject. You may use the textbook, encyclopedias, atlases, or other materials in your classroom library to complete the tasks. Be able to name your sources of information when you have finished the activity.

Pioneer's herbal medicine kit

GEOGRAPHERS Prepare fact sheets on the landforms, climate, animals, and vegetation that travelers might encounter along the Oregon Trail.

MUSICIANS Review what you have read about traveling west on the Oregon Trail. Then make up a song that pioneers might sing about life on the trail. Fit your words to a familiar tune or write a new one.

HISTORIANS Create a time capsule about life on the Oregon Trail. Use an empty coffee can as your time capsule. Put sketches, words, phrases, and "artifacts" into your time capsule to illustrate geography, people, and events along the trail. Seal your capsule and decorate the outside to identify the contents. Plan to open it at the end of the school year.

ARTISTS Choose a painting from the chapter that shows pioneers traveling west. Then find another painting showing a similar subject. Give a talk about the two paintings. What do the paintings tell you about the journey west? Are the two paintings similar? If they are different, how do you explain the differences? What are the artists trying to say in the paintings?

ACTORS Review the selections from Amelia Stewart Knight's diary on page 355. Prepare a dramatic reading of her diary. One member of the group can read from the diary while other members act out the story.

★ Make an audiotape or videotape about Traveling Along the Oregon Trail. Tape each group that performs or presents its assignment.

Butter churn

Crossing the Platte River

CHAPTER 13

The Worlds of North and South

(1820–1860)

CHAPTER OUTLINE

1 The Growth of Industry in the North

2 Life in the Industrial North

3 Cotton Becomes King

4 Life in the Cotton Kingdom

Early 1800s *Slavery ended in the North. Many free African Americans, such as this news vendor, found work in the nation's cities.*

1830s *The first commercial railroads in the United States went into service. Here, an early steam locomotive pulls into a station in Maryland.*

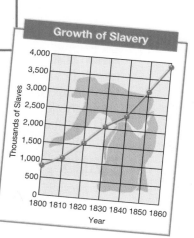

Growth of Slavery

(Graph: Thousands of Slaves vs. Year, 1800–1860)

1840s *A cotton boom in the South led to the expansion of slavery, as this graph shows.*

1820   1825   1830   1835   1840

WORLD EVENT
1840 World Anti-Slavery Convention held in Great Britain

Chapter Setting

"I was born in 1844. . . . First [thing] I remember was my ma and us [children] being sold off the [auction] block to Mistress Payne. When I was. . . too little to work in the field, I stayed at the big house most of the time and helped Mistress Payne feed the chickens, make scarecrows to keep the hawks away and put wood on the fires. After I got big enough to hoe, I went to the field same as the other[s]. . . . In the summer after the crop was laid by I helped to cut wood for winter, build fences, cut bushes. . . . I never earned any money for myself. . . . I didn't hardly know what money looked like."

In this excerpt, Jack Payne recalls his life as an enslaved person in Texas. Payne was only one of millions of African Americans throughout the South who suffered the anguish of slavery. Toiling from dawn till dusk, they had neither freedom nor rights.

By the 1840s, cotton was the South's major cash crop. Cotton plantations and slavery spread from the east coast to the Mississippi River and beyond. From plantations worked by enslaved African Americans, hundreds of thousands of cotton bales were shipped to the North.

In the North, new machines and inventions triggered the growth of factories and cities. Workers toiled long hours at low wages to make cotton into thousands of rolls of cloth. So it was that the North and South, very different in ways of life, were linked by cotton—and the evils of slavery.

ACTIVITY Study the pictures, maps, and graphs in this chapter. Then make a list of words or phrases that describe life in the North and the South in the mid-1800s. After you have read the chapter, review your list to see if you wish to make any changes.

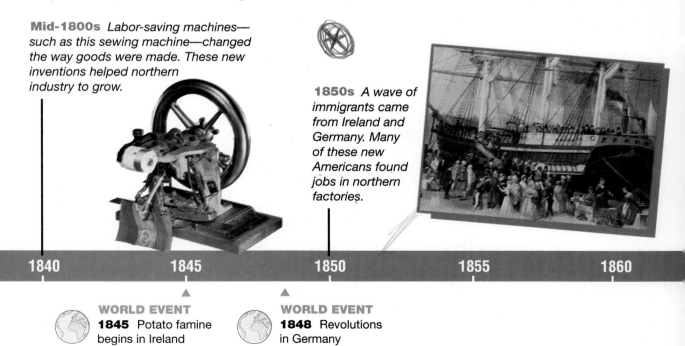

Mid-1800s *Labor-saving machines— such as this sewing machine—changed the way goods were made. These new inventions helped northern industry to grow.*

1850s *A wave of immigrants came from Ireland and Germany. Many of these new Americans found jobs in northern factories.*

1840	1845	1850	1855	1860

WORLD EVENT
1845 Potato famine begins in Ireland

WORLD EVENT
1848 Revolutions in Germany

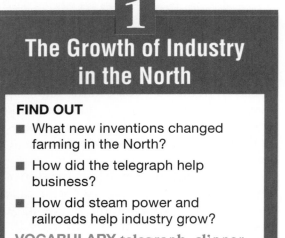

1
The Growth of Industry in the North

FIND OUT
- What new inventions changed farming in the North?
- How did the telegraph help business?
- How did steam power and railroads help industry grow?

VOCABULARY telegraph, clipper ship

In 1846, Elias Howe made a bold claim. He had built a machine, he said, that could sew a piece of clothing faster than five seamstresses combined. Scoffing at Howe's claim, a Boston clothing maker arranged a contest.

During the competition, Howe sat at a small table, calmly pumping the foot pedal that drove his machine. Nearby, the seamstresses worked feverishly with needle and thread. In the end, all agreed that Howe had won.

Soon, clothing makers had bought hundreds of Howe's sewing machines. Workers could now make dozens of jackets faster than a tailor could sew one by hand. The cost of clothing dropped. Many tailors had to find new ways to earn a living. The sewing machine was one of many new inventions that changed life in the North after 1820.

Farming Inventions

In the 1800s, the North was a seedbed for new inventions. "In Massachusetts and Connecticut," a French visitor exclaimed, "there is not a laborer who has not invented a machine or a tool."

Several inventions made work easier for farmers. John Deere invented a lightweight plow made of steel. Earlier plows made of heavy iron or wood had to be pulled by slow-moving oxen. A horse pulling a steel plow could prepare a field for planting much faster.

In 1847, Cyrus McCormick opened a factory in Chicago that manufactured mechanical reapers. The reaper was a horse-drawn machine that mowed wheat and other grains. McCormick's reaper could do the work of five people using hand tools.

The reaper and the steel plow helped farmers raise more grain with fewer hands. As a result, thousands of farm workers left the countryside. Some went west to start farms of their own. Others found jobs in new factories in northern cities.

The Telegraph

In 1844, Samuel F.B. Morse received a patent for a "talking wire," or telegraph. The **telegraph** was a device that sent electrical signals along a wire. The signals were based on a code of dots, dashes, and spaces. Later, this code became known as the Morse code.

Congress gave Morse funds to run wire from Washington, D.C., to Baltimore. On May 24, 1844, Morse set up his telegraph in the Supreme Court chamber in Washington. He tapped out a short message: "What hath God wrought!" A few seconds later, the operator in Baltimore tapped back the same message. The telegraph worked!

Morse's invention was an instant success. Telegraph companies sprang up everywhere and strung thousands of miles of wire. Newspaper reporters wired their stories in. Businesses especially gained from being able to find out instantly about supply, demand, and prices of goods in different areas. For example, western farmers might learn of a wheat shortage in New York and ship their grain east to meet the demand.

Railroads and Industry *The railroad was a key to the growth of industry in the North. Here, a freight train delivers ore to a foundry, where it will be turned into steel.* **Daily Life** *What other effects do you think the growth of railroads had on northern life?*

The First Railroads

A further boost to the economy came as transportation improved. Americans continued to build roads and canals. The greatest change, however, came with the railroads.

The first railroads were built in the early 1800s. Horses or mules pulled cars along wood rails covered with strips of iron. Then, in 1829, an English family developed a steam-powered engine to pull rail cars. The engine, called the *Rocket,* barreled along at 30 miles (48 km) per hour, an amazing speed at the time.

In the United States, some people laughed at the noisy clatter of these "iron horses." Others watched in horror as sparks flew from the smokestack, burning holes in passengers' clothing and setting barns on fire.

Many Americans believed that horse-drawn rail cars were safer and faster than trains pulled by a steam engine. In 1830, a crowd gathered in Baltimore to watch a horse-drawn rail car race the *Tom Thumb,* a steam-powered engine. At first, the horse struggled to keep up. Suddenly, *Tom Thumb* broke down, leaving the horse-drawn car to cross the finish line first.

The defeat of *Tom Thumb* did not mean the end of the steam engine. Engineers soon designed better engines and rails. Private companies began to build railroads, sometimes with help from state governments. By the 1850s, railroads linked eastern cities to Cincinnati and Chicago in the Midwest. Cities at the center of railroad hubs grew rapidly. (□ See "American Notes" on page 586.)

Yankee Clippers

Railroads boosted business inside the United States. At the same time, trade also increased between the United States and other nations. At seaports in the Northeast, captains loaded their ships with cotton, fur, wheat, lumber, and tobacco. Then they sailed to the four corners of the world.

Speed was the key to successful trade at sea. In 1845, an American named John Griffiths launched the *Rainbow,* the first of the **clipper ships.** These sleek vessels had tall

Linking Past and Present
The development of speedy clipper ships led to a new sport for the very rich—yachting. In 1851, a clipper ship named America *won a highly promoted race in England. The winning trophy became known as the America's Cup. American yachts have won 29 of 30 America's Cup challenges since the first race in 1851.*

masts and huge sails that caught every gust of wind. Their narrow hulls clipped swiftly through the water.

In the 1840s, American clipper ships broke every speed record. One clipper sped from New York to Hong Kong in 81 days, flying past older ships that took five months to reach China. The speed of the clippers helped the United States win a large share of the world's sea trade in the 1840s and 1850s.

The golden age of the clipper ship was brief. In the 1850s, Britain launched the first oceangoing steamships. These sturdy iron vessels carried more cargo and traveled even faster than clippers.

The Northern Economy Expands

In 1834, a young French engineer, Michel Chevalier, toured the North. He was most impressed by the burst of industry

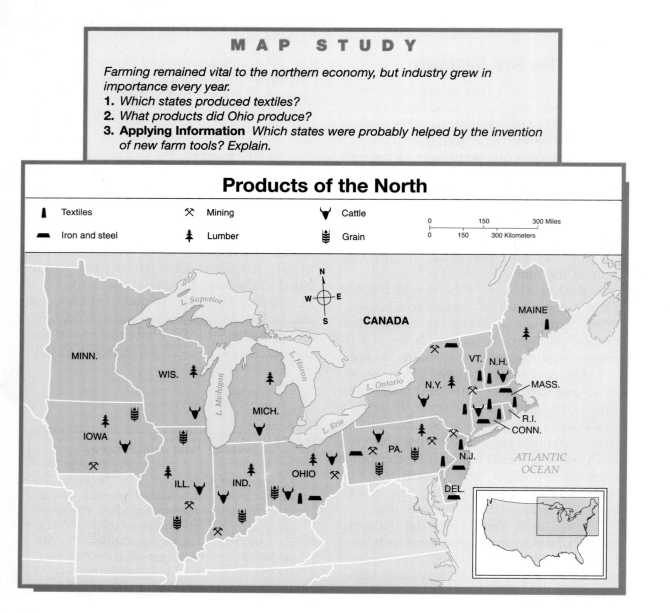

MAP STUDY

Farming remained vital to the northern economy, but industry grew in importance every year.
1. Which states produced textiles?
2. What products did Ohio produce?
3. **Applying Information** Which states were probably helped by the invention of new farm tools? Explain.

Products of the North

Textiles	Mining	Cattle
Iron and steel	Lumber	Grain

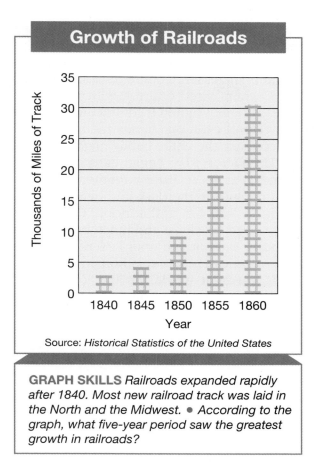

Growth of Railroads

Thousands of Miles of Track

35
30
25
20
15
10
5
0

1840 1845 1850 1855 1860

Year

Source: *Historical Statistics of the United States*

GRAPH SKILLS *Railroads expanded rapidly after 1840. Most new railroad track was laid in the North and the Midwest.* • *According to the graph, what five-year period saw the greatest growth in railroads?*

there—the textile factories, shipyards, and iron mills. He wrote:

> 66Everywhere is heard the noise of hammers, of spindles, of bells calling the hands to their work, or dismissing them from their tasks. . . . It is the peaceful hum of an industrious population, whose movements are regulated like clockwork.99

Northern industry did, in fact, grow steadily in the mid-1800s. That growth was largely due to new methods, inventions, and developments.

Advances in technology. By the 1830s, factories began to use steam power instead of water power. Machines driven by steam were powerful and cheap to run. Also, the use of steam power allowed factory owners to build factories almost anywhere they wanted, not just alongside swift-flowing rivers.

At the same time, new machines made it possible to produce goods for less. These lower-priced goods attracted eager buyers. Families no longer had to make clothing and other goods in their homes. Instead, they could buy factory-made products.

Railroads. Railroads allowed factory owners to ship raw materials and finished goods cheaply and quickly. Also, as railroads stretched across the nation, they linked distant towns with cities and factories. These towns became new markets for factory goods.

Railroads also affected northern farming. New England farmers could not compete with cheap grains and other foods that the railroads brought from the West. Many left their farms to find new jobs as factory workers, store clerks, and sailors. More and more, New Englanders turned to manufacturing and trade.

SECTION 1 REVIEW

1. **Identify:** (a) Elias Howe, (b) John Deere, (c) Cyrus McCormick, (d) Samuel F.B. Morse, (e) John Griffiths.
2. **Define:** (a) telegraph, (b) clipper ship.
3. What new inventions made work easier for farmers?
4. How did many businesses benefit from the telegraph?
5. Explain how each of the following helped industry grow: (a) steam power, (b) new machines, (c) railroads.
6. **CRITICAL THINKING Forecasting** How do you think the growth of industry affected the daily lives of people in the North?

ACTIVITY **Writing to Learn**
Imagine that you are a newspaper reporter. Write an eyewitness description of the race between *Tom Thumb* and the horse-drawn railroad car.

Life in the Industrial North

FIND OUT
- How did working conditions change in factories and shops?
- Why did skilled workers form unions?
- What newcomers arrived in the United States in the mid-1800s?
- What was life like for African Americans in the North?

VOCABULARY skilled worker, trade union, strike, unskilled worker, immigrant, famine, nativist, discrimination

Alzina Parsons never forgot her thirteenth birthday. The day began as usual, with work in the local spinning mill. Suddenly, Alzina cried out. She had caught her hand in the spinning machine, badly mangling her fingers. The foreman summoned the factory doctor. He cut off one of the injured fingers and sent the girl back to work.

In the early 1800s, such an incident probably would not have happened. Factory work was hard, but mill owners treated workers like human beings. By the 1840s, however, there was an oversupply of workers. Many factory owners now treated workers like machines.

Factory Conditions Worsen

Factories of the 1840s and 1850s were very different from earlier mills. They were larger, and they used steam-powered machines. More laborers worked longer hours for lower wages.

Cities where factories were located also changed. Factory owners no longer built planned villages with boarding houses and parks. Instead, workers lived in dark, dingy houses in the shadow of the factory.

Families in factories. The demand for workers increased as more factories sprang up. Owners hired entire families. In some cases, a family signed a contract to work for one year. If even one family member broke the contract, the entire family might be fired.

The factory day began early. A whistle sounded at 4 A.M. Father, mother, and children dressed in the dark and headed off to work. At 7:30 A.M. and at noon, the whistle announced breakfast and lunch breaks. The workday did not end until 7:30 P.M., when a final whistle sent workers home.

Hazards at work. On the job, factory workers faced discomfort and danger. Few factories had windows or heating systems. In summer, the heat and humidity were stifling. In winter, the cold chilled workers' bones and contributed to frequent sickness.

The factory's machines had no safety devices, and accidents were common. Owners ignored the hazards. There were no laws regulating factory conditions. Injured workers often lost their jobs.

Workers as machines. In 1855, a visitor to a textile mill in Fall River, Massachusetts, asked the manager of the mill how he treated his workers. The manager's reply was harsh but honest:

“I regard people just as I regard my machinery. So long as they can do my work for what I choose to pay them, I keep them, getting out of them all I can.”

Despite the long hours and dangers, factory workers in America were better off than those in Europe. American workers could find jobs and earn regular wages. European workers often had no work at all.

Factories Replace Workshops

For skilled workers, the spread of factories changed the nature of work. Skilled

CRITICAL THINKING SKILLS

Synthesizing Information

To make the best use of historical evidence, you must be able to synthesize. That is, you must put pieces of evidence together to form conclusions.

Synthesizing often requires the analysis of different types of evidence, such as graphs, pictures, and primary sources. The more evidence you examine and synthesize, the more accurate will be your impression of a certain period of history.

Study the 1830 factory work rules and the picture of the 1854 shoe factory workers below. Then follow the steps to synthesize the information.

1. **Identify key facts and ideas in each piece of evidence.** (a) When does the workday begin for workers in Amasa Whitney's mill? (b) Are workers in Amasa Whitney's mill allowed to talk while they work?

(c) Who supervised the work of the boys in the shoe factory?

2. **Compare the pieces of evidence.** (a) To what type of workplace does each piece of evidence relate? (b) Which piece of evidence provides more information? (c) Which piece of evidence gives information about the exact hours of work? (d) Which piece shows working conditions?

3. **Synthesize the evidence in order to draw conclusions.** Use both sources to draw conclusions. What do the two pieces of evidence show about life for factory workers in the mid-1800s?

ACTIVITY Look through magazines that are meant for your age group. List the subjects of the articles and the advertisements. Synthesize the information you have gathered, and draw some conclusions about young people today.

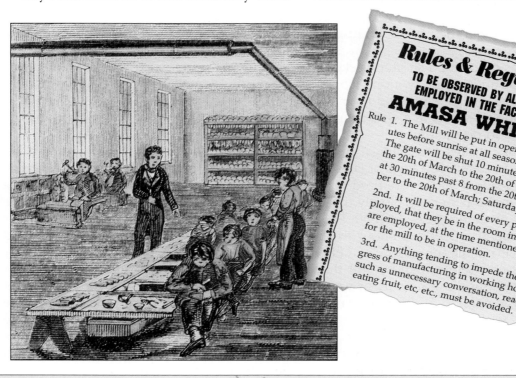

Rules & Regulations

TO BE OBSERVED BY ALL PERSONS EMPLOYED IN THE FACTORY OF

AMASA WHITNEY

Rule 1. The Mill will be put in operation 10 minutes before sunrise at all seasons of the year. The gate will be shut 10 minutes past 8 from the 20th of March to the 20th of September; at 30 minutes past 8 from the 20th of September to the 20th of March; Saturdays at sunset.

2nd. It will be required of every person employed, that they be in the room in which they are employed, at the time mentioned above for the mill to be in operation.

3rd. Anything tending to impede the progress of manufacturing in working hours, such as unnecessary conversation, reading, eating fruit, etc, etc., must be avoided.

workers are people who have learned a trade, such as carpentry or shoemaking.

The nature of work changes. In the past, a typical shoemaker had several young apprentices. The shoemaker taught the apprentices how to make shoes. After they became expert shoemakers, the apprentices would then open their own shops.

By the 1830s, the shoe trade had changed completely. Apprentices no longer learned to make an entire shoe. Instead, workers did only one part of the job. One worker sewed the sole, for example, while another tacked on the heel. The workers did not work in a shop but were crowded together in a small factory.

Other trades also changed. Shop owners saw that they could produce goods more cheaply if they hired workers with fewer skills and paid them lower wages. More and more, laborers rather than skilled workers produced clocks, barrels, and other goods.

Skilled workers unite. Skilled workers had always taken pride in their skills and independence. The factory system threatened to rob them of both. By the 1830s, skilled workers in many trades were uniting to form **trade unions.**

The unions called for a shorter workday, higher wages, and better working conditions. Sometimes, unions pressed their demands by going on strike. In a **strike,** union workers refuse to do their jobs.

At the time, strikes were illegal in the United States. Strikers faced fines or jail sentences. Strike leaders often were fired.

Workers make progress. Slowly, however, workers made progress. In 1840, President Van Buren approved a 10-hour workday for government employees. Other workers pressed their demands until they won the same hours as government workers. Workers celebrated another victory in 1842 when a Massachusetts court declared that they had the right to strike.

Skilled workers won better pay because factory owners needed their skills. Unskilled workers, however, were unable to bargain for better wages. **Unskilled workers** held jobs that required little or no training. Because these workers were easy to replace, employers did not listen to their demands.

Women Workers Organize

The success of trade unions encouraged unskilled workers to organize. Workers in New England textile mills especially were eager to protest cuts in wages and unfair work rules. Many of these workers were women.

Women workers faced special problems. First, they had always earned less money than men did. Second, most union leaders did not want women in their ranks. Like many people at the time, they believed that women should not work outside the home. In fact, the goal of many unions was to raise men's wages so that their wives could leave their factory jobs.

Despite the problems, women organized. They staged several strikes at Lowell, Massachusetts, in the 1830s. In the 1840s, Sarah Bagley organized the Lowell Female Labor Reform Association. The group gathered signatures for a petition to the state legislature demanding a 10-hour day.

Millions of New Americans

By the late 1840s, many workers in the new factories of the North were immigrants. An **immigrant** is a person who enters a new country in order to settle there. In the 1840s and 1850s, about 4 million immigrants arrived in the United States. They supplied much of the unskilled labor that helped to build the nation's growing industries.

The Irish. In the 1840s, a disease destroyed the potato crop across Europe. The loss of the crop caused a **famine,** or severe food shortage, especially in Ireland. Between 1845 and 1860, over 1.5 million Irish fled to the United States.

On Strike *Unskilled women workers organized to gain better treatment. Here, shoemakers in Lynn, Massachusetts, march to protest unfair work rules.* **Economics** *Why are employers less likely to respond to the demands of unskilled workers?*

Most of the Irish immigrants were too poor to buy farmland. They settled in the cities where their ships landed. In New York and Boston, thousands of Irish crowded into poor neighborhoods. They took any job they could find.

The Germans. Another wave of immigrants came from Germany. Nearly one million Germans arrived between 1850 and 1860. Revolutions had broken out in several parts of Germany in 1848. The rebels fought for democratic government. When the uprisings failed, thousands had to flee. Many other Germans came simply to make a better life for themselves. Those with enough money often bought farms in the Midwest. Others settled in eastern cities.

Imprint on American life. Newcomers from many lands helped the American economy grow. In New England, Irish men and women took factory jobs. Coal miners and iron workers from Britain and Germany brought useful skills to American industry.

Each group left an imprint on American life. The Irish brought lively music and dances. Germans brought the custom of decorating trees at Christmas. Immigrants from Norway, Sweden, and other countries also enriched the United States with their language, food, and customs.

A Reaction Against Immigrants

Not everyone welcomed the flood of newcomers. One group of Americans, called **nativists,** wanted to preserve the country for native-born, white citizens. Using the slogan "Americans must rule America," they called for laws to limit immigration. They also wanted to keep immigrants from voting until they had lived in the United States for 21 years. At the time, newcomers could vote after only 5 years in the country.

Some nativists protested that newcomers "stole" jobs from native-born Americans by working for lower pay. Others blamed immigrants for crime in the growing cities. Still others mistrusted the many Irish and German newcomers because they were Catholics. Until the 1840s, nearly all Americans were Protestants.

In the 1850s, nativists formed a new political party. It was called the ***Know-Nothing party*** because members answered, "I know nothing," when asked about the party. Many meetings and rituals of the party were kept secret. In 1856, the Know-Nothing candidate for President won 21 percent of the popular vote. Soon after, however, the party died out. Still, many Americans continued to blame the nation's problems on immigrants.

BIOGRAPHY William Whipper *William Whipper grew wealthy as the owner of a lumber yard in Pennsylvania. He devoted much time and money to help bring an end to slavery.* **Citizenship** *Why did many free blacks work to end slavery?*

African Americans in the North

In the nation's early years, slavery was legal in the North. By the early 1800s, however, all the northern states had outlawed slavery. As a result, thousands of free African Americans lived in the North.

Denied equal rights. Although they were free, African Americans in the North still faced discrimination. Discrimination is a policy or an attitude that denies equal rights to certain groups of people. One writer pointed out that African Americans were denied "the ballot-box, the jury box, the halls of the legislature, the army, the public lands, the school, and the church."

Even skilled African Americans had trouble finding decent jobs. One black carpenter was turned away by every furniture maker in Cincinnati. At last, he found someone willing to hire him. But when he entered the shop, the other workmen threw down their tools. Either he must leave or they would, they declared. Similar experiences occurred throughout the North.

Successful careers. Some free African Americans became wealthy businessmen. James Forten, for example, ran a successful sailmaking business in Philadelphia. Paul Cuffe went to sea at age 16. Later, he grew wealthy as a shipbuilder and owner of a small fleet of trading vessels in New Bedford, Massachusetts. Both Cuffe and Forten used the money they earned to help other African Americans gain freedom.

African Americans also made their mark in other fields. John Rock, a Massachusetts lawyer and judge, presented cases to the Supreme Court. Ira Aldridge became one of the most acclaimed actors in the world.

SECTION 2 REVIEW

1. **Identify:** (a) Know-Nothing party, (b) Sarah Bagley, (c) James Forten, (d) John Rock.
2. **Define:** (a) skilled worker, (b) trade union, (c) strike, (d) unskilled worker, (e) immigrant, (f) famine, (g) nativist, (h) discrimination.
3. How did working conditions in factories worsen in the 1840s and 1850s?
4. Name two groups of immigrants who arrived in the 1840s and 1850s.
5. (a) What problems did free African Americans face in the North? (b) What successes did they enjoy?
6. **CRITICAL THINKING Linking Past and Present** Why do you think hundreds of thousands of immigrants still come to the United States every year?

ACTIVITY **Writing to Learn**
Imagine that you are a shoemaker in the early 1830s. Write an ad for your shoes. Tell why they are better than factory-made shoes.

3

Cotton Becomes King

FIND OUT

- How did the cotton gin affect the growth of slavery?
- Why did cotton planters move westward?
- Why did the South have less industry than the North?

In 1827, an Englishman, Basil Hall, traveled through much of the South aboard a riverboat. He complained that southerners were interested in only one thing—cotton:

    66All day and almost all night long, the captain, pilot, crew and passengers were talking of nothing else; and sometimes our ears were so wearied with the sound of cotton! cotton! cotton! that we gladly hailed fresh . . . company in hopes of some change—but alas! . . . 'What's cotton at?' was the first eager inquiry. 99

Cotton became even more important to the South in the years after Hall's visit. Even though southerners grew other crops, cotton was the region's leading export. Cotton plantations—and the slave system they depended on—shaped the way of life in the South.

The Cotton Gin

New Englanders built the first American textile mills in the 1790s. These mills, along with mills in Great Britain, used raw cotton to manufacture cloth.

At first, southern planters could not keep up with the demand. They could grow cotton easily because the South's soil and climate were ideal. Removing the seeds

from the raw cotton, however, was a slow process. Planters needed a better way to clean the cotton.

In 1793, Eli Whitney, a young Connecticut schoolteacher, was traveling to Georgia. He was going to be a tutor on a plantation. When Whitney learned of the problem facing planters, he decided to build a machine to clean cotton.

In only 10 days, Whitney came up with a model. His cotton engine, or gin, had two rollers with thin wire teeth. The teeth separated the seeds from the fibers, leaving the cotton ready to be spun. (See Exploring Technology on page 388.)

The cotton gin was simple, but its effects were enormous. A worker using a gin could do the work of 50 people cleaning cotton by hand. Because of the gin, planters could now grow cotton at a huge profit.

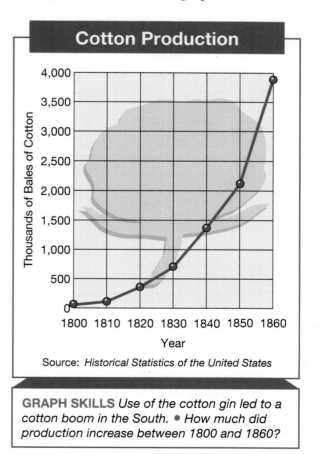

Cotton Production

Thousands of Bales of Cotton (y-axis: 0, 500, 1,000, 1,500, 2,000, 2,500, 3,000, 3,500, 4,000)

Year (x-axis: 1800, 1810, 1820, 1830, 1840, 1850, 1860)

Source: *Historical Statistics of the United States*

GRAPH SKILLS *Use of the cotton gin led to a cotton boom in the South.* • *How much did production increase between 1800 and 1860?*

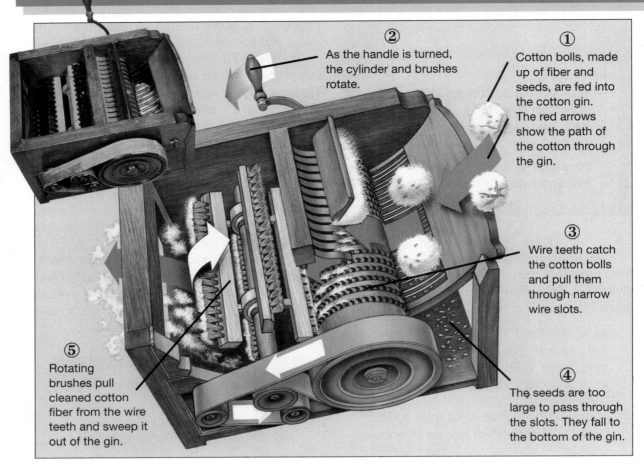

② As the handle is turned, the cylinder and brushes rotate.

① Cotton bolls, made up of fiber and seeds, are fed into the cotton gin. The red arrows show the path of the cotton through the gin.

③ Wire teeth catch the cotton bolls and pull them through narrow wire slots.

⑤ Rotating brushes pull cleaned cotton fiber from the wire teeth and sweep it out of the gin.

④ The seeds are too large to pass through the slots. They fall to the bottom of the gin.

Cotton Gin *Before the invention of the cotton "gin," or engine, cotton seeds had to be separated from the fibers by hand. It was a slow, time-consuming process, and a person could clean only a few pounds of cotton a day. A worker using the gin, however, could clean up to 50 pounds of cotton in a single day!* **Economics** *How did the cotton gin encourage the growth of slavery?*

The Cotton Boom

Planters soon found that soil wore out if planted with cotton year after year. They needed new land to cultivate. After the War of 1812, cotton planters began to move west. By the 1850s, the Cotton Kingdom extended in a wide band from South Carolina through Alabama and Mississippi to Texas.

As plantations spread across the South, cotton production increased rapidly. In 1792, cotton planters grew only 6,000 bales of cotton a year. By 1850, the figure was over 2 million bales.

The cotton boom had a tragic side, too. As the Cotton Kingdom spread, so did slavery. Even though cotton could now be cleaned by machine, it still had to be planted and picked by hand. The result was a cruel cycle. Slaves grew and picked the cotton that brought profits to planters. Planters used the profits to buy more land and more slaves.

The United States had made the slave trade with Africa illegal after 1807. As a result, planters in the new cotton regions bought slaves from planters in southeastern states. In many cases, these sales broke up slave families.

No Place for Industry

Cotton was the South's biggest cash crop. Tobacco, rice, and sugar cane also made money for planters. Southerners raised much of the nation's livestock, too.

Slaves rather than factories. Some southerners wanted to encourage industry in the South. William Gregg, for example, modeled his cotton mill in South Carolina on the mills in Lowell, Massachusetts. Gregg built houses and gardens for his workers and schools for their children.

Even so, the South lagged behind the North in manufacturing. Rich planters invested their money in land and slaves rather than in factories. Also, slavery reduced the demand for goods in the South. In the North, most people had enough money to buy manufactured goods. In the South, however, millions of slaves could not buy

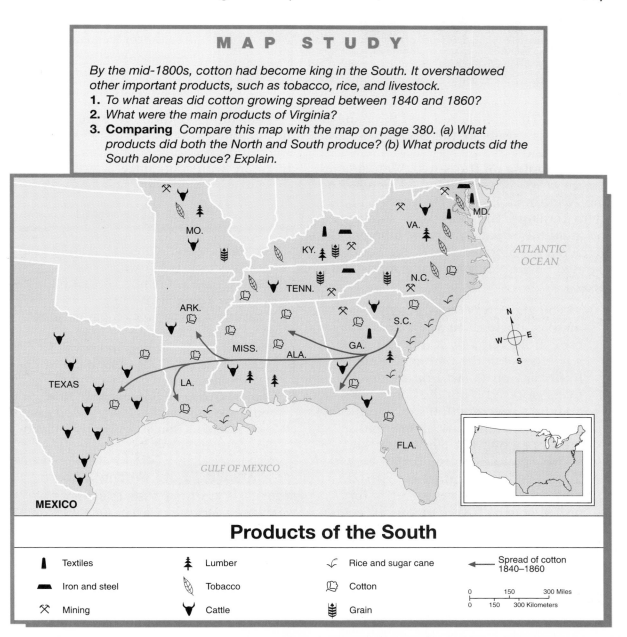

MAP STUDY

By the mid-1800s, cotton had become king in the South. It overshadowed other important products, such as tobacco, rice, and livestock.
1. To what areas did cotton growing spread between 1840 and 1860?
2. What were the main products of Virginia?
3. **Comparing** Compare this map with the map on page 380. (a) What products did both the North and South produce? (b) What products did the South alone produce? Explain.

Products of the South

Symbol	Product	Symbol	Product	Symbol	Product
▮	Textiles	🌲	Lumber	⌇	Rice and sugar cane
▬	Iron and steel	🍃	Tobacco	⬡	Cotton
⚒	Mining	⩒	Cattle	🌾	Grain

← Spread of cotton 1840–1860

0   150   300 Miles
0   150   300 Kilometers

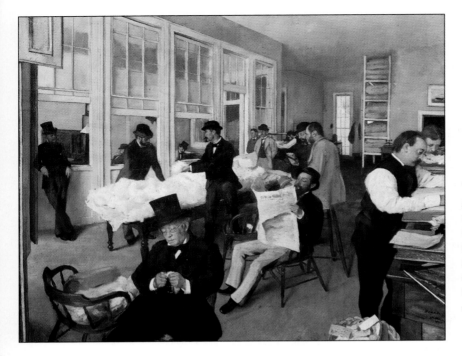

The Business of Cotton *The French artist Edgar Degas painted this scene of merchants in a New Orleans cotton market. Cotton was the South's leading export in the mid-1800s.* **Economics** *What other products were important in the southern economy?*

anything. This greatly reduced the number of products used in the South and hurt southern industry.

Depending on the North. With little industry of its own, the South depended on the North and Europe for goods such as cloth, furniture, and tools. Many southerners resented this situation. One southerner described a burial to show how the South depended on the North for many goods in the 1850s:

66 The grave was dug through solid marble, but the marble headstone came from Vermont. It was in a pine wilderness but the pine coffin came from Cincinnati. An iron mountain overshadowed it but the coffin nails and the screws and the shovel came from Pittsburgh. . . . A hickory grove grew nearby, but the pick and shovel handles came from New York. . . . That country, so rich in underdeveloped resources, furnished nothing for the funeral except the corpse and the hole in the ground. 99

Still, most southerners were proud of their booming cotton industry. As long as cotton remained king, southerners looked to the future with confidence.

SECTION 3 REVIEW

1. **Locate:** (a) South Carolina, (b) Alabama, (c) Mississippi, (d) Texas.
2. **Identify:** (a) Eli Whitney, (b) Cotton Kingdom, (c) William Gregg.
3. What effect did the cotton gin have on the southern economy?
4. Why did cotton planters move west?
5. Why did the South lag behind the North in manufacturing?
6. **CRITICAL THINKING Forecasting** How do you think southerners in the 1800s would have reacted if someone had threatened the cotton industry?

ACTIVITY **Writing to Learn**
Imagine that you own thousands of acres of wilderness in Mississippi in the 1840s. Write an advertisement to attract planters to buy your land.

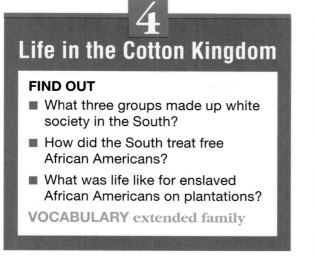

4

Life in the Cotton Kingdom

FIND OUT
- What three groups made up white society in the South?
- How did the South treat free African Americans?
- What was life like for enslaved African Americans on plantations?

VOCABULARY extended family

Solomon Northup first learned to pick cotton at age 32. Northup was born a free African American in New York. In 1841, two white men kidnapped him and sold him as a slave in the South. For the next 12 years, Northup worked on a plantation in Louisiana. Like other enslaved African Americans, he toiled in the fields from "can see to can't see," or from dawn to dusk. For supper, he ate cold bacon and corn meal. His bed was a "plank twelve inches wide and ten feet long."

Northup was not the only free African American to be captured and sold into slavery. He was fortunate, however, to be one of the few who escaped. His book *12 Years a Slave* gave northerners a first-hand look at the slave system.

White Southerners

The Old South is often pictured as a land of vast plantations worked by hundreds of slaves. Such grand estates did exist in the South. However, most white southerners were not rich planters. In fact, most whites owned no slaves at all.

The "cottonocracy." A planter was someone who owned at least 20 slaves. In 1860, there were about 2 million white families in the South. Of them, only 1 in 40, or a total of about 50,000, were families of planters. These wealthy families were called the "cottonocracy" because they made their money from cotton. Even though they were few in number, their views and way of life dominated the South.

The richest planters built elegant homes and filled them with fine European furniture. They entertained lavishly, dressing and behaving very much like European nobility.

Planters had their responsibilities, too. Because of their wealth and influence, many planters became political leaders. They devoted many hours to local, state, and national politics. To run day-to-day affairs on their plantations, planters hired overseers to manage the work of slaves.

Small farmers. Most southern whites were small farmers. These "plain folk" owned the land they farmed and perhaps

A Plantation Mistress *The wife of a planter enjoyed wealth and social position. She also had many duties, including nursing the sick and overseeing the work of house slaves.* **Economics** *Why were wealthy southern families called the "cottonocracy"?*

one or two slaves. Unlike planters, plain folk worked alongside their slaves in the cotton fields.

Small farmers in the South were not as well off as those in the North. As a result, they often helped each other out. "People who lived miles apart counted themselves as neighbors," wrote a farmer in Mississippi. "And in case of sorrow or sickness, there was no limit to the service neighbors provided."

Poor whites. At the bottom of the social ladder was a small group of poor whites. They did not own the land they farmed. Instead, they rented it, often paying the owner with part of their crop. Many barely kept their families from starving.

Poor whites often lived in the hilly, wooded areas of the South. They planted crops such as corn, potatoes, and other vegetables. They also herded cattle and pigs. Yet despite their hard lives, poor whites enjoyed rights denied to all African Americans, enslaved or free.

African Americans in the South

Both free and enslaved African Americans lived in the South. Although legally free, free African Americans faced harsh discrimination. Enslaved African Americans had no rights at all.

Free blacks. Most free African Americans were descendants of slaves freed during and after the American Revolution. Others had bought their freedom. In 1860, over 200,000 free African Americans lived in the South. Most lived in Maryland and Delaware, where slavery was in decline. Others lived in cities such as New Orleans, Richmond, and Charleston.

Slave owners did not like free African Americans living in the South. They feared that free African Americans set a bad example, encouraging slaves to rebel. Also, slave owners justified slavery on the basis that African Americans could not take care of themselves. Free African American workers proved this idea wrong.

Hauling in Cotton *For African Americans living under slavery, life was a constant round of hard work. This picture shows enslaved African Americans hauling in cotton from the fields.* **Economics** *What role did cotton play in the economy of the South?*

To discourage free African Americans, southern states passed laws that made life even harder for them. Free African Americans were not allowed to vote or travel. In some southern states, they either had to move out of the state or allow themselves to be enslaved.

Despite these limits, free African Americans made valuable contributions to southern life. For example, Norbert Rillieux (RIHL yoo) invented a machine that revolutionized sugar making. Henry Blair patented a seed planter.

Enslaved African Americans. Enslaved African Americans made up one third of the South's population by 1860. Most worked as field hands on cotton plantations. Both men and women cleared new land and planted and harvested crops. Children helped by pulling weeds, collecting wood, and carrying water to the field hands. By the time they were teenagers, they too worked between 12 and 14 hours a day.

On large plantations, some African Americans became skilled workers, such as carpenters and blacksmiths. A few worked in cities and lived almost as if they were free. Their earnings, however, belonged to their owners.

Older slaves, especially women, worked as house servants on big estates. They cooked, cleaned, and took care of children under the direction of the planter's wife.

Slave Codes

Southern states passed laws known as slave codes to keep slaves from either running away or rebelling. (See page 111.) Under the codes, enslaved African Americans were forbidden to gather in groups of more than three. They could not leave their owner's land without a written pass. They were not allowed to own guns.

Slave codes also made it a crime for slaves to learn how to read and write. Owners believed that without education enslaved African Americans would find it hard to escape. If they did not know how to read, owners reasoned, runaway slaves could not use maps or read train schedules. They would not be able to find their way north.

Some laws were meant to protect slaves, but only from the worst forms of abuse. Even so, enslaved African Americans did not have the right to testify in court. As a result, they were not able to bring charges against owners who abused them.

Enslaved African Americans had only one real protection against mistreatment. Owners looked on their slaves as valuable property. Most wanted to keep this human property healthy and productive.

Life Without Freedom

The life of African Americans varied from plantation to plantation. Some owners made sure their slaves had decent food, clean cabins, and warm clothes. Other planters spent as little as possible on their slaves.

"Work, work, work." Even the kindest owners insisted that slaves work long, hard days. Slaves worked all year round, up to 16 hours a day. Frederick Douglass, who escaped slavery, recalled:

66 We were worked in all weathers. It was never too hot or too cold; it could never rain, blow, hail, or snow too hard for us to work in the field. Work, work, work. 99

Owners and overseers whipped slaves to get a full day's work. However, the worst part of slavery was not the beatings. It was the complete loss of freedom. "It's bad to belong to folks that own you soul an' body," one slave said.

Family life. It was hard for enslaved African Americans to keep families together. Southern laws did not recognize slave mar-

History and You

Enslaved African Americans passed down family history and traditions to their children and grandchildren in oral rather than written form. What stories about your family's past have your grandparents or parents passed on to you orally? Are there some special family traditions that you hope to pass along to your children?

riages. Owners could sell a husband and wife to different buyers. Children were taken from their parents and sold.

On large plantations, many enslaved families did manage to stay together. For those African Americans, the family provided strength, pride, and love. Grandparents, parents, children, aunts, uncles, and cousins formed a close-knit group. This idea of an **extended family** had its roots in Africa.

Enslaved African Americans preserved other traditions as well. Parents taught their children traditional African stories and songs. Many African cultures used folk tales as a way to pass on their history and moral beliefs.

Religion offers hope. By the 1800s, many enslaved African Americans were devout Christians. Planters often arranged for white ministers to preach to their slaves.

African Americans also had their own preachers and beliefs. These emphasized hope in the future. The moving spirituals sung by enslaved African Americans reflected this strong hope. Like the one below, many spoke of a coming day of freedom:

66 Old Satan thought he had me fast,
Broke his old chain and free at last. 99

In later years, much popular American music would develop from African American spirituals. Jazz, blues, and rock 'n' roll all have their roots in the songs enslaved African Americans sang as they worked in the cotton fields.

Resisting Slavery

Enslaved African Americans struck back against the system that denied them both freedom and wages. Some broke tools, destroyed crops, and stole food.

Many enslaved African Americans dared to run away. Most runaways wanted to reach the North. In the end, very few of

| ARTS | SCIENCES | **GEOGRAPHY** | WORLD | ECONOMICS | CIVICS |

A Musical Debt to West Africa

Rock 'n' roll, jazz, blues, spirituals—all are "American" music. Yet these popular musical styles trace their roots to Africa.

Most of the Africans transported to the United States in the slave trade came from West Africa. They brought with them their land's rich musical heritage.

Making music is central to West African culture. West Africans use song to express their emotions. Creating and performing music is a group activity. Everyone joins in to create new verses and to expand on old ones. And everyone plays a musical instrument—drums, horns, shakers—to give the music its strong and varied rhythms.

A favorite technique is the "call and response." A soloist sings a line and the group responds. After several rounds, everyone joins in and sings the chorus.

West Africans enslaved in the United States adapted the tradi-

African horn

American banjo

tional call and response to a new musical form—the spiritual. In "Nobody Knows the Trouble I've Had," for example, the group answers the soloist's "call" with the words "Oh, yes, Lord!" Then all join in the mournful chorus:

African sculpture of a hornplayer

❝Nobody knows the
    trouble I've had,
Nobody knows but Jesus.
Nobody knows the trouble
    I've had,
Sing glory hallelu!❞

The spirituals were not written down, and different groups sang different words. The singers also made up new verses to reflect their feelings at the time.

Community participation, improvisation, varied rhythms, release of emotions—for centuries, these were part of the West African musical tradition. Today, they form an important part of the American musical tradition as well.

■ What musical traditions traveled from West Africa to the Americas? How does this illustrate the geographic theme of movement?

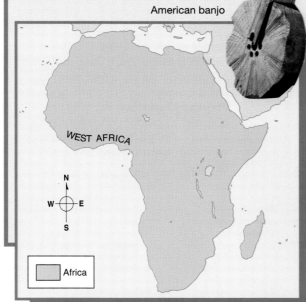

WEST AFRICA

N
W—E
S

Africa

ACTIVITY Create a song that reflects the call and response tradition of West African music. You may use a familiar tune or make up your own.

them made it to freedom. The journey was long and dangerous. Every county had slave patrols and sheriffs ready to question an unknown black person. It took courage and a great deal of luck to make it through.

Flight for Freedom

What was it like to run away from slavery? The runaway in the following account was not a real person. The description of his flight is based on reports of real runaways who made their way to freedom.

Slipping away in the dark. In the dark, on an early Sunday morning, 20-year-old Jesse Needham slipped out of his shabby cabin into the nearby cotton fields. Sunday was the best day to escape. Slaves did not work on Sunday, and there was a chance he would not be missed for 24 hours.

In an extra shirt, Jesse carried a chunk of bacon and some cornbread, stolen from the cook house. Not much food for the 300-mile journey ahead, Jesse worried.

When he reached the edge of his master's land, Jesse crossed into the woods beyond. As he well knew, without a pass, he had already broken the law.

Finding courage. By dawn, Jesse was 8 miles from the plantation. Traveling by daylight was easier, but it was too risky. He curled up under an old spruce tree to sleep.

But his mind would not rest. When dogs began barking at a nearby plantation, Jesse leaped to his feet. His heart pounded and his knees buckled. He was sure that the slave patrol's hounds had picked up his scent. To his relief, no one came.

At dusk, Jesse set out again. The countryside was becoming more and more unfamiliar. Jesse had never been so far from the plantation before. Making his way through the moonlit woods, he thought about life on the plantation—the weariness, the hunger, his bed of straw and rags. He would never go back, he vowed—never.

Thinking things through. Stopping under a tree to rest, Jesse thought about the men who would soon be hunting him. Today or tomorrow, newspapers would announce his escape. Handbills with his description would be posted and slave patrols alerted. Jesse could read—just a little—and he remembered a newspaper ad for a runaway slave:

❝TWENTY DOLLARS REWARD—the slave HERCULES. 36 years old, 5 feet 7 or 8 inches high, badly scarred with the whip. I will pay the reward if delivered to me, or lodged in jail, so that I get him.❞

Running Away *Each year, thousands of African Americans fled north to escape slavery. In this painting by Thomas Moran, two fugitives are pursued by bloodhounds through a swamp.* **Daily Life** *In what other ways did African Americans resist slavery?*

His mind racing, Jesse tried to form a plan. Perhaps he could steal some corn and roast it. No, he decided, a fire might draw attention. He had better eat the corn uncooked. Maybe other African Americans would give him food. He quickly reminded himself that going near slave quarters was a sure way to get caught. Patrols usually kept a close eye on the quarters.

The way north. As Jesse plotted, he remembered the words of a spiritual he often sang: "Follow the North Star, up to the land of freedom." Jesse looked up. There was nothing but clouds. Cold, alone, and helpless, he wondered if he was walking in a circle.

Moving on, Jesse soon spied a rutted country lane. He would leave the woods and follow it, he decided. After all, there probably would be few travelers at that hour. At every sound, Jesse ducked back into the woods, trembling.

Dawn was breaking as Jesse came to a crossroads. There, he spelled out a milestone: Richmond 27 miles. His master's brother lived in Richmond, Jesse recalled. Jesse took a deep breath. He was, indeed, headed north.

As the sun rose, Jesse returned to the woods. Kneeling at a stream, he washed and took a long drink. Then, looking up at the bright sky, he folded his hands and prayed that Jesus would help him find his way to freedom.

Did Jesse make it to the North? Like many other runaways, he was captured and returned to his owner. Now considered a troublemaker, he was sold to another owner. Other Jesses, however, would run from slavery. Despite the nearly hopeless odds, they would risk all to reach freedom. ■

Revolts Against Slavery

A few African Americans used violence to resist the brutal system they faced. Denmark Vesey, a free African American, planned a revolt in 1822. Betrayed before the revolt began, Vesey and 35 others were executed.

In 1831, an African American preacher named Nat Turner led a major revolt. Turner led his followers through Virginia, killing more than 57 whites. Terrified whites hunted the countryside for Turner. They killed many innocent African Americans before catching and hanging him.

Nat Turner's revolt increased southern fears of an uprising of enslaved African Americans. Revolts were rare, however. Since whites were cautious and well armed, a revolt had almost no chance of success.

As slavery grew, the economic ties between North and South became stronger. Northern mill owners needed southern cotton. Southerners relied on the goods from northern factories. Yet Americans in both regions knew that the North and the South had very different ways of life. The key difference seemed to be slavery. (☐ See "Contrasting North and South" on page 588.)

SECTION 4 REVIEW

1. **Identify:** (a) Norbert Rillieux, (b) Henry Blair, (c) Denmark Vesey, (d) Nat Turner.
2. **Define:** extended family.
3. Describe the classes that made up white society in the South.
4. Why did slave owners discourage free African Americans from living in the South?
5. How did African culture and religion help enslaved African Americans endure the hardships of plantation life?
6. **CRITICAL THINKING Analyzing Information** What concerns did runaway slaves like Jesse Needham have in their flight to freedom?

ACTIVITY Writing to Learn
Imagine that you are an enslaved African American on a southern plantation. Write the words for a spiritual about the coming of freedom.

Summary

- Inventions and advances in technology helped the northern economy to grow.
- Factory conditions worsened in the 1830s, and workers organized to win better working conditions.
- The cotton gin boosted cotton production and encouraged the spread of slavery.
- Southern society was made up of rich planters, small farmers, poor whites, free African Americans, and enslaved African Americans.

Reviewing the Main Ideas

1. How did the invention of labor-saving devices for farmers help spur the growth of industry?
2. How did clipper ships help the United States capture sea trade?
3. What goals did early trade unions have?
4. Why did large numbers of Irish and German immigrants come to the United States in the 1840s and 1850s?
5. Why was industry slow to grow in the South?
6. Describe the way of life of each of the following in the South: (a) rich planters, (b) small farmers, (c) poor whites.
7. (a) How did slave laws restrict the freedom of African Americans? (b) How did enslaved African Americans resist slavery?

Thinking Critically

1. **Linking Past and Present** Review the description of inventions on pages 378–379. What recent inventions have changed American life?
2. **Understanding Causes and Effects** How do you think life might have changed in a small Ohio town after a railroad linked it to New York City in the 1840s?

3. **Drawing Conclusions** Few southerners were planters. Why do you think this small group was able to dominate the political and social life of the South?

Applying Your Skills

1. **Making a Generalization** List three facts from Factory Conditions Worsen, on page 382. Then make a generalization about factory conditions in the mid-1800s.
2. **Analyzing a Quotation** In the 1840s, a southerner wrote this description of a southern gentleman: "See him with northern pen and ink, writing letters on northern paper, and sending them away in northern envelopes, sealed with northern wax, and impressed with a northern stamp." What point about the South do you think the writer was making?
3. **Reading Graphs** Study the graphs on pages 376 and 387. (a) Describe the trend in cotton production between 1800 and 1860. (b) Describe the trend in slave population between 1800 and 1860. (c) Are the two trends related? Explain.

Thinking About Geography

Match the letters on the map with the following places: **1.** Northern states, **2.** Southern states, **3.** Massachusetts, **4.** New Hampshire, **5.** Alabama, **6.** Mississippi. **Region** (a) What was the basis of the North's economy? (b) Of the South's economy?

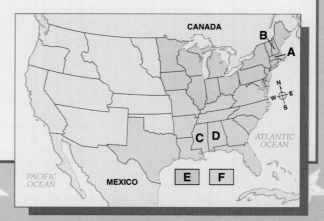

Living in the Cotton Kingdom

Form into groups to review life in the South in the 1800s. Follow the suggestions below to make, write, draw, or sing to show what you have learned about the Cotton Kingdom. You may use the textbook, encyclopedias, atlases, or other materials in your classroom library to complete the tasks. Be able to name your sources of information when you have finished the activity.

HISTORIANS AND ARTISTS Create a chart showing the social groups that made up southern society in the mid-1800s. Include a description of each class and its way of life. Illustrate the chart with original drawings or pictures cut from old magazines.

WRITERS Study the drawing and photograph of a cotton gin on page 388. Then write a description for younger readers of how a cotton gin worked. Write three questions for your readers to test whether they understand the description.

SCIENTISTS Make a museum display about growing cotton. Include facts about the soil, climate, when to plant, insect pests, harvesting, and cleaning. Include a map showing where cotton was grown in the United States in the mid-1800s. Decorate your display with samples of raw cotton, cotton cloth, and pictures of cotton growing.

ECONOMISTS AND HISTORIANS Review the positive and negative effects of cotton on life in the South. Then make a concept map to show these effects.

MUSICIANS Learn the words and music to a spiritual sung by enslaved African Americans in the 1800s. Possible songs are "Go Down, Moses," "Deep River," and "Swing Low, Sweet Chariot." Perform the spiritual for the class and then explain what the words mean. Make an audiotape of your performance to include in the Living in the Cotton Kingdom bulletin board display.

★ Create a Living in the Cotton Kingdom bulletin board display. Have each group include its completed activity.

Quilt made by an enslaved woman

A slave's wedding dress

Loading cotton in New Orleans

CHAPTER 14

A Reforming Age

(1820–1860)

CHAPTER OUTLINE

1 Liberty for All
2 Women Are Created Equal
3 Reform Sweeps the Country
4 New Voices, New Visions

Early 1800s *A powerful religious movement swept the nation. Religious leaders urged their followers to take up reform.*

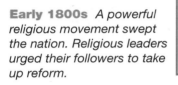

1831 *William Lloyd Garrison founded the* Liberator, *an antislavery newspaper. Garrison called for an immediate and total end to slavery.*

1820s *Northern states began requiring every town to build a grade school. This painting shows a typical schoolhouse of the period.*

1820	1825	1830	1835	1840

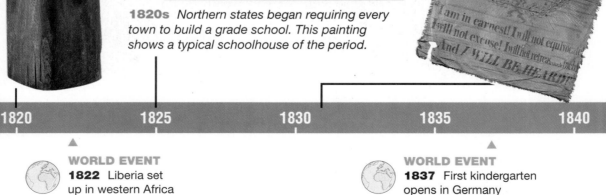

🌐 **WORLD EVENT**
1822 Liberia set up in western Africa

🌐 **WORLD EVENT**
1837 First kindergarten opens in Germany

Chapter Setting

"We are all a little wild here with numberless projects for social reform," wrote the New England author and philosopher Ralph Waldo Emerson in 1840. "But," Emerson continued, "what is man born for but to be a Re-former, a Re-maker of what man has made . . . a restorer of truth and good?"

Many other Americans in the mid-1800s shared Emerson's feelings. They were proud of what the United States had accomplished. But they believed that much remained to be done to fulfill the ideals on which the nation was founded.

The years between 1820 and 1860 were a period of great idealism in the United States. Countless reform movements sprang up to cure the nation's ills. Reformers worked to end slavery, win equal rights for women, and ensure kind treatment of prisoners and the mentally ill. They battled the evils of alcohol and fought to improve education for the nation's children. By the time this age of reform was over, Americans had worked to change every aspect of society. "Our ultimate aim," said newspaper editor Charles A. Dana, "is nothing less than Heaven on Earth."

ACTIVITY What do you think an "ideal" society would be like? Brainstorm to make a list of reforms that you think are needed in American society today.

Mid-1800s *American artists developed their own style. One group, the Hudson River School, specialized in landscapes of New York State.*

1850 *Harriet Tubman made the first of 19 trips to the South to lead slaves to freedom. In time, she helped more than 300 enslaved African Americans to escape.*

1840	1845	1850	1855	1860

WORLD EVENT
1840 World Antislavery Convention held in London

WORLD EVENT
1848 First women's college in Great Britain opens

FIND OUT

- What were the roots of the antislavery movement?
- What did reformers do to fight against slavery?
- How did Americans react to the antislavery movement?

VOCABULARY abolitionist, underground railroad

"**S**ome people of color say that they have no home, no country. I am not among that number. . . . America is my home, my country. . . . I love every inch of soil which my feet pressed in my youth, and I mourn because the accursed shade of slavery rest[s] upon it. I love my country's flag, and I hope that soon it will be cleansed of its stains, and be hailed by all nations as the emblem of freedom and independence."

Henry Highland Garnet, an African American minister and escaped slave, spoke these emotional words at a meeting of women reformers in 1848. At the time, some African Americans were beginning to lose hope of ever winning full equality in the United States.

Garnet was one of a growing number of Americans—black and white—who spoke out against slavery in the mid-1800s. Like Garnet, these Americans loved their country but wanted to make it better. Only by ending slavery, they believed, would the United States fulfill its promise to provide liberty, justice, and equality for all people.

The Issue of Slavery

The election of Andrew Jackson in 1828 unleashed a wave of democratic change in the United States. Americans pointed proudly to the growth of democracy. More people could vote and take part in government than ever before.

Yet some Americans felt that democracy was far from complete. After all, would a democracy allow people to own slaves? An English visitor summed up the American dilemma: "You will see [Americans] with one hand hoisting the cap of liberty, and with the other flogging their slaves."

A spirit of democracy. The idea that slavery was wrong had two separate elements. One element was political. The other was religious.

The political reasons for opposing slavery went back to the American Revolution. In the Declaration of Independence, Thomas Jefferson wrote that "all men are created equal." Yet many white Americans, including Jefferson himself, did not think that the statement applied to enslaved African Americans. Reformers in the 1800s disagreed.

A spirit of revival. The second reason for opposing slavery was religious. Since colonial times, Quakers had spoken out against slavery. All men and women were equal in the eyes of God, they said. It was a sin for one human being to own another.

Other religious groups also began to speak out against slavery. In the early 1800s, a powerful religious movement known as the *Second Great Awakening* swept the nation. One of its leaders was a minister named Charles Grandison Finney.

At first, Finney asked the faithful to give up sin and "walk with God." Later, he urged his followers to broaden their outlook and take up the banner of reform. He especially called on Christians to join a crusade to stamp out the evil of slavery:

Slave Auction *Despite growing antislavery feeling, a brisk trade in slaves continued. At auctions such as the one shown here, enslaved African Americans were sold to the highest bidder.* **Citizenship** *How do you think people justified the sale of human beings?*

66Let Christians of all denominations meekly but firmly come forth. . . and wash their hands of this thing. Let them give forth and write on the head and front of this great [evil], SIN.99

Slavery ends in the North. The campaign against slavery succeeded in the North. By 1804, all states from Pennsylvania north had promised to free their slaves. Of course, there were only 50,000 slaves in the North in 1800, compared to nearly 1 million in the South.

A Colony in Africa

The **American Colonization Society,** founded in 1817, proposed to end slavery by setting up a colony in Africa for freed slaves. In 1822, President Monroe helped the society establish the nation of **Liberia** in western Africa. The name Liberia comes from the Latin word meaning free.

Many white southerners supported the colonization movement. They were pleased that the society did not call for an end to slavery. Instead, it promised to pay slave owners who freed their slaves.

Our Common Heritage

If you visited Liberia today, you would find many reminders of the United States. You could visit two cities, Monrovia and Buchanan, that are named after American Presidents. You could buy things with Liberian dollars and speak English, the official language.

African Americans, on the other hand, had mixed feelings. Some, like Paul Cuffe, thought African Americans should go to Africa because they would never have equal rights in the United States. Cuffe spent $4,000 of his own money to help settle 38 free African Americans in western Africa.

Most African Americans, however, opposed colonization. They wanted to stay in the United States. After all, nearly all American blacks—slave and free—had been born in the United States, and it was their homeland. In the end, only a few thousand free African Americans settled in Liberia.

A Call to End Slavery

Supporters of colonization did not attack slavery directly. But another group of Americans did. They were abolitionists—people who wanted to end slavery in the United States.

Some abolitionists supported a gradual end to slavery. They thought slavery would die out if it were kept out of the western territories. Other abolitionists demanded that slavery end everywhere, and at once.

African American abolitionists. From the start, African Americans played an important part in the abolitionist movement. Some African Americans tried to end slavery through lawsuits and petitions. In the 1820s, Samuel Cornish and John Russwurm set up an antislavery newspaper, *Freedom's Journal*. They hoped to turn public opinion against slavery by printing stories about the brutal treatment of enslaved African Americans. James Forten and other wealthy African Americans gave generously to the paper as well as to other antislavery efforts.

In 1829, David Walker, one of the most outspoken African American abolitionists, published *Appeal to the Colored Citizens of the World*. In it, he blasted the idea of slavery and called on enslaved African Americans to free themselves by any means necessary.

Frederick Douglass speaks out. The best-known African American abolitionist was Frederick Douglass. Douglass was born into slavery in Maryland. As a child, he defied the slave codes and taught himself to read. Because enslaved African Americans could not own books, the young Douglass often picked through "the mud and filth of the gutter" to find discarded newspapers.

In 1838, Douglass escaped and made his way to Boston. One day at an antislavery

Two Fiery Abolitionists *In their fight against slavery, both Frederick Douglass (below) and William Lloyd Garrison (left) were willing to face danger. Douglass risked recapture by publicly revealing that he was an escaped slave. Garrison was almost killed by an anti-abolition mob in Boston.* **Citizenship** *What actions did Douglass and Garrison take to win support for abolition?*

meeting, he felt a powerful urge to speak. Rising to his feet, he talked about the sorrows of slavery and the meaning of freedom. The audience was moved to tears. Soon, Douglass was traveling throughout the United States and Britain, lecturing against slavery. In 1847, he began publishing an antislavery newspaper, the *North Star*.

The *Liberator*. The most outspoken white abolitionist was a fiery young man named William Lloyd Garrison. Garrison launched his antislavery paper, the *Liberator*, in 1831. In it, he proclaimed that slavery was an evil to be ended immediately. On the first page of the first issue, Garrison revealed his commitment:

> **"**I will be as harsh as truth, and as uncompromising as justice. . . . I am in earnest. . . . I will not excuse—I will not retreat a single inch—and I WILL BE HEARD.**"**

A year after starting his paper, Garrison helped to found the ***New England Anti-Slavery Society.*** Members included Theodore Weld, a young minister connected with Charles Grandison Finney. Weld brought the energy of a religious revival to antislavery meetings.

The Grimké sisters. Women also played an important role in the abolitionist cause. Angelina and Sarah Grimké were the daughters of a wealthy slaveholder in South Carolina. They came to hate slavery and moved to Philadelphia to work for abolition. Their lectures about the evils of slavery drew large crowds.

Some people, including other abolitionists, objected to women speaking out in public. But the Grimkés defended their right to do so. "To me," said Sarah, "it is perfectly clear that whatsoever it is morally right for a man to do, it is morally right for a woman to do." This belief led the Grimkés and others to start a crusade for women's rights. (See pages 408–409.)

Railroad to Freedom

Most abolitionists pursued their goals through the press and through public debate. But some risked prison and even death by helping enslaved African Americans escape from the South.

These bold men and women formed the **underground railroad.** This was not a real railroad. It was a network of abolitionists that secretly helped runaway slaves reach freedom in the North and in Canada.

Whites and free blacks served as "conductors" on the underground railroad. They guided runaway slaves to "stations" where they could spend the night. Some stations were houses of abolitionists. Others were churches, or even caves. Conductors sometimes hid runaways in wagons with false bottoms and under loads of hay.

One daring conductor, Harriet Tubman, was an escaped slave. Slave owners offered $40,000 for her capture. But Tubman paid no heed. Risking her freedom and her life, she returned to the South 19 times, conducting more than 300 slaves to freedom. On one trip, Tubman led her aged parents out of slavery. (See "Conductor on the Underground Railroad" on page 590.)

The Nation Reacts

Abolitionists like Douglass and Garrison made enemies in both the North and the South. Northern mill owners, bankers, and merchants depended on cotton from the South. They saw attacks on slavery as a threat to their livelihood.

Northern workers oppose abolition. Some northern workers also opposed the abolitionists. They feared that if slavery ended, free African Americans would come north and take their jobs by working for low pay. Henry Highland Garnet condemned northerners who "admit that slavery is wrong in the abstract, but when we ask them to help us overthrow it, they tell us it would make them beggars!"

A Time of Violent Feelings *The* Liberator *and other abolitionist newspapers stirred strong emotions. Here, an angry band of slavery supporters destroys an abolitionist printing press.* **Economics** *Why did some northerners oppose abolition?*

In New York and other northern cities, mobs sometimes broke up antislavery meetings and attacked the homes of abolitionists. At times, the attacks backfired and won support for the abolitionists. One night, a Boston mob dragged William Lloyd Garrison through the streets at the end of a rope. A doctor who saw the scene wrote, "I am an abolitionist from this very moment."

Southerners defend slavery. The antislavery movement failed to gain a foothold in the South. In fact, many slave owners reacted to the crusade by defending slavery even more. One slave owner wrote that if slaves were well fed, well housed, and well clothed, they would "love their master and serve him cheerfully, diligently, and faithfully." Other owners argued that slaves were better off than northern workers—whom they called wage slaves—who worked long hours in dusty, airless factories.

Even some southerners who owned no slaves defended slavery. To them, slavery was essential to the southern economy. Many southerners exaggerated the extent of northern support for the antislavery movement. They began to believe that northerners wanted to destroy their way of life.

SECTION 1 REVIEW

1. **Locate:** Liberia.
2. **Identify:** (a) Henry Highland Garnet, (b) Second Great Awakening, (c) American Colonization Society, (d) Frederick Douglass, (e) William Lloyd Garrison, (f) New England Anti-Slavery Society, (g) Theodore Weld, (h) Angelina and Sarah Grimké, (i) Harriet Tubman.
3. **Define:** (a) abolitionist, (b) underground railroad.
4. Give two reasons why some Americans opposed slavery.
5. Why did most African Americans oppose the colonization movement?
6. How did the abolitionist movement affect the way the South viewed northerners?
7. **CRITICAL THINKING Analyzing Information** Why do you think it was easier to end slavery in the North than in the South?

ACTIVITY Writing to Learn
Imagine that you are a reporter interviewing a slave who escaped to freedom on the underground railroad. Write five questions you would ask about the journey.

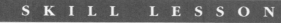

RESEARCH SKILLS
Using the Card Catalog

You will sometimes need to research information using books in the library. Most libraries have a card catalog. The card catalog helps you find the books you need.

1. **Study the parts of the card catalog.** The *card catalog* is a set of drawers holding small cards. The cards are in alphabetical order. Every nonfiction, or factual, book has at least three cards. The *author card* lists the book by the author's last name. The *title card* lists the book by its title. The *subject card* lists it by its subject.

   You can tell what kind of card it is by reading the top line. The top line will show either the author's last name, the title of the book, or the subject heading. Sometimes, author and title cards are kept together in one set of drawers and the subject cards are kept in a separate set of drawers.

   Look at Card A. (a) Is this an author, title, or subject card? (b) Who is the author of the book? (c) What is its title?

2. **Practice using the call number.** Every card for a nonfiction book has a number in the top left corner. This is the call number of the book. The *call number* tells you where you will find the book on the library shelves. Each nonfiction book has its call number printed on the spine, or narrow back edge. The letters after the number are the first letters of the author's last name. Look at Card A. (a) What is the call number of the book? (b) What do the letters printed below the call number mean?

3. **Use other cards in the card catalog.** Look at Cards B and C. (a) Is Card B an author, title, or subject card? (b) Is Card C an author, title, or subject card? (c) Why do Cards A, B, and C all have the same call number?

ACTIVITY Make up author, title, and subject cards for three books in your classroom library.

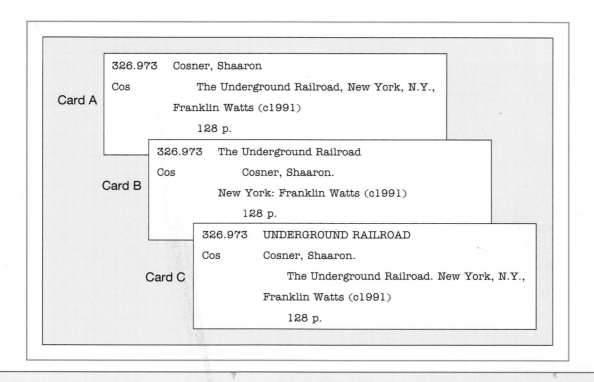

Card A
326.973　Cosner, Shaaron
Cos　　　　The Underground Railroad, New York, N.Y.,
　　　Franklin Watts (c1991)
　　　　128 p.

Card B
326.973　The Underground Railroad
Cos　　　　Cosner, Shaaron.
　　　New York: Franklin Watts (c1991)
　　　　128 p.

Card C
326.973　UNDERGROUND RAILROAD
Cos　　　　Cosner, Shaaron.
　　　　　The Underground Railroad. New York, N.Y.,
　　　Franklin Watts (c1991)
　　　　128 p.

2

Women Are Created Equal

FIND OUT

■ How did the antislavery crusade help spur the women's rights movement?

■ What did the Seneca Falls Convention demand?

■ How did opportunities for women improve in the mid-1800s?

In 1840, a group of Americans sailed to London to attend the World Antislavery Convention. Among them were two young women: Lucretia Mott and Elizabeth Cady Stanton. Once they arrived in London, however, the convention refused to let women

BIOGRAPHY Elizabeth Cady Stanton *When Elizabeth Cady Stanton was growing up, clerks in her father's law office teased her by reading her laws that denied basic rights to women. This teasing helped make Stanton a lifelong foe of inequality.* **Citizenship** *How were women's rights limited in the mid-1800s?*

take an active part in the proceedings. Convention officials even forced female delegates, including Mott and Stanton, to sit behind a curtain, hidden from view.

Mott and Stanton stayed in London for several weeks. At their hotel each evening, they debated the issue of women's rights. "[We] agreed to hold a women's rights convention," Stanton later recalled. "The men . . . had [shown] a great need for some education on that question."

An Uphill Struggle

The treatment that Mott and Stanton faced in London was not unusual for the mid-1800s. Women had few political or legal rights at the time. They could not vote or hold office. When a woman married, her husband became owner of all her property. If a woman worked outside the home, her wages belonged to her husband. A husband also had the right to hit his wife as long as he did not seriously injure her.

"Unnatural" women. Many women had joined the abolitionist movement. As these women worked to end slavery, they became aware that they lacked full social and political rights themselves. Among the first to speak out were Angelina and Sarah Grimké.

As you have read, the boldness of the Grimkés' antislavery activities shocked audiences in the North. In a newspaper editorial, a group of New England ministers scolded the sisters. "When [a woman] assumes the place and tone of a man as a public reformer," they wrote, "her character becomes unnatural."

The Grimkés and other women reformers rejected such ideas. More determined than ever, they continued their crusade. Now, however, they lectured about women's rights as well as abolition. Said Angelina Grimké:

❝The investigation of the rights of the slave has led me to a better understanding of my own.❞

"Ain't I a woman?" African American women joined the struggle for women's rights. Sojourner Truth was born into slavery in New York. She was freed by a New York law that banned slavery. Truth became active in the crusade against slavery.

Truth was a spellbinding speaker. At a meeting in 1851, she listened to a minister speak about women's need to be protected. When he was done, Truth leaped to her feet with this stinging reply:

> 66 The man over there says women need to be helped into carriages and lifted over ditches, and to have the best place everywhere. Nobody ever helps me into carriages, or over puddles, or gives me the best place. And ain't I a woman? I have ploughed and planted and gathered into barns. . . . And ain't I a woman? . . . I have borne thirteen children, and seen most of 'em sold into slavery, and when I cried out with my mother's grief, none but Jesus heard me! And ain't I a woman? 99

Others call for equal rights. After returning home from London, Lucretia Mott and Elizabeth Cady Stanton took up the cause of women's rights with new zeal. Mott was a Quaker minister and the mother of five children. A quiet speaker, she won the respect of many listeners with her logic.

Elizabeth Cady Stanton was the daughter of a well-known New York judge. Growing up, she became keenly aware that the laws denied basic rights to women.

Another tireless organizer was Susan B. Anthony. Even when audiences heckled her and threw eggs, Anthony always finished her speech. Lucy Stone and Abby Kelley also gave their energies to the movement.

A Historic Meeting

In 1840, Lucretia Mott and Elizabeth Cady Stanton decided to hold a convention

BIOGRAPHY Sojourner Truth *Born into slavery, Isabella Baumfree became one of the most powerful voices for abolition and women's rights. Taking a new name—Sojourner Truth—she "sojourned," or traveled, "up and down the land," declaring "the truth unto people."* **Daily Life** *What arguments did Truth use to show that women are as capable as men?*

to draw attention to the problems women faced. Eight years later, in 1848, in Seneca Falls, New York, that convention finally took place.

Linking Past and Present

Like many women today, Lucy Stone continued to use her own name after she married. "A wife should no more take her husband's name than he should hers," she said. Other women who kept their own names became known as "Lucy Stoners."

| ARTS | SCIENCES | GEOGRAPHY | WORLD | ECONOMICS | CIVICS |

Fashion and Women's Health

Thud! There was a faint ripple in the back of the theater as an unconscious woman was carried out. "She needs air. Give her air," the usher cried.

The scene was not unusual. Like many women of her time, this theatergoer was dressed in a tightly laced corset designed to make her waist as small as possible. On top of the corset, she wore layers of heavy, stiff petticoats, reaching to the ground. Over all this was a full-length gown. The entire outfit weighed 12 pounds (5 kg). Normal breathing was difficult.

Women reformers protested that such fashions were a threat to women's health. Doctors supported their claims. "Tight-lacers," they said, squeezed the internal organs and narrowed the pelvis. They could crush the rib cage and cause the lungs to collapse.

Elizabeth Smith Miller decided to do something about the problem. It was a spring day. Dressed in corset and petticoats, Miller struggled to bend as she planted her garden. Surely, she thought, there must be a better way for women to dress.

Miller designed a new fashion. It featured a more loosely cut top, shorter skirt, and full trousers gathered at the ankles. Trying on the new outfit, one thankful woman commented that she felt "like a captive set free from his ball and chain."

Reformer and publisher Amelia Bloomer promoted the new fashion in her journal for women. She wore it herself at public meetings. Soon, the outfit became known as "bloomers."

The new fashion did not catch on widely. Critics made fun of women who wore bloomers. They claimed the trousers were too "masculine."

Bloomers soon disappeared from the fashion scene. According to reformer Lucy Stone, they "suffered the usual fate of anything that is forty years ahead of its time."

Woman wearing bloomers

■ How did fashions in the mid-1800s threaten women's health?

ACTIVITY

Select an activity that you do every day, such as attending school, doing chores, playing ball, or working. Design an outfit that would be suitable to wear during that activity.

About 200 women and 40 men attended the **Seneca Falls Convention.** At the meeting, leaders of the women's rights movement presented a Declaration of Sentiments. Modeled on the Declaration of Independence, it proclaimed, "We hold these truths to be self-evident: that all men and women are created equal."

The women and men at Seneca Falls voted for resolutions that demanded equality for women at work, at school, and in church. All the resolutions passed without opposition except one. It demanded that women be allowed to vote in elections. Even the bold women at Seneca Falls hesitated to take this step. In the end, the resolution passed by a slim majority.

The Seneca Falls Convention marked the start of an organized women's rights movement. In the years after 1848, women worked for change in many areas. They won additional legal rights in some states. For example, New York State passed laws allowing women to keep property and wages after they married. Progress was slow, however. Many men and women opposed the goals of the women's rights movement. The struggle for equal rights would last many years.

New Opportunities for Women

The women at Seneca Falls believed that education was a key to equality. At the time, women from poor families had little hope of learning even to read and write. And while young middle-class women were often sent to school, they were taught dancing and drawing rather than mathematics and science, like their brothers. After all, people argued, women were expected to devote themselves to marriage and children. Why did they need an education?

Reformers, like Emma Willard and Mary Lyon, worked to improve education for women. Willard opened a high school for girls in Troy, New York. Here, young wom-

en studied "men's subjects," such as mathematics, physics, and philosophy.

Mary Lyon spent years raising money for Mount Holyoke Female Seminary in Massachusetts. She did not call the school a college because she knew that many people thought it was wrong for women to attend college. In fact, Mount Holyoke, which opened in 1837, was the first women's college in the United States.

At about the same time, a few men's colleges began to admit women. As women's education improved, women found jobs teaching, especially in grade schools.

A few women tried to enter fields such as medicine. Elizabeth Blackwell attended medical school at Geneva College in New York. To the surprise of school officials, she graduated first in her class. Women had practiced medicine since colonial times, but Blackwell was the first woman in the United States with a medical degree. She later set up the first nursing school in the nation.

SECTION 2 REVIEW

1. **Identify:** (a) Lucretia Mott, (b) Elizabeth Cady Stanton, (c) Sojourner Truth, (d) Susan B. Anthony, (e) Seneca Falls Convention, (f) Emma Willard, (g) Mary Lyon, (h) Elizabeth Blackwell.
2. What rights were denied to women in the early 1800s?
3. What issues did delegates at Seneca Falls vote on?
4. What type of education did most women receive in the mid-1800s?
5. **CRITICAL THINKING Understanding Causes and Effects** How was the women's rights movement a long-range effect of the antislavery movement?

ACTIVITY Writing to Learn
Imagine that you are Lucretia Mott or Elizabeth Cady Stanton. Prepare a flier announcing the women's rights convention you are organizing.

Reform Sweeps the Country

FIND OUT

- What reforms did Dorothea Dix seek?
- How did Americans improve public education in the mid-1800s?
- Why did some Americans want to ban the sale of alcohol?

VOCABULARY temperance movement

In the mid-1800s, the spirit of reform led Americans to work for change in many areas. They took to heart the words of a poem they had learned in school:

> Beautiful hands are they that do
> Deeds that are noble, good, and
>   true;
> Beautiful feet are they that go
> Swiftly to lighten another's
>   woe.

Some reformers turned their attention to what one minister called the "outsiders" in American society—criminals and the mentally ill. One of the most vigorous of these reformers was a Boston schoolteacher, Dorothea Lynde Dix.

Dorothea Dix: Helping the Helpless

Dorothea Dix was born on the Maine frontier in 1802. At age 12, her parents sent her to live with her grandmother in Boston. There, Dorothea attended school to become a teacher.

An energetic teacher. After completing eighth grade, Dix was considered qualified to teach by the standards of the time. At age 14, she opened her own grade school. A few years later, she opened another, larger school, which was a free school for poor children.

Dix amazed people with her energy and hard work. She rose each day at 4 or 5 A.M. She read, wrote, and studied until well after midnight. When the available textbooks did not provide enough material on history and science, Dix wrote her own book. Teachers throughout the nation were soon using it.

A new mission. One day in March 1841, Dix got an urgent message. A young Harvard University student had been asked to set up a Sunday School class for women in the jail at Cambridge, near Boston. The young man could not keep order among the prisoners. Did Dix know anyone who could help?

Dix took the job herself. At the Cambridge jail, she found 20 women prisoners. Some were there for stealing, others for drunkenness. But the prisoners who caught Dix's attention were those who had committed no crime. These women had been jailed because they were mentally ill.

The jailer locked the mentally ill prisoners in small, dark cells at the rear of the jail. There was no heat in the cells, and the women were half frozen. Dix demanded to know why these women were treated so cruelly. The jailer replied that "lunatics" did not feel the cold.

That moment changed Dix's life forever. By the time she left the jail, she knew she had to take action.

A shocking report. During the next 18 months, Dix visited every jail, poorhouse, and hospital in Massachusetts. Her detailed report shocked state legislators:

> I proceed, gentlemen, briefly to call your attention to the present state of Insane Persons confined within this Commonwealth, in cages, closets, cellars, stalls, pens! Chained, naked, beaten with rods, and lashed into obedience.

BIOGRAPHY Dorothea Dix *The sight of "harmless lunatics" locked in a cold, dark cell prompted Dorothea Dix to action. Largely through Dix's efforts, 28 states had established special hospitals for the care of the mentally ill by 1860.* **Citizenship** *How did Dix go about the task of achieving reform?*

Still, the legislators hesitated to raise taxes to build a new mental hospital. Dix offered her report to the newspapers. In the end, the legislature voted for the hospital.

Dix's work was not done. She inspected jails and poorhouses in Vermont, Connecticut, and New York. In time, she traveled as far as Louisiana and Illinois. In North Carolina, an angry official told Dix that "nothing can be done here." She replied, "I know no such word." In nearly every state, her reports convinced legislatures to treat the mentally ill as patients, not criminals.

Reforming prisons. Dix also spoke out against conditions in the prisons. Men, women, and children were often crammed into cold, damp rooms. If food was in short supply, prisoners went hungry unless they had money to buy meals from jailers.

In the early 1800s, five out of six people in northern jails were debtors. To Dix, jailing debtors made no sense. How could people earn money to pay back debts when they were behind bars?

Dix and others called for changes in the prison system. As a result, some states built prisons with only one or two inmates to a cell. Cruel punishments were banned, and people convicted of minor crimes received shorter sentences. Slowly, states stopped treating debtors as criminals. ■

Educating a Free People

In 1816, Thomas Jefferson wrote, "If a nation expects to be ignorant and free, it expects what never was and never will be." Jefferson knew that a democracy needed educated citizens. Reformers agreed. As more men won the right to vote in the 1820s, reformers acted to see that they were well informed.

Before the 1820s, few American children attended school. Public schools were rare. Those that did exist were usually old and run down. Teachers were poorly trained and ill paid. Students of all ages crowded together in a single room.

New public schools. New York led the way in reforming education. In the 1820s, the state ordered every town to build a school. Before long, other northern states required towns to support public schools.

In Massachusetts, Horace Mann led the fight for better schools. Mann became head of the state board of education in 1837. For 12 years, he hounded legislators to provide more money for education. Under his leadership, Massachusetts built new schools, extended the school year, gave teachers higher pay, and opened three colleges to train teachers. (☐ See "How Americans Shortchange Their Children" on page 593.)

Reformers in other states urged their legislatures to follow the lead of Massachusetts and New York. By the 1850s, most northern states had set up free tax-supported elementary schools. Schools in the South improved more slowly. In both the North and

One-Room Schoolhouse *Many Americans in the 1800s received their education in one-room schoolhouses, such as the one in this painting by Winslow Homer. The single room housed all grades, and older students helped younger ones with their lessons.* **Citizenship** *Why is education important in a democracy?*

South, schooling ended in the eighth grade. There were few public high schools.

Education for African Americans. In most areas, free African Americans had little chance to attend school. A few cities, like Boston and New York, set up separate schools for African American students. However, these schools received less money than schools for white students did.

Some African Americans went on to higher education. They attended private colleges such as Harvard, Dartmouth, and Oberlin. In the 1850s, several colleges for African Americans opened in the North. The first was Lincoln University, in Pennsylvania.

Special schools. Some reformers took steps to improve education for people with disabilities. In 1817, Thomas Gallaudet (gal uh DEHT) set up a school for people who are deaf, in Hartford, Connecticut. A few years later, Samuel Gridley Howe became director of the first American school for people who

are blind. Howe invented a way to print books with raised letters. Blind students could read the letters with their fingers.

Battling "Demon Rum"

In 1854, Timothy Shay Arthur published a book called *Ten Nights in a Barroom and What I Saw There*. It told the story of how an entire village was destroyed by "demon rum." A play based on the novel followed.

History and You
The first public schools went through only the eighth grade. If your education stopped at eighth grade, what subjects would you not learn? What types of skills would you have to learn outside of school? Which careers would it be difficult for you to pursue?

Today, the play seems somewhat silly, but it addressed a serious problem of the 1800s. Alcohol abuse was widespread at the time. At political rallies, weddings, and funerals, men, women, and sometimes even children drank heavily. Craftsworkers and apprentices often drank alcohol in their workshops. In cities, men could buy a glass of whiskey in grocery stores, candy stores, and barber shops as easily as at taverns.

Reformers linked abuse of alcohol to crime, the breakup of families, and mental illness. In the late 1820s, reformers began a campaign against drinking. It was known as the temperance movement. Some temperance groups tried to persuade people to drink less. Others demanded that states ban the sale of alcohol.

In the 1850s, temperance groups won a major victory when Maine banned the sale of alcohol. Eight other states soon passed "Maine laws." Many Americans resented the laws, and most states later repealed them. Still, temperance crusaders pressed on. They gained new strength in the late 1800s.

SECTION 3 REVIEW

1. **Identify:** (a) Dorothea Dix, (b) Horace Mann, (c) Thomas Gallaudet, (d) Samuel Gridley Howe.
2. **Define:** temperance movement.
3. Why did Dorothea Dix decide to reform Massachusetts prisons?
4. What improvements were made in public education after the 1820s?
5. Why did temperance groups want to end the drinking of alcohol?
6. **CRITICAL THINKING Understanding Causes and Effects** How would lack of educational opportunities for African Americans contribute to prejudice against them?

ACTIVITY Writing to Learn
Write the script for a TV documentary exposing one of the abuses you read about in this section.

LINKING PAST AND PRESENT

PAST

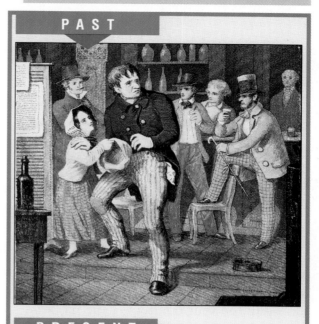

PRESENT

Fight Against Alcohol *Americans have long been concerned about the dangers of drinking alcohol. In the 1800s, temperance leaders warned that alcohol was destroying homes and families. In the 1854 engraving at top, a father is led home by his daughter after spending his pay in a saloon. Today, much of the debate about alcohol centers on drunken driving. At bottom, members of Students Against Driving Drunk (SADD) express their concern. ● How does your community fight drunken driving?*

New Voices, New Visions

FIND OUT

- Who were some of the writers and artists of the 1800s?
- How did American writers express the unique spirit of the nation?
- What styles did American painters develop?

In 1820, a Scottish minister named Sydney Smith blasted the lack of culture in the United States:

> 66 In the four quarters of the globe, who reads an American book? Or goes to an American play? Or looks at an American picture or statue? What does the world yet owe to Americans? 99

Any American artist or writer of worth, Smith went on, had been trained in the studios of Europe. The best the United States could offer, he said, was "a galaxy . . . of newspaper scribblers."

Even as Smith wrote these scornful words, a group of American writers and artists was breaking free of European traditions. These men and women created a voice and a vision that were truly American.

American Storytellers

Until the early 1800s, most American writers depended on Europe for their ideas and inspiration. In the 1820s, however, Americans began to write stories with American themes.

Washington Irving. One of the most popular American writers of the early 1800s was Washington Irving, a New Yorker. Irving first became known for *The Sketch Book,* a collection of tales published in 1820. Two of the best-loved tales are "Rip Van Winkle" and "The Legend of Sleepy Hollow."

Irving's stories amused people. They also gave Americans a sense of the richness of their past. Irving's appeal went beyond the United States, however. Irving was the first American writer to enjoy fame in Europe as well as at home.

James Fenimore Cooper. James Fenimore Cooper, another New Yorker, also published novels set in the past. In *The Deerslayer* and *The Last of the Mohicans,* Cooper gave a romantic, or idealized, view of relations between whites and Native Americans on the frontier. The stories were so full of exciting adventures, however, that few readers cared whether or not they were true to life.

Later writers. Nathaniel Hawthorne drew on the history of Puritan New England to create his novels and short stories. The Puritan past fascinated Hawthorne. *The Scarlet Letter,* his best-known novel, was published in 1850. It explores the forces of good and evil in Puritan New England.

In 1851, Herman Melville published *Moby Dick.* In this novel, Melville takes the reader on a wild voyage aboard the whaling ship *Pequod.* The crazed captain, Ahab, has vowed revenge against the white whale that years earlier bit off his leg. *Moby Dick* had only limited success when it was first published. Today, however, critics rank *Moby Dick* among the finest American novels ever written.

William Wells Brown published *Clotel,* a novel about slave life, in 1853. Brown was the nation's first published African American novelist and the first African American to earn his living as a writer.

Women Writers

By the mid-1800s, a growing number of women were publishing books. Margaret Fuller wrote *Woman in the Nineteenth Cen-*

tury. The book was an important influence on the movement for women's rights.

Many of the best-selling novels of the period were written by women. These novels often told about young women who gained wealth and happiness through honesty and self-sacrifice. Some novels were more true to life. They showed the hardships faced by widows and orphans.

Few of these novels are read today. However, writers such as Catharine Sedgwick and Fanny Fern earned far more money than Nathaniel Hawthorne or Herman Melville. In fact, Hawthorne complained bitterly about the success of women writers. "America is now wholly given over to a . . . mob of scribbling women," he once said.

Poetic Voices

John Greenleaf Whittier, a Quaker from Massachusetts, wanted to write poems about the colonial past. But his friend William Lloyd Garrison, the abolitionist, urged him to use his pen to serve the antislavery cause. In many poems, Whittier sought to make his readers aware of the evils of slavery.

The favorite poet of Americans in the mid-1800s was Henry Wadsworth Longfellow. Longfellow based many of his poems on events from the nation's past. Perhaps his best-known poem is "Paul Revere's Ride." Today, many Americans can still recite the opening lines:

> 66Listen, my children, and you
>   shall hear
> Of the midnight ride of Paul
>   Revere,
> On the eighteenth of April in
>   Seventy-five;
> Hardly a man is now alive
> Who remembers that famous day
>   and year.99

Walt Whitman published only one book of poems, *Leaves of Grass*. However, he

Women Writers
This poster shows a gathering of notable American writers of the mid-1800s. Among them are Harriet Beecher Stowe, author of Uncle Tom's Cabin, *and Julia Ward Howe, who wrote the lyrics to "The Battle Hymn of the Republic."* **Linking Past and Present** *What women writers are popular today?*

added to it over a period of 27 years. Whitman had great faith in the common people. His poetry celebrated democracy and the diverse people who made the nation great.

Some of the best poems of the period were written by Emily Dickinson. Dickinson wrote more than 1,700 poems, but only 7 were published in her lifetime. She called her poetry "my letter to the world." Today, Dickinson is considered one of the nation's greatest poets.

Emerson and Thoreau: Following the "Inner Light"

The American writer who probably had the greatest influence in the mid-1800s was Ralph Waldo Emerson. People flocked to hear him read his essays stressing the importance of the individual. Each person,

BIOGRAPHY **Walt Whitman** *"I hear America singing," wrote Walt Whitman. In his poems, Whitman celebrated Americans of all kinds—from carpenters to seamstresses to runaway slaves. This portrait of Whitman was done by Thomas Eakins, one of the great American portrait painters.* **Culture** *How did Whitman's poetry support the ideals of democracy?*

Emerson said, has an "inner light." He urged people to use this inner light to guide their lives.

Henry David Thoreau (thuh ROW), Emerson's friend and neighbor, believed that the growth of industry and the rise of cities were ruining the nation. Thoreau tried to live as simply as possible. A person's wealth, he said, is measured by the number of things he or she can do without.

Thoreau's best-known work is *Walden.* In it, he tells of a year spent alone in a cabin on Walden Pond in Massachusetts. Like Emerson, Thoreau believed that each person must decide what is right or wrong:

&& If a man does not keep pace with his companions, perhaps it is because he hears a different drummer. Let him step to the music he hears. &&

Thoreau's "different drummer" told him that slavery was wrong. He was a fierce abolitionist and served as a conductor on the underground railroad.

American Landscapes

Before the 1800s, American painters traveled to Europe to study art. Benjamin West of Philadelphia, for example, settled in London. In 1772, he was appointed historical painter to King George III.

Many American painters journeyed to London to study with West. They included Charles Willson Peale, Gilbert Stuart, and John Singleton Copley, among the best American portrait painters of the time. Both Peale and Stuart painted well-known pictures of George Washington.

By the mid-1800s, American artists began to develop their own style. The first group to do so became known as the ***Hudson River School*** because they painted landscapes of New York's Hudson River region. Two of the best-known painters of the Hudson River School were Thomas Cole and Asher B. Durand. In his murals, African American artist Robert S. Duncanson also reflected the style of this school.

Other American artists painted scenes of hard-working farm families and country people. George Caleb Bingham was inspired by his native Missouri. His paintings

Linking Past and Present
Stuart's portraits of Washington are among the most familiar images of the first President. In fact, you probably see a Stuart portrait of Washington every day—on the one-dollar bill.

Catskill Scene *Artists of the Hudson River School captured the gentle beauty of New York's Catskill Mountain region. This painting,* View of Troy, New York, *is by William Richardson Tyler.* **The Arts** *How did painters of the mid-1800s differ from earlier American painters?*

show frontier life along the rivers that feed the great Mississippi.

Several painters tried to capture the culture of Native Americans on canvas. George Catlin and Alfred Jacob Miller traveled to the Far West. Their paintings record the daily life of Indians on the Great Plains and in the Rocky Mountains.

Artists of the 1800s celebrated the vast American landscape. They expressed confidence in Americans and their future. This confidence was shared by reformers in the East and by the thousands of Americans opening up new frontiers in the West.

SECTION 4 REVIEW

1. **Identify:** (a) Washington Irving, (b) Nathaniel Hawthorne, (c) Herman Melville, (d) William Wells Brown, (e) Henry Wadsworth Longfellow, (f) Hudson River School, (g) George Catlin.
2. List the important themes that each of the following stressed in his work: (a) John Greenleaf Whittier, (b) Walt Whitman, (c) Ralph Waldo Emerson, (d) Henry David Thoreau.
3. Describe the works of each of the following: (a) Margaret Fuller, (b) Emily Dickinson.
4. What subjects did some artists paint in the 1800s?
5. **CRITICAL THINKING Drawing Conclusions** Why do you think artists and writers did not develop a unique American style until the mid-1800s?

ACTIVITY **Writing to Learn**

Imagine that you are an art critic. Write a paragraph summarizing your reaction to the painting above.

Summary

- In the mid-1800s, many Americans worked to end slavery in the United States.
- Women gained opportunities in education and other areas.
- The spirit of reform led Americans to call for better prison conditions, improvements in education and health care, and a ban on alcohol.
- American writers and artists began to use American themes in the 1800s.

Reviewing the Main Ideas

1. What were the political and religious ideas behind the antislavery movement?
2. (a) Why were some northerners opposed to the antislavery movement? (b) How did some southerners justify slavery?
3. What did women at the Seneca Falls Convention demand?
4. State the role each of the following played in the movement for women's rights: (a) Sojourner Truth, (b) Elizabeth Cady Stanton, (c) Mary Lyon.
5. How did American public schools improve in the mid-1800s?
6. How did American writers of the mid-1800s break free of European traditions?
7. What themes did American painters select in the mid-1800s?

Thinking Critically

1. **Linking Past and Present** (a) What did abolitionists do to win public support? (b) How do reform leaders today try to win support for their causes?
2. **Understanding Causes and Effects** Why do you think former slaves were especially effective speakers for the abolitionist cause?
3. **Drawing Conclusions** (a) Why do you think leaders in the women's rights move-ment believed that education was a key to winning equality? (b) What effect do you think the opening of schools for women had on the women's rights movement?
4. **Analyzing Information** American writers in the 1800s stressed the importance of the individual. How did the writers' emphasis on the individual reflect the events and themes of American history?

Applying Your Skills

1. **Finding the Main Idea** Reread the statement by Henry Highland Garnet on page 402. Then write one or two sentences summarizing the main idea.
2. **Making a Review Chart** Make a review chart with five columns and three rows. Label the columns Abolition, Women's Rights, Care for the Mentally Ill, Prison Reform, Education Reform. Label the rows Problems to Solve, Leaders, Achievements. Then complete the chart. Which movement do you think achieved the most? Explain.

Thinking About Geography

Match the letters on the map with the following places: **1.** Massachusetts, **2.** New York, **3.** South Carolina, **4.** Maryland, **5.** Connecticut, **6.** Maine. **Region** Which states identified by letters on the map were part of the slaveholding region?

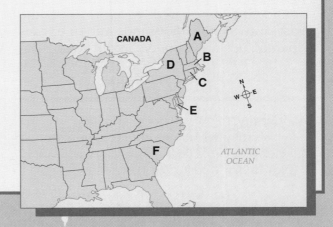

Traveling on the Underground Railroad

Form into groups to review the underground railroad. Follow the suggestions below to write, draw, dance, or give an oral presentation to show what you have learned about this famous escape route. You may use the textbook, encyclopedias, atlases, or other materials in your classroom library to complete the tasks. Be able to name your sources of information when you have finished the activity.

Harriet Tubman, at left, with people she led to freedom

CARTOGRAPHERS Create a map showing the routes taken by the underground railroad. The routes should start in the slave states of the South and extend to free states in the North as well as to Canada. Include a scale and a directional arrow.

MATHEMATICIANS Based on the map created by the cartographers, calculate the distances that escaping slaves had to travel along the different routes of the underground railroad. Then, based on people being able to walk about 10 miles a day, calculate how long it took to escape along each route. Make a chart of your statistics.

On the way to freedom

HISTORIANS Prepare brief profiles of these abolitionists: Frederick Douglass, William Lloyd Garrison, Angelina and Sarah Grimké, Sojourner Truth, Harriet Tubman, and John Greenleaf Whittier. Present your profiles in writing or as oral histories.

ARTISTS Design a mural depicting the flight of slaves on the underground railroad.

DANCERS Create a dance showing an escape along the underground railroad. Have dancers represent the "conductor" and the various escaping slaves, including mothers and children. Your dance should dramatize incidents along the escape route, as well as the feelings of the escaped slaves when they reached freedom.

"Station" on the underground railroad

 Organize a Traveling on the Underground Railroad Day and have each group present its activity to the rest of the school.

History Through

LITERATURE

A Slave *Virginia Hamilton*

Introduction The desire for freedom led many slaves to take the tremendous risk of escaping to the North. The following true story tells how the escape of Tice Davids inspired the first use of the term "underground road."

The underground road was named for the deed of an actual man born a slave who one day ran away from slavery. It became the name given to all the secret trails that led north, and to the system of human helpers of all races—who braved prison and even death to lead the running-aways to freedom.

Tice Davids inspired the first use of the term "underground road." On a day in 1831 that seemed ordinary, full of pain and hard work for him, Davids discovered that he had changed. He wondered how it had happened that on this day he could not bear to be a slave a moment longer.

It was time for him to make his way north. And so he ran.

Tice knew where he was going. There were Friends across the Ohio River, waiting. North would be somewhere there, and on and on. Word of that had come to him on the plantation. Whispers about liberty had made their way through the servants' quarters and on to the fields. They spread on the wind down to the riverbank. Tice had an idea of what it was to be free. It meant that he might rest without fear covering him like a blanket as he slept. It meant that nobody could buy or sell him.

Not all those who were slaves had the daring to escape. It wasn't that Tice was without fear. But, like others before him, given the chance, he'd take it.

There were those, black and free, who combed the riverbank, looking to help the running-aways. And there were certain Presbyterian ministers from the South who had formed a new church and had settled in the counties of southern Ohio. They were known to be friends of slaves. Like ever-present eagles with fierce, keen eyes, they too watched the great river for the running-aways.

Trusted to be a good servant, Tice had taken his life into his own hands and had run. And now he hurried, running.

"Look for the lantern!" That had been the urgent message passed along the slave quarters for those who would run at night.

"Listen for the bell!" Word was that the lone, distant sound of a bell clanging could be heard from across the wide river—when the wind was right. Other times, the bell seemed to clang up and down the shore. The river might be covered in fog. And hidden deep in the mist on the shore, a running-away could clearly hear the bell. He could follow its ringing all the way over and to a safe house.

Tice Davids would have to find a way across the great water if he was ever to be free. With luck he might find a usable boat or raft along the shore. What would he do if there was nothing to ride across on?

Capture for him was unthinkable, and he kept on running.

"Heard tell that on the other side, a slave is no longer such. They say that on the other side of the wide water, a slave is a free man."

That was the word and the truth that all Kentucky slaves believed. He kept that in mind as he ran. He looked back, knowing what he would see. There were the planter and his men, coming after him. The slave

Soaring Spirits *Slavery could chain the bodies of African Americans but not their spirits. This illustration captures the joyous dream of flying away to freedom shared by all slaves.* **Linking Past and Present** *Can you think of people today who might also dream of flying away to freedom?*

owner. Some called him master; Tice wouldn't when he could avoid it.

Friends, waiting across the river, was the word he could count on. If only he could get to the Friends!

He had been running for some time. Almost as though he were dreaming, he lifted one leg and then the other. Whatever had possessed him to try to break out?

Now he was at the Kentucky shore and it was empty. There was no boat to row, no raft to pole. The distant Ohio shore seemed farther than far. There was nothing for it but to swim.

Tice waded into the water, tired out before he began. The cold wet of the river shocked him, revived him. He knew to calm himself down and soon got his mind in hand. He began moving his arms, swimming in clean, long strokes.

About halfway across, Tice thought he heard a bell. The sound gave him strength and he swam gamely on.

It took the slave owner time to locate a skiff, but a small boat was found at last. He and his men shoved off and gave chase. The slave owner never let his slave out of his sight. Even when Tice staggered from the water onto the Ohio shore, the owner glared through the mist and pinpointed the dark, exhausted figure.

"Think we have him now," he said. He blinked to get the wet from his eyes. It was one blink too many. Tice Davids was gone. Disappeared!

"It's not believable," the owner said. "I saw him before my eyes and now he's gone. Vanished! It's not possible, but there it is."

The slave owner searched the shore every which way. He looked into ditches. He and his men beat the bushes and crept into caves and gazed up into trees. They poked the haystacks in the fields. They talked to people in the slavery-hating settlement at Ripley, Ohio, and they had their suspicions. But not one of the townsfolk would admit to having seen anybody running away. The Kentucky slave owner never again saw Tice Davids.

"Well, I'm going home," he said finally. He and his men crossed the river again and returned to Kentucky.

"Only one way to look at it," he told everyone at home, shaking his head in disbelief. "Tice must've gone on an underground road!"

Tice Davids made his way north through all of Ohio, all the way to Sandusky, on Lake Erie. There, at last, he settled, a free man— and the first to travel the underground road.

Later, the underground road took on an inspiring new name in honor of the amazing steam trains on parallel rails then coming into their own in America: *the Underground Railroad!*

Those who guided the running-aways along the highly secret system of the Underground Railroad had the cleverness to call themselves "conductors," the name used on the steam railway trains. The safe houses and secret hiding places known to the conductors were called "stations" and "depots," after railway stations and railway depots. Eventually, Tice Davids became a conductor on the Underground Railroad, helping other running-aways escape.

THINKING ABOUT LITERATURE

1. Why did Tice Davids run away?
2. How did Tice know where to go?
3. CRITICAL THINKING **Drawing Conclusions** What conclusion can you draw about the citizens of Ripley, Ohio? Explain.

ACTIVITY Imagine that you are Tice Davids. Write a first-person account of your escape from slavery.

The Nation Torn Apart

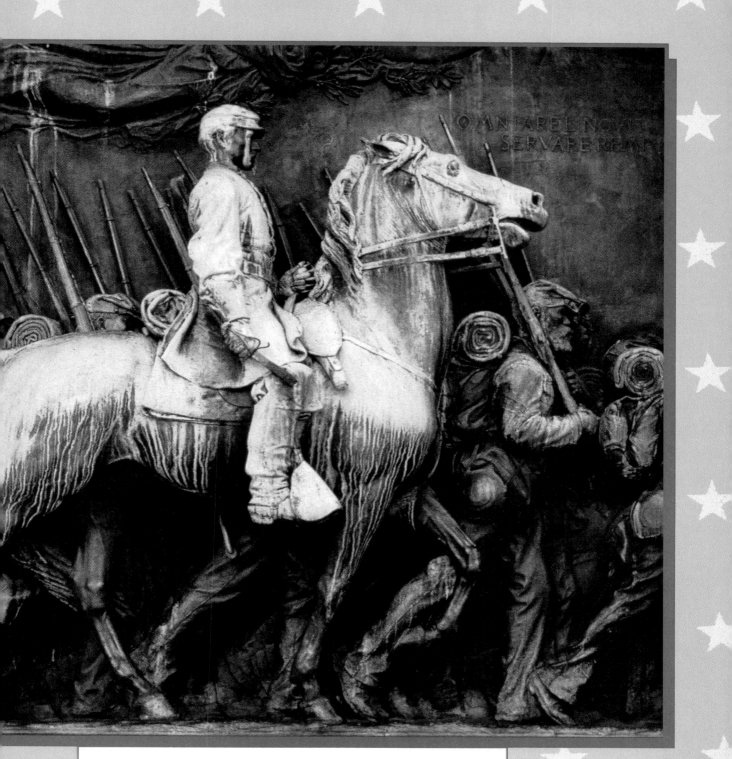

D ifferences between the North and South, especially over slavery, triggered a long and bloody civil war. This monument honors the 54th Massachusetts, an African American regiment in the war.

1820 *The Missouri Compromise extended slavery to some territories west of the Mississippi River. Here, slaves pick cotton on a plantation.*

1852 *Harriet Beecher Stowe published* Uncle Tom's Cabin. *The novel helped stir antislavery feeling in the North.*

1850 *The Fugitive Slave Law enraged northerners. The law required that all citizens help catch runaway slaves.*

| 1820 | 1848 | 1850 | 1852 | 1854 |

WORLD EVENT
1833 Slavery abolished in British Empire

WORLD EVENT
1848 France abolishes slavery in West Indian colonies

Chapter Setting

On June 16, 1858, a lawyer named Abraham Lincoln spoke before a crowded convention hall in Springfield, Illinois:

> 66 'A house divided against itself cannot stand.' I believe this government cannot endure permanently half slave and half free. I do not expect the Union to be dissolved—I do not expect the house to fall—but I do expect it will cease to be divided. It will become all one thing, or all the other. Either the opponents of slavery will arrest the further spread of it . . . or its [supporters] will push it forward till it shall become. . .lawful in all the states, old as well as new, North as well as South. 99

Lincoln had just been chosen to run as the Republican candidate for the Senate. Few people outside Illinois had heard of him. His speech, however, became famous. Soon many northerners were repeating the phrase, "A house divided against itself cannot stand." They agreed that the nation could not go on half slave and half free.

By the 1850s, more and more northerners had turned against slavery. They strongly opposed southern attempts to open the new territories of the West to slavery. Time after time, North and South clashed over this issue.

By 1861, when Abraham Lincoln became President, Americans were worried. Could the Union that had existed for nearly a century remain whole?

ACTIVITY Read the lines from Lincoln's "house divided" speech out loud. Then draw a political cartoon that expresses the main idea of Lincoln's speech.

1854 The Kansas-Nebraska Act led to violence in the Kansas Territory. Proslavery bands, like this one, clashed with antislavery forces there.

1858 Illinois Senate candidates Abraham Lincoln and Stephen Douglas debated the issue of slavery. The debates earned Lincoln nationwide fame.

1860 South Carolina became the first state to secede from the Union. South Carolinians wore palmetto leaf ribbons as a symbol of defiance.

| 1854 | 1856 | 1858 | 1860 | 1862 |

WORLD EVENT
1861 Russian ruler frees serfs

Slavery or Freedom in the West

FIND OUT

- Why did the issue of slavery flare up in 1819?
- What was the Missouri Compromise?
- What was the goal of the Free Soil party?

VOCABULARY sectionalism, popular sovereignty

In 1820, Thomas Jefferson was in his late seventies. The former President had vowed "never to write, talk, or even think of politics." Still, he voiced alarm when he heard about a fierce debate going on in Congress:

❝In the gloomiest moment of the revolutionary war, I never had any [fears] equal to what I feel from this source. . . . We have a wolf by the ears, and we can neither hold him nor safely let him go.❞

The "wolf" was the issue of slavery. Jefferson feared that the bitter quarrel would tear the country apart.

The Missouri Question

Louisiana was the first state carved out of the Louisiana Purchase, joining the Union as a slave state in 1812. Because slavery was well established there, few people protested. But when Missouri asked to join the Union as a slave state six years later, there was an uproar.

The admission of Missouri would upset the balance of power in the Senate. In 1819, there were 11 free states and 11 slave states. Each state had two senators. If Missouri became a slave state, the South would have a majority in the Senate. Determined not to lose power, northerners fought against letting Missouri enter as a slave state.

The argument over Missouri lasted many months. Finally, Senator Henry Clay proposed a compromise. During the long debate, Maine

A Slave Market As Americans debated the issue of slavery, slave auctions like the one at left went on. The numbered tags were used by owners to identify slaves they rented out. **Citizenship** How did the entry of new states into the Union affect the debate over slavery?

had also applied for statehood. Clay suggested admitting Missouri as a slave state and Maine as a free state. His plan, called the **Missouri Compromise,** kept the number of slave and free states equal.

As part of the Missouri Compromise, Congress drew an imaginary line across the southern border of Missouri at latitude 36° 30'N. Slavery was permitted in the part of the Louisiana Purchase south of that line. It was banned north of the line. The only exception was Missouri. (See the map on page 430.)

Slavery in the Mexican Cession

The Missouri Compromise applied only to the Louisiana Purchase. In 1848, the Mexican War added a vast stretch of western land to the United States. Once again, the question of slavery in the territories arose.

An antislavery plan. As you have read in Chapter 12, many northerners opposed the Mexican War. They feared that the South would extend slavery into the West. David Wilmot, a member of Congress from Pennsylvania, called for a law to ban slavery in any lands won from Mexico. Southern leaders angrily opposed the **Wilmot Proviso.** They said that Congress had no right to ban slavery in the territories.

In 1846, the House passed the Wilmot Proviso, but the Senate defeated it. As a result, Americans continued to argue about slavery in the West even while their army fought in Mexico.

Americans take sides. The Mexican War strengthened feelings of sectionalism in the North and South. Sectionalism is loyalty to a state or section, rather than to the country as a whole. Many southerners were united by their support for slavery. They saw the North as a growing threat to their way of life. Many northerners saw the South as a foreign country, where American rights and liberties did not exist.

As the debate over slavery heated up, people found it hard not to take sides. Northern abolitionists demanded that slavery be banned throughout the country. They insisted that slavery was morally wrong. By the late 1840s, a growing number of northerners agreed.

Southern slaveholders thought that slavery should be allowed in any territory. They also demanded that slaves who escaped to the North be returned to them. Even white southerners who did not own slaves agreed with these ideas.

Moderate views. Between these two extreme views were more moderate positions. Some moderates argued that the Missouri Compromise line should be extended across the Mexican Cession to the Pacific Ocean. Any new state north of the line would be a free state. Any new state south of the line could allow slavery.

Other moderates supported the idea of popular sovereignty. Popular sovereignty means control by the people. In other words, voters in a new territory would decide for themselves whether or not to allow slavery in the territory. Slaves, of course, could not vote.

A new political party. The debate over slavery led to the birth of a new political party. By 1848, many northerners in both the Democratic party and the Whig party opposed the spread of slavery. But the leaders of both parties refused to take a stand on the question. They did not want to give up their chance of winning votes in the South. Some also feared that the slavery issue would split the nation.

In 1848, antislavery members of both parties met in Buffalo, New York. There, they founded the **Free Soil party.** Their slogan was "Free soil, free speech, free labor, and free men." The main goal of the Free Soil party was to keep slavery out of the western territories. Only a few Free Soilers were abolitionists who wanted to end slavery in the South.

The Missouri Compromise—Why 36°30'?

In the Northwest Ordinance of 1787, Congress banned slavery north of the Ohio River. The ordinance applied to the newly acquired lands of the Northwest Territory. To antislavery forces, however, the Ohio River became a border between free and slave states. Before long, their decision to maintain that border was put to the test.

In 1818, Missouri applied for admission to the United States as a slave state, which caused turmoil. Antislavery forces pointed to the ban on slavery in the Northwest Ordinance. If the Ohio River line were carried westward, they pointed out, most of Missouri would lie north of it. To allow Missouri to enter as a slave state would break that line.

Debate dragged on through two sessions of Congress. When Maine applied for admission as a free state, some members of Congress saw a chance to resolve the issue.

They would allow Missouri to come in as a slave state. Then they would achieve a balance by admitting Maine as a free state. This proposal, however, failed to win enough support to be passed.

Hoping to break the deadlock, Senator Jesse B. Thomas of Illinois suggested an amendment. By the terms of Thomas's amendment, Congress would set the line 36°30'N as a permanent boundary between free and slave states west of the Mississippi River. Missouri, which already permitted slavery, would be the only exception. Thomas proposed 36°30' because it formed the southern boundary of Missouri. At the same time, it was only slightly south of 37°N, where the Ohio River ends.

Thomas's amendment turned the tide. In 1820, Congress passed the Maine-Missouri Bill. Maine entered the Union as a free state later that year. Missouri entered as a slave state in 1821.

■ Why did Congress choose the line 36°30' as the boundary between free states and slave states west of the Mississippi River?

Missouri Compromise

MAINE

NORTHWEST TERRITORY

MISSOURI Ohio R.

Missouri Compromise Line
36°30' N

Mississippi R.

N
W E
S

Free states and territories closed to slavery		Slave states and territories open to slavery

0   150   300 Miles

0   150   300 Kilometers

ACTIVITY

On an outline map of the United States, locate and label Missouri, Kansas Territory, and Nebraska Territory. Then draw the Missouri Compromise line—36°30'N. Based on this line, would Kansas and Nebraska come in as free states or as slave states? Explain.

A Three-Way Race *Slavery was an important issue in the 1848 presidential election. In this cartoon, the candidates race for the finish line—Zachary Taylor on a bloodhound, Martin Van Buren on a buffalo, and Lewis Cass on a bicycle.* **Citizenship** *What was each candidate's position on slavery?*

The Free Soil Challenge

While Americans debated the slavery question, the 1848 campaign for President took place. Free Soilers named former President Martin Van Buren as their candidate. Democrats chose Lewis Cass of Michigan. Whigs selected Zachary Taylor, a hero of the Mexican War.

For the first time, slavery was an important election issue. Van Buren called for a ban on slavery in the Mexican Cession. Cass supported popular sovereignty. Because Taylor was a slave owner from Louisiana, many southern voters assumed that he supported slavery.

In the end, Zachary Taylor won the election. Still, Van Buren took 10 percent of the popular vote. Thirteen other Free Soil candidates won seats in Congress. Only three months old, the Free Soil party had made a strong showing in the election. Their success showed that slavery had become a national issue.

SECTION 1 REVIEW

1. **Locate:** (a) Missouri, (b) Maine, (c) Missouri Compromise line.
2. **Identify:** (a) Missouri Compromise, (b) Wilmot Proviso, (c) Free Soil party, (d) Martin Van Buren, (e) Lewis Cass, (f) Zachary Taylor.
3. **Define:** (a) sectionalism, (b) popular sovereignty.
4. Why did Missouri's request to join the Union cause an uproar?
5. How did the Mexican War revive the issue of slavery?
6. **CRITICAL THINKING Analyzing Ideas** The slogan of the Free Soil party was "Free soil, free speech, free labor, and free men." Why might this slogan have appealed to voters in the North?

ACTIVITY Writing to Learn
Imagine that you are an African American living in the North in 1820. Write a letter to a newspaper to express your opinion of the Missouri Compromise.

2
Saving the Union

FIND OUT
- Why did the slavery question arise again in 1850?
- How did the North and South reach another compromise?
- How did the issue of fugitive slaves divide the North and South?

VOCABULARY fugitive, civil war

The issue of slavery in the West soon flared up again. In 1850, California asked to join the Union as a free state. Tempers raged as members of Congress tried to reach another compromise.

Senator Thomas Hart Benton of Missouri supported California's request. Most of California lay north of the Missouri Compromise line. Though a slave owner himself, Benton felt that the compromise had to be upheld. He denounced Senator Henry Foote of Mississippi for helping to block California's admission.

Foote rose angrily from his seat. Drawing a pistol, he pointed it at Benton's chest. As other senators watched in horror, Benton roared, "Let him fire! Stand out of the way and let the assassin fire!"

No blood was shed in the Senate that day. However, many Americans began to fear that a peaceful solution to the slavery issue was impossible.

Seeking a Compromise

For a time after the Missouri Compromise, both slave and free states had entered the Union peacefully. Between 1821 and 1848, Michigan, Iowa, and Wisconsin entered as free states. Arkansas, Florida, and

Texas came in as slave states. (See the graph below.)

When California requested admission as a free state, once again the balance of power in the Senate was threatened. Southerners did not want to give the North a majority in the Senate. They also feared that more free states might be carved out of the huge Mexican Cession. Some southerners even talked about seceding from the Union.

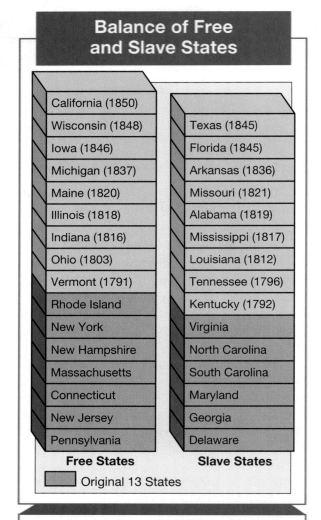

Balance of Free and Slave States

Free States	Slave States
California (1850)	
Wisconsin (1848)	Texas (1845)
Iowa (1846)	Florida (1845)
Michigan (1837)	Arkansas (1836)
Maine (1820)	Missouri (1821)
Illinois (1818)	Alabama (1819)
Indiana (1816)	Mississippi (1817)
Ohio (1803)	Louisiana (1812)
Vermont (1791)	Tennessee (1796)
Rhode Island	Kentucky (1792)
New York	Virginia
New Hampshire	North Carolina
Massachusetts	South Carolina
Connecticut	Maryland
New Jersey	Georgia
Pennsylvania	Delaware

☐ Original 13 States

GRAPH SKILLS *Both the North and the South were determined to maintain the delicate balance in the Senate between slave and free states.* • *How did the admission of California affect this balance?*

A Great Debate *The Senate debated Henry Clay's proposed Compromise of 1850 for six months. Here, Clay appeals to his fellow senators to support his plan.* **Citizenship** *What was Clay's main goal in proposing the Compromise of 1850?*

Clay pleads for compromise. To resolve the crisis, Congress turned to Senator Henry Clay. Clay had won the nickname "the Great Compromiser" for working out the Missouri Compromise. Now, nearly 30 years later, the 73-year-old Clay was frail and ill. Still, he pleaded for the North and South to reach an agreement. If they failed to do so, Clay warned, the nation could break apart.

Calhoun replies. Senator John C. Calhoun of South Carolina prepared the South's reply to Clay. Calhoun was dying of tuberculosis and could not speak loudly enough to address the Senate. Wrapped in a heavy cloak, he glared at his northern foes while another senator read his speech.

Calhoun refused to compromise. He insisted that slavery be allowed in the western territories. Calhoun also demanded that fugitive, or runaway, slaves be returned to their owners in the South. Fugitives actually were few in number and not the real issue. Calhoun really wanted northerners to admit that southern slaveholders had the right to reclaim their "property."

If the North would not agree to the South's demands, Calhoun told the Senate, "let the states . . . agree to part in peace. If you are unwilling that we should part in peace, tell us so, and we shall know what to do." Everyone knew what Calhoun meant. If an agreement could not be reached, the South would secede from the Union.

Webster calls for unity. Daniel Webster of Massachusetts spoke next. Webster had been Clay's rival for decades. Now he supported Clay's plea to save the Union. Webster stated his position clearly:

66I speak today not as a Massachusetts man, nor as a northern man, but as an American. . . . I speak today for the preservation of the Union. . . . There can be no such thing as a peaceable secession. Peaceable secession is an utter impossibility.99

Webster feared that the states could not separate without a civil war. A **civil war** is a war between people of the same country.

Like many northerners, Webster viewed slavery as evil. Disunion, however, he believed was worse. To save the Union, Webster was willing to compromise with the South. He would support the South's demand that northerners be required to return fugitive slaves.

A Compromise at Last

In 1850, while the debate raged, Calhoun died. His last words reportedly were "The South! The South! God knows what will become of her!" President Taylor also died in 1850. Taylor had opposed Clay's compromise plan. The new President, Millard Fillmore, supported it. An agreement finally seemed possible.

Henry Clay gave more than 70 speeches in favor of a compromise. At last, however, he became too sick to continue. Stephen Douglas, a young and energetic senator from Illinois, took up the fight for him. Douglas tirelessly guided each part of Clay's plan, called the *Compromise of 1850,* through Congress.

The Compromise of 1850 had four parts. First, California was allowed to enter the Union as a free state. Second, the rest of the Mexican Cession was divided into the territories of New Mexico and Utah. In each territory, voters would decide the slavery question according to popular sovereignty. Third, the slave trade was ended in Washington, D.C., the nation's capital. Congress, however, declared that it had no power to ban the slave trade between slave states. Fourth, a strict new fugitive slave law was passed.

The North and South had reached a compromise. But neither side got all that it wanted. The new Fugitive Slave Law was especially hard for northerners to accept.

The Fugitive Slave Law of 1850

Most northerners had ignored the Fugitive Slave Law of 1793. As a result, fugitive slaves often lived as free citizens in northern cities. The *Fugitive Slave Law of 1850* was harder to ignore. It required all citizens to help catch runaway slaves. People who let fugitives escape could be fined $1,000 and jailed for six months.

The new law set up special courts to handle the cases of runaways. Judges received $10 for sending an accused runaway to the South. They received only $5 for setting someone free. Lured by the extra money, some judges sent African Americans to the South whether or not they were runaways. Fearful that they would be kidnapped and enslaved under the new law, thousands of free African Americans fled to Canada.

The Fugitive Slave Law enraged northerners. By forcing them to catch runaways, the law made northerners feel they were

Denouncing the Fugitive Slave Law *Many northerners viewed the Fugitive Slave Law as an "outrage to humanity." This engraving from a Boston newspaper shows abolitionist Wendell Phillips urging a crowd to disobey the hated law.* **Citizenship** *What does this picture suggest about the opponents of the Fugitive Slave Law?*

part of the slave system. In several northern cities, crowds tried to rescue fugitive slaves from their captors. Martin R. Delany, an African American newspaper editor, spoke for many northerners, black and white:

> 66My house is my castle. . . . If any man approaches that house in search of a slave—I care not who he may be, whether constable or sheriff, magistrate or even judge of the Supreme Court. . . if he crosses the threshold of my door, and I do not lay him a lifeless corpse at my feet, I hope the grave may refuse my body a resting place. 99

Calhoun had hoped that the Fugitive Slave Law would force northerners to admit that the slave owners did indeed have rights. Instead, each time the law was enforced, it convinced more northerners that slavery was evil.

An Antislavery Bestseller

An event in 1852 added to the growing antislavery mood of the North. That year, Harriet Beecher Stowe published a novel called *Uncle Tom's Cabin*. Stowe wrote the novel to show the evils of slavery and the injustice of the Fugitive Slave Law.

Stowe told the story of Uncle Tom, an enslaved African American noted for his kindness and his devotion to his religion. Tom is bought by Simon Legree, a cruel planter who treats his slaves brutally. In the end, Legree whips Uncle Tom until he dies.

The book had wide appeal in the North. In its first year, it sold 300,000 copies. It was also published in many different languages. Soon, a play based on the novel appeared in cities around the world.

Southerners claimed that *Uncle Tom's Cabin* did not give a true picture of slave life. Indeed, Stowe had seen little of slavery firsthand. Yet the book helped to change the way northerners felt about slavery. No longer could they ignore slavery as a political problem for Congress to settle. They now saw slavery as a moral problem facing every American. For this reason, *Uncle Tom's Cabin* was one of the most important books in American history. (📖 See "Uncle Tom's Cabin" on page 595.)

SECTION 2 REVIEW

1. **Locate:** (a) California, (b) New Mexico Territory, (c) Utah Territory.
2. **Identify:** (a) Henry Clay, (b) John C. Calhoun, (c) Daniel Webster, (d) Stephen Douglas, (e) Compromise of 1850, (f) Fugitive Slave Law of 1850, (g) Harriet Beecher Stowe, (h) *Uncle Tom's Cabin*.
3. **Define:** (a) fugitive, (b) civil war.
4. Why did California's request for statehood raise the slavery issue again?
5. Why did many northerners and southerners support the Compromise of 1850?
6. What did northerners dislike about the Fugitive Slave Law of 1850?
7. **CRITICAL THINKING Forecasting** Do you think the Compromise of 1850 offered a lasting solution to the slavery question? Explain.

ACTIVITY Writing to Learn
Write a short skit showing how the Fugitive Slave Law of 1850 stirred northern feelings against slavery.

Our Common Heritage
Elizabeth Cady Stanton praised Harriet Beecher Stowe for her work as a writer. Stowe, however, did not support Stanton's work for women's rights. In fact, she later wrote a book poking fun at Stanton and Victoria Woodhull, the first woman to run for President.

Bloodshed in Kansas

FIND OUT
- What events made the issue of slavery emerge again in 1854?
- Why did proslavery and antislavery forces move into Kansas?
- How did the Dred Scott decision divide the nation?

In the mid-1850s, proslavery and antislavery forces battled for control of the territory of Kansas. An observer described election day in one Kansas district in 1855:

66On the morning of the election, before the polls were opened, some 300 or 400 Missourians and others were collected in the yard. . . where the election was to be held, armed with bowie-knives, revolvers, and clubs. They said they came to vote, and whip the. . . Yankees, and would vote without being sworn. Some said they came to have a fight, and wanted one.99

Hearing of events in Kansas, Abraham Lincoln, then a young lawyer in Illinois, predicted that "the contest will come to blows, and bloodshed." Once again, the issue of slavery in the territories divided the nation.

Kansas-Nebraska Act

Americans had hoped that the Compromise of 1850 would end debate over slavery in the West. In 1854, however, the issue of slavery in the territories surfaced yet again.

In January 1854, Senator Stephen Douglas of Illinois introduced a bill to set up a government for the Nebraska Territory. The Nebraska Territory stretched from Texas north to Canada, and from Missouri west to the Rocky Mountains.

Douglas knew that white southerners did not want to add another free state to the Union. He proposed dividing the Nebraska Territory into two territories, Kansas and Nebraska. (See the map at right.) In each territory, settlers would decide the issue of slavery by popular sovereignty. Douglas's bill was known as the *Kansas-Nebraska Act.*

Undoing the Missouri Compromise. The Kansas-Nebraska Act seemed fair to many people. After all, the Compromise of 1850 had applied popular sovereignty in New Mexico and Utah. Others felt that Kansas and Nebraska were different. The Missouri Compromise had already banned slavery in those areas, they insisted. The Kansas-Nebraska Act would, in effect, undo the Missouri Compromise.

Southern leaders supported the Kansas-Nebraska Act. They were sure that slave owners from Missouri would move across the border into Kansas. In time, they hoped, Kansas would become a slave state. President Franklin Pierce, a Democrat elected in 1852, also supported the bill. With the President's help, Douglas pushed the Kansas-Nebraska Act through Congress.

Northern outrage. Northern reaction to the Kansas-Nebraska Act was swift and angry. Opponents of slavery called the act a "criminal betrayal of precious rights." Slavery could now spread to areas that had been free for more than 30 years.

Northerners protested by challenging the Fugitive Slave Law. Two days after Congress passed the Kansas-Nebraska Act, slave catchers in Boston seized Anthony Burns, a fugitive. Citizens of Boston poured into the streets to keep Burns from being sent to the South. It took two companies of soldiers to stop the crowd from freeing Burns. Such incidents showed that antislavery feeling was rising in the North.

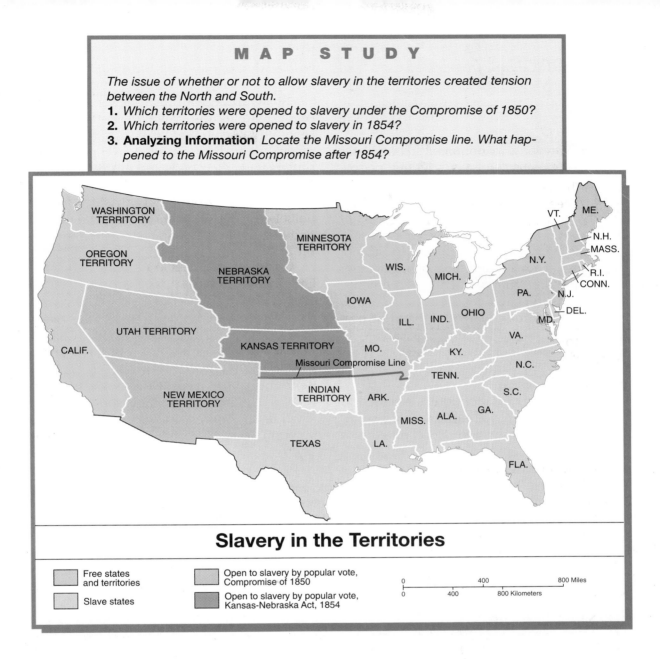

The issue of whether or not to allow slavery in the territories created tension between the North and South.
1. Which territories were opened to slavery under the Compromise of 1850?
2. Which territories were opened to slavery in 1854?
3. **Analyzing Information** Locate the Missouri Compromise line. What happened to the Missouri Compromise after 1854?

WASHINGTON TERRITORY

OREGON TERRITORY

MINNESOTA TERRITORY

NEBRASKA TERRITORY

WIS.

MICH.

VT. ME.

N.H.
MASS.

N.Y.

R.I.
CONN.

PA. N.J.

DEL.

UTAH TERRITORY

IOWA

ILL. IND. OHIO

MD.

VA.

CALIF.

KANSAS TERRITORY

MO.

KY.

Missouri Compromise Line

N.C.

TENN.

NEW MEXICO TERRITORY

INDIAN TERRITORY

ARK.

S.C.

MISS. ALA. GA.

TEXAS

LA.

FLA.

Slavery in the Territories

Free states and territories	Open to slavery by popular vote, Compromise of 1850
Slave states	Open to slavery by popular vote, Kansas-Nebraska Act, 1854

0   400   800 Miles
0   400   800 Kilometers

Kansas Explodes

Kansas now became a testing ground for popular sovereignty. Stephen Douglas hoped that settlers would decide the slavery issue peacefully on election day. Instead, proslavery and antislavery forces sent settlers to Kansas to fight for control of the territory.

Rushing to Kansas. Most of the new arrivals were farmers from neighboring states.

Their main interest in moving to Kansas was cheap land. Few of these settlers owned slaves. At the same time, abolitionists brought in more than 1,000 settlers from New England.

Proslavery settlers moved into Kansas as well. They wanted to make sure that antislavery forces did not overrun the territory. Proslavery bands from Missouri often rode across the border. These **Border Ruffians** battled the antislavery forces in Kansas.

Divided Kansas. In 1855, Kansas held elections to choose lawmakers. Hundreds of Border Ruffians crossed into Kansas and voted illegally. They helped to elect a proslavery legislature.

The new legislature quickly passed laws to support slavery. One law said that people could be put to death for helping slaves escape. Another made speaking out against slavery a crime punishable by two years of hard labor.

Antislavery settlers refused to accept these laws. They elected their own governor and legislature. With two rival governments, Kansas was in chaos.

The first shots. In 1856, a band of proslavery men raided the town of Lawrence, an antislavery stronghold. The attackers destroyed homes and smashed the press of a Free Soil newspaper.

John Brown, an abolitionist, decided to strike back. Brown had moved to Kansas to help make it a free state. He claimed that God had sent him to punish supporters of slavery.

Brown rode with his four sons and two other men to the town of Pottawatomie (paht uh WAHT uh mee) Creek. In the middle of the night, they dragged five proslavery settlers from their beds and murdered them.

The killings at Pottawatomie Creek sparked more violence. Both sides fought fiercely. By late 1856, more than 200 people had been killed. Newspapers called the territory ***Bleeding Kansas.***

Bloodshed in the Senate

Even before Brown's attack, the battle over Kansas spilled into the Senate. Charles Sumner of Massachusetts was the leading abolitionist senator. In one speech, Sumner denounced the proslavery legislature in Kansas. He then attacked his southern foes, singling out Andrew Butler, an elderly senator from South Carolina.

Bleeding Kansas *The struggle between proslavery and antislavery forces for control of Kansas erupted into violence. This eyewitness sketch shows a battle between proslavery and antislavery settlers.* **Citizenship** *How was the violence in Kansas related to the Kansas-Nebraska Act?*

Butler was not in the Senate on the day Sumner spoke. A few days later, however, Butler's nephew, Congressman Preston Brooks, marched into the Senate chamber. Using a heavy cane, Brooks beat Sumner until he fell, bloody and unconscious, to the floor.

Many southerners felt that Sumner got what was coming to him. Hundreds of people sent canes to Brooks to show their support. To northerners, however, the brutal act was just more evidence that slavery led to violence.

The Dred Scott Decision

With Congress in an uproar, many Americans looked to the Supreme Court to settle the slavery issue and restore peace. In 1857, the Court ruled on a case involving a slave named Dred Scott. But instead of bringing harmony, the Court's decision further divided North and South.

Dred Scott had lived for many years in Missouri. Later, he moved with his owner to Illinois and then to Wisconsin Territory, where slavery was not allowed. After they returned to Missouri, Scott's owner died. Antislavery lawyers helped Scott to file a lawsuit. They argued that since Scott had lived in a free territory, he was a free man.

A sweeping decision. In time, the case reached the Supreme Court. The Court's decision startled Americans. First, it ruled that Scott could not file a lawsuit because, as a

BIOGRAPHY Dred Scott *When his owner died, Dred Scott filed a lawsuit for his freedom. He argued that since he had lived in a free territory, he should be a free man. In a ruling that caused an uproar, the Supreme Court disagreed. After the Court's ruling, Scott was sold. His new owner then gave him his freedom.* **Citizenship** *How did the Dred Scott decision overturn the Missouri Compromise?*

black, he was not a citizen. The Justices also agreed that slaves were property.

The Court did not stop there. Instead, the Justices went on to make a sweeping decision about the larger issue of slavery in the territories. According to the Court, Congress did not have the power to outlaw slavery in *any* territory. The Court's ruling meant that the Missouri Compromise was unconstitutional.

The nation reacts. White southerners rejoiced at the ***Dred Scott decision.*** It meant that slavery was legal in all the territories— just what they had been demanding for years.

Our Common Heritage
As the dispute over slavery heated up, violence erupted a number of times in Congress. On one occasion, more than 20 members were brawling when someone grabbed someone else's hair. The hair turned out to be a wig! Fighting stopped as the members broke into laughter.

African Americans responded angrily to the Dred Scott decision. In the North, many held public meetings to condemn the ruling. At a meeting in Philadelphia, a speaker hoped that the Dred Scott decision would lead more whites to "join with us in our efforts to recover the long lost boon of freedom."

White northerners were also shocked by the ruling. Many had hoped that slavery would die out if it were restricted to the South. Now, however, slavery could spread throughout the West. Even northerners who disliked abolitionists felt that the Dred Scott ruling was wrong. A Cincinnati newspaper declared, "We are now one great . . . slaveholding community."

SECTION 3 REVIEW

1. **Locate:** (a) Kansas Territory, (b) Nebraska Territory.
2. **Identify:** (a) Kansas-Nebraska Act, (b) Franklin Pierce, (c) Border Ruffians, (d) John Brown, (e) Bleeding Kansas, (f) Charles Sumner, (g) Dred Scott decision.
3. How did the Kansas-Nebraska Act undo the Missouri Compromise?
4. Why did popular sovereignty lead to fighting in Kansas?
5. Explain how each of the following reacted to the Dred Scott decision: (a) white southerners, (b) African Americans, (c) white northerners.
6. CRITICAL THINKING **Analyzing a Quotation** After the Kansas-Nebraska Act was passed, Stephen Douglas stated that "the struggle for freedom was forever banished from the halls of Congress to the western plains." What did Douglas mean?

ACTIVITY Writing to Learn

Write two sets of headlines for the events in Section 3. One set should be for a northern newspaper, the other for a southern newspaper.

4 Republicans Challenge Slavery

FIND OUT
- Why did a new political party take shape in the mid-1850s?
- How did Abraham Lincoln view slavery?
- How did the raid on Harpers Ferry deepen differences between the North and South?

VOCABULARY arsenal

In the mid-1850s, people who opposed slavery in the territories were looking for a new political voice. Neither the Whig party nor the Democratic party would take a strong stand against slavery. "We have submitted to slavery long enough," an Ohio Democrat declared.

Free Soilers, northern Democrats, and antislavery Whigs met in towns and cities across the North. In 1854, a group gathered in Michigan to form the *Republican party.* The new party grew quickly. By 1856, it was ready to challenge the older parties for power.

The Republican Party

The main goal of the Republican party was to keep slavery out of the western territories. A few Republicans were abolitionists and hoped to end slavery in the South as well. Most Republicans, however, wanted only to stop the spread of slavery.

In 1856, Republicans selected John C. Frémont to run for President. Frémont was a frontiersman who had fought for California's independence. (See page 366.) He had little political experience, but he opposed the spread of slavery. In northern cities, Republicans marched through the streets singing Frémont's campaign song:

> 66Arise, arise ye brave!
>   And let our war-cry be,
>   Free speech, free press, free soil, free men,
>   Frémont and victory!99

The Whig party was very weak. Frémont's main opponent was Democrat James Buchanan. Buchanan was from Pennsylvania, but he sympathized with the southern position on slavery.

Supported by the large majority of southerners and many northerners, Buchanan won the election. Still, the Republicans made a strong showing. Without the support of a single southern state, Frémont won one third of the popular vote. Southerners worried that their influence in the national government was fading.

Abe Lincoln of Illinois

The next test for the Republican party came in 1858 in Illinois. Abraham Lincoln, a Republican, challenged Democrat Stephen Douglas for his seat in the Senate. The election captured the attention of the whole nation. Most Americans thought that Douglas would run for President in 1860.

A self-starter from Kentucky. Abraham Lincoln was born in the backcountry of Kentucky. Like many frontier people, his parents moved often to find better land. The family lived in Indiana and later in Illinois. As a child, Lincoln spent only a year in school. But he taught himself to read and spent hours reading by firelight.

After Lincoln left home, he opened a store in Illinois. There, he studied law on his own and launched a career in politics. After spending eight years in the state legislature, Lincoln served one term in Congress. Bitterly opposed to the Kansas-Nebraska Act, he decided to run for the Senate in 1858.

"Honest Abe" Abraham Lincoln often poked fun at his own plain style and appearance. "The Lord prefers common-looking people," he said. "That is why He makes so many of them." **American Traditions** Why was Lincoln popular?

"Just folks." When the race began, Lincoln was not a national figure. Still, people in Illinois knew him well and liked him. To them, he was "just folks"—someone who enjoyed picnics, wrestling contests, and all their other favorite pastimes.

People also admired his honesty and wit. His plainspoken manner made him a good speaker. Even so, a listener once complained that he could not understand one of Lincoln's speeches. "There are always some fleas a dog can't reach" was Lincoln's reply.

The Lincoln-Douglas Campaign Trail

One sunny day in August 1858, a train sped across the Illinois prairie. Inside his private railroad car sat Senator Stephen Douglas. Banners draped outside the car proudly announced the "Little Giant," as Douglas—

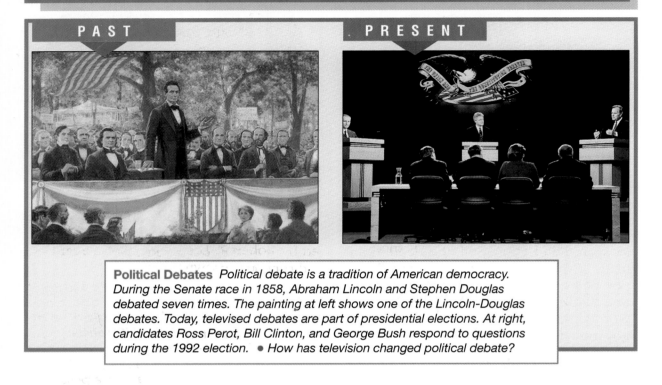

PAST

PRESENT

Political Debates *Political debate is a tradition of American democracy. During the Senate race in 1858, Abraham Lincoln and Stephen Douglas debated seven times. The painting at left shows one of the Lincoln-Douglas debates. Today, televised debates are part of presidential elections. At right, candidates Ross Perot, Bill Clinton, and George Bush respond to questions during the 1992 election.* ● *How has television changed political debate?*

only five feet tall—was called. Behind the senator's car was a flatcar mounted with a brass cannon. Whenever the train approached a station, two young men in uniform fired the cannon. Senator Douglas was coming to town!

Abraham Lincoln was traveling on the same train. Lincoln sat in a public car with other passengers. Lincoln knew that on his own he could never draw big crowds as Senator Douglas did. To remedy this, Lincoln followed his opponent around the state, answering him speech for speech.

A series of debates. To get more attention, Lincoln challenged Douglas to a series of debates. Although not really eager, Douglas agreed. During the campaign, the two men debated seven times.

The first debate took place in Ottawa, Illinois. It was a broiling-hot day. Dust clouds rose as farmers drove their wagons to town. Others floated down the Illinois

River in flatboats. Nobody minded the heat because this Senate election was especially important. Besides, politics was a favorite entertainment for Americans.

Douglas speaks. Standing before a crowd of 10,000, Douglas began his attack. Lincoln, he declared in a booming voice, was a hot-headed abolitionist who wanted blacks and whites to be complete equals— even to socialize with one another! Even worse, Douglas warned, Lincoln's call for an end to slavery would lead to war between the North and South.

Douglas then reminded the audience of his own views. Popular sovereignty, he urged, was the best way to solve the slavery crisis. Even though he personally disliked slavery, he did not care whether people in the territories voted "down or up" for it.

Lincoln replies. Lincoln rose to reply. He seemed unsure what to do with his long arms and big hands. But Lincoln's voice carried clearly to the edge of the crowd. If slavery was wrong, he said, Douglas and other Americans could not ignore it. They could not treat it as an unimportant question to be voted "down or up." On the contrary, if slavery was evil, it should be kept out of the territories.

Like nearly all whites of his day, Lincoln did not believe in "perfect equality" between blacks and whites. He did, however, believe that slavery was wrong. He declared:

> 66 There is no reason in the world why the [African American] is not entitled to all the natural rights [listed] in the Declaration of Independence, the right to life, liberty and the pursuit of happiness. I hold that he is as much entitled to these as the white man. . . . In the right to eat the bread . . . which his own hand earns, he is my equal and the equal of Judge Douglas, and the equal of every living man. 99

The debate went on for three hours. When it was over, Douglas's supporters marched away with their hero. A crowd of Republicans carried Lincoln on their shoulders, his long legs dangling to the ground.

A leader emerges. Week after week, both men spoke nearly every day to large crowds. Newspapers reprinted their speeches. The more northerners read Lincoln's speeches, the more they thought about the injustice of slavery. Many could no longer agree with Douglas that slavery was simply a political issue. Like Lincoln, they believed that "if slavery is not wrong, nothing is wrong." (📖 See "Lincoln's Warning" on page 598.)

Douglas won the election by a slim margin. Still, Lincoln was a winner, too. He was now known throughout the country. Two years later, the two rivals would again meet face to face—both seeking the office of President. ■

John Brown's Raid

In the meantime, more bloodshed pushed the North and South farther apart. In 1859, John Brown carried his antislavery campaign from Kansas to the East. He led a group of followers, including five African Americans, to Harpers Ferry, Virginia. There, they raided a federal arsenal, or gun warehouse. Brown thought that enslaved African Americans would flock to the arsenal. He planned to give them weapons and lead them in a revolt.

Seizing the arsenal. Brown quickly gained control of the arsenal. No slave uprising took place, however. Instead, troops led by Robert E. Lee killed 10 of the raiders and captured Brown.

John Brown's Farewell *John Brown was captured at Harpers Ferry and tried for murder and treason. This painting shows Brown being led to his execution, as northerners imagined the scene.* **Culture** *How do you think southerners responded to this painting?*

Most people, in both the North and the South, thought that Brown's plan to lead a slave revolt was insane. After all, there were not many enslaved African Americans in Harpers Ferry. At his trial, however, Brown seemed perfectly sane. He sat quietly as the court found him guilty of murder and treason and sentenced him to death.

Trial and death. Because he showed great dignity during his trial, Brown became a hero to many northerners. On the morning he was hanged, church bells rang solemnly throughout the North. In years to come, New Englanders would sing a popular song: "John Brown's body lies a mold'ring in the grave, but his soul is marching on."

To white southerners, the northern response to John Brown's death was outrageous. People were actually singing the praises of a man who had tried to lead a slave revolt! Many southerners became convinced that the North wanted to destroy slavery—and the South along with it. The nation was poised for a violent clash.

SECTION 4 REVIEW

1. **Identify:** (a) Republican party, (b) John C. Frémont, (c) James Buchanan, (d) Abraham Lincoln, (e) John Brown.
2. **Define:** arsenal.
3. What was the main goal of the Republican party?
4. Why did Americans pay special attention to the 1858 Senate race in Illinois?
5. Why did John Brown raid an arsenal at Harpers Ferry?
6. **CRITICAL THINKING Comparing** Compare Lincoln's and Douglas's views on slavery.

ACTIVITY Writing to Learn

Imagine that you are a lawyer at the trial of John Brown. Write a speech in which you call on the jury to reach a verdict of either guilty or not guilty.

5
The South Breaks Away

FIND OUT
■ How did the South react to Lincoln's victory in 1860?
■ What were the Confederate States of America?
■ What events led to the outbreak of the Civil War?

In May 1860, thousands of people swarmed into Chicago for the Republican convention. They filled the city's 42 hotels. When beds ran out, they slept on billiard tables. All were there to find out one thing. Who would win the Republican nomination for President—William Seward of New York or Abraham Lincoln of Illinois?

On the third day of the convention, a delegate rushed to the roof of the hall. There, a man stood waiting next to a cannon. "Fire the salute," ordered the delegate. "Old Abe is nominated!"

As the cannon fired, crowds surrounding the hall burst into cheers. Amid the celebration, a delegate from Kentucky struck a somber note. "Gentlemen, we are on the brink of a great civil war."

The Election of 1860

The Democrats held their convention in Charleston, South Carolina. Southerners wanted the party to support slavery in the territories. But Northern Democrats refused to do so. In the end, the party split in two. Northern Democrats chose Stephen Douglas to run for President. Southern Democrats picked John Breckinridge of Kentucky.

Some Americans tried to heal the split between North and South by forming a new party. The Constitutional Union party chose John Bell of Tennessee, a Whig, to run for President. Bell was a moderate who wanted to keep the Union together. He got support only in a few southern states that were still seeking a compromise.

When the votes were counted, Lincoln had carried the North and won the election. Southern votes did not affect the outcome at all. Lincoln's name was not even on the ballot in 10 southern states. Northerners outnumbered southerners and outvoted them.

The Union Is Broken

Lincoln's election brought strong reaction in the South. A South Carolina woman described how the news was received:

> **66** The excitement was very great. Everybody was talking at the same time. One, . . . more moved than the others, stood up—saying . . . 'The die is cast—No more vain regrets—Sad forebodings are useless. The stake is life or death—' . . . No doubt of it. **99**

To many southerners, Lincoln's election meant that the South no longer had a voice in national government. They believed that the President and Congress were now set against their interests—especially slavery. Even before the election, the governor of South Carolina had written to other southern governors. If Lincoln won, he wrote, it would be their duty to leave the Union.

Secession. Senator John Crittenden of Kentucky made a last effort to save the Union. In December 1860, he introduced a bill to extend the Missouri Compromise line to the Pacific. However, slavery in the West was no longer the issue. Many southerners believed that the North had put an abolitionist in the White House. They felt that secession was their only choice.

The first state to secede was South Carolina. On December 20, 1860, delegates to a convention in Charleston voted for secession. By February 1, 1861, Alabama, Florida, Georgia, Louisiana, Mississippi, and Texas had seceded. (See the map on page 453.)

A new nation. The seven states that had seceded held a convention in Montgomery, Alabama, in early 1861. They formed a new nation and named it the ***Confederate States of America.*** Jefferson Davis of Mississippi was named president of the Confederacy.

Most southerners believed that they had every right to secede. After all, the Declaration of Independence said that "it is the right of the people to alter or to abolish" a government that denies the rights of its citizens. Lincoln, they believed, would deny white southerners their right to own slaves.

Few southerners thought that the North would fight to keep the South in the Union. Should war come, however, they expected to win quickly.

War Comes

When Lincoln took the oath of office on March 4, 1861, he faced a dangerous situation. Lincoln warned that "no state . . . can lawfully get out of the Union." He pledged, however, that there would be no war unless the South started it.

Inauguration of Jefferson Davis *Southerners chose Jefferson Davis as president of the Confederate States of America. Here, a crowd watches as Davis takes the oath of office.* **Citizenship** *How was this moment a turning point for the South?*

MAP, GRAPH, AND CHART SKILLS
Reading an Election Map

Maps can show different kinds of information. The election map below shows the results of the 1860 presidential election.

Presidential election maps are useful because they show which states each candidate won. Most presidential election maps are accompanied by circle graphs to show the percentage of the popular vote and the electoral vote that each candidate won.

1. **Decide what is shown on the map and graphs.** (a) What is the subject of the map? (b) What do the four colors stand for? (c) What do the graphs at bottom right show?

2. **Practice using information from the map and graphs.** (a) Which party won nearly all the northern states? (b) Which party won nearly all the southern states? (c) What percentage of the popular vote did the Republican party receive? (d) What percentage of the electoral vote did the Republican party receive? (e) Who was the candidate of the Constitutional Union party? (f) Which states did he win?

3. **Draw conclusions about the election.** Based on the map and graphs, draw conclusions about the election of 1860. (a) How does the map show that sectionalism was important in the election? (b) What did the election show about the political voice of voters in the South?

ACTIVITY Locate the results for the most recent presidential election. Make an election map and two circle graphs for the electoral and the popular votes. Based on the map, do you think sectionalism played an important role in the results?

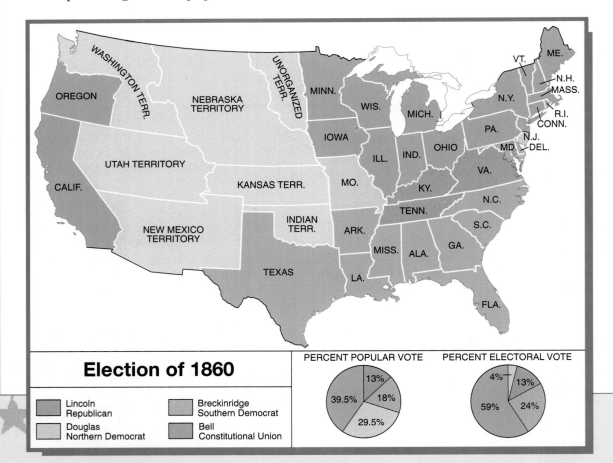

Election of 1860

PERCENT POPULAR VOTE

13%
39.5% 18%
29.5%

PERCENT ELECTORAL VOTE

4% 13%
59% 24%

Lincoln
Republican

Breckinridge
Southern Democrat

Douglas
Northern Democrat

Bell
Constitutional Union

Flags Over Fort Sumter *On April 13, 1861, Confederate troops shot down the Union flag, at right, that flew over Fort Sumter. They then raised the flag of the Confederacy over the fort, as shown in the painting.* **Geography** *Why was the location of Fort Sumter important to the Confederacy?*

Federal forts in the South. The Confederacy had already started seizing federal forts in the South. It felt that the forts were a threat because the United States was now a "foreign" power.

President Lincoln faced a difficult decision. Should he let the Confederates take over federal property? If he did, he would seem to be admitting that states had the right to leave the Union. But if he sent troops to hold the forts, he might start a war. He might also lose the support of the eight slave states that had not seceded.

In April, the Confederacy forced Lincoln to make up his mind. By then, Confederate troops controlled nearly all forts, post offices, and other federal buildings in the South. The Union held only three forts off Florida and one fort in South Carolina.

Opening shots. The fort in South Carolina, **Fort Sumter,** was important because it guarded Charleston Harbor. The Confederacy could not leave it in Union hands. On April 12, 1861, the Confederates asked for the fort's surrender.

Major Robert Anderson, the Union commander, refused to give in. Confederate guns then opened fire. Anderson and his troops quickly ran out of ammunition. On April 13, Anderson surrendered the fort. Amazingly, no one was injured.

As Confederate troops shelled Fort Sumter, people in Charleston gathered on their rooftops to watch. To many, it was like a huge fireworks display. No one knew that the fireworks marked the beginning of a terrible war that would last four years.

SECTION 5 REVIEW

1. **Identify:** (a) John Breckinridge, (b) John Bell, (c) John Crittenden, (d) Confederate States of America, (e) Jefferson Davis, (f) Fort Sumter.
2. Why did the Democratic party split in 1860?
3. What did Lincoln's victory in the 1860 election mean to the South?
4. What difficult decisions did Lincoln face when he became President?
5. Why was Fort Sumter important to the Confederacy?
6. **CRITICAL THINKING Solving Problems** Could the country have avoided war if the North and the South had reached an agreement about slavery in the territories? Explain.

ACTIVITY **Writing to Learn**
Write a campaign slogan for each of the four candidates in the presidential election of 1860.

Summary

- As settlers pushed west, the issue of slavery in the territories caused a growing division between the North and the South.
- The Fugitive Slave Law increased northern opposition to slavery.
- Proslavery and antislavery forces battled for control of Kansas Territory.
- The Republican party opposed expansion of slavery into the western territories.
- After Lincoln was elected President, seven southern states seceded from the Union.

Reviewing the Main Ideas

1. Discuss two moderate solutions to the slavery issue in the Mexican Cession.
2. List the four main parts of the Compromise of 1850.
3. How did *Uncle Tom's Cabin* affect people's view of slavery?
4. (a) What was the Dred Scott decision? (b) How did northerners and southerners view the decision?
5. (a) What plan did Stephen Douglas favor to settle the issue of slavery? (b) Why did Abraham Lincoln disagree with Douglas?
6. How did John Brown's death further divide the North and the South?
7. (a) Why did the Confederacy seize federal forts in the South? (b) Why did Lincoln hesitate to send troops to hold the forts?

Thinking Critically

1. **Linking Past and Present** (a) Why do you think it took months for Congress to pass both the Missouri Compromise and the Compromise of 1850? (b) What issues are difficult for Congress to agree on today?

2. **Defending a Position** If the United States had not expanded to the Pacific Ocean, a civil war would not have occurred. Do you agree with this statement? Explain.

3. **Forecasting** Lincoln said that "no state . . . can lawfully get out of the Union." Why do you think the North would be unwilling to let the South secede peacefully?

Applying Your Skills

1. **Analyzing a Quotation** Review Lincoln's response to Stephen Douglas on page 443. (a) According to Lincoln, what rights were slaves denied? (b) What does Lincoln mean by "the right to eat the bread. . . which his own hand earns"?

2. **Reading an Election Map** Look at the map on page 446. (a) Did Lincoln get electoral votes from states south of the Missouri Compromise line? (b) Did states on the West Coast vote the same way as the North or the South? (c) What evidence is there that border states between the North and South had a unique political outlook?

Thinking About Geography

Match the letters on the map with the following places: **1.** Missouri, **2.** Maine, **3.** California, **4.** Kansas Territory, **5.** Nebraska Territory, **6.** New Mexico Territory, **7.** Utah Territory. **Region** Which area listed above was admitted to the Union as a free state in 1850?

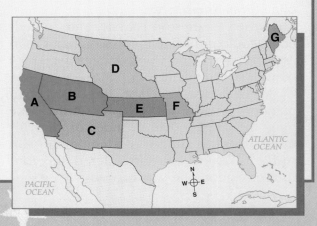

Debating Slavery in the Western Territories

Form into groups to explore the issue of slavery in the western territories. Follow the suggestions below to write, draw, or act to show what you have learned about the attempts to keep the nation together. You may use the textbook, encyclopedias, atlases, or other materials in your classroom library to complete the tasks. Be able to name your sources of information when you have finished the activity.

CARTOGRAPHERS On a large sheet of paper, create a map of the United States after the admission of California in 1850.
- Label the free states in one color.
- Label the slave states in another color.
- Add the date on which each state was admitted to the Union.

Notice of meeting to protest Fugitive Slave Law

WRITERS Form into groups to write textbook entries for a younger child in which you explain each of the following: Missouri Compromise, Compromise of 1850, Fugitive Slave Law of 1850, Kansas-Nebraska Act, Dred Scott decision. Illustrate your entries with maps, graphs, charts, and pictures.

ARTISTS Divide into two groups: northern artists and southern artists. Have each group of artists create a political cartoon from the point of view of their group about one of the following: Missouri Compromise, Compromise of 1850, Bleeding Kansas, Dred Scott decision.

Handcuffs and shackles

HISTORIANS List the important events and the attempts at compromise that led up to the Civil War, starting with the Missouri Compromise in 1820. Then use your list to make a time line of events leading to the Civil War. Be prepared to explain the significance of each event.

REPORTERS Create a "debate page" for an 1850s newspaper. Summarize background information, conduct and record "people in the street" interviews, draw cartoons, and write opposing editorials about one of the following: Missouri Compromise, Kansas-Nebraska Act, Compromise of 1850.

★ Display each group's activity on a Debating Slavery in the Western Territories bulletin board.

Border Ruffians voting in Kansas

Torn by War

(1861–1865)

1862 *Union and Confederate soldiers met in the Battle of Antietam. With over 23,000 casualties, Antietam was one of the bloodiest battles of the Civil War.*

1861 *The Civil War began when the Confederates seized Fort Sumter. The South soon adopted the "Stars and Bars" as its flag.*

1863 *President Lincoln issued the Emancipation Proclamation. It stated that all slaves in lands controlled by the Confederacy were now free.*

| 1861 | 1862 | 1863 |

WORLD EVENT
1861 Russian ruler frees serfs

WORLD EVENT
1862 Britain denies recognition to Confederacy

Chapter Setting

"I have just...heard a sermon... to the graduating class [of West Point].... There is a certain hymn that is always sung...the last Sunday that graduates attend church here. It commences 'When shall we meet again?'... And everyone felt the truth of the concluding words, 'Never, no more,' for in all probability in another year, the half of them may be in their graves...."

Tully McCrea, a young cadet, included this moving account in a letter to his sweetheart, Belle. President Lincoln had recently issued a call for troops to put down what he considered a revolt in the South. Now, the graduating class at West Point, the academy where army officers were trained, was preparing to take up arms.

The young men who had studied together would soon become enemies. Some would fight for the Union. Others would join the Confederacy.

Tully McCrea's own family was divided in its loyalties. Orphaned at a young age, Tully and a brother grew up with relatives in Ohio. Another brother and a sister grew up on a southern plantation. "My sister and aunt would rather see me dead in my grave than see me remain in the North," wrote Tully. "We are destined to have a long and bloody civil war, in which brother will be fighting against brother," he predicted.

McCrea was correct. The Civil War lasted four years. More Americans died than in any other war the nation has fought.

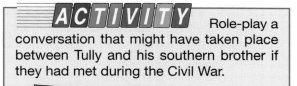

ACTIVITY Role-play a conversation that might have taken place between Tully and his southern brother if they had met during the Civil War.

1864 *News of Union victories helped Lincoln win reelection. Lincoln supporters carried lanterns like this one during nighttime parades.*

1865 *The Civil War ended with the surrender of the Confederates at Appomattox Courthouse. Here, defeated southern troops tearfully roll up their flag.*

1863

1864

1865

WORLD EVENT
1864 First Red Cross societies established in Europe

1
Preparing for War

FIND OUT

■ How did the states choose sides?

■ What resources for war did each side have?

■ Who were the leaders of each side?

A few days after Fort Sumter fell, President Lincoln called for 75,000 volunteers to serve as soldiers for 90 days in a campaign against the South. The response was overwhelming. Throughout the North, crowds cheered the Stars and Stripes and booed the southern "traitors." Said a New Englander, "The whole population, men, women, and children, seem to be in the streets. . . . The people have gone stark mad!"

In the South, the scene was much the same. Southerners rallied to the Stars and Bars, as they called the new Confederate flag. Volunteers flooded into the Confederate army.

With flags held high, both sides marched off to war. Most felt certain that a single, gallant battle would resolve the issue. Few suspected that the North and South were entering on a long civil war—the most destructive war in the nation's history.

A Nation Divided

As the war began, each side was convinced of the justice of its cause. Southerners believed that they had the right to leave the Union. In fact, they called the conflict the War for Southern Independence. Northerners believed just as firmly that they had to fight to save the Union.

Choosing sides was most difficult in the eight slave states that were still in the Union

in April 1861. (See the map at right.) Four of these states—Virginia,* North Carolina, Tennessee, and Arkansas—quickly joined the Confederacy. But in the remaining states—Delaware, Kentucky, Missouri, and Maryland—many citizens favored the Union. These states were known as the border states. From the start, Delaware supported the Union. The other border states wavered between the North and the South. In time, all three decided to remain in the Union.

The Two Sides

In 1861, neither the North nor the South was prepared to fight a war. As the two sides rushed to build their armies, each had advantages and disadvantages. (See the chart on page 454.)

The South. The South had the key advantage of fighting a defensive war. It was up to the North to attack and defeat the South. If it did not, the Confederacy would become a separate country.

Defending their homeland gave southerners a strong reason to fight. "Our men must prevail in combat," one Confederate said, "or they will lose their property, country, freedom—in short, everything."

Southerners had skills that made them good soldiers. Hunting was an important part of southern life. From an early age, boys learned to ride horses and use guns. Wealthy young men often went to military school. Before the Civil War, many of the best officers in the United States Army were from the South.

The South, however, also had serious weaknesses. It had few factories to produce weapons, railroad tracks, and other vital supplies. Before the war, southerners bought most manufactured goods from the

---

*In the western part of Virginia, many people supported the Union. When Virginia seceded, the westerners formed their own government. They joined the Union as West Virginia in 1863.

In April 1861, eight slave states were still in the Union. As war began, these states had to choose sides in the struggle.
1. Which states eventually seceded?
2. Which states stayed in the Union?
3. **Forecasting** How do you think that the decision of some slave states to remain in the Union might have affected Union goals in the war? Explain.

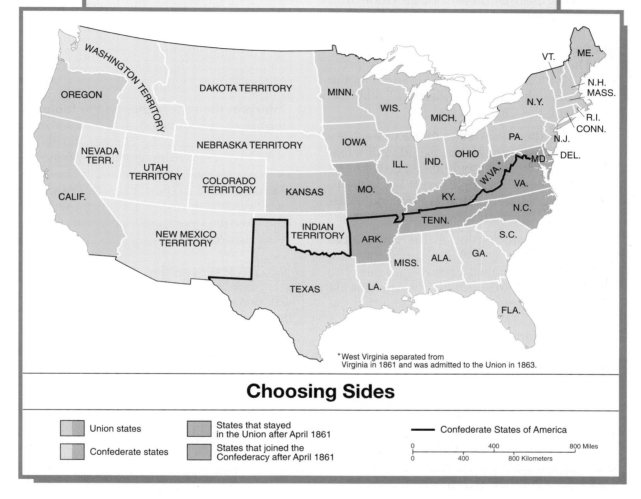

*West Virginia separated from Virginia in 1861 and was admitted to the Union in 1863.

Choosing Sides

- Union states
- Confederate states
- States that stayed in the Union after April 1861
- States that joined the Confederacy after April 1861
- —— Confederate States of America

0 400 800 Miles
0 400 800 Kilometers

North or from Europe. The South also had few railroads to move troops and supplies. The railroads that it did have often did not connect to one another.

Finally, the South had a small population. Only about 9 million people lived in the Confederacy, compared with 22 million in the Union. More than one third of the population was enslaved. As a result, the South had fewer people eligible to become soldiers or able to support the war effort.

The North. The North had almost four times as many free citizens as the South. Thus, it had a large source of volunteers. It also had many people to grow food and to work in factories making supplies.

Industry was the North's greatest resource. Northern factories made 90 percent of the nation's manufactured goods. These factories quickly began making supplies for the Union army. The North also had more than 70 percent of the nation's rail lines.

MAP, GRAPH, AND CHART SKILLS
Reading a Table

A table is used to present information in a way that is quick and easy to understand. Tables often present numbers or statistics. The numbers are set up in columns and rows.

The table below compares the resources of the North and South in 1861. Studying the table can help you to understand why the North won the Civil War.

1. **Identify the information in the table.** Note that the resources are measured in different ways. For example, population is measured in thousands of people. (a) What is the title of the table? (b) How is farmland measured? (c) How is railroad track measured?

2. **Read the information in the table.** Note that the table has five columns. The first column shows what each resource is. The second and third columns give the amount and percentage of each resource that the North had. The fourth and fifth columns give the same information for the South. (a) How many factories did the South have? (b) What percentage of the national total of factories did the South have?

(c) What percentage of the nation's railroad track did the North have?

3. **Compare the information in the table.** Use the chart to compare the resources of the North and South. (a) Which side had more workers in industry? (b) How many acres of farmland did each side have? (c) In which resource did the South come closest to equaling the North?

4. **Interpret the information in the table.** Interpret the information in the table based on your reading of the chapter. (a) Which side had the advantage in all of the resources shown? (b) How might these advantages have helped that side during the war? (c) Which resource do you think was the most important during the war? Explain your answer.

ACTIVITY Make a chart with two columns, labeled Battles Won by the North and Battles Won by the South. Include the date and location of each battle. Then make a statement that compares the two sides of the chart.

Resources of the North and South, 1861

Resources	North		South	
	Number	Percent of Total	Number	Percent of Total
Farmland	105,835 acres	65%	56,832 acres	35%
Railroad Track	21,847 miles	71%	8,947 miles	29%
Value of Manufactured Goods	$1,794,417,000	92%	$155,552,000	8%
Factories	119,500	85%	20,600	15%
Workers in Industry	1,198,000	92%	111,000	8%
Population	22,340,000	63%	9,103,000 (3,954,000 slaves)	37%

Source: *Historical Statistics of the United States*

The North also had a strong navy and a large fleet of private trading ships. With few warships and only a small commercial fleet, the South could do little to hurt the Union at sea.

Despite these advantages, the North faced a difficult military challenge. To bring the South back into the Union, northern soldiers had to conquer a huge area. Instead of defending their homes, they were invading unfamiliar land.

Wartime Leaders

The outcome of the war also depended on leadership. Presidents Abraham Lincoln in the North and Jefferson Davis in the South, as well as military leaders on both sides, played key roles in determining who won the war.

President Davis. Many people thought Davis was a stronger leader than Lincoln. Davis had attended West Point and served as an officer in the Mexican War. Later, he served as Secretary of War under President Franklin Pierce. Davis was widely respected for his honesty and courage.

Davis, however, did not like to turn over to others the details of day-to-day military planning. When Davis made a decision, he "could not understand any other man coming to a different conclusion," in the words of his wife. As a result, Davis wasted time arguing with his advisers.

President Lincoln. At first, some northerners had doubts about Abraham Lincoln's ability to lead. He had little experience in national politics or military matters. In time, however, Lincoln proved to be a patient but strong leader and a fine war planner.

Marching Off to War *Patriotic feeling was strong on both sides as the Civil War began. Here, the 7th New York Regiment marches proudly off to war.* **Citizenship** *Name two advantages the North had as war began.*

Lee and His Generals *Strong military leadership was one of the South's chief advantages in the Civil War. Here, Confederate generals meet on a hillside. Robert E. Lee is at right, on a white horse.* **Citizenship** *Why did Lee refuse when Lincoln asked him to command the Union army?*

Day by day, Lincoln gained the respect of those around him. Many especially liked his sense of humor. They noted that Lincoln even accepted criticism with a smile. When Secretary of War Edwin Stanton called Lincoln a fool, Lincoln commented, "Did Stanton say I was a fool? Then I must be one, for Stanton is generally right and he always says what he means."

Linking Past and Present
A Union official, Simon Cameron, decided to get even with Lee for siding with the Confederacy. He ordered Lee's plantation home in Arlington, Virginia, to be used as a burial ground for Union soldiers. Later, the government declared Arlington a national cemetery, and thousands of veterans of foreign wars are honored by burial there.

Choosing sides. After Fort Sumter fell, army officers in the South had to make a choice. They could stay in the Union army and fight against their home states. Or they could join the Confederate forces.

Robert E. Lee faced this kind of decision when his home state of Virginia seceded. President Lincoln asked Lee to command the Union army. Although he disliked slavery and had opposed secession, Lee refused. He explained in a letter to a friend:

> 66I cannot raise my hand against my birthplace, my home, my children. I should like, above all things, that our difficulties might be peaceably arranged. . . . What ever may be the result of the contest, I foresee that the country will have to pass through a terrible ordeal. 99

Lee later became commander of the Confederate army.

SECTION 1 REVIEW

1. **Locate:** (a) Virginia, (b) Delaware, (c) Kentucky, (d) Missouri, (e) Maryland.
2. **Identify:** (a) Jefferson Davis, (b) Edwin Stanton, (c) Robert E. Lee.
3. (a) Name the eight slave states that were still in the Union in April 1861. (b) Which of these states remained in the Union?
4. Name two strengths and two weaknesses that each of the following had as a leader: (a) Jefferson Davis, (b) Abraham Lincoln.
5. **CRITICAL THINKING Comparing** (a) Compare the advantages and disadvantages of the North and South at the beginning of the war. (b) Which side do you think was better equipped to fight a long war? Explain.

ACTIVITY **Writing to Learn**
Imagine that you are Robert E. Lee at the beginning of the Civil War. Write a diary entry exploring your feelings about the war.

2

The Struggle Begins

FIND OUT

■ What were the military aims of each side?

■ Who won the early battles?

■ How did the Union achieve two of its three war aims?

In the summer of 1861, the armies of both the North and the South marched off to war with flags flying and drums rolling. Each side expected to win and to win quickly. The reality of war soon shattered this dream. Abner Small, a volunteer from Maine, described a scene that would be repeated again and again:

    66 I can see today, as I saw then, the dead and hurt men lying limp on the ground. . . . From somewhere across the field a battery pounded us. . . . We wavered, and rallied, and fired blindly; and men fell writhing. 99

It soon became clear that there would be no quick, easy end to the war. Leaders on both sides began to plan for a long, difficult struggle.

Strategies for Victory

Fighting during the Civil War took place in three major areas: the East, the West, and at sea. Union war plans involved all three areas.

Union plans. First, the Union planned to blockade southern ports. They wanted to cut off the South's supply of manufactured goods by halting its trade with Europe. Second, in the West, the Union planned to seize control of the Mississippi River. This would keep the South from using the river to sup-

ply its troops. It would also separate Arkansas, Texas, and Louisiana from the rest of the Confederacy. Finally, in the East, Union generals wanted to seize Richmond, Virginia, and capture the Confederate government headquartered there.

Confederate plans. The South's strategy was simpler: The Confederate army would stay at home and fight a defensive war. Northerners, they believed, would quickly tire of fighting. If the war became unpopular in the North, President Lincoln would have to give up the effort to bring the South back into the Union.

Southerners counted on European money and supplies to help fight the war. Southern cotton was important to the textile mills of England and other countries. Confederates were confident that Europeans would quickly recognize the South as an independent nation and continue to buy southern cotton for their factories.

Forward to Richmond!

"Forward to Richmond! Forward to Richmond!" Every day for more than a month, the influential *New York Tribune* blazed this "Nation's War-Cry" across its front page. Throughout the North, people were impatient. Sure of a quick victory, they called for an attack on Richmond, the Confederate capital.

A clash of untrained troops. Responding to popular pressure, President Lincoln ordered the attack. In July 1861, Union soldiers set out from Washington, D.C., for Richmond, about 100 miles (160 km) away. They had barely left Washington, however, when they clashed with the Confederates. The battle took place near a small stream called Bull Run, in Virginia. (See the map on page 459.)

July 21, 1861, was a lovely summer day. Hundreds of Washingtonians rode out to watch the battle, many of them carrying picnic baskets. In a holiday mood, they spread

THE EAGLE'S NEST.
"THE UNION; IT MUST AND SHALL BE PRESERVED."

Guarding the Nest *Northerners viewed the Civil War as a fight to protect the Union from southern "traitors." In this 1861 cartoon, the American eagle reacts swiftly as dragons, serpents, and other "traitors" emerge from Confederate "eggs."* **Culture** *How did southerners view the Civil War?*

out on a grassy hilltop overlooking Bull Run. They were eager to see Union troops crush the Confederates.

The spectators, however, were disappointed. Southern troops did not turn and run as expected. Inspired by the example of General Thomas Jackson, they held their ground. A Confederate officer remarked that Jackson was standing "like a stone wall." From then on, the general was known as "Stonewall" Jackson.

A Union retreat. In the end, it was Union troops that retreated. One observer reported:

66Off they went. . . across fields, toward the woods, anywhere, everywhere, to escape. . . . To enable them better to run, they threw away their blankets, knapsacks, canteens, and finally muskets, cartridge-boxes, and everything else.99

The Confederates did not pursue the fleeing Union army. Had they done so, they might even have captured Washington, D.C. Instead, they remained behind to gather the gear thrown away by the panicked Union troops.

The ***Battle of Bull Run*** showed both sides that their soldiers needed training. It also showed that the war would be long and bloody.

"All quiet along the Potomac." After the disaster at Bull Run, President Lincoln appointed General George McClellan as commander of the Union armies. McClellan was a superb organizer. In six months, he transformed a mob of raw recruits into an army of trained soldiers.

McClellan, however, was very cautious. He delayed leading his troops into battle. Newspapers reported "all quiet along the Potomac" so often that the phrase became a national joke. Finally, President Lincoln lost patience. "If McClellan is not using the army," the President snapped, "I should like to borrow it."

A cautious move on Richmond. In March 1862, McClellan was at last ready to move. He and most of the Union army left Washington by steamboat and sailed down the Potomac River for Richmond. (See the map on page 459.) The rest of the army stayed in Washington.

Landing south of Richmond, McClellan began inching slowly toward the Confederate capital. Learning of the Union approach, General Robert E. Lee launched a series of brilliant counterattacks. Lee also sent General Stonewall Jackson north to threaten Washington. Lincoln was thus prevented from sending the rest of the Union army to help McClellan.

Cautious as usual, McClellan decided to abandon the attack and retreated. Once again, there was a lull in the war in the East.

Naval Action

Early in the war, Union ships blockaded southern ports. At first, enterprising southerners slipped through the blockade in small, fast ships. These "blockade runners" brought everything from matches to guns into the Confederacy.

In time, however, the blockade became more effective. Trade through southern ports dropped by more than 90 percent. The South desperately needed a way to break the Union blockade. One method it tried was the ironclad ship. (See Exploring Technology, on pages 460 and 461.)

At the start of the war, the Union abandoned a warship named the **Merrimack** near Portsmouth, Virginia. Confederates covered the ship with iron plates 4 inches thick and sent it into battle against the Union navy. On March 8, 1862, the *Merrimack* sank one Union ship, drove another aground, and forced a third to surrender. Their cannonballs bounced harmlessly off the *Merrimack*'s metal skin.

The Union countered with its own ironclads. One of these, the **Monitor,** struck back at the *Merrimack* in the waters off Hampton Roads, Virginia. The Confederate ship had more firepower, but the *Monitor* maneuvered more easily. In the end, neither ship seriously damaged the other, and both withdrew.

Ironclad ships changed naval warfare. Both sides rushed to build more of them. However, the South never mounted a seri-

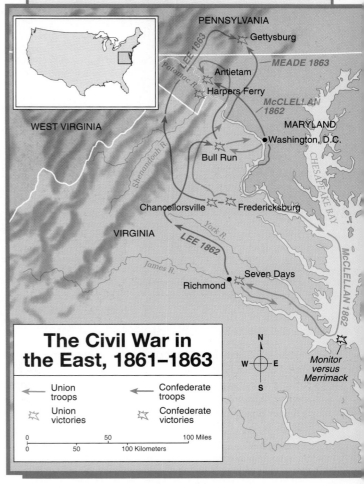

MAP STUDY

Early in the war, General Lee led the Confederate army to one victory after another in the East.
1. What victories did Lee win in the East in 1862?
2. Who claimed victory at Antietam?
3. **Applying Information** Based on the subsection Naval Action, locate Hampton Roads, Virginia, on the map.

The Civil War in the East, 1861–1863

← Union troops
← Confederate troops
✫ Union victories
✫ Confederate victories

0   50   100 Miles
0   50   100 Kilometers

ous attack against the Union navy. The Union blockade held throughout the war.

Antietam

In September 1862, General Lee took the offensive and marched his troops north into Maryland. He believed that a southern

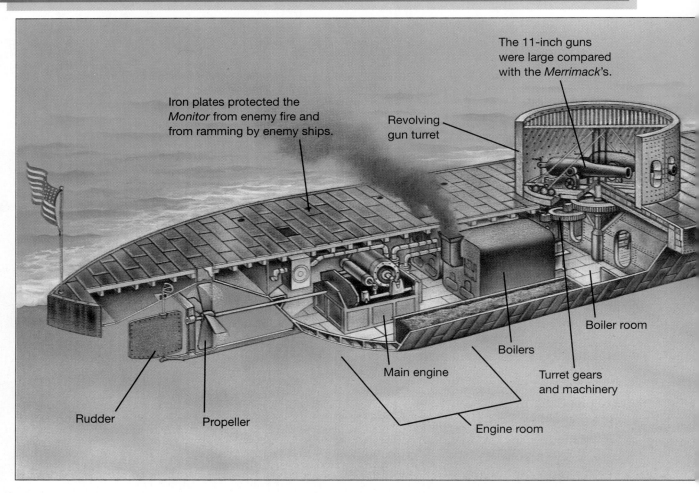

The 11-inch guns were large compared with the *Merrimack*'s.

Iron plates protected the *Monitor* from enemy fire and from ramming by enemy ships.

Revolving gun turret

Boiler room

Boilers

Turret gears and machinery

Main engine

Engine room

Rudder

Propeller

Ironclad Ship *The* Monitor, *the first Union ironclad ship, looked like a "tin can on a raft." Its most unusual feature was the revolving gun turret, which made it possible to fire at the enemy from any angle. Before this, a captain might have had to turn his entire ship around in order to reach his target. In the picture at right, the* Monitor *is shown engaging the* Merrimack, *a Confederate ironclad.* **Technology** *What other advantages did ironclads offer?*

victory on northern soil would be a great blow to northern morale. Luck was not on Lee's side, however. A Confederate messenger lost Lee's battle plans. Two Union soldiers found them and turned them over to McClellan.

Even with Lee's battle plan before him, McClellan was slow to act. After waiting a few days, he finally attacked Lee's main force at Antietam (an TEET uhm) on September 17. In the daylong battle that followed, more than 23,000 Union and Confederate soldiers were killed or wounded.

On the night of September 18, Lee ordered his troops to slip back into Virginia. The Confederates breathed a sigh of relief when they saw that McClellan was not pursuing them.

Neither side won a clear victory at the **Battle of Antietam.** Because Lee had or

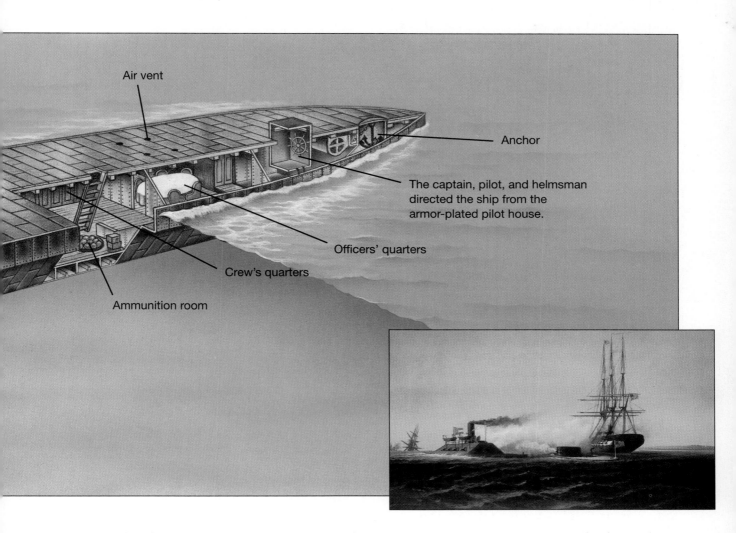

Air vent

Anchor

The captain, pilot, and helmsman directed the ship from the armor-plated pilot house.

Officers' quarters

Crew's quarters

Ammunition room

dered his forces to withdraw, however, the North claimed victory.

Winning the Mississippi

While McClellan hesitated in the East, Union forces gained ground in the West. As you have read, the Union war plan called for the North to gain control of the Mississippi River. General Ulysses S. Grant began moving toward that goal. (See the map on page 474.) In February 1862, Grant attacked and captured Fort Henry and Fort Donelson in Tennessee. These Confederate forts guarded two important tributaries of the Mississippi.

Shiloh. Grant now pushed south to Shiloh, a small village located on the Tennessee River. At Shiloh, on April 6, he was surprised by Confederate forces. Only after reinforcements arrived was Grant able to beat back the enemy.

The *Battle of Shiloh* was one of the bloodiest battles of the Civil War. More Americans were killed or wounded at Shiloh than in the American Revolution, the War of 1812, and the Mexican War combined.

The fall of Vicksburg. While Grant was fighting at Shiloh, the Union navy moved to gain control of the Mississippi River. In April 1862, Union gunboats captured the city of New Orleans. Other ships seized Memphis,

The Siege of Vicksburg *Here, Grant first attacks Vicksburg. Six weeks later, the city surrendered. Defeat was made more bitter by the date of surrender—July 4. Vicksburg did not celebrate Independence Day again until 1945.* **Geography** *Why did the Union want to control Vicksburg?*

Tennessee. The Union now controlled both ends of the river. The South could no longer use the Mississippi as a supply line.

However, the North could not safely use the river, either. Confederates still held Vicksburg, Mississippi. *Vicksburg* sat on a cliff high above the river. Cannons there could shell boats traveling between New Orleans and Memphis.

Early in 1863, Grant's forces tried again and again to seize Vicksburg. The Confederates held out bravely. At last, Grant devised a brilliant plan. Marching his troops inland, he launched a surprise attack on Jackson, Mississippi. Then, he turned and attacked Vicksburg from the rear. After a six-week siege, Vicksburg finally surrendered on July 4, 1863.

The Union had achieved two of its military goals. First, its naval blockade had cut off the South's trade with Europe. Second, by taking control of the Mississippi River, the Union had split the Confederacy into two parts.

SECTION 2 REVIEW

1. **Locate:** (a) Richmond, (b) Washington, D.C., (c) Potomac River, (d) Fort Henry, (e) Fort Donelson, (f) New Orleans, (g) Memphis, (h) Vicksburg.
2. **Identify:** (a) Stonewall Jackson, (b) Battle of Bull Run, (c) George McClellan, (d) *Merrimack,* (e) *Monitor,* (f) Battle of Antietam, (g) Ulysses S. Grant, (h) Battle of Shiloh.
3. Describe the North's three-part plan for defeating the South.
4. What did both sides learn from the Battle of Bull Run?
5. **CRITICAL THINKING Analyzing Ideas** "The South could win the war by not losing, but the North could win only by winning." What does this statement mean?

ACTIVITY **Writing to Learn**
Study the drawing of the *Monitor* on page 460. Write two sentences describing features of the ship that would make it effective in naval battles.

3
Freedom

FIND OUT
- Why did Lincoln issue the Emancipation Proclamation?
- How did Union war goals change?
- How did African Americans contribute to the Union war effort?

VOCABULARY emancipate

At first, the Civil War was not a war against slavery. Yet wherever Union troops went, enslaved African Americans rushed to them, expecting to be freed. Most were sorely disappointed. Union officers often held these runaways prisoner until their masters arrived to take them back to slavery.

Some northerners began to raise new questions. Would the North support slavery by sending runaways back to their owners? Was slavery not the root of the conflict between North and South? Had tens of thousands of men died to bring a slaveholding South back into the Union? As a result of questions such as these, the mood of the North began to change.

"Forever Free"

The Civil War began as a war to restore the Union, not to end slavery. President Lincoln made this clear in the following statement:

66 If I could save the Union without freeing any slave, I would do it; and if I could save it by freeing all the slaves, I would do it; and if I could do it by freeing some and leaving others alone, I would also do that. **99**

Lincoln had a reason for handling the slavery issue cautiously. As you have read, four slave states remained in the Union. The President did not want to do anything that might cause these states to shift their loyalty to the Confederacy. The resources of these border states might allow the South to turn the tide of the war.

Addressing the issue of slavery. By mid-1862, however, Lincoln came to believe that he could save the Union only by broadening the goals of the war. He decided to free enslaved African Americans living in the Confederacy. In the four loyal slave states, however, slaves would not be freed. Nor would slaves be freed in Confederate lands that had already been captured by the Union, such as New Orleans.

Abraham Lincoln and Son Tad *President Lincoln believed that his most important job was to save the Union, not to end slavery. He felt deeply, however, that slavery was "a moral, social, and political wrong."* **Citizenship** *Why did Lincoln handle the slavery issue cautiously?*

Lincoln had practical reasons for this approach. He wanted to weaken the Confederacy without angering slave owners in the Union. Also, Lincoln was not sure whether most northerners would support freedom for enslaved African Americans. He hoped to introduce the idea slowly, by limiting it to territory controlled by the Confederacy.

The President had another motive, too. As you have read in Chapter 15, Lincoln believed that slavery was wrong. When he felt that he could act to free slaves without threatening the Union, he did so.

Lincoln was concerned about the timing of his announcement. He did not want Americans to think he was freeing slaves as a last, desperate effort to save a losing cause. He waited for a Union victory to announce his plan. The Battle of Antietam gave Lincoln his chance.

Issuing the Proclamation. On September 22, 1862, Lincoln issued a preliminary proclamation. It warned that on January 1, 1863, anyone held as a slave in a state still in rebellion against the United States would be emancipated. To emancipate means to set free.

Then, on January 1, 1863, Lincoln issued the formal ***Emancipation Proclamation.*** The Emancipation Proclamation declared:

> **66** On the 1st day of January, in the year of our Lord 1863, all persons held as slaves within any state or. . . part of a state [whose] people. . . shall then be in rebellion against the United States, shall be then, thenceforward, and forever free. **99**

Since the rebelling states were not under Union control, no slaves actually gained freedom on January 1, 1863. Still, the Emancipation Proclamation changed the character of the war. Now, Union troops were fighting to end slavery as well as to save the Union.

Many Europeans applauded the Proclamation. As a result, it became less likely that Britain or any other European country would come to the aid of the South. The

Waiting for the Hour *The Emancipation Proclamation went into effect at midnight, January 1, 1863. This painting shows a gathering of enslaved African Americans waiting for the hour to strike.* **Citizenship** *Which slaves were affected by the Emancipation Proclamation? Which were not affected?*

Johnny Rebs *Most of the soldiers in both armies were between the ages of 18 and 21. Some were even younger. The flag bearer in this picture of a Confederate artillery unit was not yet 16 years old.* **Linking Past and Present** *Could a 16-year-old serve in the armed forces today? Explain.*

ty is a soldier who is killed or seriously wounded.

In one battle, Union troops knew that they were greatly outnumbered. Each soldier wrote his name on a slip of paper and pinned it to his uniform. The soldiers wanted to make sure that their bodies could be identified when the battle was over.

Crude medical care. Soldiers who were sick, wounded, or captured faced other horrors. Medical care on the battlefield was crude. Surgeons routinely cut off the injured arms and legs of wounded men.

Many minor wounds became infected. With no medicines to fight infection, half the wounded died. Diseases like pneumonia and malaria swept through the camps, killing more men than guns or cannons did.

Prison camps. On both sides, prisoners of war faced appalling conditions. At Andersonville, a prison camp in Georgia, more than one Union prisoner out of three died of starvation or disease. One prisoner wrote:

66There is no such thing as delicacy here.... In the middle of last night I was awakened by being kicked by a dying man. He was soon dead. I got up and moved the body off a few feet, and again went to sleep to dream of the hideous sights.99

Discord in the North

Not everyone in the North supported the war. Some northerners thought the South should be allowed to leave the Union. Others favored calling a peace conference to work out a compromise with the South. Supporters of the war called these people *Copperheads,* after the poisonous snake.

Other northerners wanted to save the Union but opposed the way Lincoln was conducting the war. In the border states, many slave owners openly supported the South.

Filling the ranks. By 1863, with no end in sight, northerners became discouraged. Soon, there were not enough volunteers to fill the ranks of the Union army. The Union had been giving $100 bounties, or payments, to men who enlisted. Now, it raised the bounty to more than $300. Still, there were not enough volunteers. The government decided to take new measures.

In 1863, Congress passed a draft law. The draft required all able-bodied males between the ages of 20 and 45 to serve in the military if they were called. A man could avoid the draft by paying the government $300 or by hiring someone to serve in his place. This angered many people who could not afford the $300. They began to see the Civil War as "a rich man's war and a poor man's fight."

Riots in the cities. The draft law went into effect just a few months after President Lincoln signed the Emancipation Proclamation. As a result, some northerners believed that they were being forced to fight to end slavery. Riots broke out in several cities.

The worst riot took place in New York City during July 1863. For four days, white workers attacked free blacks. Rioters also attacked rich New Yorkers who had paid to avoid serving in the army. At least 74 people were killed during the riot.

Lincoln moved to stop the draft riots and other "disloyal practices." Several times, he suspended habeas corpus (HAY bee uhs KOR puhs), the right to have a hearing before being jailed. When people protested his action, Lincoln referred them to the Constitution. It gave him the power, he said, to deny people their rights "when in the cases of rebellion or invasion, the public safety may require it."

Trouble in the Confederacy

The Confederacy had its share of problems, too. In some areas of the South, such as eastern Tennessee, thousands of citizens opposed the war.

Jefferson Davis faced problems in creating a strong federal government in the South. Many southerners believed strongly in the idea of states' rights. They resisted paying taxes to a central government. They also did not give full cooperation on military or other matters. At one point, Georgia threatened to secede from the Confederacy!

Like the North, the South faced a shortage of soldiers. As early as 1862, the South passed a draft law. Under the law, men who owned or supervised more than 20 slaves

Lottery Wheel *Desperate for troops, the Union passed a draft law in 1863. In Wilmington, Delaware, this glass-sided lottery wheel was used to select the names of those who would serve.* **Citizenship** *Why did the draft law lead to rioting in some cities?*

did not have to serve in the army. This caused much resentment among the South's small farmers. Most of them owned no slaves, or only a few slaves. They felt it was unfair that they had to fight to preserve slavery and slave owners did not.

Toward the end of the war, the South was unable to replace soldiers killed or wounded in battle—or the thousands who deserted. There simply were not enough white men to fill the ranks. Robert E. Lee urged the Confederacy to let enslaved African Americans serve as soldiers. The Confederate congress finally agreed to Lee's plan. However, the war ended before any enslaved people put on gray uniforms.

War Boosts the Northern Economy

The Civil War cost far more than any earlier war. Both sides needed to find ways to pay for it.

Raising money in the North. In 1861, Congress passed the nation's first income tax law. It required all workers to pay a small part of their wages to the federal government.

The North also raised money by taxing luxuries like carriages, jewelry, and billiard tables. In addition, the Union issued bonds worth millions of dollars to help finance the war. People who bought bonds were in effect lending money to the Union.

Rising prices. Even with new taxes and bonds, however, the Union did not have enough money to pay for the war. To get the funds it needed, the North printed more than $400 million in paper money. People called these dollars "greenbacks" because of their color.

The flood of greenbacks soon led to inflation, a rise in prices caused by an increase in the amount of money in circulation. As the money supply increased, each dollar was worth less. To make up for this, merchants charged more for their goods. During the war, prices for goods nearly doubled in the North.

An economic boost. In some ways, the war helped the North's economy. Because many farmers went off to fight, there was a greater need for machines to plant and harvest crops. Northern farmers bought 165,000 reapers during the war, compared to a few thousand the year before the war began. Farm production actually went up during the war.

Wartime demand for clothing, shoes, guns, and other goods brought a boom to many northern industries. Some northern manufacturers made fortunes by profiteering. Profiteers overcharged the government for goods desperately needed for the war.

Hard Times in the South

The South had great trouble raising money for the war. The Confederate congress passed an income tax as well as a tax-in-kind. The tax-in-kind required farmers to turn over one tenth of their crops to the government. The government decided to take crops because it knew that southern farmers had little cash to spare.

The economy suffers. Like the North, the South also printed paper money. It printed so much, in fact, that wild inflation set in. By 1865, one Confederate dollar was worth only two cents in gold.

The war damaged the southern economy, especially the cotton trade. Cotton was the South's main source of income. Early in the war, Jefferson Davis halted cotton shipments to Britain. He was sure that Britain would side with the South in order to get cotton. The tactic backfired, however. Britain simply bought more cotton from Egypt and India. Davis succeeded only in cutting the South's income.

Effects of the blockade. The Union blockade hurt the South badly. It created severe shortages for both soldiers and civilians. By 1865, famine stalked the Confederacy. Even the wealthy went hungry. "I had a little piece of bread and a little molasses today for my dinner," wrote South Carolina plantation mistress Mary Boykin Chesnut in her diary.

The South spent precious dollars buying weapons in Europe. However, the blockade kept most from being delivered. When the southern troops won a battle, they had to scour the field for guns and unused bullets. Southerners hurried to build weapons factories, but the shortages continued.

Even when supplies were available, the South had trouble getting them to their troops. Union armies ripped up railroad tracks, and the South had few parts to make repairs. Soldiers sometimes waited weeks for food and clothing.

Supporting the War Effort *In both the North and South, women formed aid societies to support the war effort. Women in Chicago made and sold the antislavery potholders at left. In Richmond, women crafted the Confederate flag at right out of paper roses.* **Citizenship** *Why was the support of people on the home front so important to both sides?*

Women at War

In both the North and South, women took over jobs as men left for the battlefields. "Women were in the field everywhere," wrote a northern traveler in 1863. They were "driving the reapers. . . and loading grain. . . a very unusual sight [before the war]." As the northern economy geared up for war production, women also took jobs in factories.

Soldiers and spies. There were some women who helped the war effort more directly. In April 1861, Susan Lear wrote to the governor of Virginia:

> 66 Send me a good Musket, Rifle, or double barrel Shot Gun. I think I would prefer the latter as I am acquainted with its use. I believe, Sir, if a Regiment of Yankees were to come we [women] would drive them away. 99

A few women disguised themselves as soldiers and fought in battle. Others served as spies.

Nursing the wounded. Women on both sides volunteered to work as nurses. Untrained women had served as nurses during the Revolution and in the Mexican War. During the Civil War, doctors were unwilling at first to permit even trained nurses to work in military hospitals. When wounded men began to swamp army hospitals, however, this attitude changed.

History and You
In 1863, women in Chicago collected 30,000 boxes of supplies for the Union troops. When the government did not have enough money to ship the supplies to the front, the women raised $100,000—far more than needed— by selling home-made items at a giant fair. Have you ever organized a fair or similar project to raise money for a cause?

Dorothea Dix, famous for her work reforming prisons and mental hospitals, became superintendent of nurses for the Union army. She set such strict rules for her nurses that they called her Dragon Dix. Dix, however, was just as hard on herself, toiling alongside the women she enlisted.

Clara Barton earned fame as a Civil War nurse and founder of the American Red Cross. Barton kept records on hundreds of wounded soldiers. She helped many families trace sons and husbands who were missing in action. Sojourner Truth, the antislavery leader, worked in Union hospitals and in camps for freed slaves.

In the South, Sally Louisa Tompkins opened a hospital in Richmond, Virginia. Of the 1,333 patients treated in Tompkins's hospital, only 73 died—an excellent record for the time.

SECTION 4 REVIEW

1. **Identify:** (a) Copperhead, (b) Dorothea Dix, (c) Clara Barton, (d) Sojourner Truth, (e) Sally Louisa Tompkins.
2. **Define:** (a) civilian, (b) bounty, (c) draft, (d) habeas corpus, (e) inflation, (f) profiteer, (g) tax-in-kind.
3. How did technology make Civil War battles deadlier than battles of earlier wars?
4. (a) Why did many northerners see the Civil War as "a rich man's war and a poor man's fight"? (b) Why did many southerners oppose the draft?
5. How did the Union blockade affect the South?
6. **CRITICAL THINKING Applying Information** Why were northerners who opposed the war called Copperheads?

ACTIVITY Writing to Learn
Mary Boykin Chesnut, whom you read about on page 469, kept a detailed diary throughout the Civil War. List five questions that you would ask Chesnut about her experiences during the war.

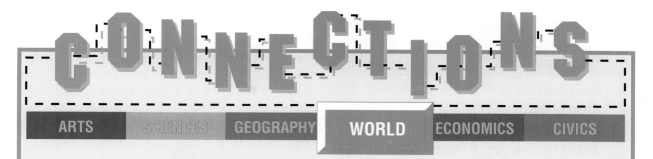

| ARTS | SCIENCES | GEOGRAPHY | **WORLD** | ECONOMICS | CIVICS |

Nurses in the Civil War

When the Civil War began, the United States was not prepared to care for the wounded. There were no ambulances to take the wounded from the battleground. There were no field hospitals to receive them, no medical corps to treat their injuries, no professional nursing staff to speed their recovery. Even a minor injury might result in death.

At first, volunteers rushed to fill the need for nurses. A few, such as the nuns from Catholic nursing orders, were trained providers of medical care. Others had been trained by Protestant nurses from the Kaiserwerth School in Germany. On the whole, however, volunteers knew little about caring for the sick or wounded.

Dorothea Dix, who was known for reforming the treatment of the mentally ill, became head of army nurses for the Union. Dix brought to the job knowledge that she had gained in Europe. Among the places she had visited was the British military hospital in Scutari, Turkey. There, she saw firsthand how famed British nurse Florence Nightingale had reformed nursing.

Inspired by Nightingale's work abroad, Dix and others attacked the greatest obstacle to effective nursing: unsanitary conditions. They ordered hospitals cleaned, kitchens established, and bath houses constructed. They provided medicines and bandages. They also fought against the dread disease of scurvy by making sure that soldiers received green vegetables to eat.

Nursing the wounded

The lack of trained nurses during the Civil War dramatized the need for change. Following the war, interest in nursing education was high, and three schools of nursing opened in the United States in 1873. At first, these schools closely followed the model that Nightingale had established in Europe. In time, however, they developed a slightly different plan to meet the special needs of nursing in the United States.

■ How was American nursing influenced by European methods?

Susie King Taylor, Union nurse

> ### ACTIVITY
> Design a series of postage stamps celebrating the achievements of nurses during the Civil War.

As you have read, the Union claimed victory at Antietam in September 1862. In the next few months, however, the Confederate army won several dazzling victories. "There never were such men in an army before," said General Lee. "They will go anywhere and do anything if properly led."

These were gloomy days in the North. Few people realized that the tide of war would soon turn and the Union would win.

Confederate Victories

The two stunning victories that gave Lee hope came in late 1862 and 1863. (See the map on page 459.) Lee won by outsmarting the Union generals who fought against him.

Fredericksburg. In December 1862, Union forces set out once again on a drive toward Richmond. This time, they were led by General Ambrose Burnside. Meeting Robert E. Lee's army outside Fredericksburg, Virginia, Burnside ordered his troops to attack.

After the two sides traded fire, Lee had his soldiers fall back, leaving the town to Burnside. The Confederates dug in at the crest of a treeless hill above Fredericksburg. There, they waited for the Yanks.

As the Union soldiers advanced, Confederate guns mowed them down by the thousands. Six times Burnside ordered his men to charge. Six times the rebels drove them back. Southerners could hardly believe the bravery of the doomed Union troops. "We forgot they were fighting us," one southerner wrote, "and cheer after cheer at their fearlessness went up along our lines." The battle was one of the Union's worst defeats.

Chancellorsville. The following May, Lee, aided by Stonewall Jackson, again outwitted the Union army. This time, the battle was fought on thickly wooded ground near Chancellorsville, Virginia. Lee and Jackson defeated the Union troops in three days.

Although the South won the battle, it suffered a severe loss. At dusk, nervous Confederate sentries fired at what they thought was a Union soldier riding toward them. The "Union soldier," it turned out, was Stonewall Jackson. Jackson died as a result of his injuries several days later. Lee said sadly, "I have lost my right arm."

Still, Lee decided to keep the Union off balance by moving north into Pennsylvania. He hoped to take the Yankees by surprise in their own backyard. If he was successful in Pennsylvania, Lee planned to swing south and capture Washington, D.C.

Lee at Gettysburg

By chance, on June 30, some of Lee's men came upon Union soldiers at the small town of Gettysburg, Pennsylvania. The two opposing sides scrambled to bring in additional troops. In the battle that followed the next day, Confederates drove the Union forces out of town. The Yankees took up strong positions on Cemetery Ridge, overlooking Gettysburg.

Cemetery Ridge. The next morning, July 2, General James Longstreet trained his field glasses on Cemetery Ridge. Longstreet, one of Lee's best generals, studied the tents, campfires, and lines of soldiers that dotted the ridge. He did not like what he saw. The Union position looked too strong to risk a battle.

Lee disagreed. "The enemy is there," Lee said, pointing to the distant hill, "and I am going to attack him there."

"If he is there," Longstreet replied, "it will be because he is anxious that we should attack him; a good reason, in my judgment, for not doing so." Longstreet urged Lee to march south, drawing the Union army after him. Then, Lee could choose more favorable ground for battle.

Lee's plan. Lee's mind was made up. His soldiers wanted to fight, not retreat. Lee hoped to destroy the Union army.

Lee ordered an attack on both ends of the long Union line. Southern troops fought hard and suffered heavy casualties. When the sun set after a day of savage fighting, however, the Union line had not broken. (See "The Killer Angels" on page 600.)

Next morning, Longstreet again argued that Lee should move south. Lee, however, was convinced that a direct assault could overwhelm the troops on Cemetery Ridge. He sent 15,000 men under General George Pickett to charge the center of the Union line on Cemetery Ridge. To reach the Yankees, the men would have to cross an open field and then run up a steep slope.

Pickett's Charge. Pickett's men waited in a shady grove as Confederate cannons tried to soften up the Union line. At 3 P.M., an unhappy Longstreet gave Pickett the signal to proceed. "My heart was heavy," Longstreet recalled. "I could see the desperate and hopeless nature of the charge and the hopeless slaughter it would cause."

Pickett gave the order to charge. As the men rushed forward, Union rifles opened fire. Row after row of Confederates dropped to the ground, bleeding. Still, the wave of

The Armies Clash at Gettysburg *The Battle of Gettysburg was a major turning point in the war. This painting shows almost the entire Gettysburg battlefield on the final day. The view is from the center of the Union line.* **Geography** *What was General Longstreet's opinion of the Union position? What was General Lee's opinion?*

men in gray surged forward. But the bullets and shells kept all but a few from reaching the top of Cemetery Ridge. A Union soldier described the terrible scene at the crest:

66Men fire into each other's faces not five feet apart. There are bayonet thrusts, saber strokes, pistol shots, men going down on their hands and knees, spinning round like tops, throwing out their arms, gulping blood, falling, legless, armless, headless. There are ghastly heaps of dead men. 99

In the end, *Pickett's Charge* failed. As the surviving rebel troops limped back, Lee rode among them. "It's all my fault," he admitted humbly. Lee had no choice but to retreat. The Confederates would never again invade the North. The war had reached its turning point. ■

Honoring the Dead at Gettysburg

The Battle of Gettysburg left more than 40,000 dead or wounded. When the soldiers who died there were buried, their graves stretched as far as the eye could see. On

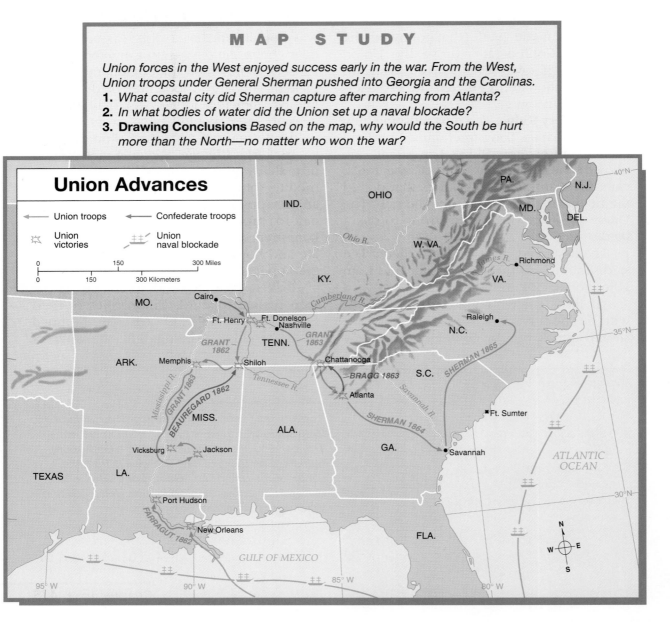

MAP STUDY

Union forces in the West enjoyed success early in the war. From the West, Union troops under General Sherman pushed into Georgia and the Carolinas.
1. What coastal city did Sherman capture after marching from Atlanta?
2. In what bodies of water did the Union set up a naval blockade?
3. Drawing Conclusions Based on the map, why would the South be hurt more than the North—no matter who won the war?

Union Advances

← Union troops ← Confederate troops

☆ Union victories   ‡‡ Union naval blockade

0   150   300 Miles
0   150   300 Kilometers

IND. OHIO PA. N.J.
Ohio R. W. VA. MD. DEL.
MO. Cairo KY. Cumberland R. VA. Richmond James R.
Ft. Henry Ft. Donelson Nashville GRANT 1863 Raleigh
GRANT 1862 TENN. N.C.
ARK. Memphis Shiloh Chattanooga SHERMAN 1865 S.C.
Tennessee R. BRAGG 1863
BEAUREGARD 1862 Atlanta
MISS. Savannah R. Ft. Sumter
Vicksburg Jackson ALA. GA. SHERMAN 1864 Savannah ATLANTIC OCEAN
Mississippi R.
TEXAS LA.
Port Hudson
FARRAGUT 1862 New Orleans FLA.
GULF OF MEXICO

40°N
35°N
30°N
95°W 90°W 85°W 80°W

N
W E
S

November 19, 1863, northerners held a ceremony to dedicate this cemetery.

President Lincoln attended, but he was not the main speaker. At the time, his popularity was quite low. Lincoln sat with his hands folded as another speaker talked for two hours. Then, the President rose and spoke for about three minutes.

In his *Gettysburg Address,* Lincoln said that the Civil War was a test of whether or not a democratic nation could survive. He reminded Americans that their nation was founded on the belief that "all men are created equal." Looking out at the thousands of graves, Lincoln told the audience:

    66 We here highly resolve that these dead shall not have died in vain— that this nation, under God, shall have a new birth of freedom—and that government of the people, by the people, for the people, shall not perish from the earth. 99

Few listened to Lincoln. Newspapers gave his speech little attention. "It is a flat failure," Lincoln said. "The people are disappointed." Later generations, however, have honored Lincoln's brief address as a profound statement of American ideals.

Total War

For three years, Lincoln had searched for a general who could lead the Union to victory. More and more, he thought of Ulysses S. Grant, who continued to win battles in the West. In 1864, after Grant's victory at Vicksburg, Lincoln appointed him commander of the Union forces.

Sheridan in the Shenandoah. Grant had a plan for ending the war. He wanted to destroy the South's ability to fight. Grant sent General Philip Sheridan and his cavalry into the rich farmland of Virginia's Shenandoah Valley. He instructed Sheridan:

    66 Leave nothing to invite the enemy to return. Destroy whatever cannot

BIOGRAPHY **Ulysses S. Grant** *Many northerners questioned President Lincoln's choice of Ulysses S. Grant to lead the Union troops. Grant's stubbly beard and casual clothing gave him a scruffy, nonmilitary look. Lincoln, however, believed in Grant's ability to win. "I can't spare this man," he said. "He fights."* **Citizenship** *How did Grant wage total war against the South?*

be consumed. Let the valley be left so that crows flying over it will have to carry their rations along with them. 99

Sheridan obeyed. In the summer and fall of 1864, he marched through the valley, destroying farms and livestock.

Marching through Georgia. Grant also sent General William Tecumseh Sherman to capture Atlanta, Georgia, and then march to the Atlantic coast. Like Sheridan, Sherman had orders to destroy everything useful to the South. Sherman's troops captured Atlanta in September 1864. They burned the city in November when Sherman began his "march to the sea."

Sherman's troops ripped up railroad tracks, built bonfires from the ties, then heated and twisted the rails. They burned barns, homes, and factories.

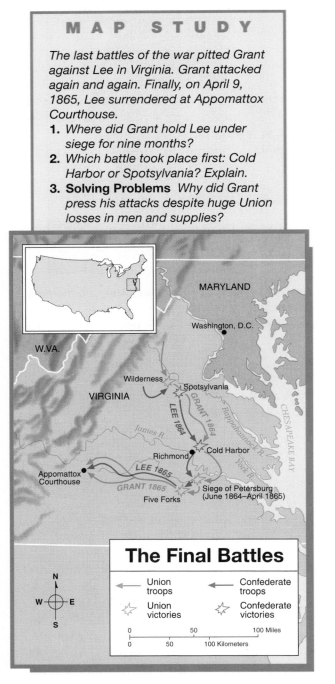

M A P   S T U D Y

The last battles of the war pitted Grant against Lee in Virginia. Grant attacked again and again. Finally, on April 9, 1865, Lee surrendered at Appomattox Courthouse.
1. Where did Grant hold Lee under siege for nine months?
2. Which battle took place first: Cold Harbor or Spotsylvania? Explain.
3. **Solving Problems** Why did Grant press his attacks despite huge Union losses in men and supplies?

MARYLAND

Washington, D.C.

W.VA.

Wilderness

Spotsylvania

VIRGINIA

LEE 1864

GRANT 1864

Rappahannock R.

CHESAPEAKE BAY

James R.

Richmond

Cold Harbor

LEE 1865

York R.

Appomattox Courthouse

GRANT 1865

Siege of Petersburg (June 1864–April 1865)

Five Forks

The Final Battles

→ Union troops → Confederate troops

☆ Union victories ☆ Confederate victories

N W E S

0   50   100 Miles
0   50   100 Kilometers

A new type of combat. Grant, Sherman, and Sheridan had created a new type of combat called total war. In the past, only soldiers were involved in wars. In total war, however, everyone was affected as the army destroyed food and equipment that might be useful to the enemy. As a result of the Union decision to wage total war, civilians in the South suffered the same hardships as soldiers.

Lincoln Is Reelected

In 1864, Lincoln ran for reelection. At first, his defeat seemed, in his own words, "extremely probable." Before the capture of Atlanta, Union chances for victory looked bleak. Lincoln knew that many northerners were unhappy with his handling of the war.

The Democrats nominated General George McClellan to oppose Lincoln. Although he had commanded the Union army, McClellan was more willing than Lincoln to compromise with the South. If peace could be achieved, he was ready to restore slavery.

When Sherman took Atlanta in September, the North rallied around Lincoln. Sheridan's smashing victories in the Shenandoah Valley in October further increased Lincoln's popular support. In the election in November, the vote was close, but Lincoln remained President.

The War Ends

Grant had begun a drive to capture Richmond in May 1864. Throughout the spring and summer, he and Lee fought a series of costly battles. Northerners read with horror that Grant had lost 60,000 dead and wounded in a single month at the battles of the Wilderness, Spotsylvania, and Cold Harbor. (See the map at left.) Still, Grant pressed on. He knew that the Union could replace men and supplies. The South could not.

Richmond falls. As Grant knew, Lee's army was shrinking. To prevent further losses, Lee dug in at Petersburg, near Richmond. Here, Grant kept Lee under siege for nine months. At last, with a fresh supply of troops, Grant took Petersburg on April 2, 1865. The same day, Richmond fell.

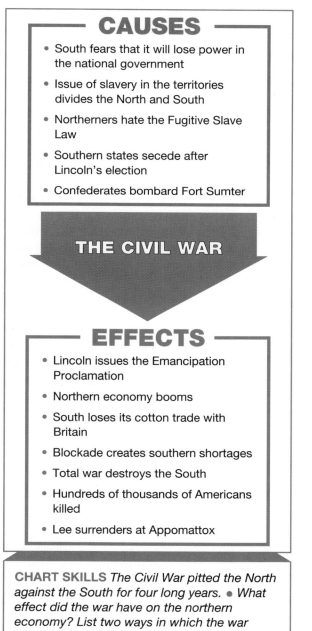

CAUSES

- South fears that it will lose power in the national government
- Issue of slavery in the territories divides the North and South
- Northerners hate the Fugitive Slave Law
- Southern states secede after Lincoln's election
- Confederates bombard Fort Sumter

THE CIVIL WAR

EFFECTS

- Lincoln issues the Emancipation Proclamation
- Northern economy booms
- South loses its cotton trade with Britain
- Blockade creates southern shortages
- Total war destroys the South
- Hundreds of thousands of Americans killed
- Lee surrenders at Appomattox

CHART SKILLS *The Civil War pitted the North against the South for four long years.* • *What effect did the war have on the northern economy? List two ways in which the war affected life in the South.*

Lee surrenders. Lee and his army withdrew to a small Virginia town called Appomattox Courthouse. There, they were trapped by Union troops. Lee knew his men would be slaughtered if he kept fighting. On April 9, 1865, he surrendered. (⬚ See "Lee, Dignified in Defeat" on page 602.)

At Appomattox Courthouse, Grant offered the defeated Confederate army generous terms of surrender. Soldiers were required to turn over their rifles, but officers were allowed to keep their pistols. Soldiers who had horses could keep them. Grant knew that southerners would need the animals for spring plowing.

As the Confederates surrendered, Union soldiers began to cheer. Grant ordered them to be silent. "The war is over," he said. "The rebels are our countrymen again."

SECTION 5 REVIEW

1. **Locate:** (a) Fredericksburg, (b) Chancellorsville, (c) Gettysburg, (d) Atlanta, (e) Appomattox Courthouse.
2. **Identify:** (a) Pickett's Charge, (b) Gettysburg Address, (c) Ulysses S. Grant, (d) Philip Sheridan, (e) William Tecumseh Sherman.
3. (a) What victories in late 1862 and early 1863 encouraged the Confederates? (b) What battle marked the turning point of the war?
4. What was Grant's plan for ending the war?
5. Why was Grant better able than Lee to withstand tremendous losses?
6. **CRITICAL THINKING Making Decisions** How might Lee's brilliant successes at Fredericksburg and Chancellorsville have contributed to his defeat at Gettysburg?

ACTIVITY Writing to Learn
Use the maps on pages 474 and 476 and your text to describe the troop movements of one Union general.

Summary

- Neither the Union nor the Confederacy was prepared for war, but the Union possessed important material advantages.
- The North had three war goals: to blockade the southern ports, to control the Mississippi, and to capture Richmond. The South planned to fight a defensive war.
- Lincoln broadened Union war goals by issuing the Emancipation Proclamation.
- Both sides experienced divisions over the war, resentments concerning the draft, and inflation.
- The tide of war turned at Gettysburg in 1863, and in 1865 Lee surrendered at Appomattox Courthouse.

Reviewing the Main Ideas

1. (a) What advantages did each side have as war began? (b) What weaknesses?
2. (a) Which battles did Grant win in the West? (b) Which war goals had the North achieved by 1863?
3. (a) What did the Emancipation Proclamation provide? (b) How did it change the nature of the war?
4. Why did some northerners oppose the war?
5. (a) How did each side raise money to fight the war? (b) How did the war affect the economy of each side?
6. How did women contribute to the war effort?
7. How did the Union wage total war on the South in 1864 and 1865?

Thinking Critically

1. **Linking Past and Present** (a) What advances in technology made Civil War battles deadly? (b) How would a war today be even more deadly?

2. **Making Decisions** Some people believe that Grant's decision to wage total war on the South was wrong because it hurt civilians as much as it hurt Confederate soldiers. Do you agree or disagree? Explain.

Applying Your Skills

1. **Analyzing a Quotation** In 1861, antislavery leader Frederick Douglass said: "This is no time to fight with one hand when both are needed. This is no time to fight with only your white hand, and allow your black hand to remain tied!" (a) What did Douglass mean by this statement? (b) What evidence from the chapter shows that the government came to agree with Douglass?

2. **Making a Generalization** General Robert E. Lee said of his soldiers: "There never were such men in an army before. They will go anywhere and do anything if properly led." List two facts to show that his generalization might also apply to Union forces.

Thinking About Geography

Match the letters on the map with the following places: **1.** Atlanta, **2.** Bull Run, **3.** Vicksburg, **4.** Gettysburg, **5.** Appomattox, **6.** Confederate states, **7.** Union states. **Location** Which battles shown on the map were fought in the Confederate states?

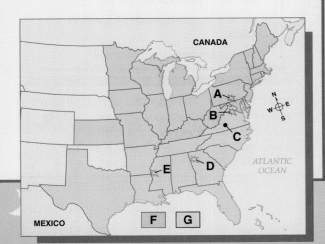

Fighting With the Blue and the Gray

Form into groups to review battlefield scenes during the Civil War. Follow the suggestions below to write, draw maps, plot graphs, or organize an exhibit to show what you have learned. You may use the textbook, encyclopedias, atlases, or other materials in your classroom library to complete the tasks. Be able to name your sources of information when you have finished the activity.

Drum of a Union regiment

GEOGRAPHERS Imagine that you have been ordered to make a report for General Lee before the Battle of Gettysburg. Find out more about the geography of Gettysburg. Then draw a map showing main roads, bodies of water, hills, valleys, and major towns in the area. Include a scale and a directional arrow. Write a short report explaining the key points on your map and giving suggestions for winning the coming battle.

SCIENTISTS Prepare fact sheets on medical care for soldiers during the Civil War. Include information on battle-field hospitals; diseases such as malaria, dysentery, and typhoid; and people who nursed the wounded, such as Clara Barton, Sojourner Truth, Sally Louisa Tompkins, and Dorothea Dix.

Confederate battle surgeon's field kit

WRITERS Imagine that you are an African American soldier fighting in the Union army. Write a series of diary entries describing your experiences and your feelings about the war.

MATHEMATICIANS Choose five major battles of the Civil War. Find out the casualties suffered by the North and South in each battle. Then use the information to make bar graphs showing northern and southern casualties.

ARTISTS Organize an exhibit of Civil War photographs and paintings. Prepare a catalog for your exhibit. Include information about each photograph and painting, and explain how it adds to your understanding of the war.

★ Set up a Fighting With the Blue and the Gray corner in your classroom. Display each group's finished activity or a description of it.

Family visit in a Union camp

Rebuilding the Nation

(1864–1877)

1865 *Abraham Lincoln was assassinated. Across the nation, stunned Americans mourned the President's death.*

1867 *Congress passed the first Reconstruction Act. Under this law, southern states had to allow African American men to vote.*

1868 *Andrew Johnson was impeached. The trial created a furor, and spectators needed tickets to get in. In the end, the President was acquitted.*

1864	1866	1868	1870

▲ **WORLD EVENT**
1867 Britain establishes the Dominion of Canada

Chapter Setting

"With malice toward none; with charity for all; with firmness in the right, as God gives us to see the right, let us strive on to finish the work we are in; to bind up the nation's wounds; to care for him who shall have borne the battle and for his widow, and his orphan—to do all which may achieve and cherish a just and lasting peace among ourselves, and with all nations."

President Abraham Lincoln spoke these words on March 4, 1865, as part of his second inaugural address. In the South, cannons still roared and soldiers still died on the battlefield. Yet Americans knew that the Civil War was nearly over. Soon, it would be time to rebuild and reunite the nation.

Lincoln wanted all Americans to work together at this huge task. In his speech, he urged northerners to forgive the South. He called on northerners and southerners to build a "union of the hearts."

Not all northerners shared Lincoln's forgiving spirit. The South had caused the Civil War, they said, and the South should be punished for it. Some wanted Confederate leaders to stand trial for treason. Others wanted to seize southern plantations, break them up, and give the land to newly freed slaves.

Americans faced hard decisions in the years following the Civil War. The fighting ended in 1865, but the North and the South still had many problems to resolve before they could truly be reunited.

ACTIVITY List possible goals for rebuilding the South. Then choose one goal and brainstorm ways that this goal could best be achieved.

1870 *Congress outlawed the use of force to keep people from voting. They hoped to stop groups that used acts of terror to keep African Americans from the polls.*

1872 *President Ulysses S. Grant was reelected. Widespread corruption in Grant's government helped weaken support for Reconstruction policies.*

THE WORKING MAN'S BANNER.
FOR PRESIDENT. FOR VICE-PRESIDENT.

ULYSSES S. GRANT
"The Galena Tanner"

HENRY WILSON
"The Natick Shoemaker"

1877 *Rutherford B. Hayes became President after a disputed election. His decision to remove remaining federal troops from the South ended Reconstruction.*

REPUBLICAN CANDIDATES.
PRESIDENT. VICE PRESIDENT.
R.B. HAYES of Ohio. W.A. WHEELER of New York.

| 1870 | 1872 | 1874 | 1876 |

WORLD EVENT 1870 Italy unified

WORLD EVENT 1871 Germany unified

First Steps Toward Reunion

The North lost more soldiers in the Civil War than the South did. Still, northern farms and cities were hardly touched by the war. As one returning Union soldier remarked, "It seemed . . . as if I had been away only a day or two, and had just taken up . . . where I had left off."

Confederate soldiers, however, had little chance of taking up where they had left off. The South faced staggering problems after the war. Southern cities and farmlands lay in ruins, and a whole way of life had ended. All southerners—rich and poor, black and white—faced a long, uphill struggle to rebuild their lives.

The Defeated South

Shortly after the Civil War ended, an Englishman visited the South. He was horrified by the destruction he saw:

66 [The land consists of] plantations in a state of semi-ruin, and plantations of which the ruin is for the present total and complete. . . . The trail of war is visible . . . in burnt-up [cotton gins], ruined bridges, mills, and factories . . . and in large tracts of once cultivated land stripped of every vestige of fencing. The roads, long neglected, are in disorder, and . . . in many places . . . impassable. 99

Except for the battles of Gettysburg and Antietam, all the fighting of the war took place in the South. In some areas, every house, barn, and bridge had been destroyed. Two thirds of the South's railroad tracks had been turned into twisted heaps of scrap. The cities of Charleston, Richmond, Savannah, and Atlanta had been leveled. A quarter of a million Confederate soldiers died in the war. Thousands more were disabled by their wounds.

The war wrecked the South's financial system. After the war, Confederate money was worthless. People who lent money to the Confederacy were never repaid. Many southern banks closed, and depositors lost their savings.

Southern society was changed forever by the war. No longer were there white owners and black slaves. Nearly 4 million freedmen—men and women who had been slaves—now lived in the South. Most had no land, no jobs, and no education. Under slavery, they had been forbidden to own property and to learn to read and write. What would become of them?

Rival Plans for the South

Even before the war ended, President Lincoln worried about rebuilding the South. He wanted to make it reasonably easy for southerners to rejoin the Union. The sooner the nation was reunited, Lincoln believed, the faster the South would be able to rebuild.

As early as 1863, Lincoln outlined a plan for **Reconstruction.** Reconstruction refers to the period when the South was rebuilt, as well as to the federal government's program to rebuild it. Under Lincoln's **Ten Percent Plan,** as it was called, a southern state

Lincoln Visits Richmond *In the final days of the Civil War, President Lincoln visited the captured Confederate capital of Richmond, Virginia. Many war-weary residents of the city, as well as African Americans eager for freedom, welcomed the Union President.* **Daily Life** *How does the painting show the damage that Richmond suffered during the war?*

could form a new government after 10 percent of its voters swore an oath of loyalty to the United States. Once it was formed, the new government had to abolish slavery. Voters could then elect members of Congress and take part in the national government once again.

Many Republicans in Congress thought Lincoln's plan was too generous toward the South. In 1864, they passed a rival plan for Reconstruction. The **Wade-Davis Bill** required a majority of white men in each southern state to swear loyalty to the Union. It also denied the right to vote or hold office to anyone who had volunteered to fight for the Confederacy.

Help for Freedmen

Lincoln refused to sign the Wade-Davis Bill because he felt it was too harsh. Congress and the President did agree on one proposal, however. A month before Lee surrendered, Congress passed a bill creating the **Freedmen's Bureau.** Lincoln quickly signed it.

Providing food and clothing. The Freedmen's Bureau provided food and clothing to freedmen. It tried to find them jobs. The bureau also helped poor whites. It provided medical care for more than a million people. One former Confederate was amazed to see "a Government which was lately fighting us . . . now generously feeding our poor and distressed." (See "Out From This Place" on page 604.)

Setting up schools. One of the bureau's most important tasks was to set up schools for freed slaves in the South. By 1869, about 300,000 African Americans attended bureau schools. Most of the teachers were volunteers—often women—from the North.

Both old and young students were eager to learn. Grandmothers and granddaughters sat side by side in the classroom. One bureau agent in South Carolina observed that freedmen "will starve themselves, and go without clothes, in order to send their children to school."

The Freedmen's Bureau laid the foundation for the South's public school system. It set up more than 4,300 grade schools. It also created colleges and universities for African American students, including Howard, Morehouse, Fisk, and Hampton Institute. Many graduates of these schools became teachers themselves. By the 1870s, African Americans were teaching in grade schools throughout the South.

Charlotte Forten and African American Education

For former slaves, attending school was one of freedom's most precious gifts. Even before the Freedmen's Bureau began setting up schools, newly freed African Americans built schools on their masters' abandoned lands. Many teachers from the North came to help in these schools. Among these teachers was a young woman named Charlotte Forten.

Forten volunteers. Charlotte Forten came from a wealthy African American family in Philadelphia. As a young girl, she was educated by private tutors. Later, she attended a teacher-training school. A strong abolitionist, Forten devoted her life to helping African Americans improve the quality of their lives through education.

During the Civil War, Forten was eager to serve. She got her chance early in the war, after Union troops captured the Sea Islands, off the coast of South Carolina. Plantation owners fled, but their slaves refused to go with them. Instead, they planted crops, built a church, and established a school. In 1862, when she was 25 years old, Charlotte Forten joined a group of northern teachers who came to help the Sea Islanders with their school.

Forten faced a stiff challenge. She was to teach reading, writing, spelling, history, and arithmetic. Yet there were few books or other supplies. Classes were large and included students of all ages. Still, Forten was excited by the willingness and enthusiasm of her students. She wrote:

66 I never before saw children so eager to learn. . . . They come here as other children go to play. The older ones . . . work in the fields . . . and then come to school, after their hard toil in the hot sun, as bright and as anxious to learn as ever. . . . It is wonderful how a people who have been so long crushed to the earth . . . can have so great a desire for knowl-

Learning to Read *"My Lord, Ma'am, what a great thing learning is!" a South Carolina freedman told a northern teacher. This painting shows a Virginia family using their new skills to read the Bible.* **Citizenship** *How did the Freedmen's Bureau help African Americans get an education?*

edge, and such a capacity for attaining it. "

Forten loved her work as a teacher, and her students made good progress. She assisted the tiny community in other ways, too. She cared for sick babies, and from time to time even tended a local store.

Recruiting for the Freedmen's Bureau. After two years, poor health forced Charlotte Forten to return to the North. There, after the Civil War, she helped to recruit teachers for the Freedmen's Bureau schools that were opening throughout the South. The diary she kept of her experiences on the Sea Islands was later published as a book. ■

Lincoln Is Assassinated

President Lincoln hoped to convince Congress to accept his Reconstruction plan. Whether he would have succeeded will never be known.

On April 14, 1865, just five days after Lee's surrender, the President attended a play at Ford's Theater in Washington, D.C. As Lincoln watched the play, John Wilkes Booth, an actor, crept into the President's box. Booth, a southerner, blamed Lincoln for the South's crushing defeat. Now, taking careful aim, he shot Lincoln in the head. Within a few hours, the President was dead.

The relief felt at the end of the war suddenly turned to shock. Millions mourned Lincoln's death. Booth, meanwhile, fled Washington. He was later caught and killed in a barn outside the city.

Linking Past and Present
Today, Ford's Theater is a national monument. It houses a collection of items related to Lincoln's life and death. The theater has also been restored, and since 1968 has reopened for dramatic performances.

A New President, A New Plan

Vice President Andrew Johnson became President when Lincoln died. Johnson had served as governor of Tennessee and had represented that state in Congress. When Tennessee seceded in 1861, Johnson had remained loyal to the Union.

At first, many Republicans in Congress were pleased when Johnson became President. They believed that he would support a strict Reconstruction plan. After all, Johnson had stated that "traitors must be punished." As it turned out, Johnson's plan for Reconstruction was almost as mild as Lincoln's.

Johnson called for a majority of voters in each southern state to pledge loyalty to the United States. He also demanded that each state ratify the *Thirteenth Amendment,* which banned slavery throughout the nation. Congress had passed the Thirteenth Amendment in January 1865.

Rebellion in Congress

The southern states did what Johnson asked. In late 1865, the President approved their new state governments. Southern voters then elected new members of Congress. Many of those elected had held high office in the Confederacy. Alexander Stephens, the former vice president of the Confederacy, was elected senator from Georgia.

Republicans in Congress were outraged. The men who had led the South out of the Union were now being elected to the House and Senate. Also, nowhere in the South had African Americans been allowed to vote.

When Congress met in December 1865, many Republicans refused to let southern representatives take their seats. Instead, Republicans set up a Joint Committee on Reconstruction to draw up a new plan for the South. The stage was set for a showdown between Congress and the President.

SECTION 1 REVIEW

1. **Identify:** (a) Reconstruction, (b) Ten Percent Plan, (c) Wade-Davis Bill, (d) Freedmen's Bureau, (e) Charlotte Forten, (f) Andrew Johnson, (g) Thirteenth Amendment.
2. **Define:** freedman.
3. Name two problems the South faced after the Civil War.
4. What did the Freedmen's Bureau do?
5. Why did Republicans in Congress refuse to seat the South's representatives?
6. **CRITICAL THINKING Analyzing Information** Could Charlotte Forten have taught African Americans in the South to read and write before the Civil War? Explain.

ACTIVITY Writing to Learn
Write newspaper headlines for three events discussed in Section 1.

2
Congress Takes Charge

FIND OUT

- How did white southerners try to limit the rights of freedmen?
- What were the goals of Radical Republicans?
- Why did Congress try to remove President Johnson from office?
- What were the Fourteenth and Fifteenth amendments?

VOCABULARY black codes

In the spring of 1866, disturbing reports trickled in to Congress. In some southern cities, peddlers openly sold Confederate flags. A New Orleans restaurant featured "Stonewall Jackson soup" and "Confederate hash." Throughout the South, people sang a new song. "I'm a good old rebel," it declared, "and I don't want no pardon for anything I done."

These reports confirmed what many Republicans had suspected. Under President Johnson's plan, there was "evidence of an intense hostility to the federal union and an equally intense love of the late Confederacy." "The rebellion has not ended," declared one angry Republican. "It has only changed its weapons!"

A New Kind of Bondage in the South

Most southern states had ratified the Thirteenth Amendment, which banned slavery. However, most white southerners did not want to give African Americans real freedom. Southern legislatures passed black codes, laws that severely limited the rights of freedmen.

Black codes forbade African Americans to vote, own guns, or serve on juries. In some states, African Americans were permitted to work only as servants or farm laborers. In others, the codes required freedmen to sign contracts agreeing to work for a year at a time. Those without contracts could be arrested and sentenced to work on a plantation.

Black codes, however, gave African Americans some rights they did not have before the Civil War. For example, African Americans could legally marry and own some kinds of property. Still, the codes were clearly meant to keep freedmen from gaining political or economic power. As one African American veteran wrote, "If you call this Freedom, what do you call Slavery?"

The North Reacts

Republicans were angered by the black codes and the election of former Confederate leaders to Congress. The Joint Commit-

Starting a New Life *Left without homes or work, newly freed slaves had to find ways to support themselves. In this painting by Thomas P. Anshutz, a family tends their small cabbage patch.* **Citizenship** *How did southern legislatures limit the rights of African Americans after the Civil War?*

tee on Reconstruction sent President Johnson a report condemning southern practices. "There is yet among the southern people," the report said, "a desire to preserve slavery in its original form as much and as long as possible." When Johnson ignored the report, members of Congress vowed to take Reconstruction out of the President's hands.

Radicals. Those who led the opposition to President Johnson were called ***Radical Republicans,*** often shortened to Radicals.*

---

*A radical is a person who wants to make drastic changes in society.

Thaddeus Stevens of Pennsylvania led the Radicals in the House. Charles Sumner of Massachusetts was the chief Radical Republican voice in the Senate.

Radical Republicans had two main goals. First, they wanted to break the power of the rich planters who had ruled the South for years. These "aristocrats," Radicals believed, had caused the Civil War. Second, Radicals wanted to ensure that freedmen received the right to vote.

Moderates. Radical Republicans did not control Congress. To accomplish their goals, the Radicals needed the help of moderate Republicans, who made up the largest group in Congress.

Moderates and Radicals did not agree on all issues. However, they shared a strong political motive for favoring a strict policy toward the South. Most southerners were Democrats. With southerners barred from Congress, Republicans easily controlled both the House and the Senate. If southern Democrats were seated, Republicans might lose their power.

The President and Congress Clash

The conflict between President Johnson and Congress came to a head in 1866. In April, Congress passed the Civil Rights Act. The act gave citizenship to African Americans. By passing it, Congress hoped to combat the black codes and secure for African Americans the rights denied them by southern states. President Johnson vetoed the bill. But Republicans in Congress overrode the veto.

Citizenship for African Americans. Some Republicans worried that the Supreme Court might declare the Civil Rights Act unconstitutional. They remembered that in the Dred Scott decision in 1857, the Court had ruled that African Americans were not citizens. Hoping to avoid a similar legal challenge, Republicans now proposed the Fourteenth Amendment to the Constitution.

The *Fourteenth Amendment* granted citizenship to all persons born in the United States. This included nearly all African Americans. It also guaranteed all citizens "equal protection of the laws" and declared that no state could "deprive any person of life, liberty, or property without due process of law." This provision made it illegal for states to discriminate against an individual on unreasonable grounds such as the color of a person's skin.

Political rights for African Americans. In addition, the Fourteenth Amendment provided that any state that denied African Americans the right to vote would have its representation in Congress reduced. Republicans believed that freedmen would be able to defend their rights if they could vote.

With the Fourteenth Amendment, Republicans tried to secure basic political rights for African Americans in the South. In fact, the nation had far to go before all Americans achieved equality. Over the next 100 years, citizens would seek to obtain their rights by asking the courts to enforce the Fourteenth Amendment.

Election of 1866. President Johnson was furious. He violently opposed the Fourteenth Amendment and urged the former Confederate states to reject it. In time, all did so except Tennessee.

Johnson decided to make the Fourteenth Amendment an issue in the November 1866 congressional elections. Traveling through the North, the President called on voters to reject the Radical Republicans and endorse his plan for Reconstruction.

In many towns, audiences heckled the President. Losing his temper, Johnson yelled back. One heckler shouted that Johnson should hang Jefferson Davis. "Why not hang Thad Stevens?" the President replied. Many northerners criticized Johnson for acting in an undignified manner.

In July, white mobs rioted in New Orleans, Louisiana, killing 34 African Amer-

icans. This convinced many northerners that Johnson's policies were not succeeding. They felt that stronger measures were needed to protect freedmen.

The election results were a disaster for Johnson. Republicans won majorities in both houses of Congress. They also won every northern governorship and majorities in every northern state legislature.

The Radical Program

Republicans in Congress now prepared to take charge of Reconstruction. With overwhelming majorities in both the House and Senate, they could override Johnson's vetoes. The President, one Republican commented, was the "dead dog in the White House." The period that followed is often called *Radical Reconstruction.*

Radical Reconstruction begins. Congress passed the first *Reconstruction Act* over Johnson's veto in March 1867. The Reconstruction Act threw out the southern state governments that had refused to ratify the Fourteenth Amendment—all the former Confederate states except Tennessee. The act also divided the South into five military districts. Each district was commanded by an army general. Said one Radical senator, "This bill sets out by laying its hand on the rebel governments and taking the very life out of them."

The Reconstruction Act required the former Confederate states to write new constitutions. Congress also required the new state governments to ratify the Fourteenth Amendment before rejoining the Union. Most important, the act stated that African Americans must be allowed to vote in all southern states.

Elections in the South. Once the new constitutions were in place, the reconstructed states held elections to set up new state governments. To show their disgust with Radical Reconstruction policies, many white

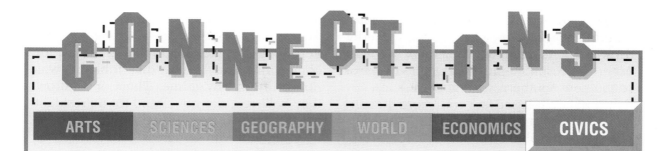

| ARTS | SCIENCES | GEOGRAPHY | WORLD | ECONOMICS | **CIVICS** |

Letter to a Former Owner

During Reconstruction, some freedmen stayed in the South with their former owners. They worked the land for a share of the crops they raised. Others left for the North and the dream of a better life. The following letter was written from Ohio in 1865. In it, freedman Jourdon Anderson responds to his former owner's request that he return to the South.

❝SIR: I got your letter, and was glad to find that you had not forgotten Jourdon, and that you wanted me to come back and live with you again. . . .

I am doing tolerably well here. I get twenty-five dollars a month, with [food] and clothing; have a comfortable home for Mandy—the folks call her Mrs. Anderson—and the children . . . go to school and are learning well. . . .

Mandy says she would be afraid to go back without some proof that you were disposed to treat us justly and kindly, and we have concluded to test your sincerity by asking you to send us our wages for the time we served you. . . . I served you faithfully for thirty-two years, and Mandy for twenty years . . . . If you fail to pay us for our faithful labors in the past, we can have little faith in your promises in the future. . . . We trust the good Maker has opened your eyes to the wrongs which you and your fathers have done to me and my fathers, in making us toil for you for generations without [pay]. . . .

In answering this letter, please state . . . if there has been any schools opened for the colored children in your neighborhood. The great desire of my life now is to give my children an education.

From your old servant,
—JOURDON ANDERSON❞

■ What rights did the Anderson family gain by their move?

A schoolroom during Reconstruction

Form to help freedmen keep family records

ACTIVITY Imagine that you are Jourdon Anderson. Describe what freedom means to you in terms of your five senses: Freedom looks like —, sounds like —, feels like —, smells likes —, tastes like —.

southerners stayed away from the polls. Freedmen, on the other hand, proudly turned out to exercise their new right to vote. As a result, Republicans gained control of the new southern state governments.

Congress passed several more Reconstruction acts, each time over Johnson's veto. It was Johnson's duty, as President, to enforce these laws. However, many Republicans feared he would not do so. Republicans in Congress decided to remove the President from office.

Showdown

On February 24, 1868, the House of Representatives voted to impeach President Johnson. As you have read, to impeach means to bring formal charges of wrongdoing against an elected official. According to the Constitution, the House can impeach the President only for "high crimes and misdemeanors." The case is tried in the Senate. The President is removed from office only if found guilty by two thirds of the senators.

During the trial, it became clear that the President was not guilty of high crimes and misdemeanors. Even Charles Sumner, Johnson's bitter foe, admitted that the charges were "political in character."

In the end, the Senate vote was 35 to 19. This was just one vote short of the two-thirds majority needed to remove Johnson from office. Despite intense pressure, seven Republican senators had refused to vote for conviction. They knew that Johnson was not guilty of any crime. The Constitution, they believed, did not intend for a President to be removed from office simply because he disagreed with Congress. Johnson served out the few months that were left in his term.

Grant Becomes President

In 1868, Republicans nominated General Ulysses S. Grant as their candidate for President. Grant was the Union's greatest hero in the Civil War.

By election day in November 1868, most of the southern states had rejoined the Union. As Congress demanded, the new southern governments allowed African Americans to vote. About 700,000 blacks went to the polls in the 1868 election. Nearly all cast their votes for Grant. He easily defeated his opponent, Democrat Horatio Seymour of New York.

The Fifteenth Amendment

In 1869, Republicans in Congress proposed another amendment to the Constitution. The *Fifteenth Amendment* forbade any

Lining Up to Vote *Throughout the South, African Americans exercised their newly won right to vote. In this picture, a federal soldier supervises an election in Richmond, Virginia.* **Citizenship** *Why do you think a soldier was present at this election?*

state from denying African Americans the right to vote because of their race.

Some Republicans supported the Fifteenth Amendment for political reasons. African American votes had brought Republicans victory in the South. If African Americans could also vote in the North, Republicans realized, they would help Republicans to win elections there, too.

Many Republicans had other reasons for supporting the Fifteenth Amendment. They remembered the great sacrifices that were made by African American soldiers in the Civil War. They felt it was wrong to let African Americans vote in the South but not in the North.

The Fifteenth Amendment was ratified in 1870. At last, all African American men over age 21 had the right to vote.

SECTION 2 REVIEW

1. **Identify:** (a) Radical Republicans, (b) Thaddeus Stevens, (c) Charles Sumner, (d) Fourteenth Amendment, (e) Radical Reconstruction, (f) Reconstruction Act, (g) Fifteenth Amendment.
2. **Define:** black codes.
3. How did southern legislatures limit the rights of freedmen?
4. Describe the Reconstruction plan adopted by Congress in 1867.
5. (a) Why did Republicans impeach Johnson? (b) What was the result?
6. **CRITICAL THINKING Analyzing Ideas** A senator who voted against the removal of President Johnson later said that he did not vote in favor of Johnson but in favor of the presidency. What do you think the senator meant?

ACTIVITY Writing to Learn
Take the position of either a radical or a moderate in the conflict over Reconstruction. Write a speech presenting your point of view.

3
The Reconstruction South

FIND OUT
- What groups dominated southern politics during Reconstruction?
- How did some white southerners use terror to regain control of the South?
- What did Reconstruction governments do to rebuild the South?
- What was life like for freedmen and poor whites during Reconstruction?

VOCABULARY scalawag, carpetbagger, sharecropper

By 1867, life in the South had changed dramatically. Gone forever were slave auctions and the hated slave patrols. African Americans were free—free to work for themselves, to vote, and to run for office. In Alabama, a group of freedmen drew up this ringing declaration:

> ❝We claim exactly *the same rights, privileges and immunities as are enjoyed by white men.* . . . The law no longer knows white nor black, but simply men, and consequently we are entitled to. . . hold office, sit on juries and do everything else which we have in the past been prevented from doing solely on the ground of color. ❞

Before the Civil War, a small group of rich planters controlled southern politics. During Reconstruction, however, new groups dominated state governments. They tried to reshape the politics of the South.

Forces in Southern Politics

The state governments created during Radical Reconstruction were different from any the South had known before. The old leaders had lost much of their influence. Three groups stepped in to take their place. These were white southerners who supported the Republicans, northerners who moved south after the war, and freedmen.

Scalawags and carpetbaggers. Some white southerners supported the new Republican governments. Many were business people who had opposed secession in 1860. Now, they wanted to forget the war and get on with rebuilding the South. Many whites felt that any southerner who helped the Republicans was a traitor. They called white southern Republicans scalawags, a word used for small, scruffy horses.

Northerners who moved south after the war were another important force. White southerners called them carpetbaggers. They said that carpetbaggers had left in a hurry to get rich in the South. They had time only to fling a few clothes into cheap cloth suitcases, called carpetbags.

In fact, northerners went south for a number of reasons. A few were fortune hunters who hoped to profit as the South was being rebuilt. Many more were Union soldiers who had grown to love the South's rich land. Others, including many African Americans, were reformers who wanted to help the freedmen.

African Americans in public life. Freedmen were the third major group in southern politics during Reconstruction. Under slavery, African Americans had no voice in government. Now, they not only voted in large numbers, but they also ran for and were elected to public office.

African Americans became sheriffs, mayors, and legislators in the South's new local and state governments. Between 1869 and 1880, 16 African Americans were elected to Congress. Hiram Revels and Blanche K. Bruce, both from Mississippi, won seats in the United States Senate.

BIOGRAPHY Blanche K. Bruce *The first African American to serve a full term in the Senate was Blanche K. Bruce. As senator from Mississippi, Bruce worked to improve conditions not only for African Americans but for Asians and Native Americans as well.* ***Citizenship*** *What personal traits do you think Bruce needed to succeed?*

White Southerners Fight Back

From the start, most southerners who had held power before the Civil War resisted Reconstruction. Nearly all were Democrats. These white southerners, known as *Conservatives,* wanted the South to change as little as possible. They were only willing to let African Americans vote and hold a few offices as long as real power remained in the hands of whites.

Spreading terror. Other white southerners took a harsher view. Some were wealthy planters who wanted to force African Americans back to work on plantations. Others were small farmers and laborers who felt threatened by the millions of freedmen who now competed with them for land and power. These whites declared war on anyone who worked with the Republican party. As Senator Ben Tillman of South Carolina recalled:

66 We reorganized the Democratic party with one plank, and only one plank, namely, that 'this is a white man's country, and white men must govern it.' Under that banner we went to battle. 99

RESEARCH SKILLS
Finding Information in the Library

You can find information in the library in many sources—such as books, encyclopedias, and magazines. In Skill Lesson 14 (page 407), you learned how to use the card catalog to find books in the library. Most libraries have several encyclopedias. Encyclopedias present useful overviews of many subjects. ***Periodicals,*** or magazines and newspapers, offer up-to-date articles on many subjects.

1. **Find information in an encyclopedia.** Encyclopedia articles are arranged in alphabetical order. At the end of each article are ***cross-references*** that tell you which other articles in the encyclopedia have information about the subject you are researching.

   Using an encyclopedia in your classroom or library, look up Andrew Johnson. (a) Are there any cross-references at the end of the article? (b) To what articles do the cross-references refer you?

2. **Practice using the *Readers' Guide*.** The *Readers' Guide to Periodical Literature* is an index, or list, of articles that appear in popular magazines. The *Readers' Guide* lists every article at least twice—once by the author's last name and again by the subject. Look at the sample from the *Readers' Guide* below. (a) What subject entries are shown? (b) Which article appears under an author entry? (c) What was the author's name?

3. **Look for information in the *Readers' Guide*.** Each subject entry in the *Readers' Guide* tells you the title of the article, the name of the author (for signed articles), and the title of the magazine. The entry lists the volume number of the magazine, the first page number of the article, and the date of the magazine. The date is in abbreviated form. At the front of the *Readers' Guide* is a list that tells you what the abbreviation stands for.

   Look at the sample from the *Readers' Guide*. (a) In which volume of *Ebony* did the article "The 100 most influential black Americans" appear? (b) On what page did the article begin? (c) In what magazine did the article "Five blacks seeking S. C. Congress seat" appear? (d) What was the date of the magazine in which the article appeared? (e) What date do you think is indicated by the abbreviation S '92?

ACTIVITY On October 5, 1992, *U.S. News & World Report* printed an article on pages 70–77 entitled "Who Was Lincoln?" The article was written by Gerald Parshall and appeared in volume 113 of the magazine. Write a *Readers' Guide* subject entry and author entry for this article.

Volume: page number	BLACK POLITICAL CANDIDATES Five blacks seeking S. C. Congress seat. il *Jet* 82:7 Ag 17 '92
Magazine title	BLACKMON, DOUGLAS A. The resegregation of a southern school. *Harper's* 285:14-16+ S '92
Abbreviated date (May 1992)	BLACKS The 100 most influential black Americans. il *Ebony* 47:62+ My '92

White southerners formed secret societies to help them regain power. The most dangerous was the **Ku Klux Klan,** or KKK. The Klan worked to keep blacks and white Republicans out of office.

Dressed in white robes and hoods to hide their identity, Klansmen rode at night to the homes of African American voters, shouting threats and burning wooden crosses. When threats did not work, the Klan used violence. Klan members murdered hundreds of African Americans and their white allies.

Congress responds. Many moderate southerners condemned the violence of the Klan. Yet they could do little to stop the Klan's reign of terror. Freedmen turned to the federal government for help. In Kentucky, African American voters sent a letter to Congress. They wrote:

66We believe you are not familiar with the Ku Klux Klan's riding nightly over the country spreading terror wherever they go by robbing, whipping, and killing our people without provocation.99

Congress acted to stop the Klan's violence. In 1870, Congress made it a crime to use force to keep people from voting. As a result, Klan activities decreased, but the threat of violence lingered. Some African

Spreading Terror *The Ku Klux Klan used acts of terror against blacks and their supporters. Sometimes they left miniature coffins, like the one at right, on the doorsteps of their enemies. Hoods, like the one at left, gave Klansmen a frightening appearance.* **Citizenship** *What was the goal of groups like the Ku Klux Klan?*

Americans continued to vote and hold office despite the risk. Many others, however, stayed away from the ballot box.

The Difficult Task of Rebuilding

Despite political problems, Reconstruction governments tried to rebuild the South. They built public schools for both black and white children. Many states gave women the right to own property. In addition, Reconstruction governments rebuilt railroads, telegraph lines, bridges, and roads. Between 1865 and 1879, the South laid 7,000 miles (11,200 km) of railroad track.

Rebuilding the economy. Cotton production, long the basis of the South's economy, recovered slowly. However, by 1880 planters were growing as much cotton as they had in 1860.

Industry also grew during Reconstruction. Birmingham, Alabama, became an important iron and steel center. It was often called the "Pittsburgh of the South." Still, the South lagged behind the rest of the nation in industry. By the end of the century, the South was actually producing a smaller part of the nation's manufactured goods than it had in 1860.

Problems of taxes and corruption. Rebuilding cost money. Before the war, south-

Our Common Heritage
When Hiram Revels won election as the first African American senator, he took over the seat that had been held by Jefferson Davis. Davis had resigned the seat in 1861 to become president of the Confederacy.

erners had paid very low taxes. Reconstruction governments raised taxes sharply. Higher taxes created discontent among many southern whites.

Southerners were further angered by widespread corruption in the Reconstruction governments. One state legislature, for example, voted $1,000 to cover a member's bet on a horse race. Other items billed to the state included hams, perfume, clothing, champagne, and a coffin.

Corruption was not limited to the South. After the Civil War, dishonesty plagued northern governments, too. In fact, most southern officeholders served their states well and honestly.

A Cycle of Poverty

In the first months after the war, freedmen left the plantations on which they had lived and worked. For many, moving away was a sign of freedom. As one woman said, "I must go. If I stay here, I'll never know I am free." Freedmen found few opportunities, however.

"Nothing but freedom." Some Radical Republicans talked about giving each freedman "40 acres and a mule." Thaddeus Stevens suggested breaking up big plantations and distributing the land. Most Americans opposed the plan, however. In the end, former slaves received—in the words of a freedman—"nothing but freedom."

Through hard work or good luck, some freedmen did become landowners. Most, however, had little choice but to return to where they had lived in slavery. Lizzie Atkins, a former slave from Texas, explained, "We was almost forced to stay on there with [Master], because no other white man would hire us or give us a place to stay."

Sharecropping. Some large planters had held onto their land and wealth through the war. Now, they had huge amounts of land but no slaves to work it. In the hard times of Reconstruction, many freedmen and poor whites went to work for the large

Back to the Plantation *For many African Americans, life changed little after the Civil War. Here, freedmen on a South Carolina plantation haul in the day's harvest of cotton, just as they had done as slaves.* **Daily Life** *Why did many freedmen go to work on plantations?*

planters. They farmed the planters' land, using seed, fertilizer, and tools that the planters provided. In return, they gave the landowners a share of the crop at harvest time. For this reason, these landless farmers were called **sharecroppers.**

Sharecroppers hoped to own their own land one day. In the meantime, most faced a day-to-day struggle just to survive. They did well if they had enough food for themselves and their families. For many, sharecropping was another form of slavery.

Even farmers who owned land faced hard times. Each spring, farmers received supplies on credit from a store owner. In the fall, they had to repay what they had borrowed. Often, the harvest did not cover the whole debt. As they sank deeper into debt, many farmers lost their land and became sharecroppers themselves. Much of the South became locked into a cycle of poverty.

SECTION 3 REVIEW

1. **Identify:** (a) Blanche K. Bruce, (b) Hiram Revels, (c) Conservatives, (d) Ku Klux Klan.
2. **Define:** (a) scalawag, (b) carpetbagger, (c) sharecropper.
3. What role did African Americans play in Reconstruction governments?
4. (a) What were two accomplishments of Reconstruction governments? (b) What were two problems?
5. Why did many African Americans and poor whites in the South become sharecroppers?
6. **CRITICAL THINKING Drawing Conclusions** Why do you think groups like the Ku Klux Klan did not exist before the Civil War?

ACTIVITY Writing to Learn
Draw a political cartoon about scalawags, carpetbaggers, the Ku Klux Klan, or another aspect of Reconstruction.

4
End of an Era

FIND OUT
- Why did northerners lose interest in Reconstruction?
- What happened in the election of 1876?
- How did white Conservatives tighten their control over the South?
- What did the Supreme Court rule in *Plessy* v. *Ferguson*?

VOCABULARY poll tax, literacy test, grandfather clause, segregation

In 1876, millions of Americans traveled to a great Centennial Exposition in Philadelphia. The fair celebrated the first hundred years of the United States. Visitors gazed at the latest wonders of modern industry— such as the telephone, the elevator, and a giant steam engine four stories high.

As Americans looked to the future, they lost interest in Reconstruction. By the late 1870s, conservative whites had regained control of the South.

Radicals in Decline

By the 1870s, Radical Republicans were losing power in Congress. Many northerners grew weary of trying to change the South. It was time to forget the Civil War, they believed, and let southerners run their own governments—even if that meant African Americans might lose the rights they had so recently gained.

Republicans were also hurt by widespread corruption in the government of President Grant. The President had appointed many friends to office. Some used their jobs to steal. Although Grant was reelected, many people had lost faith in Republicans.

In 1872, Congress pardoned former Confederate officials. As a result, nearly all white southerners could vote again. They voted solidly Democratic. At the same time, southern whites terrorized African Americans who tried to vote. One by one, Republican governments in the South fell. By 1876, only three southern states were under Republican control: South Carolina, Florida, and Louisiana. (📖 See "Abandoning Black Citizens" on page 606.)

The End of Reconstruction

The end of Reconstruction came with the election of 1876. Democrats nominated Samuel Tilden, governor of New York, for President. Tilden was known for fighting corruption. The Republican candidate was Rutherford B. Hayes, governor of Ohio. Like Tilden, Hayes vowed to fight dishonesty in government.

When the votes were tallied, Tilden had 250,000 more popular votes than Hayes. But Tilden had only 184 electoral votes—one

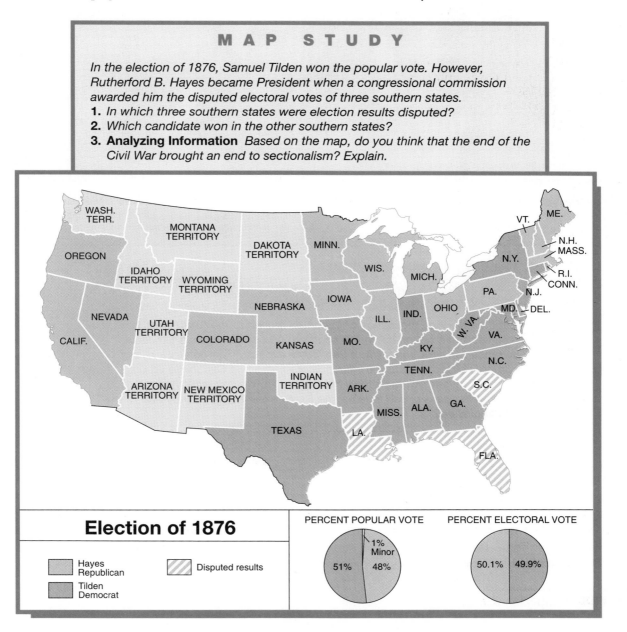

MAP STUDY

In the election of 1876, Samuel Tilden won the popular vote. However, Rutherford B. Hayes became President when a congressional commission awarded him the disputed electoral votes of three southern states.

1. *In which three southern states were election results disputed?*

2. *Which candidate won in the other southern states?*

3. Analyzing Information *Based on the map, do you think that the end of the Civil War brought an end to sectionalism? Explain.*

Election of 1876

Hayes Republican

Tilden Democrat

Disputed results

PERCENT POPULAR VOTE

51%   48%   1% Minor

PERCENT ELECTORAL VOTE

50.1%   49.9%

ART GALLERY: OUR COMMON HERITAGE

JACOB LAWRENCE
Frederick Douglass Series, No. 31 , 1938–1939

After the Civil War, thousands of freedmen moved to the North and West, seeking a better life. In this painting, African American artist Jacob Lawrence captured the spirit of this "black exodus." The bold colors and geometric shapes reflect the influence of African and Caribbean art on Lawrence's work. **Multicultural Heritage** *Why do you think many African Americans chose to leave the South even though slavery had been abolished?*

vote short of the number needed to win the election. Twenty other votes were in dispute. The outcome of the election hung on these votes. All but one of the disputed votes came from Florida, Louisiana, and South Carolina—the three southern states still controlled by Republicans.

As inauguration day drew near, the nation still had no one to swear in as President. Congress set up a special commission to settle the crisis. A majority of the commission members were Republicans. The commission decided to give all the disputed electoral votes to Hayes.

Southern Democrats could have fought the election of Hayes. But Hayes had privately agreed to end Reconstruction. Once in office, he removed all remaining federal troops from South Carolina, Florida, and Louisiana. Reconstruction was over.

Separate but Not Equal

With the North out of southern affairs, white Conservatives tightened their grip on southern governments. Some whites continued to use violence to keep African Americans from voting. Southern states also found other ways to keep African Americans from exercising their rights.

Voting restrictions. By the late 1880s, many southern states had passed poll taxes. Poll taxes required voters to pay a fee each time they voted. Because of the poll taxes, poor freedmen could rarely afford to vote.

Literacy tests required voters to read and explain a difficult part of the Constitution. Since freedmen had little education, such tests kept them away from the polls. Many southern whites were poor and illiterate, too. Some were not allowed to vote. Others were allowed to vote anyway by friendly white officials.

To allow more whites to vote, states passed grandfather clauses. If a voter's father or grandfather had been eligible to vote on January 1, 1867, the voter did not have to take a literacy test. Since no African Americans in the South could vote before 1868, grandfather clauses were a way to ensure that only white men could vote.

History and You
Lucy Hayes, who became First Lady in 1877, set an example for women of her time. She was the first First Lady to have attended college. She was also a strong supporter of temperance. Does the First Lady today set an example that Americans want to follow?

Jim Crow. At the same time that African Americans were losing the right to vote, segregation became the law of the South. Segregation means separating people of different races. Southern states passed laws that separated blacks and whites in schools, restaurants, theaters, trains, streetcars, playgrounds, hospitals, and even cemeteries. The laws were called *Jim Crow laws.*

African Americans brought lawsuits to challenge segregation. In 1896, the Supreme Court upheld segregation in *Plessy v. Ferguson.* The Court ruled that segregation was legal so long as facilities for blacks and whites were equal. In fact, facilities were rarely equal. For example, southern states spent much less on schools for blacks than they did on schools for whites.

Reconstruction was a time of both success and failure. Southerners, especially African Americans, faced hard times. But at last, all African Americans were citizens. Laws passed during Reconstruction, such as the Fourteenth Amendment, became the basis of the civil rights movement almost 100 years later.

SECTION 4 REVIEW

1. **Identify:** (a) Samuel Tilden, (b) Rutherford B. Hayes, (c) Jim Crow laws, (d) *Plessy* v. *Ferguson.*
2. **Define:** (a) poll tax, (b) literacy test, (c) grandfather clause, (d) segregation.
3. Why did Republicans lose support in the North?
4. How did Hayes gain southern support in the election of 1876?
5. CRITICAL THINKING **Evaluating Information** Do you think African Americans in the South benefited from Reconstruction?

ACTIVITY Writing to Learn
Imagine that you are an African American teenager in the South in the late 1880s. Describe five ways that Jim Crow laws might affect your life.

Working in Factories *Many children helped their families by going out to work in the 1830s. In this spinning mill, a young boy is working under the machine at left.*

Learning a Trade *Training for a trade began at an early age. Here, a young workman learns how to sharpen a scythe.*

A Game of Lacrosse *Traditional activities continued to play an important role in the lives of young Native Americans. Here, youths enjoy a game of lacrosse.*

Teenage Soldier *Boys as young as 14 or 15 fought in the Civil War. In this painting, Winslow Homer captures the innocence of a young Union soldier.*

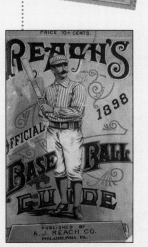

A Wild West Show
Americans of all ages flocked to see Buffalo Bill Cody's rollicking Wild West Show.

A Board Game
Manufactured toys and games became popular in the late 1800s. This board game was inspired by the adventures of newspaper reporter Nellie Bly.

Baseball *By the 1890s, baseball had become the nation's favorite sport. Americans followed the progress of professional baseball players such as the one shown here.*

Picturing the Past

Young Americans in the 1800s

As the nation expanded in the 1800s, so did the world of young Americans. Home and family were still the center of life. However, more young people began to find amusement and employment in the outside world. The Industrial Revolution, the Civil War, and the growth of cities all brought major changes in the lives of the nation's young people. ■ *Which activities shown here are still part of the lives of young Americans today?*

Summary

- President Lincoln and President Johnson urged generous treatment for the South, but Congress rejected their proposals.
- Under Radical Reconstruction, Congress tried to break the power of rich planters and ensure that freedmen received the right to vote.
- Reconstruction governments made slow progress in rebuilding the South, and many southerners became caught in a cycle of poverty.
- Reconstruction ended in 1877, and African Americans lost many of their new-found freedoms.

Reviewing the Main Ideas

1. (a) What was Lincoln's plan for Reconstruction? (b) Why did some Republicans oppose it?
2. What did Radical Republicans want to achieve during Reconstruction?
3. What did the Reconstruction Act provide?
4. What three groups dominated southern governments during Reconstruction?
5. What problems did freedmen face?
6. Why did many southerners sink into a cycle of poverty during Reconstruction?
7. How did Hayes win the election of 1876 even though he received fewer popular votes than Tilden did?

Thinking Critically

1. **Forecasting** How might the history of Reconstruction have been different if Lincoln had not been assassinated?
2. **Linking Past and Present** Many white southerners were angered by high taxes imposed by Reconstruction governments. (a) How do voters today feel about paying high taxes for services? (b) Are there services that should be provided even if they require high taxes? Explain.
3. **Understanding Causes and Effects** Read the three statements that follow. Decide which one is an effect and which two are causes. Explain how the causes and the effect are connected. (a) Southern states passed black codes. (b) Southern states elected former Confederates to Congress. (c) Republicans opposed Johnson's plan to readmit southern states.

Applying Your Skills

1. **Making a Generalization** Reread the discussion of conditions in the South after the Civil War, on page 482. (a) List three facts about the South after the war. (b) Based on your list, make a generalization about the South after the war.
2. **Making a Review Chart** Make a chart with three columns. Label the columns Lincoln, Johnson, Radical Republicans. Then list the major points of the Reconstruction plan that each proposed. (a) Which plan was strictest? (b) Which plan was least strict? (c) Based on what you have read, how would you explain the differences?

Thinking About Geography

Match the letters on the map with the following places: **1.** South Carolina, **2.** Florida, **3.** Louisiana, **4.** Ohio, **5.** New York. **Region** Which southern states were under Republican control in 1876?

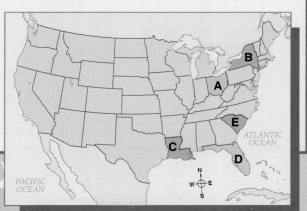

Looking Back at Reconstruction

Form into groups to review Reconstruction after the Civil War. Follow the suggestions below to write, draw, or act to show what you have learned about this period. You may use the textbook, encyclopedias, atlases, or other materials in your classroom library to complete the tasks. Be able to name your sources of information when you have finished the activity.

LANGUAGE EXPERTS AND ARTISTS List the Reconstruction terms and words you have learned. Then organize them into a Reconstruction Glossary. Use original drawings or pictures cut from magazines to illustrate your glossary.

President Andrew Johnson

ARTISTS Review the goals of the Freedmen's Bureau. Then create a poster advertising the Bureau's work and encouraging people to participate.

ACTORS Find out more about the events and issues leading up to the trial of President Andrew Johnson. Then prepare a skit in which you act out Johnson's trial in the United States Senate.

CITIZENS Study the text of the Thirteenth, Fourteenth, and Fifteenth amendments printed in the Reference Section. Then divide into groups to create a concept map for each amendment. Include the main ideas of each amendment and show how it affects the daily lives of Americans today. Illustrate your concept map with original drawings or pictures cut from magazines.

A carpetbag

HISTORIANS Design a trivia game based on what you have learned about Reconstruction in Chapter 17. Include individuals, places, and events.

★ Organize a Looking Back at Reconstruction bulletin board. Include an example or summary of each group's work.

Celebrating the Fifteenth Amendment

LITERATURE

The Red Badge of Courage

Stephen Crane

Introduction *The Red Badge of Courage* tells the story of Henry Fleming, a young volunteer for the Union army during the Civil War. The following passage is from an early chapter in the novel. It describes Henry's departure from home and his early days in the army.

Vocabulary Before you read the selection, find the meaning of these words in a dictionary: **doggedly, shirking, monotonous, province, pickets, philosophical, reflectively, reproached, infantile, assurance**

When [Henry] had stood in the doorway with his soldier's clothes on his back, and with the light of excitement and expectancy in his eyes almost defeating the glow of regret for the home bonds, he had seen two tears leaving their trails on his mother's scarred cheeks.

Still, she had disappointed him by saying nothing whatever about returning with his shield or on it. He had privately primed himself for a beautiful scene. He had prepared certain sentences which he thought could be used with touching effect. But her words destroyed his plans. She had doggedly peeled potatoes and addressed him as follows: "You watch out, Henry, an' take good care of yerself in this here fighting business—you watch out, an' take good care of yerself. Don't go a-thinkin' you can lick the hull rebel army at the start, because yeh can't. Yer jest one little feller amongst a hull lot of others, and yeh've got to keep quiet an' do what they tell yeh. I know how you are, Henry.

"I've knet yeh eight pair of socks, Henry, and I've put in all yer best shirts, because I want my boy to be jest as warm and comf'able as anybody in the army. Whenever they get holes in 'em, I want yeh to send 'em rightaway back to me, so's I kin dern 'em.

"An' allus be careful an' choose yer comp'ny. There's lots of bad men in the army, Henry. The army makes 'em wild, and they like nothing better than the job of leading off a young feller like you, as ain't never been away from home much and has allus had a mother, an' a-learning 'em to drink and swear. Keep clear of them folks, Henry. . . .

"I don't know what else to tell yeh, Henry, excepting that yeh must never do no shirking, child, on my account. If so be a time comes when yeh have to be kilt or do a mean thing, why, Henry, don't think of anything 'cept what's right, because there's many a woman has to bear up 'ginst sech things these times, and the Lord'll take keer of us all.

"Don't forget about the socks and the shirts, child; and I've put a cup of blackberry jam with yer bundle, because I know

Prisoners From the Front
The Civil War was long and bloody. More Americans died in it than in any other war. In Prisoners From the Front, *Winslow Homer shows some of the sadness of the war.* **American Traditions** *Why do you think soldiers on both sides would have mixed feelings about the war?*

yeh like it above all things. Good-by, Henry. Watch out, and be a good boy."

He had, of course, been impatient under the ordeal of this speech. It had not been quite what he expected, and he had borne it with an air of irritation. He departed feeling vague relief.

Still, when he had looked back from the gate, he had seen his mother kneeling among the potato parings. Her brown face, upraised, was stained with tears, and her spare form was quivering. He bowed his head and went on, feeling suddenly ashamed of his purposes. . . .

After complicated journeyings with many pauses, there had come months of monotonous life in a camp. He had had the belief that real war was a series of death struggles with small time in between for sleep and meals; but since his regiment had come to the field the army had done little but sit still and try to keep warm. . . .

He had grown to regard himself merely as a part of a vast blue demonstration. His province was to look out, as far as he could, for his personal comfort. For recreation he could twiddle his thumbs and speculate on the thoughts which must agitate the minds of the generals. Also, he was drilled and drilled and reviewed, and drilled and drilled and reviewed.

The only foes he had seen were some pickets along the river bank. They were a sun-tanned, philosophical lot, who sometimes shot reflectively at the blue pickets. When reproached for this afterward, they usually expressed sorrow, and swore by their gods that the guns had exploded without their permission. The youth, on guard duty one night, conversed across the stream with one of them. He was a slightly ragged man, who spat skillfully between his shoes and possessed a great fund of bland and infantile assurance. The youth liked him personally.

"Yank," the other had informed him, "yer a right dum good feller." This sentiment, floating to him upon the still air, had made him temporarily regret war.

THINKING ABOUT LITERATURE

1. What advice did Henry's mother give him?
2. How was a soldier's life different from what Henry expected?
3. **CRITICAL THINKING Analyzing Information** What does Henry's experience with the enemy picket reveal about the special problems of fighting a civil war?

ACTIVITY Imagine that you are a recruitment officer for the Union army. Create a poster that will convince people to join the Union cause.

Shaping the Future

(1877–Present)

> ### CHAPTER OUTLINE
>
> **1** A Nation of Nations
>
> **2** The New Industrial America
>
> **3** A Changing Government
>
> **4** Looking Abroad

Late 1800s *Inventions and transcontinental railroads spurred the growth of industry and big business. For many Americans, John D. Rockefeller, drawn here in an oil barrel and oil-lamp hat, represented the oil industry and new ways of doing business.*

Early 1900s *After the Spanish-American War, the United States became a world power. Shown here as an eagle, it extended its influence to the Caribbean Sea and the Pacific Ocean.*

Late 1800s *Millions of new immigrants from Eastern Europe entered the United States. The Statue of Liberty in New York harbor, shown here, welcomed them to their new land.*

| 1870 | 1895 | 1920 | 1945 |

WORLD EVENT
1914 World War I begins

WORLD EVENT
1945 World War II ends

Chapter Setting

With fear and hope, Rosa Cristoforo left her village in Italy in 1884 to join her husband in "l'America." She journeyed to the French port of Le Havre, where she boarded a steamship for the long voyage across the Atlantic Ocean. Rosa lived below deck "in a big dark room" with many other poor immigrants. After two weeks, she finally caught sight of land. She never forgot that moment.

❝I stood and watched the hills and the land come nearer. Other poor people, dressed in their best clothes and loaded down with bundles, crowded around. America! The country where everyone could find work! Where wages were so high no one had to go hungry! Where all men were free and equal and where even the poor could own land! But now we were so near it seemed too much to believe. Everyone stood silent—like in prayer.**❞**

Hopes for a better life brought millions of immigrants to the United States in the late 1800s. That new life did not always match the newcomers' dreams. Yet the ideals of freedom and equality inspired Americans to work to shape their nation's future, bringing it ever closer to their dreams. Over time, the people who came helped to build a strong and diverse nation.

> **ACTIVITY** Take a survey of class members to find out what national or ethnic backgrounds are represented. Then locate the nations or regions on a map.

1945 *The United States entered the Cold War with the Soviet Union. For 40 years, the two superpowers were military and political rivals. This French poster shows the Soviet military threat to Europe.*

1990s *The United States increased efforts to compete in a global economy. NAFTA, shown here as puzzle pieces, joined the United States, Canada, and Mexico in a free trade agreement.*

1950s *A civil rights movement spurred the federal government to support equal treatment under the law. Here, a mother and daughter share the news of a Supreme Court ruling that school segregation is illegal.*

1945	1970	1995	PRESENT

WORLD EVENT
1960s Many African nations win independence

WORLD EVENT
1990s Ethnic conflict in former Soviet republics grows

A Nation of Nations

FIND OUT

- What immigrants have come to the United States?
- How did cities change after the Civil War?
- How have advances in technology and communication affected American life?

"The United States themselves are essentially the greatest poem." So wrote Walt Whitman, the author of *Leaves of Grass*. In this volume of poetry, published in 1855, Whitman hailed the bustling, growing United States.

Whitman's praise included the many different peoples and regions that gave the nation its strength and life. "Here is not merely a nation but a teeming nation of nations," Whitman said. In Leaves of Grass, he celebrated all Americans who made up the "teeming nation":

66The spinning-girl retreats and
    advances to the hum of the big
    wheel, . . .
The machinist rolls up his
    sleeves, . . .
The groups of newly-come immi-
    grants cover the wharf or
    levee, . . .
The squaw wrapt in her yellow-
    hemmed cloth is offering moc-
    casins and bead bags for sale, . . .
The President holding a cabinet
    council is surrounded by the
    great Secretaries, . . .
The Missourian crosses the plains
    toting his wares and his cattle, . . .

And of these one and all I weave
    the song of myself. 99

In the years since the Civil War, the United States has continued to live up to Whitman's vision. Still a "teeming nation of nations," it reflects the influence of many cultures and backgrounds. The result has been the creation of a unique people—Americans.

The Tide of Immigration

After the Civil War, immigrants continued to enter the United States. In the 1880s, the number of newcomers rose sharply to almost half a million a year.

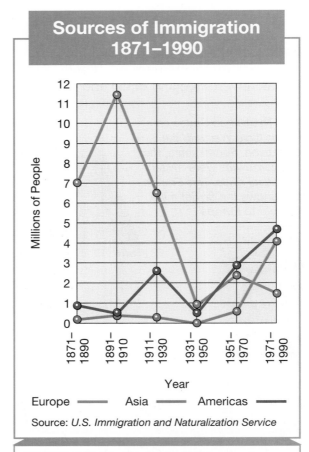

Sources of Immigration 1871–1990

Millions of People

Year

Europe — Asia — Americas —

Source: *U.S. Immigration and Naturalization Service*

GRAPH SKILLS *The United States is often called a nation of immigrants.* • *Where did the largest number of immigrants come from in the period between 1871 and 1890? Between 1971 and 1990?*

Gateway to a New World *Millions of families like this one entered the United States through Ellis Island. They brought with them all their worldly belongings, including treasured items such as the embroidered vest above.* **Multicultural Heritage** *How do you think immigrants contributed to American culture?*

The "new" immigrants. Many of these immigrants came from countries in Southern and Eastern Europe, such as Italy, Poland, Russia, and Hungary. They included many Catholics, as well as Jews fleeing persecution in Eastern Europe.

The "new" immigrants from Southern and Eastern Europe faced great hardships to reach the United States. Uprooted from their families and homes, they flocked to European ports, sometimes sneaking past guarded borders. Like Rosa Cristoforo, many endured a rough voyage across the Atlantic.

Ports of entry. The most famous port for European immigrants was Ellis Island, near the Statue of Liberty in New York. Thousands of other immigrants arrived elsewhere, however.

As immigration increased after 1900, the city of Galveston, Texas, took many immigrants that Ellis Island could not handle. On the West Coast, immigrants from China, Japan, and Korea entered through San Francisco, California, as well as Seattle, Washington, and Oahu, Hawaii. From Mexico, families traveled north to El Paso and Laredo in Texas.

The pain of discrimination. Like the Irish and Germans who arrived in the 1840s and 1850s, the new immigrants faced discrimination. Their religious beliefs, customs, and languages seemed strange to many Americans. In the 1920s, Congress cut back sharply the number of immigrants who were allowed to enter the United States.

Despite the new restrictions, people from all over the world still dreamed of coming to the United States. They, too, wanted to share in the American dream of freedom and opportunity.

A Young Filipino in America

In the 1920s, the United States governed the Philippines as a territory. During those years, young Filipinos came to work in the United States. One, Carlos Bulosan, later wrote a book about his experiences. Not all of the events described in it actually happened to Bulosan himself. Still, they give a vivid picture of what life was like for Filipinos like "Carlos."

Carlos Bulosan *In* America Is in the Heart, *Carlos Bulosan writes about the hardships and discrimination that Filipinos faced in the United States. Still, he praises the American dream. "America," he tells readers, "is not a land of one race or one class. . . . We are all Americans."* **American Traditions** *What famous American inspired "Carlos" in Bulosan's book?*

Dreams of America. Growing up as a young boy in the Philippines, Carlos worked as a houseboy for an American woman. In time, he learned more and more about the United States—or America, as it was commonly called.

In his spare hours, Carlos often walked to a nearby lake with his friend Dalmacio (dahl MAH see oh). There, Carlos and Dalmacio shared their dream of starting a new life in America. The two boys practiced their English by reading aloud to each other from a book about Abraham Lincoln.

"Who is this Abraham Lincoln?" Carlos asked.

"He was a poor boy who became President of the United States," replied Dalmacio. "He was born in a log cabin and walked miles and miles to borrow a book so that he would know more about his country." Lincoln's story fascinated Carlos. Determined to learn more, he borrowed other books from the local library.

In the golden land. By age 17, Carlos had saved enough money to buy a ticket to Seattle, Washington. He had to ride with 200 other Filipinos in steerage—the hot, dark, lower section of the boat.

Carlos arrived in Seattle in June 1930, with only 20 cents. For a day or two, he stayed at a hotel in Chinatown. When he could not pay for his room, the hotel owner appeared with an older Filipino.

"You are working for me now," the man told Carlos. "Get your hat and follow me." The man sent him to Alaska to work in a fish-canning factory.

The jobs in Alaska required long hours and hard work. Sometimes, they were dangerous. One day, Carlos saw a worker lose his arm in a cutting machine. Still, he and other workers found some enjoyment. Because summer days were very long in Alaska, they stayed up very late to play baseball after work.

Carlos had arrived in the United States during the Great Depression of the 1930s. Jobs were scarce. After returning from Alaska, he and other Filipinos took whatever work they could find. In the Yakima Valley of Washington, they picked apples. In California, they gathered winter peas and oranges.

Too often, Carlos and other workers met with discrimination. When Carlos tried to rent an apartment in a "whites only" district in Los Angeles, the landlady pulled down the "For Rent" sign. Another time, he was beaten by antiunion people for trying to join a farm workers' union.

Eventually, Bulosan found good American friends. When he fell ill from tuberculosis, they encouraged him to write about his experiences.

In 1943, Bulosan completed his book, *America Is in the Heart.* He wanted his Filipino friends and all Americans to understand that everyone could contribute to "this vast land"—just as Abraham Lincoln had:

> 66 America is not a land of one race or one class. . . . We are all Americans that have toiled and suffered and known oppression and defeat, from the first Indian that offered peace in Manhattan to the last Filipino peapickers. America is not bound by geographical latitudes. America is not merely a land or an institution. America is in the hearts of men that died for freedom; it is also in the eyes of men that are building a new world. 99 ■

Recent Newcomers

In 1965, Congress revised the immigration laws so that more people could enter the country. Many more immigrants from Latin America arrived, including Mexicans and Cubans.

During the 1970s and 1980s, the number of immigrants from Asia rose sharply as well. Most were Filipinos, Chinese, and Koreans. During and after the Vietnam War, many Vietnamese and Cambodians also sought new homes in the United States.

In the 1980s, about 6 million immigrants entered the United States legally. Another 3 to 5 million crossed American borders without official papers. Together, those totals are higher than in any previous decade in American history.

In 1986, Congress took steps to control illegal immigration. An amnesty or pardon, however, was granted to illegal aliens who had been in the country before January 1, 1982. During the 1990s, legal immigration continued to rise. By 1995, legal immigrants were applying for citizenship in record numbers.

Each wave of immigrants has enriched American life. Over the years, immigrants have helped to build railroads, subways, and factories. They have worked on farms, built skyscrapers, and started new businesses. Their foods, songs, stories, and customs have helped to make American culture richer and more vibrant.

The Rise of Cities

The growth of cities has also brought changes in American life. At the end of Reconstruction, less than one quarter of all Americans lived in cities. Between 1880 and 1900, the number of people living in cities doubled. By 1920, a majority of Americans made their homes in cities or suburbs. By 1990, nearly 80 percent of all Americans lived in metropolitan areas.

The move to the cities changed American culture. City newspapers printed more interesting—and sometimes more sensational—news stories. Huge department stores such as Macy's in New York offered a full range of goods. Subways and trolleys whisked people from one side of town to the other. Professional sports, especially baseball, became popular pastimes.

During the 1970s and 1980s, older cities of the East and Midwest actually lost population. People left those regions and moved to the Sunbelt, as the states of the Southeast and Southwest are called. Many went in search of jobs. The sunny climate with mild winters also was an attraction. By 1990, the 30 fastest-growing urban areas in the nation were all in the South and the West.

A People and Their Music

The richness of American life has always been expressed in music. Since colonial times, folk songs have been popular. Some were the ballads of Irish and Scottish immigrants. Some were spirituals sung in slave

The Morning News *Big-city newspapers of the early 1900s attracted readers with stories of crime, sports, and gossip. Here, New Yorkers crowded into a trolley eagerly read the morning news.* **Linking Past and Present** *How do people keep informed about the news today?*

quarters. Others were banjo tunes from the gold fields of California.

As the United States changed, so did its music. In the early 1900s, a new kind of music, called jazz, was heard in the South. It drew on the rhythms brought from West Africa by slaves. African American musicians like Louis Armstrong and "Jelly Roll" Morton were the founders of jazz. Jazz musicians often improvise, or make up, variations on a song as they play it.

In the 1950s, another sound swept the nation—rock 'n' roll. Artists like Chuck Berry, Little Richard, and Bill Haley used drums and electric guitars to create music with a strong, lively beat. Buddy Holly and Elvis Presley also became teenager favorites.

Over the past 40 years, popular music has taken many forms. Americans of all ages and backgrounds have enjoyed country and western, rhythm and blues, heavy metal, new wave, jazz, and rap. Music superstars like Pearl Jam, Garth Brooks, Madonna, and Queen Latifah have sold millions of albums.

Radio, Film, and Television

Advances in communication have transformed American life since the late 1800s. Radio, film, and television all have brought Americans closer together.

Radio. During the 1920s, radio stations began to broadcast across the nation. They brought news, sports, and entertainment into American homes. Today, radios and cassette recorders almost as small as a credit card allow people to listen to music anywhere.

Movies. Motion-picture film revolutionized American culture as well. The first movie theaters opened in the early 1900s. Until 1927, movies were silent—that is, they had no sound track. Audiences read subtitles to follow the plot. Today, most movie theaters offer a choice of several different movies.

Television. Television began in the United States in the late 1940s. By the 1950s, millions of Americans began to buy television sets. Today, almost every home has at least one set. Also, many people own videocassette recorders, which allow them to record programs or rent movies to watch at home.

Radio, movies, and television allow Americans to share experiences. They also help to inform the public. For example, millions of Americans can watch candidates for President debate on television. This information often helps viewers to decide for whom they will vote in an upcoming election.

Cable television. At the same time, the growing number of television channels has increased the variety of programs available. Cable television offers programs for country-and-western music fans, home shoppers, and comedy lovers. Local channels allow ordinary citizens a chance to air their own programs. Channels like Univision (UNI), which broadcasts in Spanish, serve a variety of specific audiences and groups.

Technology and Tomorrow

In July 1969, American astronaut Neil Armstrong stepped out of a lunar landing craft onto the surface of the moon. "That's one small step for a man, one giant leap for mankind," he announced. Armstrong was the first person to walk on the moon. The moon landing was only one example of the effects of advanced technology.

Since the 1940s, a revolution in processing information by computer has affected every part of American life. Businesses use computers to print documents, keep bank records, or program factory robots. Personal computers at home help students to write papers and parents to balance checkbooks and keep records. CD-ROM drives can play back sounds and movie clips, display pictures, or store an encyclopedia on one disk.

Technology has helped to tie together a diverse nation. As American society becomes more complex, the nation needs ways to weave together its many different regions, groups, and traditions. Even more than in Walt Whitman's day, we are a "teeming nation of nations."

SECTION 1 REVIEW

1. **Locate:** (a) Italy, (b) Poland, (c) Russia, (d) Hungary, (e) China, (f) Japan (g) Korea, (h) Philippine Islands, (i) Vietnam.
2. **Identify:** (a) Carlos Bulosan, (b) Neil Armstrong.
3. Why did immigrants of the late 1800s face discrimination?
4. Why did people move to the Sunbelt in the 1970s and 1980s?
5. How have computers affected American life?
6. **CRITICAL THINKING Comparing** How are Walt Whitman's and Carlos Bulosan's views of America similar?

ACTIVITY Writing to Learn

Imagine that you are a 13-year-old immigrant in the late 1800s. Jot down 10 words that describe your feelings about coming to the United States.

Traffic Report *Advances in communication have changed the way Americans live. Here, a helicopter pilot reports on traffic conditions for station KRON-TV during rush hour in San Francisco.* **Daily Life** *How have improved communications helped to bring Americans together?*

2
The New Industrial America

FIND OUT
- How did railroads boost industry?
- What changes in business took place after the Civil War?
- How have jobs changed in the 1900s?

VOCABULARY corporation, monopoly

At the end of the Civil War, taking a train usually meant inconvenience and delay. Passengers had no place to eat or sleep. More often than not, they would have to wait while workers fixed a derailed car or changed a locomotive.

Less than 20 years later, American railroads had been transformed. T. S. Hudson, a British tourist, boasted about his "scamper through America." In 1882, he boarded a train outfitted with luxurious Pullman sleeping cars. For 75 cents, he bought on board a breakfast of hot breads, eggs, sausage, oysters, and trout. One new river bridge after another allowed the train to speed westward without delay.

The much-improved railroads benefited businesses as well as passengers. By the 1900s, the United States had become a leader in industry. Able to move equipment and products quickly from one place to another, railroads were the key to linking together distant sections of the new industrial nation.

Linking the Nation Together

After 1865, the railroad system expanded quickly. Railroad owners combined small lines with large systems. Cornelius Vanderbilt, for example, bought up all the rail lines between New York City and Chicago. This meant that goods loaded in Chicago rode on the same car of the New York Central Railroad all the way to New York City. As a result, the cost of shipping freight by rail dropped sharply.

Transcontinental railroads. In 1869, the first railroad to span the country was completed. Heading west, workers for the Union Pacific Railroad laid tracks from Omaha, across the Great Plains, and through the Rocky Mountains. Meanwhile, crews of the Central Pacific Railroad began in San Francisco and hacked through the granite peaks of the Sierra Nevada. The two railroads joined their routes at Promontory Point, Utah.

By 1893, five cross-country railroads spanned the nation. These railroads opened the West to settlement by cattle ranchers and farmers. As settlers from the East moved into the Great Plains and the Far West, war broke out with Native Americans living there. In the end, the United States Army was victorious. Forced to move onto reservations, western Indians adapted to the wrenching changes in their ways of life.

The expanding rail system gave a boost to industry. Construction of the railroads created a huge demand for coal, iron, steel, and lumber. Also, the railroads opened up new markets in towns and villages across the nation.

The automobile. A second revolution in transportation came in the 1900s, with the coming of automobiles, trucks, and airplanes. In 1900, cars were still novelties. Only 4,000 "horseless carriages" chugged along the nation's dirt roads. Henry Ford soon developed an assembly line that made it possible to put cars together quickly and efficiently. He compared making a car with making any other product:

"The way to make automobiles is to make one automobile like another automobile . . . just as one pin is like another pin when it comes from a pin factory, or one match is like another match when it comes from a match factory."

The assembly line reduced costs so that more people could afford a car. By 1920, more than 9 million cars were on the roads. By the mid-1980s, that number had skyrocketed to more than 320 million.

The airplane. In 1903, two bicycle mechanics, Orville and Wilbur Wright, built the first successful airplane. The first passenger airline in the United States began service in 1914. Airplanes were also used during World War I (1914–1918).

After the war, planes moved more and more mail, freight, and passengers. During World War II (1939–1945), jet engines were first developed. Today, jets carry goods and people to all parts of the world in very little time. Wide-bodied jumbo jets carry 500 people at one time. Military jets fly faster than the speed of sound.

A Flood of Inventions

The automobile and airplane were only two of the many inventions that fueled the development of American industry. From 1860 to 1890, the United States patent office issued more than half a million patents for new inventions.

A boost for the steel industry. Some inventions, such as the automobile, led to the creation of new industries. Others made it possible to produce vital goods more quickly and cheaply. For example, in the 1850s, a new way to produce steel was developed. With the Bessemer process, as it was called, high-grade steel could be made much more cheaply than before.

The new steel found many uses. Long-lasting steel rails replaced iron rails on the nation's railroads. Strong steel girders supported skyscrapers, or buildings of 20 stories or more. Steel also was used for smaller items such as nails, screws, needles, bolts, barrel hoops, and barbed wire. Today, steel remains an important material in automobiles and buildings as well as in consumer goods such as stainless-steel pans and tableware.

End of a Way of Life *The arrival of white settlers brought an end to the Plains Indians' way of life. Here, a Plains Indian stares in despair at what has happened to the lands that once belonged to his people.* **Daily Life** *What features in the painting represent changes brought by white settlers?*

Advances in the laboratory. No one did more to organize inventing into a scientific system than Thomas Alva Edison. During the late 1800s, Edison set up the first modern research laboratory.

Out of the laboratory came hundreds of new products, including the phonograph, sound motion picture, and electric light bulb. Edison also developed the first electric power plant. Soon after, streets, businesses, and houses were lit by electric lights. Today, many companies have huge research laboratories that produce thousands of inventions every year.

New Business Ways

Before the Civil War, most businesses were small and often run by a single family. They usually sold their products in their

A Nation of Inventors

Inventor	Date	Invention
Anna Baldwin	1878	milking machine
Thomas Alva Edison	1879	incandescent bulb
James Ritty	1879	cash register
Jan E. Matzeliger	1882	shoemaking machine
Lewis E. Waterman	1884	fountain pen
Elihu Thomas	1886	electric welding machine
Granville Woods	1887	automatic air brake
King C. Gillette	1888	safety razor with throwaway blades
George H. Wheeler and Jesse W. Reno	1892	escalator
Charles and J. Frank Duryea	1893	gasoline-powered car
Leo H. Baekeland	1909	plastic
Willis Carrier	1911	air conditioner
Vladimir Kosma Zworykin	1923	video camera
Bell Telephone Laboratories	1947	transistor
Edwin Herbert Land	1947	instant camera
Francis Melvin Rogallo	1948	hang glider
Clarence Birdseye	1949	food-dehydrating process
IBM	1965	word processor
Robert Jarvik	1982	artificial heart
Richard Bruno	1986	compact disc interactive

CHART SKILLS *Americans have been pioneers in scientific research and practical inventions. • Which invention shown on the chart do you think had the greatest impact on American life? Explain.*

own or neighboring villages, towns, and cities. After the Civil War, demands for products caused businesses to grow.

A new age of corporations. During the late 1800s, businesses developed new ways to run more efficiently. Many businesses became corporations. A corporation is a business owned by investors who buy shares of stock. By allowing thousands of investors to buy stock, corporations can raise the millions of dollars they need to build huge factories and hire hundreds of workers.

The rapid growth of industry in the late 1800s caused problems, however. In many industries, single companies became large enough to force almost all other companies out of business. When one company gained control of a certain industry, it became a monopoly. Monopolies dominated steel, oil, and sugar production, as well as other industries.

Government regulation. Reformers in the late 1800s and early 1900s fought for government regulation of industry to prevent the abuses of monopolies. Many monopolies were broken up under Presidents Theodore Roosevelt, William Howard Taft, and Woodrow Wilson.

Today, government regulations prevent any one company from gaining a monopoly in an industry. Yet many modern companies are far larger than the monopolies of the late 1800s. Often, a single corporation owns a large number of smaller companies in different fields. For example, one conglomerate, as it is called, might own a bus company, a cosmetics company, a toy company, a frozen-food company, and a football team.

The Labor Force

The rise of large industries changed the American workplace. Many of the new factories were dangerous places to work. They were poorly lighted and had few windows so there was little fresh air. Textile workers inhaled dust and fibers. In steel mills, workers stood only inches away from vats of hissing, molten steel. Children often worked long hours in strenuous jobs like coal mining.

The first labor unions. Like business leaders, workers pioneered new organizations. To protect themselves against poor working conditions and long hours, some workers joined together in labor unions. The first national union of skilled and unskilled workers, the Knights of Labor, was founded in 1869.

The early labor unions were unpopular with factory owners and much of the American public. Strikers in the late 1800s often were arrested—and sometimes fired at—by police or army troops.

Slowly, unions won acceptance in many industries. In 1935, during the Great Depression, Congress passed a law making it legal for workers to form unions to bargain with factory owners. By 1940, there were 9 million union workers. Large labor unions, like large corporations, became an accepted part of American business.

A shifting job market. Today, economic changes are again affecting the work that people do. In some industries, computers direct the operation of labor-saving robots. Skilled workers program the computers and maintain the equipment. In other industries, newly developed chemicals are possible hazards for workers. Often, the long-range health effects of new products are not known for many years.

More people today are working in white-collar, or professional, occupations and service jobs. They sell insurance, electronic equipment, and automobiles. They program computers, create advertising, maintain jetliners, and do medical research.

Foreign Competition

In the 1900s, the United States developed a healthy foreign trade. It exported far more goods than it imported.

At Work in a Textile Mill *Factory work has changed greatly since the late 1800s. Early factories were dangerous, and the labor force was often made up of children. Today, improvements in technology have made factory work safer, and child labor is forbidden by law. These pictures of a textile mill of the late 1800s, at left, and a similar mill today show some of the changes that have occurred.* **Technology** *How has technology made factory work safer?*

By the 1980s, however, American industries faced greater competition from other countries. In Japan, for example, factories were newer and more efficient. Also, wages were lower. Japan, therefore, was able to produce and sell goods more cheaply.

American industries have taken steps to meet foreign competition. Many have improved their plants and products. Some have asked the government to limit foreign imports by imposing tariffs.

Today, industries across the world are linked in a global economy. Many nations have signed trade agreements that allow them to compete more fairly. In 1993, for example, the United States, Canada, and Mexico ratified the North American Free Trade Agreement, or NAFTA. NAFTA reduced or eliminated many tariffs between the three countries. Worldwide trade agreements are put into place by an agency set up under the General Agreement on Tariffs and Trade, or GATT.

SECTION 2 REVIEW

1. **Identify:** (a) Henry Ford, (b) Orville and Wilbur Wright, (c) Thomas Alva Edison, (d) Knights of Labor.
2. **Define:** (a) corporation, (b) monopoly.
3. (a) How did transcontinental railroads affect the West? (b) How did railroads boost industry?
4. (a) How did monopolies grow? (b) Why are there no monopolies today?
5. Why did the first labor unions form?
6. What changes have affected work today?
7. **CRITICAL THINKING Synthesizing Information** How did inventions affect economic growth?

ACTIVITY **Writing to Learn**
Choose an invention of the 1800s from the chart on page 516. Imagine that you live in that time. Describe your reaction when you see the invention for the first time. How would it help you?

3

A Changing Government

FIND OUT

■ How have the rights of African Americans changed since the Civil War?

■ How did women gain suffrage?

■ Why did the federal government expand its role in the economy?

VOCABULARY initiative, referendum, recall

In December 1916, President Woodrow Wilson appeared in the House of Representatives to read his annual message to Congress. The members listened quietly. Suddenly, in the front row of the visitors' gallery above, six women leaned over the balcony and unrolled a yellow banner. In bold letters it read, "Mr. President, what will you do for woman suffrage?"

Wilson smiled faintly and continued his speech. The doorkeeper for the House, however, ran angrily up the aisle and jumped to pull the banner down. On the third try, he succeeded. Still, the women had made their point. Newspapers carried the story across the nation.

These and other actions by women finally convinced President Wilson to join the campaign to give women the vote. In the years after the Civil War, many citizens worked to broaden rights for individuals and reform government in other ways.

Winning the Full Rights of Citizenship

Today, all American citizens over age 18 have the right to vote. In 1860, however, only white men age 21 or over could vote. Winning the right to vote, as well as other rights of citizenship, for other groups of Americans became an ongoing struggle.

Rights for African Americans. The Fifteenth Amendment, ratified in 1870, stated that an adult male citizen could not be prevented from voting because of race. This officially extended the right to vote to black men.

After Reconstruction, however, southern states passed laws to make it difficult or impossible for African Americans to vote. Other laws kept blacks and whites from associating in public places. In the North, too, African Americans faced discrimination.

Even though many could not vote, African Americans fought in World War I and World War II. They were forced to serve

African American Soldiers in World War I *Until the late 1940s, the United States armed forces rigidly separated black and white troops. In his painting* War Knows No Color Line, *modern African American artist E. Sims Campbell pays tribute to the courage and sacrifice of black soldiers in World War I.* **Multicultural Heritage** *What do you think is the meaning of the title of Campbell's painting?*

WAR KNOWS NO COLOR LINE

in segregated regiments, however. Not until 1948 was the military integrated, by order of President Harry Truman.

Civil rights movement. In the 1950s and 1960s, African Americans began new campaigns for equal treatment under the law. The Reverend Martin Luther King, Jr., led nonviolent protests against segregation. His marches often met violent opposition. The resistance only increased his support, however. Time after time, King encouraged his followers to keep up their efforts:

> **"**If we protest courageously, and yet with dignity and Christian love, when the future history books are written, somebody will have to say, 'There lived a race of people, of black people, of people who had the moral courage to stand up for their rights.'**"**

In response, Congress passed civil rights laws to help end racial segregation and discrimination. The Voting Rights Act of 1965 protected African Americans who wanted to register to vote. In 1964, only 35 percent of southern African Americans were registered. By the early 1990s about 7,500 African Americans held elected office in the United States. They included over 330 mayors and 26 members of Congress.

Citizenship for Asian immigrants. Most immigrants who came to the United States could become naturalized citizens after a number of years. A law passed in 1790, however, allowed only "white" immigrants to become naturalized citizens.

Under this system, Asian immigrants were denied full participation in American life. Unlike other immigrants, they could not become citizens and vote. In states that allowed only citizens to own property, Asian immigrants could not own farms, businesses, or even their own homes.

Takao Ozawa, a Japanese immigrant who had lived in the United States more than 20 years, challenged the law as unfair. In 1922, however, the Supreme Court ruled against him. Only in 1952 did Congress allow Asian immigrants to become naturalized citizens.

Women's rights. Women won the right to vote when the Nineteenth Amendment was ratified in 1920. In fact, the struggle had begun much earlier. The Seneca Falls Convention in 1848 passed a resolution demanding suffrage for women. (See page

San Francisco's Chinatown *San Francisco, California, has one of the largest Chinese communities outside Asia. Many of the city's first Chinese came during the Gold Rush in 1849. This painting shows a street market in San Francisco's Chinatown in the mid-1800s.* **Citizenship** *How were Asians treated differently from other immigrants?*

Representative Nydia Velázquez *Women have made important gains in many areas in recent years. In 1992, Nydia Velázquez became the first Puerto Rican woman elected to the House of Representatives.* **Local History** *What women hold political office in your state?*

411.) During the late 1800s and early 1900s, women's organizations continued the campaign for the vote.

The campaign was often long and hard. Across the country, "suffragettes" tried to win support wherever they could. One suffragette told of her campaign on a train trip in Kansas:

66About a dozen passengers were in the caboose . . . and we held a meeting and discussion which lasted about 45 minutes. Upon reaching Osborne at three o'clock I found about 100 people assembled for an auction sale in the middle of the street. . . The temptation to hold a meeting overcame fatigue. I jumped into an automobile nearby and had a most interested crowd until the auctioneer came.99

By 1919, women in many states could vote in state and local elections. The Nineteenth Amendment gave women the right to vote in presidential elections as well.

During the 1960s, women won greater civil and economic rights. Federal laws made it illegal to favor men over women when hir-ing or paying wages. In the 1970s and 1980s, women made important gains in politics. In 1993, Ruth Bader Ginsburg became the second woman to sit on the Supreme Court, joining Sandra Day O'Connor.

The vote for 18-year-olds. In March 1971, Congress passed the Twenty-sixth Amendment. This amendment guaranteed the right to vote to persons age 18 or older. At the time, soldiers as young as age 18 were fighting and dying in the Vietnam War but were not allowed to vote until age 21. The amendment won strong support, and it was ratified in less than four months.

A Growing Role for Voters

As new groups of Americans gained the right to vote, voters also won new powers. Today, voters in some states can introduce a bill to the legislature by collecting signatures on a petition. This process is called an **initiative.** In a **referendum,** people vote directly on a bill. In some states, voters also have the power to remove a person from office in a **recall election.**

The initiative, referendum, and recall were ideas supported by reformers in the early 1900s. These reformers were called Progressives. Progressives also supported primary elections and direct election of senators. In a primary, voters from each political party decide who will be their party's candidate in the general election. The creation of primaries meant that political bosses could no longer handpick candidates.

The Constitution originally called for senators to be chosen by state legislatures. The Seventeenth Amendment, which was ratified in 1913, gave voters in each state the right to elect two senators.

A More Active Federal Government

As the nation has expanded, the role of the federal government has grown. Often, the government has stepped in to help or protect Americans.

Regulation of business. In the late 1800s, for example, the growth of industry created large businesses worth millions of dollars. These businesses sometimes used their power and influence unfairly. Reformers called on Congress to regulate large businesses and protect ordinary workers and citizens. Congress created the Interstate Commerce Commission, or ICC, in 1887. The ICC investigated complaints and took some big companies to court.

Government-sponsored programs. During the 1900s, the government became increasingly involved in the lives of Americans. One of the major turning points grew out of the Great Depression of the 1930s. During the depression, millions of workers were thrown out of work, and many farmers lost their land.

In 1933, when the depression was at its worst, Franklin Delano Roosevelt became President. With the help of Congress, he set up many new programs to relieve the suffering of the unemployed. The government also sponsored public-works programs. These put unemployed men and women to work on projects such as the creation of dams, schools, and parks.

Questions about regulation. Since the 1930s, government has been faced with other questions. Should it regulate the dangerous gases that pour from factory smokestacks? Should it protect consumers from foods and medicines that might be harmful? Should it inspect shops and factories to make sure they are safe for workers? The federal government now regulates each of these areas, as well as many others.

Research for Space and Ecology *In the airtight chamber shown here, NASA space scientists are developing a "closed-loop life support system." Just by breathing, astronauts will supply enough carbon dioxide to sustain a collection of plants. The plants, in turn, will give off enough oxygen to sustain the astronauts. Closer to home, this project offers valuable insights into ways to protect the Earth's fragile ecology.* **Daily Life** *What other steps have Americans taken to protect the environment?*

In the 1970s, concerns about the environment led Congress to pass laws cleaning up polluted rivers and smog-filled air. During the 1980s and 1990s, some scientists suggested that human activities such as cutting down forests and burning gas, oil, and coal may be causing a dangerous increase in the Earth's temperatures. Americans are coming to realize that the way they live has long-term effects on the Earth.

Americans also began to worry about the high costs of government programs and of enforcing government regulations. They worried, too, that the federal government had too much power. In 1980, Americans elected Ronald Reagan to be President, in part because he promised to cut taxes and reduce government regulation. In 1995, the newly elected Republican Congress began a campaign to cut the size of the federal government. Still, the government continues to play an active role in many areas of American life.

SECTION 3 REVIEW

1. **Identify:** (a) Martin Luther King, Jr., (b) Voting Rights Act of 1965, (c) Ruth Bader Ginsburg, (d) Sandra Day O'Connor.
2. **Define:** (a) initiative, (b) referendum, (c) recall.
3. What were the goals of the civil rights movement of the 1950s and 1960s?
4. How did women win the right to vote?
5. How did the federal government help to relieve unemployment in the 1930s?
6. CRITICAL THINKING **Defending a Position** Why do you think the initiative and the recall make for a more democratic government?

ACTIVITY **Writing to Learn** Imagine that you are a woman or an 18-year-old at a time before you had the right to vote. Write a speech to inspire others to support your right.

4
Looking Abroad

FIND OUT
- Why did the United States become more active in world affairs?
- What part did the United States play in the two world wars?
- How has American foreign policy changed since the end of World War II?

In 1858, New Yorkers paraded through their city streets amid bonfires and fireworks. The celebration was in honor of Cyrus Field, who had just laid the first successful wire cable across the Atlantic Ocean.

For the first time, telegraph messages passed instantly between England and the United States. But the celebration had begun too soon. A few weeks later, the telegraph was silent. Somewhere in the deep Atlantic, the cable had broken.

In 1866, however, Field tried again. He hired the largest steamship in the world, the *Great Eastern*, to set a course east from Ireland. Powered by huge paddle wheels, the *Great Eastern* carefully lowered a total of 1,900 miles (3,058 km) of wire into the ocean. This time, the line did not break.

In the years after the Civil War, Field's transatlantic cable drew the nations of the world together. Railroads and oceangoing steamers also cut travel time on land and sea. Because of these and other changes, the United States became more involved in world affairs.

Growing Involvement in World Affairs

During its first 100 years, the United States paid little attention to world affairs. Washington, Jefferson, and other Presidents hoped that the nation could grow and prosper without becoming entangled in foreign wars or other disputes.

Foreign trade. Over the years, however, the United States increased its export of food and manufactured goods to foreign countries. Europe was the most important market. After the Civil War, trade with China, Japan, Korea, and Latin America also grew.

In 1853, for example, Isaac Singer opened a factory that manufactured sewing machines. He soon saw that his machines would be in demand in Europe as well as in the United States. By 1900, more than 60,000 Singer sewing machine agents were located throughout the world, including China and the islands of the South Pacific.

Trade with Asia. As American trade grew, European countries were building empires in Africa and Asia. These empires increased the power and wealth of European nations. American business leaders feared that they would be squeezed out of many new foreign markets, especially in Asia. In Congress, Senator Albert Beveridge of Indiana urged an increase in trade:

> 66Our largest trade henceforth must be with Asia. The Pacific is our ocean. . . . China is our natural customer. . . . That statesman commits a crime against American trade . . . who fails to put America where she may command that trade.99

In 1898, the United States annexed Hawaii, whose fine harbors in the Pacific Ocean provided a base for the United States Navy. With a safe harbor in Hawaii, the United States could more easily open and protect markets in Asia.

New territories. The Spanish-American War of 1898 also gave the United States new territories. The war broke out as a result of a dispute over Spanish actions in Cuba. American troops quickly defeated the Spanish.

Under the peace treaty, the formerly Spanish islands of Puerto Rico in the Caribbean and Guam and the Philippines in the Pacific became United States territories. Cuba became independent.

Relations With Latin America

The United States also took a more active role in Latin America. In 1901, Theodore Roosevelt became President. His motto was "Speak softly, but carry a big stick." By this, he meant that the United States would strive for peace but not shy away from using force when necessary.

Roosevelt used the "big stick" in Latin America. Several European countries were trying to influence Venezuela and the Dominican Republic. Roosevelt reminded them that under President Monroe, the United States had warned against European powers meddling in the Americas. (See page 319.) Roosevelt was the second President to use

Teddy Roosevelt Wields the "Big Stick" *President Theodore Roosevelt believed that the United States had the "regrettable but necessary . . . duty" to act as an international policeman. In this 1904 cartoon, TR, as he was called, uses his "big stick" to maintain order around the world.* ***United States and the World*** *How do Americans feel today about the policies of a "big stick"?*

Americans in World War II *World War II was fought in both Europe and the Pacific. This painting by Dwight Shepler shows the landing of American forces on the tiny island of Corregidor, in the Philippines.* ***United States and the World*** *What event led the United States to enter World War II?*

the Monroe Doctrine as an active policy in the region.

Throughout the 1900s, the United States has intervened in Latin America in order to protect American interests. President William Howard Taft, for example, sent troops into Nicaragua and Honduras. President Woodrow Wilson sent marines to Haiti. President Ronald Reagan ordered troops to invade Grenada. And more recently, President Bill Clinton sent troops to Haiti.

Over the years, Americans have debated the policies of a "big stick." Opponents argue that the United States has made enemies by intervening in the internal affairs of weaker nations. Supporters respond that the United States has served as a needed police officer in Latin America.

The World at War

In 1914, World War I broke out in Europe. At first, President Wilson declared neutrality. Then, in 1917, the United States entered the war on the side of Britain and its allies. When peace came in 1918, many Americans no longer wanted to be involved in world affairs. These people were called isolationists.

In the 1930s, the nations of Europe again moved toward war. In Germany, the dictator Adolf Hitler ruled with absolute power. In 1939, war broke out when Hitler invaded neighboring Poland. Italy and Japan sided with Hitler, forming the Axis powers. They fought against the Allies, which included Britain, France, and the Soviet Union.

Again, the United States tried to remain neutral. On December 7, 1941, however, the Japanese launched a surprise attack on Pearl Harbor in Hawaii. Congress quickly declared war on Japan. Days later, Italy and Germany declared war on the United States. After four years of war and millions of deaths, the Allies defeated Germany and Italy. The war against Japan did not end until American planes dropped atomic bombs on the Japanese cities of Hiroshima and Nagasaki.

The United States as a World Power

At the end of World War II, much of Europe lay in ashes. Homes had no heat, city streets were dark, and the war-weary were starving. To help Europe's battered economy, the United States created the Marshall Plan. Under the plan, the United States gave billions of dollars to rebuild factories and railroads in Europe.

Rivalry with the Soviet Union. Soon after the end of World War II, the United States became concerned about the Soviet Union. The two nations had been allies during the war. After the war, however, the Soviet dictator Joseph Stalin helped communists to take over countries in Eastern Europe. To contain Soviet influence, the United States and the nations of Western Europe formed the North Atlantic Treaty Organization, or NATO.

Rivalry between the United States and the Soviet Union never broke out into armed conflict. With nuclear missiles pointed at each other, that prospect became too frightening. Yet the tension and hostility between the two superpowers became known as the Cold War.

Wars in Asia. Twice, American troops fought wars to contain communist expansion. The United Nations, an international peacekeeping organization set up in 1945, commanded American troops from 1950 to 1953 to turn back an invasion of South Korea by communist North Korea.

In the 1960s and 1970s, American soldiers fought in Vietnam against communist rebels. Many Americans, especially young people, protested. They said that the conflict in Vietnam was a civil war and that it did not threaten American security. In the early 1970s, the troops finally returned home. But more than 57,000 Americans had lost their lives in the nation's longest war.

Hopes for peace and democracy. After 1985, superpower tensions eased as Premier Mikhail Gorbachev (mee kah EEL gor buh

CHAWF) launched economic and democratic reforms in the Soviet Union. In 1989, countries in Eastern Europe rejected their communist governments.

Two years later an even more startling event took place. The Soviet Union itself broke up. Some of the former republics became independent nations. Others, including Russia, formed a new Commonwealth of Independent States. The Cold War was over, although smaller conflicts continued to break out around the world.

Regional Involvement

The United States has been involved in other troubled regions of the world. In the Middle East, it has tried to bring about peace between its chief ally in the region, Israel, and Israel's Arab neighbors.

In 1990, new tensions broke out in the Middle East. Iraq invaded the oil-rich kingdom of Kuwait. When Iraq refused to withdraw from Kuwait, the United Nations Security Council authorized the use of force. In 1991, the United States and its allies went to war and defeated Iraq.

Americans have tried to help other peoples in developing nations. Developing nations include many countries in Africa, Asia, and Latin America that are beginning to

Historic Handshake *In the mid-1990s, Israel and the PLO stunned the world by signing peace agreements. Here, President Clinton watches as Israeli Prime Minister Yitzhak Rabin, left, shakes hands with PLO leader Yasir Arafat, right.* **United States and the World** *How could the United States continue to aid the peace process?*

Ready for the Future *The United States faces many challenges as it approaches a new century. Still, Americans, like these people proudly displaying the flag, look to the future with confidence in themselves and their nation.* **Citizenship** *What do you think is the greatest challenge the nation faces in the next century? How can Americans meet the challenge?*

industrialize. The United States gives billions of dollars every year to help developing nations build their economies. Yet the problems of these countries are hard to solve.

The United States has given foreign aid in part because poverty can cause political problems. In poor countries, rebels have often won the support of the people by promising to distribute the wealth more evenly. In 1959 in Cuba, Fidel Castro led a successful revolution. After winning power, he angered the United States because his socialist government became a strong ally of the Soviet Union. Today, Cuba's economy has worsened, leaving it close to collapse.

As citizens of a superpower, Americans face a world filled with difficult problems. People do not always agree on what action to take. But Americans no longer expect to return to the days when a nation could ignore events in the rest of the world.

The Future of a Free People

In this book, you have read about the many individuals, groups, and cultures who helped create a new republic, the United States. The progress of that nation, through 1877, was never easy. Americans were called upon to stand up for their rights and to fight a revolution. Even four years of civil war challenged the nation to forge a freer and more perfect union.

What does the future hold? Since 1877, the United States has become an industrial power and a world leader. It can continue as one only if every American works to preserve the age-old opportunities of life, liberty, and the pursuit of happiness. Your generation holds the power to shape America's future.

SECTION 4 REVIEW

1. **Locate:** (a) Hawaii, (b) Puerto Rico, (c) Cuba, (d) Israel, (e) Iraq, (f) Kuwait.
2. **Identify:** (a) Cyrus Field, (b) Theodore Roosevelt, (c) Adolf Hitler, (d) Joseph Stalin, (e) Mikhail Gorbachev.
3. How did the United States acquire Puerto Rico, Guam, and the Philippines?
4. What was President Theodore Roosevelt's policy in Latin America?
5. (a) How did Americans feel about world involvement after World War I? (b) How did the United States help Europe after World War II?
6. **Synthesizing Information** Do you think it is possible for the United States to be isolationist today? Explain.

ACTIVITY **Writing to Learn**
Write newspaper headlines for five events that demonstrate American involvement in world affairs since 1877.

Presidents of the United States, 1877–Present

President	Dates	Major Events
Rutherford B. Hayes	1877–1881	Reconstruction ends; light bulb invented; millions of European immigrants arrive
James A. Garfield	1881	Booker T. Washington founds Tuskegee Institute; Garfield assassinated
Chester A. Arthur	1881–1885	First electric power plant and skyscraper; Civil Service Commission curbs spoils system
Grover Cleveland	1885–1889	Statue of Liberty unveiled; Interstate Commerce Commission orders railroads to set "reasonable and just rates"
Benjamin Harrison	1889–1893	Sherman Antitrust Act prohibits monopolies
Grover Cleveland	1893–1897	Cuba revolts against Spain; Supreme Court upholds racial segregation in *Plessy* v. *Ferguson*
William McKinley	1897–1901	United States acquires Philippines, Guam, and Puerto Rico; McKinley assassinated
Theodore Roosevelt	1901–1909	Roosevelt defends striking coal workers; Panama grants United States the Canal Zone; Pure Food and Drug Act protects consumers
William H. Taft	1909–1913	National Association for the Advancement of Colored People founded; Pan American Union (21 republics) acts on mutual concerns
Woodrow Wilson	1913–1921	Panama Canal opened; World War I
Warren G. Harding	1921–1923	Harlem Renaissance flourishes; Harding dies
Calvin Coolidge	1923–1929	Lindbergh flies Atlantic; Kellogg-Briand Pact outlaws war except in self-defense
Herbert C. Hoover	1929–1933	Stock market crashes; Great Depression begins; Hitler gains power in Germany
Franklin D. Roosevelt	1933–1945	New Deal creates employment; World War II; Roosevelt dies
Harry S. Truman	1945–1953	United Nations seeks peaceful solutions to international disputes; NATO provides mutual defense for some European nations; Korean War
Dwight D. Eisenhower	1953–1961	Civil rights sit-in movement begins
John F. Kennedy	1961–1963	First American in space; Cuban missile crisis; John Kennedy assassinated
Lyndon B. Johnson	1963–1969	Civil Rights Act bans job discrimination; bombing of North Vietnam begins; Martin Luther King, Jr., and Robert Kennedy assassinated
Richard M. Nixon	1969–1974	Moon landing; Vietnam cease-fire; Watergate hearings; Nixon resigns
Gerald R. Ford	1974–1977	Ford pardons Nixon; Vietnam War ends
Jimmy Carter	1977–1981	Egypt and Israel sign Camp David peace agreement; Iranians seize American hostages
Ronald W. Reagan	1981–1989	First woman justice appointed to Supreme Court; United States and Soviet Union reduce nuclear forces
George Bush	1989–1993	Eastern European nations seek democracy; Iraq invades Kuwait; Persian Gulf War
Bill Clinton	1993–	Successful peace initiatives in Northern Ireland and the Middle East; diplomatic recognition of Vietnam; NATO peacekeeping forces sent to Bosnia

CHART SKILLS *This chart shows the Presidents from Reconstruction to the present. • Who was President during World War I? World War II?*

Summary

- Immigrants from all over the world have increased the nation's diversity and enriched its culture. Advances in communications and technology have helped to tie together the diverse nation.
- Advances in transportation, inventions, and new methods of doing business led the United States to become an industrial giant. Economic changes have caused more Americans to work in skilled occupations or white-collar professions.
- Women and other groups of Americans have all gained important civil rights, including the right to vote. Recently, Americans have questioned the large role of government in Americans' lives.
- Increased foreign trade forced the United States into a more active role in world affairs. After World War II, the United States became a world leader.

Reviewing the Main Ideas

1. (a) What "new" immigrants arrived in the late 1800s and early 1900s? (b) What new waves of immigrants arrived in the 1970s, 1980s, and 1990s? (c) How have immigrants contributed to the United States?
2. What advances in communication have affected American culture?
3. How did the Bessemer process affect American industry?
4. What changes have taken place in American business since the late 1800s?
5. How did each of the following amendments extend voting rights: (a) Fifteenth; (b) Nineteenth; (c) Twenty-sixth?
6. How has the federal government expanded its role in the economy since the Civil War?

7. Why did the United States seek to increase trade with Asia in the late 1800s?
8. (a) What role did the United States play in World War I and World War II? (b) How has the United States tried to help developing countries?

Thinking Critically

1. **Linking Past and Present** Compare the dangers that workers faced in factories of the late 1800s and the hazards that workers face today.
2. **Analyzing Ideas** The Reverend Martin Luther King, Jr., led nonviolent protests against segregation. Why do you think this method of protest was successful?
3. **Defending a Position** Do you think the United States should follow a "big stick" policy in Latin America? Explain.
4. **Synthesizing Information** Imagine that you lived in the United States in the late 1800s. What changes would you see taking place in the nation?

Applying Your Skills

1. **Skimming a Chapter** (a) What does the chapter outline tell you about this chapter? (b) List the main topics in Section 3.
2. **Using Photographs as a Primary Source.** Study the photographs on page 518. (a) What is the subject of the photographs? (b) Describe the workers and the machinery shown in the photographs. (c) Based on the photographs, do you think factory conditions are better today than they were 100 years ago? Explain.
3. **Ranking** Make a list of 10 events since the Civil War. Rank them according to the impact you think each has had on American history, beginning with the one with the greatest impact.

Getting Involved

Y ou have just finished a year's study of American history. You have learned about the people and events that have shaped our nation. You have also tried to connect those past events with your life today.

At the beginning of your study, you were introduced to five major issues of American history: Multicultural Nation, Spirit of Democracy, Changing Economy, Environment, and Global Interdependence. These issues, as you recall, help tie the facts of American history together. Tracing these issues helped you to understand not just *what happened* in American history but *why* and *how* it happened.

On the following pages, you will have a chance to explore these issues of American history in a slightly different way. First, Milestones lists the major events and dates related to each issue. A Case Study tells how people your age turned ideas about each issue into action. Finally, a suggested activity related to the issue gives you a chance to *get involved*.

Issues for Today

Multicultural Nation

CASE STUDY
Helping Immigrant Children

Every year, thousands of immigrants enter the United States from all over the world. The new arrivals have to learn a new language, find a place to live, get a job. Children have to make new friends and attend American schools, which may seem strange to them. For many, the first years in their new land can be lonely and confusing.

In New York City, members of the City Volunteer Corps (CVC) wondered if they could do something to help new immigrants. CVC is a youth service group that works to improve the quality of life in the city. CVC members come from many different cultural backgrounds, and many are recent immigrants themselves.

The CVC group volunteered in a Korean Youth Center that served some of New York City's large Korean population. The volunteers tutored children in the center's after-school program. They helped the children to read English, to complete their homework assignments, and to improve their conversational skills. They also organized games and activities.

The CVC members helped hundreds of Korean children adapt to their new lives in the United States. Their work had another effect, too. Their daily contacts with the Korean children gave the young CVC members a chance to know and appreciate people of another culture.

Getting Involved

Work with your classmates to find out if there are immigrants or other new residents in your community. What problems do these people face? Do they need help with language or customs? Do they need advice about finding homes, jobs, stores, or schools? Identify ways in which you can help. Then organize a program to help the newcomers feel more at home.

MILESTONES

70,000–50,000 years ago
First Americans arrive from Asia

1500s–1700s
Europeans found colonies

1619
Africans arrive in Virginia

1840s
Immigration from Northern Europe continues

1880s
Immigration from Southern and Eastern Europe begins

1980s
Immigration from Latin America, Asia, and Caribbean increases

Spirit of Democracy

CASE STUDY
Celebrating the First Amendment

In 1989, a group of students from Scottsdale, Arizona, visited the Lincoln Memorial in Washington, D.C. They recalled that Martin Luther King, Jr., had delivered a now-famous speech on the steps of the Memorial in 1963. Before a hushed crowd of 200,000 people, King spoke of his dream: a United States in which all people were truly equal.

Inspired by this memory, the students came up with the idea of setting up a museum in vacant exhibit space at the Lincoln Memorial. The exhibit would honor Dr. King's speech.

To promote their plan, the students created information packets and wrote letters to officials. They rounded up the support of local officials, civic groups, and the press. Finally, they made another trip to Washington to meet with the National Park Service and a subcommittee of the House of Representatives.

The group's hard work paid off. The plan was approved. A new exhibit, informally called the Legacy of Lincoln, opened at the Lincoln Memorial in September of 1994.

The exhibit honors rights guaranteed by the First Amendment to the Constitution—freedom of speech, religion, press, assembly, and petition. It includes displays showing the many ways in which those rights have been expressed at the Lincoln Memorial. Among these are video excerpts of Dr. King's 1963 speech.

Getting Involved

Find out when your representative to Congress will be in your area. Then arrange a class visit to the representative's district office. Plan for the visit by researching several issues that Congress is currently debating. Make a list of questions to ask your representative about these issues.

Changing Economy

CASE STUDY
Volunteering in a Children's Center

Volunteers have always been a part of American life. By giving their time to hospitals, libraries, schools, and fire departments, they have enabled their communities to expand services without increasing costs. Today, volunteers are more important than ever. Their services form an important part of the economy.

One volunteer who made a difference in his community is 14-year-old Dennis Chisholm, Jr. Dennis lives in Winston-Salem, North Carolina. He volunteered to work at the Children's Center for the Physically Handicapped. He gave his time during summer vacations and after school.

Dennis performed a variety of tasks at the center. He helped feed the children and assisted them with physical therapy. He also helped adapt computer equipment and software for their use. He even started a weekly newsletter and encouraged the children to act as reporters.

For the children at the center, Dennis was a valuable friend and helper. For the people who run the center, he was an important resource. Like many of the nation's social agencies, Winston-Salem's Children's Center had suffered severe cutbacks in spending. Only with help from volunteers like Dennis can the center fulfill its goal of service.

Getting Involved

With your class, set up a service to run errands or do other chores for elderly or shut-in members of your community. Possible services can include mailing letters, shopping, light cleaning, or simply reading to people. Create and distribute a flyer advertising your service. Provide a telephone number where you can be reached. Take turns processing the calls and assigning volunteers to do the work.

MILESTONES

5,000 years ago
Farming in Americas

1600s
Farming and trade in colonies

1790
First factory

1800
Interchangeable parts

Early 1800s
Internal improvements

1869
Transcontinental railroad

Late 1800s
Rise of industry and big business

1890s
Overseas trade increases

1913
Assembly line

1930s
Government role increases

1970s
Computer Age

1980s
Shift from manufacturing to services

1993
NAFTA

Environment

CASE STUDY
Setting Up a Recycling Center

The people of Sprague, Washington, had never paid much attention to all the talk about recycling. They simply saved up their trash and then took it to the local dump. Getting rid of garbage this way was easy—and cheap.

Then the dump closed. Sprague residents had to hire a company to collect their garbage. They were shocked at the cost. For the first time, garbage became an issue in the tiny farming town.

Chris Victor, a local teenager, decided to act. Chris belonged to a community service group called Camp Fire. He suggested that the group set up a recycling center in Sprague. He pointed out that they could reduce garbage collection bills *and* help the environment.

The teens set to work. First, they scouted possible places for the center. They decided that an unused portion of Sprague's senior citizen's center would be a good location. The group then presented their plan to the mayor, who gave his approval.

Next, the group set up bins for glass, aluminum, paper, and cardboard. They also made a video to educate the town about the program. When the program was underway, the group emptied the bins once a month. They hauled the contents to a nearby recycling plant.

From the start, the program was a great success. In the first month alone, the center collected 1,500 pounds of paper, 500 pounds of glass, 100 pounds of aluminum cans, and 1,000 pounds of cardboard!

Getting Involved

With your classmates, set up a recycling program for your school. First, decide what you will recycle and where. Then present your plan to the teacher for approval. Finally, create a poster explaining your program. Arrange to bring what you collect to a recycling plant.

CASE STUDY
Protecting the World's Children

Eighth graders in Readington, New Jersey, were studying about children in different parts of the world. As part of their studies, they read about the United Nations Convention on the Rights of the Child. This international treaty is designed to protect the basic rights of all children. These rights include the right to food, shelter, and health care. They also include freedom of speech and freedom from discrimination.

The Readington students were troubled to think that some children in the world were denied these basic rights. "We wanted to help them," they said. They set out to learn more about the UN treaty.

The students discovered that 102 nations had ratified the Convention on the Rights of the Child. The United States, however, was not one of them. The students decided to try to change that.

The class wrote a petition urging the United States to approve the treaty. They sent the petition to more than 40 schools, asking other students to support their campaign. More than 2,000 students signed the petition! They also wrote letters to government leaders and to local newspapers, calling for approval of the treaty.

By the end of the school year, the United States had still not ratified the treaty. The Readington students were encouraged, however. They had made people aware of the treaty to protect the rights of children around the world.

Getting Involved

Contact an international agency such as the UN or the Red Cross to find out what you might do to help children in troubled areas of the world. For example, you might collect and sort needed items such as clothing, food, medical supplies, books, and so on. Form into groups and assign members tasks needed to carry out the project.

MILESTONES

1492
Columbian Exchange begins

1823
Monroe Doctrine

1854
Trade opens with Japan

1914
Panama Canal

1933
Good Neighbor Policy

1945
United Nations

1948
Marshall Plan

1949
NATO

1961
Peace Corps

1961
Alliance for Progress

1975
Helsinki Agreement

1993
NAFTA

Source Readings and Art

UNIT 1

A Meeting of Different Worlds

A Majestic Landscape *Among the many striking features of the diverse North American landscape are snow-capped mountains, thick pine forests, and breathtaking canyons. This painting by Karl Bodmer captures the rugged beauty and splendor of the high plains.* **Linking Past and Present** *This picture was painted during the 1800s. How might this landscape have changed since the picture was painted? Why?*

CHAPTER 1 Geography of the Americas
(Prehistory–Present)

■ 1-1 This Land Is Your Land

LITERATURE

INTRODUCTION Anyone who has ever traveled across America has been impressed by the country's immense size and beauty and by the tremendous variety of its geographic features. During his youth, songwriter Woody Guthrie visited many parts of America. In this song, "This Land Is Your Land," Guthrie draws upon his memories of those travels. The song provides a sense of the scope of America and praises the beauty of its mighty rivers, towering mountains, and fertile valleys.

VOCABULARY Before you read the selection, find the meaning of these words in a dictionary: rambled, chanting.

As I was walking that ribbon of highway
I saw above me that endless skyway
I saw below me that golden valley
This land was made for you and me.

Chorus: This land is your land
    This land is my land from
      California to the New York island
    From the red wood forest to the Gulf
      Stream waters
    This land was made for you and me.

I've roamed and rambled and followed
    my footsteps
to the sparkling sands of her diamond
    deserts

And all around me a voice was sounding
This land was made for you and me.

Chorus: This land is your land
    This land is my land from
        California to the New York island
    From the red wood forest to the
        Gulf Stream waters
        This land was made for you and me.

When the sun comes shining and I was
    strolling
and the wheat fields waving and the dust
    clouds rolling
As the fog was lifting a voice was chanting
This land was made for you and me.

Chorus: This land is your land
    This land is my land from
        California to the New York island

From the red wood forest to the
    Gulf Stream waters
This land was made for you and
me.

"This Land Is Your Land" by Woody Guthrie. TRO © Copyright 1956 (renewed), 1958 (renewed) and 1970 Ludlow Music, Inc., New York, NY. Used by permission of Ludlow Music, Inc.

■ THINKING ABOUT THE SELECTION

1. How does the songwriter convey a sense of America's vast size?

2. Which physical regions of North America are mentioned in the song?

3. CRITICAL THINKING **Applying Information** Use the map on pages 612–613 to locate places named or referred to in "This Land Is Your Land."

The Rugged Coast of Maine *Many features of the American landscape reveal the tremendous power of nature. In this painting, Paul Dougherty portrays the beauty and ruggedness of the Maine coast.* **Geography** *How do you think the harshness of the Maine landscape affected the lives of the people who settled there?*

INTRODUCTION Americans like to speak of conquering the wilderness. Indeed, after Europeans began settling North America, that is what they did, from the coastal plains bordering the Atlantic Ocean to the mountain ranges along the Pacific. But many beautiful areas of wilderness remain. Here Minnesota writer Paul Gruchow, who has hiked throughout the West, explains why we need to preserve these empty places.

VOCABULARY Before you read the selection, find the meaning of these words in a dictionary: pika, evoke, perseveres, parsimonious, persistence, arduous, void.

Walkers use the . . . maps published by the United States Department of the Interior Geological Survey, on which five and a quarter inches represent a mile. These maps are marvels of clarity and economy. They are printed in four colors: black for place names, brown for contour lines, blue for water, green for forests. The contour lines record every forty-foot change in elevation. Where the going gets rough, the brown lines crowd

Traveling by Dog Sled *To survive in the American wilderness, people had to adapt to their environments. As this painting by Paul Kane shows, Native Americans on the northern plains sometimes traveled over the snow-covered land by dog sled.* **Geography** *Why were dog sleds an especially effective method of transportation for people living in northern climates?*

more and more closely together; in the steepest places, they make almost solid bands of brown. The places I look for on the topographic maps are the ones with lots of brown lines and no green. They will prove rugged and rocky, flowerful in summer and swarming with insects, boggy with meltwater in places and still snowcovered in others, ringing with the bright whistles of pikas.

The maps, I suppose, compromise the idea of wilderness even as they help to evoke it. How absolutely wild can a place be that has already been reduced symbolically to . . . a topographic map? But the maps reassured us that we were headed, at least, toward houseless, roadless, trailless places, toward empty places.

In empty places life perseveres against harsh restrictions of climate or topography. In a sense they always were empty. The places that survive now as wilderness are by nature demanding, uncompromising, parsimonious. The green and rich wilderness places have long since been claimed for human purposes. I like the brittle and severe qualities of the places that remain empty. I like life that has braved the odds, made the best of little, come to terms with conditions that frustrate life in general.

I see, too, an appealing youthfulness in such places. Most of the places on the maps that remain empty are, by geologic measure, very young. The sparse North American grasslands, the Nebraska sandhills, the Sonoran desert, the tundra-covered mountaintops: all are communities that have developed in the recent geologic past. . . .

I like too the idea of life lived at the edge. A spruce tree at the upper limits of a mountain treeline, thick and misshapen, shorn of its branches on its windward side, no more than shoulder high although it may be a century old, such a spruce speaks powerfully of the persistence of life. Every person who enters the wilderness goes in search of the same speech. A journey into the wilderness is a test of the will against the odds. Going into the wilderness, any wilderness, is a way of opening yourself to the possibility of danger and to the likelihood of discomfort, at the least. There is the possibility of getting lost, of being trapped in a storm, of confronting an angry animal, of falling. There are the certain hardships of arduous walks, of exposure to cold, heat, wind, rain, of sleeping on the ground, of solitude. To be alone is sometimes the most difficult challenge of all. . . . Just as the tortured spruce tree at the edge of the upper forest enlarges and frees the world for trees, so our encounters with wilderness widen and free us.

Empty: unoccupied. . . . Empty is one of those words that reveals unspoken attitudes. Lacking people, it means. No humans equals nothing. . . .

Nevertheless some value and meaning clearly resides in such places, as in all places. Despite ourselves and our beliefs, some among us continue . . . to seek them out. We go to a mountaintop, or retreat to the desert, or . . . to some lonely cove along the wide and empty sea. We are drawn toward wildness as water is toward the level. And there we find that something that we cannot name. We find ourselves, we say. But I suppose that what we really find is the void within ourselves, the loneliness, the surviving heart of wildness, that binds us to all the living earth.

From *The Necessity of Empty Places* by Paul Gruchow. Copyright © 1988 by Paul Gruchow. Reprinted by permission of St. Martin's Press, Inc., New York, NY.

■ THINKING ABOUT THE SELECTION

1. How does Gruchow use the map to plan where he will hike?

2. What does the author like about wilderness regions?

3. CRITICAL THINKING **Expressing an Opinion** What are your feelings about "empty places"? Why?

CHAPTER 2 The First Americans
(Prehistory–1600)

■ 2-1 "I'm Indian and That's It"

INTRODUCTION For some Native American groups, the traditional customs died out after Europeans came to America. Many peoples, however, preserved their traditions—not just ways of doing things, but also ways of thinking and believing. Among them are the Chippewa (or Ojibwa), who lived, and still live, near the shores of Lake Superior. Elizabeth Gurno, a Chippewa, was born in Minnesota in the early 1900s. In this selection, she talks about some Native American traditions and what they mean.

VOCABULARY Before you read the selection, find the meaning of these words in a dictionary: mainstay, eyesore.

The Indians survived with their hunting and their garden produce. And years ago there was plenty of wild rice. . . . Wild rice has always been our mainstay of life. If you have rice, you are not hungry. Indians believed that at one time or another, we came from the water. Therefore, anything in the water is edible. You can eat it if you know how to cook it.

And then we made maple sugar. . . . Indians took things from Mother Earth. She gave us maple syrup. But with the left hand, we thanked her. I still do this in my family. We had quite a ceremony about that when I was growing up. Same with rice. Even if you don't ask everybody on the reservation to come in and join you, you ask a few people to come in and you give thanks. And with this wild rice, you save up enough maple syrup or sugar to mix with it. Just the two things mixed together. You eat that. That's a thanksgiving for what Mother Nature has given to you. . . .

There are many things in Indian life that nowadays you'd say don't make sense. We are associated with drums and feathers and that sort of thing. . . . [A] feather in our culture has to be earned. We are born with one feather. That is a gift from our parents. Now my father told me he was given a feather at his birth, and a blanket. And the blanket did not come from J. C. Penney. It was homemade out of rabbit hide. And the mother took nine months to make it. She finished her last stitch the day the baby was born. That was her gift to the baby. . . .

And now these feathers weren't just crow feathers or robin. They were eagle. Years ago, eagles were plentiful, but as the non-Indians moved in with all their concrete, the eagles went other places. . . .

And then we decorated things with porcupine quills. Those quills are very dangerous, but then they were used to decorate anything made out of birch bark. The ends have to be bent. They can go through human flesh. . . . They were dyed with chokecherries and raspberries for red, or pitch from the base of a balsam tree or a beech tree. . . . My grandmother had an art with birch bark that she chewed a design into the thin bark that my uncle would then in turn sew onto another basket. . . .

And she worked in the true Indian spirit. An Indian always has several things in mind when he does things: first, that he's busy with his hands doing something and not wasting his or anybody else's time. Then that he's making something useful and something beautiful to look at—not just an eyesore. And then that he's making something that will tell a story. It had to have meaning. . . .

A Rich Artistic Tradition *Many Native American groups looked to nature for art as well as survival. This elaborately decorated coffin is the work of the Haidas, a group that lives in what is now Alaska and British Columbia.* **Culture** *What do you think might be the purpose of the face carved into the coffin? Explain.*

The sacred colors are white, red, black, yellow, and blue. White is for the north, for the white snow. That, in turn, gives you strength. Red is the east for the sun. Yellow is for the south—for the heat that ripens our staff of life, the corn. And black is for the west. If a storm is coming, look to the west and there will be black clouds. The storm originates in the west. And blue represents man. So in doing any type of work, we try to include one or all of the colors depending on what we're making. . . .

Years back, it was a downright sin to be known as an Indian. It was something to be ashamed of. I couldn't go along with that because my grandmother spoke nothing but Chippewa. I lived in an Indian home. That's the way I breathed. The others picked up English. Then they in turn didn't want their children to speak Chippewa because the government agent told us that was wrong: "You don't look like a white man, but you got to live like one. You have to live like a white man now."

But I'm an Indian. I believe Indian ways. They know I'm Indian and that's it. I cannot erase me. I'm here to stay.

From *I Wish I Could Give My Son a Wild Raccoon* by Eliot Wigginton. Copyright © 1976 by Reading Is Fundamental. Used by permission of Doubleday, a division of Bantam Doubleday Dell Publishing Group, Inc.

■ THINKING ABOUT THE SELECTION

1. What Native American customs involving food does the author, Elizabeth Gurno, describe?

2. According to Gurno, what is the "true Indian spirit" of workmanship?

3. CRITICAL THINKING **Analyzing a Quotation** In speaking of her Native American heritage, Gurno says "That's the way I breathed." What do you think she means by that? In what, if any, traditional way do you "breathe"?

■ 2-2   How Fire Came to the Six Nations   LITERATURE

INTRODUCTION Information about the lives and beliefs of Native Americans is provided by their legends and folk tales. These stories were passed by word of mouth from generation to generation. Often, such legends were told to explain forces in nature that are difficult to understand. The Mohawks, one of the Iroquois nations, told the following tale about how humans discovered fire. As you read the selection, you will see that it supplies many details about the Mohawk way of life.

VOCABULARY Before you read the selection, find the meaning of these words in a dictionary: attained, ceaseless, balsam, resinous.

Three Arrows was a boy of the Mohawk tribe. Although he had not yet seen fourteen winters he was already known among the Iroquois for his skill and daring. His arrows sped true to their mark. His name was given him when with three bone-tipped arrows he brought down three flying wild geese from the same flock. He could travel in the forest

An Algonquin of the Carolinas *Much information about the clothing and traditions of the Algonquin people was preserved in a series of watercolors by John White, an early English settler. In this painting, White shows an Algonquin man in typical clothing.* **Local History** *Why are paintings and sketches an effective means of preserving history?*

as softly as the south wind and he was a skillful hunter, but he never killed a bird or animal unless his clan needed food. He was well-versed in woodcraft, fleet of foot, and a clever wrestler. His people said, "Soon he will be a chief like his father."

The sun shone strong in the heart of Three Arrows, because soon he would have to meet the test of strength and endurance through which the boys of his clan attained manhood. He had no fear of the outcome of the dream fast which he was so soon to take. His father was a great chief and a good man, and the boy's life had been patterned after that of his father.

When the grass was knee-high, Three Arrows left his village with his father. They climbed to a sacred place in the mountains. They found a narrow cave at the back of a little plateau. Here Three Arrows decided to live for his few days of prayer and vigil. He was not permitted to eat anything during the days and nights of his dream fast. He had no weapons, and his only clothing was a breechclout* and moccasins. His father left the boy with a promise that he would visit him every day that the ceremony lasted, at dawn.

Three Arrows prayed to the Great Spirit. He begged that soon his clan spirit would appear in a dream and tell him what his guardian animal or bird was to be. When he knew this, he would adopt that bird or animal as his special guardian for the rest of his life. When the dream came he would be free to return to his people, his dream fast successfully achieved.

For five suns Three Arrows spent his days and nights on the rocky plateau, only climbing down to a little spring for water after each sunset. His heart was filled with a dark cloud because that morning his father had sadly warned him that the next day, the sixth sun, he must return to his village even

*loincloth

if no dream had come to him in the night. This meant returning to his people in disgrace without the chance of taking another dream fast.

That night Three Arrows, weak from hunger and weary from ceaseless watch, cried out to the Great Mystery. "O Great Spirit, have pity on him who stands humbly before Thee. Let his clan spirit or a sign from beyond the thunderbird come to him before tomorrow's sunrise, if it be Thy will." As he prayed, the wind suddenly veered from east to north. This cheered Three Arrows because the wind was now the wind of the great bear, and the bear was the totem of his clan.

When he entered the cavern he smelled for the first time the unmistakable odor of a bear: this was strong medicine. He crouched at the opening of the cave, too excited to lie down although his tired body craved rest. As he gazed out into the night he heard the rumble of thunder, saw the lightning flash, and felt the fierce breath of the wind from the north. Suddenly a vision came to him, and a gigantic bear stood beside him in the cave. Then Three Arrows heard it say, "Listen well, Mohawk. Your clan spirit has heard your prayer. Tonight you will learn a great mystery which will bring help and gladness to all your people." A terrible clash of thunder brought the dazed boy to his feet as the bear disappeared. He looked from the cave just as a streak of lightning flashed across the sky in the form of a blazing arrow. Was this the sign from the thunderbird?

Suddenly the air was filled with a fearful sound. A shrill shrieking came from the ledge just above the cave. It sounded as though mountain lions fought in the storm; yet Three Arrows felt no fear as he climbed toward the ledge. As his keen eyes grew accustomed to the dim light, he saw that the force of the wind was causing two young balsam trees to rub violently against each other. The strange noise was caused by

friction, and as he listened and watched fear filled his heart, for, from where the two trees rubbed together a flash of lightning showed smoke.

Fascinated, he watched until flickers of flame followed the smoke. He had never seen fire of any kind at close range nor had any of his people. He scrambled down to the cave and covered his eyes in dread of this strange magic. Then he smelt bear again and he thought of his vision, his clan spirit, the bear, and its message. This was the mystery he was to reveal to his people. The blazing arrow in the sky was to be his totem, and his new name—Blazing Arrow.

At daybreak, Blazing Arrow climbed onto the ledge and broke two dried sticks from what remained of one of the balsams. He rubbed them violently together, but nothing happened. "The magic is too powerful for me," he thought. Then a picture of his clan and village formed in his mind, and he patiently rubbed the hot sticks together again. His will power took the place of his tired muscles. Soon a little wisp of smoke greeted his renewed efforts, then came a bright spark on one of the sticks. Blazing Arrow waved it as he had seen the fiery arrow wave in the night sky. A resinous blister on the stick glowed, then flamed—fire had come to the Six Nations!

Source: Allan A. Macfarlan, *Fireside Book of North American Indian Folktales* (Harrisburg, PA: Stackpole Books, 1974).

■ THINKING ABOUT THE SELECTION

1. What test did the boys of Three Arrows' tribe have to pass in order to attain manhood?

2. Why did Three Arrows think he was about to receive a sign from the thunderbird?

3. CRITICAL THINKING Drawing Conclusions Why was Three Arrows afraid when he saw fire?

CHAPTER 3 Europeans Reach the Americas
(1000–1650)

■ 3-1 Cortés and Montezuma

INTRODUCTION When Cortés and his soldiers landed in Mexico, the Aztec emperor Montezuma showered them with gifts. In the following essay, William Carlos Williams (1883-1963), a famous American poet and writer who had a great interest in history, describes those lavish gifts. He also paints a vivid picture of the Aztec capital city Tenochtitlán and of the first meeting between Cortés and Montezuma. Yet Williams does not offer an interpretation of the events. He believed in presenting vivid images that speak for themselves.

VOCABULARY Before you read the selection, find the meaning of these words in a dictionary: whetted, hewn, interceded, palpable, sally, semblance, aborigines, regent.

Montezuma immediately sent gifts, at the same time begging the Spaniard not to risk coming up into the back country: a gold necklace of seven pieces, set with many gems like small rubies, a hundred and eighty-three emeralds and ten fine pearls, and hung with twenty-seven little bells of gold. Two wheels, one of gold like the sun and the other of silver, with the image of the moon upon it. . . . A shield of wood and leather, with little bells hanging to it and covered with plates of gold, in the middle of which was cut the image of the god of war between four heads of a lion, a tiger, an éagle, and an owl represented alive with their hair and feathers. Twenty-four curious and beautiful shields of gold, of feathers and very small pearls, and four of feathers and silver only. Four fishes, two ducks and some other birds of molten gold. . . . And books made of tablets with a smooth surface for writing, which being joined might be folded together or stretched out to a considerable length, "the characters inscribed thereon resembling nothing so much as Egyptian hieroglyphics."

But Cortez* was unwilling to turn back; rather these things whetted his appetite for the adventure. Without more ado he sent letters to his king advising him that having come to these lands to conquer them, in the royal name and that of the true church, he would forthwith proceed to take Montezuma, dead or alive, unless he should accept the faith and acknowledge himself a subject to the Spanish throne.

The advance was like any similar military enterprise: it accomplished its purpose. . . . Montezuma seeing that there was nothing else for it, sent envoys accompanied by three hundred warriors, who met the Spaniard advancing on the lake road and there welcomed him to the district with great ceremony and show of friendliness. . . .

The following day at noon [Cortez] arrived at the end of his journey. There it lay! a city as large as Cordova or Seville, entirely within the lake two miles from the mainland: Tenochtitlán. Four avenues or entrances led to it, all formed of artificial causeways. Along the most easterly of these, constructed of great beams perfectly hewn and fitted together, and measuring two spears-lengths in width, the Christian advanced. Running in at one side of the city and out at the other, this avenue constituted at the same time its principal street.

_____
*alternative spelling of Cortés

As Cortez drew nearer he saw, right and left, magnificent houses and temples, close to the walls of which . . . moved parallel rows of priests in black robes, and, between them, supported by two attendants, Montezuma, on foot, down the center of the roadway. Cortez stepped forward but the attendants interceded. The Emperor then advanced alone and with great simpleness of manner placed a golden chain about the Christian's neck. Then taking him by the hand, and the whole procession following, he conducted him to the quarters which had been chosen for the visitors, a great building close to the royal palaces in the center of the city. . . .

Montezuma spoke: "They have told you that I possess houses with walls of gold and many other such things and that I am a god or make myself one. The houses you see are of stone and lime and earth." Then opening his robe: "You see that I am composed of flesh and bone like yourself and that I am mortal and palpable to the touch." To this smiling sally, so full of gentleness and amused irony, Cortez could reply nothing save to demand that the man declare himself a subject to the Spanish King forthwith and that, furthermore, he should then and there announce publicly his allegiance to the new power.

Whatever the Aztec may have felt during the weeks of Cortez' slow advance upon his capital from the seashore, nothing at the present moment seemed to disturb his aristocratic reserve. He had thought and he had made up his mind. Without semblance of anger, fear or impatience . . . he spoke again. He explained that his people were not the aborigines of the land but that they had emigrated there in times past and ended by accepting the Spanish Monarch as his rightful and hereditary master. After due announcements and explanations had been made to the people, Cortez became the

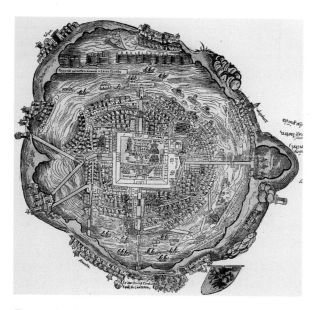

Tenochtitlán at the Time of the Spanish Conquest
Tenochtitlán, the Aztec capital, was built on an island in the center of a lake. Filled with exquisite houses and temples, it was the largest and most elaborate city in the Americas. This woodcut from a letter Cortés sent to the Spanish king shows the plan of the city at the time of his arrival. **Geography** *Why do you think the Aztecs chose to build their capital on an island?*

acknowledged regent, in the name of Castile* and the true church, for all that country.

William Carlos Williams. "The Destruction of Tenochtitlan," *In the American Grain.* Copyright © 1933 by William Carlos Williams. Reprinted by permission of New Directions Publishing Corporation.

■ THINKING ABOUT THE SELECTION

1. What kinds of gifts did Montezuma send to Cortés?

2. What demands did Cortés make?

3. **CRITICAL THINKING Drawing Conclusions** (a) Why do you think Montezuma sent such elaborate gifts to the Spanish? (b) Did Cortés react to the gifts as Montezuma hoped he would?

---

*a region and former kingdom in northern and central Spain

INTRODUCTION   Like its European neighbors, France wanted to find a northwest passage through or around America in order to reach Asia. This was the aim of Giovanni da Verrazano, an Italian explorer sent westward by the French king in 1524. Verrazano's ship, the *Dauphine*, first sighted land off the Carolinas and then sailed northward along the Atlantic coast. In these passages, the explorer describes the Native Americans, the land, and New York Harbor.

VOCABULARY   Before you read the selection, find the meaning of these words in a dictionary: russet, multitude, esteem, trifles, piteously.

The people are of color russet, and not much unlike the Saracens*—their hair is black, thick and not very long, which they tie together in a knot behind and wear it like a little tail. They are well featured in their limbs, of average stature, and commonly somewhat bigger than we. . . . We saw many of them handsome, having black and great eyes, with a cheerful and steady look, sharp witted, nimble and exceeding great runners, as far as we could learn by experience. In those two last qualities, they are like the people of the East parts of the world, and especially those of the uttermost parts of China. We could not learn of this people their manner of living, nor their particular customs, by reason of the short time we spent on the shore. . . .

Sailing forwards, we found certain small rivers . . . washing the shore on both sides as the coast lines. And beyond this we saw the open country rising above the sandy shore with many fair fields and plains, full of mighty great woods, some very thick, and some thin. . . . And the land is full of many

---

*a tribe from Syria

beasts—stags, deer and hares, and likewise of lakes and pools of fresh water, with great plenty of fowls, convenient for all kind of pleasant game.

We departed from this place, still running along the coast, . . . we saw everywhere very great fires, by reason of the multitude of inhabitants. . . .

[With the intention of sending them] things, which the Indians commonly desire and esteem, [such] as sheets of paper, glasses, bells, and such like trifles, we sent a young man, one of our mariners ashore. . . . Swimming towards them and . . . not trusting them, he cast the things upon the sand. Seeking afterwards to return to the ship, he was [beaten upon the shore by violent waves], so bruised that he lay there almost dead.

The Indians . . . ran to catch him, and drawing him out, they carried him a little way off from the sea. The young man being at first dismayed, began then greatly to fear, and cried out piteously. The Indians which did accompany him went about to cheer him and to give him courage. . . . Then setting him on the ground at the foot of a little hill against the sun, they began to behold him with great admiration, marvelling at the whiteness of his flesh. . . . They made him warm at a great fire, not without our great fear who remained in the boat, that they would have roasted him at that fire, and have eaten him.

The young man having recovered his strength, and having stayed a while with them, showed them by signs that he [wanted] to return to the ship. They with great love clapping him fast about with many embracings, accompanied him to the sea. [Then to reassure him], they went unto a high ground and stood there, beholding him until he entered the boat. . . .

Having made our abode three days in this country, and riding on the coast for want of harbors, we [traveled] along the shore . . . sailing only in the daytime, and riding at anchor by night. In the space of 100 leagues sailing, we found a very pleasant place situated among certain little steep hills.* From amidst the hills there ran down into the sea an exceeding great stream of water, which in the mouth was very deep, . . .

We [passed into] the said river, and saw the country very well peopled. . . . [But because of a sudden contrary wind coming from the sea], we were forced to return to our ship, leaving this land to our great

discontentment, for the great pleasantness thereof, which we suppose is not without some riches, all the hills showing mineral matters in them.

Source: *The New Land,* compiled and edited by Phillip Viereck (New York: The John Day Company, 1967).

■ THINKING ABOUT THE SELECTION

1. What features of the North American landscape most impressed Verrazano?

2. What does the incident described here suggest about the Indians' treatment of Verrazano's expedition?

3. **CRITICAL THINKING Drawing Conclusions** Which parts of Verrazano's narrative do you think would have been most likely to encourage further exploration?

---

*Verrazano is describing the lower bay of New York Harbor.

Discovery of the Hudson River *European explorers made repeated attempts to find a northwest passage through the Americas to Asia. This painting by Albert Bierstadt depicts the expedition of the English navigator Henry Hudson, who had been hired by the Dutch. Although Hudson did not find a northwest passage, he did discover the river that now bears his name.* **Geography** *What obstacles do you imagine Hudson and his crew faced as they sailed up the river?*

CHAPTER 4

The 13 English Colonies
(1630–1750)

■ 4-1 Forefathers' Song

INTRODUCTION A ballad is a type of song that tells a story and provides many descriptive details. "Forefathers' Song" is a ballad from early colonial New England. Written around 1630, it tells in plain language what life was like in the English colonies in America. Climate, food, and clothing are some of the topics discussed. Through the words of the song, you will learn more about colonial life.

VOCABULARY Before you read the selection, find the meaning of these words in a dictionary: ponder, forfeits, clout, pottage.

New England's annoyances you that would
   know them,
Pray ponder these verses which briefly
   doth show them.
The place where we live is a wilderness
   wood,
Where grass is much wanting that's fruitful
   and good:
Our mountains and hills and our valleys
   below,
Being commonly covered with ice and
   with snow;
And when the north-west wind with
   violence blows,
Then every man pulls his cap over his
   nose:
But if any's so hardy and will it withstand,
He forfeits a finger, a foot or a hand.

But when the Spring opens we then take
   the hoe,
And make the ground ready to plant and
   to sow;
Our corn being planted and seed being
   sown,
The worms destroy much before it is
   grown;

And when it is growing, some spoil there is
   made
By birds and by squirrels that pluck up the
   blade;
And when it is come to full corn in the
   ear,
It is often destroyed by raccoon and by
   deer.

And now our garments begin to grow
   thin,
And wool is much wanted to card and to
   spin;
If we can get a garment to cover without,
Our other in-garments are clout upon
   clout:
Our clothes we brought with us are apt to
   be torn,
They need to be clouted soon after they're
   worn,
But clouting our garments they hinder us
   nothing,
Clouts double are warmer than single
   whole clothing.

If fresh meat be wanting to fill up our
   dish,
We have carrots and turnips as much as
   we wish:
And if there's a mind for a delicate dish
We repair to the clam-banks, and there we
   catch fish.
Instead of pottage and puddings and
   custards and pies,
Our pumpkins and parsnips are common
   supplies;
We have pumpkins at morning and
   pumpkins at noon,
If it was not for pumpkins we should be
   undone!

* * *

The Beginning of New England *Settlers throughout the New England colonies faced monumental tasks in clearing land, planting crops, and building homes. When they survived despite formidable odds, they took time to express thanks to God. This painting by Jennie Brownscombe shows the most famous of those celebrations—the first Thanksgiving at Plymouth.* **Daily Life** *What information does the painting provide about life in early New England?*

But you whom the Lord intends hither to
    bring,
Forsake not the honey for fear of the
    sting;
But bring both a quiet and contented
    mind,
And all needful blessings you surely will
    find.

Source: "Forefathers' Song," a traditional ballad.

■ THINKING ABOUT THE SELECTION

1. What difficulties did the early New Englanders face in trying to grow crops?

2. Why did the colonists' clothes need to be "clouted"?

3. CRITICAL THINKING **Drawing Conclusions** Despite the hardships the colonists faced, what attitude is expressed in the last stanza of the "Forefathers' Song"?

■ 4-2   A Complaint From Virginia

FIRST PERSON

INTRODUCTION Like other colonizing countries, England established settlements abroad in order to benefit its own economy. As far as trade was concerned, the policy was simple. The colonies were to ship raw materials to England, in return for which England would sell the colonies its manufactured goods.

Many colonists resented England's trade policy. In 1697, three Virginians sent a petition to the Board of Trade, the English government office that supervised the colonies. The

English seemed to want nothing from Virginia but tobacco. These Virginians had other ideas. They list the colony's resources and natural advantages, and suggest problems.

VOCABULARY Before you read the selection, find the meaning of these words in a dictionary: judicious, commodity.

It is astonishing to hear what contrary descriptions are given of the country of Virginia, even by those who have often seen it, and know it very well; some of them representing it as the best, others as the worst country in the world. Perhaps they are both in the right. For the most general true character of Virginia is this, that as to the natural advantages of a country, it is one of the best; but as to the improved ones, one of the worst of all the English settlements in America. When one considers the wholesomeness of its air, the fertility of its soil . . . and the temperature of its climate . . . it is certainly one of the best countries in the world. But on the other hand, if we inquire for well-built towns, for convenient ports and markets, for plenty of ships and seamen, for well improved trades and manufactures, for well-educated children, for an industrious and thriving people, or for a happy government in church and state, . . . it is certainly, for all these things, one of the poorest, miserablest, and worst countries in all America that is inhabited by Christians. . . .

It is impossible to reckon up all the improvements which might be made in such a country, where many useful inventions would present themselves to the industrious. The following ones are such as naturally offer to any judicious spectator.

The manufacture of iron and other minerals, with which that country, to all appearance, is well stored, together with all the advantages of wood to burn them, and water to make the transportation easy. . . .

It is likewise very fit for potash for soap, by reason of the infinite numbers of trees, which make that country more to resemble a forest than one of the countries of Europe.

It abounds also in pitch, tar, rosin, masts, and all timbers for shipping. . . .

Wheat, rye, Indian corn, oats, barley, pease, and many other sorts of edible seeds grow there in great plenty. . . .

The country has also great advantages for the making of cider, oil, figs, raisins, and conserved fruits. . . .

We need not mention tobacco, which would likewise be an excellent staple commodity of that country, if they would make it good, without trash; but so it is at present, that tobacco swallows up all other things, everything else is neglected, and all markets are often so glutted with bad tobacco, that it becomes a mere drug, and will not clear the freight and custom*. . . .

But now, if it be inquired, what sort of a country it is? After all this, we must represent it after a quite different manner from what might be expected from the first and eldest of all the English settlements in America. . . .

The inhabitants are of three sorts, planters, tradesmen, and merchants.

Though the planters are the most numerous, perhaps not the hundredth part of the country is yet cleared from the woods, and not one foot of the marsh and swamp drained. As fast as the ground is worn out with tobacco and corn, it runs up again in underwoods. . . .

For want of towns, markets, and money, there is but little encouragement for tradesmen and skilled workers, and therefore little choice of them, and their labour very dear in the country. . . .

*That is, it will not bring enough return to pay for transportation and taxes.

Life on a Southern Plantation *The first African slaves were brought to Virginia during the early 1600s to work on large plantations, growing tobacco. Wealthy planters also had slaves who tended to household duties, including caring for the children. In this painting by Payne Limner, a boy, returning from a hunt, is greeted by his younger brother and the child's nurse.* **Daily Life** *How do you think the lives of the boys in this painting would differ from the lives of the children living in the house on page 551?*

The merchants live the best of any in that country; but yet are subject to great inconveniencies in the way of their trade, which might be avoided if they had towns, markets, and money. . . .

If towns and ports can be brought to bear, the chief obstruction to the improvement of that country will be removed. It is certain that little help towards it is to be expected from the General Assembly; unless they should come to have a Governor, in whom they have a most mighty confidence, that he acts for the public good. . . . But the members of the assembly are daily more and more adverse to living in towns together; the major part of the House of Burgesses consisting of Virginians that never saw a town, nor have no notion of the conveniency of any other but a country life.

Source: "Large and True Account of the Present State of Virginia," Massachusetts Historical Collections (Boston, 1789).

■ THINKING ABOUT THE SELECTION

1. According to the authors, why is Virginia both one of the best and one of the worst regions in the world?

2. What solution does the petition recommend for Virginia's problems?

3. **CRITICAL THINKING Analyzing Ideas** According to the authors, why is the government of Virginia unable to solve the colony's difficulties?

Crossing the Delaware *This painting by Thomas Sully shows General George Washington just before crossing the Delaware River in December 1776. Washington and his troops launched a successful surprise attack on the British at Trenton, New Jersey.* **American Traditions** *What impact do you think that the victory at Trenton had on the colonial army? Why?*

CHAPTER 5 The Road to Revolution
(1745–1775)

■ 5-1 What Should Colonists Do?   FIRST PERSON

INTRODUCTION Britain's policy of taxing the colonists, begun in the 1760s, stirred up tremendous opposition. One of the many American critics was John Dickinson. His protests took the form of 12 weekly letters published in a Pennsylvania newspaper beginning in December 1767. Dickinson signed himself "a farmer in Pennsylvania." He did own country property, but he was also a lawyer and state assemblyman. The selections here are from his last letter.

VOCABULARY Before you read the selection, find the meaning of these words in a dictionary: indelibly, frugal, goads, prudent, posterity, magnanimity.

Let these truths be indelibly impressed on our minds: that we cannot be happy without being free; that we cannot be free without being secure in our property; that we cannot be secure in our property, if, without our consent, others may take it away; that taxes imposed on us by parliament, do thus take it away; that duties* laid for the sole purposes of raising money are taxes; that attempts to lay such duties should be instantly and firmly opposed; that this opposition can never be effective, unless it is the united effort of these provinces. . . .

_____
*Duties are taxes on imported goods. For example, the taxes imposed by the Townshend Acts were duties.

As long as the products of our labours and the rewards of our care can properly be called our own, so long will it be worth our while to be industrious and frugal. But if when we plow, sow, reap, gather, and thresh, we find, that we plow, sow, reap, gather, and thresh for others, whose pleasure is to be the sole limit on how much they shall take, and how much they shall leave, why should we repeat the unprofitable toil? Horses and oxen are content with that portion of the fruits of their work, which their owners assign to them, in order to keep them strong enough to raise successive crops. But even these beasts will not submit to draw for their masters, until they are subdued with whips and goads. Let us take care of our rights, and we therein take care of our property. . . .

I shall be extremely sorry if any man mistakes my meaning in any thing I have said. Officers employed by the crown are entitled to legal obedience and sincere respect. These it is a duty to give them, and these no good or prudent person will withhold. But when these officers, through rashness or design, endeavour to enlarge their authority beyond its due limits . . . their attempts should be considered as equal injuries to the crown and people, and should be courageously and constantly opposed. . . .

You will be a "Band of brothers" cemented by the dearest ties, confederated in a good cause. Your honour and welfare will be, as they now are, most intimately concerned; and besides—you are assigned by Divine Providence, in the appointed order of things, the protectors of unborn ages, whose fate depends upon your virtue. . . .

To discharge this double duty to yourselves and to your posterity; you have nothing to do, but to call forth into use the

Landing of the British Troops *In 1768, the British army occupied Boston to enforce the writs of assistance. These documents gave customs officers the right to inspect a ship's cargo without reason. This engraving by Paul Revere shows the British army arriving at Boston harbor.* **American Traditions** *What does the British action suggest about Britain's expectations of the colonists' response to the writs of assistance? How do you think colonists reacted to Revere's engraving?*

good sense and spirit, of which you are possessed. You have nothing to do, but to conduct your affairs peaceably, prudently, firmly, jointly. By these means you will support the character of freemen, without losing that of faithful subjects. . . . You will prove that Americans have that true magnanimity of soul, that can resent injuries without falling into rage; and that tho' your devotion to Great Britain is the most affectionate, yet you can make proper distinctions, and know what you owe to yourselves as well as to her. You will, at the same time that you advance your interests, advance your reputation. You will convince the world of the justice of your demands, and the purity of your intentions—while all mankind must with unceasing applause

confess, that you indeed deserve liberty, who so well understand it, so passionately love it, so temperately enjoy it, and so wisely, bravely, and virtuously, assert, maintain, and defend it.

Source: John Dickinson, *Letters from a Farmer in Pennsylvania* (New York: Outlook Company, 1903).

■ THINKING ABOUT THE SELECTION

1. How does Dickinson advise the colonists to behave?

2. What is Dickinson's attitude toward British officials?

3. CRITICAL THINKING **Drawing Conclusions** Is Dickinson urging colonists to revolt? Provide reasons to support your answer.

■ 5-2 Early Thunder

LITERATURE

INTRODUCTION In a historical novel called *Early Thunder*, Jean Fritz explores the mood of Salem, Massachusetts, in the spring of 1774. The people of Salem, waiting to learn of Parliament's reaction to the Boston Tea Party, find themselves divided into two groups. There are Tories, who believe in unquestioning loyalty to the king, and Whigs, who think unjust laws should not be obeyed.

Finally, the town receives news of the Intolerable Acts. As part of the punishment, Parliament has decreed that the people of Massachusetts cannot call town meetings without the governor's permission. The Whigs in Salem decide to call a meeting anyway.

Fourteen-year-old Daniel West, the central figure in the novel, comes from a Tory family. After he learns of the punishments imposed by Parliament, he finds his beliefs changing. He agrees less with the Tories and more with the Whigs. In the following passage, Daniel struggles to tell his best friend, Beckett, about his change of heart.

VOCABULARY Before you read the selection, find the meaning of these words in a dictionary: cascaded, oration, ordinance, cringing.

He'd have to tell Beckett. The thought was a coldness inside him. He tried out different speeches but it was as if it were someone else talking. How could he tell Beckett he was deserting a cause they'd upheld together, . . . a cause they'd upheld through taunts and insults and opposition?

The day of the town meeting came and still Daniel hadn't told but he promised himself that at the noon recess, when the meeting would be either over or called off, he'd tell—Beckett first and later in the day he'd tell Charlie and Benjie [fellow students, who were Whigs]. With school in session, there would be no opportunity to go to the Town House and watch what went on, but people didn't expect trouble. The governor was reported to be angry but he'd done nothing to stop the meeting and no one supposed he would now.

It rained the morning of the meeting, one of those long, hard rains determined, it seems, to turn the land back over to the sea. Rivers of water rushed down the streets, sheets of water cascaded down roofs, walls of water flung themselves so fiercely at Daniel and Beckett on the way to school that there was no opportunity to talk about the town meeting or anything else. When they finally got into the schoolroom, they found themselves alone except for Mr. Nicholls, who remarked rather testily that although he'd been able to get to school on time, he supposed the rain was delaying the others. But as time went on, it became clear that the others weren't coming and Daniel knew it wasn't because of the rain. They were playing hooky. Perhaps they'd heard something concerning the town meeting; Charlie's father was, after all, a Committee member.

With the classroom all but empty, Daniel took a seat by the window instead of his customary one in the middle of the room, thinking that he might see activity of some kind that would give him a hint of what was going on. The ledge of the window, however, was so high he couldn't see the street unless he stood up. He waited until Mr. Nicholls seemed absorbed in his droning and carefully raised up and looked out. Only rain; nothing more. It was after he'd stood up the third time that Mr. Nicholls slammed down his book.

"Since you're determined to be on your feet, Daniel West," he said, "you can stay there and translate the next passage for us."

Daniel picked up his book but before looking at it, he took another quick glance outside and it was then he saw Mr. Carver, one of the most hotheaded of the local Whigs. He was running through the rain and he held a gun in his hand.

"We're waiting," Mr. Nicholls said.

The passage was from Cicero's [a Roman statesman] first oration against Cataline [a political opponent of Cicero]. Daniel tried to

Paul Revere's Ride *Relations between Britain and the colonies grew steadily worse as news of the Intolerable Acts spread. On April 18, 1775, Paul Revere, shown here in this drawing by J. Steeple Davis, galloped along the road to Lexington, warning the colonists that the British were advancing. Thanks to Revere's warning, the minutemen were prepared for the arrival of the British forces.* **American Traditions** *What do you think would have happened if Revere had never embarked on his ride?*

put his mind to it. "What an age is ours!" he read. "You are attacking our whole constitution." He looked out the window. Mr. Carver was out of sight. "And our immortal gods," he went on. He stumbled and hesitated. "The houses of our city and the lives of our citizens." He glanced up again but when he looked back, he'd lost his place.

"It seems," Mr. Nicholls said icily, "that not only are five of our members physically absent, a sixth one might as well not be here. For tomorrow I assign you a double translation. To be written out. As for now, it hardly seems profitable to continue. Class is dismissed." He'd barely finished his words when he was out of the room and Daniel and Beckett were left alone.

"What did you see?" Beckett asked.

Daniel went to the window. "Mr. Carver. He had a gun in his hand."

"Headed toward the Town House?"

"Yes." There was no avoiding it, Daniel thought. He'd have to tell Beckett now. They couldn't go to the Town House together with Beckett thinking that they shared the same views and that things were the same as always. He went to the hook for his coat.

"Beckett," he said slowly, "what do you think of the Committee calling this town meeting?"

"What do you suppose I think?" Beckett was bent over, adjusting his boots. "It was a mistake. Right from the beginning. If there's trouble, it's their doing."

"You go along with the ordinance against the town meetings?"

"I don't like it but I go along. Of course I go along. It's the king's orders. And I'm his subject. Every time folks differ, they can't take things into their own hands."

"Right or wrong, you go along with anything the king says?"

"I may disagree but then maybe the king knows more than I do." Beckett straightened. "Yes, I go along. Right or wrong, I'm with the king and Parliament. And so are you, Daniel West, so stop your foolishness."

"Sometimes I put right before the king. If the right is big enough." Daniel's voice sounded small, not proud the way he'd meant it to. He had one arm in his coat; he let the other sleeve dangle. "I've come around to putting freedom before the empire." He watched Beckett lower himself into one of the classroom seats. "We have to have meetings. We have to have a say in how our lives are run. We have to talk as long as talking's possible. And if that doesn't work and if there's no other way—"

"What?"

Daniel felt himself cringing, his back up against a wall. "If they start to fight, we'll have to fight."

Beckett's face was unbelieving. "You're not trying to tell me, are you, that you've *turned?*"

Daniel winced. "I've changed. I'm a—" He stopped and then started the sentence again. "I'm no longer a Tory."

"Well." Beckett's hands lay loosely on his knees. He stared down at the floor.

"We've always said we respected other people's opinions even if they differ from ours. We've always said we didn't see why politics should interfere with friendship."

"Yes, that's what we've said." Beckett didn't look up.

"I don't want things to change between us, Beckett."

"Well." Beckett kept studying the floor. "You've got a right to change, I guess. I'll get used to it. I don't hold it against you." For the first time Beckett looked up. His face was miserable. "It's not *me* that's going to come between us, Daniel. It's *them*. They'll try to turn you against me."

Daniel thrust his arm into the sleeve of his coat. "Well, they won't succeed. . . ."

They walked together to the door. Beckett put his hand on the latch and then he hesitated. He took a deep breath and let it out slowly. "We just won't talk politics, Daniel. There are other things to talk about. . . ."

From *Early Thunder* by Jean Fritz. Copyright © 1967 by Jean Fritz. Reprinted by permission of Coward-McCann, Inc.

■ THINKING ABOUT THE SELECTION

1. What did Daniel have to tell his friend Beckett? Why was he worried about telling him?

2. How did Beckett react to Daniel's new beliefs?

3. CRITICAL THINKING **Recognizing Points of View** Daniel and Beckett have different ideas about whether colonists should always obey the king. Explain each position.

■ 6-1   A Teenage Prisoner of War

INTRODUCTION In 1774, when he was only 15, John Adlum joined a company of militia. Two years later he was called to active duty. Adlum fought at Fort Washington, in northern Manhattan, which fell to the British in November 1776. Along with some 2,800 other American soldiers, Adlum was taken prisoner. This selection from his memoirs begins as he talks to a British guard.

VOCABULARY Before you read the selection, find the meaning of these words in a dictionary: cannonade, provincial.

I had a curiosity what they thought of our defense and observed to him that they made a great haul of us that day, to which he replied yes but it could not well be otherwise as our lines were not half manned.

"Then you think if we had more men we would have made a better defense?"

"To be sure you would."

"There was a very great noise made with the artillery today."

"Yes, I was in the last war in Germany and I think I never heard so brisk a cannonade in my life."

"Then you think we behaved tolerably well?"

"Yes, considering your numbers and the badness of your cause you have done as well as could be expected." . . .

"You say you were in Germany in the last war. Were you in any of the great battles there?"

"Yes."

"From the quantity of firing with small arms, did they in Germany do as much execution* as we do?"

---
*that is, kill as many soldiers

"No, they do not. I was in the battle of Bunker's Hill and there was more execution done there for the quantity of firing than I ever knew or heard of, except once where our regiment was attacked and, supported by some Grenadiers, we in about fifteen minutes killed near seven hundred Frenchmen."

Battle of Bunker Hill *As this painting by Alonzo Chappel suggests, the American forces fiercely resisted the British advance in the Battle of Bunker Hill. Although the British eventually won, the American army proved that it was a force to be reckoned with.* **Linking Past and Present** *How does this battle scene differ from the way battles have been portrayed in recent wars? What accounts for these differences?*

"Then you think that we might fight pretty hard upon an occasion?"

"Yes, if you were well disciplined and commanded by British officers."

"Why British officers and not our own?"

"Because there is but very few of them that appear gentlemen, consequently they cannot have a proper sense of honor."

I felt the hit and did not ask him any more questions. . . .

[Later Adlum struck up another conversation with a British sergeant.] He observed to me, "You appear to be very young to be embarked in so bad a cause but," continued he, "I suppose you were forced into the service as most of you are."

I replied that he was mistaken and that so far from being forced there was more offered their services than arms could be procured for.

"Why," said he, "I understood that it was otherwise." He said he regretted to see so young a lad as I appeared to be opposing his King and if I would look back and see the great number of prisoners following I must be satisfied that the war was near its end, and that by the next spring we would have no troops to resist the powerful armies of the King, that this affair would prevent any but mad men from joining in the service and that he did not believe there would be much further resistance; that he remembered General Washington when he was a provincial colonel, and he regretted that so good a man should meet the fate that awaited him.

I replied (being pretty much of an enthusiast) that the reason they beat us on Long Island and now at Fort Washington was because we could not run away [to regroup] and that their shipping was the cause of all their success, and that he might depend upon it that whenever we got them from their shipping and in the country we would beat them wherever we met them. . . .

The sergeant said I was very much mistaken and he was sorry to see so young a lad as I appeared to be have such an opinion of the irresistible power of the British King, and that our fate was inevitable, for the next spring we would be a conquered people.

"But," says he, "I have no idea that many will suffer, none but the principal officers and the leading men in Congress. As for the privates and small fry, they will be treated with humanity while prisoners and will be supplied with all their wants. I shall not be surprised that after you are well fed and clothed to see General Howe send you all home with more favorable sentiments toward us (the British) than you now seem to be possessed of." But the sergeant was woefully mistaken; he calculated upon a humanity that neither General Howe nor his [troops] possessed or ever felt.

Source: Howard H. Peckham, ed., *Memoirs of the Life of John Adlum in the Revolutionary War* (Chicago: William L. Clements Library, 1968).

■ THINKING ABOUT THE SELECTION

1. What does the first British guard think about the colonial army's fighting ability?

2. What are the guards' attitudes toward the American cause?

3. CRITICAL THINKING **Defending a Position** Explain whether or not you think Adlum does a good job defending the American position.

■ 6-2   **Marion's Men**   LITERATURE

INTRODUCTION Fighting on their own soil, the Americans enjoyed a distinct advantage over the British. One military leader who used that advantage was Francis Marion, the Swamp Fox. He used guerrilla tactics in skirmishes and battles throughout South Carolina. The greatest weapons his small army had were its speed and the element of surprise. Sleeping by day and striking at night, Marion's army was very successful against the British. The following song, "Marion's Men," gives an idea of what life was like for the followers of the Swamp Fox.

VOCABULARY Before you read the selection, find the meaning of these words in a dictionary: legions, saber, coax, steeds, coursers.

We follow where the Swamp Fox guides,
His friends and merry men are we,
And when the Tory Legions ride
We burrow in the cypress trees.
The gloomy swampland is our bed,
Our home is in the red deer's den,
Our roof, the treetop overhead,
For we are wild and hunted men.

    Chorus: We ride, we hide, we strike
        again,
          For we are Marion's men.

We fly by day and shun its light,
But, prompt to strike the sudden blow,
We mount, and start with early night,

And through the forest track our foe,
And soon he hears our chargers leap,
And flashing saber blinds his eyes,
And ere he drives away his sleep,
And rushes from his camp, he dies.

    Chorus: We ride, we hide, we strike
        again,
          For we are Marion's men.

Now pile the brush and roll the log,
Hard pillow, but a soldier's head,
That's half the time in brake and bog,
Must never think of softer bed,
The owl is hooting to the night,
The cooter crawling o'er the bank,
And in that pond the plashing light,
Tells where the alligator sank.

    Chorus: We ride, we hide, we strike
        again,
          For we are Marion's men.

The Swamp Fox whistles to the scouts,
You hear his order calm and low,

A Victory at Cowpens *Like Francis Marion, General Daniel Morgan was successful against the British in the South. Americans under Morgan's command dealt the British a "very unexpected and severe blow" at Cowpens, South Carolina. This painting of the Battle of Cowpens is by William Ranney, well known for his scenes of the Revolution.* **Citizenship** *Why did the British decide to shift their efforts to the South?*

Come, wave your torch across the dark,
We shall not be the last to go,
Have courage, comrades, Marion leads,
The Swamp Fox takes us out tonight,
So clear your swords and coax your steeds,
Tonight we right, tonight we fight.

> Chorus: We ride, we hide, we strike
> again,
> For we are Marion's men.

We follow where the Swamp Fox guides,
We leave the swamp and cypress tree,
Our spurs are in our coursers' sides,
And ready for the strife are we.
The Tory camp is now in sight,
And there he cowers within his den,
He hears our shout, he dreads the fight,
He fears, and flies from Marion's men.

> Chorus: We ride, we hide, we strike
> again,
> For we are Marion's men.

"Marion's Men" (lyrics only) from *SONGS OF '76: A Folksinger's History of the Revolution* by Oscar Brand. Copyright © 1972 by Oscar Brand. Reprinted by permission of the publisher, M. Evans & Co., Inc.

■ THINKING ABOUT THE SELECTION

1. Explain the meaning of the line "We fly by day and shun its light."

2. What clues do such words as *bog, pond,* and *alligator* give about the songwriter's surroundings?

3. CRITICAL THINKING **Linking Past and Present** Give an example of a place in the world today where guerrilla fighting is taking place.

CHAPTER 7 Creating a Republic
(1776–1790)

■ 7-1 Comments From a German Visitor   FIRST PERSON

INTRODUCTION Under the Articles of Confederation, the United States set up a very weak national government. One European visitor who saw it in action was Johann David Schoepf from Germany. He first came to America during the Revolutionary War as a physician for Britain's Hessian troops. After the war, he spent two years traveling about the country.

VOCABULARY Before you read the selection, find the meaning of these words in a dictionary: vexations, prerogatives, sovereign, indignation.

The Congress has neither the necessary weight nor the necessary solidity. It is therefore, in the very restricted range of its activities, exposed to all manner of grievous vexations. It was to be expected of a people so enthusiastic for liberty that they should grant their Congress only a shadow of dignity, and watch its proceedings with a jealous eye.

The real business and the prerogatives of the Congress, insofar as it represents the common power of the United States, are: To declare war and conclude peace, to raise armies and give them orders, to contract alliances with foreign powers, to oversee the constitutions of all the states and preserve their relations to the whole; to call for and administer the revenues necessary to these ends, and to make public debts.

Insofar its activities may be compared with those of other sovereign powers, the Congress being bound to exercise care for the well-being and the safety of the community. But as regards the application of

Celebrating a New Plan of Government *Faced with the weaknesses of the Articles of Confederation, delegates to a "grand convention" wrote a new Constitution in the summer of 1787. Americans celebrated ratification of that Constitution with huge parades and other festivities. The banner shown here was carried in one of those parades by members of the Society of Pewterers.* **Citizenship** *The United States is still governed under the Constitution that was adopted in 1788. What does that tell you about the document?*

the means needed, there are a thousand difficulties in the way. Thus the United States authorized the Congress to borrow money and to pledge the honor of the nation. But to pay these debts, there is no authority granted. Each individual state has its own independent government which is concerned for its especial welfare and inner security; its own laws, police, and execution of justice. . . .

Nothing has so much damaged faith in the Congress, . . . and nothing has caused more general and bitter indignation against it, than the debts heaped by it upon the states, and especially the woeful pains left by the paper-money issued under its authority, which . . . has been the occasion of the loss of a great part or all of the property of so many once prosperous families and individuals. . . .

There was a time when printed bits of paper were to the people as valuable as hard coin. . . . At that time the paper-money issued by the Congress and the states was wholly esteemed and was reckoned without question as equal to silver and gold. But this kind of mintage was found to be so easy that new millions were struck off on all occasions in payment of the costs of the war. Thus, credit began to weaken. . . .

The value of the paper had already considerably fallen, when it was proclaimed that in the payment of old debts paper-money should be legally accepted at its full nominal value, paper dollars at the time being about as 50 to 1 of silver. Thus whoever before the war, owed 50 hard dollars could now come off by the payment of 50 paper dollars, the fiftieth part of the true worth. . . . It may easily be fancied to what great injustice and oppression such a decree must have given rise with the paper-money of the Congress sinking at last to nothing.

Source: Adapted from Johann David Schoepf, *Travels in the Confederation* (Philadelphia: William J. Campbell, 1911).

■ THINKING ABOUT THE SELECTION

1. What are the main powers of Congress under the Articles? What important power does it lack?

2. Why did paper money issued by the Congress lose value?

3. **CRITICAL THINKING Understanding Causes and Effects** Why would worthless paper money cause "once prosperous families and individuals" to lose all of their property?

INTRODUCTION Novelist Conrad Richter (1890–1968) drew on letters and personal records to create authentic accounts of life in the Northwest Territory. Best known is his trilogy *The Awakening Land,* about the hardships and struggles of a pioneer family in Ohio. The trilogy begins with the novel *The Trees.*

When Sayward Luckett, the central character of *The Trees,* is only 15 years old, her parents decide to move from Pennsylvania to the wilderness of the Northwest Territory. There she will face obstacles and challenges not ordinarily encountered by young people.

In the passage that follows, Sayward, her parents, and her young brother and sisters have begun their journey west. As they travel, Sayward recalls the discussion between her father and mother, Worth and Jary Luckett, about whether the move was necessary. Sayward's daydream is interrupted, however, as the family gets its first view of the Ohio wilderness.

VOCABULARY Before you read the selection, find the meaning of these words in a dictionary: hickory, glinted, puncheon, whittled, loom, unbeknownst, illimitable, foliage, billows, habitation, melancholy, caterwauling, fetor, ranker, gat.

Jary sat quiet on her homemade hickory rocker. Oh, she knew how bad Worth wanted an excuse to get away from here. Her eyes slanted down toward the clay floor. Her mouth rounded a bit as if she took all things, good, bad, and indifferent, and was running them quietly around inside her lips. Her mouth was so gentle and yet could shut like a mussel shell. She looked up and there was no telling what lay in her mind.

"You're aimin' to cross the Ohio?" she asked, and her eyes glinted a moment dangerously at her man.

He gave a nod. Even her father, Sayward saw, didn't know what she'd say or do. He took out his clay pipe and made to fill it, but his eyes never stopped watching her face. The young ones could hardly stand the waiting now.

Their mother went on grimly.

"I told you I'd never go way back there." Hope died in the young faces. She dropped her eyes and stared a long time across the doorsill, then around the cabin room at the familiar slab stools and puncheon table, the hand-whittled loom and wheel, and across the doorsill again to the mite of a grave in the clearing. None of these things could they take with them. "And yit," back in her mouth she complained, "what's a body to do if the game's left the country?"

* * * * *

Now they had crossed the Ohio on a pole ferry and the mud on their feet was no longer the familiar red and brown earth of Pennsylvania. . . .

They rounded a high ridge. . . . Here was something Worth had not told them about.

For a moment Sayward reckoned that her father had fetched them unbeknownst to the Western ocean and what lay beneath was the late sun glittering on green-black water. Then she saw that what they looked down on was a dark, illimitable expanse of wilderness. It was a sea of solid treetops broken only by some gash where deep beneath the foliage an unknown stream made its way. As far as the eye could reach, this lonely forest sea rolled on and on till its faint blue billows broke against an incredibly distant horizon.

They had all stopped with a common notion and stood looking out. Sayward saw her mother's eyes search with the hope of finding some settlement or leastwise a settler's clearing. But over that vasty solitude no wisp of smoke arose. Though they waited here till night, the girl knew that no light of

New Cities on the Frontier *Passage of the Northwest Ordinance sparked the growth of new settlements in the Northwest Territory. Some of these settlements eventually grew into large cities. One of these was Cincinnati, which is shown as it appeared in 1835 in this painting by John Casper Wild.* **Local History** *What government policies have had an important impact on the town or city in which you live? Explain.*

human habitation would appear except the solitary red spark of some Delaware or Shawnee campfire. Already the lowering sun slanted melancholy rays over the scene, and as it sank, the shadows of those far hills reached out with long fingers.

It was a picture Sayward was to carry to her grave, although she didn't know it then. In later years when it was all to go so that her own father wouldn't know the place if he rose from his bury hole, she was to call the scene to mind. This is the way it was, she would say to herself. Nowhere else but in the American wilderness could it have been.

The sun was gone now. Far out they heard the yelping of a wolf and nearer the caterwauling of a panther. Worth stood leaning on his long Lancaster rifle, his nose wrinkling like a hound's.

"You kin smell the game!" he said hungrily.

Sayward sniffed. All she could [smell] was the scent of wild herbs and leaves mingled with the faint strange fetor of ranker, blacker earth than she knew in Pennsylvania. She looked at her brother and sisters. They stood with young eyes drinking in this place and it was plain as if drawn on shell-bark that what they saw were otters coasting down muddy slides and gray moose crashing through the woods and fat beaver cracking down their broad tails on gat water like pistol shots. They could see skins drying on the log walls of a cabin yet unbuilt and skins in a heavy pack on their father's shoulders and skins handed over the counter of a trader's post along the Scioto or Ohio [rivers] where the shelves hung heavy with black and white English blankets, Turkey red calico, bolts of Merrimac blue, shawls with fringes, brass bound muskets and buckets of white beads.

"We [might] even git rich and have shoes!" Sulie spoke out.

That broke the tension. They all looked down on her and smiled.

From *The Trees* by Conrad Richter. Copyright 1940 and renewed 1968 by Conrad Richter. Reprinted by permission of Alfred A. Knopf, Inc.

■ THINKING ABOUT THE SELECTION

1. What reason did Sayward's father give for wanting to move his family to the Northwest Territory?

2. What was Sayward's first impression of the region?

3. **CRITICAL THINKING Drawing Conclusions** Predict how you think the region was going to change as more settlers moved in.

UNIT

3

The New Republic

Daily Life in the New Nation *After winning their fight for independence, the people of the United States began forging a way of life that was distinctly American. Writers and artists created works that captured the American spirit. This painting by Francis Guy shows daily life in Brooklyn, New York, during the early 1800s.* **Linking Past and Present** *How do you imagine this part of Brooklyn has changed since the time of the painting? Explain.*

CHAPTER 8 The New Government Begins
(1789–1800)

■ 8-1 Jefferson Describes Washington

FIRST PERSON

INTRODUCTION Probably any American of the 1790s could identify George Washington as the commander of the American forces in the American Revolution and the first President of the United States. How many people, however, could explain what George Washington was *really* like? In the late 1790s, a biographer turned to the people who knew Washington best and asked them to describe his character. The following excerpt is from a letter Thomas Jefferson wrote in response to the biographer's request.

Jefferson's letter is very candid. It provides interesting insights into Washington's strengths and weaknesses.

VOCABULARY Before you read the selection, find the meaning of these words in a dictionary: delineate, deranged, prudence, integrity, consanguinity, ascendency, stature, deportment, mediocrity, copiousness, diffusely, extensive, constellation, destiny, scrupulously, vouch, cordial, verily.

I think I knew General Washington intimately and thoroughly; and were I called on to delineate his character, it should be in terms like these.

His mind was great and powerful, without being of the very first order. His penetration [was] strong, though not so acute as that of a Newton, Bacon, or Locke. . . . As far as he saw, no judgment was ever sounder. [His mind] was slow in operation, being little aided by invention or imagination, but sure in conclusion. Hence the common remark of his officers, of the advantage he derived from councils of war, where hearing all suggestions, he selected whatever was best. . . . But if deranged during the course of the action, . . . he was slow in re-adjustment. The consequence was, that he often failed in the field, and rarely against an enemy in station, as at Boston and York. He was incapable of fear, meeting personal dangers with the calmest unconcern.

Perhaps the strongest feature in his character was prudence. [He] never [acted] until every circumstance, every consideration, was maturely weighed; refraining if he saw a doubt. . . . Once decided, [he went] through with his purpose, whatever obstacles opposed. His integrity was the most pure, his justice the most inflexible I have ever known. No motives of interest or consanguinity, of friendship or hatred, [could] bias his decision. He was, indeed, in every sense of the words, a wise, a good, and a great man.

His temper was naturally high toned, but [he] had obtained a firm and habitual ascendency over it. If ever, however, it broke its bonds, he was most tremendous in his wrath. . . .

His person, you know, was fine, his stature exactly what one would wish, his deportment easy, erect and noble. [He was] the best horseman of his age. . . . Although in the circle of his friends, where he might be unreserved with safety, he took a free share in conversation, his [abilities in informal discussion] were not above mediocrity, possessing neither copiousness of ideas, nor fluency of words. In public, when called on for a sudden opinion, he was unready, short and embarrassed. Yet he wrote readily, rather diffusely, in an easy and correct style. This he had acquired by conversation with the world, for his education was merely reading, writing and common arithmetic, to which he added surveying at a later day.

His time was employed in action chiefly, reading little, and that only in agriculture and English history. His correspondence became necessarily extensive, and, with journalizing his agricultural proceedings, occupied most of his leisure hours within doors.

On the whole, his character was, in its mass, perfect, in nothing bad, in few points indifferent. It may truly be said, that never did nature and fortune combine more perfectly to make a man great, and to place him in the same constellation with whatever worthies have merited from man an everlasting remembrance. For his was the singular destiny and merit of leading the armies of his country successfully through . . . war, [establishing] its independence; . . . conducting its councils through the birth of a

The Father of His Country *George Washington retired from public life in 1797. Both this inaugural mug and this watercolor of George and Martha Washington by an unknown artist symbolize the love and admiration Americans felt for the leader who had been "first in war, first in peace, and first in the hearts of his countrymen."* **American Traditions** *What are some ways our nation continues to honor George Washington?*

government, new in its forms and principles, until it had settled down into a quiet and orderly train; and of scrupulously obeying the laws through the whole of his career, civil and military, of which the history of the world furnishes no other example. . . .

These are my opinions of General Washington, which I would vouch at the judgment seat of God, having been formed on an acquaintance of thirty years. I served with him in the Virginia legislature from 1769 to the Revolutionary war, and again, a short time in Congress, until he left us to take command of the army. During the war and after it we corresponded occasionally, and in the four years of my continuance in the office of Secretary of State, our [interaction] was daily, confidential and cordial. . . .

I felt on his death, with my countrymen that "verily a great man hath fallen this day in Israel."

Excerpts from *Eyewitnesses and Others: Readings in American History, Volume I: Beginning to 1865*, copyright 1991 by Holt, Rinehart and Winston, Inc., reprinted by permission of the publisher.

■ THINKING ABOUT THE SELECTION

1. In Jefferson's opinion, why was he qualified to evaluate Washington's character?

2. According to Jefferson, what were some of Washington's strengths? What were some of his weaknesses?

3. **CRITICAL THINKING Expressing an Opinion** Which of Washington's characteristics do you think made him a good general? Which made him a good President?

■ 8-2   Great Little Madison   LITERATURE

INTRODUCTION One of the fiercest debates to take place in the first Congress concerned the funding of the debt from the Revolution. On one side of the issue was Secretary of the Treasury Alexander Hamilton. Hamilton wanted to issue new bonds to pay the national debt, and he wanted the national government to assume state debts. This plan was opposed by James Madison. Madison and others believed that assuming the states' debts was unfair to states like Virginia that had already repaid their debts. The following selection from Jean Fritz's biography of Madison presents this debate and its resolution.

VOCABULARY Before you read the selection, find the meaning of these words in a dictionary: thronged, sheaf, secede, speculators, site.

When the debate hit the floor of the House, the country learned for the first time that Congress could at a moment's notice turn into a theater. Senators took time off so they could listen to the proceedings. Abigail Adams (wife of the vice president) and her lady friends thronged into the galleries.

Alexander Hamilton could not argue his case himself, because he was not a member of the House. Still, it was clearly a fight between two of the country's leaders: Hamilton's supporters on one side, Madison and his men on the other. Spectators looked forward particularly to the times when Mr. Madison spoke. He would shuffle a sheaf of papers, stand up, and clear his throat as if he were alerting the audience that though it might be difficult to hear him, he had something to say. Softspoken as he was, he tore into Mr. Hamilton's plan as if it offended every nerve in his body. And when he was reminded that this system had worked in England—well, that's when Madison's face reddened and when he began rocking back and forth in his old tense way. Who needed England to show them how to run their country? he would snap. Madison may still have borne old grudges against England, but what he particularly resented now was the way England continued to act as if the United States were a second-rate nation, hardly worth anyone's attention.

Veterans Return From the War
The Revolution was over, and veterans, like those in this painting by William Ranney, headed home. But when they arrived, they found that the nation they had fought to create had no money to pay them their wages. **Economics** *To whom else did the United States owe money?*

On the other hand, when Madison presented his plan for raising money, he, too, was shouted down. Why couldn't they sell land in the western territories that would eventually become part of the United States? he asked. George Clymer of Pennsylvania, a follower of Hamilton, snorted at the idea. It was "romantic," he said, to suppose that the western territories would ever agree to come into the United States. Then consider taxes. Consider tariffs, Madison suggested, Why not a whisky tax? Why not a higher tariff on American ships trading with countries having no commerical agreements with us? By this Madison meant Great Britain, which had refused to sign such an agreement, but there was an immediate outcry from New England representatives. They were the ones who did most of the trading with England; they were the ones most partial to their former enemy.

It was toward the end of the debate that Thomas Jefferson arrived back from Paris, back also from a long visit to Monticello, where Madison had seen him over the Christmas holidays. At the first opportunity Hamilton cornered him, explaining how serious the debt problem had become. Particularly the question of the nation taking over state debts. There were some states threatening to secede from the Union, he explained, if the nation did not assume their debts.

Jefferson invited Hamilton to dinner the next night. He would invite Madison too, he said.

By this time Madison realized that he could not win the debate over the funding system. Some of the speculators were themselves members of Congress. Moreover, if the country's money was largely in the hands of those who were wealthy and able to speculate, the stability of the country would be assured. That was what many believed. There remained, however, the delicate question of state debts. Hamilton needed only a few more votes to get his way on this. While Madison had no notion of changing his vote, he did agree that he might possibly arrange among his supporters to give Hamilton his victory. *If,* he said. If Hamilton for his part would see that the vote on the location of the national capital went as Madison wanted it. The Potomac River as the permanent site. A ten-year temporary site at Philadelphia. Hamilton agreed.

Still, at the end of the evening James Madison . . . felt betrayed. Perhaps he should have paid more attention to Hamilton's outburst at the Constitutional Convention. Loyal as he was to the American cause, Hamilton, born and brought up on a British island in the West Indies, obviously still held an undue admiration for British aristocracy. He was an ambitious man, Alexander Hamilton, handsome and charming with the ability to manipulate people. . . . And Madison worried about his influence over President Washington.

Actually Alexander Hamilton may himself have felt betrayed. He and Madison had both promoted the idea of a strong central government, yet in this crucial case Madison did not seem to be behind it. Madison could have pointed out, however, that he had not changed. First and foremost, he was in favor of a balance of power. If one branch of government seemed to be showing too much power, if the central government seemed to be dominating the states, he would always try to tip the scales. A few months later he would oppose Hamilton again when he succeeded in establishing a national bank. Madison advised Washington that the bank was unconstitutional and he shouldn't sign the bill. But Washington listened to Hamilton instead, just as Madison feared. And he did sign the bill.

From *The Great Little Madison* by Jean Fritz. Copyright © 1989 by Jean Fritz. Reprinted by permission of G.P. Putnam's Sons.

■ THINKING ABOUT THE SELECTION

1. What objection did Madison raise to Hamilton's plan?

2. (a) Explain Madison's plan for raising money. (b) Why was Madison's plan "shouted down"?

3. CRITICAL THINKING **Synthesizing Information** Briefly summarize the debt issue, James Madison's and Alexander Hamilton's position, and the outcome of the debate.

CHAPTER 9 The Jefferson Era
(1801–1816)

■ 9-1   The Man Without a Country   LITERATURE

INTRODUCTION During Jefferson's second term as President, his former Vice President, Aaron Burr, became involved in an unsuccessful plot to create a separate country out of lands west of the Mississippi River. Writer Edward Everett Hale used the outcome of Burr's plot as the background for his story, "The Man Without a Country." It tells of the life of Lieutenant Philip Nolan, a young soldier who became part of Burr's scheme. When Nolan was on trial for his involvement, he cried out in anger, "I wish I may never hear of the United States again." For his punishment, the court granted Nolan's wish. The remainder of his life was spent aboard ships of the United States Navy. For more than 50 years, he was not allowed to set foot on American soil, and no one ever spoke to him of the United States.

The following passage is taken from the conclusion of the story. Lieutenant Nolan, aware that he is near death, begs the captain of his ship to tell him everything that has happened in his former country, which he has come to love.

An American Seascape *Following the War of 1812, the United States entered an "Era of Good Feelings." Most Americans were filled with a deep love for their country. Many American artists expressed this feeling by painting pictures that captured the beauty of the American landscape. For instance, this painting by Fitz Hugh Lane highlights the tranquil beauty of Cape Ann, Massachusetts.* **Linking Past and Present** *What are some of the ways in which Americans today express feelings of patriotism?*

VOCABULARY Before you read the selection, find the meaning of these words in a dictionary: triced, sovereignty, tyrant, expiated, manifold, transgressions.

Dear Fred: I try to find heart and life to tell you that it is all over with dear old Nolan. I have been with him on this voyage more than I ever was, and I can understand wholly now the way in which you used to speak of the dear old fellow. I could see that he was not strong, but I had no idea the end was so near. . . . Well, I went in, and there, to be sure, the poor fellow lay in his berth, smiling pleasantly as he gave me his hand, but looking very frail. I could not help a glance round, which showed me what a little shrine he had made of the box he was lying in. The stars and stripes were triced up above and around a picture of Washington and he had painted a majestic eagle, with lightnings blazing from his beak and his foot just clasping the whole globe, which his wings overshadowed. The dear old boy saw my glance, and said, with a sad smile, "Here, you see. I have a country! And then he pointed to the foot of his bed, where I had not seen before a great map of the United States, as he had drawn it from memory, and which he had there to look upon as he lay. Quaint, queer old names were on it, in large letters: "Indiana Territory," "Mississippi Territory," and "Louisiana Territory," as I suppose our fathers learned such things; but the old fellow had patched in Texas, too; he had carried his western boundary all the way to the Pacific, but on that shore he had defined nothing.

"O Captain," he said, "I know I am dying. I cannot get home. Surely you will tell me something now? . . . Do not speak till I say what I am sure you know, that there is not in this ship, that there is not in America—God bless her!—a more loyal man than I. There cannot be a man who loves the old flag as I do, or prays for it as I do, or hopes for it as I do. There are thirty-four stars in it now, Danforth. I thank God for that, though I do not know what their names are. There has never been one taken away; I thank God for that. I know by that that there has never been any successful Burr. O Danforth, Danforth," he sighed out, "how like a wretched night's dream a boy's idea of personal fame or of separate sovereignty seems, when one looks back on it after such a life as mine! But tell me—tell me something—tell me everything, Danforth, before I die."

Ingham, I swear to you that I felt like a monster that I had not told him everything before . . . Who was I, that I should have been acting the tyrant all this time over this . . . old man, who had years ago expiated, in his whole manhood's life, the madness of a boy's treason? "Mr. Nolan," said I, "I will tell you everything you ask about. Only, where shall I begin?". . . "God bless you! Tell me their names," he said, and he pointed to the stars on the flag. "The last I know is Ohio. . . ."

I told him the names in as good order as I could, and he bade me take down his beautiful map and draw them in as I best could with my pencil. He was wild with delight about Texas, told me . . . he had guessed at Texas. Then he was delighted as he saw California and Oregon—that, he said, he had suspected partly, because he had never been permitted to land on that shore, though the ships were there so much. . . . Then he settled down more quietly, and very happily, to hear me tell in an hour the history of fifty years.

How I wished it had been somebody who knew something! But I did as well as I could. I told him of the English war. I told him about Fulton and the steamboat beginning. I told him about old Scott, and Jackson; told him all I could think of about the Mississippi, and New Orleans, and Texas and his own old Kentucky. . . .

I tell you, Ingham, it was a hard thing to condense the history of half a century into that talk with a sick man. And I do not now know what I told him—of emigration, and the means of it—of steamboats, and railroads, and telegraphs—of inventions, and books, and literature of colleges, and West Point, and the Naval School—but with the queerest interruptions that ever you heard. You see it was Robinson Crusoe asking all the accumulated questions of fifty-six years! . . .

And he drank it in and enjoyed it as I cannot tell you. He grew more and more silent, yet I never thought he was tired or faint. I gave him a glass of water, but he just wet his lips, and told me not to go away. Then he asked me to bring the Presbyterian

"Book of Public Prayer" which lay there, and said, with a smile, that it would open at the right place and so it did. . . . I knelt down and read, and he repeated with me, "For ourselves and our country, O gracious God, we thank Thee, that, notwithstanding our manifold transgressions of Thy holy laws, Thou hast continued to us Thy marvelous kindness." . . . "Danforth," said he, "I have repeated those prayers night and morning, it is now fifty-five years." And then he said he would go to sleep. He bent me down over him and said, "Look in my Bible, Captain, when I am gone." And I went away.

In an hour, when the doctor went in gently, he found Nolan had breathed his life away with a smile. He had something pressed close to his lips. It was his father's badge of the Order of the Cincinnati.

We looked in his Bible, and there was a slip of paper. . . . On this slip of paper he had written:

Bury me in the sea; it has been my home, and I love it. But will not some one set up a stone for my memory at Fort Adams or at Orleans, that my disgrace may not be more than I ought to bear? Say on it:

In Memory of
PHILIP NOLAN

Lieutenant in the Army
of the United States

He loved his country as no other man has loved her; but no man deserved less at her hands

Source: Edward Everett Hale, "The Man Without a Country," 1863.

■ THINKING ABOUT THE SELECTION

1. How does Nolan convey the love he has developed for his former country?

2. What did Nolan want Captain Danforth to tell him?

3. CRITICAL THINKING **Defending a Position** Do you think Nolan's punishment was fair? Why or why not?

INTRODUCTION One of the most vivid accounts of the Battle of New Orleans was written by a rifleman who took part in it. All that is known about the author is that he came from Kentucky.

VOCABULARY Before you read the selection, find the meaning of these words in a dictionary: apprehend, breastwork, epaulets, cadaverous, prostrate, levee.

The official report said the action lasted two hours and five minutes, but it did not seem half that length of time to me. It was so dark that little could be seen, until just about the time the battle ceased. The morning had dawned, to be sure, but the smoke was so thick that everything seemed to be covered up in it. Our men did not seem to apprehend any danger, but would load and fire as fast as they could, talking, swearing, and joking all the time. All ranks and sections were soon broken up. After the first shot, everyone loaded and banged away on his own hook. Henry Spillman did not load and fire quite so often as some of the rest, but every time he did fire he would go up to the breastwork, look over until he could see something to shoot at, and then take deliberate aim and crack away. Lieut. Ashby was as busy as a nailor* and it was evident that the River Raisin was uppermost in his mind all the time.** He kept dashing about and every now and then he would call out, with an oath, "We'll pay you now for the River Raisin! We'll give you something to remember the River Raisin!" When the British had come up to the opposite side of the breastwork, having no gun, he picked up an empty barrel and flung it at them. Then

---

*"Busy as a nailor (nailer)" was an expression of the time meaning someone who was very active.

**A force of Kentuckians had fought, and lost, the Battle of Frenchtown, on the Raisin River near Detroit, early in 1813.

The Battle of Baltimore *This painting by Thomas Ruckle, Sr., shows American troops assembling prior to the Battle of Baltimore during the War of 1812. After launching a successful assault on Washington, D.C., the British army had begun advancing toward Baltimore. The American forces were well prepared, however, and were able to halt the British advance.* **American Traditions** *Why is the Battle of Baltimore considered a turning point in the War of 1812?*

finding an iron bar, he jumped up on the works and hove that at them. . . .

During the action, a number of the Tennessee men got mixed with ours. One of them was killed about five or six yards from where I stood. I did not know his name. A ball passed through his head and he fell against Ensign Weller. . . . This was the only man killed near where I was stationed.

It was near the close of the firing. About the time that I observed three or four men carrying his body away or directly after, there was a white flag raised on the opposite side of the breastwork and the firing ceased.

The white flag, before mentioned, was raised about ten or twelve feet from where I stood, close to the breastwork and a little to the right. It was a white handkerchief, or something of the kind, on a sword or stick. It was waved several times, and as soon as it was perceived, we ceased firing. Just then the wind got up a little and blew the smoke off, so that we could see the field. It then appeared that the flag had been raised by a British Officer wearing epaulets. It was told he was a Major. He stepped over the breastwork and came into our lines. Among the Tennesseeans who had got mixed with us during the fight, there was a little fellow whose name I do not know; but he was a cadaverous looking chap and went by [the name] of Paleface. As the British Officer came in, Paleface demanded his sword. He hesitated about giving it to him, probably thinking it was [insulting] to his dignity, to surrender to a private all over begrimed with dust and powder and that some Officer should show him the courtesy to receive it. Just at that moment, Col. Smiley came up and cried, with a harsh oath, "Give it up— give it up to him in a minute!" The British Officer quickly handed his weapon to Paleface, holding it in both hands and making a very polite bow. . . .

When the smoke had cleared away and we could obtain a fair view of the field, it looked, at the first glance, like a sea of blood. It was not blood itself which gave it this appearance but the red coats in which the British soldiers were dressed. Straight out before our position, for about the width of space which we supposed had been occupied by the British column, the field was entirely covered with prostrate bodies. In some places they were laying in piles of several, one on top of the other. On either side, there was an interval more thinly sprinkled with the slain; and then two other dense rows, one near the levee and the other towards the swamp. About two hundred yards off, directly in front of our position, lay a large dapple gray horse, which we understood to have been Pakenham's. . . .*

When we first got a fair view of the field in our front, individuals could be seen in every possible attitude. Some laying quite dead, others mortally wounded, pitching and tumbling about in the agonies of death. Some had their heads shot off, some their legs, some their arms. Some were laughing, some crying, some groaning, and some screaming. There was every variety of sight and sound.

Source: "A Contemporary Account of the Battle of New Orleans by a Soldier in the Ranks," *Louisiana Historical Quarterly*, January 1926.

■ THINKING ABOUT THE SELECTION

1. What aspects of the battle action does the author stress?

2. How does the author describe the battle-field after the firing stopped?

3. CRITICAL THINKING Expressing an Opinion On the basis of this selection, do you think the author was a careful observer? Why or why not?

---

*Sir Edward Pakenham was the general commanding the British forces. He was killed in the battle.

■ **10-1   Traveling Westward**   FIRST PERSON

INTRODUCTION   Charles Fenno Hoffman, a New Yorker, was one of the first professional writers in the United States. He was also a hardy man. Despite the fact that he had only one leg (the result of a childhood accident), he journeyed on horseback throughout the Northwest Territory in the early 1800s. In the following selection from his book *A Winter in the West*, he describes the National Road and the pioneer families who traveled along it as they headed westward to forge new lives on the frontier.

VOCABULARY   Before you read the selection, find the meaning of these words in a dictionary: emigrants, foraging, arduous, traverse, allude.

By far the greatest portion of travellers one meets with . . . consists of teamsters and the emigrants. The former generally drive six horses before their enormous wagons—stout, heavy-looking beasts, descended, it is said, from the famous [draft] horses of Normandy. They go about twenty miles a day. . . .

   As for the emigrants, it would astonish you to witness how they get along. A covered one-horse wagon generally contains the whole worldly substance of a family consisting not infrequently of a dozen members. The tolls are so high along this western turnpike, and horses are comparatively so cheap in the region whither the emigrant is bound, that he rarely provides more than one miserable [horse] to transport his whole family to the far west. The strength of the poor animal is of course half the time unequal to the demand upon it, and you will, therefore, unless it be raining very hard, rarely see anyone in the wagon, except perhaps some child overtaken by sickness, or a mother nursing a young infant. The head of the family walks by the horse, cheering and encouraging him on his way. The good woman, when not engaged as hinted above, either trudges along with her husband, or, leading some weary little traveller by the hand far behind, endeavors to keep the rest of her charge from loitering by the wayside. The old house-dog—if not chained beneath the wagon to prevent the half-starved brute from foraging too freely in a friendly country—brings up the rear. . . .

   The hardships of such a tour must form no bad preparatory school for the arduous life which the new settler has afterward to enter upon. Their horses, of course, frequently give out on the road; and in companies so numerous, sickness must

Making Travel Faster and Easier *The westward expansion of the United States was made easier by many improvements in transportation during the early 1800s. This painting by Lars Sellstedt shows two steamships leaving Buffalo harbor and a canal boat being pulled into the harbor.* **Linking Past and Present** *What important advances in transportation have occurred during the 1900s?*

frequently overtake some of the members. . . . About thirty miles from Wheeling we first struck the national road. It appears to have been originally constructed of large round stones, thrown without much arrangement on the surface of the soil, after the road was first levelled. These are now being plowed up, and a thin layer of broken stones is in many places spread over the renovated surface. I hope the roadmakers have not the conscience to call this Macadamizing.* It yields like snow-drift to the heavy wheels which traverse it, and the very best parts of the road that I saw are not to be compared with a Long-Island turnpike. Two-thirds indeed of the extent we traversed were worse than any artificial road I ever travelled, except perhaps the log causeways among the new settlements in northern New York. The ruts are worn so broad and deep by heavy travel, that an army of pigmies might march into the bosom of the country under the cover they would afford. . . .

---

*Macadam roads, developed about 1815, were constructed of crushed stones. They were named after their inventor, a Scot named John McAdam.

There is one feature, however, in this national work which is truly fine—I allude to the massive stone bridges which form a part of it. They occur, as the road crosses a winding creek, a dozen times within twice as many miles. They consist either of one, two, or three arches; the centre arch being sprung a foot or two higher than those on either side. Their thick walls projecting above the road, their round stone buttresses, and carved key-stones combine to give them an air of Roman solidity and strength. They are monuments of taste and power that will speak well for the country when the brick towns they bind together shall have crumbled in the dust.

Source: Charles Fenno Hoffman, *A Winter in the West*, 1835.

■ **THINKING ABOUT THE SELECTION**

1. Describe a typical pioneer family as seen by Hoffman.

2. (a) What does Hoffman dislike about the National Road? (b) What does he like?

3. **CRITICAL THINKING Defending a Position** As Hoffman describes them, do the settlers moving westward seem admirable? Give reasons for your answer.

■ 10-2   **Life on the Mississippi**   LITERATURE

INTRODUCTION   One of the most popular writers in American literature was Mark Twain (1835–1910). Twain drew heavily on his personal experience—including his four years as an apprentice steamboat pilot on the Mississippi River—in his writing. In his most popular novels *The Adventures of Tom Sawyer* and *The Adventures of Huckleberry Finn* as well as in *Life on the Mississippi*, he makes the West "come alive." The following passage from *Life on the Mississippi* recalls a scene from Twain's boyhood.

VOCABULARY   Before you read the selection, find the meaning of these words in a dic-

tionary: ambition, comrades, transient, minstrel, gaudy, drowsing, drayman, prodigious, gilded, facilitate.

When I was a boy, there was but one permanent ambition among my comrades in our village on the west bank of the Mississippi River. That was, to be a steamboat-man. We had transient ambitions of other sorts, but they were only transient.

When a circus came and went, it left us all burning to become clowns: the first . . . minstrel show that came to our section left us all suffering to try that kind of life: now and then we had a hope that if we lived and were good, God would permit us to be pirates. These ambitions faded out, each in its turn; but the ambition to be a steamboat-man always remained.

Once a day a cheap gaudy packet arrived upward from St. Louis, and another downward from Keokuk. Before these events, the day was glorious with expectancy: after them, the day was a dead and empty thing. Not only the boys, but the whole village, felt this.

After all these years I can picture that old time to myself now, just as it was then: the white town drowsing in the sunshine of a summer's morning: the streets empty, or pretty nearly so: one or two clerks sitting in front of the Water Street stores, with their splint-bottomed chairs tilted back against the wall, chins on breasts, hats slouched over their faces, asleep—with shingle shaving enough around to show what broke them down. . . .

Presently a film of dark smoke appears above one of those remote points: instantly a . . . drayman, famous for his quick eye and prodigious voice, lifts up the cry, "S-t-e-a-m-b-o-a-t a-comin'!" and the scene changes! The . . . clerks wake up, a furious clatter of drays follows, every house and store pours out a human contribution, and all in a twinkling the dead town is alive and moving.

Drays, men, boys, all go hurrying from many quarters to a common center, the wharf. Assembled there, the people fasten their eyes upon the coming boat as upon a wonder they are seeing for the first time.

And the boat is rather a handsome sight, too. She is long and sharp and trim and pretty: she has two tall, fancy-topped chimneys, with a gilded device of some kind swung between them: a fanciful pilothouse, all glass and gingerbread, perched on top of the deck behind them; the paddleboxes are gorgeous with a picture or with gilded rays above the boat's name. . . .

The captain lifts his hand, a bell rings, the wheels stop; then they turn back, churning the water to foam, and the steamer is at rest. Then such a scramble as there is to get aboard, and to get ashore, and to take in freight and to discharge freight, all at one and the same time; and such a yelling and cursing as the mates facilitate it all with! Ten minutes later the steamer is under way again. . . . After ten more minutes the town is dead again.

Source: Mark Twain, *Life on the Mississippi*, 1883.

■ THINKING ABOUT THE SELECTION

1. What effect did the daily arrival of the steamboat have on the town in which Twain lived?

2. What did the steamboat symbolize to Twain and his boyhood friends?

3. CRITICAL THINKING **Linking Past and Present** Do you think there is something that means as much to people today as that steamboat meant to Twain and his companions? Explain.

Loading a Steamboat at New Orleans *Great flat-bottomed steamboats turned the rivers of the West into busy routes for traders and travelers. Here, workers load goods onto the steamboat* Gipsy *at New Orleans.* **Geography** *How was the design of these steamboats suited to western rivers?*

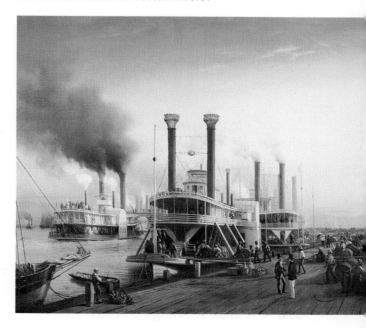

Forging Trails Across the Frontier *During the early and mid-1800s, the United States grew rapidly. A steady flow of pioneers headed westward, hoping to start new lives on the frontier. In this painting, Albert Bierstadt shows a surveying expedition heading into the Rocky Mountains.* **American Traditions** *What do you imagine it might have been like to have been one of the first settlers to arrive in the Rocky Mountains? Explain.*

CHAPTER 11 The Jackson Era
(1824–1840)

■ **11-1 The President's Lady**   LITERATURE

INTRODUCTION Irving Stone's biographical novel *The President's Lady* tells the story of Andrew Jackson and his wife, Rachel, from their first meeting until Rachel's death just before her husband's inauguration. The following passage from the novel tells of Jackson's reaction to the outcome of the presidential election of 1824.

VOCABULARY Before you read the selection, find the meaning of these words in a dictionary: donned, greatcoat, prodigious, chagrin, castigation, morosely, pilloried, tumultuous, maraudings, ardent, booty, garner.

They awakened on the morning of February 9, the day of decision, to find snow falling

heavily. Andrew donned a greatcoat and boots and left the hotel in time to reach the Capitol by noon, so that he might participate in the senatorial count which would name John Calhoun as vice-president. When Rachel asked if he were intending to remain after the Senate adjourned and the House took its seat to vote for president he replied that he did not think it proper for him to be in the House while the members were being polled.

He was back shortly after one o'clock, ordering dinner sent up to their room so they could avoid the milling crowds below in the tavern. The first course had just been set on their parlor table when Andy came in, the expression on his face clearer than any marked ballot: Mr. Adams had been elected on the first count! By prodigious efforts and brilliant maneuvering Henry Clay, single-handed, had swung Kentucky, Ohio and Missouri behind Adams.

John Eaton [Jackson's assistant] stormed in, his face black with disappointment and chagrin, and proceeded to give Henry Clay a thorough castigation. Andrew heard him out, then said quietly:

"That's not altogether fair to Mr. Clay, John. He has a right to throw his influence to the man he thinks best for the job. You remember he once accused me, right on the floor of the House, of being a 'military chieftain who would overthrow the liberties of the people.'"

That evening they attended the last of President Monroe's regular Wednesday levees. Andrew congratulated Mr. Adams cordially. While riding back to the hotel in the Jackson carriage, John Eaton commented on how quiet the city was: no bonfires, no victory celebrations or cheering crowds.

"They wanted you, General," Eaton concluded morosely. "They feel cheated."

But nothing could shake Andrew's calm acceptance. For her own part, Rachel was content. On the whole it had been a decent election; the predictions that the Republic would fall into ruin because its Chief Executive was to be chosen by popular vote had failed to materialize; and so had her own fears of being pilloried by the opposition.

"Well, Rachel, my dear, I tried to make you First Lady of the land. You are not too disappointed, are you?"

She smiled inwardly. . . .

"Whatever disappointment I may feel is for you."

"Well, then, I'll be happy to get back to the Hermitage."

"For how long?" she asked softly. ". . . until the next election?"

His eyes met hers. They were stern.

"I will be fifty-eight in a month. Mr. Adams is certain to serve the regular two terms. Surely you don't think at the age of sixty-six . . . ? This is *forever!*"

He used that word to me at home, thought Rachel, but this time he means it. Perhaps at long last he will be content to remain a gentleman planter.

Forever lasted five days. On February 14, President-elect Adams offered the post of Secretary of State to Henry Clay. All hell broke loose, in Washington and across the nation. . . .

Every ounce of Andrew's calm and acceptance vanished. She knew from the sense of outrage that shook his long lean frame that nothing in his tumultuous career,

Andrew Jackson *A self-made man and a war hero, Andrew Jackson, shown here in a portrait by Ralph E. W. Earl, won the loyal support of common Americans. His election in 1828 was regarded as evidence of a growing spirit of equality.* **Linking Past and Present** *How important is it for politicians today to win the support of average Americans?*

always excepting the maraudings of the British, had ever made him so utterly determined to avenge a wrong. As he stood in the far corner of the room surrounded by his most ardent supporters, she heard him cry:

"So the Judas of the West has closed the contract and will receive the thirty pieces of silver? The end will be the same. Was there ever witnessed such a barefaced corruption before?"

A dozen voices answered him at once.

"But surely Mr. Clay will know that the whole country is outraged?" "He can't be so stupid as to accept . . ."

"What, refuse his part of the booty?" Andrew's voice, as it penetrated to her, was shrill and cold. "But he must go before the Senate for confirmation. By the Eternal, gentlemen, I still have a vote here, and I pledge you my word that I shall unbosom myself. This barter of votes is sheer bribery, and if allowed to continue will destroy our form of government."

Three weeks later, in a slanting rain-storm, the family left the capital, all four riding in the carriage with the extra horses tied behind. Andrew was silent, his head on his chest, his eyes closed; he was still smarting from his defeat in the Senate where he had been able to garner only fourteen votes against the appointment of Mr. Clay. She had persuaded him that, as a matter of form, he should attend the inauguration. He had complained to her that Mr. Adams "had been escorted to the Capitol with the pomp and ceremony of guns and drums, which is not consistent with the character of the occasion." However, he had been among the first to shake hands with Mr. Adams, and had administered the oath to Calhoun, the new Vice-President, in the Senate.

From *The President's Lady* by Irving Stone. Copyright 1951 by Irving Stone. Used by permission of Doubleday, a division of Bantam Doubleday Dell Publishing Group, Inc.

■ THINKING ABOUT THE SELECTION

1. Why did Andrew Jackson defend Clay against John Eaton's charges?

2. What event caused Jackson to charge that there had been corruption in the election?

3. CRITICAL THINKING **Making Inferences** What effect do you think the election of 1824 had on Andrew Jackson's campaign for President in 1828? Explain.

■ **11-2 Campaign Hoopla**

INTRODUCTION In the presidential campaign of 1840, few Whigs were more enthusiastic than a prosperous New York merchant named Philip Hone. Having lost a great deal of money in the depression of the 1830s, Hone hated the Democrats. In his diary, he admiringly describes some of the meetings and parades in honor of "Tippecanoe and Tyler too."

VOCABULARY Before you read the selection, find the meaning of these words in a dictionary: paraphernalia, appellation, scepter, prodigious, decorous.

BOSTON, THURSDAY, SEPT. 8.—The great day is over, and how shall I attempt to describe it? The weather, which was doubtful last night, was bright this morning, and the delegates from other States and from the different towns in Massachusetts began to assemble on the Common at nine o'clock, with their standards, badges, and other paraphernalia. The scene began to be very soon of the most exciting character. Crowds were pressing toward the spot from every quarter. The windows of the fine houses which surround the Common were filled with well-dressed ladies. Horsemen were

A Country Celebration *During the Jackson administration and the years that followed, many American painters celebrated the life of the common people. For example, this painting by William Sidney Mount shows a lively country dance.* **American Traditions** *Why is it not surprising that many American artists celebrated the lives of average Americans during the age of Jackson?*

galloping to and fro, and Old Men of the Revolution tottering toward the places allotted to them. . . . I was directed to join the other invited guests at the State House, where I met Mr. [Daniel] Webster, the President of the day, and many other distinguished men. The procession did not begin to move until twelve o'clock. . . .

The procession moved up Beacon Street and down the other side of the Common . . . proceeded through Charlestown and arrived at Bunker Hill after a march of two hours and a half. . . . The ceremonies were commenced by a short address from Mr. Webster . . . after which several of the distinguished visitors were introduced to the audience, and each in turn made a short speech much to the purpose.

This honor was conferred upon me. Mr. Webster presented me as his friend, and informed the people that I was the person who first distinguished the party by the appellation of Whigs.* I spoke a few minutes and then concluded by saying that it appeared to me that all the men in the United States were present, and that they had better cut the matter short by going into the

*Hone claimed to have been the first to use the term "Whigs" for the party of those who opposed Jackson.

election at once. "As many of you, therefore," I said at the top of my voice, "as are willing to have William Henry Harrison for your President will please to say aye." This was responded to by a shout that rent the skies, and I came off with flying colors. . . .

WEDNESDAY, DEC. 2—*Presidential Election.** This is the day which decides the fate of Mr. Van Buren and his Administration. The electors of President and Vice-President meet simultaneously in each of the States of the Union, and will quietly and in discharge of the constitutional rights of the people, deposit 234 votes for William Henry Harrison for President, . . . and 60 votes for Martin Van Buren for President. . . .

The party which has been in power forty years yields the scepter to its adversary, . . .

_____

*This was not when balloting took place, but rather the day when state electors met to confirm the popular vote.

There is not probably a country in the world where a change of such prodigious magnitude could have been effected in the same time, with so little apparent machinery, and in so orderly and decorous a manner.

Source: Allan Nevins, ed., *The Diary of Philip Hone* (New York: Dodd, Mead and Company, 1927).

■ THINKING ABOUT THE SELECTION

1. Describe Philip Hone's role in the Boston meeting.

2. Which aspects of the Boston meeting seem most important to Hone?

3. CRITICAL THINKING **Drawing Conclusions** (a) How does the election make Hone feel about the American system of government? (b) Do you think he would have felt the same way if Harrison had lost? Why or why not?

CHAPTER **12** From Sea to Shining Sea
(1820–1860)

■ 12-1 Death Comes for the Archbishop LITERATURE

INTRODUCTION Many of the novels and stories of Willa Cather (1873–1947) focus on pioneer life in the Great Plains. In *Death Comes for the Archbishop*, however, her setting is the American Southwest during the 1850s. The book's main character, Bishop Latour, journeys with his Native American guide Jacinto throughout New Mexico and Arizona and is deeply influenced by the environment and the culture of the region. In the following selection, Father Latour and Jacinto camp for the night during a journey to a distant mission.

VOCABULARY Before you read the selection, find the meaning of these words in a dictionary: firmament, proposition, vehement.

Jacinto got firewood and good water from the Lagunas, and they made their camp in a pleasant spot on the rocks north of the village. As the sun dropped low, the light brought the white church and the yellow adobe houses up into relief from the flat ledges. Behind their camp, not far away, lay a group of great mesas. The Bishop asked Jacinto if he knew the name of the one nearest them.

"No, I do not know any name," he shook his head. "I know Indian name," he added, as if, for once, he were thinking aloud.

"And what is the Indian name?"

"The Laguna Indians call Snow-Bird mountain." He spoke somewhat unwillingly.

Life in San Antonio *During the mid-1800s, settlers flooded into the Southwest. By the 1840s, the population of Texas alone had swelled to 140,000. Many of these people settled in emerging cities. This painting by William G. M. Samuel shows downtown San Antonio in 1849.* **Daily Life** *How might life in San Antonio during the mid-1800s have differed from life in the large eastern cities of the time?*

"That is very nice," said the Bishop musingly. "Yes, that is a pretty name. . . ."

The two companions sat, each thinking his own thoughts as night closed in about them; a blue night set with stars, the bulk of solitary mesas cutting into the firmament. The Bishop seldom questioned Jacinto about his thoughts or beliefs. He didn't think it polite, and he believed it to be useless. There was no way he could transfer his own memories of European civilization into the Indian mind, and he was quite willing to believe that behind Jacinto there was a long tradition, a store of experience, which no language could translate to him. A chill came with the darkness. Father Latour put on his old fur-lined cloak, and Jacinto, loosening the blanket tied about his loins, drew it up over his head and shoulders.

"Many stars," he said presently. "What you think about the stars, Padre?"

"The wise men tell us they are worlds, like ours, Jacinto."

. . . "I think not," he said in the tone of one who has considered a proposition fairly and rejected it. "I think they are leaders— great spirits."

"Perhaps they are," said the Bishop with a sigh. "Whatever they are, they are great. Let us say *Our Father*, and go to sleep, my boy."

Kneeling on either side of the embers they repeated the prayer together and then rolled up in their blankets. The Bishop went to sleep thinking with satisfaction that he was beginning to have some sort of human companionship with his Indian boy. One called the young Indians "boys," perhaps because there was something youthful and elastic in their bodies. Certainly about their behavior there was nothing boyish in the American sense, nor even in the European sense. Jacinto was never, by any chance, [naive]; he was never taken by surprise. One felt that his training, whatever it had been, had prepared him to meet any situation which might confront him. He was as much at home in the Bishop's study as in his own pueblo—and he was never too much at home anywhere. Father Latour felt he had gone a good way toward gaining his guide's friendship, though he did not know how.

The truth was, Jacinto liked the Bishop's way of meeting people; thought he had the right tone with Padre Gallegos, the right tone with Padre Jesus, and that he had good manners with the Indians. In his experience, white people, when they addressed Indians, always put on a false face. There were many kinds of false faces; Father Vaillant's, for example, was kindly but too vehement. The Bishop put on none at all. He stood straight and turned to the Governor of Laguna, and his face underwent no change. Jacinto thought this remarkable.

From *Death Comes for the Archbishop* by Willa Cather. Copyright 1927 by Willa Cather and renewed 1955 by the Executors of the Estate of Willa Cather. Reprinted by permission of Alfred A. Knopf, Inc.

■ THINKING ABOUT THE SELECTION

1. Why did the Bishop hardly ever question Jacinto about his beliefs?

2. How had the Bishop gained Jacinto's trust?

3. **CRITICAL THINKING Comparing** (a) Compare the Bishop's and Jacinto's beliefs concerning the stars. (b) What did each man think of the other's belief?

■ 12-2 In the Gold Fields of California

FIRST PERSON

INTRODUCTION One of the thousands of forty-niners drawn west by the Gold Rush was Elisha Douglass Perkins. At the age of twenty-five, he left Marietta, Ohio, to try his luck in the California gold fields. After a difficult cross-country trip that took more than four months, Perkins and the friends he was traveling with arrived in Sacramento in the fall of 1849. Soon afterward, they tried their luck prospecting. Perkins's diary ends a few months after these entries. He died in California in 1852, having never returned to Ohio.

VOCABULARY Before you read the selection, find the meaning of these words in a dictionary: adz, commenced, sundries, accumulating, bilious.

November 1. Well here we are in the gold mines of California, & mining has been tried

"& found wanting!" We left Sac. City [Sacramento] October 18, with our provisions &c in Chapins wagons en route for the Cosumne River distant some 28 or 30 miles & arrived here the 21. We are about S.E. from the city, in a rolling country & on a small rapid stream tumbling over a rocky bed. The appearance of the country through which we passed was somewhat better than that down the Sac. River, as we saw it, but yet I have not been in any part of the "beautiful valley" of which we used to hear. On locating here we immediately went to work making "washers."* Doe & John being somewhat "under the weather" I did nearly all the work on the mine alone. I cut down a

---

*These were wooden troughs through which water was poured to wash out sand and pebbles, leaving the heavier gold behind.

pine tree, cut it off the proper length peeled & cut down one side & with axe & adz hollowed it out till I reduced it to about 1/2 inch in thickness by nearly two days of hard labor & blistering of hands &c. . . .

The first three days Doc took hold with pick & shovel we excavated a hole about 4 feet deep & made in that time about 2.00! Here Doc broke down & was taken sick & John being about [recovered] he commenced with me in another place & we have made something everyday, the highest 11.00 lowest 3 each. This won't do & we shall probably leave soon for richer diggings next week. Tis terrible hard work, & such a backache as we have every night! We are below the bed of the creek & have to bale out water from our "hole" every hour, & work in the mud & wet at the bottom.

I am pretty well satisfied that fortunes in Cal. as anywhere else, with some exceptions, take time & hard work to get, & I must go home without mine I'm afraid, as I would hardly lead this kind of life 5 years for any fortune, & I certainly would not be separated from H. [Harriet] for that length of time. Since we have been here every man of our company has been sick but myself. . . .

Thursday Nov. Still in our camp on the Cosumne & poor as the "diggings" have proved are likely to remain here all winter. The rains have set in in earnest & teams cannot travel. Chapins teams went to town for our provisions & sundries & are stuck fast about 5 miles from here, not able to move a step. I fear we may have difficulty in getting anything to eat. Doc has finally left us for good, & will probably go home in the next steamer, couldn't stand the hard work & went to town last week. His leaving puts the finishing stroke to my list of disappointments "& now I'm all alone." Shall have to give up my expectations of accumulating sufficient to carry me home in the spring & be thankful if I get enough to pay my expenses this winter. Well I'm here & must take the country as I find it. . . .

Gold Rush Sketches *Following the discovery of gold in 1848, people poured into California from all over the world. In 1849, more than 80,000 people arrived, hoping to strike it rich. These drawings by O.C. Seltzer provide a glimpse of the daily lives of prospectors.* **Linking Past and Present** *California's population has continued to grow throughout the 1900s. How might you explain this growth?*

Christmas Day, 1849. Oh how I wish I could spend this day at home, what a "merry Christmas" I would have of it, & what happy faces I should see instead of these of the disappointed set now around me. The day here ushered in by firing of guns pistols &c & some blasting of heavy logs in lieu of cannon & this is about the amount of our celebrating. . . .

January 8, 1850, Thursday P.M. Have just returned from assisting in the performance of the last sad duties for one of our little party which left Marietta last spring so full of health & high hopes. S. E. Cross was taken sick about two weeks since with a bilious fever. . . . Although every thing was done for him which our means permitted, [the illness] proved fatal yesterday January 7, at about 11 o'clock P.M. & we buried him today upon the hillside overlooking our little settlement. The death of one of our number here so far away

Source Readings and Art • **585**

from home & all that makes life dear, casts a gloom on all the survivors & we cannot but think of the possibility of a like fate being reserved for ourselves, & oh how terrible the thought. If I must die, let me but get home & die in the arms of my friends, & I'll not complain, but here with no one to care for me, or shed a tear of affection as my spirit takes its flight, tis horrible. . . . California has been, & will be the cause of many broken hearts & much grief, & I look forward to my release from it with great anxiety.

Source: Thomas D. Clark, ed., *Gold Rush Diary: Being the Journal of Elisha Douglass Perkins on the Overland Trail in the Spring and Summer of 1849* (Lexington, KY: University of Kentucky Press, 1967).

■ THINKING ABOUT THE SELECTION

1. What circumstances made gold mining especially difficult for Perkins and his companions?

2. What seems to have been Perkins's worst fear?

3. CRITICAL THINKING **Drawing Conclusions** If Perkins's diary entries had been printed in the Marietta newspaper, what effect do you think they might have had on other people eager to journey to California?

CHAPTER **13** The Worlds of North and South
(1820–1860)

■ **13-1 American Notes**

INTRODUCTION Charles Dickens, a famous English novelist, visited the United States for six months in 1842. During that time he traveled to Boston, New York, Philadelphia, Washington, St. Louis, and Cincinnati and journeyed on the Mississippi River. Dickens's keen powers of observation and subtle sense of humor are evident throughout his account of this trip. In the following selection, Dickens describes the American railroad of the 1840s.

VOCABULARY Before you read the selection, find the meaning of these words in a dictionary: omnibuses, caravan, anthracite, interrogatively, enumerate, hewn, stagnant.

I made acquaintance with an American railroad, on this occasion, for the first time. As these works are pretty much alike all through the States, their general characteristics are easily described.

There are no first and second class carriages as with us; but there is a gentle-men's car and a ladies' car: the main distinction between which is that in the first, everybody smokes; and in the second, nobody does. As a black man never travels with a white one, there is also a negro car; . . . There is a great deal of jolting, a great deal of noise, a great deal of wail, not much window, a locomotive engine, a shriek, and a bell.

The cars are like shabby omnibuses, but larger: holding thirty, forty, fifty, people. The seats, instead of stretching from end to end, are placed crosswise. Each seat holds two persons. There is a long row of them on each side of the caravan, a narrow passage up the middle, and a door at both ends. In the centre of the carriage there is usually a stove, fed with charcoal or anthracite coal; which is for the most part red-hot. It is insufferably close; and you see the hot air fluttering between yourself and any other object you may happen to look at, like the ghost of smoke.

In the ladies' car, there are a great many gentlemen who have ladies with them. There are also a great many ladies who have nobody with them: for any lady may travel alone, from one end of the United States to the other, and be certain of the most courteous and considerate treatment everywhere. The conductor or check-taker, or guard, or whatever he may be, wears no uniform. He walks up and down the car, and in and out of it, as his fancy dictates; leans against the door with his hands in his pockets and stares at you, if you chance to be a stranger; or enters into conversation with the passengers about him. A great many newspapers are pulled out, and a few of them are read. Everybody talks to you, or to anybody else who hits his fancy. If you are an Englishman, he expects that the railroad is pretty much like an English railroad. If you say "No," he says "Yes?" (interrogatively), and asks in what respect they differ. You enumerate the heads of difference, one by one, and he says "Yes?" (still interrogatively) to each. Then he guesses that you don't travel faster in England; and on your replying that you do, says, "Yes?" again (still interrogatively), and it is quite evident, doesn't believe it. . . .

Except when a branch road joins the main one, there is seldom more than one track of rails; so that the road is very narrow, and the view, where there is a deep cutting, by no means extensive. When there is not, the character of the scenery is always the same. Mile after mile of stunted trees: some hewn down by the axe, some blown down by the wind, some half fallen and resting on their neighbours, many mere logs half hidden in the swamp, others mouldered away to spongy chips. . . . Now you emerge for a few brief minutes on an open country, glittering with some bright lake or pool, broad as many an English river, but so small here that it scarcely has a name; now catch hasty glimpses of a distant town, with its clean white houses and their cool piazzas, its

The Transportation Revolution *Many advances in transportation occurred during the mid-1800s. The most significant of these was the railroad. This painted tin tray shows an early train traveling through the countryside.* **Linking Past and Present** *What do you consider to be the most important advance in transportation in the 1900s? Why?*

prim New England church and schoolhouse; when whir-r-r-r! almost before you have seen them, comes the same dark screen: the stunted trees, the stumps, the logs, the stagnant water—all so like the last that you seem to have been transported back again by magic.

The train calls at stations in the woods, where the wild impossibility of anybody having the smallest reason to get out, is only to be equalled by the apparently desperate hopelessness of there being anybody to get in. It rushes across the turnpike road, where there is no gate, no policeman, no signal: nothing but a rough wooden arch, on which is painted "When the Bell Rings, Look Out For The Locomotive." On it whirls headlong, dives through the woods again, emerges in the light, clatters over frail arches, rumbles upon the heavy ground, shoots beneath a wooden bridge which intercepts the light for a second like a wink, suddenly awakens all the slumbering echoes in the main street of a large town, and dashes on haphazard, pell-mell, neck-or-nothing, down the middle of the road. There—with mechanics working at their trades, and people leaning from their doors and windows, and boys flying kites and playing marbles, and men smoking, and women talking, and children crawling, and pigs burrowing, and unaccustomed horses plunging and rearing, close to the very rails—there—on, on, on—tears the mad dragon of an engine with its train of cars; scattering in all directions a shower of burning sparks from its wood fire; screeching, hissing, yelling, panting; until at last the thirsty monster stops beneath a covered way to drink, the people cluster round, and you have time to breathe again.

Source: Charles Dickens, *American Notes*, 1842.

■ **THINKING ABOUT THE SELECTION**

1. According to Dickens, what is the most noticeable distinction between the men's car and the ladies' car?

2. (a) What impression does Dickens convey of the interiors of the railroad cars? (b) Which details in his account contribute to this impression?

3. **CRITICAL THINKING Comparing** According to Dickens, how were American railroads different from those in England?

■ 13-2   Contrasting North and South
FIRST PERSON

INTRODUCTION Harriet Martineau of England, who traveled widely in the United States in the 1830s, was an acute observer of the American scene. In the following passage from her book *Society in America*, she presents her contrasting impressions of the North and the South. As you read the selection, note how Martineau's personal opinions color her writing.

VOCABULARY Before you read the selection, find the meaning of these words in a dictionary: preclude, predicament, servile, debasement, degradation, incessant.

In the north, the children all go to school, and work there, more or less. As they grow up, they part off into the greatest variety of employments. The youths must, without exception, work hard; or they had better drown themselves. Whether they are to be lawyers, or otherwise professional; or merchants, manufacturers, farmers, or citizens, they have everything to do for themselves. A very large proportion of them have, while learning their future business, to earn the means of learning. There is much manual labour in the country colleges; much teaching in the vacations done by students. Many a great man in Congress was seen in his boyhood leading his father's horses to water; and, in his youth, guiding the plow in his father's field. There is probably hardly a man in New England who cannot ride, drive, and tend his own horse. . . .

There are a few young men, esteemed the least happy members of the community, who inherit wealth. The time will come, when the society is somewhat older, when it will be understood that wealth need not preclude work. But at present, there are no individuals so forlorn, in the northern States, as young men of fortune. Men who have shown energy and skill in working their way in society are preferred for political representatives. There is no scientific or literary class, for such individuals to fall into: all the world is busy around them, and they are reduced to the predicament, unhappily the most dreaded of all in the United States, of standing alone. . . .

Women Heading to the Factory *As northern industries grew, thousands of women went to work in factories. In this painting by Winslow Homer, several women are heading to work, carrying their lunch pails. The wooded setting of the factory was typical of many New England factories of the time. Yet the women who worked there usually endured harsh conditions and were badly underpaid.* **Daily Life** *What do you imagine a typical day was like for the women in this painting?*

As for the women of the northern States, most have the blessing of work, though not of the extent and variety which will hereafter be seen to be necessary for the happiness of their lives. All married women, except the ladies of rich merchants and others, are liable to have their hands full of household occupation, from the uncertainty of domestic service. . . . Women who do not marry have, in many instances, to work for their support. . . .

What is life in the slave States, in respect of work?

There are two classes, the servile and the [master], between whom there is a great gulf fixed. The servile class has not even the benefit of hearty toil. No solemn truths sink down into them, to cheer their hearts, stimulate their minds, and nerve their hands. Their wretched lives are passed between an utter debasement of the will, and a conflict of the will with external force.

The other class is in circumstances as unfavourable as the least happy order of persons in the old world. The means of educating children are so meagre that young people begin life under great disadvantages. The vicious fundamental principle of morals in a slave country, that labour is disgraceful, taints the infant mind with a stain which is fatal in the world of spirits. . . . When children at school call everything that pleases them "gentlemanly," and pity all (but slaves) who have to work, and talk of marrying early for a [home], it is all over with them. A more hopeless state of degradation can hardly be conceived of, however they may ride, and play the harp, and sing Italian, and teach their slaves what they call religion. . . .

The wives of slave-holders are, as they and their husbands declare, as much slaves as their negroes. If they will not have everything go to rack and ruin around them, they must superintend every household operation, from the cellar to the garrets. . . . The lady of the house carries her huge bunch of keys, (for every consumable thing must be locked up,) and has to give out, on incessant requests, whatever is wanted for the household. She is for ever superintending, and trying to keep things straight, without the slightest hope of attaining anything like leisure and comfort. What is there in . . . the reputation of ease and luxury, which can compensate for toils and cares of this nature?

Source: Harriet Martineau, *Society in America*, 1837.

■ THINKING ABOUT THE SELECTION

1. What, according to Harriet Martineau, is the most striking feature of life in the North?

2. Why does Martineau think the circumstances of the southern slave owners are unfavorable?

3. CRITICAL THINKING **Drawing Conclusions** (a) What overall impression of life in the United States does Martineau convey? (b) Do you think that most Americans of the time would have agreed with her? Why or why not? (c) Do you agree? Explain.

CHAPTER **14** A Reforming Age
(1820–1860)

■ **14-1 Conductor on the Underground Railroad** LITERATURE

INTRODUCTION Harriet Tubman, who was born a slave, escaped to freedom in 1849. Anxious for others to enjoy that same freedom, she became a "conductor" for the underground railroad, escorting fugitive slaves to Canada. On one very important journey in 1854, three of her brothers were among the group of people she helped escape. The following passage from Ann Petry's biography of Tubman describes part of that journey. When it begins, Harriet and her brothers are hiding on the plantation where their parents, Daddy Ben and Old Rit, are slaves.

VOCABULARY Before you read the selection, find the meaning of these words in a dictionary: fodder, chinks, detain, jouncing.

It was still raining. From the dark, heavy look of the sky, visible through the roof of the fodder house, it would be an all-day rain. Christmas Day. And a Sunday. The beat

of the rain against the roof of the fodder house, against its sides, would be their only Christmas greeting. She hoped they wouldn't resent it too much.

There were wide chinks in the walls. Through them she could see the swaybacked cabin where Daddy Ben and Old Rit lived. It looked exactly like the cabin on the Brodas plantation where she was born. A whole row of these sway-backed cabins here, too. Smoke kept pouring out of the clay-daubed chimney, hanging heavy in the air. Old Rit had probably killed her pig, and was cooking it for the Christmas dinner. The master gave her a baby pig every year, and she fattened it, saving food from her own plate to feed the pig, so that she could feed her family with a lavish hand on this one day. She'd have pork and sausage and bacon. Plenty of food. The boys said that Old Rit was expecting them for dinner. They always spent Christmas Day with her.

She had to figure out some way of letting Ben know that she was here, that the boys were with her and that they needed food. It would never do to let Old Rit know this. She would laugh and shout. Then when she learned, as she certainly would, that the boys were running away, going North, she would try to detain them, would create such an uproar that the entire quarter would know their secret.

Harriet remembered the two men, John Chase and Peter Jackson. They were strangers. She asked them to go to the cabin, to tell Ben that his children were in the fodder house, badly in need of food. She warned them not to let Old Rit overhear what they said.

John and Peter did exactly as she told them. She watched them knock on the ramshackle door of the cabin, saw the door open, saw Old Ben standing in the doorway. The men motioned to him to come outside. They talked to him. Ben nodded his head. His expression did not change at all. She thought, how wonderful he is. Then he went back inside the cabin.

Late in the afternoon, he tapped on the side of the fodder house, and then opened the door, and put part of the Christmas dinner—cooked bacon, hoecake, fried pork and roasted yams—inside on the floor. He did not look at them. He said, "I know what'll come of this and I ain't goin' *to see my children*, nohow."

Harriet remembered his reputation for truthfulness. His word had always been accepted on the plantation because he was never known to tell a lie. She felt a kind of wondering admiration for him. He had become an old man in the five years since she had seen him—an old man. Yet the integrity and the strength of his character had not changed. How badly he must have wanted to see them, four of his children, there in the fodder house, on Christmas Day; but he would not lie, and so he would not look at them. Thus, if he was questioned as

Publicizing the Abolitionist Cause *Printing played a major role in the abolition movement. Antislavery newspapers, such as* Freedom's Journal *and* The Liberator, *helped to convince thousands of Americans to join the cause. This portrait by Robert Street shows a typical printer hard at work in his shop.* **Linking Past and Present** *What impact do newspapers have on the views of Americans today? What other media also affect our views?*

to the whereabouts of his boys, he could say that he had not seen them.

He made three trips from the cabin to the fodder house. Each time he put a small bundle of food inside the door until he must have given them most of the food intended for the Christmas dinner. Harriet noticed how slow his movements were. He was stooped over. He had aged fast. She would have to come back soon for him and Old Rit. Some time very soon. She remembered his great strength, and his love for his broadax, and the stories he used to tell her about the wonderful things to be seen in the woods.

She wanted to put her arms around him and look deep into his eyes and didn't because she respected his right to make this self-sacrificing contribution to their safety. How he must have wanted to look at them, especially at the daughter whom he had not seen for five long years.

They stayed in the fodder house all that day, lying on the top of the corn, listening to the drip of the rain, waiting for dark, when they would set out. They spoke in whispers.

Harriet kept reassuring them. They were perfectly safe. They would not be missed for at least two days. At Christmas everyone was busy, dancing, laughing. The masters were entertaining their friends and relatives in their big, comfortable houses. The slaves were not required to work—as long as the Yule logs burned in the fireplaces. She had never lost a passenger, never run her train off the track, they were safe with her, the Lord would see them through.

She knew they did not like this long rainy day spent inside a fodder house, rain coming through the chinks in the boards. Dainty, pretty Catherine, who had been a house servant, complained bitterly. She objected to the rough feel of the corn. She said she thought she heard the sound of rats, a dry scrabbling sound.

Harriet laughed at her, and told her this was easy, just sitting around like this, that the Underground Railroad wasn't any train ride. It means walking, and sometimes running, and being hungry, and sometimes jouncing up and down in the bottom of a farmer's wagon, but more walking than riding, rain or dry, through woods and swamps and briars and hiding anywhere that the earth offered a little shelter against prying eyes and listening ears. It meant not enough sleep because the walking had to be done at night and the sleeping during the day. Before the journey ended, Catherine would be able to sleep anywhere, on the ground, in a haystack, under a bush, and this rat-infested fodder house would loom in her memory like a king's palace. . . .

Late in the afternoon, Ben made one more trip. He pushed another bundle of food inside the door. He kept his eyes closed, tight shut. He said he would be back when it got dark and would walk with them just a little way, to visit with them. . . .

When night came, Ben tapped at the door. He had tied a bandanna tight around his eyes. Harriet took one of his arms and one of the boys took him by the other arm. They started out, walking slowly.

Harriet answered Ben's questions as fast as she could, she told him a little about the other trips she had made, said that she would be back again to get him and Old Rit, told him where some of the people were that she had piloted North, what the North was like, cold in winter, yes, but there were worse things in the world than cold. She told him about St. Catharines, in Canada, and said that she would be back—soon.

They parted from him reluctantly. Ben stood in the middle of the road, listening to the sound of their footsteps. They kept looking back at him. He did not remove the blindfold until he was certain they were out of sight. When he could hear no sound of movement, he untied the bandanna and went back to the cabin.

From *Harriet Tubman: Conductor on the Underground Railroad* by Ann Petry. Copyright © 1955 by Ann Petry, copyright renewed 1983 by Ann Petry. Reprinted by permission of Russell & Volkening as agents for the author.

■ THINKING ABOUT THE SELECTION

1. Why did Harriet not want Old Rit to know that she and her brothers were hiding in the barn?

2. Why did Old Ben refuse to look at his children?

3. CRITICAL THINKING Summarizing Based on what Harriet said to Catherine, explain how the underground railroad worked.

INTRODUCTION Horace Mann had a mission. He was determined to make education in Massachusetts—and everywhere else in the United States, for that matter—worthy of a democratic people. In lectures and books, he made eloquent appeals for improvements in everything from textbooks to classrooms. This extract is from one of Mann's lectures.

VOCABULARY Before you read the selection, find the meaning of these words in a dictionary: remuneration, vestments, embodiment, subordinate.

Compare the salaries given to engineers, to superintendents of railroads, to agents and overseers of manufacturing establishments, to cashiers of banks, and so forth, with the customary rates of remuneration given to teachers. Yet, does it deserve a more liberal [payment], does it require greater natural talents . . . to run cotton or woollen machinery, or to keep a locomotive from

Scenes From Daily Life *During the mid-1800s, American painters known as* genre *painters* focused on realistic scenes. One of the best known was William Sidney Mount, who painted these two pictures. Mount was the first American artist to show African Americans in a dignified manner. **American Traditions** *What can you learn about life in the 1800s from paintings such as these?*

running off the track, than it does to preserve this wonderfully constructed and complicated machine of the human body in health and vigor; or to prevent the spiritual nature—that vehicle which carries all our hopes—from whirling to its ruin, or from dashing madly to some fatal collision? . . .

The compensation which we give with the hand is a true representation of the value which we affix in the mind; and how much more liberally and cordially do we [pay] those who prepare outward and perishable garments for the persons of our children, than those whose office it is to [provide] their spirits with the immortal vestments of virtue? . . .

Our *works* are the visible embodiment and representation of our *feelings*. . . . Tried by this unerring standard in human nature, our *Schoolhouses* are a fair index . . . of our interest in Public Education. Suppose, at this moment, some potent enchanter, by the waving of his magic wand, should take up all the twenty-eight hundred schoolhouses of Massachusetts . . . and, whirling them through the [terrifying] air, should set them all down, visibly, round about us, in this place. . . . I ask, my friends, if, in this new spectacle under the sun, with its motley hues of red and gray, and . . . with its shingles and clapboards flapping and clattering in the wind, as if giving public notice that they were about to depart,—I ask, if, in this indescribable and unnamable group of architecture, we should not see the true image, reflection and embodiment of our own love, attachment, and regard for Public Schools and Public Education, as, in a mirror, face to face? But, however neglected, forgotten, forlorn, these [buildings] may be, yet within their walls is contained the young and blooming creation of God. In them are our hope, the hopes of the earth. . . . Our dearest treasures do not consist in lands and [buildings], in railroads and banks, in warehouses or in ships upon every sea; they are within these doors, beneath these humble roofs; and is it not our solemn duty to hold every other earthly interest subordinate to their welfare? . . .

Within the last three years, the treasury of the Commonwealth has dispensed a bounty of about twenty-five thousand dollars to encourage the growth of wheat,—and within the last two years, of about five thousand dollars for the culture of silk,—for those goods which perish with the using; while it has not contributed one cent towards satisfying the pressing demand for apparatus and libraries for our schools, by which the imperishable treasures of knowledge and virtue would be increased a hundred-fold. The State has provided for the [free] distribution of a manual, descriptive of the art and processes of silk-culture, but made no provision for the distribution of any manual on that most difficult of all arts—the art of Education,—as though silk-culture were more important and more difficult than soul-culture.

Source: Horace Mann, *Life and Works of Horace Mann*, 1891.

■ THINKING ABOUT THE SELECTION

1. What three aspects of the American attitude toward education does Mann criticize?

2. What terms does Mann use to indicate that he values children?

3. **CRITICAL THINKING Defending a Position** Do you agree with Mann's claim that "the compensation which we give with the hand is a true representation of the value which we affix in the mind"? Explain.

5

The Nation Torn Apart

The Drums of War *When the tension between North and South erupted into war, people rushed to enlist. Many of those who volunteered were young boys, such as the one in this painting by William Morris Hunt. Tragically, tens of thousands of these boys lost their lives.* **Citizenship** *Do you think that young men under eighteen should have been allowed to fight in the Civil War? Why or why not?*

CHAPTER **15** The Road to Civil War
(1820–1861)

■ **15-1 Uncle Tom's Cabin**   LITERATURE

INTRODUCTION Harriet Beecher Stowe's (1811–1896) novel *Uncle Tom's Cabin* is sometimes cited as an underlying cause of the Civil War. The poignant and dramatic story of Uncle Tom, a gentle, elderly slave sold to a cruel master, Simon Legree, did arouse very strong antislavery feelings in many Americans. In the following passage, Legree is furious and threatens to kill Uncle Tom because he has helped two slaves escape.

VOCABULARY Before you read the selection, find the meaning of these words in a dictionary: surly, perdition, rend, ironic, despotic, degradation, paroxysm, tempest, probation, irresolute.

The escape of Cassy and Emmeline irritated the before surly temper of Legree to the last degree; and his fury, as was to be expected, fell upon the defenseless head of Tom. When he hurriedly announced the tidings among his hands, there was a sudden light in Tom's eye, a sudden upraising of his hands, that did not escape him. He saw that he did not join the muster of the pursuers. He thought of forcing him to do it; but, having had, of old, experience of his inflexibility when commanded to take part in any deed of inhumanity, he would not, in his hurry, stop to enter into any conflict with him.

Bidding for Slaves *At slave markets, such as the one in this painting by Eyre Crowe, members of slave families were often sold to different people and separated forever. The worst fate, however, was to be "sold down the river" to a plantation in the Deep South, where the working conditions for slaves were especially harsh.* **Geography** *Why do you think that working conditions for slaves tended to be especially harsh in the Deep South?*

Tom, therefore, remained behind, with a few who had learned of him to pray . . . for the escape of the fugitives.

When Legree returned, baffled and disappointed, all the long-working hatred of his soul towards his slave began to gather in a deadly and desperate form. Had not this man braved him,—steadily, powerfully, resistlessly,—ever since he bought him? Was there not a spirit in him which, silent as it was, burned on him like the fires of perdition?

"I *hate* him!" said Legree, that night, as he sat up in his bed; "I *hate* him! And isn't he mine? Can't I do what I like with him? Who's to hinder, I wonder?"

But, then, Tom was a faithful, valuable servant; and, although Legree hated him the more for that, yet the consideration was still somewhat of a restraint to him.

The next morning, he determined to say nothing, as yet; to assemble a party, from some neighboring plantations, with dogs and guns; to surround the swamp, and go about the hunt systematically. If it succeeded, well and good; if not, he would summon Tom before him, and—his teeth clenched and his blood boiled—*then* he would break that fellow down. . . .

The hunt was long, animated, and thorough, but unsuccessful. . . . Legree, . . . weary and dispirited, . . . alighted from his horse.

"Now, Quimbo," said Legree, as he stretched himself down in the sittingroom, "you jest go and walk that Tom up here, right away! The old cuss is at the bottom of this yer whole matter; and I'll have it out of his old black hide, or I'll know the reason why!". . .

Tom heard the message with a forewarning heart; for he knew all the plan of the fugitives' escape, and the place of their present concealment;—he knew the deadly character of the man he had to deal with, and his despotic power. But he felt strong in God to meet death, rather than betray the helpless.

He sat his basket down by the row, and, looking up, said, "Into thy hands I commend my spirit! Thou has redeemed me, oh Lord God of truth!" and then quietly yielded himself to the rough, brutal grasp with which Quimbo seized him.

"Ay, ay!" said the giant, as he dragged him along; "ye'll cotch it, now! I'll boun' Mas'r's back's up *high*! No sneaking out, now! Tell ye, ye'll get it, and no mistake! See how ye'll look, now, helpin' [them] to run away! See what ye'll get!"

The savage words none of them reached that ear!—a higher voice there was saying, "Fear not them that kill the body, and, after that, have no more that they can do." Nerve and bone of that poor man's body vibrated to those words, as if touched by the finger of God; and he felt the strength of a thousand souls in one. As he passed along, the trees and bushes, the huts of his servitude, the whole scene of his degradation, seemed to whirl by him as the landscape by the rushing ear. His soul throbbed,—his home was in sight,—and the hour of release seemed at hand.

"Well, Tom!" said Legree, walking up, and seizing him grimly by the collar of his coat, and speaking through his teeth, in a paroxysm of determined rage, "do you know I've made up my mind to kill you?"

"It's very likely, Mas'r," said Tom, calmly.

"*I have*," said Legree, with grim, terrible calmness, "*done-just-that-thing*, Tom, unless you'll tell me what you know about these yer gals!"

Tom stood silent.

"D'ye hear?" said Legree, stamping, with a roar like that of an incensed lion. "Speak!"

"Speak!" thundered Legree, striking him furiously. "Do you know anything?"

"I know, Mas'r; but I can't tell anything. *I can die!*"

Legree drew in a long breath; and, suppressing his rage, took Tom by the arm, and, approaching his face almost to his, said, in a terrible voice, "Hark 'e, Tom!—ye think, 'cause I've let you off before, I don't mean what I say; but, this time, I've *made up my mind*, and counted the cost. You've always stood it out agin' me: now, *I'll conquer ye, or kill ye!*—one or t'other. I'll count every drop of blood there is in you, and take 'em, one by one, till ye give up!"

Tom looked up to his master, and answered, "Mas'r, if you was sick, or in trouble, or dying, I could save ye, I'd give ye my heart's blood; and, if taking every drop of blood in this poor old body would save your precious soul, I'd give 'em freely, as the Lord gave his for me. O, Mas'r, don't bring this great sin on your soul! It will hurt you more than't will me! Do the worst you can, my troubles'll be over soon; but, if ye don't repent, yours won't never end."

Like a strange snatch of heavenly music, heard in the lull of a tempest, this burst of feeling made a moment's blank pause. Legree stood aghast, and looked at Tom; and there was such a silence, that the tick of the old clock could be heard, measuring, with silent touch, the last moments of mercy and probation to that hardened heart.

It was but a moment. There was one hesitating pause,—one irresolute, relenting thrill,—and the spirit of evil came back, with seven-fold vehemence; and Legree, foaming with rage, smote his victim to the ground.

Source: Harriet Beecher Stowe, *Uncle Tom's Cabin*, 1852.

■ THINKING ABOUT THE SELECTION

1. Why did Simon Legree hate Tom?

2. Why did Tom refuse to tell Legree where the runaways were hiding?

3. **CRITICAL THINKING Recognizing Points of View** Do you think Harriet Beecher Stowe was concerned about the accuracy of her portrayal of slavery? Why or why not?

INTRODUCTION Abraham Lincoln delivered one of his most famous speeches in his home town of Springfield, Illinois, on June 16, 1858. He had just been nominated by the Republicans to run for the Senate against Stephen A. Douglas. Lincoln attacked not only his Democratic opponent, but also the policies of the present and previous presidential administrations. He cited specific provisions of the Kansas-Nebraska Act and of the Supreme Court's Dred Scott ruling. Here are some of the highlights of Lincoln's address, which came to be known as his "house divided" speech.

VOCABULARY Before you read the selection, find the meaning of these words in a dictionary: premise, augmented, extinction, auxiliary, niche.

If we could first know *where* we are, and *whither* we are tending, we would then better judge *what* to do, and *how* to do it. We are now far into the *fifth* year, since a policy was initiated, with the *avowed* object, and *confident* premise, of putting an end to slavery agitation.*

Under the operation of that policy, that agitation has not only, *not ceased*, but has *constantly augmented*.

In *my* opinion, it *will* not cease, until a *crisis* shall have been reached, and passed.

"A house divided against itself cannot stand."

I believe this government cannot endure, permanently half *slave* and half *free*.

I do not expect the Union to be *dissolved*—I do not expect the house to *fall*—but I *do* expect it will cease to be divided.

It will become *all* one thing, or *all* the other.

Either the *opponents* of slavery, will arrest the further spread of it, and place it

*Lincoln is referring here to the passage of the Kansas-Nebraska Act, in 1854.

where the public mind shall rest in the belief that it is in course of ultimate extinction; or its *advocates* will push it forward, till it shall become alike lawful in *all* the States, *old* as well as *new*—*North* as well as *South*.

Have we no *tendency* to the latter condition?

Let any one who doubts, carefully contemplate that now almost complete legal combination—piece of *machinery* so to speak—compounded of the Nebraska doctrine, and the Dred Scott decision. . . .

The *working* points of that machinery are:

First, that no negro slave, imported as such from Africa, and no descendant of such slave can ever be a *citizen* of any State, in the sense of that term as used in the Constitution of the United States. This point is made in order to deprive the Negro, in every possible event, of the benefit of that provision of the United States Constitution that declares "the citizens of each state shall be entitled to all the privileges and immunities of citizens in the several states."

Secondly, that "subject to the Constitution of the United States," neither Congress nor a *Territorial Legislature* can exclude slavery from any United States territory. This point is made in order that individual men may fill up the territories with slaves, without danger of losing them as property, and thus enhance the chances of permanency to the institution through all the future.

Thirdly, that whether the holding a negro in actual slavery in a free State, makes him free, as against the holder, the United States courts will not decide, but will leave to be decided by the courts of any slave State the negro may be forced into by the master. . . .

Auxiliary to all this, and working hand in hand with it, the Nebraska doctrine, or what is left of it, is to *educate* and *mould* public

Violence in Kansas *During the 1850s, bloody battles erupted in Kansas over the issue of slavery. This eyewitness sketch shows the Battle of Hickory Point, one of many skirmishes between proslavery and antislavery settlers in 1856.* **American Traditions** *Why did the question of slavery provoke such strong reactions from people?*

opinion, at least *Northern* public opinion, to not *care* whether slavery is voted *down* or voted up.

This shows exactly where we now *are*; and *partially* also, whither we are tending....

It should not be overlooked that, by the Nebraska bill, the people of a *State* as well as *Territory*, were to be left *"perfectly free,"* [to adopt slavery] *"subject only to the Constitution."*

Why mention a *State*? They were legislating for *territories*, and not *for* or *about* States. . . . Put that and that together, and we have another nice little niche, which we may, ere long, see filled with another Supreme Court decision, declaring that the Constitution of the United States does not permit a *State* to exclude slavery from its limits. . . .

We shall *lie down* pleasantly dreaming that the people of *Missouri* are on the verge of making their State *free*; and we shall *awake* to the *reality*, instead, that the *Supreme* Court has made *Illinois* a *slave* State.

Source: Abraham Lincoln, Speech in Springfield, Illinois, June 16, 1858.

■ THINKING ABOUT THE SELECTION

1. As Lincoln sees it, what are the two alternatives the United States faces concerning slavery?

2. What legal "machinery" was set up by the Kansas-Nebraska Act and the Dred Scott decision?

3. CRITICAL THINKING **Evaluating Information** In Lincoln's view, what danger confronts the free states?

■ 16-1 The Killer Angels

INTRODUCTION In July 1863, Union and Confederate forces met in the decisive Battle of Gettysburg. Author Michael Shaara attempted to write the story of that battle in a way that would make the reader know what it was like to have been there. Shaara relied heavily on the diaries and letters of the Union and Confederate soldiers who fought in the battle. The following excerpt is from *The Killer Angels,* Shaara's fictionalized account of Gettysburg. It tells about the events of July 2, 1863, from the point of view of Joshua Lawrence Chamberlain, a colonel in the Union army.

VOCABULARY Before you read the selection, find the meaning of these words in a dictionary: crest, gaunt, flank, enormity, recourse, bayonets, volley, bawled, saber, crouch.

He limped along the line. Signs of exhaustion. Men down, everywhere. He thought: we cannot hold.

Looked up toward the crest. Fire still hot there, still hot everywhere. Down into the dark. They are . . . good men, those Rebs. Rebs, I salute you. I don't think we can hold you.

He gathered with Spear and Kilrain back behind the line. He saw another long gap, sent Ruel Thomas to this one. Spear made count.

"We've lost a third of the men, Colonel. Over a hundred down. The left is too thin."

"How's the ammunition?"

"I'm checking."

A new face, dirt-stained, bloody: Homan Melcher, Lieutenant, Company F, a gaunt boy with buck teeth.

"Colonel? Request permission to go pick up some of our wounded. We left a few boys out there."

"Wait," Chamberlain said.

Spear came back, shaking his head. "We're out." Alarm stained his face, a grayness in his cheeks.

"Some of the boys have nothing at all."

"Nothing," Chamberlain said.

Officers were coming from the right. Down to a round or two per man. And now there was a silence around him. No man spoke. They stood and looked at him, and then looked down into the dark and then looked back at Chamberlain. One man said, "Sir, I guess we ought to pull out."

Chamberlain said, "Can't do that."

Spear: "We won't hold 'em again. Colonel, you know we can't hold 'em again."

Chamberlain: "If we don't hold, they go right on by and over the hill and the whole flank caves in."

He looked from face to face. The enormity of it, the weight of the line, was a mass too great to express. But he could see it as clearly as in a broad wide vision, a Biblical dream: If the line broke here, then the hill was gone, all these boys from Pennsylvania, New York, hit from behind, above. Once the hill went, the flank of the army went. Good God! He could see the troops running; he could see the blue flood, the bloody tide.

Kilrain: "Colonel, they're coming."

Chamberlain marveled. But we're not so bad ourselves. One recourse: Can't go back. Can't stay where we are. Results: inevitable.

The idea formed.

"Let's fix bayonets," Chamberlain said.

For a moment no one moved.

"We'll have the advantage of moving downhill," he said.

Spear understood. His eyes saw; he nodded automatically. The men coming up the hill stopped to volley; weak fire came in return. Chamberlain said, "They've got to be tired, those Rebs. They've got to be close to the end. Fix bayonets. Wait. Ellis, you take the left wing. . . ."

"Well," Ellis Spear said. He shook his head. "Well."

"Let's go." Chamberlain raised his saber, bawled at the top of his voice, "Fix bayonets!"

He was thinking: We don't have two hundred men left. Not two hundred. More than that coming at us. . . . He stepped out into the open, balanced on the gray rock. Tozier had lifted the colors into the clear. The Rebs were thirty yards off. Chamberlain raised his saber, let loose the shout that was the greatest sound he could make, boiling the yell up from his chest: *Fix bayonets! Charge! Fix bayonets! Charge! Fix bayonets! Charge!* He leaped down from the boulder, still screaming, his voice beginning to crack and give, and all round him his men were roaring animal screams, and he saw the whole Regiment rising and pouring over the wall and beginning to bound down through the dark bushes, over the dead and dying and wounded, hats coming off, hair flying, mouths making sounds, one man firing as he ran, the last bullet, last round. Chamberlain saw gray men below stop, freeze, crouch, then quickly turn. The move was so quick he could not believe it. Men were turning and running. Some were stopping to fire. There was the yellow flash and then they turned. Chamberlain saw a man drop a rifle and run. . . .

The Rebs had begun to fall back; now they were running. He had never seen them run; he stared, began limping forward to see. Great cries, incredible sounds, firing and yelling. The Regiment was driving a line, swinging to the fight, into the dark valley. Men were surrendering. . . . At that moment a new wave of firing broke out on the other side of the gray mass. He saw a line of white smoke erupt, the gray troops waver and move back this way, stop, rifles begin to fall, men begin to run to the right, trying to get away. . . . Came upon Ellis Spear, grinning crazily, foolishly, face stretched and glowing with a wondrous light.

"By God, Colonel, by God, by God," Spear said. He pointed. Men were running off down the valley. The Regiment was moving across the front of the 83rd Pennsylvania. He looked up the hill and saw them waving and cheering. Chamberlain said, aloud, "I'll be . . . ."

Making Socks for Soldiers *During the Civil War, civilians banded together to provide much-needed food, clothing, and medical supplies. Posters and advertisements helped stir public support for the war effort. This poster, for example, urged women to knit socks for soldiers.* **Citizenship** *Why was the support of people on the home front so important to both sides?*

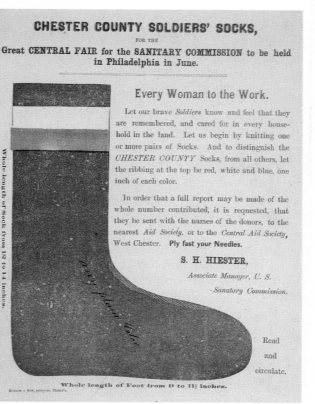

The Regiment had not stopped, was chasing the Rebs down the long valley between the hills. Rebs had stopped everywhere, surrendering. Chamberlain said to Spear, "Go on up and stop the boys. They've gone far enough."

"Yes, sir. But they're on their way to Richmond."

"Not today," Chamberlain said. "They've done enough today."

From *The Killer Angels* by Michael Shaara. Copyright © 1974 by Michael Shaara. Reprinted by permission of David McKay Co., a Division of Random House Inc.

■ THINKING ABOUT THE SELECTION

1. Why did Chamberlain give the order to fix bayonets and charge the attacking Confederate soldiers?

2. What do Chamberlain and his men think about the skill and courage of the Confederate soldiers?

3. **CRITICAL THINKING Defending a Position** Do you think the outcome of the battle would have been different if Chamberlain had not made the decisions he made? Defend your position.

■ 16-2   Lee, Dignified in Defeat

FIRST PERSON

INTRODUCTION General Robert E. Lee was one of the few Civil War leaders admired and respected by both southerners and northerners. The following first-hand description of the Confederate commander the day after his surrender was written by Theodore Lyman, an aide-de-camp to Union General George Meade.

VOCABULARY Before you read the selection, find the meaning of these words in a dictionary: florid, countenance, eccentricity, impoverished, pittance.

Monday April 10 is a day worthy of description, because I saw the remains of our great opponent, the Army of Northern Virginia. The General [Meade] proposed to ride through the Rebel lines to General Grant, who was at Appomattox Court House; and he took George and myself as aides; a great chance! for the rest were not allowed to go, no communication being permitted between the armies. At 10:30 we rode off, . . . We rode about a mile and then turned off to General Lee's Headquarters, which consisted in one fly [tent] with a campfire in front. I believe he had lost most of his baggage in some of the trains, though his establishment is at all times modest. . . . As he rode up General Meade took off his cap

and said: "Good-morning, General." Lee, however, did not recognize him, and, when he found who it was, said: "But what are you doing with all that grey in your beard?" To which Meade promptly replied: "You have to answer for most of it!"

Lee is, as all agree, a stately-looking man; tall, erect and strongly built, with a full chest. His hair and closely trimmed beard, though thick, are now nearly white. He has a large and well-shaped head, with a brown, clear eye, of unusual depth. His face is sunburnt and rather florid. In manner he is exceedingly grave and dignified—this, I believe, he always has; but there was evidently added an extreme depression, which gave him the air of a man who kept up his pride to the last, but who was entirely overwhelmed. From his speech I judge he was inclined to wander in his thoughts. You would not have recognized a Confederate officer from his dress, which was a blue military overcoat, a high grey hat, and well-brushed riding boots.

As General Meade introduced his two aides, Lee put out his hand and saluted us with all the air of the oldest blood in the world.* I did not think, when I left, in '63, for Germantown, that I should ever shake

---

*That is, with an aristocratic air.

the hand of Robert E. Lee, prisoner of war! He held a long conference with General Meade, while I stood over a fire, with his officers, in the rain. . . .

We were talking there together, when there appeared a great oddity—an old man, with an angular, much-wrinkled face, and long, thick white hair, brushed *à la* Calhoun; a pair of silver spectacles and a high felt hat further set off the countenance, while the legs kept up their claim of eccentricity by encasing themselves in grey blankets, tied somewhat in a bandit fashion. The whole made up no less a person than Henry A. Wise, once Governor of the loyal state of Virginia, now Brigadier-General and prisoner of war. By his first wife he is Meade's brother-in-law, and had been sent for to see him. I think he is punished enough: old, sick, impoverished, a prisoner, with nothing to live for, not even his son, who was killed at Roanoke Island, he stood there in his old, wet, grey blanket, glad to accept at our

hands a pittance of biscuit and coffee, to save him and his Staff from starvation! . . .

We left Lee, and kept on through the sad remnants of an army that has its place in history. It would have looked a mighty host, if the ghosts of all its soldiers that now sleep between Gettysburg and Lynchburg could have stood there in the lines, beside the living.

Source: George R. Agassiz, ed., *Meade's Headquarters 1863–1865: Letters of Colonel Theodore Lyman from the Wilderness to Appomattox* (Boston: Little Brown & Company, 1922).

■ THINKING ABOUT THE SELECTION

1. How does Lyman describe Lee?

2. What does the description of Wise indicate about the state of the Confederate army at this time?

3. **CRITICAL THINKING Drawing Conclusions** On the basis of this selection, do you think Lyman felt vindictive toward the defeated South? Give reasons for your answer.

Guerrilla Warfare *As Union troops advanced through the South, they were plagued by attacks from Confederate guerrillas. The guerrillas were semi-independent fighters who raided Union outposts and disrupted enemy communications and supply lines. This painting by Albert Bierstadt shows a group of Union soldiers firing at a band of Confederate guerrillas.* **Geography** *What advantages do you think the guerrillas might have had over the Union troops they fought against? Why?*

CHAPTER 17 Rebuilding the Nation
(1864–1877)

■ 17-1 Out From This Place

INTRODUCTION In the novel *Out From This Place*, by Joyce Hansen, Easter is a fourteen-year-old former slave who escapes to the Sea Islands. She is determined to find her friend Obi, who had joined the Union army. Easter eagerly anticipates her life as a freedwoman when she, Obi, and their young friend Jason can finally become a family.

In her search for Obi, Easter turns for help to the Freedmen's Bureau, which assisted in locating missing persons. The excerpt that follows describes Easter's visit to the Freedmen's Bureau office in Elenaville and its unsuccessful outcome.

VOCABULARY Before you read the selection, find the meaning of these words in a dictionary: destitute, prosperous, rations, inquiries.

May 1865

Easter walked quickly past the former slave market in town, imagining a long white arm pulling her inside its dark corners. The sidewalk was choked with people: men and women, whites and blacks, destitute families, prosperous-looking men who seemed not to have been touched by war at all, and Union soldiers. . . .

This was the third time since the war ended in April that she, Sarah, and some of the other people from the plantation had come to the Freedmen's Bureau office in Elenaville to inquire about relatives. Easter came seeking information about Obi. Brother Thomas [leader of the freedmen and women on the Sea Island plantation where Easter lived] still warned them, "Don't walk—especially through them woods—an' get back here before dark." James drove them.

Passengers riding in the wagon paid him ten cents to carry them back and forth. Once the war was over and people from the plantation started traveling to town more often, Jason constantly begged her to take him to Elenaville. She couldn't come without him.

Easter hurried to catch up with the others. The office of the Freedmen's Bureau was packed with people, outside and in. There were whites sprinkled among the blacks.

"Can I stay outside?" Jason asked when Easter was able to enter the building after waiting for two hours on one of the lines outside.

"Yes, but you stay right here on this street. Don't go runnin' off. . . ."

"Listen to Easter and stay close by," Sarah added.

"I will! I will!" he shouted excitedly.

People sat and stood in every corner of the large room, which had once been used as a warehouse for storing cotton. A few bales were still stacked along a wall. A woman and two men sat behind separate desks. They took care of supplying people with emergency rations of food and money, helping people find lost family members, and even starting schools. They also made sure that the work contracts that were being used to hire the freedmen and freedwomen to work on the plantations were in order.

Easter sat on the floor with Sarah and the rest of the people and waited, hoping that this time someone would be able to tell her where Obi was. Time seemed to stop in the crowded room, and when her turn came to talk to one of the agents, she had a pounding headache.

Reconstructing the South *Southern cities and farmlands were devastated by the war. In 1867, Congress instituted a Reconstruction plan that punished the South and made its recovery even more difficult. Yet the South still managed to rebuild, as shown in this 1872 painting of Charlestown Square by Charles Hamilton.* **Citizenship** *How might a more lenient plan for Reconstruction have affected the South differently?*

"Afternoon, ma'am," she said politely as she sat down. The woman's brown wavy hair reminded her of Miss Grantley [a woman from the North who had taught Easter to read and write]. Easter repeated her scanty information about Obi once again. Her headache eased as she talked. The woman thumbed through a thick record book.

"Oh yes, you were here two weeks ago. I'm sorry, we have no record of anyone by that name."

Easter sighed deeply.

"I'm very sorry," the woman repeated. "You said he escaped here to the Sea Islands. We wrote to the Freedmen's Bureau in Georgetown, but there's no response from them yet. We're attempting to make inquiries with the army, but they have so much to do, don't you know."

Easter tried to contain the horrible thought that Obi had been killed in battle and left dead somewhere. "Ma'am, does the army know all the soldiers that die . . . ?"

"Of course. Unfortunately, sometimes soldiers are missing, but the army keeps track of everyone as best they can. You say your former master's name is Jennings? Your friend may have taken that name. We'll make another inquiry and find out whether they have a soldier named Obi Jennings."

"Thank you, ma'am," Easter said dully. When she left the building the sun was red and sinking. . . .

She made up her mind not to return to the Freedmen's Bureau. . . . She . . . would . . . look for Obi herself.

From *Out From This Place* by Joyce Hansen. Copyright © 1988 by Joyce Hansen. Reprinted by permission of Walker & Company.

■ THINKING ABOUT THE SELECTION

1. According to the passage, what type of assistance did the Freedmen's Bureau provide?

2. What did Easter fear might have happened to Obi?

3. CRITICAL THINKING **Making Inferences** List some of the difficulties that faced people who worked in the Freedmen's Bureau.

INTRODUCTION The end of Reconstruction came at a high cost for African Americans living in the South. When Democrats returned to power in the South and systematically deprived blacks of their rights, few Americans protested. What this abandonment felt like is described here by John R. Lynch, an African American from Mississippi who served in his state legislature and in Congress during Reconstruction. He later fought in the Spanish-American War and was commissioned a second lieutenant on the battlefield for gallantry in action.

VOCABULARY Before you read the selection, find the meaning of these words in a dictionary: ostracized, forfeited, odium, affiliation, oblivion, devoid.

In the elections of 1872 nearly every State in the Union went Republican. In the State and Congressional elections of 1874 the result was the reverse of what it was two years before,—nearly every State going Democratic. . . . It was the State and Congressional elections of 1874 that proved to be the death of the Republican party in the South. . . .

[After] 1872 and prior to 1875. . . a Southern white man could become a Republican without being socially ostracized. Such a man was no longer looked upon as a traitor to his people, or false to his race. He no longer forfeited the respect, confidence, good-will, and favorable opinion of his friends and neighbors. . . . But after the State and Congressional elections of 1874 there was a complete change of front. The new order of things was then set aside. . . .

It soon developed that all that was left of the once promising and flourishing Republican party at the South was the true, faithful, loyal, and sincere colored men,—who remained Republican from necessity as well as from choice,—and a few white men, who were Republicans from principle and

conviction, and who were willing to incur the odium, run the risks, take the chances, and pay the penalty that every white Republican who had the courage of his convictions must then pay. . . .

The writer cannot resist the temptation to bring to the notice of the reader [a scene] . . . of which he had personal knowledge. Colonel James Lusk had been a prominent, conspicuous and influential representative of the Southern aristocracy of ante-bellum days. He enjoyed the respect and confidence of the community in which he lived,—especially of the colored people. He, like thousands of others of his class, had identified himself with the Republican party. . . .

After the Congressional elections of 1874 Colonel Lusk decided that he would return to the ranks of the Democracy.* Before making public announcement of that fact he decided . . . that his faithful friend and loyal supporter, Sam Henry,** should be the first to whom that announcement should be made. When he had finished, Henry was visibly affected.

"Oh! no, Colonel," he cried, breaking down completely, "I beg of you do not leave us. You are our chief, if not sole dependence. You are our Moses. If you leave us, hundreds of others in our immediate neighborhood will be sure to follow your lead. We will thus be left without solid and substantial friends. I admit that with you party affiliation is optional. With me it is not. You can be either a Republican or a Democrat, and be honored and supported by the party to which you may belong. With me it is different. I must remain a Republican whether I want to or

*That is, the Democratic party.

**Sam Henry, an African American, was president of the local Republican organization.

Harvesting Cotton *When the Civil War ended, freedmen and women had to start new lives. In this painting by Winslow Homer, freed slaves harvest cotton on a plantation.* **Daily Life** *In what ways do you think the daily lives of former slaves were changed when they won their freedom? In what ways were their lives unchanged?*

not. . . . Colonel, I beg of you, I plead with you, don't go!" . . .

Henry's remarks made a deep and profound impression upon Colonel Lusk. He informed Henry that no step he could take was more painful to him than this. He assured Henry that this act on his part was from necessity and not from choice.

"The statement you have made, Henry, that party affiliation with me is optional," he answered, "is presumed to be true; but, in point of fact, it is not. No white man can live in the South in the future and act with any other than the Democratic party unless he is willing and prepared to live a life of social isolation and remain in political oblivion. While I am somewhat advanced in years, I am not so old as to be devoid of political ambition. Besides I have two grown sons. There is, no doubt, a bright, brilliant and successful future before them if they are Democrats; otherwise, not. . . . I must yield to the inevitable and surrender my convictions upon the altar of my family's good,—the outgrowth of circumstances and conditions which I am powerless to prevent and cannot control. . . . If I could see my way clear to pursue a different course it would be done; but my decision is based upon careful and thoughtful consideration and it must stand."

Source: John R. Lynch, *The Facts of Reconstruction* (New York: Neale Publishing Company, 1913).

■ THINKING ABOUT THE SELECTION

1. How did the political situation change for southern whites between 1872 and 1875?

2. According to Lynch, why did southern blacks have no choice but to belong to the Republican party?

3. **CRITICAL THINKING Defending a Position** What are your reactions to the story of Colonel Lusk and Sam Henry? Explain.

BILL
OF
RIGHTS

FREEDOM of SPEECH

FREEDOM of ASSEMBLY

FREEDOM of RELIGION

FREEDOM of The PRESS

150 YEARS

Reference Section

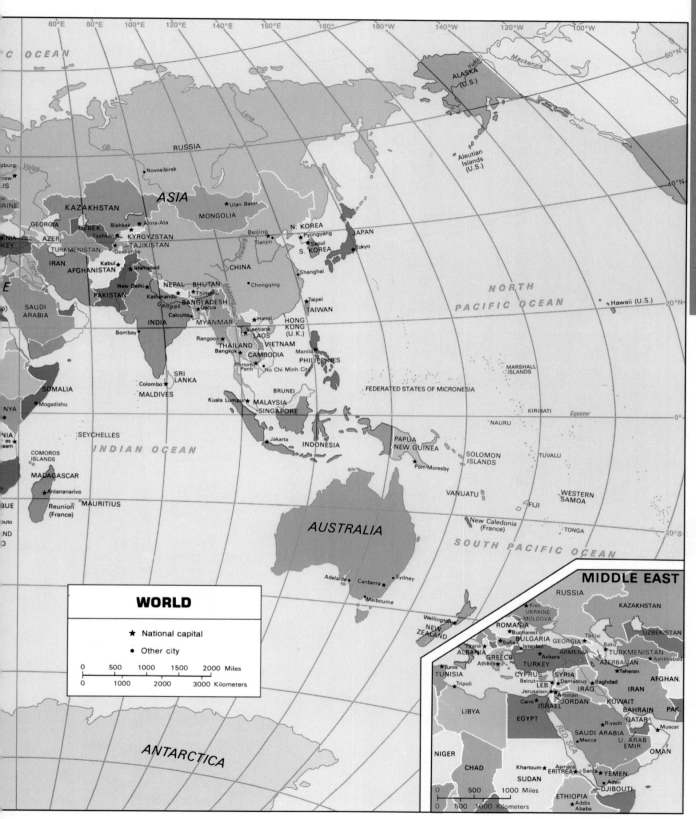

°C OCEAN

60°E   80°E   100°E   120°E   140°E   160°E   180°   160°W   140°W   120°W   100°W

60°N

RUSSIA

Ob

Novosibirsk

ASIA

40°N

KAZAKHSTAN

MONGOLIA   Ulan Bator

GEORGIA

AZER.   UZBEK.   Bishkek   Alma-Ata   Beijing   N. KOREA

KEY   Tashkent   KYRGYZSTAN   Tianjin   Pyongyang   JAPAN

TURKMENISTAN   TAJIKISTAN   S. KOREA   Seoul   Tokyo

Dushanbe   CHINA

IRAN   Kabul   Islamabad   Shanghai

AFGHANISTAN   Chongqing

PAKISTAN   New Delhi   NEPAL   BHUTAN   Taipei   20°N

Kathmandu   Thimphu   TAIWAN

SAUDI   Ganges   BANGLADESH   Hanoi   HONG

ARABIA   Calcutta   Dacca   Vientiane   KONG

Bombay   INDIA   MYANMAR   LAOS   (U.K.)

Rangoon   THAILAND   VIETNAM

NORTH

PACIFIC OCEAN

Hawaii (U.S.)

SOMALIA   Bangkok   CAMBODIA   Manila

NYA   Colombo   SRI   Phnom   PHILIPPINES

Mogadishu   LANKA   Penh   Ho Chi Minh City

MALDIVES   MARSHALL   ISLANDS

SEYCHELLES   BRUNEI

FEDERATED STATES OF MICRONESIA

Kuala Lumpur   MALAYSIA

SINGAPORE   KIRIBATI   Equator   0°

NIA   INDIAN OCEAN   NAURU

COMOROS   Jakarta   INDONESIA   PAPUA

ISLANDS   NEW GUINEA   SOLOMON   TUVALU

MADAGASCAR   ISLANDS

Port Moresby   VANUATU   WESTERN

Antananarivo   SAMOA

Reunion   MAURITIUS   New Caledonia

(France)   (France)   FIJI   20°S

AUSTRALIA   TONGA

SOUTH PACIFIC OCEAN

Adelaide   Canberra   Sydney

Melbourne

WORLD

★ National capital

• Other city

0   500   1000   1500   2000 Miles

0   1000   2000   3000 Kilometers

Wellington   NEW   ZEALAND

ANTARCTICA

MIDDLE EAST

RUSSIA

KAZAKHSTAN

Kiev   UKRAINE   UZBEKISTAN

MOLDOVA

ROMANIA   Tbilisi   Baku

Bucharest   GEORGIA   TURKMENISTAN

Tirane   Sofia   BULGARIA   GEORGIA   ARMENIA   Ashkhabad

ALBANIA   Istanbul   Ankara   AZERBAIJAN   Teheran

GREECE   TURKEY

Tunis   Athens   CYPRUS   SYRIA   IRAN   AFGHAN.

TUNISIA   Beirut   Damascus   Baghdad

Tripoli   LEB.   IRAQ   PAK.

Jerusalem   Amman   KUWAIT

Cairo   ISRAEL   JORDAN   BAHRAIN

LIBYA   EGYPT   QATAR   Muscat

Riyadh   U. ARAB   OMAN

Mecca   EMIR.

NIGER   SAUDI ARABIA

CHAD   Khartoum   Asmara   Sana   YEMEN

ERITREA   Aden   DJIBOUTI

SUDAN

0   500   1000 Miles   ETHIOPIA   Addis

0   500   1000 Kilometers   Ababa

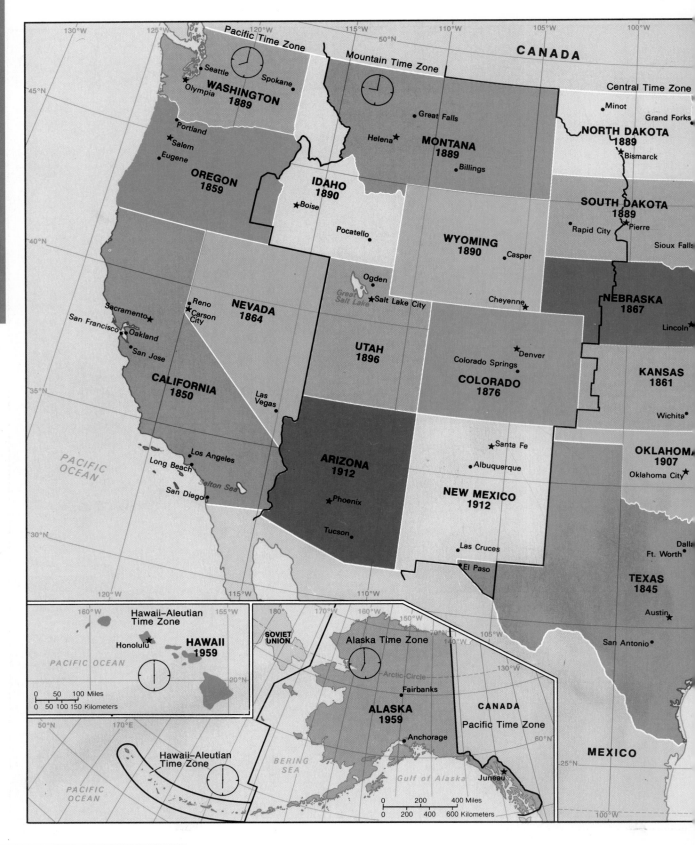

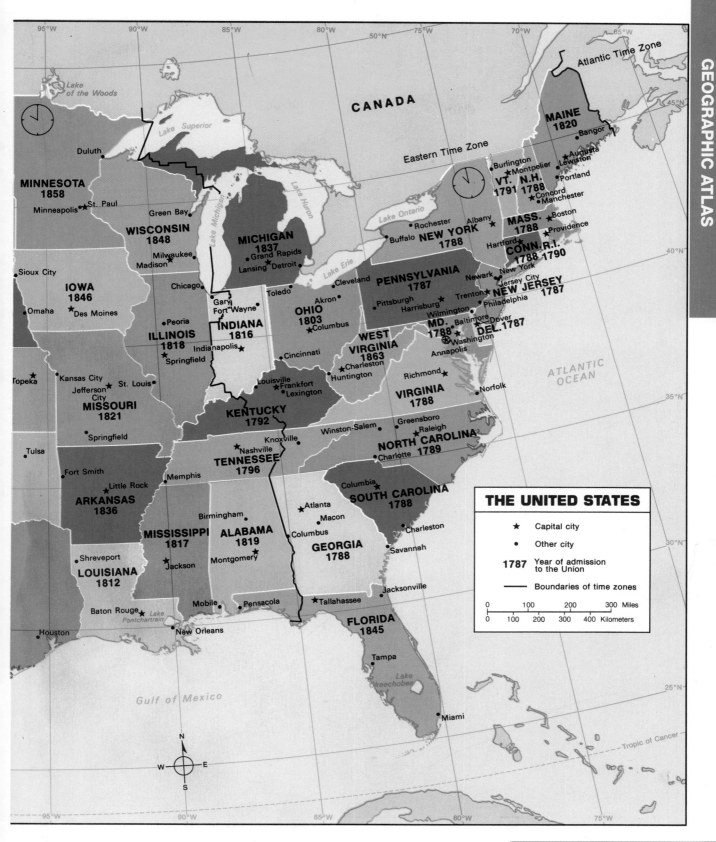

Atlantic Time Zone

CANADA

Eastern Time Zone

MAINE 1820
Bangor

Duluth

MINNESOTA 1858

Burlington
Montpelier
VT. N.H. 1791 1788
Augusta
Lewiston
Portland
Concord
Manchester

Minneapolis
St. Paul

WISCONSIN 1848

Green Bay

MICHIGAN 1837
Grand Rapids
Lansing Detroit

Rochester
Albany
MASS. 1788
Boston
Providence

Buffalo
NEW YORK 1788

Hartford
CONN. R.I. 1788 1790

Milwaukee
Madison

IOWA 1846

Sioux City

Chicago

Gary
Fort Wayne

Toledo

Cleveland

PENNSYLVANIA 1787
Pittsburgh
Harrisburg

Newark
New York
Jersey City
NEW JERSEY 1787
Trenton
Philadelphia
Wilmington
DEL. 1787
Dover

Omaha
Des Moines

Peoria

INDIANA 1816

OHIO 1803
Columbus

MD. 1788
Baltimore
Washington
Annapolis

ILLINOIS 1818
Indianapolis
Springfield

Cincinnati

WEST VIRGINIA 1863
Charleston
Huntington

Richmond

Norfolk

ATLANTIC OCEAN

Topeka
Kansas City
Jefferson City
St. Louis

Louisville
Frankfort
Lexington

MISSOURI 1821
Springfield

KENTUCKY 1792

VIRGINIA 1788

Winston-Salem
Greensboro
Raleigh

Knoxville
Nashville
TENNESSEE 1796

NORTH CAROLINA 1789
Charlotte

Tulsa

Fort Smith
Little Rock

Memphis

ARKANSAS 1836

Columbia

SOUTH CAROLINA 1788

Atlanta
Macon

Charleston

Birmingham

MISSISSIPPI 1817
Jackson

ALABAMA 1819
Montgomery
Columbus

GEORGIA 1788

Savannah

LOUISIANA 1812
Baton Rouge
New Orleans

Shreveport

Mobile
Pensacola

Tallahassee

Jacksonville

Houston

Lake Pontchartrain

Gulf of Mexico

FLORIDA 1845

Tampa
Lake Okeechobee

Miami

Tropic of Cancer

Lake of the Woods
Lake Superior
Lake Michigan
Lake Huron
Lake Erie
Lake Ontario

THE UNITED STATES	
★	Capital city
•	Other city
1787	Year of admission to the Union
—	Boundaries of time zones

0   100   200   300 Miles
0 100 200 300 400 Kilometers

N
W   E
S

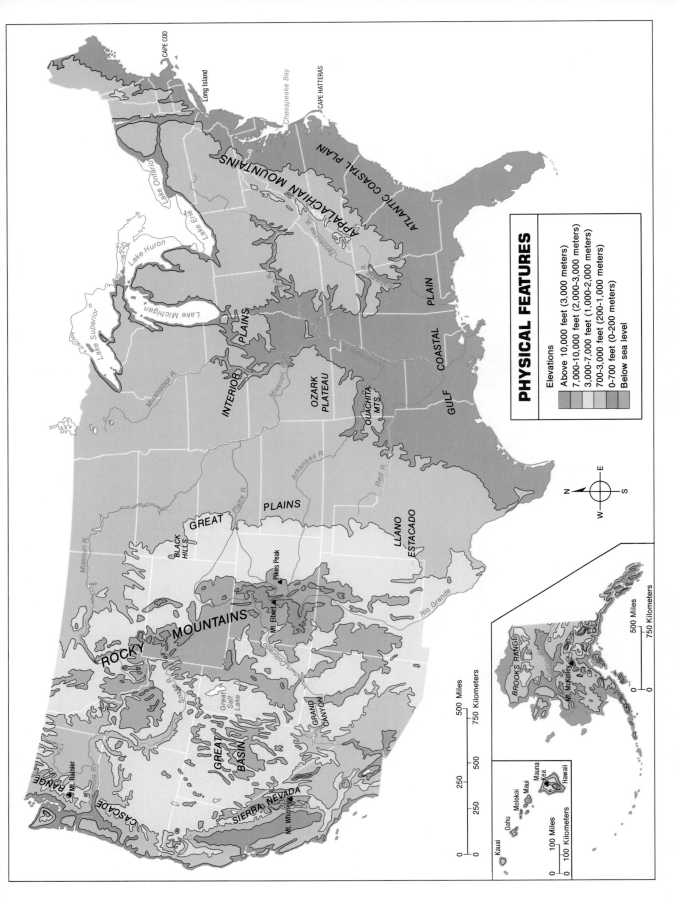

GEOGRAPHIC ATLAS

PHYSICAL FEATURES

Elevations

Above 10,000 feet (3,000 meters)
7,000-10,000 feet (2,000-3,000 meters)
3,000-7,000 feet (1,000-2,000 meters)
700-3,000 feet (200-1,000 meters)
0-700 feet (0-200 meters)
Below sea level

CAPE COD

Long Island

Chesapeake Bay

CAPE HATTERAS

APPALACHIAN MOUNTAINS

ATLANTIC COASTAL PLAIN

Lake Ontario

Lake Erie

Lake Huron

Lake Michigan

Lake Superior

Tennessee R.

Ohio R.

COASTAL

PLAIN

GULF

INTERIOR

PLAINS

Mississippi R.

Missouri R.

OZARK
PLATEAU

OUACHITA
MTS.

Arkansas R.

Red R.

GREAT

PLAINS

BLACK
HILLS

Platte R.

Pikes Peak

Mt. Elbert

ROCKY

MOUNTAINS

LLANO
ESTACADO

Rio Grande

Colorado R.

Snake R.

Great
Salt
Lake

GREAT

BASIN

GRAND
CANYON

Columbia R.

Mt. Rainier

CASCADE
RANGE

SIERRA NEVADA

Mt. Whitney

N
E
S
W

BROOKS RANGE

Yukon R.

Mt. McKinley

500 Miles

750 Kilometers

0

250 500 Miles

250 500 750 Kilometers

0

Kauai
Oahu
Molokai
Maui
Mauna
Kea
Hawaii

100 Miles

100 Kilometers

0

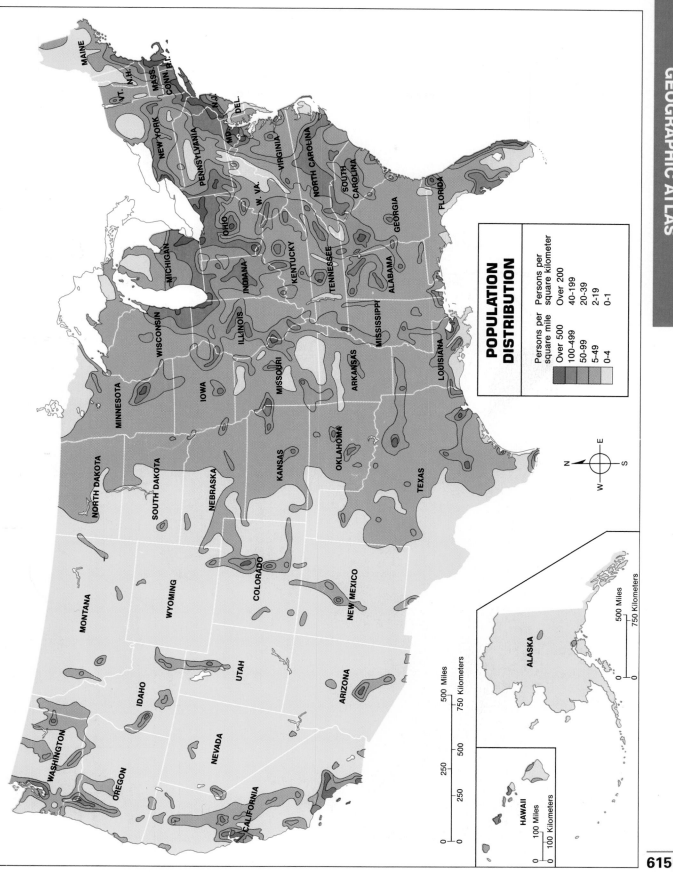

POPULATION DISTRIBUTION

Persons per square mile	Persons per square kilometer
Over 500	Over 200
100-499	40-199
50-99	20-39
5-49	2-19
0-4	0-1

MAINE

N.H.

VT.

MASS.

CONN. R.I.

NEW YORK

PENNSYLVANIA

N.J.

DEL.

MD.

OHIO

W. VA.

VIRGINIA

NORTH CAROLINA

SOUTH CAROLINA

GEORGIA

FLORIDA

MICHIGAN

INDIANA

KENTUCKY

TENNESSEE

ALABAMA

MISSISSIPPI

WISCONSIN

ILLINOIS

IOWA

MISSOURI

ARKANSAS

LOUISIANA

MINNESOTA

NORTH DAKOTA

SOUTH DAKOTA

NEBRASKA

KANSAS

OKLAHOMA

TEXAS

MONTANA

WYOMING

COLORADO

NEW MEXICO

WASHINGTON

OREGON

IDAHO

UTAH

NEVADA

ARIZONA

CALIFORNIA

N
E
S
W

ALASKA

HAWAII

500 Miles
750 Kilometers

500 Miles
750 Kilometers

100 Miles
100 Kilometers

250   500
250   500   750 Kilometers

0   0

615

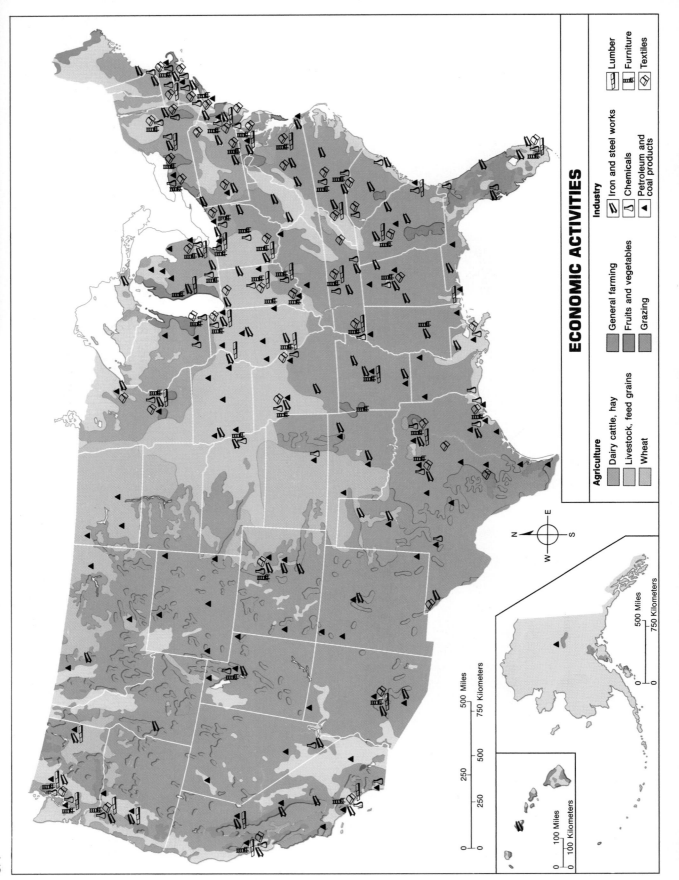

ECONOMIC ACTIVITIES

Agriculture

Dairy cattle, hay

Livestock, feed grains

Wheat

General farming

Fruits and vegetables

Grazing

Industry

Iron and steel works

Chemicals

Petroleum and coal products

Lumber

Furniture

Textiles

500 Miles

250   250

500   750 Kilometers

N
W — E
S

500 Miles

250   500   750 Kilometers

100 Miles

100 Kilometers

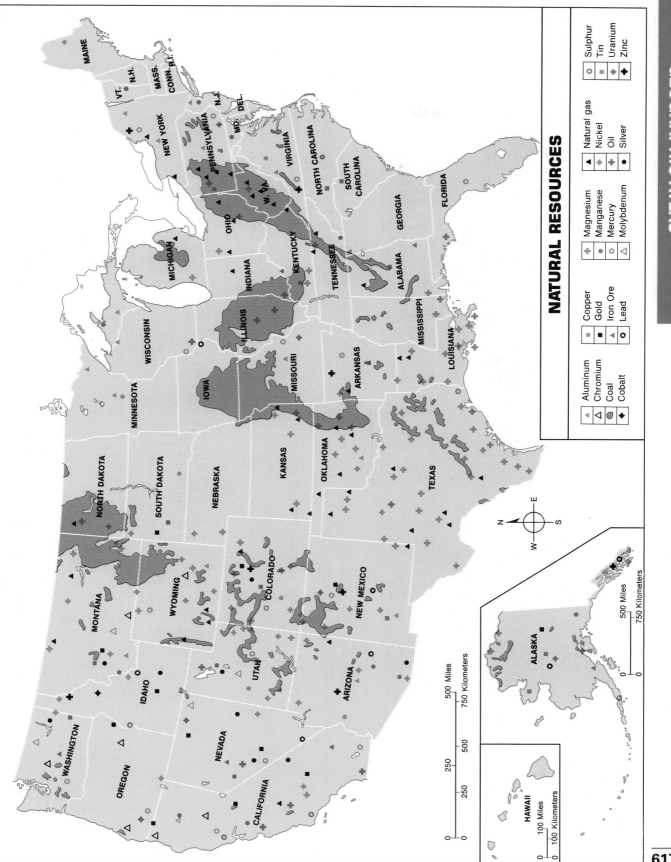

NATURAL RESOURCES

GEOGRAPHIC ATLAS

Legend:

◄	Aluminum
△	Chromium
◖	Coal
◆	Cobalt

●	Copper
■	Gold
▲	Iron Ore
◎	Lead

✚	Magnesium
●	Manganese
◎	Mercury
△	Molybdenum

◄	Natural gas
◆	Nickel
✚	Oil
●	Silver

◎	Sulphur
■	Tin
◆	Uranium
✚	Zinc

Map labels:

MAINE, N.H., VT., MASS., CONN., R.I., NEW YORK, N.J., DEL., PENNSYLVANIA, MD., OHIO, W. VA., VIRGINIA, NORTH CAROLINA, SOUTH CAROLINA, FLORIDA, GEORGIA, ALABAMA, MISSISSIPPI, LOUISIANA, TENNESSEE, KENTUCKY, INDIANA, ILLINOIS, MICHIGAN, WISCONSIN, MINNESOTA, IOWA, MISSOURI, ARKANSAS, OKLAHOMA, KANSAS, TEXAS, NEBRASKA, SOUTH DAKOTA, NORTH DAKOTA, MONTANA, WYOMING, COLORADO, NEW MEXICO, UTAH, ARIZONA, IDAHO, NEVADA, CALIFORNIA, OREGON, WASHINGTON

ALASKA, HAWAII

Scale bars:
250, 500, 750 Kilometers
250, 500 Miles

100 Kilometers / 100 Miles (Hawaii)

500 Miles / 750 Kilometers (Alaska)

N E S W compass

617

The Fifty States

State	Date of Entry to Union (Order of Entry)	Area in Square Miles	Population 1995* (In Thousands)	Number of Representatives in House	Capital	Largest City
Alabama	1819 (22)	51,705	4,274	7	Montgomery	Birmingham
Alaska	1959 (49)	591,004	634	1	Juneau	Anchorage
Arizona	1912 (48)	114,000	4,072	6	Phoenix	Phoenix
Arkansas	1836 (25)	53,187	2,438	4	Little Rock	Little Rock
California	1850 (31)	158,706	32,398	52	Sacramento	Los Angeles
Colorado	1876 (38)	104,091	3,710	6	Denver	Denver
Connecticut	1788 (5)	5,018	3,274	6	Hartford	Bridgeport
Delaware	1787 (1)	2,044	718	1	Dover	Wilmington
Florida	1845 (27)	58,664	14,210	23	Tallahassee	Jacksonville
Georgia	1788 (4)	58,910	7,102	11	Atlanta	Atlanta
Hawaii	1959 (50)	6,471	1,221	2	Honolulu	Honolulu
Idaho	1890 (43)	83,564	1,156	2	Boise	Boise
Illinois	1818 (21)	56,345	11,853	20	Springfield	Chicago
Indiana	1816 (19)	36,185	5,820	10	Indianapolis	Indianapolis
Iowa	1846 (29)	56,275	2,861	5	Des Moines	Des Moines
Kansas	1861 (34)	82,277	2,601	4	Topeka	Wichita
Kentucky	1792 (15)	40,409	3,851	6	Frankfort	Louisville
Louisiana	1812 (18)	47,751	4,358	7	Baton Rouge	New Orleans
Maine	1820 (23)	33,265	1,236	2	Augusta	Portland
Maryland	1788 (7)	10,460	5,078	8	Annapolis	Baltimore
Massachusetts	1788 (6)	8,284	5,976	10	Boston	Boston
Michigan	1837 (26)	58,527	9,575	16	Lansing	Detroit
Minnesota	1858 (32)	84,402	4,619	8	St. Paul	Minneapolis
Mississippi	1817 (20)	47,689	2,666	5	Jackson	Jackson
Missouri	1821 (24)	69,697	5,286	9	Jefferson City	Kansas City
Montana	1889 (41)	147,046	862	1	Helena	Billings
Nebraska	1867 (37)	77,355	1,644	3	Lincoln	Omaha
Nevada	1864 (36)	110,561	1,477	2	Carson City	Las Vegas
New Hampshire	1788 (9)	9,279	1,132	2	Concord	Manchester
New Jersey	1787 (3)	7,787	7,931	13	Trenton	Newark
New Mexico	1912 (47)	121,593	1,676	3	Santa Fe	Albuquerque
New York	1788 (11)	49,108	18,178	31	Albany	New York
North Carolina	1789 (12)	52,669	7,150	12	Raleigh	Charlotte
North Dakota	1889 (39)	70,703	637	1	Bismarck	Fargo
Ohio	1803 (17)	41,330	11,203	19	Columbus	Columbus
Oklahoma	1907 (46)	69,956	3,271	6	Oklahoma City	Oklahoma City
Oregon	1859 (33)	97,073	3,141	5	Salem	Portland
Pennsylvania	1787 (2)	45,308	12,134	21	Harrisburg	Philadelphia
Rhode Island	1790 (13)	1,212	1,001	2	Providence	Providence
South Carolina	1788 (8)	31,113	3,732	6	Columbia	Columbia
South Dakota	1889 (40)	77,116	735	1	Pierre	Sioux Falls
Tennessee	1796 (16)	42,144	5,226	9	Nashville	Memphis
Texas	1845 (28)	266,807	18,592	30	Austin	Houston
Utah	1896 (45)	84,899	1,944	3	Salt Lake City	Salt Lake City
Vermont	1791 (14)	9,614	579	1	Montpelier	Burlington
Virginia	1788 (10)	40,767	6,646	11	Richmond	Virginia Beach
Washington	1889 (42)	68,138	5,497	9	Olympia	Seattle
West Virginia	1863 (35)	24,231	1,824	3	Charleston	Charleston
Wisconsin	1848 (30)	56,153	5,159	9	Madison	Milwaukee
Wyoming	1890 (44)	97,809	487	1	Cheyenne	Cheyenne
District of Columbia		69	559	1 (nonvoting)		

Self-Governing Areas, Possessions, and Dependencies	Area in Square Miles	Population (in Thousands)	Capital
Puerto Rico	3,515	3,662	San Juan
Guam	209	128	Agana
U.S. Virgin Islands	132	106	Charlotte Amalie
American Samoa	77	47	Pago Pago

*1995 population statistics are projections prepared by the Bureau of the Census.

THE FIFTY STATES

This gazetteer, or geographical dictionary, lists places that are important in American history. The approximate latitude and longitude are given for cities, towns, and other specific locations. See text page 4 for information about latitude and longitude. In the Gazetteer, after the description of each place, there are usually two numbers in parentheses. The first number refers to the text page where you can find out more about the place. The second appears in slanted, or *italic,* type and refers to a map *(m)* where the place is shown.

A

Africa Second largest continent in the world. (p. 65, *m66*)

Alabama 22nd state. Nicknamed the Heart of Dixie or the Cotton State. (p. 618, *m612–613*)

Alamo (29°N/99°W) Mission in San Antonio, Texas, where 183 rebels died during the Texas war for independence. (p. 358, *m357*)

Alaska 49th state. Largest in size but one of the least populated states. (p. 618, *m612–613*)

Albany (43°N/74°W) Capital of New York State. Called Fort Orange by the Dutch of New Netherland. (p. 171, *m170*)

Andes Rugged mountain chain in South America. (p. 52, *m51*)

Appalachian Mountains Heavily forested mountain chain that stretches from Georgia to Maine and Canada. A barrier to colonial expansion. (p. 18, *m19*)

Appomattox Courthouse (37°N/79°W) Small town in Virginia where Lee surrendered to Grant on April 9, 1865. (p. 477, *m476*)

Argentina Country in South America. Gained independence from Spain in 1816. (p. 317, *m315*)

Arizona 48th state. Nicknamed the Grand Canyon State. (p. 618, *m612–613*)

Arkansas 25th state. Nicknamed the Land of Opportunity. (p. 618, *m612–613*)

Asia Largest of the world's continents. (p. 62, *m11*)

Atlanta (34°N/84°W) Capital and largest city of Georgia. Burned by Sherman during the Civil War. (p. 475, *m474*)

Atlantic Ocean World's second largest ocean. (p. 15, *m11*)

B

Baltimore (39°N/77°W) Port city in Maryland. (p. 289, *m288*)

Barbary States North African nations Morocco, Algiers, Tunis, and Tripoli. Americans paid a tribute to their rulers so they would not attack American ships. (p. 279, *m280*)

Bering Sea Narrow sea between Asia and North America. Scientists think a land bridge existed here during the last ice age. (p. 32, *m33*)

Boston (42°N/71°W) Seaport and industrial city in Massachusetts. (p. 95, *m96*)

Brazil Largest country in South America. Gained independence from Portugal in 1822. (p. 317, *m315*)

Breed's Hill (42°N/71°W) Overlooks Boston harbor. Site of fighting during the Battle of Bunker Hill. (p. 162)

Buena Vista (26°N/101°W) Site of an American victory in the Mexican War. (p. 366, *m365*)

Buffalo (43°N/79°W) Industrial city in New York State on Lake Erie. Free Soil party was founded there in 1848. (p. 429, *m612–613*)

Bunker Hill (42°N/71°W) Overlooks Boston harbor. Site of first major battle of the Revolution. (p. 161)

C

Cahokia (39°N/90°W) Fur-trading post in southwestern Illinois in the 1700s. Captured by George Rogers Clark in 1778 during the Revolution. (p. 176, *m175*)

GAZETTEER

California 31st state. Nicknamed the Golden State. Ceded to the United States by Mexico in 1848. (p. 366, *m437*)

Canada Northern neighbor of the United States. Second largest nation in the world. Made up of 10 provinces: Ontario, Quebec, Nova Scotia, New Brunswick, Alberta, British Columbia, Manitoba, Newfoundland and Labrador, Prince Edward Island, and Saskatchewan. (p. 133, *m610–611*)

Canadian Shield Lowland region that lies mostly in eastern Canada. Its low hills and plains are rich in minerals. (p. 19, *m19*)

Chancellorsville (38°N/78°W) Site of a Confederate victory in 1863. (p. 472, *m459*)

Charleston (33°N/80°W) City in South Carolina. Site of a British victory in the American Revolution. (p. 180, *m181*)

Chesapeake Bay Large inlet of the Atlantic Ocean in Virginia and Maryland. (p. 289, *m288*)

Chicago (42°N/88°W) Third largest city in the United States. Developed as a railroad and meatpacking center in the late 1800s. (p. 18, *m612–613*)

Coastal Plains Region consisting of the Atlantic Plain on the east coast and the Gulf Plain which lies along the Gulf of Mexico. (p. 20, *m19*)

Colorado 38th state. Nicknamed the Centennial State. (p. 618, *m612–613*)

Columbia River Chief river of the Pacific Northwest. (p. 352, *m353*)

Concord (43°N/71°W) Village near Boston, Massachusetts. Site of the first fighting in the American Revolution on April 19, 1775. (p. 155, *m163*)

Connecticut One of the original 13 states. Nicknamed the Constitution State or the Nutmeg State. (p. 95, *m96*)

Cowpens (35°N/82°W) Located in South Carolina. Site of a decisive American victory in 1781 during the Revolution. (p. 181, *m181*)

Cuba (22°N/79°W) Island nation in the Caribbean. Gained independence from Spain in 1898. Strongly influenced by the United States until Fidel Castro established communist control in 1959. (p. 527, *m610–611*)

Cumberland Gap (37°N/84°W) Pass in the Appalachian Mountains near the border of Virginia, Kentucky, and Tennessee. (p. 304, *m306*)

Cuzco (14°S/72°W) Inca capital located high in the Andes Mountains of Peru. (p. 52, *m51*)

D

Delaware One of the original 13 states. Nicknamed the First State or the Diamond State. (p. 103, *m102*)

Delaware River Flows into the Atlantic Ocean through Delaware Bay. (p. 171, *m170*)

Detroit (42°N/83°W) Largest city in Michigan. (p. 287, *m288*)

District of Columbia Located on the Potomac River. Seat of the federal government of the United States. (p. 247, *m612–613*)

E

East Indies Islands in Southeast Asia that are now part of Indonesia. Source of spices in the 1500s and 1600s. (p. 65)

England Part of Great Britain. (p. 65, *m80*)

Equator Line of latitude labeled 0°. Separates the Northern Hemisphere and Southern Hemisphere. (p. 11, *m11*)

Erie Canal Linked the Hudson and Mohawk rivers with Buffalo and Lake Erie. Built between 1817 and 1825. (p. 308, *m308*)

Europe Smallest continent except for Australia. (p. 62, *m11*)

F

Florida 27th state. Nicknamed the Sunshine State. (p. 618, *m612–613*)

Fort Donelson (37°N/88°W) Located in Tennessee. Captured by Grant in 1862. (p. 461, *m474*)

Fort Henry (37°N/88°W) Located in Tennessee. Captured by Grant in 1862. (p. 461, *m474*)

Fort McHenry (39°N/77°W) Located in Baltimore harbor. British bombardment there in 1814 inspired Francis Scott Key to write "The Star-Spangled Banner." (p. 289)

Fort Necessity (40°N/79°W) Makeshift stockade built by the British near the Monongahela River during the French and Indian War. (p. 136, *m139*)

Fort Pitt (40°N/80°W) British name for Fort Duquesne after its capture from the French in 1758. (p. 140, *m175*)

Fort Sumter (33°N/80°W) Guarded the entrance to Charleston harbor in South Carolina. Confederates fired the first shots of the Civil War at the fort in 1861. (p. 447, *m474*)

Fort Ticonderoga (44°N/74°W) Originally French, then British fort at the south end of Lake Champlain. Captured by Ethan Allen in 1775. (p. 160, *m163*)

France Country in Western Europe. First ally of the United States. Scene of heavy fighting in both World Wars. (p. 65, *m610–611*)

Fredericksburg (38°N/78°W) Located in eastern Virginia. Site of a Confederate victory in 1862. (p. 472, *m459*)

G

Gadsden Purchase Land purchased from Mexico in 1853. Now part of Arizona and New Mexico. (p. 366, *m367*)

Georgia One of the original 13 states. Nicknamed the Peach State or the Empire State of the South. (p. 618, *m612–613*)

Gettysburg (40°N/77°W) Small town in southern Pennsylvania. Site of a Union victory in 1863 and Lincoln's Gettysburg Address. (p. 473, *m459*)

Gonzales (29°N/97°W) City in Texas near San Antonio. Site of the first Texan victory over Mexico in 1835. (p. 357, *m357*)

Great Britain Island nation of Western Europe. Includes England, Scotland, Wales, and Northern Ireland. (p. 136, *m610–612*)

Great Lakes Group of five freshwater lakes in the heart of the United States. (p. 21, *m19*)

Great Plains Western part of the Interior Plains. Once grazed by large herds of buffalo. Now an important wheat-growing and ranching region. (p. 18, *m19*)

Great Wagon Road Early pioneer route across the Appalachians. (p. 105, *m102*)

Grenada (12°N/61°W) Island nation in the Caribbean. Invaded by the United States in 1983 to end the threat of communist influence there. (p. 525, *m610–611*)

Guam (14°N/143°E) Island in the Pacific Ocean. Territory of the United States. Acquired from Spain in 1898. (p. 524)

Guatemala Country in Central America. Gained independence from Spain in 1821. Mayas built an advanced civilization there over 3,000 years ago. (p. 48, *m610–611*)

Gulf of Mexico Body of water along the southern coast of the United States. (p. 133, *m133*)

H

Haiti Country in the West Indies. Won independence from France in the early 1800s. Occupied by United States troops from 1915 to 1934. For six months in 1994 and 1995, United States peacekeeping forces helped restore the democratically elected president, Jean-Bertrand Aristide, to power in Haiti.(p. 272, *m610–611*)

Harpers Ferry (39°N/78°W) Town in West Virginia. Abolitionist John Brown raided the arsenal there in 1859. (p. 443, *m459*)

Hawaii Newest of the 50 states. Nicknamed the Aloha State. (p. 618, *m612–613*)

Hawaiian Islands Region composed of a group of eight large islands and many small islands. The islands are the tops of volcanoes that erupted through the floor of the Pacific Ocean. (p. 20, *m19*)

Hiroshima (34°N/133°E) City in southern Japan. Mostly destroyed by an atomic bomb dropped there on August 6, 1945. Largely rebuilt since 1950. (p. 525)

Hudson Bay Large inlet of the Arctic Ocean. Named for the explorer Henry Hudson. (p. 78, *m80*)

Hudson River Largest river in New York State. Explored by Henry Hudson in 1609. (p. 78, *m87*)

I

Idaho 43rd state. Nicknamed the Gem State. Acquired by the United States as part of the Oregon Territory. (p. 618, *m612–613*)

Illinois 21st state. Nicknamed the Inland Empire. Settled as part of the Northwest Territory. (p. 618, *m612–613*)

GAZETTEER

Independence (37°N/96°W) City in Missouri. Starting point of the Oregon Trail. (p. 353, *m361*)

Indiana 19th state. Nicknamed the Hoosier State. Settled as part of the Northwest Territory. (p. 618, *m612–613*)

Interior Plains Region of the central United States that stretches from the Rockies to the Appalachians. (p. 18, *m19*)

Intermountain Region Rugged and mostly dry region from the Rocky Mountains to the Sierra Nevada and coastal mountains of the western United States. (p. 18, *m19*)

Iowa 29th state. Nicknamed the Hawkeye State. Acquired by the United States as part of the Louisiana Purchase. (p. 618, *m612–613*)

J

Jamestown (37°N/77°W) First successful English colony in North America. (p. 85, *m87*)

Japan Densely populated industrial nation in East Asia. Opened up to trade with the West by Commodore Matthew Perry. One of the Axis Powers in World War II. (p. 525, *m610–611*)

K

Kansas 34th state. Nicknamed the Sunflower State. Acquired by the United States as part of the Louisiana Purchase. (p. 618, *m612–613*)

Kaskaskia (38°N/90°W) Fur-trading post on an island in the Mississippi River. Captured by George Rogers Clark in 1778. First state capital of Illinois. (p. 176, *m175*)

Kentucky 15th state. Nicknamed the Bluegrass State. Was the first area west of the Appalachians to be settled by early pioneers. (p. 618, *m612–613*)

Kilwa (8°S/39°E) East African trading state in the 1400s. (p. 66, *m66*)

King's Mountain (35°N/81°W) Located in South Carolina. Site of an American victory in the Revolution. (p. 179, *m181*)

Kuwait Oil-rich country in the Middle East. Invaded by Iraq in 1990. (p. 526, *m610–611*)

L

Lancaster Turnpike Road built in the 1790s linking Philadelphia and Lancaster, Pennsylvania. (p. 305, *m306*)

Latin America Name for those parts of the Western Hemisphere where Latin languages such as Spanish, French, and Portuguese are spoken. Includes Mexico, Central and South America, and the West Indies. (p. 315, *m315*)

Lexington (42°N/71°W) Site of the first clash between minutemen and British troops in 1775. Now a suburb of Boston. (p. 155, *m163*)

Liberia Country in West Africa. Set up in 1822 as a colony for free African Americans. (p. 403, *m610–611*)

Long Island Located in New York. Site of a British victory in the Revolution. (p. 169, *m170*)

Louisbourg (46°N/60°W) French fort in eastern Canada. Changed hands several times between France and Britain. (p. 139, *m139*)

Louisiana 18th state. Nicknamed the Pelican State. First state created out of the Louisiana Purchase. (p. 618, *m612–613*)

Louisiana Purchase Region between the Mississippi River and the Rocky Mountains that was purchased from France in 1803. (p. 273, *m273*)

M

Maine 23rd state. Nicknamed the Pine Tree State. Originally part of Massachusetts, Maine gained separate statehood in 1820 under the terms of the Missouri Compromise. (p. 618, *m612–613*)

Mali Kingdom in West Africa that reached its peak between 1200 and 1400. (p. 66, *m66*)

Maryland One of the original 13 states. Nicknamed the Old Line State or the Free State. (p. 618, *m612–613*)

Mason-Dixon Line 244-mile boundary between Pennsylvania and Maryland surveyed and marked by Charles Mason and Jeremiah Dixon. (p. 106)

Massachusetts One of the original 13 states. Nicknamed the Bay State or the Old Colony. (p. 618, *m612–613*)

Memphis (35°N/90°W) City in Tennessee on the Mississippi River. Captured by Grant in 1862. (p. 461, *m474*)

Mexican Cession Lands acquired by the United States from Mexico under the Treaty of Guadalupe Hidalgo in 1848. (p. 366, *m367*)

Mexico Southern neighbor of the United States. Gained independence from Spain in 1821. (p. 315, *m315*)

Mexico City (19°N/99°W) Capital of Mexico. Was the capital of New Spain. Site of the ancient Aztec city of Tenochtitlán. (p. 366, *m365*)

Michigan 26th state. Nicknamed the Great Lake State or the Wolverine State. Settled as part of the Northwest Territory. (p. 618, *m612–613*)

Middle East Region at the eastern end of the Mediterranean Sea. Source of much of the world's oil. (p. 63, *m610–611*)

Minnesota 32nd state. Nicknamed the Gopher State. Most of it was acquired by the United States as part of the Louisiana Purchase. (p. 618, *m612–613*)

Mississippi 20th state. Nicknamed the Magnolia State. (p. 618, *m612–613*)

Mississippi River Longest river in the United States. Links the Great Lakes with the Gulf of Mexico. (p. 20, *m19*)

Missouri 24th state. Nicknamed the Show Me State. Acquired by the United States as part of the Louisiana Purchase. (p. 618, *m612–613*)

Missouri Compromise Line Line drawn across the Louisiana Purchase at latitude 36°/30′N to divide free states from slave states. (p. 429, *m430*)

Missouri River Second longest river in the United States. Rises in the northern Rocky Mountains and joins the Mississippi River near St. Louis. (p. 274, *m273*)

Mogadishu (2°N/45°E) East African trading state in the 1400s. (p. 66, *m66*)

Montana 41st state. Nicknamed the Treasure State. Acquired by the United States in part through the Louisiana Purchase. (p. 618, *m612–613*)

Montreal (46°N/74°W) Major city in Canada. Located on the St. Lawrence River. Settled by the French. (p. 163, *m163*)

N

Nagasaki (33°N/130°E) Japanese port city. Largely destroyed by the atomic bomb dropped on August 9, 1945. (p. 525)

National Road Early road to the West that began in Cumberland, Maryland. Now part of U.S. Highway 40. (p. 306, *m306*)

Nauvoo (41°N/91°W) Town founded by the Mormons in Illinois in the 1840s. (p. 369)

Nebraska 37th state. Nicknamed the Cornhusker State. Acquired by the United States as part of the Louisiana Purchase. (p. 618, *m612–613*)

Nevada 36th state. Nicknamed the Sagebrush State or the Battle Born State. Acquired by the United States at the end of the Mexican War. (p. 618, *m612–613*)

Newfoundland (48°N/57°W) Island at the mouth of the St. Lawrence River. Part of Canada. (p. 78, *m80*)

New France Colony established by France in North America. (p. 80, *m80*)

New Hampshire One of the original 13 states. Nicknamed the Granite State. (p. 618, *m612–613*)

New Jersey One of the original 13 states. Nicknamed the Garden State. (p. 618, *m612–613*)

New Mexico 47th state. Nicknamed the Land of Enchantment. Acquired by the United States at the end of the Mexican War. (p. 618, *m612–613*)

New Netherland Dutch colony on the Hudson River. Taken over by the English and renamed New York in 1664. (p. 82)

New Orleans (30°N/90°W) Port city in Louisiana near the mouth of the Mississippi River. Settled by the French in the 1600s. Site of a battle between the Americans and the British at the end of the War of 1812. (p. 272, *m273*)

New Spain Area ruled by Spain for 300 years. Included colonies in the West Indies, Central America, and North America. (p. 74, *m72*)

New York One of the original 13 states. Nicknamed the Empire State. (p. 618, *m612–613*)

GAZETTEER

New York City (41°N/74°W) Port city at the mouth of the Hudson River. Founded by the Dutch as New Amsterdam. First capital of the United States. (p. 169, *m170*)

North America World's third largest continent. Separated from South America by the Isthmus of Panama. (p. 15, *m11*)

North Carolina One of the original 13 states. Nicknamed the Tar Heel State or the Old North State. (p. 618, *m612–613*)

North Dakota 39th state. Nicknamed the Sioux State or the Flickertail State. Acquired by the United States as part of the Louisiana Purchase. (p. 618, *m612–613*)

Northwest Territory Name for lands north of the Ohio River and east of the Mississippi River. Acquired by the United States by the Treaty of Paris in 1783. (p. 191, *m192*)

Nueces River Claimed by Mexico in the Mexican War as the southern border of Texas. (p. 364, *m365*)

O

Ohio 17th state. Nicknamed the Buckeye State. Settled as part of the Northwest Territory. (p. 618, *m612–613*)

Ohio River Important transportation route. Begins at Pittsburgh and joins the Mississippi River at Cairo, Illinois. (p. 133, *m133*)

Oklahoma 46th State. Nicknamed the Sooner State. Acquired by the United States as part of the Louisiana Purchase. (p. 618, *m612–613*)

Oregon 33rd state. Nicknamed the Beaver State. Acquired by the United States as part of the Oregon Territory. (p. 618, *m612–613*)

Oregon Country Area in the Pacific Northwest. Claimed by the United States, Britain, Spain, and Russia in the early 1800s. (p. 350, *m353*)

Oregon Trail Overland route from Independence, Missouri, on the Missouri River to the Columbia River valley. (p. 353, *m353*)

P

Pacific Coast Highest and most rugged region of the United States. Includes the Cascades and the Sierra Nevada. (p. 18, *m19*)

Pacific Ocean World's largest ocean. (p. 15, *m11*)

Pennsylvania One of the original 13 states. Nicknamed the Keystone State. (p. 618, *m612–613*)

Peru Country in South America. Gained independence from Spain in 1821. (p. 74, *m610–611*)

Philadelphia (40°N/75°W) Major port and chief city in Pennsylvania. Second capital of the United States. (p. 103, *m102*)

Philippine Islands (14°N/125°E) Group of islands in the Pacific Ocean. Acquired by the United States in 1898. Gained independence in 1946. (p. 71, *m610–611*)

Pikes Peak (39°N/105°W) Mountain located in the Rocky Mountains of central Colorado. (p. 278, *m273*)

Plymouth (42°N/71°W) New England colony founded in 1620 by Pilgrims. Absorbed by the Massachusetts Bay Colony in 1691. (p. 89, *m87*)

Port Royal (45°N/65°W) Permanent colony founded by Champlain in Nova Scotia. (p. 80, *m139*)

Portugal Country in Western Europe. In the 1400s, sailors set out from there to explore the coast of Africa. (p. 65, *m66*)

Potomac River Forms part of the Maryland-Virginia border. Flows through Washington, D.C., and into Chesapeake Bay. (p. 458, *m459*)

Prime Meridian Line of longitude labeled 0°. (p. 11, *m11*)

Princeton (40°N/75°W) City in New Jersey. Site of an American victory during the Revolution. (p. 171, *m170*)

Promontory Point (42°N/112°W) Located just north of the Great Salt Lake. Place where the Central Pacific and the Union Pacific railroads were joined to form the first transcontinental railroad. (p. 514)

Puerto Rico (18°N/67°W) Island in the Caribbean Sea. A self-governing commonwealth of the United States. (p. 71, *m610–611*)

Q

Quebec (47°N/71°W) City in eastern Canada on the St. Lawrence River. Founded in 1608 by the French explorer Samuel de Champlain. (p. 80, *m80*)

R

Rhode Island One of the original 13 states. Nicknamed Little Rhody or the Ocean State. (p. 618, *m612–613*)

Richmond (38°N/78°W) Located on the James River. Capital of Virginia. Capital of the Confederacy during the Civil War. (p. 458, *m459*)

Rio Grande River that forms the border between the United States and Mexico. (p. 364, *m365*)

Roanoke Island (36°N/76°W) Island off the coast of North Carolina. Site of the "lost colony" founded in 1587. (p. 84, *m87*)

Rocky Mountains Mountains extending through the western United States. Barrier to travel in pioneer days. (p. 18, *m19*)

Russia Largest country in the world, spanning Europe and Asia. A communist revolution took place there in 1917. Part of the Soviet Union until 1991. (p. 526, *m610–611*)

S

Sacramento (39°N/122°W) Capital of California. Developed as a gold rush boom town. (p. 369, *m612–613*)

St. Augustine (30°N/81°W) City in Florida. Founded by Spain in 1565. Oldest European settlement in the United States. (p. 75, *m75*)

St. Lawrence River Waterway leading from the Great Lakes to the Atlantic Ocean. Forms part of the border between the United States and Canada. (p. 78, *m80*)

St. Louis (38°N/90°W) City in Missouri on the Mississippi River. Lewis and Clark began their expedition there. (p. 274, *m273*)

Salt Lake City (41°N/112°W) Largest city in Utah. Founded in 1847 by Mormons. (p. 370, *m612–613*)

San Antonio (29°N/99°W) City in southern Texas. Chief Texan settlement in Spanish and Mexican days. Site of the Alamo. (p. 357, *m357*)

San Diego (33°N/117°W) City in southern California. Founded as the first Spanish mission in California. (p. 362, *m361*)

San Francisco (38°N/122°W) City in northern California. Boom town of the California gold rush. (p. 370, *m612–613*)

Santa Fe (35°N/106°W) Capital of New Mexico. First settled by the Spanish. (p. 361, *m361*)

Santa Fe Trail Overland trail from Independence to Santa Fe. Opened in 1821. (p. 362, *m361*)

Saratoga (43°N/75°W) City in eastern New York. The American victory there in 1777 was a turning point in the American Revolution. (p. 172, *m170*)

Savannah (32°N/81°W) Oldest city in Georgia. Founded in 1733. (p. 180, *m181*)

Sierra Nevada Mountain range mostly in California. (p. 18, *m19*)

Songhai West African kingdom in the 1400s. (p. 66, *m66*)

South America World's fourth largest continent. Part of the Western Hemisphere. (p. 15, *m11*)

South Carolina One of the original 13 states. Nicknamed the Palmetto State. (p. 618, *m612–613*)

South Dakota 40th state. Nicknamed the Coyote State or the Sunshine State. Acquired by the United States as part of the Louisiana Purchase. (p. 618, *m612–613*)

Spain Country in southwestern Europe. Columbus sailed from Spain in 1492. (p. 65, *m610–611*)

Spanish borderlands Area that spanned the present-day United States from Florida to California. (p. 72, *m75*)

Spanish Florida Part of New Spain. Purchased by the United States in 1821. (p. 282, *m273*)

Strait of Magellan (53°S/69°W) Narrow water route at the tip of South America. (p. 15)

T

Tennessee 16th state. Nicknamed the Volunteer State. Gained statehood after North Carolina ceded its western lands to the United States. (p. 618, *m612–613*)

Tenochtitlán (19°N/99°W) Capital of the Aztec empire. Now part of Mexico City. (p. 50, *m51*)

Texas 28th state. Nicknamed the Lone Star State. Proclaimed independence from Mexico in 1836. Was a separate republic until 1845. (p. 618, *m612–613*)

Tikal (17°N/90°W) Ancient Mayan city. (p. 48, *m51*)

Timbuktu (17°N/3°W) City on the Niger River in Africa. Flourished as a center of trade and learning. (p. 66, *m66*)

GAZETTEER

Trenton (41°N/74°W) Capital of New Jersey. Site of an American victory in the Revolution. (p. 171, *m170*)

U

Utah 45th state. Nicknamed the Beehive State. Settled by Mormons. (p. 618, *m612–613*)

V

Valley Forge (40°N/76°W) Winter headquarters for the Continental Army in 1777–1778. Located near Philadelphia. (p. 172, *m170*)

Veracruz (19°N/96°W) Port city in Mexico on the Gulf of Mexico. (p. 366, *m365*)

Vermont 14th state. Nicknamed the Green Mountain State. First new state to join the Union after the American Revolution. (p. 618, *m612–613*)

Vicksburg (42°N/86°W) City on a high cliff overlooking the Mississippi River. Site of a Union victory in 1863. (p. 462, *m474*)

Vincennes (39°N/88°W) City in Indiana. Settled by the French. British fort there was captured by George Rogers Clark in 1779. (p. 176, *m175*)

Vinland Viking settlement in present-day Newfoundland. (p. 54)

Virgin Islands (18°N/64°W) Territory of the United States. Purchased from Denmark in 1917. (p. 618, *m610–611*)

Virginia One of the original 13 states. Site of the first English settlements in the Americas. Nicknamed the Old Dominion. (p. 618, *m612–613*)

W

Washington 42nd state. Nicknamed the Evergreen State. Acquired by the United States as part of Oregon Territory. (p. 618, *m612–613*)

Washington, D.C. (39°N/77°W) Capital of the United States since 1800. Called Federal City until it was renamed for George Washington in 1799. (p. 289, *m288*)

Western Hemisphere Western half of the world. Includes North and South America. (p. 15, *m610–611*)

West Indies Islands in the Caribbean Sea. Explored by Columbus in 1492. (p. 67, *m72*)

West Virginia 35th state. Nicknamed the Mountain State. Separated from Virginia early in the Civil War. (p. 618, *m612–613*)

Willamette River Flows across fertile farmlands in northern Oregon to join the Columbia River. (p. 350, *m353*)

Wisconsin 30th state. Nicknamed the Badger State. Settled as part of the Northwest Territory. (p. 618, *m612–613*)

Wyoming 44th state. Nicknamed the Equality State. (p. 618, *m612–613*)

Y

Yorktown (37°N/76°W) Town in Virginia near the York River. Site of the surrender of Cornwallis to the Americans in 1781. (p. 181, *m181*)

Glossary

This glossary defines all vocabulary words and many important historical terms and phrases. These words and terms appear in blue or dark slanted type the first time that they are used in the text. The page number after each definition refers to the page on which the word or phrase is first discussed in the text. For other references, see the Index.

Pronunciation Key

When difficult names or terms first appear in the text, they are respelled to help you with pronunciation. A syllable printed in SMALL CAPITAL LETTERS receives the greatest stress. The pronunciation key below lists the letters and symbols that will help you pronounce the word. It also includes examples of words using each sound and showing how they would be pronounced.

Symbol	Example	Respelling
a	hat	(hat)
ay	pay, late	(pay), (layt)
ah	star, hot	(stahr), (haht)
ai	air, dare	(air), (dair)
aw	law, all	(law), (awl)
eh	met	(meht)
ee	bee, eat	(bee), (eet)
er	learn, sir, fur	(lern), (ser), (fer)
ih	fit	(fiht)
ī	mile	(mīl)
ir	ear	(ir)
oh	no	(noh)
oi	soil, boy	(soil), (boi)
oo	root, rule	(root), (rool)
or	born, door	(born), (dor)
ow	plow, out	(plow), (owt)

Symbol	Example	Respelling
u	put, book	(put), (buk)
uh	fun	(fuhn)
yoo	few, use	(fyoo), (yooz)
ch	chill, reach	(chihl), (reech)
g	go, dig	(goh), (dihg)
j	jet, gently bridge	(jeht), (JEHNT lee), (brihj)
k	kite, cup	(kit), (kuhp)
ks	mix	(mihks)
kw	quick	(kwihk)
ng	bring	(brihng)
s	say, cent	(say), (sehnt)
sh	she, crash	(shee), (krash)
th	three	(three)
y	yet, onion	(yeht), (UHN yuhn)
z	zip, always	(zihp), (AWL wayz)
zh	treasure	(TREH zher)

A

abolitionist person who wanted to end slavery in the United States. (p. 404)

Act of Toleration (1649) law that gave religious freedom to all Christians in Maryland. (p. 107)

Adams-Onís Treaty agreement by which Spain gave Florida to the United States. (p. 319)

adobe sundried clay brick. (p. 36)

Albany Plan of Union Benjamin Franklin's plan for a Grand Council to make laws, raise taxes, and set up defense of the colonies. (p. 137)

alien foreigner. (p. 260)

Alien Act (1798) law that allowed the President to expel foreigners thought to be dangerous to the country. (p. 260)

altitude height above sea level. (p. 22)

amend change. (p. 207)

amendment formal written change. (p. 225)

American Colonization Society group founded in 1817 to set up a colony for free blacks in Africa. (p. 403)

American System plan devised by Henry Clay providing for high tariffs and internal improvements to promote economic growth. (p. 313)

annex add on, such as territory. (p. 360)

Antifederalist person opposed to the Constitution during the ratification debate in 1787. (p. 205)

appeal ask that a decision be reviewed by a higher court. (p. 234)

apprentice person who learns a trade or craft from a master craftsworker. (p. 121)

Reference Section • **627**

appropriate set aside money for a special purpose. (p. 230)

archaeology study of evidence left by early peoples. (p. 34)

arsenal gun warehouse. (p. 443)

Articles of Confederation first constitution of the United States. (p. 189)

artifact object made by humans and used by archaeologists to recreate a picture of the past. (p. 34)

astrolabe instrument used by sailors to measure the positions of stars and figure out their latitude at sea. (p. 63)

B

backcountry area along the eastern slopes of the Appalachian Mountains. (p. 105)

Bacon's Rebellion uprising led by Nathaniel Bacon against Native American villages in 1676. (p. 107)

Bank of the United States national bank set up by Congress in 1791. (p. 248)

Bear Flag Republic country set up in 1845 by Americans in California. (p. 366)

bill proposed law. (pp. 203, 223)

bill of rights document that lists freedoms the government promises to protect. (p. 189)

Bill of Rights first 10 amendments to the Constitution. (p. 207)

black code laws that limited the rights of freedmen in the South after the Civil War. (p. 486)

Bleeding Kansas name given to the Kansas Territory by newspapers because of the violence there over slavery. (p. 438)

blockade shutting off a port by ships to keep people or supplies from moving in or out. (p. 163)

bond certificate that promises to pay the holder the money loaned plus interest on a certain date. (p. 245)

Border Ruffians proslavery bands from Missouri who battled antislavery forces in Kansas. (p. 437)

Boston Massacre shooting of five Bostonians by British soldiers on March 5, 1770. (p. 149)

Boston Tea Party protest in which Bostonians dressed as Indians dumped British tea into the harbor. (p. 153)

bounty payment made to men who joined the Union army. (p. 467)

boycott to refuse to buy certain goods or services. (p. 144)

burgess representative to the colonial assembly of Virginia. (p. 86)

C

Cabinet group of officials who head government departments and advise the President. (pp. 227, 245)

canal channel dug out and filled with water to allow ships to cross a stretch of land. (p. 307)

capitalist person who invests money in a business to make a profit. (p. 297)

caravel ship with a steering rudder and triangular sails. (p. 65)

carpetbagger name for a northerner who went to the South during Reconstruction. (p. 492)

cartographer mapmaker. (p. 8)

cash crop surplus of crops sold for money on the world market. (p. 104)

caucus private meeting of political party leaders to choose a candidate. (p. 330)

cavalry troops on horseback. (p. 174)

cede give up, as land. (p. 366)

charter legal document giving certain rights to a person or company. (p. 85)

checks and balances system set up by the Constitution in which each branch of the federal government has the power to check, or control, the actions of the other branches. (p. 203)

civilian person not in the military. (p. 466)

civilization advanced culture. (p. 48)

civil war war between people of the same country. (p. 433)

climate average weather of a place over a period of 20 or 30 years. (p. 22)

clipper ship fast-sailing ship of the mid-1800s. (p. 379)

colony group of people settled in a distant land who are ruled by the government of their native land. (p. 68)

committee of correspondence group of colonists who wrote letters and pamphlets to inform and unite colonists against British rule. (p. 147)

compromise settlement in which each side gives up some of its demands in order to reach an agreement. (p. 197)

Compromise of 1850 agreement over slavery that admitted California to the Union as a free state, allowed popular sovereignty in New Mexico and Utah, banned the slave trade in Washington, D.C., and passed a strict fugitive slave law. (p. 434)

Confederate States of America nation formed by the states that seceded from the Union in 1860 and 1861. (p. 445)

conquistador Spanish word for conqueror. (p. 70)

constituent person who elects a representative to office. (p. 232)

constitution document that sets out the laws and principles of a government. (p. 188)

Constitutional Convention meeting of delegates from 12 states who wrote a constitution for the United States in 1787. (p. 195)

Continental Army army set up by the Second Continental Congress to fight the British. (p. 161)

continental divide mountain ridge that separates river systems. (p. 276)

Convention of 1800 document in which Napoleon Bonaparte agreed to stop seizing American ships in the West Indies. (p. 260)

Copperhead northerner who thought the South should be allowed to leave the Union. (p. 467)

corduroy road log road. (p. 306)

corporation business owned by investors who buy shares of stock. (p. 517)

cotton gin invention of Eli Whitney's that speeded the cleaning of cotton fibers. (p. 296)

Cotton Kingdom in the 1850s, region where large plantations produced cotton. Stretched from South Carolina to Texas. (p. 388)

coureur de bois French phrase meaning runner of the woods. Trapper or trader in New France. (p. 81)

creole person born in the Americas to Spanish parents. (p. 76)

culture entire way of life of a people. (p. 34)

culture area region in which people share a similar way of life. (p. 37)

D

Daughters of Liberty group of colonial women who protested the Stamp Act. (p. 145)

Declaration of Independence (1776) document that stated that the colonies had become a free and independent nation. (p. 166)

democratic ensuring that all people have the same rights. (p. 268)

discrimination policy or attitude that denies equal rights to certain groups of people. (p. 386)

domestic tranquillity peace at home. (p. 217)

draft law requiring men of a certain age to serve in the military. (p. 467)

Dred Scott decision Supreme Court decision in 1857 that stated slaves were property, not citizens. (p. 439)

drought long dry spell. (p. 36)

due process of law right of every citizen to the same fair rules in all cases brought to trial. (pp. 208, 236)

dumping selling goods in another country at very low prices. (p. 312)

E

economic depression period during which business activity slows, prices and wages fall, and unemployment rises. (p. 194)

electoral college group of electors from each state that meets every four years to vote for the President and Vice President. (p. 203)

elevation height above the surface of the Earth. (p. 16)

emancipate set free. (p. 464)

Emancipation Proclamation (1863) President Lincoln's declaration freeing slaves in the Confederacy. (p. 464)

embargo ban on trade with another country. (p. 281)

Embargo Act (1807) law forbidding Americans to export or import any goods. (p. 281)

encomienda right to demand taxes or labor from Native Americans in the Spanish colonies. (p. 76)

English Bill of Rights (1689) document that protected the rights of English citizens. (p. 116)

equator imaginary line that lies at 0° latitude and divides the Earth into the Northern and Southern hemispheres. (p. 11)

execute carry out. (p. 189)

executive agreement informal agreement made by the President of the United States with other heads of state. (p. 232)

executive branch part of a government that carries out the laws. (p. 197)

export trade goods sent to markets outside a country. (p. 113)

extended family close-knit family group that includes grandparents, parents, children, aunts, uncles, and cousins. (p. 394)

F

factory system method of producing goods that brings workers and machines together in one place. (p. 297)

famine severe shortage of food. (p. 384)

federal national. (p. 221)

federalism division of power between the states and the national government. (p. 201)

Federalist supporter of the Constitution in the ratification debate in 1787. Favored a strong national government. (p. 205)

GLOSSARY

feudalism system of rule by lords who owed loyalty to their king. (p. 62)

Fifteenth Amendment constitutional amendment that gave African Americans the right to vote in all states. (p. 490)

First Continental Congress meeting of delegates from 12 colonies in Philadelphia in September 1774. (p. 154)

forty-niner person who went to California during the Gold Rush in 1849. (p. 370)

Fourteenth Amendment constitutional amendment that granted citizenship to all persons born in the United States. (p. 488)

freedman freed slave. (p. 482)

Freedmen's Bureau government agency that helped former slaves. (p. 483)

Free Soil party political party founded in 1848 by antislavery Whigs and Democrats. (p. 429)

French and Indian War conflict between the French and British in North America. Fought from 1754 to 1763. (p. 136)

fugitive runaway, such as an escaped slave in the 1800s. (p. 433)

Fugitive Slave Law of 1850 law that required all citizens to help catch runaway slaves. (p. 434)

G

General Court representative assembly in the Massachusetts Bay Colony. (p. 95)

general welfare wellbeing of all the people. (p. 218)

gentry highest social class in the 13 English colonies. (p. 118)

geography study of people, their environments, and their resources. (p. 4)

Gettysburg Address speech given by President Lincoln in 1863 after the Battle of Gettysburg. (p. 475)

glacier thick sheet of ice. (p. 32)

grandfather clause law passed by southern states after the Civil War. Excused a voter from a poll tax or literacy test if his father or grandfather had voted before 1867. Kept most African Americans from voting. (p. 499)

Great Awakening religious movement in the colonies in the 1730s and 1740s. (p. 120)

Great Compromise Roger Sherman's plan at the Constitutional Convention for a two-house legislature. Settled differences between large and small states. (p. 198)

H

habeas corpus right to have charges filed or a hearing before being jailed. (p. 468)

hemisphere half of the Earth. (p. 11)

hieroglyphics system of writing that uses pictures to represent words and ideas. (p. 49)

hill area of raised land. Lower, less steep, and more rounded than a mountain. (p. 16)

history account of what has happened in the lives of different peoples. (p. 4)

hogan Navajo house built of mud plaster over a framework of wooden poles. (p. 40)

House of Burgesses representative assembly in colonial Virginia. (p. 86)

House of Representatives lower house of Congress. Each state is represented according to its population. (p. 228)

I

igloo Inuit house made of snow and ice. (p. 38)

immigrant person who enters a country in order to settle there. (p. 384)

impeach bring formal charges against an official such as the President. (pp. 203, 231)

import trade good brought into a country. (p. 113)

impressment act of seizing men from a ship or village and forcing them to serve in the navy. (p. 280)

indentured servant person who signed a contract to work for a certain length of time in exchange for passage to the colonies. (p. 118)

Indian Removal Act (1830) law that forced Native Americans to sign treaties agreeing to move west of the Mississippi. (p. 339)

Industrial Revolution process by which machines replaced hand tools, and new sources of power, such as steam and electricity, replaced human and animal power. Caused a shift from farming to manufacturing. (p. 296)

inflation economic cycle in which the value of money falls and the prices of goods rise. (p. 469)

initiative procedure that allows voters to introduce a bill by collecting signatures on a petition. (p. 521)

interchangeable parts identical parts of a tool or instrument that are made by machine. (p. 301)

Intolerable Acts laws passed by Parliament in 1774 to punish colonists for the Boston Tea Party. (p. 153)

irrigate bring water to an area. (p. 6)

isthmus narrow strip of land. (p. 16)

J

Jay's Treaty (1795) agreement to stop British attacks on American merchant ships and settle other differences between the two nations. (p. 252)

Jim Crow law law passed by southerners that segregated public places. (p. 499)

joint committee group made up of members of both the House of Representatives and the Senate. (p. 230)

judicial branch part of a government that decides if laws are carried out fairly. (p. 197)

judicial review power of the Supreme Court to decide whether laws passed by Congress are constitutional. (pp. 228, 270)

Judiciary Act (1789) law that organized the federal court system into district and circuit courts. (p. 245)

jury panel of citizens. (p. 234)

justice fairness. (p. 216)

K

kachina masked dancer who represented the spirits in Pueblo religious ceremonies. (p. 40)

Kansas-Nebraska Act (1854) law that divided Nebraska into two territories. Provided for the question of slavery in the territories to be decided by popular sovereignty. (p. 436)

kayak small boat made of animal skins. (p. 38)

Kentucky and Virginia resolutions (1798, 1799) declarations that states had the right to declare a law unconstitutional. (p. 260)

kitchen cabinet group of unofficial advisers to President Andrew Jackson. (p. 334)

kiva underground chamber where Pueblo men held religious ceremonies. (p. 40)

Know-Nothing party political party organized by nativists in the 1850s. (p. 385)

Ku Klux Klan secret group first set up in the South after the Civil War. Members terrorized African Americans and other minority groups. (p. 494)

L

laissez faire (lehs ay fayr) French term meaning let alone. Referred to the idea that government should play as small a role as possible in economic affairs. (p. 269)

Land Ordinance of 1785 law that set up a system for settling the Northwest Territory. (p. 192)

latitude distance north or south from the Equator. (p. 4)

League of the Iroquois alliance of the five Iroquois nations. Formed in 1570. (p. 46)

legislative branch part of a government that passes laws. (p. 197)

legislature group of people with power to make laws for a country or colony. (p. 115)

liberty freedom to live as you please as long as you obey the laws and respect the rights of others. (p. 218)

literacy test examination to see if a person can read and write. (p. 499)

long house Iroquois dwelling. (p. 46)

longitude distance east or west from the Prime Meridian. (p. 4)

Louisiana Purchase large territory purchased from France in 1803. (p. 273)

Loyalist colonist who stayed loyal to Great Britain during the American Revolution. (p. 167)

M

Magna Carta document that guaranteed rights to English nobles in 1215. (p. 86)

magnetic compass device that shows which direction is north. (p. 63)

Manifest Destiny belief that the United States had the right to all the land between the Atlantic and Pacific oceans. (p. 363)

manor part of a lord's holding in the Middle Ages, including the castle, peasants' huts, and surrounding villages or fields. (p. 62)

map projection way of drawing the Earth on a flat surface. (p. 8)

Marbury* v. *Madison (1803) Supreme Court case that set the precedent of judicial review. (p. 270)

Mayflower Compact (1620) agreement signed by Pilgrims before they landed at Plymouth. (p. 89)

mercantilism economic theory that a nation's strength came from building up its gold supplies and expanding its trade. (p. 112)

mestizo person in the Spanish colonies of mixed Spanish and Indian background. (p. 76)

Middle Ages period from about 500 to 1350 in Europe. (p. 62)

Middle Colonies colonies of New York, New Jersey, Pennsylvania, and Delaware. (p. 100)

Middle Passage ocean trip from Africa to the Americas in which thousands of slaves died. (p. 111)

militia army of citizens who serve as soldiers during an emergency. (p. 154)

minuteman volunteer who trained to fight the British in 1775. (p. 154)

mission religious settlement. Run by Catholic priests and friars in the Spanish colonies. (p. 75)

Missouri Compromise (1820) plan proposed by Henry Clay to keep the number of slave and free states equal. (p. 429)

monopoly company that completely controls the market of a certain industry. (p. 517)

Monroe Doctrine policy statement of President James Monroe in 1823. Warned European nations not to interfere in Latin America. (p. 319)

Mormon member of the Church of Jesus Christ of Latter-day Saints. (p. 369)

Mound Builders Native Americans who built thousands of huge earth mounds from eastern Oklahoma to the Atlantic. (p. 34)

mountain high, rugged land usually at least 1,000 feet (300 m) above the surrounding land. (p. 16)

Mountain Man trapper in the West in the early 1800s. (p. 351)

N

national debt total sum of money a government owes. (p. 245)

nationalism pride in or devotion to one's country. (p. 282)

Native American descendant of people who reached the Americas thousands of years ago. (p. 33)

nativist person who wanted to limit immigration and preserve the United States for native-born white Americans. (p. 385)

Navigation Acts laws that governed trade between England and its colonies. (p. 114)

neutral choosing not to fight on either side in a war. (p. 174)

New England Colonies colonies of Massachusetts, New Hampshire, Connecticut, and Rhode Island. (p. 94)

nominating convention meeting at which a political party selects a candidate for President. (p. 330)

nonimportation agreement promise of colonial merchants and planters to stop importing goods taxed by the Townshend Acts. (p. 145)

Northwest Ordinance (1787) law that set up a government for the Northwest Territory. It also set up a way for new states to be admitted to the United States. (p. 192)

northwest passage waterway through or around North America. (p. 78)

nullification idea of declaring a federal law illegal. (p. 337)

nullify cancel. (p. 260)

O

override overrule. Congress can override a President's veto if two thirds of both houses vote to do so. (pp. 203, 223)

P

Patriot colonist who supported the American Revolution. (p. 167)

patroon rich landowner in the Dutch colonies. (p. 101)

peninsulare person sent from Spain to rule the Spanish colonies. (p. 76)

pet bank state bank used by President Jackson and Roger Taney to deposit government money. (p. 336)

Pilgrims group of English settlers who sought religious freedom in the Americas. (p. 87)

plain broad area of fairly level land. (p. 16)

plantation large estate farmed by many workers. (p. 76)

plateau large raised area of flat or gently rolling land. (p. 18)

Plessy* v. *Ferguson (1896) ruling by the Supreme Court that segregation was legal as long as facilities for blacks and whites were equal. (p. 499)

poll tax fee paid by a voter in order to vote. (p. 499)

popular sovereignty control by the people; allowing each territory to decide for itself whether or not to allow slavery. (p. 429)

potlatch ceremonial dinner among some Native Americans of the Northwest Coast. (p. 39)

preamble an opening statement. (p. 216)

precedent act or decision that sets an example for others to follow. (pp. 227, 244)

precipitation water that falls from the sky in the form of rain or snow. (p. 22)

presidio fort that housed soldiers in the Spanish colonies. (p. 74)

Proclamation of 1763 British law that forbade American colonists to settle west of a line that ran along the Appalachian Mountains. (p. 143)

profiteer person who takes advantage of an emergency to make money. (p. 469)

proprietary colony English colony in which the king gave land to proprietors in exchange for a yearly payment. (p. 101)

protective tariff tax placed on imported goods to protect from foreign competition. (p. 248)

public school school supported by taxes. (p. 121)

pueblo adobe dwelling of the Anasazis; Spanish word for village or town. (pp. 36, 74)

Puritans group of English Protestants who settled in Massachusetts. (p. 94)

Q

Quakers Protestant reformers who settled in Pennsylvania. (p. 102)

Quartering Act (1765) law that required English colonists to provide housing, candles, bedding, and beverages to British soldiers stationed in the colonies. (p. 147)

R

racism belief that one race is superior to another. (p. 111)

Radical Reconstruction period after the Civil War when Republicans controlled Congress and passed strict laws affecting the South. (p. 488)

Radical Republicans group of Republicans in Congress who wanted to protect the rights of freedmen in the South and keep rich southern planters out of power. (p. 487)

ratify approve. (pp. 182, 220)

recall special election that allows voters to remove an elected official from office. (p. 521)

Reconstruction period after the Civil War when the South was rebuilt; also, the federal program to rebuild it. (p. 482)

referendum process by which people can vote directly on a bill. (p. 521)

relief difference in height of land. (p. 16)

rendezvous yearly meeting where Mountain Men traded furs for supplies. (p. 351)

repeal cancel. (p. 145)

representative government system of government in which voters elect representatives to make laws for them. (pp. 86, 220)

republic nation in which voters elect representatives to govern them. (p. 199)

Republican party political party formed in 1854 by a group of Free Soilers, northern Democrats, and antislavery Whigs. (p. 440)

S

sachem tribal chief of the Iroquois. (p. 46)

scalawag white southerner who supported Radical Republicans. (p. 492)

secede withdraw. (p. 338)

Second Great Awakening religious movement that swept the nation in the early 1800s. (p. 402)

sectionalism loyalty to a state or section rather than to the whole country. (p. 429)

sedition stirring up rebellion against a government. (p. 260)

Sedition Act (1798) law that allowed citizens to be fined or jailed for criticizing public officials. (p. 260)

segregation separation of people of different races. (p. 499)

Senate upper house of Congress. Each state is represented by two senators. (p. 230)

Seneca Falls Convention (1848) meeting at which leaders of the women's rights movement voted on a plan for achieving equality. (p. 411)

separation of powers system in which the power of a government is divided among separate branches. (p. 201)

serf peasant who was bound to the land for life. (p. 62)

sharecropper farmer who works land owned by another and gives the landowner part of the harvest. (p. 496)

Shays' Rebellion (1786) revolt of Massachusetts farmers against increased taxes. (p. 194)

skilled worker person with a trade, such as a carpenter, a printer, or a shoemaker. (p. 382)

slave code laws that controlled behavior of slaves and denied them basic rights. (p. 111)

Sons of Liberty group of colonial men who joined together to protest the Stamp Act and protect colonial liberties. (p. 145)

Southern Colonies colonies of Maryland, Virginia, North and South Carolina, and Georgia. (p. 106)

speculator person who invests in a risky venture in the hope of making a large profit. (p. 247)

spinning jenny machine that let a person spin several threads at once. (p. 296)

spoils system practice of rewarding supporters with government jobs. (p. 334)

Stamp Act (1765) law passed by Parliament that taxed legal documents, newspapers, almanacs, playing cards, and dice. (p. 143)

standard time zone one of the 24 time divisions of the world as measured from the Prime Meridian. (p. 13)

standing committee permanent committee in the House of Representatives or the Senate. (p. 230)

states' rights idea that individual states have the right to limit the power of the federal government. (p. 337)

strike refusal by union workers to do their jobs until their demands are met. (p. 384)

suffrage right to vote. (p. 330)

Supreme Court highest court in the United States. (p. 234)

T

tariff tax on foreign goods brought into a country. (p. 248)

Tariff of Abominations name given by southerners to the Tariff of 1828. (p. 336)

tax-in-kind tax paid with goods rather than money. (p. 469)

Tea Act (1773) British law that let the British East India Company sell tea directly to colonists. (p. 150)

GLOSSARY

telegraph device that sends electrical signals along a wire. (p. 378)

temperance movement campaign against the sale or drinking of alcohol. (p. 415)

tepee cone-shaped tent made of buffalo hides. (p. 41)

Thirteenth Amendment (1865) constitutional amendment that banned slavery in the United States. (p. 485)

Three-Fifths Compromise agreement of delegates to the Constitutional Convention that three fifths of the slaves in any state be counted in its population. (p. 198)

toleration willingness to let others practice their own beliefs. (p. 96)

Townshend Acts (1767) British laws that taxed goods such as glass, paint, paper, silk, and tea. (p. 145)

trade union association of workers formed to win better wages and working conditions. (p. 384)

Trail of Tears forced march of Native Americans to lands west of the Mississippi. (p. 340)

traitor person who betrays his or her country. (p. 165)

travois sled used by Plains people to haul gear. (p. 43)

Treaty of Ghent (1814) treaty that ended the War of 1812 between Britain and the United States. (p. 291)

Treaty of Greenville (1795) treaty between the United States and 12 Indian nations of the Northwest Territory. (p. 252)

Treaty of Paris (1763) treaty that ended the French and Indian War. (p. 141)

Treaty of Paris (1783) treaty that ended the American Revolution. (p. 182)

triangular trade colonial trade route between New England, the West Indies, and Africa. (p. 114)

tributary branch of a river. (p. 20)

turnpike road built by a private company. Charged tolls to those using it. (p. 306)

tyranny cruel and unjust government. (p. 220)

U

unconstitutional not permitted by the Constitution. (pp. 223, 255)

underground railroad secret network of people who helped runaway slaves to reach freedom in the North or Canada. (p. 405)

unskilled worker person who does a job that requires little or no special training. (p. 384)

V

veto reject. (pp. 203, 223)

viceroy official who rules an area in the name of a king or queen. (p. 96)

vigilante self-appointed law enforcer who deals out punishment without holding a trial. (p. 371)

W

Wade-Davis Bill Reconstruction plan passed by Republicans in Congress in July 1864. Vetoed by President Lincoln. (p. 483)

War Hawks members of Congress who wanted war with Britain in 1812. (p. 282)

weather condition of the Earth's atmosphere at any given time and place. (p. 22)

Whiskey Rebellion (1794) revolt of farmers to protest the tax on whiskey. (p. 250)

writ of assistance legal document that let a British customs officer inspect a ship's cargo without giving any reason for the search. (p. 145)

X

XYZ Affair (1797) incident in which French agents asked American ambassadors in Paris for a bribe. (p. 259)

Y

Yankee nickname given to merchants from New England. (p. 114)

Connections With Literature

*The page references to Prentice Hall Literature are from the Paramount Edition.

Connections With Science

Connections With Mathematics

Topic	See Prentice Hall Middle Grades Mathematics

UNIT 1 A Meeting of Different Worlds

Location, pages 4–5
  (latitude and longitude)
Maps and Globes, page 8

Time Zones, page 13
Early Cultures of the Southwest, pages 35–36
  (converting Fahrenheit to Celsius)
Cultural Exchange, pages 54–56
  (reading a line graph)

Course 1, Graphing on the Coordinate Plane,
  pages 469–470
Course 2, Exploring Maps and Scale Drawings,
  pages 382–384
Course 1, Time Zones, page 462
Course 1, Changing Celsius to Fahrenheit,
  page 446
Course 1, Reading and Understanding Graphs,
  page 21
Course 2, Line Graph, page 10

UNIT 2 From Revolution to Republic

Taking a Stand at Bunker Hill, pages 161–162
  (Bunker Hill Memorial)
Serious Challenges for the Articles of Confederation,
  pages 190–191 (money and trade)

A Farsighted Policy for Western Lands, pages 191–194
  (townships and sections)

Course 3, Indirect Measurement, page 359

Course 1, Keeping Track of Your Savings,
  pages 120–122
Course 1, Estimating with Percents, pages 391–394
Course 1, Area of Rectangles and Squares,
  pages 233–236
Course 2, Estimating Length and Area,
  pages193–194

UNIT 3 The New Republic

Hamilton and the National Debt, page 245
  (national currency)
Opposition to Hamilton's Plan, pages 245–248
  (the District of Columbia)
Lewis and Clark's Assignment, page 274
  (maps, scale drawings)

Course 3, Government Spending, page 245
Course 3, Solving Proportions, page 347
Course 3, Municipal Geometry, page 97

Course 2, Exploring Maps and Scale Drawings,
  pages 382–384
Course 3, Using a Proportion, page 354

UNIT 4 An Expanding Nation

The Log Cabin Campaign, pages 343–345
  (reading a circle graph)

Wagon Trains West, pages 353–354
  (converting miles to km)
The First Railroads, page 379
  (determining distance)

Course 1, Constructing a Circle Graph,
  pages 399–400
Course 2, Circle Graphs, pages 406–409
Course 1, Metric Length, pages 124–127

Course 3, Formulas, page 169

UNIT 5 The Nation Torn Apart

The Election of 1860, pages 444–445, 446
  (reading circle graphs)
The Two Sides, pages 452–455
  (reading a table)
Rival Plans for the South, pages 482–483
  (Ten Percent Plan)

Showdown, page 490
  (two-thirds majority)

Course 2, Using Statistics to Persuade, pages 34–37

Course 1, Make a Table, pages 8–10
Course 2, Making a Table, page 167
Course 1, Percent Sense, page 384–386
Course 2, Modeling Percents, pages 385–386
Course 3, Percents and Proportions, pages 430–431
Course 2, Fractions, Decimals, and Percents,
  pages 388–389

CONNECTIONS WITH MATHEMATICS

Connections With Fine Art

* This is a partial list of the fine art found in *The American Nation: Beginnings to 1877.*
For source information for all works, see the illustration credits on pages 686–690.

CONNECTIONS WITH FINE ART

Connections With Music

CONNECTIONS WITH MUSIC

Presidents of the United States

1

2

PRESIDENTS OF THE UNITED STATES

1. **George Washington** (1732–1799)
   Years in office: 1789–1797
   No political party
   Elected from: Virginia
   Vice Pres.: John Adams

2. **John Adams** (1735–1826)
   Years in office: 1797–1801
   Federalist party
   Elected from: Massachusetts
   Vice Pres.: Thomas Jefferson

3. **Thomas Jefferson** (1743–1826)
   Years in office: 1801–1809
   Democratic Republican party
   Elected from: Virginia
   Vice Pres.: Aaron Burr, George Clinton

4. **James Madison** (1751–1836)
   Years in office: 1809–1817
   Democratic Republican party
   Elected from: Virginia
   Vice Pres.: George Clinton,
            Elbridge Gerry

5. **James Monroe** (1758–1831)
   Years in office: 1817–1825
   Democratic Republican party
   Elected from: Virginia
   Vice Pres.: Daniel Tompkins

6. **John Quincy Adams** (1767–1848)
   Years in office: 1825–1829
   National Republican party
   Elected from: Massachusetts
   Vice Pres.: John Calhoun

7. **Andrew Jackson** (1767–1845)
   Years in office: 1829–1837
   Democratic party
   Elected from: Tennessee
   Vice Pres.: John Calhoun,
            Martin Van Buren

8. **Martin Van Buren** (1782–1862)
   Years in office: 1837–1841
   Democratic party
   Elected from: New York
   Vice Pres.: Richard Johnson

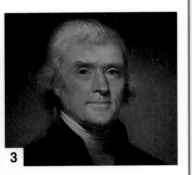

3

4

5

6

7

8

9

9. **William Henry Harrison*** (1773–1841)
      Years in office: 1841
      Whig party
      Elected from: Ohio
      Vice Pres.: John Tyler

10. **John Tyler** (1790–1862)
      Years in office: 1841–1845
      Whig party
      Elected from: Virginia
      Vice Pres.: none

11. **James K. Polk** (1795–1849)
      Years in office: 1845–1849
      Democratic party
      Elected from: Tennessee
      Vice Pres.: George Dallas

12. **Zachary Taylor*** (1784–1850)
      Years in office: 1849–1850
      Whig party
      Elected from: Louisiana
      Vice Pres.: Millard Fillmore

13. **Millard Fillmore** (1800–1874)
      Years in office: 1850–1853
      Whig party
      Elected from: New York
      Vice Pres.: none

14. **Franklin Pierce** (1804–1869)
      Years in office: 1853–1857
      Democratic party
      Elected from: New Hampshire
      Vice Pres.: William King

15. **James Buchanan** (1791–1868)
      Years in office: 1857–1861
      Democratic party
      Elected from: Pennsylvania
      Vice Pres.: John Breckinridge

16. **Abraham Lincoln**** (1809–1865)
      Years in office: 1861–1865
      Republican party
      Elected from: Illinois
      Vice Pres.: Hannibal Hamlin,
                 Andrew Johnson

10

11

12

13

14

15

16

*Died in office   **Assassinated

PRESIDENTS OF THE UNITED STATES

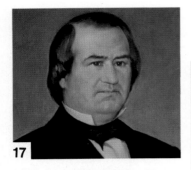

17

19

21

23

25

17. **Andrew Johnson** (1808–1875)
   Years in office: 1865–1869
   Republican party
   Elected from: Tennessee
   Vice Pres.: none

18. **Ulysses S. Grant** (1822–1885)
   Years in office: 1869–1877
   Republican party
   Elected from: Illinois
   Vice Pres.: Schuyler Colfax,
      Henry Wilson

19. **Rutherford B. Hayes** (1822–1893)
   Years in office: 1877–1881
   Republican party
   Elected from: Ohio
   Vice Pres.: William Wheeler

20. **James A. Garfield** (1831–1881)
   Years in office: 1881
   Republican party
   Elected from: Ohio
   Vice Pres.: Chester A. Arthur

21. **Chester A. Arthur** (1830–1886)
   Years in office: 1881–1885
   Republican party
   Elected from: New York
   Vice Pres.: none

22. **Grover Cleveland** (1837–1908)
   Years in office: 1885–1889
   Democratic party
   Elected from: New York
   Vice Pres.: Thomas Hendricks

23. **Benjamin Harrison** (1833–1901)
   Years in office: 1889–1893
   Republican party
   Elected from: Indiana
   Vice Pres.: Levi Morton

24. **Grover Cleveland** (1837–1908)
   Years in office: 1893–1897
   Democratic party
   Elected from: New York
   Vice Pres.: Adlai Stevenson

25. **William McKinley**** (1843–1901)
   Years in office: 1897–1901
   Republican party
   Elected from: Ohio
   Vice Pres.: Garret Hobart,
      Theodore Roosevelt

26. **Theodore Roosevelt** (1858–1919)
   Years in office: 1901–1909
   Republican party
   Elected from: New York
   Vice Pres.: Charles Fairbanks

18

20

22

24

26

27

28

29

30

31

32

33

34

35

36

27. **William Howard Taft** (1857–1930)
Years in office: 1909–1913
Republican party
Elected from: Ohio
Vice Pres.: James Sherman

28. **Woodrow Wilson** (1856–1924)
Years in office: 1913–1921
Democratic party
Elected from: New Jersey
Vice Pres.: Thomas Marshall

29. **Warren G. Harding*** (1865–1923)
Years in office: 1921–1923
Republican party
Elected from: Ohio
Vice Pres.: Calvin Coolidge

30. **Calvin Coolidge** (1872–1933)
Years in office: 1923–1929
Republican party
Elected from: Massachusetts
Vice Pres.: Charles Dawes

31. **Herbert C. Hoover** (1874–1964)
Years in office: 1929–1933
Republican party
Elected from: California
Vice Pres.: Charles Curtis

32. **Franklin D. Roosevelt*** (1882–1945)
Years in office: 1933–1945
Democratic party
Elected from: New York
Vice Pres.: John Garner, Henry
    Wallace, Harry S. Truman

33. **Harry S. Truman** (1884–1972)
Years in office: 1945–1953
Democratic party
Elected from: Missouri
Vice Pres.: Alben Barkley

34. **Dwight D. Eisenhower** (1890–1969)
Years in office: 1953–1961
Republican party
Elected from: New York
Vice Pres.: Richard M. Nixon

35. **John F. Kennedy**** (1917–1963)
Years in office: 1961–1963
Democratic party
Elected from: Massachusetts
Vice Pres.: Lyndon B. Johnson

36. **Lyndon B. Johnson** (1908–1973)
Years in office: 1963–1969
Democratic party
Elected from: Texas
Vice Pres.: Hubert Humphrey

*Died in office   **Assassinated

PRESIDENTS OF THE UNITED STATES

37

39

41

37. **Richard M. Nixon***** (1913–1994)
    Years in office: 1969–1974
    Republican party
    Elected from: New York
    Vice Pres.: Spiro Agnew,
        Gerald R. Ford

38. **Gerald R. Ford** (1913–   )
    Years in office: 1974–1977
    Republican party
    Elected from: Michigan
    Vice Pres.: Nelson Rockefeller

39. **Jimmy Carter** (1924–   )
    Years in office: 1977–1981
    Democratic party
    Elected from: Georgia
    Vice Pres.: Walter Mondale

40. **Ronald W. Reagan** (1911–   )
    Years in office: 1981–1989
    Republican party
    Elected from: California
    Vice Pres.: George H.W. Bush

41. **George H.W. Bush** (1924–   )
    Years in office: 1989–1993
    Republican party
    Elected from: Texas
    Vice Pres.: J. Danforth Quayle

42. **William J. Clinton** (1946–   )
    Years in office: 1993–
    Democratic party
    Elected from: Arkansas
    Vice Pres.: Albert Gore, Jr.

38

40

42

***Resigned

★ All pictures in Presidents of the United States are official portraits.

The Declaration of Independence

On June 7, 1776, the Continental Congress approved the resolution that "these United Colonies are, and of right ought to be, free and independent States." Congress then appointed a committee to write a declaration of independence. The committee members were John Adams, Benjamin Franklin, Robert Livingston, Roger Sherman, and Thomas Jefferson.

Jefferson actually wrote the Declaration, but he got advice from the others. On July 2, Congress discussed the Declaration and made some changes. On July 4, 1776, it adopted the Declaration of Independence in its final form.

The Declaration is printed in black. The headings have been added to show the parts of the Declaration. They are not part of the original text. Annotations, or explanations, are on the tan side of the page. Page numbers in the annotations show where a subject is discussed in the text. Difficult words are defined.

When in the course of human events it becomes necessary for one people to dissolve the political bands which have connected them with another and to assume, among the powers of the earth, the separate and equal station to which the laws of nature and of nature's God entitle them, a decent respect to the opinions of mankind requires that they should declare the causes which impel them to the separation.

dissolve: break **powers of the earth:** other nations **station:** place **impel:** force

The colonists feel that they must explain to the world the reasons why they are breaking away from England.

The Purpose of Government Is to Protect Basic Rights

We hold these truths to be self-evident, that all men are created equal; that they are endowed by their Creator with certain unalienable rights; that among these are life, liberty, and the pursuit of happiness. That, to secure these rights, governments are instituted among men, deriving their just powers from the consent of the governed; that, whenever any form of government becomes destructive of these ends, it is the right of the people to alter or to abolish it, and to institute a new government, laying its foundation on such principles and organizing its powers in such form, as to them shall seem most likely to effect their safety and happiness. Prudence, indeed, will dictate that governments long established should not be changed for light and transient causes; and, accordingly, all experience hath shown that mankind are more disposed to suffer, while evils are sufferable, than to right themselves by abolishing the forms to which they are accustomed. But when a long train of abuses and usurpations, pursuing invariably the same object, evinces a design to reduce them under absolute despotism, it is their right, it is their duty, to throw off such government and to provide new guards for their future security. Such has been the patient sufferance of these colonies, and such is now the necessity which constrains them to alter their former systems of government. The history of the present King of Great Britain is a history of repeated injuries and usurpations, all having, in direct object, the establishment of an absolute

endowed: given **unalienable rights:** so basic that they cannot be taken away **secure:** protect **instituted:** set up **deriving:** getting **alter:** change **effect:** bring about

People set up governments to protect their basic rights. Governments get their power from the consent of the governed. If a government takes away the basic rights of the people, the people have the right to change the government.

prudence: wisdom **transient:** temporary, passing **disposed:** likely **usurpations:** taking and using powers that do not belong to a person **invariably:** always **evinces a design to reduce them under absolute despotism:** makes a clear plan to put them under complete and unjust control **sufferance:** endurance **constrains:** forces **absolute tyranny:** harsh and unjust government *candid:* free from prejudice

People do not change governments for slight reasons. But they are forced to do so when a government becomes tyrannical. King George III has a long record of abusing his power.

assent: approval *relinquish:* give up
inestimable: too great a value to be measured *formidable:* causing fear

This part of the Declaration spells out three sets of wrongs that led the colonists to break with Britain.

The first set of wrongs is the king's unjust use of power. The king refused to approve laws that are needed. He has tried to control the colonial legislatures.

depository: central storehouse *fatiguing:* tiring out *compliance:* giving in
dissolved: broken up *annihilation:* total destruction *convulsions:* disturbances

The king has tried to force colonial legislatures into doing his will by wearing them out. He has dissolved legislatures (such as those of New York and Massachusetts). (See pages 149 and 153.)

endeavored: tried *obstructing:* blocking
naturalization: process of becoming a citizen
migration: moving *hither:* here
appropriations: grants *obstructed the administration of justice:* prevented justice from being done *judiciary powers:* system of law courts *tenure:* term (of office)
erected: set up *multitude:* large number
swarms: huge crowds *harass:* cause trouble *render:* make

Among other wrongs, he has refused to let settlers move west to take up new land. He has prevented justice from being done. Also, he has sent large numbers of customs officials to cause problems for the colonists.

jurisdiction: authority *quartering:* housing
mock: false

The king has joined with others, meaning Parliament, to make laws for the colonies. The Declaration then lists the second set of wrongs—unjust acts of Parliament.

tyranny over these States. To prove this, let facts be submitted to a candid world:

Wrongs Done by the King

He has refused his assent to laws the most wholesome and necessary for the public good.

He has forbidden his governors to pass laws of immediate and pressing importance, unless suspended in their operation till his assent should be obtained; and, when so suspended, he has utterly neglected to attend to them.

He has refused to pass other laws for the accommodation of the large districts of people, unless those people would relinquish the right of representation in the legislature; a right inestimable to them and formidable to tyrants only.

He has called together legislative bodies at places unusual, uncomfortable, and distant from the depository of their public records, for the sole purpose of fatiguing them into compliance with his measures.

He has dissolved representative houses, repeatedly for opposing, with manly firmness, his invasions on the rights of the people.

He has refused, for a long time after such dissolutions, to cause others to be elected: whereby the legislative powers, incapable of annihilation, have returned to the people at large for their exercise; the state remaining, in the meantime, exposed to all the danger of invasion from without and convulsions within.

He has endeavored to prevent the population of these States; for that purpose, obstructing the laws for naturalization of foreigners, refusing to pass others to encourage their migration hither, and raising the conditions of new appropriations of lands.

He has obstructed the administration of justice by refusing his assent to laws for establishing judiciary powers.

He has made judges dependent on his will alone for the tenure of their offices and the amount and payment of their salaries.

He has erected a multitude of new offices and sent hither swarms of officers to harass our people and eat out their substance.

He has kept among us, in time of peace, standing armies, without the consent of our legislatures.

He has affected to render the military independent of, and superior to, the civil power.

He has combined with others to subject us to a jurisdiction foreign to our Constitution and unacknowledged by our laws, giving his assent to their acts of pretended legislation—

For quartering large bodies of armed troops among us;

For protecting them by a mock trial from punishment for any murders which they should commit on the inhabitants of these States;

For cutting off our trade with all parts of the world;

For imposing taxes on us without our consent;

For depriving us, in many cases, of the benefit of trial by jury;

For transporting us beyond seas to be tried for pretended offences;

For abolishing the free system of English laws in a neighboring province, establishing therein an arbitrary government, and enlarging its boundaries, so as to render it at once an example and fit instrument for introducing the same absolute rule into these colonies;

For taking away our charters, abolishing our most valuable laws, and altering, fundamentally, the powers of our governments;

For suspending our own legislatures and declaring themselves invested with power to legislate for us in all cases whatsoever.

He has abdicated government here by declaring us out of his protection and waging war against us.

He has plundered our seas, ravaged our coasts, burnt out towns, and destroyed the lives of our people.

He is, at this time, transporting large armies of foreign mercenaries to complete the works of death, desolation, and tyranny already begun with circumstances of cruelty and perifidy scarcely paralleled in the most barbarous ages, and totally unworthy, the head of a civilized nation.

He has constrained our fellow citizens, taken captive on the high seas, to bear arms against their country, to become the executioners of their friends and brethren, or to fall themselves by their hands.

He has excited domestic insurrections amongst us and has endeavored to bring on the inhabitants of our frontiers, the merciless Indian savages, whose known rule of warfare is an undistinguished destruction of all ages, sexes, and conditions.

In every state of these oppressions, we have petitioned for redress in the most humble terms; our repeated petitions have been answered only by repeated injury. A prince whose character is thus marked by every act which may define a tyrant is unfit to be the ruler of a free people.

Nor have we been wanting in attention to our British brethren. We have warned them, from time to time, of attempts made by their legislature to extend an unwarrantable jurisdiction over us. We have reminded them of the circumstances of our emigration and settlement here. We have appealed to their native justice and magnanimity, and we have conjured them, by the ties of our common kindred, to disavow these usurpations, which would inevitably interrupt our connections and correspondence. They, too, have been deaf to the voice of justice and consanguinity. We must, therefore, acquiesce in the necessity which denounces our separation, and hold them, as we hold the rest of mankind, enemies in war, in peace, friends.

imposing: forcing   **depriving:** taking away
transporting us beyond seas: sending colonists to England for trial   **neighboring province:** Quebec   **arbitrary government:** unjust rule   **fit instrument:** suitable tool
invested with power: having the power

During the years leading up to 1776, the colonists claimed that Parliament had no right to make laws for them because they were not represented in Parliament. Here, the colonists object to recent laws of Parliament, such as the Quartering Act and the blockade of colonial ports (page 153), which cut off their trade. They also object to Parliament's claim that it had the right to tax them without their consent.

abdicated: given up   **plundered:** robbed
ravaged: attacked   **mercenaries:** hired soldiers   **desolation:** misery   **perfidy:** falseness   **barbarous:** uncivilized
constrained: forced   **brethren:** brothers
domestic insurrections: internal revolts

Here, the Declaration lists the third set of wrongs—warlike acts of the king. Instead of listening to the colonists, the king has made war on them. He has hired soldiers to fight in America (page 163).

oppressions: harsh rule   **petitioned:** asked
redress: relief   **unwarrantable jurisdiction over:** unfair authority   **magnanimity:** generosity   **conjured:** called upon
common kindred: relatives   **disavow:** turn away from   **consanguinity:** blood relationships, kinship   **acquiesce:** agree
denounces: speaks out against

During this time, colonists have repeatedly asked for relief. But their requests have brought only more suffering. They have appealed to the British people but received no help. So they are forced to separate.

DECLARATION OF INDEPENDENCE

Colonies Declare Independence

We, therefore, the representatives of the United States of America, in general Congress assembled, appealing to the Supreme Judge of the world for the rectitude of our intentions, do, in the name and by the authority of the good people of these colonies, solemnly publish and declare, that these united colonies are, and of right ought to be, free and independent states: that they are absolved from all allegiance to the British Crown, and that all political connections between them and the state of Great Britain is, and ought to be, totally dissolved; and that, as free and independent states, they have full power to levy war, conclude peace, contract alliances, establish commerce, and to do all other acts and things which independent states may of right do. And, for the support of this declaration, with a firm reliance on the protection of Divine Providence, we mutually pledge to each other our lives, our fortunes, and our sacred honor.

Signers of the Declaration of Independence

John Hancock, President
Charles Thomson, Secretary

New Hampshire
Josiah Bartlett
William Whipple
Matthew Thornton

Massachusetts
Samuel Adams
John Adams
Robert Treat Paine
Elbridge Gerry

Rhode Island
Stephen Hopkins
William Ellery

Connecticut
Roger Sherman
Samuel Huntington
William Williams
Oliver Wolcott

Delaware
Caesar Rodney
George Read
Thomas McKean

New York
William Floyd
Philip Livingston
Francis Lewis
Lewis Morris

New Jersey
Richard Stockton
John Witherspoon
Francis Hopkinson
John Hart
Abraham Clark

Georgia
Button Gwinnett
Lyman Hall
George Walton

Maryland
Samuel Chase
William Paca
Thomas Stone
Charles Carroll

North Carolina
William Hooper
Joseph Hewes
John Penn

Virginia
George Wythe
Richard Henry Lee
Thomas Jefferson
Benjamin Harrison
Thomas Nelson, Jr.
Francis Lightfoot Lee
Carter Braxton

South Carolina
Edward Rutledge
Thomas Heyward, Jr.
Thomas Lynch, Jr.
Arthur Middleton

Pennsylvania
Robert Morris
Benjamin Rush
Benjamin Franklin
John Morton
George Clymer
James Smith
George Taylor
James Wilson
George Ross

DECLARATION OF INDEPENDENCE

The Constitution of the United States of America

The Constitution is printed in black. The titles of articles, sections, and clauses are not part of the original document. They have been added to help you find information in the Constitution. Some words or lines are crossed out because they have been changed by amendments or no longer apply. Annotations, or explanations, are on the tan side of the page. Page numbers in the annotations show where a subject is discussed in the text. Difficult words are defined.

Preamble

We the people of the United States, in order to form a more perfect Union, establish justice, insure domestic tranquillity, provide for the common defense, promote the general welfare, and secure the blessings of liberty to ourselves and our posterity, do ordain and establish this Constitution for the United States of America.

The Preamble describes the purpose of the government set up by the Constitution. Americans expect their government to defend justice and liberty and provide peace and safety from foreign enemies.

Article 1. The Legislative Branch

Section 1. A Two-House Legislature

All legislative powers herein granted shall be vested in a Congress of the United States, which shall consist of a Senate and House of Representatives.

The Constitution gives Congress the power to make laws. Congress is divided into the Senate and the House of Representatives.

Section 2. House of Representatives

1. Election of Members The House of Representatives shall be composed of members chosen every second year by the people of the several states, and the electors in each state shall have the qualifications requisite for electors of the most numerous branch of the state legislature.

Clause 1 *Electors* refers to voters. Members of the House of Representatives are elected every two years. Any citizen allowed to vote for members of the larger house of the state legislature can also vote for members of the House.

2. Qualifications No person shall be a Representative who shall not have attained to the age of twenty-five years, and been seven years a citizen of the United States, and who shall not, when elected, be an inhabitant of that state in which he shall be chosen.

Clause 2 A member of the House of Representatives must be at least 25 years old, an American citizen for 7 years, and a resident of the state he or she represents.

3. Determining Representation Representatives ~~and direct taxes~~ shall be apportioned among the several states which may be included within this Union, according to their respective numbers ~~which shall be determined by adding to the whole number of free persons, including those bound to service for a term of years, and excluding Indians not taxed, three-fifths of all other persons.~~ The actual enumeration shall be made within three years after the first meeting of the Congress of the United States, and within every subsequent term of ten years, in such manner as they shall by law direct. The number of Representatives shall not exceed one for every 30,000, but each state shall have at least one Representative; ~~and until such enumeration shall be made, the state of New Hampshire shall be entitled to choose three; Massachusetts, eight; Rhode Island and Providence Plantations, one; Connecticut, five; New York, six; New Jersey, four; Pennsylvania, eight; Delaware, one; Maryland, six; Virginia, ten; North Carolina, five; South Carolina, five; and Georgia, three.~~

Clause 3 The number of representatives each state elects is based on its population. An *enumeration,* or census, must be taken every 10 years to determine population. Today, the number of representatives in the House is fixed at 435.

This is the famous Three-Fifths Compromise worked out at the Constitutional Convention (page 198). *Persons bound to service* meant indentured servants. *All other persons* meant slaves. All free people in a state were counted. However, only three fifths of the slaves were included in the population count. This three-fifths clause became meaningless when slaves were freed by the Thirteenth Amendment.

Clause 4 *Executive authority* means the governor of a state. If a member of the House leaves office before his or her term ends, the governor must call a special election to fill the seat.

Clause 5 The House elects a speaker. Today, the speaker is usually chosen by the party that has a majority in the House. Also, only the House has the power to *impeach,* or accuse, a federal official of wrongdoing.

Clause 1 Each state has two senators. Senators serve for six-year terms. The Seventeenth Amendment changed the way senators were elected.

Clause 2 Every two years, one third of the senators run for reelection. Thus, the makeup of the Senate is never totally changed by any one election. The Seventeenth Amendment changed the way of filling *vacancies,* or empty seats. Today, the governor of a state must choose a senator to fill a vacancy that occurs between elections.

Clause 3 A senator must be at least 30 years old, an American citizen for 9 years, and a resident of the state he or she represents.

Clause 4 The Vice President presides over Senate meetings, but he or she can vote only to break a tie.

Clause 5 *Pro tempore* means temporary. The Senate chooses one of its members to serve as president pro tempore when the Vice President is absent.

Clause 6 The Senate acts as a jury if the House impeaches a federal official. The Chief Justice of the Supreme Court presides if the President is on trial. Two thirds of all senators present must vote for *conviction,* or finding the accused guilty. No President has ever been convicted. The House impeached President Andrew Johnson in 1868, but the Senate acquitted him of the charges (page 490). In 1974, President Richard Nixon resigned before he could be impeached.

Clause 7 If an official is found guilty by the Senate, he or she can be removed from office and barred from holding federal office in the future. These are the only punishments the Senate can impose. However, the convicted official can still be tried in a criminal court.

4. Filling Vacancies When vacancies happen in the representation from any state, the executive authority thereof shall issue writs of election to fill such vacancies.

5. Selection of Officers; Power of Impeachment The House of Representatives shall choose their Speaker and other officers; and shall have the sole power of impeachment.

Section 3. The Senate

1. Selection of Members The Senate of the United States shall be composed of two Senators from each state ~~chosen by the legislature thereof,~~ for six years, and each Senator shall have one vote.

2. Alternating Terms; Filling Vacancies Immediately after they shall be assembled in consequence of the first election, they shall be divided as equally as may be into three classes. ~~The seats of the Senators of the first class shall be vacated at the expiration of the second year, of the second class at the expiration of the fourth year, and of the third class at the expiration of the sixth year,~~ so that one-third may be chosen every second year; ~~and if vacancies happen by resignation, or otherwise, during the recess of the legislature of any state, the executive thereof may make temporary appointments until the next meeting of the legislature, which shall then fill such vacancies.~~

3. Qualifications No person shall be a Senator who shall not have attained to the age of thirty years, and been nine years a citizen of the United States, and who shall not, when elected, be an inhabitant of that state for which he shall be chosen.

4. President of the Senate The Vice-President of the United States shall be president of the Senate, but shall have no vote, unless they be equally divided.

5. Election of Senate Officers The Senate shall choose their other officers, and also a president *pro tempore,* in the absence of the Vice-President, or when he shall exercise the office of the President of the United States.

6. Impeachment Trials The Senate shall have the sole power to try all impeachments. When sitting for that purpose, they shall be on oath or affirmation. When the President of the United States is tried, the Chief Justice shall preside; and no person shall be convicted without the concurrence of two-thirds of the members present.

7. Penalties Upon Conviction Judgment in cases of impeachment shall not extend further than to removal from office, and disqualification to hold and enjoy any office of honor, trust, or profit under the United States; but the party convicted shall nevertheless be liable and subject to indictment, trial, judgment, and punishment, according to law.

Section 4. Elections and Meetings

1. Election of Congress The times, places, and manner of holding elections for Senators and Representatives shall be prescribed in each state by the legislature thereof; but the Congress may at any time by law make or alter such regulations, except as to the places of choosing Senators.

2. Annual Sessions The Congress shall assemble at least once in every year, ~~and such meeting shall be on the first Monday in December, unless they shall by law appoint a different day.~~

Section 5. Rules for the Conduct of Business

1. Organization Each house shall be the judge of the elections, returns, and qualifications of its own members, and a majority of each shall constitute a quorum to do business; but a smaller number may adjourn from day to day, and may be authorized to compel the attendance of absent members, in such manner, and under such penalties, as each house may provide.

2. Procedures Each house may determine the rules of its proceedings, punish its members for disorderly behavior, and with the concurrence of two-thirds, expel a member.

3. A Written Record Each house shall keep a journal of its proceedings, and from time to time publish the same, excepting such parts as may in their judgment require secrecy; and the yeas and nays of the members of either house on any question shall, at the desire of one-fifth of those present, be entered on the journal.

4. Rules for Adjournment Neither house, during the session of Congress, shall, without the consent of the other, adjourn for more than three days, nor to any other place than that in which the two houses shall be sitting.

Section 6. Privileges and Restrictions

1. Salaries and Immunities The Senators and Representatives shall receive a compensation for their services, to be ascertained by law and paid out of the Treasury of the United States. They shall in all cases, except treason, felony, and breach of the peace, be privileged from arrest during their attendance at the session of their respective houses, and in going to and returning from the same; and for any speech or debate in either house, they shall not be questioned in any other place.

2. Restrictions on Other Employment No Senator or Representative shall, during the time for which he was elected, be appointed to any civil office under the authority of the United States, which shall have been created, or the emoluments whereof shall have been increased, during such time; and no person holding any office under the United States shall be a member of either house during his continuance in office.

Clause 1 Each state legislature can decide when and how congressional elections take place, but Congress can overrule these decisions. In 1842, Congress required each state to set up congressional districts with one representative elected from each district. In 1872, Congress decided that congressional elections must be held in every state on the same date in even-numbered years.

Clause 2 Congress must meet at least once a year. The Twentieth Amendment moved the opening date of Congress to January 3.

Clause 1 Each house decides whether a member has the qualifications for office set by the Constitution. A *quorum* is the smallest number of members who must be present for business to be conducted. Each house can set its own rules about absent members.

Clause 2 Each house can make rules for the conduct of members. It can only expel a member by a two-thirds vote.

Clause 3 Each house keeps a record of its meetings. *The Congressional Record* is published every day with excerpts from speeches made in each house. It also records the votes of each member.

Clause 4 Neither house can *adjourn,* or stop meeting, for more than three days unless the other house approves. Both houses of Congress must meet in the same city.

Clause 1 *Compensation* means salary. Congress decides the salary for its members. While Congress is in session, a member is free from arrest in civil cases and cannot be sued for anything he or she says on the floor of Congress. This allows for freedom of debate. However, a member can be arrested for a criminal offense.

Clause 2 *Emolument* also means salary. A member of Congress cannot hold another federal office during his or her term. A former member of Congress cannot hold an office created while he or she was in Congress. An official in another branch of government cannot serve at the same time in Congress. This strengthens the separation of powers.

Clause 1 *Revenue* is money raised by the government through taxes. Tax bills must be introduced in the House. The Senate, however, can make changes in tax bills. This clause protects the principle that people can be taxed only with their consent.

Clause 2 A *bill,* or proposed law, that is passed by a majority of the House and Senate is sent to the President. If the President signs the bill, it becomes law.

A bill can also become law without the President's signature. The President can refuse to act on a bill. If Congress is in session at the time, the bill becomes law 10 days after the President receives it.

The President can *veto,* or reject, a bill by sending it back to the house where it was introduced. Or if the President refuses to act on a bill and Congress adjourns within 10 days, then the bill dies. This way of killing a bill without taking action is called the *pocket veto.*

Congress can override the President's veto if each house of Congress passes the bill again by a two-thirds vote. This clause is an important part of the system of checks and balances (page 203).

Clause 3 Congress can pass resolutions or orders that have the same force as laws. Any such resolution or order must be signed by the President (except on questions of adjournment). Thus, this clause prevents Congress from bypassing the President simply by calling a bill by another name.

Clause 1 *Duties* are tariffs. *Imposts* are taxes in general. *Excises* are taxes on the production or sale of certain goods. Congress has the power to tax and spend tax money. Taxes must be the same in all parts of the country.

Clause 2 Congress can borrow money for the United States. The government often borrows money by selling *bonds,* or certificates that promise to pay the holder a certain sum of money on a certain date (page 245).

Clause 3 Only Congress has the power to regulate foreign and *interstate trade,* or trade between states. Disagreements over interstate trade was a major problem with the Articles of Confederation (pages 190–191).

Section 7. Law-Making Process

1. Tax Bills All bills for raising revenue shall originate in the House of Representatives; but the Senate may propose or concur with amendments as on other bills.

2. How a Bill Becomes a Law Every bill which shall have passed the House of Representatives and the Senate shall, before it become a law, be presented to the President of the United States; if he approve, he shall sign it, but if not, he shall return it, with his objections, to that house in which it shall have originated, who shall enter the objections at large on their journal, and proceed to reconsider it. If after such reconsideration two-thirds of that house shall agree to pass the bill, it shall be sent, together with the objections, to the other house, by which it shall likewise be reconsidered, and, if approved by two-thirds of that house, it shall become a law. But in all such cases the votes of both houses shall be determined by yeas and nays, and the names of the persons voting for and against the bill shall be entered on the journal of each house respectively. If any bill shall not be returned by the President within ten days (Sundays excepted) after it shall have been presented to him, the same bill shall be a law, in like manner as if he had signed it, unless the Congress by their adjournment prevent its return, in which case it shall not be a law.

3. Resolutions Passed by Congress Every order, resolution, or vote to which the concurrence of the Senate and House of Representatives may be necessary (except on a question of adjournment) shall be presented to the President of the United States; and before the same shall take effect, shall be approved by him, or being disapproved by him, shall be repassed by two-thirds of the Senate and House of Representatives, according to the rules and limitations prescribed in the case of a bill.

Section 8. Powers Delegated to Congress

The Congress shall have power

1. Taxes To lay and collect taxes, duties, imposts, and excises, to pay the debts and provide for the common defense and general welfare of the United States; but all duties, imposts, and excises shall be uniform throughout the United States;

2. Borrowing To borrow money on the credit of the United States;

3. Commerce To regulate commerce with foreign nations, and among the several states, and with the Indian tribes;

4. Naturalization; Bankruptcy To establish a uniform rule of naturalization, and uniform laws on the subject of bankruptcies throughout the United States;

5. Coins; Weights; Measures To coin money, regulate the value thereof, and of foreign coin, and fix the standard of weights and measures;

6. Counterfeiting To provide for the punishment of counterfeiting the securities and current coin of the United States;

7. Post Offices To establish post offices and post roads;

8. Copyrights; Patents To promote the progress of science and useful arts by securing for limited times to authors and inventors the exclusive right to their respective writings and discoveries;

9. Federal Courts To constitute tribunals inferior to the Supreme Court;

10. Piracy To define and punish piracies and felonies committed on the high seas and offenses against the law of nations;

11. Declarations of War To declare war, ~~grant letters of marque and reprisal~~, and make rules concerning captures on land and water;

12. Army To raise and support armies, but no appropriation of money to that use shall be for a longer term than two years;

13. Navy To provide and maintain a navy;

14. Rules for the Military To make rules for the government and regulation of the land and naval forces;

15. Militia To provide for calling forth the militia to execute the laws of the Union, suppress insurrections, and repel invasions;

16. Rules for the Militia To provide for organizing, arming, and disciplining the militia, and for governing such part of them as may be employed in the service of the United States, reserving to the states, respectively, the appointment of the officers, and the authority of training the militia according to the discipline prescribed by Congress;

17. National Capital To exercise exclusive legislation in all cases whatsoever, over such district (not exceeding ten miles square) as may, by cession of particular states, and the acceptance of Congress, become the seat of government of the United States, and to exercise like authority over all places purchased by the

Clause 4 *Naturalization* is the process whereby a foreigner becomes a citizen. *Bankruptcy* is the condition in which a person or business cannot pay its debts. Congress has the power to pass laws on these two issues. The laws must be the same in all parts of the country.

Clause 5 Congress has the power to coin money and set its value. Congress has set up the National Bureau of Standards to regulate weights and measures.

Clause 6 *Counterfeiting* is the making of imitation money. *Securities* are bonds. Congress can make laws to punish counterfeiters.

Clause 7 Congress has the power to set up and control the delivery of mail.

Clause 8 Congress may pass copyright and patent laws. A *copyright* protects an author. A patent makes an inventor the sole owner of his or her work for a limited time.

Clause 9 Congress has the power to set up *inferior,* or lower, federal courts under the Supreme Court.

Clause 10 Congress can punish *piracy,* or the robbing of ships at sea.

Clause 11 Only Congress can declare war. Declarations of war are granted at the request of the President. *Letters of marque and reprisal* were documents issued by a government allowing merchant ships to arm themselves and attack ships of an enemy nation. They are no longer issued.

Clauses 12, 13, 14 These clauses place the army and navy under the control of Congress. Congress decides on the size of the armed forces and the amount of money to spend on the army and navy. It also has the power to write rules governing the armed forces.

Clauses 15, 16 The *militia* is a body of citizen soldiers. Congress can call up the militia to put down rebellions or fight foreign invaders. Each state has its own militia, today called the National Guard. Normally, the militia is under the command of a state's governor. However, it can be placed under the command of the President.

Clause 17 Congress controls the district around the national capital. In 1790, Congress made Washington, D.C., the nation's capital (page 247). In 1973, it gave residents of the District the right to elect local officials.

Clause 18 Clauses 1–17 list the powers delegated to Congress. The writers of the Constitution added Clause 18 so that Congress could deal with the changing needs of the nation. It gives Congress the power to make laws as needed to carry out the first 17 clauses. Clause 18 is sometimes called the elastic clause because it lets Congress stretch the meaning of its power.

Clause 1 *Such persons* means slaves. This clause resulted from a compromise between the supporters and the opponents of the slave trade (page 198). In 1808, as soon as Congress was permitted to abolish the slave trade, it did so. The $10 import tax was never imposed.

Clause 2 A *writ of habeas corpus* is a court order requiring government officials to bring a prisoner to court and explain why he or she is being held. A writ of habeas corpus protects people from unlawful imprisonment. The government cannot suspend this right except in times of rebellion or invasion.

Clause 3 A *bill of attainder* is a law declaring that a person is guilty of a particular crime. An *ex post facto law* punishes an act which was not illegal when it was committed. Congress cannot pass a bill of attainder or ex post facto laws.

Clause 4 A *capitation tax* is a tax placed directly on each person. *Direct taxes* are taxes on people or on land. They can be passed only if they are divided among the states according to population. The Sixteenth Amendment allowed Congress to tax income without regard to the population of the states.

Clause 5 This clause forbids Congress to tax exports. In 1787, southerners insisted on this clause because their economy depended on exports.

Clause 6 Congress cannot make laws that favor one state over another in trade and commerce. Also, states cannot place tariffs on interstate trade.

Clause 7 The federal government cannot spend money unless Congress *appropriates* it, or passes a law allowing it. This clause gives Congress an important check on the President by controlling the money he or she can spend. The government must publish a statement showing how it spends public funds.

consent of the legislature of the state in which the same shall be, for the erection of forts, magazines, arsenals, dock-yards, and other needful buildings; —and

18. Necessary Laws To make all laws which shall be necessary and proper for carrying into execution the foregoing powers, and all other powers vested by this Constitution in the government of the United States, or in any department or officer thereof.

Section 9. Powers Denied to the Federal Government

1. The Slave Trade ~~The migration or importation of such persons as any of the states now existing shall think proper to admit shall not be prohibited by the Congress prior to the year 1808; but a tax or duty may be imposed on such importation, not exceeding $10 for each person.~~

2. Writ of Habeas Corpus The privilege of the writ of habeas corpus shall not be suspended, unless when in cases of rebellion or invasion the public safety may require it.

3. Bills of Attainder and Ex Post Facto Laws No bill of attainder or *ex post facto* law shall be passed.

4. Apportionment of Direct Taxes ~~No capitation or other direct tax shall be laid, unless in proportion to the census or enumeration herein before directed to be taken.~~

5. Taxes on Exports No tax or duty shall be laid on articles exported from any state.

6. Special Preference for Trade No preference shall be given any regulation of commerce or revenue to the ports of one state over those of another; nor shall vessels bound to, or from, one state, be obliged to enter, clear, or pay duties in another.

7. Spending No money shall be drawn from the Treasury, but in consequence of appropriations made by law; and a regular statement and account of the receipts and expenditures of all public money shall be published from time to time.

THE CONSTITUTION

8. Creation of Titles of Nobility No title of nobility shall be granted by the United States; and no person holding any office of profit or trust under them, shall, without the consent of the Congress, accept of any present, emolument, office, or title, of any kind whatever, from any king, prince, or foreign state.

Section 10. Powers Denied to the States

1. Unconditional Prohibitions No state shall enter into any treaty, alliance, or confederation; grant letters of marque and reprisal; coin money; emit bills of credit; make anything but gold and silver coin a tender in payment of debts; pass any bill of attainder, *ex post facto* law, or law impairing the obligation of contracts, or grant any title of nobility.

2. Powers Conditionally Denied No state shall, without the consent of the Congress, lay any imposts or duties on imports or exports, except what may be absolutely necessary for executing its inspection laws; and the net produce of all duties and imposts, laid by any state on imports or exports, shall be for the use of the Treasury of the United States; and all such laws shall be subject to the revision and control of the Congress.

3. Other Denied Powers No state shall, without the consent of Congress, lay any duty of tonnage, keep troops, or ships of war in time of peace, enter into any agreement or compact with another state, or with a foreign power, or engage in war, unless actually invaded, or in such imminent danger as will not admit of delay.

Article 2. The Executive Branch

Section 1. President and Vice-President

1. Chief Executive The executive power shall be vested in a President of the United States of America. He shall hold his office during the term of four years, and together with the Vice-President, chosen for the same term, be elected as follows:

2. Selection of Electors Each state shall appoint, in such manner as the legislature thereof may direct, a number of electors, equal to the whole number of Senators and Representatives to which the state may be entitled in the Congress; but no Senator or Representative, or person holding an office or trust or profit under the United States, shall be appointed an elector.

3. Electoral College Procedures ~~The electors shall meet in their respective states, and vote by ballot for two persons, of whom one at least shall not be an inhabitant of the same state with themselves. And they shall make a list of all the persons voted for, and of the number of votes for each; which list they shall sign and certify, and transmit sealed to the seat of the government of the United States, directed to the president of the Senate. The president of the Senate shall, in the presence of the Senate and House of Representatives, open all the certificates, and the votes shall then be counted. The person having the greatest number of votes shall be President, if such number be a majority of the whole number of electors appointed; and if there be more than one who have such majority, and have an equal number of votes, then the House of Representatives shall immediately choose by~~

Clause 8 The government cannot award titles of nobility, such as Duke or Duchess. American citizens cannot accept titles of nobility from foreign governments without the consent of Congress.

Clause 1 The writers of the Constitution did not want the states to act like separate nations. So they prohibited states from making treaties or coining money. Some powers denied to the federal government are also denied to the states. For example, states cannot pass ex post facto laws.

Clauses 2, 3 Powers listed here are forbidden to the states, but Congress can lift these prohibitions by passing laws that give these powers to the states.

Clause 2 forbids states from taxing imports and exports without the consent of Congress. States may charge inspection fees on goods entering the states. Any profit from these fees must be turned over to the United States Treasury.

Clause 3 forbids states from keeping an army or navy without the consent of Congress. States cannot make treaties or declare war unless an enemy invades or is about to invade.

Clause 1 The President is responsible for **executing,** or carrying out, laws passed by Congress.

Clauses 2, 3 Some writers of the Constitution were afraid to allow the people to elect the President directly (page 203). Therefore, the Constitutional Convention set up the electoral college. Clause 2 directs each state to choose electors, or delegates to the electoral college, to vote for President. A state's electoral vote is equal to the combined number of senators and representatives. Each state may decide how to choose its electors. Members of Congress and federal officeholders may not serve as electors. This much of the original electoral college system is still in effect.

Clause 3 called upon each elector to vote for two candidates. The candidate who received a majority of the electoral votes would become President. The runner-up would become Vice President. If no candidate won a majority, the House would choose the President. The Senate would choose the Vice President.

The election of 1800 showed a problem with the original electoral college system (page

261). Thomas Jefferson was the Republican candidate for President, and Aaron Burr was the Republican candidate for Vice President. In the electoral college, the vote ended in a tie. The election was finally decided in the House, where Jefferson was chosen President. The Twelfth Amendment changed the electoral college system so that this could not happen again.

ballot one of them for President; and if no person have a majority, then from the five highest on the list the said House shall in like manner choose the President. But in choosing the President the votes shall be taken by states, the representation from each state having one vote. A quorum for this purpose shall consist of a member or members from two-thirds of the states, and a majority of all the states shall be necessary to a choice. In every case, after the choice of the President, the person having the greatest number of votes of the electors shall be the Vice-President. But if there should remain two or more who have equal votes, the Senate shall choose from them by ballot the Vice-President.

Clause 4 Under a law passed in 1792, electors are chosen on the Tuesday following the first Monday of November every four years. Electors from each state meet to vote in December.

Today, voters in each state choose **slates,** or groups, of electors who are pledged to a candidate for President. The candidate for President who wins the popular vote in each state wins that state's electoral vote.

4. Time of Elections The Congress may determine the time of choosing the electors, and the day on which they shall give their votes; which day shall be the same throughout the United States.

Clause 5 The President must be a citizen of the United States from birth, at least 35 years old, and a resident of the country for 14 years. The first seven Presidents of the United States were born under British rule, but they were allowed to hold office because they were citizens at the time the Constitution was adopted.

5. Qualifications for President No person except a natural-born citizen or a citizen of the United States, at the time of the adoption of this Constitution, shall be eligible to the office of the President; neither shall any person be eligible to that office who shall not have attained to the age of thirty-five years, and been fourteen years a resident within the United States.

Clause 6 The powers of the President pass to the Vice President if the President leaves office or cannot discharge his or her duties. The wording of this clause caused confusion the first time a President died in office. When President William Henry Harrison died, it was uncertain whether Vice President John Tyler should remain Vice President and act as President or whether he should be sworn in as President. Tyler persuaded a federal judge to swear him in. So he set the precedent that the Vice President assumes the office of President when it becomes vacant. The Twenty-fifth Amendment replaced this clause.

6. Presidential Succession In case of the removal of the President from office, or of his death, resignation, or inability to discharge the powers and duties of the said office, the same shall devolve on the Vice-President, and the Congress may by law provide for the case of removal, death, resignation, or inability, both of the President and Vice-President, declaring what officer shall then act as President, and such officer shall act accordingly, until the disability be removed, or a President shall be elected.

Clause 7 The President is paid a salary. It cannot be raised or lowered during his or her term of office. The President is not allowed to hold any other federal or state position while in office. Today, the President's salary is $200,000 a year.

7. Salary The President shall, at stated times, receive for his services, a compensation, which shall neither be increased nor diminished during the period for which he shall have been elected, and he shall not receive within that period any other emolument from the United States, or any of them.

Clause 8 Before taking office, the President must promise to protect and defend the Constitution. Usually, the Chief Justice of the Supreme Court administers the oath of office to the President.

8. Oath of Office Before he enter on the execution of his office, he shall take the following oath or affirmation:—"I do solemnly swear (or affirm) that I will faithfully execute the office of President of the United States, and will to the best of my ability, preserve, protect, and defend the Constitution of the United States."

Section 2. Powers of the President

1. Commander in Chief of the Armed Forces The President shall be Commander in Chief of the Army and Navy of the United States, and of the militia of the several states, when called into the actual service of the United States; he may require the opinion, in writing, of the principal officer in each of the executive departments, upon any subject relating to the duties of their respective offices, and he shall have power to grant reprieves and pardons for offenses against the United States, except in cases of impeachment.

2. Making Treaties and Nominations He shall have power, by and with the advice and consent of the Senate, to make treaties, provided two-thirds of the Senators present concur; and he shall nominate, and by and with the advice and consent of the Senate, shall appoint ambassadors, other public ministers and consuls, judges of the Supreme Court, and all other officers of the United States, whose appointments are not herein otherwise provided for, and which shall be established by law; but the Congress may by law vest the appointment of such inferior officers, as they think proper, in the President alone, in the courts of law, or in the heads of departments.

3. Temporary Appointments The President shall have power to fill up all vacancies that may happen during the recess of the Senate, by granting commissions which shall expire at the end of their next session.

Section 3. Duties

He shall from time to time give to the Congress information of the state of the Union, and recommend to their consideration such measures as he shall judge necessary and expedient; he may, on extraordinary occasions, convene both houses, or either of them, and in case of disagreement between them, with respect to the time of adjournment, he may adjourn them to such time as he shall think proper; he shall receive ambassadors and other public ministers; he shall take care that the laws be faithfully executed, and shall commission all the officers of the United States.

Section 4. Impeachment and Removal From Office

The President, Vice-President, and all civil officers of the United States, shall be removed from office on impeachment for, and conviction of, treason, bribery, or other high crimes or misdemeanors.

Article 3. The Judicial Branch

Section 1. Federal Courts

The judicial power of the United States shall be vested in one Supreme Court, and in such inferior courts as the Congress may from time to time ordain and establish. The judges, both of the Supreme and inferior courts, shall hold their offices during good

Clause 1 The President is head of the armed forces and the state militias when they are called into national service. So the military is under **civilian,** or nonmilitary, control.

The President can get advice from the heads of executive departments. In most cases, the President has the power to grant a reprieve or pardon. A **reprieve** suspends punishment ordered by law. A **pardon** prevents prosecution for a crime or overrides the judgment of a court.

Clause 2 The President has the power to make treaties with other nations. Under the system of checks and balances, all treaties must be approved by two thirds of the Senate. Today, the President also makes agreements with foreign governments. These executive agreements do not need Senate approval.

The President has the power to appoint ambassadors to foreign countries and to appoint other high officials. The Senate must **confirm,** or approve, these appointments.

Clause 3 If the Senate is in **recess,** or not meeting, the President may fill vacant government posts by making temporary appointments.

The President must give Congress a report on the condition of the nation every year. This report is now called the State of the Union Address. Since 1913, the President has given this speech in person each January.

The President can call a special session of Congress and can adjourn Congress if necessary. The President has the power to receive, or recognize, foreign ambassadors.

The President must carry out the laws. Today, many government agencies oversee the execution of laws.

Civil officers include federal judges and members of the Cabinet. **High crimes** are major crimes. **Misdemeanors** are lesser crimes. The President, Vice President, and others can be forced out of office if impeached and found guilty of certain crimes. Andrew Johnson is the only President to have been impeached.

Judicial power means the right of the courts to decide legal cases. The Constitution creates the Supreme Court but lets Congress decide on the size of the Supreme Court. Congress has the power to set up inferior, or lower, courts. The Judiciary Act of 1789 (page 245) set up a system of district and circuit courts, or courts of appeal. Today, there are 95 district courts and 11 courts of appeal. All federal judges serve for life.

Clause 1 *Jurisdiction* refers to the right of a court to hear a case. Federal courts have jurisdiction over cases that involve the Constitution, federal laws, treaties, foreign ambassadors and diplomats, naval and maritime laws, disagreements between states or between citizens from different states, and disputes between a state or citizen and a foreign state or citizen.

In *Marbury* v. *Madison* (page 270), the Supreme Court established the right to judge whether a law is constitutional.

Clause 2 *Original jurisdiction* means the power of a court to hear a case where it first arises. The Supreme Court has original jurisdiction over only a few cases, such as those involving foreign diplomats. More often, the Supreme Court acts as an appellate court. An *appellate court* does not decide guilt. It decides whether the lower court trial was properly conducted and reviews the lower court's decision.

Clause 3 This clause guarantees the right to a jury trial for anyone accused of a federal crime. The only exceptions are impeachment cases. The trial must be held in the state where the crime was committed.

Clause 1 Treason is clearly defined. An *overt act* is an actual action. A person cannot be convicted of treason for what he or she thinks. A person can be convicted of treason only if he or she confesses or two witnesses testify to it.

Clause 2 Congress has the power to set the punishment for traitors. Congress may not punish the children of convicted traitors by taking away their civil rights or property.

Each state must recognize the official acts and records of any other state. For example, each state must recognize marriage certificates issued by another state. Congress can pass laws to ensure this.

behavior, and shall, at stated times, receive for their services a compensation, which shall not be diminished during their continuance in office.

Section 2. Jurisdiction of Federal Courts

1. Scope of Judicial Power The judicial power shall extend to all cases, in law and equity, arising under this Constitution, the laws of the United States, and treaties made or which shall be made, under their authority; to all cases affecting ambassadors, other public ministers and consuls; to all cases of admiralty and maritime jurisdiction; to controversies to which the United States shall be a party; to controversies between two or more states; between a state and citizens of another state; between citizens of the same state claiming lands under grants of different states, and between a state or the citizens thereof, and foreign states, citizens, or subjects.

2. The Supreme Court In all cases affecting ambassadors, other public ministers and consuls, and those in which a state shall be a party, the Supreme Court shall have original jurisdiction. In all the other cases before mentioned, the Supreme Court shall have appellate jurisdiction, both as to law and fact, with such exceptions, and under such regulations as the Congress shall make.

3. Trial by Jury The trial of all crimes, except in cases of impeachment, shall be by jury; and such trial shall be held in the state where the said crimes shall have been committed; but when not committed within any state, the trial shall be at such place or places as the Congress may by law have directed.

Section 3. Treason

1. Definition Treason against the United States shall consist only in levying war against them, or in adhering to their enemies, giving them aid and comfort. No person shall be convicted of treason unless on the testimony of two witnesses to the same overt act, or on confession in open court.

2. Punishment The Congress shall have power to declare the punishment of treason, but no attainder of treason shall work corruption of blood or forfeiture except during the life of the person attainted.

Article 4. Relations Among the States

Section 1. Official Records and Acts

Full faith and credit shall be given in each state to the public acts, records, and judicial proceedings of every other state. And the Congress may by general laws prescribe the manner in which such acts, records, and proceedings shall be proved, and the effect thereof.

Section 2. Privileges of Citizens

1. Privileges The citizens of each state shall be entitled to all privileges and immunities of citizens in the several states.

2. Extradition A person charged in any state with treason, felony, or other crime, who shall flee from justice, and be found in another state, shall on demand of the executive authority of the state from which he fled, be delivered up, to be removed to the state having jurisdiction of the crime.

3. Return of Fugitive Slaves ~~No person held to service or labor in one state, under the laws thereof, escaping into another, shall in consequence of any law or regulation therein, be discharged from such service or labor, but shall be delivered up on claim of the party to whom such service or labor may be due.~~

Section 3. New States and Territories

1. New States New states may be admitted by the Congress into this Union; but no new state shall be formed or erected within the jurisdiction of any other state; nor any state be formed by the junction of two of more states, or parts of states, without the consent of the legislatures of the states concerned as well as of the Congress.

2. Federal Lands The Congress shall have power to dispose of and make all needful rules and regulations respecting the territory or other property belonging to the United States; and nothing in this Constitution shall be so construed as to prejudice any claims of the United States, or of any particular state.

Section 4. Guarantees to the States

The United States shall guarantee to every state in this Union a republican form of government, and shall protect each of them against invasion; and on application of the legislature, or of the executive (when the legislature cannot be convened) against domestic violence.

Article 5. Amending the Constitution

The Congress, whenever two-thirds of both houses shall deem it necessary, shall propose amendments to this Constitution, or, on the application of the legislatures of two-thirds of the several states, shall call a convention for proposing amendments, which, in either case, shall be valid to all intents and purposes, as part of this Constitution, when ratified by the legislatures of three-fourths of the several states, or by conventions in three-fourths thereof, as the one or the other mode of ratification may be proposed by the Congress; provided that ~~no amendments which may be made prior to the year 1808 shall in any manner affect the first and fourth clauses in the Ninth Section of the First Article;~~ and that no state, without its consent, shall be deprived of its equal suffrage in the Senate.

Clause 1 All states must treat citizens of another state in the same way it treats its own citizens. However, the courts have allowed states to give residents certain privileges, such as lower tuition rates.

Clause 2 *Extradition* means the act of returning a suspected criminal or escaped prisoner to a state where he or she is wanted. State governors must return a suspect to another state. However, the Supreme Court has ruled that a governor cannot be forced to do so if he or she feels that justice will not be done.

Clause 3 *Persons held to service or labor* refers to slaves or indentured servants. This clause required states to return runaway slaves to their owners. The Thirteenth Amendment replaces this clause.

Clause 1 Congress has the power to admit new states to the Union. Existing states cannot be split up or joined together to form new states unless both Congress and the state legislatures approve. New states are equal to all other states.

Clause 2 Congress can make rules for managing and governing land owned by the United States. This includes territories not organized into states, such as Puerto Rico and Guam, and federal lands within a state.

In a *republic,* voters choose representatives to govern them. The federal government must protect the states from foreign invasion and from *domestic,* or internal, disorder if asked to do so by a state.

The Constitution can be *amended,* or changed, if necessary. An amendment can be proposed by (1) a two-thirds vote of both houses of Congress or (2) a national convention called by Congress at the request of two thirds of the state legislatures. (This second method has never been used.) An amendment must be *ratified,* or approved, by (1) three fourths of the state legislatures or (2) special conventions in three fourths of the states. Congress decides which method will be used.

Article 6. National Supremacy

Section 1. Prior Public Debts

The United States government promised to pay all debts and honor all agreements made under the Articles of Confederation.

All debts contracted and engagements entered into, before the adoption of this Constitution, shall be as valid against the United States under this Constitution, as under the Confederation.

Section 2. Supreme Law of the Land

The Constitution, federal laws, and treaties that the Senate has ratified are the supreme, or highest, law of the land. Thus, they outweigh state laws. A state judge must overturn a state law that conflicts with the Constitution or with a federal law.

This Constitution, and the laws of the United States which shall be made in pursuance thereof, and all treaties made, or which shall be made, under the authority of the United States, shall be the supreme law of the land; and the judges in every state shall be bound thereby, anything in the constitution or laws of any state to the contrary notwithstanding.

Section 3. Oaths of Office

State and federal officeholders take an oath, or solemn promise, to support the Constitution. However, this clause forbids the use of religious tests for officeholders. During the colonial period, every colony except Rhode Island required a religious test for officeholders.

The Senators and Representatives before mentioned, and the members of the several state legislatures, and all executive and judicial officers, both of the United States and of the several states, shall be bound by oath or affirmation, to support this Constitution; but no religious test shall ever be required as a qualification to any office or public trust under the United States.

Article 7. Ratification

During 1787 and 1788, states held special conventions. By October 1788, the required nine states had ratified the Constitution.

The ratification of the convention of nine states shall be sufficient for the establishment of the Constitution between the states so ratifying the same.

Done in Convention, by the unanimous consent of the states present, the seventeenth day of September, in the year of our Lord one thousand seven hundred and eighty-seven, and of the independence of the United States of America the twelfth. *In Witness* whereof, we have hereunto subscribed our names.

Attest: William Jackson
Secretary

George Washington
President and Deputy from Virginia

New Hampshire
John Langdon
Nicholas Gilman

Massachusetts
Nathaniel Gorham
Rufus King

Connecticut
William Samuel Johnson
Roger Sherman

New York
Alexander Hamilton

New Jersey
William Livingston
David Brearley
William Paterson
Jonathan Dayton

Pennsylvania
Benjamin Franklin
Thomas Mifflin
Robert Morris
George Clymer
Thomas Fitzsimons
Jared Ingersoll
James Wilson
Gouverneur Morris

Delaware
George Read
Gunning Bedford, Jr.
John Dickinson
Richard Bassett
Jacob Broom

Maryland
James McHenry
Dan of St. Thomas Jennifer
Daniel Carroll

Virginia
John Blair
James Madison, Jr.

North Carolina
William Blount
Richard Dobbs Spaight
Hugh Williamson

South Carolina
John Rutledge
Charles Cotesworth Pinckney
Charles Pinckney
Pierce Butler

Georgia
William Few
Abraham Baldwin

Amendments to the Constitution

The first ten amendments, which were added to the Constitution in 1791, are called the Bill of Rights. Originally, the Bill of Rights applied only to actions of the federal government. However, the Supreme Court has used the due process clause of the Fourteenth Amendment to extend many of the rights to protect individuals against action by the states.

Amendment 1
Freedoms of Religion, Speech, Press, Assembly, and Petition

Congress shall make no law respecting an establishment of religion, or prohibiting the free exercise thereof; or abridging the freedom of speech, or of the press; or the right of the people peaceably to assemble, and to petition the government for a redress of grievances.

The First Amendment protects five basic rights: freedom of religion, speech, the press, assembly, and petition. Congress cannot set up an established, or official, church or religion for the nation. During the colonial period, most colonies had established churches. However, the authors of the First Amendment wanted to keep government and religion separate.

Congress may not **abridge,** or limit, the freedom to speak and write freely. The government may not censor, or review, books and newspapers before they are printed. This amendment also protects the right to assemble, or hold public meetings. **Petition** means ask. **Redress** means to correct. **Grievances** are wrongs. The people have the right to ask the government for wrongs to be corrected.

Amendment 2
Right to Bear Arms

A well-regulated militia, being necessary to the security of a free state, the right of the people to keep and bear arms shall not be infringed.

State militia, such as the National Guard, have the right to bear arms, or keep weapons. Courts have generally ruled that the government can regulate the ownership of guns by private citizens.

Amendment 3
Lodging Troops in Private Homes

No soldier shall, in time of peace, be quartered in any house, without the consent of the owner; nor in time of war, but in a manner to be prescribed by law.

During the colonial period, the British quartered, or housed, soldiers in private homes without the permission of the owners (page 153). This amendment limits the government's right to use private homes to house soldiers.

Amendment 4
Search and Seizure

The right of the people to be secure in their persons, houses, papers, and effects, against unreasonable searches and seizures, shall not be violated; and no warrants shall issue but upon probable cause, supported by oath or affirmation, and particularly describing the place to be searched, and the persons or things to be seized.

This amendment protects Americans from unreasonable searches and seizures. Search and seizure are permitted only if a judge has issued a **warrant,** or written court order. A warrant is issued only if there is probable cause. This means an officer must show that it is probable, or likely, that the search will produce evidence of a crime. A search warrant must name the exact place to be searched and the things to be seized.

THE CONSTITUTION

In some cases, courts have ruled that searches can take place without a warrant. For example, police may search a person who is under arrest. However, evidence found during an unlawful search cannot be used in a trial.

This amendment protects the rights of the accused. *Capital crimes* are those that can be punished with death. *Infamous crimes* are those that can be punished with prison or loss of rights. The federal government must obtain an *indictment,* or formal accusation, from a grand jury to prosecute anyone for such crimes. A *grand jury* is a panel of between 12 and 23 citizens who decide if the government has enough evidence to justify a trial. This procedure prevents the government from prosecuting people with little or no evidence of guilt. (Soldiers and the militia in wartime are not covered by this rule.)

    Double jeopardy is forbidden by this amendment. This means that a person cannot be tried twice for the same crime. However, if a court sets aside a conviction because of a legal error, the accused can be tried again. A person on trial cannot be forced to testify, or give evidence, against himself or herself. A person accused of a crime is entitled to *due process of law,* or a fair hearing or trial.

    Finally, the government cannot seize private property for public use without paying the owner a fair price for it.

In criminal cases, the jury must be *impartial,* or not favor either side. The accused is guaranteed the right to a trial by jury. The trial must be speedy. If the government purposely postpones the trial so that it becomes hard for the person to get a fair hearing, the charge may be dismissed. The accused must be told the charges against him or her and be allowed to question prosecution witnesses. Witnesses who can help the accused can be ordered to appear in court.

    The accused must be allowed a lawyer. Since 1942, the federal government has been required to provide a lawyer if the accused cannot afford one. In 1963, the Supreme Court decided that states must also provide lawyers for a defendant too poor to pay for one.

Common law refers to rules of law established by judges in past cases. This amendment guarantees the right to a jury trial in lawsuits where the sum of money at stake is more than $20. An appeals court cannot change a verdict because it disagrees with the decision of the jury. It can set aside a verdict only if legal errors made the trial unfair.

Amendment 5
Rights of the Accused

No person shall be held to answer for a capital, or otherwise infamous, crime, unless on a presentment or indictment of a grand jury, except in cases arising in the land or naval forces, or in the militia, when in actual service in time of war or public danger; nor shall any person be subject for the same offense to be twice put in jeopardy of life and limb; nor shall be compelled, in any criminal case, to be a witness against himself; nor be deprived of life, liberty, or property, without due process of law; nor shall private property be taken for public use, without just compensation.

Amendment 6
Right to Speedy Trial by Jury

In all criminal prosecutions, the accused shall enjoy the right to a speedy and public trial, by an impartial jury of the state and district wherein the crime shall have been committed, which district shall have been previously ascertained by law, and to be informed of the nature and cause of the accusation; to be confronted with the witnesses against him; to have compulsory process for obtaining witnesses in his favor, and to have the assistance of counsel for his defense.

Amendment 7
Jury Trial in Civil Cases

In suits at common law, where the value in controversy shall exceed $20, the right of trial by jury shall be preserved, and no fact tried by a jury shall be otherwise re-examined in any court of the United States than according to the rules of the common law.

Amendment 8
Bail and Punishment

Excessive bail shall not be required, nor excessive fines imposed, nor cruel and unusual punishments inflicted.

Bail is money the accused leaves with the court as a pledge that he or she will appear for trial. If the accused does not appear for trial, the court keeps the money. *Excessive* means too high. This amendment forbids courts to set unreasonably high bail. The amount of bail usually depends on the seriousness of the charge and whether the accused is likely to appear for the trial. The amendment also forbids cruel and unusual punishments such as mental and physical abuse.

Amendment 9
Powers Reserved to the People

The enumeration in the Constitution, of certain rights, shall not be construed to deny or disparage others retained by the people.

The people have rights that are not listed in the Constitution. This amendment was added because some people feared that the Bill of Rights would be used to limit rights to those actually listed.

Amendment 10
Powers Reserved to the States

The powers not delegated to the United States by the Constitution, nor prohibited by it to the states, are reserved to the states respectively, or to the people.

This amendment limits the power of the federal government. Powers not given to the federal government belong to the states. The powers reserved to the states are not listed in the Constitution.

Amendment 11
Suits Against States

Passed by Congress on March 4, 1794. Ratified on January 23, 1795.

The judicial power of the United States shall not be construed to extend to any suit in law or equity, commenced or prosecuted against one of the United States, by citizens of another state, or by citizens or subjects of any foreign state.

This amendment changed part of Article 3, Section 2, Clause 1. As a result, a private citizen from one state cannot sue the government of another state in federal court. However, a citizen can sue a state government in a state court.

Amendment 12
Election of President and Vice-President

Passed by Congress on December 9, 1803. Ratified on June 15, 1804.

The electors shall meet in their respective states, and vote by ballot for President and Vice-President, one of whom, at least, shall not be an inhabitant of the same state with themselves; they shall name in their ballots the person voted for as President, and in distinct ballots the person voted for as Vice-President, and they shall make distinct lists of all persons voted for as President, and of all persons voted for as Vice-President, and of the number of votes for each, which lists they shall sign and certify, and transmit, sealed, to the seat of government of the United States, directed to the President of the Senate; the President of the Senate shall, in the presence of the Senate and House of Representatives, open all the certificates and the votes shall then be counted; the person having the greatest number of votes for President shall be the

This amendment changed the way the electoral college voted. Before the amendment was adopted, each elector simply voted for two people. The candidate with the most votes became President. The runner-up became Vice President. In the election of 1800, however, a tie vote resulted between Thomas Jefferson and Aaron Burr (page 261).

In such a case, the Constitution required the House of Representatives to elect the President. Federalists had a majority in the House. They tried to keep Jefferson out of office by voting for Burr. It took 35 ballots in the House before Jefferson was elected President.

THE CONSTITUTION

To keep this from happening again, the Twelfth Amendment was passed and ratified in time for the election of 1804.

This amendment provides that each elector choose one candidate for President and one candidate for Vice President. If no candidate for President receives a majority of electoral votes, the House of Representatives chooses the President. If no candidate for Vice President receives a majority, the Senate elects the Vice President. The Vice President must be a person who is eligible to be President.

This system is still in use today. However, it is possible for a candidate to win the popular vote and lose in the electoral college. This happened in 1876 (pages 497–499).

President, if such number be a majority of the whole number of electors appointed; and if no person have such majority, then from the persons having the highest numbers not exceeding three on the list of those voted for as President, the House of Representatives shall choose immediately, by ballot, the President. But in choosing the President, the votes shall be taken by the states, the representation from each state having one vote; a quorum for this purpose shall consist of a member or members from two-thirds of the states, and a majority of all the states shall be necessary to a choice. And if the House of Representatives shall not choose a President whenever the right of choice shall devolve upon them, before the fourth day of March next following, then the Vice-President shall act as President, as in the case of the death or other constitutional disability of the President. The person having the greatest number of votes as Vice-President, shall be the Vice-President, if such number be a majority of the whole number of electors appointed, and if no person have a majority, then, from the two highest numbers on the list, the Senate shall choose the Vice-President; a quorum for the purpose shall consist of two-thirds of the whole number of Senators, and a majority of the whole number shall be necessary to a choice. But no person constitutionally ineligible to the office of President shall be eligible to that of Vice-President of the United States.

Amendment 13
Abolition of Slavery
Passed by Congress on January 31, 1865. Ratified on December 6, 1865.

The Emancipation Proclamation (1863) freed slaves only in areas controlled by the Confederacy (pages 464–465). This amendment freed all slaves. It also forbids **involuntary servitude,** or labor done against one's will. However, it does not prevent prison wardens from making prisoners work.

Congress can pass laws to carry out this amendment.

Section 1. Neither slavery nor involuntary servitude, except as a punishment for crime whereof the party shall have been duly convicted, shall exist within the United States, or any place subject to their jurisdiction.

Section 2. Congress shall have power to enforce this article by appropriate legislation.

Amendment 14
Rights of Citizens
Passed by Congress on June 13, 1866. Ratified on July 9, 1868.

This section defines citizenship for the first time in the Constitution, and it extends citizenship to blacks. It also prohibits states from denying the rights and privileges of citizenship to any citizen. This section also forbids states to deny due process of law.

Section 1 guarantees all citizens "equal protection under the law." For a long time, however, the Fourteenth Amendment did not protect blacks from discrimination. After Reconstruction, separate facilities for blacks and whites sprang up (page 499). In 1954, the Supreme Court ruled that separate facilities for blacks and whites were by their nature unequal. This ruling, in the case of Brown v. Board of Education, made school segregation illegal.

Section 1. Citizenship All persons born or naturalized in the United States and subject to the jurisdiction thereof, are citizens of the United States and of the state wherein they reside. No state shall make or enforce any law which shall abridge the privileges or immunities of citizens of the United States; nor shall any state deprive any person of life, liberty, or property, without due process of law; nor deny to any person within its jurisdiction the equal protection of the laws.

THE CONSTITUTION

Section 2. Apportionment of Representatives Representatives shall be apportioned among the several states according to their respective numbers, counting the whole number of persons in each state, excluding Indians not taxed. But when the right to vote at any election for the choice of electors for President and Vice-President of the United States, Representatives in Congress, the executive and judicial officers of a state, or the members of the legislature thereof, is denied to any of the male inhabitants of such state, being twenty-one years of age and citizens of the United States, or in any way abridged, except for participation in rebellion, or other crime, the basis of representation therein shall be reduced in the proportion which the number of such male citizens shall bear to the whole number of male citizens twenty-one years of age in such state.

Section 3. Former Confederate Officials No person shall be a Senator or Representative in Congress, or elector of President and Vice-President, or hold any office, civil or military, under the United States, or under any state, who, having previously taken an oath, as a member of Congress, or as an officer of the United States, or as a member of any state legislature, or as an executive or judicial officer of any state, to support the Constitution of the United States, shall have engaged in insurrection or rebellion against the same, or given aid or comfort to the enemies thereof. But Congress may, by vote of two-thirds of each house, remove such disability.

Section 4. Government Debt The validity of the public debt of the United States, authorized by law, including debts incurred for payment of pensions and bounties for services in suppressing insurrection or rebellion, shall not be questioned. But neither the United States nor any state shall assume or pay any debt or obligation incurred in aid of insurrection or rebellion against the United States or any claim for the loss or emancipation of any slave; but all such debts, obligations, and claims shall be held illegal and void.

Section 5. Enforcement The Congress shall have power to enforce, by appropriate legislation, the provisions of this article.

Amendment 15
Voting Rights
Passed by Congress on February 26, 1869. Ratified on February 2, 1870.

Section 1. Extending the Right to Vote The right of citizens of the United States to vote shall not be denied or abridged by the United States or any state on account of race, color, or previous condition of servitude.

Section 2. Enforcement The Congress shall have power to enforce this article by appropriate legislation.

This section replaced the three-fifths clause. It provides that representation in the House of Representatives is decided on the basis of the number of people in the state. It also provides that states which deny the vote to male citizens over age 21 will be punished by losing part of their representation in the House. This provision has never been enforced.

Despite this clause, black citizens were often prevented from voting. In the 1960s, federal laws were passed to end voting discrimination.

This section prohibited people who had been federal or state officials before the Civil War and who had joined the Confederate cause from serving again as government officials. In 1872, Congress restored the rights of former Confederate officials.

This section recognized that the United States must repay its debts from the Civil War. However, it forbade the repayment of debts of the Confederacy. This meant that people who had loaned money to the Confederacy would not be repaid. Also, states were not allowed to pay former slave owners for the loss of slaves.

Congress can pass laws to carry out this amendment.

Previous condition of servitude refers to slavery. This amendment gave blacks, both former slaves and free blacks, the right to vote. In the late 1800s, southern states used grandfather clauses, literacy tests, and poll taxes to keep blacks from voting (page 499).

Congress can pass laws to carry out this amendment. The Twenty-fourth Amendment barred the use of poll taxes in national elections. The Voting Rights Act of 1965 gave federal officials the power to register voters in places where there was voting discrimination.

THE CONSTITUTION

Amendment 16
The Income Tax
Passed by Congress on July 12, 1909. Ratified on February 3, 1913.

The Congress shall have power to lay and collect taxes on incomes, from whatever source derived, without apportionment among the several states, and without regard to any census or enumeration.

Congress has the power to collect taxes on people's income. An income tax can be collected without regard to a state's population. This amendment changed Article 1, Section 9, Clause 4.

Amendment 17
Direct Election of Senators
Passed by Congress on May 13, 1912. Ratified on April 8, 1913.

Section 1. Method of Election The Senate of the United States shall be composed of two Senators from each state, elected by the people thereof, for six years; and each Senator shall have one vote. The electors in each state shall have the qualifications requisite for electors of the most numerous branch of the state legislatures.

This amendment replaced Article 1, Section 2, Clause 1. Before it was adopted, state legislatures chose senators. This amendment provides that senators are directly elected by the people of each state.

Section 2. Vacancies When vacancies happen in the representation of any state in the Senate, the executive authority of such state shall issue writs of election to fill such vacancies: *Provided* that the legislature of any state may empower the executive thereof to make temporary appointments until the people fill the vacancies by election as the legislature may direct.

When a Senate seat becomes vacant, the governor of the state must order an election to fill the seat. The state legislature can give the governor power to fill the seat until an election is held.

Section 3. Exception This amendment shall not be so construed as to affect the election or term of any Senator chosen before it becomes valid as part of the Constitution.

Senators who had already been elected by the state legislatures were not affected by this amendment.

Amendment 18
Prohibition of Alcoholic Beverages
Passed by Congress on December 18, 1917. Ratified on January 16, 1919.

Section 1. Ban on Alcohol After one year from the ratification of this article the manufacture, sale, or transportation of intoxicating liquors within, the importation thereof into, or the exportation thereof from, the United States and all territory subject to the jurisdiction thereof for beverage purposes is hereby prohibited.

This amendment, known as **Prohibition,** banned the making, selling, or transporting of alcoholic beverages in the United States. Later, the Twenty-first Amendment **repealed,** or canceled, this amendment.

Section 2. Enforcement The Congress and the several states shall have concurrent power to enforce this article by appropriate legislation.

Both the states and the federal government had the power to pass laws to enforce this amendment.

Section 3. Method of Ratification This article shall be inoperative unless it shall have been ratified as an amendment to the Constitution by the legislatures of the several states, as provided in the Constitution, within seven years from the date of the submission hereof to the states by the Congress.

This amendment had to be approved within seven years. The Eighteenth Amendment was the first amendment to include a time limit for ratification.

THE CONSTITUTION

Amendment 19
Women's Suffrage
Passed by Congress on June 4, 1919. Ratified on August 18, 1920.

Section 1. The Right to Vote The right of citizens of the United States to vote shall not be denied or abridged by the United States or by any state on account of sex.

Neither the federal government nor state governments can deny the right to vote on account of sex. Thus, women won **suffrage,** or the right to vote. Before 1920, some states had allowed women to vote in state elections.

Section 2. Enforcement Congress shall have power to enforce this article by appropriate legislation.

Congress can pass laws to carry out this amendment.

Amendment 20
Presidential Terms; Sessions of Congress
Passed by Congress on March 2, 1932. Ratified on January 23, 1933.

Section 1. Beginning of Term The terms of the President and Vice-President shall end at noon on the 20th day of January, and the terms of Senators and Representatives at noon on the 3rd day of January, of the years in which such terms would have ended if this article had not been ratified; and the terms of their successors shall then begin.

The date for the President and Vice President to take office is January 20. Members of Congress begin their terms of office on January 3. Before this amendment was adopted, these terms of office began on March 4.

Section 2. Congressional Sessions The Congress shall assemble at least once in every year, and such meeting shall begin at noon on the 3rd day of January, unless they shall by law appoint a different day.

Congress must meet at least once a year. The new session of Congress begins on January 3. Before this amendment, members of Congress who had been defeated in November continued to hold office until the following March. Such members were known as **lame ducks.**

Section 3. Presidential Succession If at the time fixed for the beginning of the term of the President, the President-elect shall have died, the Vice-President-elect shall become President. If a President shall not have been chosen before the time fixed for the beginning of his term, or if the President-elect shall have failed to qualify, then the Vice-President-elect shall act as President until a President shall have qualified; and the Congress may by law provide for the case wherein neither a President-elect nor a Vice-President-elect shall have qualified, declaring who shall then act as President, or the manner in which one who is to act shall be selected, and such person shall act accordingly until a President or Vice-President shall have qualified.

If the President-elect dies before taking office, the Vice President-elect becomes President. If no President has been chosen by January 20 or if the elected candidate fails to qualify for office, the Vice President-elect acts as President, but only until a qualified President is chosen.
    Finally, Congress has the power to choose a person to act as President if neither the President-elect or Vice President-elect is qualified to take office.

Section 4. Elections Decided by Congress The Congress may by law provide for the case of the death of any of the persons from whom the House of Representatives may choose a President whenever the right of choice shall have devolved upon them, and for the case of the death of any of the persons from whom the Senate may choose a Vice-President whenever the right of choice shall have devolved upon them.

Congress can pass laws in cases where a presidential candidate dies while an election is being decided in the House. Congress has similar power in cases where a candidate for Vice President dies while an election is being decided in the Senate.

Section 5. Date of Implementation ~~Sections 1 and 2 shall take effect on the 15th day of October following the ratification of this article.~~

Section 5 sets the date for the amendment to become effective.

THE CONSTITUTION

Section 6 sets a time limit for ratification.

Section 6. Ratification Period ~~This article shall be inoperative unless it shall have been ratified as an amendment to the Constitution by the legislatures of three-fourths of the several states within seven years from the date of its submission.~~

Amendment 21
Repeal of Prohibition
Passed by Congress on February 20, 1933. Ratified on December 5, 1933.

The Eighteenth Amendment is repealed, making it legal to make and sell alcoholic beverages. Prohibition ended December 5, 1933.

Section 1. Repeal of National Prohibition The eighteenth article of amendment to the Constitution of the United States is hereby repealed.

Each state was free to ban the making and selling of alcoholic drink within its borders. This section makes bringing liquor into a "dry" state a federal offense.

Section 2. State Laws The transportation or importation into any state, territory, or possession of the United States for delivery or use therein of intoxicating liquors, in violation of the laws thereof, is hereby prohibited.

Special state conventions were called to ratify this amendment. This is the only time an amendment was ratified by state conventions rather than state legislatures.

Section 3. Ratification Period ~~This article shall be inoperative unless it shall have been ratified as an amendment to the Constitution by conventions in the several states, as provided in the Constitution, within seven years from the date of the submission hereof to the states by the Congress.~~

Amendment 22
Limit on Number of President's Terms
Passed by Congress on March 12, 1947. Ratified on March 1, 1951.

Before Franklin Roosevelt became President, no President served more than two terms in office. Roosevelt broke with this custom and was elected to four terms. This amendment provides that no President may serve more than two terms. A President who has already served more than half of someone else's term can serve only one more full term. However, the amendment did not apply to Harry Truman, who had become President after Franklin Roosevelt's death in 1945.

Section 1. Two-Term Limit No person shall be elected to the office of the President more than twice, and no person who has held the office of President, or acted as President, for more than two years of a term to which some other person was elected President shall be elected to the office of the President more than once. ~~But this Article shall not apply to any person holding the office of President when this Article was proposed by the Congress, and shall not prevent any person who may be holding the office of President, or acting as President, during the term within which this Article becomes operative from holding the office of President or acting as President during the remainder of such term.~~

A seven-year time limit is set for ratification.

Section 2. Ratification Period ~~This Article shall be inoperative unless it shall have been ratified as an amendment to the Constitution by the legislatures of three-fourths of the several states within seven years from the date of its submission to the states by the Congress.~~

THE CONSTITUTION

Amendment 23
Presidential Electors for District of Columbia
Passed by Congress on June 16, 1960. Ratified on April 3, 1961.

Section 1. Determining the Number of Electors The District constituting the seat of Government of the United States shall appoint in such manner as the Congress may direct:
A number of electors of President and Vice-President equal to the whole number of Senators and Representatives in Congress to which the District would be entitled if it were a State, but in no event more than the least populous State; they shall be in addition to those appointed by the States, but they shall be considered, for the purposes of the election of President and Vice-President, to be electors appointed by a State; and they shall meet in the District and perform such duties as provided by the twelfth article of amendment.

This amendment gives residents of Washington, D.C., the right to vote in presidential elections. Until this amendment was adopted, people living in Washington, D.C., could not vote for President because the Constitution had made no provision for choosing electors from the nation's capital. Washington, D.C., has three electoral votes.

Section 2. Enforcement The Congress shall have power to enforce this article by appropriate legislation.

Congress can pass laws to carry out this amendment.

Amendment 24
Abolition of Poll Tax in National Elections
Passed by Congress on August 27, 1962. Ratified on January 23, 1964.

Section 1. Poll Tax Banned The right of citizens of the United States to vote in any primary or other election for President or Vice-President, for electors for President or Vice-President, or for Senator or Representative in Congress, shall not be denied or abridged by the United States or any state by reason of failure to pay any poll tax or other tax.

A **poll tax** is a tax on voters. This amendment bans poll taxes in national elections. Some states used poll taxes to keep blacks from voting. In 1966, the Supreme Court struck down poll taxes in state elections, also.

Section 2. Enforcement The Congress shall have the power to enforce this article by appropriate legislation.

Congress can pass laws to carry out this amendment.

Amendment 25
Presidential Succession and Disability
Passed by Congress on July 6, 1965. Ratified on February 11, 1967.

Section 1. President's Death or Resignation In case of the removal of the President from office or his death or resignation, the Vice-President shall become President.

If the President dies or resigns, the Vice President becomes President. This section clarifies Article 2, Section 1, Clause 6.

Section 2. Vacancies in Vice-Presidency Whenever there is a vacancy in the office of the Vice-President, the President shall nominate a Vice-President who shall take the office upon confirmation by a majority vote of both houses of Congress.

When a Vice President takes over the office of President, he or she appoints a Vice President who must be approved by a majority vote of both houses of Congress. This section was first applied after Vice President Spiro Agnew resigned in 1973. President Richard Nixon appointed Gerald Ford as Vice President.

If the President declares in writing that he or she is unable to perform the duties of office, the Vice President serves as Acting President until the President recovers.

Two Presidents, Woodrow Wilson and Dwight Eisenhower, have fallen gravely ill while in office. The Constitution contained no provision for this kind of emergency.

Section 3 provided that the President can inform Congress that he or she is too sick to perform the duties of office. However, if the President is unconscious or refuses to admit to a disabling illness, Section 4 provides that the Vice President and Cabinet may declare the President disabled. The Vice President becomes Acting President until the President can return to the duties of office. In case of a disagreement between the President and the Vice President and Cabinet over the President's ability to perform the duties of office, Congress must decide the issue. A two-thirds vote of both houses is needed to find the President is disabled or unable to fulfill the duties of office.

In 1970, Congress passed a law allowing 18-year-olds to vote. However, the Supreme Court decided that Congress could not set a minimum age for state elections. So this amendment was passed and ratified.

Congress can pass laws to carry out this amendment.

If members of Congress vote themselves a pay increase, it cannot go into effect until after the next congressional election. This amendment was proposed in 1789. In 1992, Michigan became the thirty-eighth state to ratify it. Congress had placed no time limit on ratification.

Section 3. Disability of the President Whenever the President transmits to the President pro tempore of the Senate and the Speaker of the House of Representatives his written declaration that he is unable to discharge the powers and duties of his office, and until he transmits to them a written declaration to the contrary, such powers and duties shall be discharged by the Vice-President as Acting President.

Section 4. Whenever the Vice-President and a majority of either the principal officers of the executive departments or of such other body as Congress may by law provide, transmit to the President pro tempore of the Senate and the Speaker of the House of Representatives their written declaration that the President is unable to discharge the powers and duties of his office, the Vice-President shall immediately assume the powers and duties of the office as Acting President.

Thereafter, when the President transmits to the President pro tempore of the Senate and the Speaker of the House of Representatives his written declaration that no inability exists, he shall resume the powers and duties of his office unless the Vice-President and a majority of either the principal officers of the executive department or of such other body as Congress may by law provide, transmit within four days to the President pro tempore of the Senate and the Speaker of the House of Representatives their written declaration that the President is unable to discharge the powers and duties of his office. Thereupon Congress shall decide the issue, assembling within 48 hours for that purpose if not in session. If the Congress, within 21 days after receipt of the latter written declaration, or, if Congress is not in session, within 21 days after Congress is required to assemble, determines by two-thirds vote of both houses that the President is unable to discharge the powers and duties of his office, the Vice-President shall continue to discharge the same as Acting President; otherwise, the President shall assume the powers and duties of his office.

Amendment 26
Voting Age
Passed by Congress on March 23, 1971. Ratified on July 1, 1971.

Section 1. Lowering of Voting Age The right of citizens of the United States, who are 18 years of age or older, to vote shall not be denied or abridged by the United States or any state on account of age.

Section 2. Enforcement The Congress shall have the power to enforce this article by appropriate legislation.

Amendment 27
Congressional Pay Increases
Ratified on May 7, 1992.

No law varying the compensation for the services of the Senators and Representatives shall take effect, until an election of Representatives shall have intervened.

THE CONSTITUTION

Index

Page numbers that are *italicized* refer to illustrations. An *m, c,* or *p* before a page number refers to a map (*m*), chart (*c*), or picture (*p*) on that page. An *n* after a page number refers to a footnote.

A

Abolition movement, activists in, 404–405, *p404;* Dred Scott decision, 439–40; John Brown, 438; Kansas, 436–39, *p438;* Lincoln-Douglas Senate race, 441–43, *p441–42;* political parties, 440–41; religious influences, 402–403; underground railroad, 405, 407, *p421;* writers, 417–18. *See also* Antislavery movement; Slavery.

Acomas, 40

Act of Toleration, 107

Adams, Abigail, 147, 168, 328

Adams, John, 328; American Revolution, 161; Declaration of Independence, 165–66, *p166,* 645; election of 1800, 261; French Revolution, 251; on government, 189; as President, 243, 258–60, *p259,* 269, 329–30, *p640;* taxation opposition, 147, 149–50, *p152;* Treaty of Paris, 182; as Vice President, 207

Adams, John Quincy, 360, *p640;* election of 1824, 328, *p328;* election of 1828, 329–30, *m329;* as Secretary of State, 319; Treaty of Ghent, 291

Adams, Samuel, 147, *p147,* 152–53, 161

Adams-Onís Treaty, 319

Adobe, 36

AFL. *See* American Federation of Labor (AFL).

Africa, *m610–11;* African trading states, 65–67, *m66, p67;* Barbary States, 279–80, *m280;* Portuguese slave trade, 67; return of African Americans, 403–404

African Americans, in American Revolution, 155, 176–77, *p176,* 182; black codes, 486; "black Seminoles," 317–18, *p318;* in Canada, 314; in Civil War, *p424–25,* 465; in colonies, 86–87, 116, 119–20, *p121;* cultural influences, 119–20, *m120, p247;* discrimination against, 386, 494, *p494,* 499; education, 414; Fifteenth Amendment, 490–91; first church, *p208;* Fourteenth Amendment, 227, 236, 487–88; freedmen, 95–96, 176–77, *p176,* 189, 391, 392–93, 397, 403–404, 414, 465, 482, 483–85, *p484,* 486, *p487,* 492, *p495;* gold rush, 372; Jim Crow laws, 499; Ku Klux Klan (KKK), 494, *p494;* Negro Election Day, 93; in North, 386; painters, 418; in politics, 492, *p492;* return to Africa, 403–404; voting rights, 86–87, 189, *c220,* 227, 330, 331, 488, 490–91, *p490,* 499, 519–20; War of 1812, 290; *Who Is Carrie?,* 322–23. *See also* Civil rights movement; Equality; Slavery.

Agriculture. *See* Farming.

Airplane, 515

Alabama, 57, 304, 444, *m445, m612–13, c618*

Alamo, *m357,* 358–59, *p359*

Alaska, *c16, m19, m612–13, c618;* land bridge of, 32, *m33;* land and climate of, 18, *m19,* 22, *m23,* 24

Albany, N.Y., 137–38, *m170,* 171–72

Aldridge, Ira, 386

Algonquins, *m42,* 83, 134, 174

Alien and Sedition acts, 260, 269

Allen, Ethan, 160–61, *p160*

Allen, Richard, *p208*

Alvarado, Pedro de, *p71*

Amazon River, 21, 25

Amendments, constitutional, 207, *c224,* 225–27, *p226,* 659–70. *See also* specific amendment.

American Colonization Society, 403–404

American Revolution, advantages, disadvantages, both sides, 160; African Americans in, 176–77, *p176,* 182; causes and effects, *c183;* debt from, 245, 247, 269, 322–33; early battles of, 160–64, *p160, m163;* end of, 181, *m181;* events leading to, 143–55; France in, 172, 174, 181, *m181,* 183; independence declared, 164–67, *p165–66;* in Middle Colonies, 169–74, *m170, p171;* money printed in, 191, *p191;* Native Americans, 175–76; peace treaty, 141, *m141,* 142–43; at sea, 176; in South, 180–81, *p180, m181;* in West, 175–76, *m175;* women in, 177–78, *p177–78*

American System, 313

Amherst, Jeffrey, 139

Anasazis, 35–36, *p36,* 40

Anderson, Robert, 447

Andes Mountains, 21, 25, 52, *p52*

Annexation, 360

Anthony, Susan B., 409

Antietam, Battle of, 459–61, *m459,* 464, 473

Antislavery movement, 408–409, *p408–409,* 435, 436. *See also* Abolition movement.

Apaches, *m42,* 361

Apalachicola River, Fla., 318

Appalachian Mountains, 18–19, *m19, m102*

Appeal to the Colored Citizens of the World (Walker), 404

Appomattox Courthouse, Va., *m476,* 477

Apprentice, 121–22

Appropriate, money by Congress, 230

Arapahos, *m42*

Archaeology, 34–36, *p35*

Arctic (culture area), 37–38, *m42*

Arctic Ocean, 15, *m19*

Argentina, 25, *m315,* 317, *m610–11*

Arizona, 24, 35, 40, *m42,* 75, *m75,* 133, 360, *m361, m612–13, c618*

Arkansas, 432, *c432,* 452, *m452, m612–13, c618*

Arkwright, Richard, 296

Armed forces, commander in chief, 233; Constitution, 216–17, 649; discrimination in, 519. *See also* Draft; specific wars.

Armstrong, Neil, 513

Arnold, Benedict, 164, 172, 180

Arsenal, 443

Arthur, Chester, *c528, p642*

Arthur, Timothy Shay, 414

Articles of Confederation, 192–94, *m192,* 196–97, 200, *c204,* 216, 220

Artifacts, 34, *p36, p38–39*

Arts, Connections With: the Erie Canal, 309; Paul Revere's engraving of the Boston Massacre, *p148*

Arts: literature, 416–17, *p417;* painting, 418–19; poets, 417–18, *p418;* women writers, 416–17, *p417. See also* Culture; specific artists.

Asia, *m66, m610–11;* land bridge to North America from, 32, *m33. See also* specific countries.

Astrolabe, 63, *p65*

Astronauts, *p68*

Atlanta, Ga., 475–76

Atlantic Ocean, 15, *m19*

Austin, Stephen, 357

Automobile, 514–15

Aztecs, 50–52, *p50, m51,* 69, 71–72, *p71*

INDEX

INDEX

INDEX

INDEX

Credits

Acknowledgments

Cover Illustration by Kazuhiko Sano. Concept by Michel Tcherevkoff **Editorial Services** Maryellen Cancellieri, McCormick Associates **Visual Research** Melissa Shustyk, Maureen Raymond, Melanie Jones, Omni-Photo Communications

Text Credits

Page 126 From *The Double Life of Pocahontas* by Jean Fritz. Copyright ©1983 by Jean Fritz. Reprinted by permission of G. P. Putnam's Sons. **Page 212** From *Johnny Tremain* by Esther Forbes. Copyright ©1943 by Esther Forbes Hoskins. Copyright © renewed 1971 by Linwood M. Erskine, Jr., Executor of the Estate. Reprinted by permission of Houghton Mifflin Company. All rights reserved. **Page 322** From *Who Is Carrie?* by James Lincoln Collier and Christopher Collier. Copyright ©1984 by James Lincoln Collier and Christopher Collier. Used by permission of Dell Books, a division of Bantam, Doubleday, Dell Publishing Group, Inc. **Page 422** "A Slave" from *Many Thousand Gone* by Virginia Hamilton. Text copyright ©1993 by Virginia Hamilton. Reprinted by permission of Alfred A. Knopf, Inc.

Illustration Credits

Frequently cited sources are abbreviated as follows: AR Art Resource, NY; **Culver** Culver Pictures, Inc.; **GC** The Granger Collection, New York; **LC** Courtesy of the Library of Congress; **OPC** Omni-Photo Communications, Inc.

Page vi *l* Colonial Williamsburg Foundation; *r* GC **vii** M. & M. Karolik Collection, Courtesy, Museum of Fine Arts, Boston; *b* Maryland Historical Society, Baltimore **viii** Courtesy Museum of New Mexico **ix** Chicago Historical Society, 1969.1737 **x** *t* Atwater Kent Museum, Philadelphia PA; *b* Chicago Historical Society **xi** *l* Giraudon/AR, NY; *r* LC **xii** *t* Joan Landis Baum, Photograph courtesy of the Museum of American Folk Art, New York; *bc* LC; *b* ©1985 Leo and Diane Dillon **xiii** *l* Colonial Williamsburg Foundation; *c* LC; *r* Reuters/Bettmann **xviii–xix** John Lei/OPC **xx-xxi** background ©Grace Davies/OPC **xx** *t* Martin Kurzweil; *b* John Lei/OPC; **xxi** *tl* Superstock; *tr* George Goodwin/Monkmeyer Press; *cr* ©Joyce Photographics/Photo Researchers, Inc.; *bl* John Lei/OPC; *br* ©Lenore Weber/OPC **xxii** *t* Kathryn DePue/Binney & Smith; *b* John Lei/OPC **xxiii** *tr* Sam C. Pierson, Jr./Photo Researchers, Inc.; *tl* Conklin/Monkmeyer Press; *c* From the *Rotarian,* June 1972. By permission of the publisher; *bl* Larry Voigt/Photo Researchers, Inc.; *br* John Lei/OPC **xxiv** *t–b* Anthony Puopolo; John Lei/OPC **xxv** *tl* Superstock; *tr* ©1993 Robert Mankoff and The Cartoon Bank, Inc.; *c* Grant Heilman Photography; *b* John Lei/OPC **xxvi-xxvii** background ©Fotopic/OPC **xxvi** *t*

Jennifer Hodgkins/Binney & Smith; *b* John Lei/OPC **xxvii** *tl* ©1993, Benita L. Epstein; *tr* ©92 Lightscapes/The Stock Market; *c* ©Bill Nation/Sygma; *bl* NASA/Mark Marten/Photo Researchers, Inc.; *br* John Lei/OPC **xxviii/xxix** background Superstock **xxviii** *t* Laura Rigolo; *b* John Lei/OPC **xxix** *tl* Stamp Design ©1993 United States Postal Service; *tr* Wesley Bocxe/Photo Researchers, Inc. bottom *l–r* Vladimir Paperny/The Image Bank; Rogers/Monkmeyer Press; John Lei/OPC

UNIT 1 Page 1 The Huntington Library, San Marino, California **2** *c* Courtesy of the Wheelwright Museum of the American Indian, P12 #12; *r* Trans. no. T.I. 170 (Photo by E. Sackler), Courtesy Department of Library Services, American Museum of Natural History **3** *l* National Museum of American Art, Washington, D.C./AR; *r* Ken Karp/OPC **5** Ann Hagen Griffiths/OPC **6** Jack Parsons/OPC **7** Gary Gay/The Image Bank **12** Comstock, Inc. **14** NASA/OPC **17** Rod Walker/Mountain Stock **20** *l* Harald Sund/The Image Bank; *r* ©David Muench 1994 **24** *t* Anne Rippy/The Image Bank; *b* Stephen J. Krasemann/Photo Researchers, Inc. **29** *t, c* Photo by John Lei/OPC; *b* Buffalo Bill Historical Center, Cody, WY, Gertrude Vanderbilt Whitney Trust Fund, Purchase **30** *l* Denver Art Museum; *c* Dallas Museum of Art, Gift of Mr. and Mrs. Raymond D. Nasher; *r* Ohio Historical Society, Photo by Dirk Bakker **31** *l* The Bodleian Library, Oxford; *c* ©Loren McIntyre/Woodfin Camp & Associates; *r* Courtesy of the Royal Ontario Museum, Toronto, Canada **32** Smithsonian Institution, Photo by Chip Clark **35** *l* The Saint Louis Art Museum, Purchase, Eliza McMillan Fund; *r* Superstock **36** *l* Tom Till Photography; *r* Trans. no. 3519(2) (Photo by P. Hollembeak/J. Beckett), Courtesy Department of Library Services, American Museum of Natural History **38** Denver Art Museum **39** Trans. no. 1428(2), Courtesy Department of Library Services, American Museum of Natural History **41** Courtesy of The National Museum of the American Indian/Smithsonian Institution, 23/4131 **43** The Thomas Gilcrease Institute of Art, Tulsa, Oklahoma, 0236.10754, Photograph Courtesy of The New York State Museum **47** *t* Rochester Museum & Science Center, Rochester, New York; *b* Trans. no. K10302, Courtesy Department of Library Services, American Museum of Natural History; Cranbrook Institute of Science (inset) **48** Peabody Museum, Harvard University **50** Laurie Platt Winfrey, Inc. **52** ©Kal Muller/Woodfin Camp & Associates **56** New York Public Library **57** GC **59** ©Loren McIntyre/Woodfin Camp & Associates **60** *l* Werner Forman Archive/AR; *c* Museum Fue Volkerkunde; *r* Lee Boltin Picture Library **61** *l* Jean Loup Charmet/Science Photo Library/Photo Researchers, Inc.; *c* Courtesy of the Pilgrim Society, Plymouth, Massachusetts; *r* National Archives of Canada, Ottawa, Neg.# C-429 **62** Bridgeman/AR **65** *l* The Metropolitan Museum of Art, The Edward C. Moore Collection, Bequest of Edward C. Moore, 1891, Copyright ©1980 The Metropolitan Museum of Art; *r*

Researchers, Inc. **226** *l* P. F. Gero/Sygma; *r* Michal Heron **227** Michael L. Abramson **230** *l* Paul S. Conklin; *r* Shepard Sherbell/SABA **231** Dennis Brack/Black Star **233** *l* Jeffrey; Markowitz/Sygma; *r* Diana Walker/ Gamma-Liaison, Inc. **234** Reuters/Bettmann **237** John Lei/OPC **239** *t* John Lei/OPC; *b* Susan Steinkamp

UNIT 3 Page 240 Courtesy of The New-York Historical Society, New York, NY **242** *l* Index of American Design, ©1993 National Gallery of Art, Washington; *r* LC **243** *l* ©Michael Freeman; *c* The Bettmann Archive; *r* National Museum of American History, Smithsonian Institution, Photo no. 49455-A **244** *l* Collection of The New-York Historical Society, New York, NY; *r* The Museum of American Political Life, University of Hartford **246** *t* Copyrighted by the White House Historical Association, Photograph by the National Geographic Society; *c* Courtesy of The Mount Vernon Ladies' Association; *b* The Brooklyn Museum **247** LC **249** Courtesy, Winterthur Museum **251** Giraudon/AR **253** *l* Chicago Historical Society; *r* Courtesy National Archives **255** Abby Aldrich Rockefeller Folk Art Center **256** Yale University Art Gallery **259** *l* Stock Montage; *r* Copyrighted by the White House Historical Association; Photograph by the National Geographic Society **261** Smithsonian Institution, Photo No. 45553 **262** *tl* Collection of The New-York Historical Society, New York, NY; *tr* The New York Public Library, Rare Book Division; *cl* The Library Company of Philadelphia; *cr* Abby Aldrich Rockefeller Folk Art Center; *b* Yale University Art Gallery **263** *tl* Canadian Museum of Civilization, 111-I-508; *tr* Glenbow Museum; *c* Courtesy, Winterthur Museum; *b* Colonial Williamsburg Foundation **265** *t* The Library Company of Philadelphia; *c* The Museum of American Political Life, University of Hartford; *b* Courtesy, Independence National Historical Park **266** *l* Smithsonian Institution, Photo No. 74-3510; *r* GC **267** *l* Canadian Parks Service: Fort Malden National Historic Site; *c* Smithsonian Institution, Photo No. 81-512; *r* Smithsonian Institution, Photo No. 88-11731 **268** *t* Copyrighted by the White House Historical Association; Photograph by the National Geographic Society; *b* Monticello, Thomas Jefferson Memorial Foundation, Inc. **270** Boston Athenaeum **271** Maryland Historical Society, Baltimore **272** GC **275** *t* Peabody Museum of Archaeology and Ethnology, Harvard University, Photo by Hillel Burger; *b* National Museum of American Art, Washington, D.C./AR **276** Smithsonian Institution, Photo No. 103598 **279** *tl* Courtesy, Peabody & Essex Museum, Salem, Massachusetts, Photo by Mark Sexton; *tr* ©George Hall/Woodfin Camp & Associates; *b* The Historical Society of Pennsylvania **284** *l* Field Museum of Natural History; *r* National Museum of American Art, Smithsonian Institution, Gift of Mrs. Joseph Harrison, Jr. **287** Gift of Edgar William and Bernice Chrysler Garbisch, 1962, Copyright ©1981 By The Metropolitan Museum of Art **289** Virginia State Historical Society, Richmond, Virginia **290** LC **291** *l* The New York Public Library, Stokes Collection; *r* Lee Boltin Picture Library **293** *t* Missouri Historical Society; *bl* Lewis and Clark on the

Lower Columbia, 1905, Charles M. Russell, gouache, watercolor, and graphite on paper, Amon Carter Museum, Fort Worth, 1961.195; *br* Missouri Historical Society **294** *l* Florida State Archives; *c* Smithsonian Institution; *r* The Metropolitan Museum of Art, Rogers Fund, 1942 (42.95.11), Copyright ©The Metropolitan Museum of Art **295** *l* National Museum of American Art, Smithsonian Institution; *c* LC, Photo by M. Rudolph Vetter; *r* Samuel S. Spaulding Collection, Buffalo and Erie County Historical Society **297** M. & M. Karolik Collection, Courtesy, Museum of Fine Arts, Boston **300** Museum of American Textile History **302** Museum of the City of New York **305** Joan Landis Baum, Photograph courtesy of the Museum of American Folk Art, New York **309** *l* Courtesy of The New-York Historical Society, New York, NY; *r* LC **311** *l*, *r* Collection of The New-York Historical Society, New York, NY; *c* Yale University Art Gallery **313** The Metropolitan Museum of Art, Rogers Fund, 1942 (42.95.7), Copyright ©The Metropolitan Museum of Art **316** Laurie Platt Winfrey, Inc. **318** Florida State Archives **321** *t* Robert Fulton, Design for Steamboat Engine, 1808, Solomon Alofsen Collection, New Jersey Historical Society; *bl* Museum of Connecticut History; *br* New York State Historical Association, Cooperstown **323** Chicago Historical Society

UNIT 4 Page 324 (detail) The Metropolitan Museum of Art, Rogers Fund, 1907 (07.123), Photograph by Geoffrey Clements, Copyright ©1985 The Metropolitan Museum of Art **326** *l–r* Walters Art Gallery, Baltimore; The Museum of American Political Life, University of Hartford, Photo by Steven Laschever; Woolaroc Museum, Bartlesville, Oklahoma **327** *l–r* LC; Trans. no. 909, Courtesy Department of Library Services, American Museum of Natural History; GC **328** National Portrait Gallery, Smithsonian Institution/AR **331** GC **332** The Nelson-Atkins Museum of Art, Kansas City, Missouri, (Purchase: Nelson Trust), 54-9 **333** *l* Andrew Jackson, Thomas Sully, Andrew W. Mellon Collection, ©1993 National Gallery of Art, Washington; *r* Tennessee State Museum, Tennessee Historical Society Collection, Photo by June Dorman **334** GC **335** LC **337** The Bettmann Archive **338** LC **339** Chris Wolf Edmonds, Lawrence, Kansas **342** Cincinnati Art Museum **343** *l* LC; *r* Corning Museum of Glass **347** *t* Museum of the City of New York, Gift of The Seawanhaka Corinthia Yacht Club; *c* Smithsonian Institution, Photo No. 78-9138; *b* The Bettmann Archive **348** *l* The New York Public Library; *r* The Center for American History, The University of Texas at Austin **349** *l* Courtesy John Zimmerman, Lane County Historical Museum, Eugene, Oregon, 49; *c* The Lundoff Collection; *r* Seaver Center for Western History Research, Natural History Museum of Los Angeles County **351** Courtesy, Colorado Historical Society **352** Joslyn Art Museum, Omaha, Nebraska **354** The Thomas Gilcrease Institute of Art, Tulsa, Oklahoma, 126.2261 **356** *Pleasant Grove—Residence of Mr. J. Morrison, Texas,* 1853–1854, Sarah Ann Lily Bumstead Hardinge Daniels, watercolor, gouache, and graphite on paper, Amon Carter Museum,

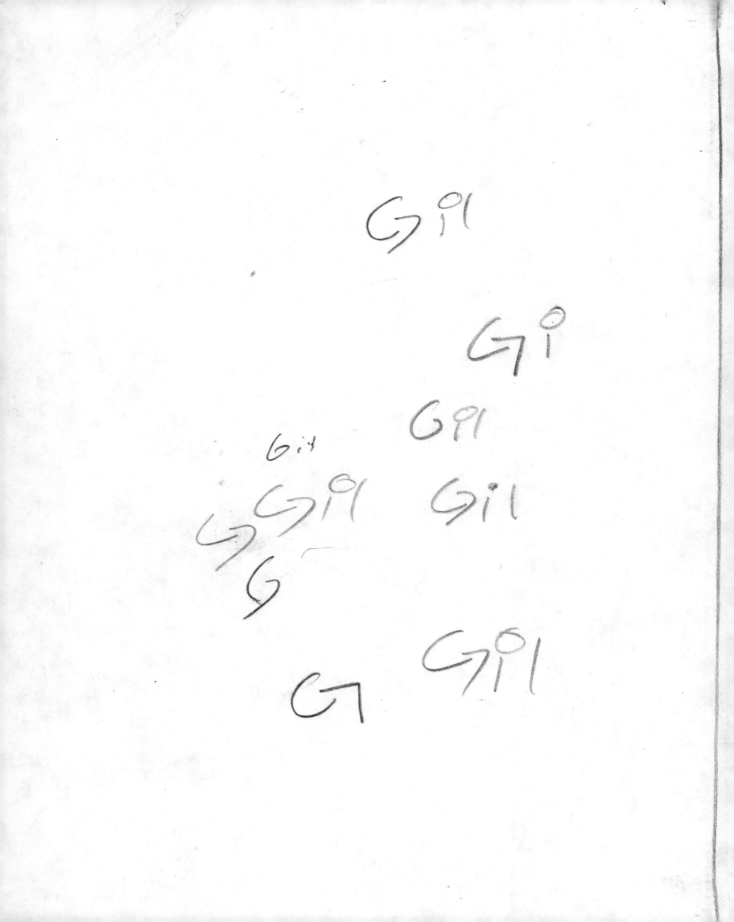